# CRITICAL SURVEY OF

# Poetry

## *Fourth Edition*

## British, Irish, and Commonwealth Poets

# CRITICAL SURVEY OF
# Poetry
## *Fourth Edition*

# British, Irish, and Commonwealth Poets

## Volume 3
John Oldham—Edward Young
Resources
Indexes

*Editor, Fourth Edition*
## Rosemary M. Canfield Reisman
*Charleston Southern University*

SALEM PRESS
Pasadena, California
Hackensack, New Jersey

*Editor in Chief:* Dawn P. Dawson

*Editorial Director:* Christina J. Moose    *Research Supervisor:* Jeffry Jensen
*Development Editor:* Tracy Irons-Georges    *Research Assistant:* Keli Trousdale
*Project Editor:* Rowena Wildin    *Production Editor:* Andrea E. Miller
*Manuscript Editor:* Desiree Dreeuws    *Page Desion:* James Hutson
*Acquisitions Editor:* Mark Rehn    *Layout:* Mary Overell
*Editorial Assistant:* Brett S. Weisberg    *Photo Editor:* Cynthia Breslin Beres

*Cover photo:* Thomas Hardy (The Granger Collection, New York)

Some of the essays in this work, which have been updated, originally appeared in the following Salem Press publications, *Critical Survey of Poetry, English Language Series* (1983), *Critical Survey of Poetry: Foreign Language Series* (1984), *Critical Survey of Poetry, Supplement* (1987), *Critical Survey of Poetry, English Language Series, Revised Edition,* (1992; preceding volumes edited by Frank N. Magill), *Critical Survey of Poetry, Second Revised Edition* (2003; edited by Philip K. Jason).

∞ The paper used in these volumes conforms to the American National Standard for Permanence of Paper for Printed Library Materials, X39.48-1992 (R1997).

**Library of Congress Cataloging-in-Publication Data**

Critical survey of poetry. — 4th ed. / editor, Rosemary M. Canfield Reisman.
    v. cm.
Includes bibliographical references and index.
    ISBN 978-1-58765-582-1 (set : alk. paper) — ISBN 978-1-58765-588-3 (set : Brit., Irish, Comm. poets : alk. paper) — ISBN 978-1-58765-589-0 (v. 1 : Brit., Irish, Comm. poets : alk. paper) — ISBN 978-1-58765-590-6 (v. 2 : Brit., Irish, Comm. poets : alk. paper) — ISBN 978-1-58765-591-3 (v. 3 : Brit., Irish, Comm. poets : alk. paper)
1. Poetry—History and criticism—Dictionaries. 2. Poetry—Bio-bibliography. 3. Poets—Biography—Dictionaries. I. Reisman, Rosemary M. Canfield.
PN1021.C7 2011
809.1'003--dc22

        2010045095

First Printing

# CONTENTS

# COMPLETE LIST OF CONTENTS

## Volume 1

# VOLUME 2

# VOLUME 3

# PRONUNCIATION KEY

To help users of the *Critical Survey of Poetry* pronounce unfamiliar names of profiled poets correctly, phonetic spellings using the character symbols listed below appear in parentheses immediately after the first mention of the poet's name in the narrative text. Stressed syllables are indicated in capital letters, and syllables are separated by hyphens.

## VOWEL SOUNDS

| Symbol | Spelled (Pronounced) |
|---|---|
| a | answer (AN-suhr), laugh (laf), sample (SAM-puhl), that (that) |
| ah | father (FAH-thur), hospital (HAHS-pih-tuhl) |
| aw | awful (AW-fuhl), caught (kawt) |
| ay | blaze (blayz), fade (fayd), waiter (WAYT-ur), weigh (way) |
| eh | bed (behd), head (hehd), said (sehd) |
| ee | believe (bee-LEEV), cedar (SEE-dur), leader (LEED-ur), liter (LEE-tur) |
| ew | boot (bewt), lose (lewz) |
| i | buy (bi), height (hit), lie (li), surprise (sur-PRIZ) |
| ih | bitter (BIH-tur), pill (pihl) |
| o | cotton (KO-tuhn), hot (hot) |
| oh | below (bee-LOH), coat (koht), note (noht), wholesome (HOHL-suhm) |
| oo | good (good), look (look) |
| ow | couch (kowch), how (how) |
| oy | boy (boy), coin (koyn) |
| uh | about (uh-BOWT), butter (BUH-tuhr), enough (ee-NUHF), other (UH-thur) |

## CONSONANT SOUNDS

| Symbol | Spelled (Pronounced) |
|---|---|
| ch | beach (beech), chimp (chihmp) |
| g | beg (behg), disguise (dihs-GIZ), get (geht) |
| j | digit (DIH-juht), edge (ehj), jet (jeht) |
| k | cat (kat), kitten (KIH-tuhn), hex (hehks) |
| s | cellar (SEHL-ur), save (sayv), scent (sehnt) |
| sh | champagne (sham-PAYN), issue (IH-shew), shop (shop) |
| ur | birth (burth), disturb (dihs-TURB), earth (urth), letter (LEH-tur) |
| y | useful (YEWS-fuhl), young (yuhng) |
| z | business (BIHZ-nehs), zest (zehst) |
| zh | vision (VIH-zhuhn) |

# CRITICAL SURVEY OF
# Poetry

## *Fourth Edition*

# British, Irish, and Commonwealth Poets

# *O*

## JOHN OLDHAM

**Born:** Shipton Moyne, Gloucestershire, England;
August 9, 1653
**Died:** Holm Pierrepont, near Nottingham, England;
December 9, 1683

PRINCIPAL POETRY

*A Satyr Against Vertue*, 1679
*Satyrs upon the Jesuits*, 1681
*Some New Pieces Never Before Publisht*, 1681
*Poems and Translations*, 1683
*Selected Poems*, 1980 (Ken Robinson, editor)
*The Poems of John Oldham*, 1986 (Raman Selden
and Harold F. Brooks, editors)

OTHER LITERARY FORMS

The literary output of John Oldham (OHL-duhm)
was restricted to verse and verse imitation. Nevertheless, his influence in these forms produced a shaping
force in English literature.

ACHIEVEMENTS

As a notably influential although minor literary figure, John Oldham is probably less recognized for any
single achievement of his own than for the way he
helped to shape the development of seventeenth and
eighteenth century verse satire. The two major phases
of his brief literary career reflect two very different satiric styles: the harshness of Juvenalian invective and
the more tempered voice of Horatian conversation. Although his *Satyrs upon the Jesuits*, the harshest of
the Juvenalian satires, contains Oldham's most well-
known and frequently anthologized pieces, his later
satires reflect a comparatively moderate tone and are
now recognized as his best poems. Among these, his
"imitations" of such figures as Horace, Juvenal, and
Nicolas Boileau-Despréaux were formative in establishing a loose form of verse translation in which the

original appeared in a contemporary social and literary
context.

Oldham's severity in his early satires looks back to
the extreme style of sixteenth century satirists; his
somewhat more tempered voice in the later verses
looks forward to the moderation of John Dryden and
Alexander Pope. When Oldham died at the age of
thirty, he had already won a firm position for himself in
the development of English literature. He failed, however, to produce a satire to rival those of the great satirists who followed him and who were indebted to his
limited though influential literary achievement.

Although no complete edition of Oldham's poetry
exists, several partial editions are available, notably the
Centaur edition of 1960 and Ken Robinson's facsimile
edition of 1980. *The Poems of John Oldham*, edited by
Raman Selden and Harold F. Brooks, corrects errors
found in the previous editions.

BIOGRAPHY

John Oldham was born in the English countryside on August 9, 1653, the son of a dissenting minister.
He received a solid education both at home and in
grammar school, entered St. Edmund's Hall, Oxford,
when he was seventeen and took his bachelor's degree
in May, 1674. Sometime during this period, Oldham
wrote his first poem, a long Pindaric ode "To the Memory of My Dear Friend, Mr. Charles Morwent." By this
time he had confirmed, at least to himself, a lifelong
commitment to the writing of poetry.

Because it was impossible to make a living from
one's pen without the aid of a literary patron, Oldham
assumed the position of "usher" (assistant master) in
Whitgift's school, Croyden, where he remained in em-
ployment from 1674 to 1677. Although the aspiring
poet had written several poems since his first ode, it
was during these years that he wrote his first verse satire, *A Satyr Against Vertue*. It was also during the years
at Croyden that Oldham was recognized by the more
prominent Restoration wits, notably the earls of Rochester and Dorset, and Sir Charles Sedley.

As his poetic reputation grew, so did Oldham's dissatisfaction with his position at Whitgift's. Considering his tutoring duties to be little more than menial labor, in 1678, he accepted a position as a private tutor,

which he kept until 1680 when he decided to move to London and become part of the literati of Restoration society. A year before the move to London, his *Satyrs upon the Jesuits* had been piratically printed, and Oldham's reputation as a promising young verse satirist was already established.

Not much is known of the time Oldham spent in London. He studied medicine for about a year, but then devoted himself wholly to poetry. He admitted to adopting the lifestyle of the Restoration town gentleman, engaging in drinking and debauchery, although he was quick to feel the pangs of conscience when reflecting on his excesses. During these three final years of his life, his health declined, and finally he retired to Nottinghamshire, residence of the young earl of Kingston, who offered the poet a comfortable home where he might pursue his literary career.

It was here that, free from the social and literary demands that London society placed on him, Oldham produced some of his finest satires and imitations. In 1683, however, only three years after he had moved to London in pursuit of literary fame, Oldham contracted smallpox. He died on December 9 of that year.

ANALYSIS

John Oldham's calling was not to the polite muse. Instead, he saw himself as inheriting the role of the poet who rails against the faults and vices of the age. His harsh Juvenalian satires and lively verse imitations were quick to attack what was wrong with society. Oldham's tone was rugged yet sharp; his poetic attitude was one of indignation. He mastered the art of the cankered muse, and left behind him some of the finest examples of vituperative verse satire.

The subjects, themes, and satirical approaches that Oldham adopted account for much of the bite in his work. Early in his career, when he wrote his most severe satires, Oldham typically addressed himself to issues that were either personally or socially repulsive to him. In *A Satyr Against Vertue*, for example, he rails against affected notions of virtue that "plague our happy state;" in the "Satire Addressed to a Friend," he complains about his own personal circumstances; and in his *Satyrs upon the Jesuits*, he vents his indignation about a subject that aroused some of the most heated political and religious controversy of the age. Unlike many of his more witty contemporaries who were content to treat their subjects with humor and objectivity, Oldham focused directly on the victims of his satire—cursing them for their actions, condemning the society in which they thrived, and depicting them in the most offensive ways. While John Dryden or even the earl of Rochester might dexterously mix censure with praise, there is no mistaking the focus of Oldham's direct accusations.

Both personal and social circumstances might account for the severity of Oldham's satiric tone. His strong sense of individualism made him an unsuitable candidate for the system of patronage, and what he perceived as the declining position of literature in Restoration England only served to confirm his individualism. It is not surprising that Oldham wrote some of his best verses after he had left London and retired to the English countryside, detached from the environment of "hack" writers and commercial values. Yet it was that very society that gave him the subjects for his satires. Political disputes between Tories and Whigs, religious controversy between Catholics and Protestants, and what many perceived as the general decadent atmosphere of London society supplied him with his best materials.

### SATYRS UPON THE JESUITS

Oldham's *Satyrs upon the Jesuits*, probably written shortly before his move to London, typifies the kind of invective and raillery for which he has become so famous. In the prologue, Oldham describes satire as his weapon and indignation as his muse; in each of the four satires, he adopts the perspective of a different speaker who functions as the vehicle of his satiric lashes. This satiric approach made it possible for him to focus directly on his victims and at the same time vary his tone so that the satire might remain consistent in its attack and yet flexible in its point of view. The ghost of Henry Garnet, a provincial of the Jesuits who was executed in 1606 for his role in the Gunpowder Plot, speaks in the first satire, urging the Jesuits to kill and plunder, to create another "inquisition." When Oldham speaks in his own voice in the second satire, he then vents his own rage against the Jesuits with the same vigor that "Garnet's Ghost" used to plot against king and nation.

Perspective shifts again in the third satire, "Loyola's Will," where Oldham speaks through the voice of Saint Ignatius of Loyola himself, founder of the Jesuit order. Here Saint Ignatius, pictured on his deathbed, passes on to his followers the "hidden rules" and "secrets" of villainy. In the final satire, the perspective is even more removed as the wooden image of Saint Ignatius assumes the satiric voice, exposing its own worthlessness and the emptiness of Catholic ritual.

The Juvenalian rant of the *Satyrs upon the Jesuits* has its source not only in the different perspectives that Oldham adopted in each satire, constantly allowing him to shift the focus of his invective, but also in the details of each speaker's remarks. One of the most savage passages of "Garnet's Ghost," for example, is filled with specific instructions on how to murder priests, mothers, unborn children, infants, young virgins, the aged, and the crippled. In "Loyola's Will," readers are given a gruesome picture of the dying Jesuit leader as he "heaves" and "pants" on his deathbed. The picture becomes even more gruesome in the final satire where spiders and rats find "refuge" and "religious sanctuary" in the decaying body of Saint Ignatius. In depicting such scenes, Oldham was extending himself far beyond the lines of general religious satire: The Jesuits are not merely criticized; they are portrayed and condemned in vicious terms.

### TRANSLATIONS AND IMITATIONS

*Satyrs upon the Jesuits* was Oldham's masterpiece in his harsh Juvenalian mode. His verse translations and imitations, however, which began to consume his poetic energies, were more temperate and moderate. Several critics believe that the very act of imitation helped tame Oldham's sharp satiric voice. Even the last of the *Satyrs upon the Jesuits*, spoken from the perspective of a dead, wooden image, was modeled in part on one of Horace's satires and is more distant and mocking in its manner.

With the verse imitations, Oldham entered the most influential phase of his brief literary career. The refined Horatian style of the translations looked forward to the moderation of Dryden and Alexander Pope. Equally influential was the theory of imitation that Oldham practiced: Instead of translating the original in its own historical context, he rendered it in a contemporary English setting—at once making the classics more alive and immediate, and making his own contemporary verse more intellectually respectable. Again, both Dryden and Pope in their own imitations were to follow Oldham's practice.

Among Oldham's early imitations were "Bion's Lamentation for Adonis," which was his elegy on Rochester, and the renditions of two odes of Horace. His outstanding satiric imitations, of Horace, Juvenal, and Boileau, were to follow in 1681 and 1682. The art of translation and imitation dominated this final phase of Oldham's career; even poems that were not strict imitations nevertheless drew on classical sources. "Spenser's Ghost" and "Satire Addressed to a Friend," two of his outstanding satires of this period, both draw on Juvenal's seventh satire. The three imitations generally considered to be Oldham's masterpieces are his renditions of Horace's ninth satire, first book (1681), Juvenal's third satire (1682), and Boileau's eighth satire (1682).

The conversational tone and comic subject of the Horatian imitation immediately distinguishes it from Oldham's earlier satiric invective. Instead of writing about plots and murder and villainy, Oldham's subject here is the poet's encounter with a bore whom he cannot manage to escape. The story is humorous, not vengeful; the "tedious chat" of the bore clearly contrasts with the bitter pleas of "Garnet's Ghost" and the deathbed speech of Saint Ignatius. Contemporary social issues are satirized, but only mildly, at times almost with understatement. The Popish Plot, for example, which fired much of Oldham's invective in his *Satyrs upon the Jesuits*, becomes in the imitation a bothersome issue that the poet would just as soon dismiss. In his translation of Horace, Oldham was not only imitating the Horatian style, but also adopting and perfecting a very different kind of satiric voice for himself.

The imitations of Juvenal and Boileau exemplify Oldham's mastery of this new satiric voice. Although the subject of each of these imitations is more serious than that of the Horatian piece, Oldham continues to treat his subject with a notably lighter tone. The criticism of London in his translation of Juvenal, for instance, describes the "nauseous town" as totally lacking any value or worth, but the details of the satire are often comic, especially in the portraits of the city's hairdressers, plotters, and courtiers. When Oldham describes England as the "common sewer" for France, his portraits of fops and their fashions are more often the object of humor than of indignation. The situation is much the same in his rendition of Boileau's eighth satire, which often exaggerates comedy to the point of absurdity. In this dispute between doctor and poet, man's position in the animal kingdom becomes a playful issue that Oldham easily exploits for his satiric purposes. Urbane conversation and pointed ridicule allow Oldham to treat the satire with humor: While the doctor defends, for example, humankind's serious position as "Lord of the Universe," the poet luxuriates in descriptions of tigers creating plots and factions, or "Whig and Tory lions" engaging in political disputes. The poet's final sustained comparison of humankind with an "ass" may not convince the doctor, but it makes Oldham's satire all the more engaging for its fine sense of wit.

### VIGOROUS INVECTIVE

Despite this change in tone, Oldham never lost his ability to write fiercely vigorous invective. This ability was, after all, his distinguishing achievement as a satirist and is almost always apparent in the details of his verse. One passage in the Juvenal imitation, for example, portrays London society as enslaved to money. Oldham describes everything, from court favors to the consent of lovers, as the object of purchase. London becomes more than merely an "expensive town"; it is depicted as a society that thrives on a system of social prostitution. Another passage, in the Boileau imitation, relies on the intrusion of a notably harsh subject in the midst of comparatively light satire. As the poet proceeds to ridicule humankind by contrasting him with animals, he pauses to make an accusation that recalls the subject matter of *Satyrs upon the Jesuits*: the "trade of cutting throats" and the "arts" of warfare and murder. Although in his best imitations Oldham had learned to moderate his depiction of the gruesome details of these arts, passages of this kind are reminders that he never entirely abandoned the cankered muse.

### DRYDEN'S "TO THE MEMORY OF MR. OLDHAM"

Oldham will be remembered for the invective of his *Satyrs upon the Jesuits* and his contributions to the art of verse imitation. He will probably be better remembered, however, as the subject of one of Dryden's finest poems, "To the Memory of Mr. Oldham." It is an appropriate memorial, for Dryden knew only too well both Oldham's shortcomings and his achievements. The harshness of Oldham's satire, Dryden says, was a "noble error," one that could not conceal what Dryden saw as Oldham's distinguishing qualities, the "wit" and "quickness" of his best verse. "To the Memory of Mr. Oldham" both praises the poet and laments his early death, reflecting the double poetic legacy which Oldham left behind: the accomplishments of an outstanding satirist, and the promise of literary distinction that an untimely death prevented.

### BIBLIOGRAPHY

Brooks, Harold F. "The Poetry of John Oldham." In *Restoration Literature: Critical Approaches*, edited by Harold Love. London: Methuen, 1972. Brooks discusses Oldham's poetry in terms of his life, contemporaries, sources, and genres; no Oldham poem receives extended explication. The essay is, however, valuable in terms of providing information about Abraham Cowley's influence on Oldham and the evaluation of Oldham as a better satirist than Metaphysical poet.

Griffin, Julia. "John Oldham and the Smithfield Crickets." *Notes and Queries* 45, no. 1 (March, 1998): 64-65. An etymological study of Oldham's "Some New Pieces."

Hammond, Paul. *John Oldham and the Renewal of Classical Culture*. New York: Cambridge University Press, 1983. In his revaluation of Oldham, Hammond uses the Rawlinson manuscripts to show how Oldham composed his best poems. Focuses on his subject's early indebtedness to Abraham Cowley and on the translations from Horace, Juvenal, and Nicolas Boileau-Despréaux. For Hammond, Oldham prepared the way for the work of Samuel Johnson, John Dryden, and Alexander Pope. The book contains a biographical chapter, a chronology, and a bibliography.

Malekin, Peter. *Liberty and Love: English Literature and Society, 1640-88*. New York: St. Martin's Press, 1981. In a chapter on the satirical aftermath of the Popish Plot, Malekin analyzes Oldham's religious satire, particularly his four satires directed at the Jesuits. For Malekin, Oldham's abusive and bitter satires, written in the Juvenalian manner, created emotional prejudice, but the lack of humor and subtlety dates and thereby weakens the poems.

Selden, Raman. "Oldham, Pope, and Restoration Satire." In *English Satire and the Satiric Tradition*, edited by Claude Rawson. Malden, Mass.: Basil Blackwell, 1984. Selden discusses Oldham's wide range of poetry (Rochesterian, Metaphysical, Ovidian, pastoral, and irony) and demonstrates, through parallel passages, Alexander Pope's extensive knowledge of Oldham's poetry. It is Oldham's rough wit that constitutes the Restoration strain in Pope's eighteenth century poetry.

_____. "Oldham's Versions of the Classics." In *Poetry and Drama, 1570-1700: Essays in Honour of Harold F. Brooks*, edited by Antony Coleman and Antony Hammond. London: Methuen, 1981. Selden describes Oldham as the most "adventurous of Augustan classicists" in his imitations of Roman satiric verse and love poetry. There are many comparisons not only between Oldham's poems and their sources but also between Oldham's versions and those of his contemporaries.

Zigerell, John. *John Oldham*. Boston: Twayne, 1983. A standard biography of Oldham that covers his life and works.

*Ruth Salvaggio*

# MICHAEL ONDAATJE

**Born:** Colombo, Ceylon (now in Sri Lanka); September 12, 1943

PRINCIPAL POETRY

*The Dainty Monsters*, 1967
*The Man with Seven Toes*, 1969
*The Collected Works of Billy the Kid: Left Handed Poems*, 1970
*Rat Jelly*, 1973
*Elimination Dance*, 1978, 1980
*There's a Trick with a Knife I'm Learning to Do: Poems, 1963-1978*, 1979
*Secular Love*, 1984
*The Cinnamon Peeler: Selected Poems*, 1989
*Handwriting*, 1998

OTHER LITERARY FORMS

Michael Ondaatje (on-DAHT-chee) has published several novels, a memoir about his childhood in Sri Lanka, and literary criticism. He has also transformed two of his works into plays: *The Collected Works of Billy the Kid* was produced in Stratford, Ontario, in 1973, in New York City in 1974, and in London in 1984; and *In the Skin of a Lion* was produced as a play in 1987. He is the editor of several anthologies of fiction and poetry as well.

Ondaatje has also exercised his writing talents in cinema, which has always fascinated him. After making *Sons of Captain Poetry* (1969), a short film about poet B. P. Nichol (Barrie Phillip Nichol), and *The Clinton Special* (1972), a longer documentary that explores the relationship between living and performing, he was invited by director Norman Jewison to join the Canadian Centre for Advanced Film Studies; there he wrote the script for *Love Clinic*, a short film.

ACHIEVEMENTS

Michael Ondaatje has been the recipient of numerous literary honors, among them the Ralph Gustafson Award (1965), the Epstein Award (1966), the E. J. Pratt Medal (1966), President's Medal of the University of Western Ontario (1967), the Governor-General's Literary Award (awarded by the Canadian Council for the Arts; 1971, 1980, 1992, 2000, 2007), the Books in Canada First Novel Award (1976), the Canada-Australia Prize (1980), the Toronto Book Award (1988), the Trillium Award (1992), and the prestigious Booker McConnell Prize (1992), awarded by the British Book Trust for his novel *The English Patient* (1992)—the first Canadian to receive this coveted prize for the best literary work in the British Commonwealth. In 2000, he won the Giller Prize, the Kinyama Pacific Rim Book Prize, and the Prix Médicis.

Though his fiction has received the most critical attention, his poetry has won its share of accolades. He received the Chalmers Award for *The Collected Works of Billy the Kid* and the du Maurier Award for poetry.

## BIOGRAPHY

Michael Ondaatje was born Philip Michael Ondaatje on a tea plantation in Colombo, Ceylon (now Sri Lanka). Philip Mervyn Ondaatje, his father, was descended from a wealthy family that can be traced back to 1600. By the time Ondaatje was born, however, his father had sold most of the family's holdings; two years later (1945) his father and mother, Enid Doris Gratiaen, were divorced. His mother went to England and sent him to St. Thomas's College Boys' School in Colombo, a school modeled on English boarding schools. By 1952, his mother had earned enough money to bring him to England, where he continued his education at Dulwich College before he immigrated in 1962 to Lennoxville, Quebec, Canada. There he attended Bishop's Univer-

*Michael Ondaatje* (Courtesy, Picador Publicity Department, London)

sity and won the President's Prize for English. After marrying Betty Jane Kimbark (Kim Jones) in 1964, he transferred to University College, University of Toronto, where he won the Ralph Gustafson Award and received a B.A. degree. While working on his M.A. degree at Queen's University in Kingston, he had some poems included in *New Wave Canada*, an anthology, which tied for the E. J. Pratt Medal, and won the Epstein Award.

After receiving his M.A. and publishing *The Dainty Monsters*, he began teaching at the University of Western Ontario, but despite publishing a critical study of Leonard Cohen and the critically acclaimed *The Collected Works of Billy the Kid*, Ondaatje was fired for lack of "academic" publications. He was then hired by the Glendon College English Department at York University. During the 1970's, Ondaatje worked in film and translated some of his work to the stage. He received awards for both poetry and fiction.

When Ondaatje served as a visiting professor at the University of Hawaii in 1981, he met Linda Spalding and separated from his wife. With Linda Spalding, he coedited *The Brick Reader* (1991). After that he published several volumes of verse, including *Secular Love*, *The Cinnamon Peeler*, and *Handwriting*. It is his fiction, however, that has received the most critical recognition. The novel *The English Patient* established him as an international literary figure with much the same stature Margaret Atwood enjoys. The novel was adapted into an award-winning film in 1996.

## ANALYSIS

Perhaps no other Canadian writer, with the exception of Atwood, has written well in such a variety of genres and received the international acclaim accorded Michael Ondaatje. This "international" reputation is hardly surprising, given his Sri Lankan heritage, his thoroughly "British" schooling, and the foreign teaching positions he has held. In fact, since *Coming Through Slaughter* and *The Collected Works of Billy the Kid* have distinctly American themes (the first about jazz man Buddy Bolden; the second about a Western cultural icon), there has been a tendency to deny Ondaatje Canadian status. Similarly, given the unconventional nature of the narrative in *Coming Through Slaughter* and the blending of poetry and prose in *The Collected Works of Billy the Kid* (which some critics have categorized as fiction or "other"), Ondaatje's writing tends to blur, if not to obscure, conventional distinctions between fiction and poetry.

## THE DAINTY MONSTERS

*The Dainty Monsters*, Ondaatje's first volume of verse, contains many poems about animals and birds. "Description Is a Bird" is the first of eight poems in the collection. For the most part, humans are absent from these poems; the animals seem to serve as symbols but resist interpretation, leaving room for various responses. Douglas Barbour reads the poem as follows: "Love is a performance against solitude which demands discipline in the midst of apparent chaos." The birds' actions describe love. Barbour feels that poems like these, those that allow "closure," were omitted in later collections because "Ondaatje's restless imagination" found them "too confining."

## THE COLLECTED WORKS OF BILLY THE KID

In 1970, three years after *The Dainty Monsters*, Ondaatje published *The Collected Works of Billy the Kid*, a hybrid book containing some lyric poems but also photographs, a fictional newspaper account, ballads, and selections from real documents. For Dennis Lee, "this polyphony introduces an exuberant flow into the book's movement, which carries a reader with ease through the discontinuities of the plot." In the book, civilization and nature are at odds, and Billy dehumanizes himself by becoming a killing machine. Constantly on edge, Billy is the outsider constrained by boundaries which he crosses or observes. The volume begins with an empty square that represents a picture of Billy, but the prose passage alludes to moving pictures. In fact, the book contains references and descriptions that suggest that Billy is a camera, observing angles and distances, or a motion picture camera, describing actions as one would write a screenplay:

> Garrett smiles, pokes his gun towards the door.
> The others melt and
> surround.
> All this I would have seen if I was on the roof looking.

As a filmmaker, Billy, like Ondaatje, is an artist; and in this volume, as in his other works, Ondaatje tends to resemble his protagonist.

## "LETTERS AND OTHER WORLDS"

In "Letters and Other Worlds" (*Rat Jelly*), which Stephen Scobie has described as "the greatest single poem in Canadian literature," Ondaatje attempts to come to terms with his absentee father, a recurrent figure in his work. The poem recounts his father's drinking bouts, his self-destructive behavior, and his self-imposed isolation in a room with bottles of liquor. The poem is at once amusing and tragic, like his father's life: "His early life was a terrifying comedy." Ondaatje jokes that his father's "falling/ dead drunk onto the street" and stopping the Perahara procession was "a crucial/ turning point" that "led to Ceylon's independence in 1948" because his father was a "semi-official, and semi-white at that."

The last verse paragraph presents, through balancing imagery, the tenuous hold his father had on his life. In his room, Ondaatje's father wrote apologies, "Letters in a clear hand of the most complete empathy." While his heart widened to accept "all manner of change in his children and friends," he "himself edged/ into the terrible acute hatred/ of his own privacy." Fearful (earlier Ondaatje writes, "My father's body was a globe of fear") of accepting and forgiving himself, "he balanced and fell."

## "LIGHT"

Ondaatje often used mythology in his early poems, but in the later ones, he tends to mythologize domesticity. Community becomes a major concern as he probes relationships with friends and family. In "Light" (*There's a Trick with a Knife I'm Learning to Do*), dedicated to his mother, as he sits through a midnight summer storm, he sees the slides "re-shot from old minute photographs" projected on the wall. His relatives "stand/ complex ambiguous grainy," at several removes from reality. The complexity and ambiguity are reflected in memories of eccentric but endearing behavior (his Aunt Christie thought Harold MacMillan was "communicating with her through pictures in the newspapers"). The pictures, like the various pieces that comprise *The Collected Works of Billy the Kid*, are "fragments, all I remember"; but Ondaatje can see his family not only reflected in himself and in his children, but also as a "parade in my brain" and make connections between "expanding stories," partly of his creation, and "the grey grainy pictures." Like the trees around his house, they "Haven't moved an inch from me."

### SECULAR LOVE

In *Secular Love*, Ondaatje became more autobiographical, more intimate, and more confessional, in the manner of poets like Robert Lowell. The volume describes the disintegration of a marriage, a near mental breakdown, "Rock Bottom" (the title of one of the four sections), and recovery and new love. Although the poems are part of a whole and are, for the most part, interdependent, "To a Sad Daughter," which has been anthologized, stands on its own. It is a secular love poem-lecture to a daughter who is not what he "expected." She delights in violent sports, retreats into "purple moods," and finds his expression of "love" embarrassing, but he likes this behavior. Uncomfortable with the role of father and not good at giving advice, he nevertheless gives her a "lecture" which is poignant and life-affirming (perhaps the advice applies to his own life). Using myth, he advises her to listen to the song of the sirens, to not be fooled by anyone but herself, and to "break going out not in." The poem ends on a quasi-religious note ("suburban annunciation") and suggests that love may lie beneath a violent exterior: "Your goalie/ in his frightening mask/ dreams perhaps/ of gentleness."

### HANDWRITING

In this volume of poetry, Ondaatje turns his attention to Sri Lanka, to Sri Lankan culture, and to the writing process. The poem that begins "What we lost" best describes how Sri Lankan culture has deteriorated. The poet describes the loss of the "interior love poem," the "dates when the abandonment/ of certain principles occurred." The principles involve courtesy, the arts, and "Lyrics that rose/ from love/ back into the air." The nuances of human communication, the harmony between humans and nature, and the tie between nature and religion—"All this we burned or traded for power and wealth." In this volume Ondaatje addresses the political problems of Sri Lanka as he juxtaposes "men carrying recumbent Buddhas/ or men carrying mortars."

### OTHER MAJOR WORKS

LONG FICTION: *Coming Through Slaughter*, 1976; *In the Skin of a Lion*, 1987; *The English Patient*, 1992; *Anil's Ghost*, 2000; *Divisadero*, 2007.

PLAYS: *The Collected Works of Billy the Kid*, pr. 1973 (adaptation of his poetry); *In the Skin of a Lion*, pr. 1987 (adaptation of his novel).

NONFICTION: *Leonard Cohen*, 1970; *Claude Glass*, 1979; *Running in the Family*, 1982.

EDITED TEXTS: *The Long Poem Anthology*, 1979; *The Faber Book of Contemporary Canadian Short Stories*, 1990; *From Ink Lake: Canadian Stories*, 1990; *The Brick Reader*, 1991 (with Linda Spalding); *An H in the Heart*, 1994 (of B. P. Nichol's work; with George Bowering); *Lost Classics*, 2000; *The Conversations: Walter Murch and the Art of Editing Film*, 2002.

MISCELLANEOUS: *Vintage Ondaatje*, 2004.

### BIBLIOGRAPHY

Barbour, Douglas. *Michael Ondaatje*. New York: Twayne, 1993. An early book-length study of Ondaatje's work, it provides a careful reading and useful analysis of both the early and later poetry and the prose works through *The English Patient*. Devoting a chapter to each of the major works, Barbour makes a strong case for Ondaatje as an important postmodern, postcolonial writer based on his keen perception, imaginative intensity, and eloquence.

Clarke, George Elliott. "Michael Ondaatje and the Production of Myth." *Studies in Canadian Literature* 16, no. 1 (1991): 1-21. Clarke offers an interpretation of the idea of myth that he then applies to Ondaatje's works from *The Dainty Monsters* to *Secular Love*.

Heble, Ajay. "'The Widening Rise of Surprise': Containment and Transgression in the Poetry of Michael Ondaatje." *Wascana Review* 26 (Spring-Fall, 1991): 117-127. Heble examines the unexpected pairings, the jarring juxtapositions, and the abrupt shifts in tone in Ondaatje's poetry. His explication of "Letter and Other Worlds" is especially interesting since it deals with Ondaatje's father. In the poem Heble demonstrates how the poet transforms a bit of personal history, his father's drunken fall, into local mythology, a factor in the Home Rule movement. Using the line "My father's body was a globe of fear/ His body was a town we never knew," Heble shows how private body and public space coalesce.

Hillger, Annick. *Not Needing All the Words: Michael Ondaatje's Literature of Silence*. Ithaca, N.Y.: McGill-Queen's University Press, 2006. The author analyzes numerous poems and argues that Ondaatje is trying to find a ground for the self beyond the realm of language.

Jaumain, Serge, and Marc Maufort, eds. *The Guises of Canadian Diversity: New European Perspectives / Les masques de la Diversite Canadienne: Nouvelles perspectives europeenes*. Amsterdam: Rodopi, 1995. This is a diverse collection of essays by graduate students in Canadian studies at several European universities. Contains three essays on Ondaatje, focusing on his creative use of history, art, and autobiography.

Jewinski, Ed. *Michael Ondaatje: Express Yourself Beautifully*. Toronto, Ont.: ECW Press, 1994. This short, illustrated biography, written without the cooperation of its subject, portrays Ondaatje's life as a series of abrupt and dramatic incidents. It relates the writer's early life experiences to later imaginative works, such as *Running in the Family* and *The English Patient*.

Solecki, Sam, ed. *Spider Blues: Essays on Michael Ondaatje*. Montreal: Véhicule Press, 1985. This collection contains many interesting early essays on Ondaatje. It covers a wide range of approaches and perspectives, from interviews and reviews to essays on his use of autobiography, postmodern poetics, and myth.

Tötösy de Zepetnek, Steven, ed. *Comparative Cultural Studies and Michael Ondaatje's Writing*. West Lafayette, Ind.: Purdue University Press, 2005. This collection of essays by scholars of English-Canadian literature examine Ondaatje and his works.

*Thomas L. Erskine*

# WILFRED OWEN

**Born:** Oswestry, England; March 18, 1893
**Died:** Sambre Canal, France; November 4, 1918

PRINCIPAL POETRY

*Poems by Wilfred Owen*, 1920 (Siegfried Sassoon, editor)
*The Poems of Wilfred Owen*, 1931 (Edmund Charles Blunden, editor)
*The Collected Poems of Wilfred Owen*, 1963 (Cecil Day Lewis, editor)
*Wilfred Owen: War Poems and Others*, 1973 (Dominic Hibberd, editor)

OTHER LITERARY FORMS

Like many of the poets and artists of his time, Wilfred Owen professed a strong interest in the theater and supposedly drafted a play while recovering from shell shock in Craiglockhart military hospital in 1917, although no manuscript has appeared. Owen's letters, which have been collected, deserve mention for two reasons. First, the style reflects both the poetic temper of the man and the adherence to detail reflective of an age of correspondence that will probably never return. Second, and perhaps more important, Owen's letters record the transitions typical of most British soldiers who survived on the front for a long time: from resolve to do the soldier's duty, to disgust, fear, and depression, to the solemn acceptance of fate that extended service produced. One is fascinated by Owen's attempt to depict his life on the front for his naïve family and friends, as well as his ability to do so in spite of censorship.

ACHIEVEMENTS

Many commentators have emphasized that Wilfred Owen exhibited more potential to continue and enlarge the craft of poetry than any of the soldier-poets of World War I. He was a technician, an innovator, a "poet's poet" long before he was a proud soldier, a horrified combatant, and a victim. The kinds of criticisms applied to Rupert Brooke (immature, too much style, and too little substance) or Siegfried Sassoon (limited, more propaganda than art) have little validity when it comes to Owen. Indeed, in spite of his early death and limited canon, several twentieth century poets (among them W. H. Auden and Stephen Spender) have publicly stated their admiration for Owen's work or have used or expanded his methods. A notable dissenting voice is that of William Butler Yeats, who shocked many writers and critics by excluding Owen's work from his *Oxford Book of Modern Verse* (1936). Yeats defended his decision in a famous venomous blast, writing to Dorothy Wellesley that Owen was "unworthy of the poet's corner of a country newspaper. He is all blood, dirt, and sucked sugar stick . . . (he calls poets, 'bards,' a girl a 'maid,' and talks about 'Titanic wars'). There is every excuse for him, but none for those who like him."

Owen's champions, however, far outnumber his detractors. It is true that all his work, from earliest to latest, is characterized by a kind of romantic embellishment, an intensity that borders on parody. This was more of a problem early in his career; as he matured, he assimilated the devices of John Keats, Percy Bysshe Shelley, and Lord Byron (among others), creating effective juxtapositions and dramatic tensions. This change was perhaps a result of the sophisticated and shocking material he found in his war experience.

Shocking the war poems are. Certainly among the most descriptive and horrifying of their era, they continue to penetrate minds supposedly benumbed by exposure to the twentieth century. In what became the preface to his first published volume of poetry, Owen wrote: "Above all, I am not concerned with Poetry. My subject is War, and the pity of War. The Poetry is in the pity." Indeed it appears true; of the many horrifying experiences suffered by the artists who recorded their experience in World War I (Robert Graves, Sassoon, Isaac Rosenberg, Edward Thomas, Brooke, and others), it is Owen's cries that are the loudest and most anguished. Owen seems to have been more outraged than most by the lamentable tragedy of fine young men lost in the struggle. What is surprising, however, is that the resultant verse is never self-indulgent, self-pitying; rather, Owen was able to focus his vision outward. He concluded sadly in the preface previously cited that "all a poet can do today is warn." Owen's disgust with the war he experienced and despised is readily apparent, but it goes beyond immediacy and is elevated to prophecy as well.

Another of Owen's goals, through all the years of fighting and suffering, was to cling to his artistic voice, to expand his abilities, to become a better poet. He sought new ways to use language, and his mastery of alliteration, onomatopoeia, assonance, and dissonance have been often cited. Perhaps his most consistently brilliant device was the use of slant rhyme (or "half rhyme" or "pararhyme" as it has been called), the subtle and effective mixture of vowel dissonance and consonant assonance most often effectively employed at the end of his lines (for example, "cold" and "killed").

The effect of Owen's expert use of form (he was a master of sonnets and elegiac mood) and his fluency (both traditional and experimental) was to suggest a poet who would have been very much at home with modernism, but who never would have forgotten his literary heritage. In fact, an observation often made concerning the poetry of Thomas Hardy, that his was the soul of the nineteenth century anticipating twentieth century innovations, applies equally well to Owen. That Owen was able to sustain his brilliance under the stress of battle makes the reader appreciate his achievement all the more.

BIOGRAPHY

Wilfred Edward Salter Owen was born in Oswestry, Shropshire, England, on March 18, 1893, the first child of Tom and Susan Owen. Owen's mother was a devout and cautious woman; his father was an active, rough-hewn, hardworking sort who was nostalgically attracted to the sea and those who sailed it. The early years of their marriage and Owen's childhood were sometimes difficult, characterized by several moves, frequent if not severe financial difficulties, and tensions produced by his parents' conflicting characters. Their union produced four children. Owen's younger brother Harold became a successful artist and devoted much of his adult life to chronicling the life of his more famous war-poet brother.

Owen was sent to Birkenhead Institute for his first years of schooling; his father approved of the discipline for which the school was noted, but Owen probably profited most from an adoring teacher and early exposure to the pleasures of literature. He also showed a great interest in religious matters, much to the delight of his mother. In 1907, the family moved to Shrewsbury, where Owen enrolled in the technical school. There he read diligently and began to compose serious essays (some on politics, some on art theory) and put down his first attempts at verse.

Somewhat confused about his future after his matriculation examination at London University in 1911, Owen accepted an opportunity to become a lay assistant to the Vicar of Dunsden. His activities were many-faceted, from the intellectual (extensive reading and attending lectures) to the practical affairs of the parish (playing with children and assisting the poor). His poetry began to mature, not so much in its subject matter as in its increasing flexibility of language. For reasons that remain unclear, Owen became disenchanted with his commitment to the vicarage and left Dunsden. After a period of contemplation, during which he struggled with his health, he was offered, and he accepted, a post to teach English at the Berlitz School in Bordeaux. He enjoyed the experience and the climate was beneficial, even as the clouds of war gathered over Europe.

Because Owen was in France during the "exhilarating" first part of the war, a time when nationalism and enthusiasm for battle possessed young men like him in England, his wavering emotions regarding the conflict are understandable. He had left his job in late 1915 to assume a position as a private tutor to a well-to-do family in Merignac, France. His correspondence reveals a confused but honor-bound attitude toward his own responsibilities: appalled at the destruction and suffering so near by, confident and proud of his ability to serve, excited at the prospect of taking his gift for poetry into battle. He briefly investigated business opportunities, flirted with but rejected the idea of joining either the French army or the Italian cavalry, and in September, 1915, returned to England, where he enlisted with the Artists' Rifles.

During his training, he sought not only to become a fine soldier but also to become familiar with many people active in the literary circles of London. He met Harold Monro of the *Poetry Review* and lived briefly in a flat adjacent to the magazine's offices. Owen performed admirably as a soldier and claimed to enjoy his work, though he appeared uncomfortable, out of place with his peers. He was well liked, however, and in June,

*Wilfred Owen* (Library of Congress)

1916, Second Lieutenant Owen was attached to the Fifth Battalion of the Manchester Regiment.

After a few months of polishing, Owen was sent with thousands of his fellows to the front. The Somme offensive, begun in July, 1916, had been stalled tragically for several months, and war planners had determined to begin another push as the new year began. Immediately, Owen was struck by the difference between the grotesque reality of the war zone and the appallingly inaccurate depictions of the war at home. These sentiments, together with supportive vivid details, were relayed home regularly. Still, he took comfort in his devotion to duty and in writing, criticizing, and discussing poetry, pleasures that he never neglected.

Writing and fighting with distinction for six months, Owen showed signs of suffering from the strain and was finally sent to Craiglockhart military hospital, where he was diagnosed as suffering from neurasthenia, or shell shock. His stay there was to be crucial, not only for his health but for his poetic and intellectual development as well. Owen participated in many of the therapeutic activities offered by the hospital. Also at Craiglockhart was Siegfried Sassoon, the distinguished soldier, poet, and most recently a virulent antiwar spokesperson. The two became friends and eventually Sassoon became audience and critic for the work that began to reveal Owen's growing artistry. Robert Graves, a friend of Sassoon and a regular visitor to the hospital, also encouraged Owen to continue his work. In December, Owen was dismissed and returned to London, where he pursued other contacts in the literary establishment. (Later, in 1920, Sassoon became responsible for collecting and publishing selections of Owen's poetry.)

In spite of his increasing disgust at the carnage of battle, amply evident in his poems of this time, Owen was compelled to return to the war, and during the summer of 1918, he was granted permission to cross to France. Participating in the heavy fighting preceding and during the armistice talks, Owen became a respected and competent soldier, winning the military cross. Invigorated artistically by his friendship with prominent writers during his recuperation, he sent poems and lively letters back to England. On November 4, 1918, one week before the armistice, Owen was killed while leading his troops across the Sambre Canal.

ANALYSIS

Wilfred Owen's most memorable, and often cited, works reveal several characteristic traits. Romantic imagery dominates his work, regardless of whether it is war-inspired. Owen was a passionate disciple of Keats; he made pilgrimages to Keats's shrines and felt a personal affinity for the great Romantic poet. There is also brutal realism in Owen's war descriptions. Had Owen not been there himself, the reader might be tempted to believe the verse exaggerated, such is its power. The poetry is also characterized by the sensual glorification of male beauty and bravery, and the hideous waste of wartime slaughter. Such elements have prompted a plentitude of conjecture about Owen's personal relationships; but the sentiment with which he glorifies male qualities in his early years and the depth with which he expressed his concern for his fellows in his war years are not, in his case, cause for prurient speculation by the psychological critics. The simple fact concerning Owen's poetry is that he wrote about his comrades in ways that were never offensive and always eloquent.

"TO POESY"

Innovations and experiments with the potential of language give Owen's best work a quality that is more of the modernistic than the Edwardian or Georgian temper. In spite of its strength and ferocity, however, there is an equally noticeable fragility. Owen's earliest extant attempts at poetry (according to Jon Stallworthy, it is probable that his first efforts were burned by his mother at his death, at the poet's request) reflect a somewhat awkward sentimentalism. He laboriously expresses his adoration for the muse in "To Poesy." The poem, an odd beginning for one who would later write that he was "not concerned with poetry," contains a variety of religious, erotic quest images (none very effective) designed to signify the "purer love" of his aesthetic principles. Also noticeable at this time in Owen's poetic infancy are poems and fragments that either imitate Keats or illustrate his exultant emotions after having visited locales associated with Keats's life and work. Again, the sentiments are apparent, if hardly laudable artistically, as in "SONNET, written at Teignmouth, on a Pilgrimage to Keats's House." Its sestet begins: "Eternally may sad waves wail his death,/ Choke in their grief 'mongst rocks where he has lain." Still, the young poet shows signs of searching for more sophisticated methods. A revealing fragment from an early manuscript shows that Owen had penciled in lines to attract attention to the interesting effect of half-rhymed words, "tomb, home," "thou, below," "spirit, inherit."

"DULCE ET DECORUM EST"

The effect that one experiences when turning from Owen's earlier works to his mature verse is dramatic indeed. "Bent double, like old beggars under sacks,/ Knock-kneed, coughing like hags, we cursed through sludge," begins "Dulce et Decorum Est," one of his most often cited depictions of the reality of war. An interesting juxtaposition established at the beginning is that of the simple exhaustion of the troops who "marched asleep . . . lame . . . blind . . . drunk with fatigue," and the nightmarish, almost surreal atmosphere of the battle, lighted by "haunting flares," pierced by the "hoots" of artillery fire, and pervaded by the sickening presence of gas. The soldier who has donned his gas mask looks through "misty panes" at thick green light, as if submerged in a "green sea." The nightmare is unrelieved by the passage of battle as the persona sees "in all my dreams," without relief, a comrade who was unable to survive the attack, who lurches grotesquely, "guttering, choking, drowning."

After witnessing these events, the reader is drawn more intimately into the scene, as the persona uses the second person, asking directly if "you too" could imagine witnessing eyes "writhing in his face" and blood that "gargles from froth-corrupted lungs." As Owen builds the intensity and visceral detail of his description, he is preparing the reader for the ironic and bitter conclusion that uses a tag from Horace (*Odes*, 23 B.C.E., 13 B.C.E.; English translation, 1621), familiar to schoolboys and used to glorify the war effort: *Dulce et decorum est pro patria mori* (it is sweet and honorable and proper to die for your country). For Owen, however, the sentiments expressed in the phrase can now only be considered an "old lie" that cannot honestly be told to children anymore. Owen brilliantly half-rhymes in the last three lines the words "glory" (what children seek) and "mori" (what happens to them in war).

### "STRANGE MEETING"

Another nightmare vision serves as the stimulus for a greatly admired work. "Strange Meeting" recounts a frightful reverie, an encounter between two soldiers in hell. Their confrontation, unified by dramatic dialogue, is inspired by the horrors of war, but it also serves as an occasion for Owen to comment on poetic principles and to prophesy (quite accurately and depressingly) on the nature of the new century.

Owen begins by describing his descent down "some profound dull tunnel," arriving at a shattered place where "encumbered sleepers groaned." He is surprised when one of these fellows jumps up; there is a moment of recognition not only between them but also of their mutual circumstance, standing "in Hell." Owen comforts his opposite in a dramatic understatement, suggesting that even here, dead, in hell, there "is no cause to mourn." Such was the gruesome reality above ground, alive, in battle. The stranger is in no mood to be assuaged, because he too had been a poet who ventured and strove for "the wildest beauty in the world." Thus,

the poet's life is lost, but that loss is not to be lamented nearly as much as the loss of the truth he might have written, the "truth untold." The ultimate tragedy is not temporary, but lasting, as future generations will be unaware of the truth of war that the poet could have recorded. Instead of rejecting the past, those generations will embrace it, probably with devastating efficiency. Had he lived, the poet would also have battled, not with instruments of war, but with his "courage" and "wisdom." His would have been a war to dominate men's minds, fought when men wearied of bleeding and death, a soothing message of "truths that lie too deep for taint" that would have flowed from his "spirit."

Owen does not wish to end the poem at this abstract level, seeking instead to pull the reader back to the immediacy of war. Even though the setting is highly contrived, Owen provides a "surprise ending" that serves two purposes: to impress upon the reader the brutal infighting characteristic of many World War I battles, and to ridicule the notion of nationalism and emphasize the common humanity of all the war's combatants. The early "recognition," a foreshadowing device, had not been between friends but between enemies, as the poet-narrator had evidently slain the poet-prophet with a bayonet. Rather than continuing either the hostilities or the discussion, the soldier who had been thus murdered offers a simpler, but more final and disturbing alternative: "Let us sleep now. . . ."

### "ARMS AND THE BOY"

In other poems, Owen draws attention to the waste of young men slaughtered. "Arms and the Boy" (an ironic revision of the opening of Vergil's *Aeneid*, (c. 29-19 B.C.E.; English translation, 1553; "Arms and the Man I sing. . . .") is a three-stanza portrait of youthful innocence confronting the awful mysteries of the instruments of war. He emphasizes the apparent discomfort as a boy tests a bayonet "keen with hunger for flesh" and caresses a bullet that seeks "to nuzzle in the hearts of lads." These gestures are not natural for youngsters whose "teeth seem for laughing round an apple" (the immediate thought here is of a soldier's death-grimace). Moreover, the human animal was not designed for battle; there are "no claws behind his fingers supple." His appearance is of gentle, delicate demeanor, a face framed with "curls," as opposed to the brutish nobility of animals that possess "talons" and "antlers."

### "ANTHEM FOR DOOMED YOUTH"

Similar sentiments, now supported by religious imagery, are expressed in "Anthem for Doomed Youth," a sonnet that illustrates Owen's fusion of the traditional elegiac mood with the realities of modern warfare. The opening question serves as an example: "What passing-bells for these who die as cattle?" The answer is that the only possible form of lamentation for the war dead is the cacophonous sounds of war, "the stuttering rifle's rapid rattle." Not only are religious ceremonies out of the question, but they would also be a "mockery." Here Owen shows the extent to which his disillusionment with organized religion had gone. Instead of the glow of holy candles, the poet finds light in "their eyes." They will wear no "pall," but will be recognized and remembered through the "pallor of girl's brows." The essence of this poem is that in such times as these, Christianity seems incapable of providing its traditional comfort. The memorial of the dead soldiers will not be "flowers" but memories held by "patient minds." Their legacy, sadly and not of their making, is but darkness, at "each slow dusk a drawing-down of blinds."

In a sense, Owen's poetic legacy can also inspire darkness for the reader. His work is highly educational, however, and thus valuable, especially when read in the context of World War I and in contrast to that of some of his fellow soldier-poets. The reader, ultimately grateful for the work that Owen left, is intrigued by what he might have become.

### OTHER MAJOR WORKS

NONFICTION: *Collected Letters*, 1967 (Harold Owen and John Bell, editors); *Selected Letters*, 1998 (Bell, editor).

### BIBLIOGRAPHY

Breen, Jennifer. *Wilfred Owen: Selected Poetry and Prose*. London: Routledge, Chapman & Hall, 1988. Breen does an excellent job of giving a brief analysis of Owen's major poems and supports her opinions by subjectively looking at his personal correspondence to gain insight for her analysis. Contains a limited bibliography.

Hibberd, Dominic. *Wilfred Owen: A New Biography*. Chicago: I. R. Dee, 2003. A fine biography, well-documented and engaging. Hibberd's detailed look at Owen's life discusses previously unexplored territory.

Hipp, Daniel. *The Poetry of Shell Shock: Wartime Trauma and Healing in Wilfred Owen, Ivor Gurney, and Siegfried Sassoon*. Jefferson, N.C.: McFarland, 2005. Contains a chapter on Owen, focusing on the topic of shell shock in his poetry.

Owen, Wilfred. *Wilfred Owen: Collected Letters*. Edited by Harold Owen and John Bell. New York: Oxford University Press, 1967. Follows the life of Owen from the time he was five until his death at the age of twenty-five, through his letters to his family and friends. Includes an index.

Purkis, John. *A Preface to Wilfred Owen*. London: Longman, 1999. A brief biographical and critical introduction to Owen and his work. Includes bibliographical references and an index.

Simcox, Kenneth. *Wilfred Owen: Anthem for a Doomed Youth*. London: Woburn, 1987. Begins with Owen's interaction with his family, focusing on his influential mother. His religious background is highlighted as Simcox reviews the major issues in Owen's poetry, amply augmented with examples from his primary works. Includes an index.

Stallworthy, Jon, ed. *The Poems of Wilfred Owen*. New York: W. W. Norton, 1985. An intensive study into the chronological sequence of 103 poems and 12 fragments by Owen. Factual footnotes allow readers a concise foundation from which to formulate their own explications.

_____. *Wilfred Owen*. New York: Oxford University Press, 1995. A full and sensitive illustrated biography of the short-lived poet and war hero. Appendixes offer genealogies, fragments of previously unpublished poems, a bibliography of Owen's library, and an index.

White, Gertrude. *Wilfred Owen*. New York: Twayne, 1969. Traces Owen's maturation as a poet from dreamy, romantic imagery to the harsh realities of World War I. Includes a bibliography and an index.

*Robert Edward Graalman, Jr.*

# P

## COVENTRY PATMORE

**Born:** Woodford, Essex, England; July 23, 1823
**Died:** Lymington, Hampshire, England; November 26, 1896

### PRINCIPAL POETRY

*Poems*, 1844
*Tamerton Church-Tower, and Other Poems*, 1853
*The Angel in the House*, 1854-1862 (2 volumes; includes *The Betrothal*, 1854; *The Espousals*, 1856; *Faithful for Ever*, 1860; and *The Victories of Love*, 1862)
*Odes*, 1868
*The Unknown Eros, and Other Odes*, 1877, 1878 (2 volumes)
*Amelia*, 1878
*Selected Poems of Coventry Patmore*, 1931 (Derek Patmore, editor)
*A Selection of Poems*, 1948 (Patmore, editor)
*The Poems of Coventry Patmore*, 1949

### OTHER LITERARY FORMS

The prose works of Coventry Patmore (PAHT-mohr) include essays, a biography, numerous letters, and aphoristic collections. His *Essay on English Metrical Law* was published in 1856 (a critical edition was published in 1961). More than twenty years later, he published his first book of prose, a biography of the poet Barry Cornwall titled *Bryan Waller Procter* (1877). He published an account of his success in managing his estate at Heron's Ghyll in *How I Managed and Improved My Estate* (1888). His major collections of prose are: *Principle in Art* (1889); *Religio Poetæ* (1893); and *Rod, Root, and Flower* (1895).

A five-volume edition of his *Works* was published in London in 1907. No edition of his letters exists, but many can be found in Basil Champneys's *Memoirs and Correspondence of Coventry Patmore* (1900) and in *Further Letters of Gerard Manley Hopkins* (1956, Claude C. Abbott, editor), the latter volume containing Patmore's correspondence with Hopkins.

### ACHIEVEMENTS

Coventry Patmore has often been referred to as a man and a poet of contradictions, and his achievements—as both—are equally contradictory. He was one of the most popular of all Victorian poets. *The Angel in the House* had gone into a sixth edition by 1885, and by the time of his death in 1896, it had sold more than 250,000 copies. He was widely read throughout the British Empire as well as in the United States and other countries. He was also, however, one the most quickly forgotten of Victorian poets. His reputation went into eclipse in the late 1860's and early 1870's, enjoyed a brief revival in the late 1870's and early 1880's, and then fell into a critical and popular decline that has never been reversed.

### BIOGRAPHY

Coventry Kersey Dighton Patmore's life falls roughly into four periods, the latter three of which correspond to his three marriages. The first period, up to his first marriage, was dominated by his father, Peter George Patmore. Peter Patmore was a man devoted to the arts, intent on social climbing, and steadfast in his devotion to friends. His life, unfortunately, was beset with problems and scandals. Peter was the man to whom William Hazlitt wrote some of the letters later published in *Liber Amoris* (1823), letters in which the married Hazlitt confessed to a degrading love affair with a young girl. When the book was published, both author and recipients were critically condemned for, at least, a serious breach of taste. Two years earlier, in 1821, Peter had been a second in a duel during which his principal was killed, there being reason to believe that Peter's ignorance of the rules of dueling led to the death. In any event, he was condemned for his role in the affair and actually left the country to avoid prosecution. On his return, Peter married Eliza Robertson, a young Scotswoman of strict religious beliefs and practices.

Peter later speculated in railway shares, lost a great deal of money, and fled to the Continent, leaving the twenty-two-year-old Coventry and his siblings without support. Finally, in 1854, Peter published *My Friends and Acquaintances*, a book of memoirs that was poorly received and that managed to rekindle the flame of controversy surrounding the duel of years earlier. Peter died the following year.

Despite his tumultuous life, Peter was a father who encouraged Coventry's poetic gifts early in life, insisting that his son publish his first volume of poems when he was only twenty-one. Peter had always encouraged Coventry's love of literature, and the two often read and discussed various authors. Perhaps in response to his wife's stern religious beliefs, Peter offered his children no religious training, preferring to treat the Bible as merely a work in the body of literature for which he had much respect. Peter was concerned enough with Coventry's education, however, to send him to Paris in 1839 to improve his French. There Coventry fell in love with the daughter of Mrs. Gore, an English novelist who had a salon in the Place Vendôme. His love, however, was not reciprocated, and the bitterness of the af-

*Coventry Patmore* (Getty Images)

fair became entangled with his bitterly anti-French sentiments, feelings that lasted most of his lifetime. While in Paris, Coventry began to explore the question of religious belief, seeking principles by which he could live and to which he could devote his work.

In 1842, Coventry visited Edinburgh and the home of his mother's family. There the religious questioning that had begun in Paris was intensified by a personal experience that brought him in contact with the Free Kirk piety and severity that surrounded him. This discomfiting episode became entangled with his anti-Scottish sentiment, also a feeling that lasted all his life.

For some time afterward, Patmore dabbled in reading, painting, and chemistry, conducting experiments in his own laboratory. He earned a meager living by translating and writing for the periodical reviews. In 1844, at the insistence of his father, he published his first volume, *Poems*. In 1846, he was given a post at the Library of the British Museum. Two years later, he became engaged to Emily Augusta Andrews, the daughter of a Congregational minister. They were married in Hampstead in 1847.

The Patmores settled in Highgate, where they entertained such visitors as Robert Browning, Alfred, Lord Tennyson, Thomas Carlyle, and John Ruskin, not to mention Dante Gabriel Rossetti and others of the Pre-Raphaelite Brotherhood. They were very popular with their visitors and seemed to enjoy their "court" in this suburb of London.

Patmore continued his work at the British Museum, and Emily bore six children over the course of their marriage. From all that can be learned, this was indeed a happy marriage, one in which Emily felt the joys of love, home, and motherhood as much as Patmore reveled in being the "breadwinner," patron, and husband to such a family. One record of the marriage is, of course, *The Angel in the House*; the first two parts, *The Betrothal* and *The Espousals*, dealing with courtship and marriage, were published in 1854 and 1856. The second installment in this poem, titled *The Victories of Love*, was also published in two parts: *Faithful for Ever* in 1860 and *The Victories of Love* in 1862. This work anticipates and reflects the event that shattered the happiness of Patmore's fifteen years of marriage: In 1862, Emily died of tuberculosis.

Patmore never recovered from the death of his first wife. In spite of his two later marriages, it was to his first wife and marriage that he always looked when he sought inspiration. The emotional and spiritual completion—as well as the physical ecstacy—that he celebrated in *The Angel in the House* and later poems was never duplicated in his other unions.

For two years after Emily's death, Patmore continued to work at the British Museum and sought to provide the warmth and guidance for his children that would have been given by Emily. In February, 1864, at the insistence of his friend Aubrey de Vere, he obtained a leave of absence and journeyed to Rome. There, the leanings he had felt even during his marriage to the stringently anti-Catholic Emily became irresistible and he converted to the Catholic Church, being received by a Jesuit, Father Cardella.

While in Rome, Patmore met his second wife, Marianne Byles. In a small comedy of errors, Patmore first proposed to her and then learned of her personal vow to become a nun. Thinking the vow irrevocable, he withdrew his proposal. When he learned that she could easily obtain a dispensation to revoke the vow, he proposed again and was accepted. Then he learned that she was not, as he had first assumed, the poor traveling companion of a wealthy woman but was the wealthy heiress herself. Again, he withdrew to protect his freedom of idea and propriety. His friends, however, urged him to reconsider, and he agreed to the marriage. He returned to England before Mary (as she was known) to prepare his children for their new mother. In July, 1864, they were married.

This second marriage produced no children, but it provided Patmore with the opportunity to purchase an estate of four hundred acres near Uckfield in Sussex, known as Heron's Ghyll, into which his family and new wife moved in 1868; he had resigned from the British Museum in 1865. For six years, Patmore ran the estate successfully, surrounding himself with the comforts of the country and spending happy hours with his children and wife. He continued writing poetry and encouraged his wife in her literary project, a translation of Saint Bernard's *On the Necessity of Loving God* (c. 1126-1141), which was later published. In 1874, Patmore sold Heron's Ghyll to the duke of Norfolk for £27,000,

realizing a profit of £8,500; he even published a pamphlet on his success as an estate manager. In 1875, the family moved to Hastings and remained there until 1891.

In 1877, Patmore published *The Unknown Eros, and Other Odes*, a series of odes dealing primarily with the nature of human and divine love. In the same year, he made a pilgrimage to Lourdes, after which he more fully devoted himself to the Blessed Virgin. In 1878, he published his final collection of poems, *Amelia*. After 1879, he wrote virtually no poetry, concentrating rather on expressing his difficult philosophy in prose.

Mary died in 1880. In 1881, Patmore married Harriet Robson, who had entered the household as a domestic during Mary's final illness. In 1882, Emily, Patmore's daughter, who had become a sister of the Society of the Holy Child Jesus, died. One year later, Henry, the youngest of the six children by Emily, died. In that same year, Harriet gave birth to a child, Francis Epiphanius, known as Piffie. Patmore, already sixty, greatly enjoyed the delights of the child—delights that helped to offset the grief he suffered at the death of so many of his loved ones.

In 1891, the Patmores moved to Lymington, where Patmore spent the remaining five years of his life in virtual seclusion. He made occasional trips to London, wrote reviews and columns for the *St. James's Gazette*, and continued writing prose, the first collection of which had been published in 1889 and the last of which would be published in 1895, a year before his death in 1896.

ANALYSIS

The reasons for the oddly varying extremes of Coventry Patmore's reputation are not hard to find. True to his contradictory nature, Patmore was a poet who could and did speak to the "common reader" in an intelligible manner, but he often spoke of mystical and esoteric subjects far beyond the grasp—or even concern—of that same reader. He gave his audience vignettes of domestic bliss—usually of the upper-middle-class variety—offering comfort in times that seemed to threaten the nuclear family and even the British Empire's economic underpinnings, yet he included in these vignettes stark confrontations with emotional and spiritual absurdities intimately connected with the vicissitudes of love. Most significant, perhaps, he was able to couch profound psychological and emotional insights in apparently simple—and simplistic—aphorisms.

Patmore's poetry gained for him his great popularity, but his thoughts were often more adaptable to prose. It was in his poetry, however, that he was best able to reveal his artistry and his philosophy in a harmonious blend of lyrical beauty and rich perception. His poetry had for its subject one idea: love. In fact, at least 95 percent of his poems deal with love in one form or another. From his earliest musings to his last philosophical treatises in verse, he was preoccupied with the manifestations of divine and human love.

Patmore's early work betrayed his affinity with the Pre-Raphaelites in its overindulgence in description for description's sake, especially in the overabundant use of adjectives before nouns and in the awkward use of Nature as a substantive character. By the time Patmore wrote *The Angel in the House*, however, he had much better control of his language. His style underwent further change and refinement so that by the time of *The Unknown Eros, and Other Odes* he had eliminated virtually all the verbal "deadwood" from his work; even when the language fails in concision, it is usually because the thought attempted is, in itself, incommunicable. Along with control of style, Patmore gained control of emotion. His late poetry best reveals this control when he treats subjects that would easily lend themselves to the worst excesses of Victorian sentimentalism.

Although Patmore was not a systematic philosopher, he was a profound and comprehensive thinker. He undertook to explain—as well as such a phenomenon could be explained—the very idea of love, easily the most irrational, mysterious, and misunderstood of human emotions. He went even further and attempted to explain the love between God and human beings in terms of human love. What Patmore attempted was explanation and not merely the ecstatic recounting of mystical experience. In order to explain, he believed that he first had to experience and then to know his subject (ironically, a very scientific attitude for someone who despised science). He used his life as such an experiment, and his poetry is his record of the results.

## EARLY POEMS

Patmore began his poetic career, as did many of his contemporaries, under the influence of the burgeoning interest in the Middle Ages that had forced its way into many poems of the period. The poems in his first two volumes, published in 1844 and 1853, are filled with knights (both ancient and modern), long journeys on horseback through lush and wild countryside, and, of course, maidens and damsels in need of love or rescue. These early works are quite conventional and, frankly, dull. They attempt to deal with his favorite topic, love, but they stand too much in awe of the subject, afraid to assert with conviction any insight the young poet might have had. Rather, they present lovers meeting, wooing, wedding, and dying—and little else.

These poems are of interest, however, for what they reveal about Patmore's increasing poetic abilities. The earliest of them, especially, are filled with excesses of description that reflect the poet's immaturity and uncertainty. One example, from "The River," will suffice;

> The leafy summer-time is young;
> The yearling lambs are strong;
> The sunlight glances merrily;
> The trees are full of song;
> The valley-loving river flows
> Contentedly along.

It is significant to note that within six lines there are eight modifiers, words attempting to convey complete pictures in themselves but that, through their conventionality, become clichés. The diction fails to "paint" the kind of vivid word-picture the poet was aiming for. Between this early style and that of *The Angel in the House*, there is a tremendous gap—and one that shows how far Patmore had progressed by the time he published his most popular poem.

## "A LONDON FÊTE"

Of the early poems, however, one demands special attention. Titled "A London Fête," this work of forty-seven lines of four-stress iamb rhymed variously in open quatrains and couplets is unusual for Patmore. The subject is a hanging at Newgate, attended by a mob of curious and excited people. The poem is stark and realistic in its presentation of the bloodthirsty nature of the people "enjoying" this spectacle. Mothers jostle with other mothers to give their babes a good view; young girls tear their garments to provide themselves with rags to wave; sots yell out the doomed man's fate in Hell. The execution takes place, and the crowd releases a cry of joy. As they leave, one baby strings its doll to a stick, and the mother praises this "pretty trick." Two children catch and hang a cat. A pickpocket slinks off to ply his trade elsewhere. Two friends chat amicably. Two people, who fought over the best vantage point, leave to settle their score "with murderous faces."

The poem is an early revelation of Patmore's elitist politics. Throughout his life, he feared (even hated) the idea of democracy and its resultant "mob." The people depicted in this poem are that very mob: drunks, thieves, murderers, and, worst of all, mothers who do not know what is best for their children, or do not care. Although the poem gives voice to Patmore's political prejudices, it is extremely effective nevertheless. Its style is compact and journalistic; its impact is heightened by its one figure of speech: a simile comparing the howling mob to the mob of damned souls in Hell as they rejoice over the addition of another to their fold. The condemnation conveyed is so complete as to disallow any attempt at rebuttal, poetic or otherwise. What is unusual about the poem, in addition to its not being about love, is that it is concerned with one specific event treated as such and left to stand on its own. Later in his career, Patmore seemed unable to isolate and then reincorporate specific events in his poetry. In seeking the significance of the event, he sometimes felt obliged to introduce a prologue (or several) or to elaborate on the event immediately on his telling it. One of the faults of *The Angel in the House* is this insistence on commentary of occasionally excessive length. That fault, however, is nowhere to be found in this early, and quite moving, poem of political and social contempt.

### THE ANGEL IN THE HOUSE

Patmore's popularity as a poet was achieved with the publication of *The Angel in the House*. This was to be his epic poem celebrating love, woman, home, and God in six books. He finished only four of them, published separately between 1854 and 1862: *The Betrothal*, *The Espousals*, *Faithful for Ever*, and *The Victories of Love*, collectively published together as *The Angel of the House* in 1863. The first two books concern a happy marriage between two true lovers; the second two books concern a marriage that begins without mutual love but ends in a state of shared happiness; the final two books, one can conjecture, would have dealt with a good marriage gone bad or a bad marriage that remained bad.

*The Angel in the House* (the title applies to the first two books, *The Betrothal* and *The Espousals*, as well as to all four) is the story of the courtship and marriage of Felix and Honoria. The poem begins with a prologue set on their eighth anniversary and ends on their tenth. The two books, with their twelve cantos each, cover, respectively, the betrothal and the marriage. The poem is Felix's gift to his wife, as a celebration of the bliss they have enjoyed and as a record of the emotions both felt throughout the course of their love and courtship. Each canto consists of a number of preludes (usually two, but no more than five) followed by an ode that contains the main "episode" or occurrence of that canto. These odes are divided into smaller numbered units. The rhyme is open quatrain and the meter is four-stress lines, usually iambic.

The cantos provide a roughly chronological account of the courtship and marriage; the chronologically arranged material falls within the odes, while the preludes range freely, dealing with any number of questions pertaining to love but always applying them to the coming incident. How this schema works can be seen, for example, in canto 6 of book 1, "The Dean," in which Felix asks the Dean for his daughter's hand in marriage. The first prelude, "Perfect Love Rare," is a meditation on and apostrophe to love as well as a lament that, indeed, perfect (that is, pure) love is a "privilege high" to be enjoyed by only the few who merit such reward. The poet goes on to add that

> A day [in love's] delicious life
>    Though full of terrors, full of tears,
> Is better than of other life
>    A hundred thousand million years.

Thus, the opening prelude, through its conventional hyperbole, offers "evidence" of the rarity of perfect love (but, of course, hints that such rarity will be achieved in the coming match).

The next prelude, "Love Justified," is simply that, a

justification of the poet's choice of a mate—as much choice, that is, as love allows. The poet concludes the prelude by claiming that his song will prove that "This little germ of nuptial love,/ . . ./ The root is . . ./ Of all our love to man and God." From the seeking of the rare in the first prelude, the poet carries his readers in the second into the realm of the earthly and attainable and offers a "logical" justification for the action.

The third prelude, "Love Serviceable," is an even more intense call to action. Here the poet asserts that the noble lover does not care about his own fate but only about the happiness of his beloved. His quest for her is, after all, to make her happy; failure in that quest would result in both his and her lack of fulfillment and joy. Thus, he must devote his full attention to obtaining his goal, for "He does not rightly love himself/ Who does not love another more." Another strong reason for taking action is offered in this prelude as the canto progresses to the ode containing the action.

There is, however, one final prelude, "A Riddle Solved," that reads:

> Kind souls, you wonder why, love you,
>     When you, you wonder why, love none.
>     We love, Fool, for the good we do,
> Not that which unto us is done!

The riddle thus solved by the altruistic nature of true love, the canto moves to the ode, divided into four parts. Felix is visiting the Dean's family. In the first part of the ode, the ladies leave to take tea outside. In the second part, the Dean and Felix make small talk over trifling matters. In the third part, Felix makes his plea for the daughter's hand. In the fourth part, the Dean, giving him his best wishes, sends him out to woo Honoria, who is having tea. Thus, the canto focuses on the act of Felix's seeking Honoria's hand but prefaces that act with observations on the rarity of perfect love, justifications for pursuing such a rare phenomenon, and insights into the nature of true love in such pursuit. The reader is, then, quite prepared for the act and its outcome by these philosophical probings that stand at the head of each canto.

The relationship among the preludes and between the preludes and odes is well handled by Patmore and provides much of the structural integrity of this long,

thoughtful poem. By including such preludes, Patmore is able to take incidents with apparent meaning and amplify or alter such meaning to suit his didactic purpose. Usually behind such manipulation is the motive of revealing something to the readers that should have been quite obvious but was hidden by the mundaneness of the everyday occurrence. Such insight is one of the strengths of the poem.

The mundaneness of the subject matter, however, contributes to the poem's major flaw, and it is a significant one. Patmore was attempting to mold the everyday to the poetic and the poetic to the everyday. By further attempting to imitate the epic mode, he was forcing a gravity and significance on his subject matter that it simply could not bear.

The poem's other principal fault—especially from a modern reader's point of view—is the philosophy on which it is built, an extreme Victorian male chauvinism. Throughout the cantos there is constant reference to the most offensive stereotypes of women; they are foreign lands, whose customs can never be understood by men; they are frail children in need of paternalistic husbands; they are empty-headed vessels in need of men's intelligence; they are objects to be sought and possessed; they are long-suffering companions put on earth to please their men; they are parts in need of a whole. In fairness to Patmore, it must be admitted that he viewed man as equally incomplete and dependent on woman for completion, but the poet insisted on basing his philosophy on "unequal equality," and, to echo George Orwell, man was "more equal than woman"— at least in Patmore's conservative worldview.

### THE VICTORIES OF LOVE

This male chauvinism is also apparent in *The Victories of Love* (the title used to refer collectively to the third and fourth books of *The Angel in the House*, *Faithful for Ever* and *The Victories of Love*). The poem, written as a series of verse letters, is not as successful as its predecessor. It lacks a true emotional focus, its style is much less direct, and its structure is not as tightly controlled. The two books consist of nineteen and thirteen letters, respectively, written in four-stress couplets. The effect of such a scheme is monotony, which further undercuts the impact of the poem.

The "victories" of the title refer to the effort of the

two lovers whose story is unfolded through the many letters. Frederick Graham, a cousin of Honoria, is deeply in love with her when she weds Felix (at the close of *The Angel in the House*). He embarks on a long sea voyage to try to overcome his passion, but as his letters to his mother show, he is unable to do so. In desperation for "a change," he marries Jane, whom he does not really love, although she grows to love him. The remainder of the poem recounts their marriage, the births and deaths of some of their children, and their "victories" in establishing first respect, then concern, and finally love for each other. Unfortunately, Jane dies, leaving Frederick with a still-unabated passion for Honoria, a passion he again tries to lose by going to sea. He does, however, see his remaining child married to Honoria's (the subjects, perhaps, of the unwritten fifth and sixth books of the epic).

In this poem, Patmore attempts far too much. He tries to imitate prattling, gossipy old ladies in strictly rhymed couplets; he tries to convey genuine emotions regarding love and honor and felicity in verse letters; and he tries, again, to justify his view of women by placing too much of the philosophical burden on the shoulders of poor dying Jane, whose letters to her mother, mother-in-law, and husband just before her death do not escape the maudlin extremes that Patmore was usually able to avoid. Jane pleads with Frederick to accept that: "Image and glory of the man,/ As he of God, is woman. Can/ This holy, sweet proportion die/ Into a dull equality?" Perhaps Patmore himself realized the significant falling-off in effectiveness in these two books of his projected six and abandoned the idea of an epic on the Household of Love.

### THE UNKNOWN EROS, AND OTHER ODES

If *The Angel in the House* proved to be Patmore's most popular work, his final major volume of poetry, *The Unknown Eros, and Other Odes*, has certainly proved to be his best collection. This volume, also published in two parts, consists of two books, the first containing a proem and twenty-four odes, the second eighteen odes. In these odes, Patmore, loosening the hold of traditional prosody, uses a variety of meters and rhyme schemes to treat his favorite topic—love—and his next-favorite topic—the political and social decline of England and its empire. As a poet of analogies, Patmore

saw the similarities in his love for woman and for God and his love for his country. Likewise, he saw the decline and death of his beloved as a reflection of the decline and death of his beloved country, and vice versa. These analogies appear throughout the odes, both explicitly and implicitly. In fact, the poet boldly announces in the proem that it may be "England's parting soul that nerves [his] tongue" and gives him the impetus to break his years of silence with these odes designed to restore to his beloved (woman and country) some of the luster lost by either death or dying.

Part of the strength of these odes lies in their variety of subject and mode. Here Patmore's prosody, more relaxed and much more colloquial, comes closer to capturing the essence of speech he so vainly sought in his earlier works; these odes seem almost effortless in their flow and offer no resistance to the reader in terms of language. They may, however, continue to resist the reader in terms of the density of their thought, the political theories expounded, or the philosophical basis of the majority of the observations. In spite of such barriers, these odes succeed as no other of Patmore's poems do in their eloquence, their emotional impact, and their profundity.

The first twelve odes in the first book form a thematic unit on love and denial of love by death; the odes are probably based on Patmore's experience with his first wife, Emily. The first few odes focus on time and its passage. Beginning with the fifth ode, there is a distinct unit on his loss at the death of his wife, on his memory of her, on his fears and hopes, and on his remarriage. These poems are some of the finest Patmore wrote, containing emotions that manage to travel more than a century between then and now with grace and meaning. "The Azalea," "Departure," and, especially, "The Toys" show Patmore at his most mature and controlled; he is able, as few of his contemporaries were, to touch a poignant note lightly enough to allow the reverberations to have their full impact on the reader. There is moralizing here, and some preaching as well, but all is blended with a sensitivity unsurpassed in his other work, including his best prose. That sensitivity is well reflected in his superbly economical style; here is one example from "Eurydice," in which he addresses his lost mate:

Thee, whom ev'n more than Heaven loved I have,
And yet have not been true
Even to thee,
I dreaming, night by night, seek now to see,
And, in a mortal sorrow, still pursue
Thro' sordid streets and lanes. . . .

Here, as in his earliest work, there is an abundance of modifiers; but now each one is charged with meaning, effectively holding readers before allowing them to move on to the next complementary and expansive link in an emotional chain.

True to his extremes, Patmore balances his best with some of his worst poetry in these odes. His political odes are not nearly as successful as the personal, nor are they, in themselves, good verse. They are marred by long-windedness, awkward lines, and, too often, repugnant ideas.

The second book of odes continues the mixture of personal and political observations but contains some of his most difficult work, the odes in which he uses the classical myths to expound his ideas on human and divine love. Some of them simply do not fulfill their intention, and most of the political odes are also unsuccessful. The personal poems, however, such as "The Child's Purchase," are generally very moving.

### LATER POEMS

After *The Unknown Eros, and Other Odes*, Patmore wrote very few poems, and these are generally rather bland when they are not offensive. For example, *Amelia* returns to the theme of the sacrificing woman and has a young girl weep over the grave of her lover's former betrothed; that, however, is not enough: She actually takes the dead woman's ring and swears to wear it for her sake because "dear to maidens are their rivals dead." Here Patmore succeeds in straining—some would say rupturing—plausibility, as he does in "The Girl of All Periods," in which a "feminist" who smokes cigarettes and reads George Sand is "put in her place" by a few sly male compliments.

Patmore insisted that his poetry was not original, in meter or insight. He even abhorred the charge of "originality" when he heard it applied to himself. By this insistence on drawing from wells already much frequented, Patmore placed himself as a poet in a very

vulnerable position. Even profound insights can become monotonous if they are constantly delivered in simple aphorisms. To that temptation to be aphoristic, Patmore too often succumbed. It is unfortunate that so much of his best poetry and his best thought lie buried. Whether this arch-conservative Victorian poet's work will again be popularly read is open to question. What is certain is this: His works deserve attention.

### OTHER MAJOR WORKS

NONFICTION: *Essay on English Metrical Law*, 1856; *Bryan Waller Procter*, 1877; *How I Managed and Improved My Estate*, 1888; *Principle in Art*, 1889; *Religio Poetæ*, 1893; *Rod, Root, and Flower*, 1895; *Memoirs and Correspondence of Coventry Patmore*, 1900 (Basil Champneys, editor).

MISCELLANEOUS: *Works*, 1907.

### BIBLIOGRAPHY

Anstruther, Ian. *Coventry Patmore's Angel: A Study of Coventry Patmore, His Wife Emily, and "The Angel in the House."* London: Haggerston Press, 1992. A short biographical study of Patmore and his wife. Includes bibliographical references and index.

Crook, J. Mordaunt. "Coventry Patmore and the Aesthetics of Architecture." *Victorian Poetry* 34, no. 4 (Winter, 1996): 519-543. Crook discusses Patmore as an architectural critic of extraordinary power and perhaps the most eloquent expositor of architectural style.

Fisher, Benjamin F. "The Supernatural in Patmore's Poetry." *Victorian Poetry* 34, no. 4 (Winter, 1996): 544-557. An examination of supernaturalism in Patmore's work. Suggests that careful readers will discover ghosts, vampires, and hauntings recurring in Patmore's poetry.

Fontana, Ernest. "Patmore and Dickinson: Angels, Cochineal, and Polar Expiation." *Emily Dickinson Journal* 13, no. 1 (2004): 1-18. Discusses Emily Dickinson's familiarity with Patmore's *The Angel in the House* and several poems she may have written in response to what she read in that collection.

Gosse, Edmund. *Coventry Patmore.* New York: Charles Scribner's Sons, 1905. The earliest book-length critical study published on Patmore, designed to complement the "official" biography of the Patmore family published by Basil Champneys. Full of anecdotes and personal accounts, it is nevertheless an important critical work on Patmore.

Oliver, E. J. *Coventry Patmore*. New York: Sheed & Ward, 1956. A short, accessible biography on Patmore. Discusses love as the focus of his life, his family, and his mystical leanings that put him at odds with clericalism. Examines the importance of place and background in his poems.

Pinch, Adela. "Love Thinking." *Victorian Studies* 50, no. 3 (Spring, 2008): 379-397. This article on love in the Victorian era uses "The Kiss" from *The Angel in the House* as a starting point. Pinch does not like Patmore's poetry and criticizes his choice of meter.

Reid, John Cowie. *Mind and Art of Coventry Patmore*. London: Routledge & Kegan Paul, 1957. This full-length study of Patmore explores the influences on Patmore and his thought, and his "doctrine" of love as expressed in his poems. Particularly noteworthy is the chapter on the odes. Includes an extensive bibliography.

Weinig, Mary Anthony. *Coventry Patmore*. Boston: Twayne, 1981. An appreciative introduction to Patmore, noting that his poems are "rooted in immediate experience of life and love and marriage." Contains strong critical commentary on *The Angel in the House* and *Faithful for Ever*. Includes a separate section on his odes, which Weinig considers the best access to Patmore for the modern reader.

*Richard F. Giles*

---

# PEARL-POET

**Flourished:** England(?); fl. latter half of the fourteenth century
**Also known as:** Gawain-Poet

PRINCIPAL POETRY

*Saint Erkenwald*, 1386? or late fifteenth century (if earlier date, often attributed to the Pearl-Poet)
*Cleanness*, c. 1400 (also known as *Purity*)

*Patience*, c. 1400
*Pearl*, c. 1400
*Sir Gawain and the Green Knight*, c. 1400

OTHER LITERARY FORMS

Even though the Pearl-Poet experimented with a variety of genres, he is best remembered for his four Middle English poems.

ACHIEVEMENTS

The work of the Pearl-Poet (also called the Gawain-Poet after his other major poem) was essentially lost until the nineteenth century. *Sir Gawain and the Green Knight* was first edited in 1839, to be followed twenty-five years later by the other three poems of the manuscript. Over the past hundred years, these poems (whose titles are modern, not found in the manuscript) have gained a secure place in Middle English poetry. Although attention has focused on *Pearl* and *Sir Gawain and the Green Knight*, considered masterpieces of their respective genres, the two verse homilies have more recently been the objects of much critical study as well.

A contemporary of Geoffrey Chaucer, the Pearl-Poet has often been compared to medieval England's most famous poet. Like Chaucer, he worked in a variety of genres and experimented with various verse forms. His poetry, like Chaucer's, shows a knowledge not only of the Bible and its commentaries but also of the new vernacular literature of the Continent. Again like Chaucer, he analyzes moral issues in narratives that create characters who are often unaware or confused by their situations. However, the Pearl-Poet must be judged apart from Chaucer, for he worked in a distinctly different poetic tradition, that of the alliterative revival, not Chaucer's French courtly style.

The poetry that flourished in northern and western England in the second half of the fourteenth century probably continued and modified (rather than reinvented) the Old English accentual and alliterative line. In contrast to the verse forms employed by Chaucer, which became the usual patterns of most English poetry after his time, the alliterative long line concentrates on stresses alone and does not count syllables. The unrhymed long lines of *Cleanness* and *Patience*, for example, include four key stresses generally separated into two half lines by a caesura, the first three stresses falling on alliterating syllables. The pattern may be diagramed as follows: Á Á ns Á X́. These alliterative long lines (sometimes grouped in quatrains), skillfully developed by the Pearl-Poet, impart a surprisingly dramatic and active feeling to *Cleanness* and *Patience*. The alliterative tendency toward variation and realistic description prevents the verse homilies from disappearing into the mist of abstraction.

In *Sir Gawain and the Green Knight*, the poet turns again to this traditional form, but arranges the lines in descriptive and narrative stanzas of varying length, rounded off by five shorter alliterating lines comprising a "bob and wheel," a device not unique to the poet but most skillfully employed by him. The one-stress line of the "bob" and the four three-stressed lines of the "wheel" rhyme *ababa*. These rhyming lines impart rhythmic variety to the poem and serve to sum up the major topic of the stanza and to emphasize key images and themes.

The mixture of alliteration and rhyme is more thorough in *Pearl*. Departing more freely from the tradition of the alliterative long line in the direction of the octosyllabic line of Chaucer's early poetry, *Pearl* is composed of 101 twelve-line stanzas, which resemble in both form and spirit the sonnet of later English poetry. Each stanza develops three rhymes in linked quatrains (*ababababbcbc*). These tightly structured stanzas are further grouped into twenty larger sections through the concluding repetition of key words and phrases forming a refrain for each stanza. The larger sections are also linked by concatenation, the device of repeating a key word from the final line of a previous stanza in the first line of a following stanza. These intricate poetic devices perfectly mirror the intricacy of the themes and arguments of the *Pearl*, a poem highly admired for its form and considered by Thorlac Turville-Petre in *The Alliterative Revival* (1977) to be "the finest of all the poems in rhyming alliterative stanzas."

In addition to the four poems that constitute the unique British Library manuscript, Cotton Nero A.x. (c. 1400), *Saint Erkenwald*, an alliterative poem describing the miraculous life of a seventh century bishop of London, has been attributed to the Pearl-Poet. Since 1882, scholars have argued that *Saint Erkenwald* shares a common diction, a similar style and dialect, and a peculiar phraseology with the poems of the Pearl-Poet. They further argue that *Saint Erkenwald* may be dated 1386, when the feast days of the bishop saint were given special status in London, thus making it contemporary with the Cotton Nero poems.

One modern editor of *Saint Erkenwald*, Clifford Peterson, however, has suggested an early fifteenth century date for the poem, which is extant only in a late fifteenth century manuscript. Scholarship, furthermore, has cast doubt on the attribution by showing that the common language is not unique to these poems and by arguing that the similar stylistic elements are best understood as reflecting the formulaic character of alliterative poetry. Therefore, it is best to limit the corpus of the Pearl-Poet to the four poems of the Cotton Nero manuscript.

BIOGRAPHY

As W. A. Davenport has aptly remarked, "Though the Gawain-poet may not have existed, it has proved necessary to invent him." Certainly, there is no external evidence to "prove" that the four poems found only in a single manuscript are by a single poet. It may be that the poems were crafted by a small school of poets working together closely at a court in the northwest Midlands during the late fourteenth century. As A. C. Spearing has argued, however, the principle of Ockham's razor suggests that it is more reasonable to postulate that the Pearl-Poet was a single poet of genius writing in a unique Middle English dialect (probably north Cheshire or south Lancashire, but with Scottish, French, and Scandinavian forms). The poems share to a remarkable extent imagery, diction, and stylistic features that cannot be entirely accounted for by a common alliterative tradition. More important, readers of the four poems are continually impressed by what Malcolm Andrew and Ronald Waldron, two of the poems' editors, have called a "conviction of an individual poetic personality" and an "unbroken consistency of thought." The analysis of the four poems below will suggest, moreover, that they are thematically related.

Nevertheless, the Pearl-Poet remains unknown. The manuscript can help scholars locate him approximately in place and time, and the poems can provide clues to his interests and knowledge. Like other poets working in the alliterative revival, he perhaps was attached to the household of an aristocrat of the northwest Midlands. The manuscript (probably not in the poet's hand) includes twelve rough illustrations of the four poems (published in Charles Moorman's 1977 edition of the manuscript), suggesting to some that the poet may have had the support of a wealthy patron. Certainly, the poems reflect a familiar knowledge of court life, as well as an interest in contemporary religious issues, a thorough knowledge of the Vulgate Bible and its commentaries, and some awareness of French poetry and perhaps even the poetry of Dante and Giovanni Boccaccio. Some scholars have argued that the descriptions, debates, and specialized diction of the poems suggest that the poet was trained as a priest or a lawyer, that he may have sailed or been, like Chaucer, on a diplomatic mission. Such arguments, however, deduced as they are from the four poems, provide little help in understanding his poetry.

Even more fruitless and really very misleading are the various attempts to identify the poet with certain historical figures of the late fourteenth century. These nominees have included Ralph Strode, the Oxford philosopher referred to by Chaucer in *Troilus and Criseyde* (1382); the poet Huchown of the Awle Ryale; and other names from the period, such as John Erghome, John Prat, and Hugo de Mascy or John Massey or simply the "maister Massy" praised by Thomas Hoccleve. What readers would gain should such scholarly speculation finally attach a name to the Pearl-Poet is not clear, for modern interest in the poet is the result of interest in his superb poetry, and it is unlikely that the little which is known about these candidates for poetic fame will affect interpretations of the poems.

*An eighteenth century illustration from Pearl-Poet's* Sir Gawain and the Green Knight *(c. 1400).* (Hulton Archive/Getty Images)

ANALYSIS

All four poems attributed to the Pearl-Poet reflect a great concern with establishing the distinctions between the temporal and sublunary viewpoint of human beings and the eternal and unvarying positions of God. This outlook is not uncommon in the art and thought of the later Middle Ages. It is the foundation of scholastic thought. Like scholasticism, furthermore, the arts were not content to establish only the distinctions between human and divine; they sought also to merge and synthesize the sacred and the secular. As long as the hierarchy of values was kept clear, allegiance to the divine and the human need not be in contradiction; it was possible to serve, for example, both the Virgin Mary and the courtly lady. However, if human sinfulness and obstinacy reversed the hierarchy, placing the earthly garden of delights above the promise of paradise regained, then the synthesis of earthly and divine was shattered and humans were left to inherit the results of their folly.

The Pearl-Poet was thus an artist of his time not only in distinguishing between the earthly and the heavenly but also in showing how the two spheres could merge and interrelate. His greatness, however, lies in his sympathetic investigation of humanity's situation in the face of the divine. Humans as creatures are subordinate to their creator, and there is no room for doubt that human rebelliousness is disastrous, because the Lord can become "wonder wroth." However, as Andrew and Waldron conclude, the poet shares "a spirit of sympathetic identification with human frailty besides a zealous dedication to ideal virtue."

The distinctions between, yet juxtaposition of, human desires and divine standards are explored by the Pearl-Poet by concentrating on three ideals. These encompass a variety of social and Christian values, best summed up by the concepts of cleanness (understood as the divine requirement of purity in both body and soul), of truthfulness to duty and to God (and thus including loyalty, obedience, and faithfulness), and of courtesy (a chivalric ideal given religious significance by the poet).

In three of the four poems, the poet creates a major character with whom readers sympathize yet who must come to learn of the differing values of humankind and the divine. In these poems, the major characters undergo a three-part mysterious journey: in *Patience*, a voyage in the belly of a whale; in *Pearl*, a visionary pilgrimage glimpsing the New Jerusalem; and in *Sir Gawain and the Green Knight*, a fantastic quest to meet an enchanted opponent. The characters face a divine or supernatural demand or challenge and are left quite befuddled, surprised, or overwhelmed by what they experience. More important, in each poem, the character is moved from a narrowly human and basically self-centered outlook to an awareness of humanity's essentially subordinate and often ignorant position in relation to the divine. Surprisingly, none of the characters has changed drastically by the end of the poems, although readers are left to assume that the new perspectives they have gained will lead to such change.

The fourth poem, *Cleanness*, also shares this three-part movement, but it presents not a journey of a single character to a mysterious or foreign land, but the history of humankind as outlined in the Old Testament and interpreted within the context of the New Testament. By concentrating on three key moments when the di-

vine intervened in human history, the poem highlights the results of humanity's unwillingness to conform to the divine.

The four poems of the Pearl-Poet are of great artistic merit. In verse of great beauty, they include passages of vigorous narrative, realistic description, and dramatic intensity. They describe extremely violent situations as well as peaceful gardens, sailors as well as an enchanted green knight, the suffering of the dying as well as the joy of the saved. Drawing from a wide range of sources yet including much that is original, the poems are carefully crafted and structured. They are compelling not only for their presentation of deeply moral and human concerns, but also for their imaginative power.

### PATIENCE

The Pearl-Poet's shortest and most simply structured poem, *Patience*, is a verse homily teaching the need for humans to submit their will to God and to act faithfully and humbly. Like traditional medieval sermons, it establishes this theme in an introductory prologue and illustrates it in an exemplum, a narrative example intended to support the preacher's main argument. In the case of *Patience*, the narrative centers on the prophet Jonah. It is a dramatic expansion of the biblical account found in the Book of Jonah.

The poet's choice of Jonah may seem odd, since the usual Old Testament figure representing patience is Job. The poet may have felt that the best way to explore the virtue of patience (which might be viewed as rather passive and uninteresting) was through negative examples (as, again, in *Cleanness*). Certainly Jonah's sulking pride and abortive attempt to flee from the command of God serve as examples of what patience is not. It may also be that Jonah was selected because, although his human rationalizing and severely limited understanding of God's nature place him in conflict with the divine, he does ultimately accept the will of God. Finally, Jonah's figurative significance in medieval exegesis as an Old Testament type of Christ may be significant. As evident in numerous commentaries and sermons, and in popular literature, Jonah's three-day entombment within the belly of the whale typifies the death of Christ and his resurrection on the third day.

The association of Old Testament story with New Testament event is not unusual in medieval poetry. Medieval theology understood the Old Testament as pre-figuring the New, and often interpreted the stories of the Jewish people as signifying Christian belief. The story of Jonah is thus told by the poet to exemplify the beatitudes preached by Christ in the Sermon on the Mount. These are recited in the prologue of *Patience*, and it is the last beatitude, interpreted as Christ's promise of heaven for those who endure patiently, that provides the poet's theme. The beatitudes certainly are classic examples of Christ's teaching that false earthly goals and aspirations are not to be confused with the true ideals of Heaven. Whereas humans seek riches, boldness, pleasure, and power, Christ praises poverty, meekness, purity, and patience. *Patience* tells how Jonah must come to recognize the distinction between human and divine to act truthfully and to obtain the mercy of God.

Although the four divisions of *Patience* in the manuscript accord with the four chapters of the biblical account, the poem's narrative actually moves in three parts: First, Jonah desperately attempts to avoid the command of God, rejects his role as prophet, and sets sail to escape the power of God; second, after being swallowed by the whale, he accepts his duty and faithfully obeys God and prophesies the destruction of Nineveh; third, while sulking because Nineveh is not destroyed, he learns of God's grace, love, and mercy.

Jonah is at first the epitome of humanity's foolish opposition to God. The poet sympathetically imagines Jonah's motives for rejecting the prophetic mission and presents his fear as understandable; nevertheless, Jonah's flight from God, his attempt to hide, is obviously ridiculous. The God who created the world, the poet ironically comments, has no power over the sea. The power of the creator over his creation, however, becomes clear to all. Even the pagan sailors who at first pray to Diana and Neptune learn to worship the Hebrew God. At the height of the storm, Jonah, wakened from his unnatural sleep, recognizes the Creator's power and identifies himself to the sailors as a follower of the world's Creator. From this point, Jonah submits himself to the will of God and, in the belly of the whale, learns to act faithfully as a prophet.

He also prays for mercy, but it is not until the third part of the story, after Jonah has prophesied the destruc-tion of Nineveh and its citizens actually repent, that the prophet of God learns the true nature of God's grace. Although now aware of the awesome power of God over his creation, Jonah remains earthbound in his attitudes. When Nineveh is saved, he feels humiliated. Again, rather than accepting God's will (the ultimate meaning of patience for the Pearl-Poet), Jonah reacts angrily, sulks childishly, and wishes he were dead. His wish does not come true, however, and through the remainder of the narrative Jonah learns that God not only controls but also loves his creatures.

Interestingly, in condemning what he does not understand, Jonah sets forth one of the major themes developed in the works of the Pearl-Poet: the bounty of God's grace. This grace is described in chivalric terms, as God's courtesy, and is linked to God's patience. Jonah prays for mercy in the belly of the whale, but now desires—because of his pride in preaching the very prophecy that he sought to avoid—that God turn against the repentant Nineveh and destroy the city. While the Lord patiently seeks to change him, Jonah's final attitude is not made clear, since the poet suddenly concludes with his epilogue urging patient acceptance of one's position and mission in life. The last lines of the narrative are the words of God, whose patience is displayed not only toward Nineveh but also toward Jonah. Thus, although the career of Jonah may be a negative example of patience, the courtesy of God reflected in his patience and grace becomes the positive representation of ideal patience.

### CLEANNESS

The poet's much longer verse homily *Cleanness* (sometimes called *Purity*) also mixes negative and positive examples, although there is no doubt that the negative receives the bulk of his attention and that God's righteous wrath, rather than his patience, becomes most evident. Again, one of Christ's beatitudes provides the theme: "Blessed is he whose heart is clean for he shall look on the Lord." The promise to the blessed clean, however, is not developed as much as the threat of damnation for the unclean. In his prologue, for example, the poet concentrates on yet another New Testament passage, Christ's parable of the wedding feast. This rather harsh analogy comparing the kingdom of heaven to a king who has a guest thrown out of a wedding feast because he is improperly dressed receives a lengthy exposition, concluding with a list of the forms of uncleanness by which humans hurl themselves into the devil's throat.

In his conclusion, the poet notes that he has given three examples of how uncleanness drives the Lord to wrath. These three Old Testament examples are arranged in chronological order, thus establishing the poem's three-part movement through the history of salvation: from the destruction of the world by the Flood, through the annihilation of Sodom and Gomorrah by fire, and finally to the overpowering of "the bold Belshazzar." The three are linked by shorter Old Testament stories as well. The Flood is introduced by the fall of Lucifer and the angels, leading to the fall of Adam; the destruction of the two cities is preceded by the stories of Abraham and Lot and their two wives; and Belshazzar's feast is interwoven with the fall of Jerusalem under Nebuchadnezzar and his eventual conversion.

Like the story of Jonah, the Old Testament stories retold in *Cleanness* have typological significance in medieval theology. Each of the three major examples of God's wrath prefigures the Last Judgment. Combined with accounts of the fall of Lucifer and the origin of sin, this typological significance gives the poem a universal sweep from creation to doomsday, symbolically encompassing the entire Christian understanding of history. The emphasis, however, is on judgment, which is clearly the moral of the introductory parable of the wedding feast: "Many are called but few are chosen."

Judgment is particularly severe against the unclean, for the Lord of heaven "hates hell no more than them that are filthy." The concept of cleanness includes innocence, ceremonial propriety, decency and naturalness, physical cleanliness, and moral righteousness. Their opposites are encompassed by the concept of filth, which includes all manner of vices, sacrilege, sodomy, lust, and the arrogance of spirit that elevates humanity's earthly desires above God's requirement of truthfulness. God floods the world because sinfulness is out of control. Not only did humanity sin against nature, but devils copulated with human beings, engendering a breed of violent giants as well. Similarly, the Sodom-

ites practiced unnatural vices, filling a land that was once like paradise thick with filth so that it sunk into the earth under the weight of its own sins. The Lord is equally angered by blasphemy and sacrilege, as Belshazzar learns when he defiles the vessels of the temple in "unclean vanity."

Lack of truthfulness, although not arousing the violent wrath of God to the same extent as lack of cleanness, is represented in the minor exempla of the poem. The stories of Lucifer and Adam exemplify the results of disobedience. Sarah's mocking the word of God when told she would bear a child reflects human lack of faith, for she prefers worldly reason to divine wisdom. Lot's wife is turned into a pillar of salt for two faults, the results of her "mistruth." She disobeyed a direct command not to look at the doomed Sodom, and she set salted food before the two angels, thus angering the Lord for her ritual uncleanness. King Zedekiah and the Jewish nation were similarly found untruthful; they proved disloyal to their duties as God's chosen people and blasphemously worshiped idols.

The minor examples suggest that the lack of truthfulness is the cause of the uncleanness that ultimately leads to humankind's doom. They also expand the concept of filth beyond sexual misconduct to include the improper relationship between the natural and the supernatural, leading to unnatural perversion and sacrilege. Thus, the sexual intercourse of fallen angels and sinful human beings is punished by the Flood because it represents unnaturalness on a cosmic scale. The Sodomite attempt to attack sexually the two angels visiting Lot is the most villainous example of their sacrilege. Although Lot's attempt to shift their lust from the angels to his two virgin daughters seems horrible, it is an attempt to keep the city's perversion on a human scale. Belshazzar's profanation of the sacred vessels consecrated to God is the final example of humanity's blasphemous desire to overturn the proper relationship between the human and the divine.

This long series of Old Testament stories linking untruthfulness to uncleanness is, luckily, broken by a few representatives of truth and cleanness: Noah, Abraham, Lot in his hospitality, the prophet Daniel, and Nebuchadnezzar after his conversion. This right relationship between humanity and God evident in truth and cleanness is, furthermore, described by the poet in terms of courtesy. After the Flood, for example, God promises never to send another universal deluge and establishes humans once again as they were before the Fall—as ruler over Earth. This new covenant between God and Noah is described by the poet as spoken in courteous words. As in *Patience*, the Pearl-Poet understands God's mercy and grace as reflecting divine courtesy. Early in the Introduction to *Cleanness*, for example, he couples the need for purity with courtesy. Similarly, when explaining how the divine became human, the poet notes that Christ came in both cleanness and courtesy, accepting and healing all who "called on that courtesy and claimed his grace." Here, then, is the key to the right relationship between the human and the divine.

## PEARL

Less overtly didactic than *Cleanness* and *Patience*, *Pearl* sets forth its main ideas by creating two characters: a dreamer who mourns the loss of a pearl and a beautiful young girl who speaks in a dream from the vantage of heaven. The dreamer, who narrates the poem in the first person, is earthbound in his outlook, mourning and complaining, like Jonah in *Patience*, against his fate. He rather foolishly debates theological issues with the visionary maiden, who speaks with divine wisdom. This relationship between a naïve narrator and an authority figure representing truthfulness is typical of the poem's genre: the dream vision. Such is evident in the early but highly influential *De consolatione philosophiae* (523; *The Consolation of Philosophy*, late ninth century) by the philosopher Boethius, as well as in the masterpiece of the genre, William Langland's *The Vision of William Concerning Piers the Plowman* (c. 1362, A Text; c. 1377, B Text; c. 1393, C Text; also known as *Piers Plowman*). The human dreamer, schooled by the agent of the divine, is also a feature of the New Testament Book of Revelation, the poem's most important source. However, the rather passive role of John during his apocalyptic visions is avoided by the poet. *Pearl*, as Spearing and others have noted, presents its teachings by means of "a dramatic encounter."

Unfortunately, attention has been diverted from analysis of this dramatic encounter by the scholarly arguments attempting to identify the meaning of the lost pearl. According to some scholars, the lost pearl represents the poet's daughter (and the poem thus is an elegy in her memory), who died at a "young and tender age" before she was two. Postulating such an occurrence may help explain the dreamer's mourning at the beginning of the poem, but the problem with reading the poem as an elegy is that it identifies the foolish narrator with the poet and equates the dream's fiction with historical and biographical events about which nothing is known. Certainly it is not the case, as A. C. Cawley writes in the introduction to his edition of the poem, that "there would be no poem" if the poet's daughter had not died—or that the poet in *Pearl* "was recording an actual vision he had experienced."

On the other hand, rejecting the naïve biographical reading of the poem as an elegy for the poet's daughter need not imply that those who argue that the poem is an allegory are closer to the truth. This reading interprets the pearl as representing some Christian concept or ideal that has been lost or misunderstood. Identifications, all with limitations, include the purified soul, virginity and innocence, the grace of God, and even the Eucharist. However, *Pearl* is not a consistent allegory in the tradition of *Everyman* or John Bunyan's *The Pilgrim's Progress* (1678, 1684). Its characters and objects are not static but dynamic, symbols that shift as the dreamer gains fuller self-knowledge and greater awareness of the divine.

The growth in the dreamer's knowledge takes place as the poem moves through three settings. The narrator at first describes a beautiful garden, luxurious in its growth. This ideal earthly garden is nevertheless time-bound. In August at the height of the season, it blooms with flowers and natural beauty, but the garden is subject to change and all will decay. It is here that the narrator has lost his pearl, here that he comes to mourn, mortally wounded by his loss, and here that he falls asleep, his spirit setting forth on a marvelous adventure while his body remains in the garden. At this point, the pearl is to be understood as a lost jewel, "pleasant for a prince," perfect, round, radiant, smooth, and without spot. The narrator's grief over the loss of this precious but earthly object, however, is to be judged as excessive. The narrator seems vaguely aware of his problem, since he refers to his "wretched will," but he must learn to put his treasure in heavenly, not earthly, things.

The second setting is introduced immediately. Now the dreamer finds himself in another garden, even more radiant and dazzling than the first. The dreamer is in a garden that is beyond change, a beautiful setting that makes him forget all grief. This is the Earthly Paradise lost by Adam for his sin and reached by Dante near the conclusion of his ascension through Purgatory in *La divina commedia* (c. 1320, 3 volumes; *The Divine Comedy*, 1802), a possible source for *Pearl*. Here, the dreamer comes to a river which he cannot cross and on the far bank sees a beautiful, gleaming maiden dressed in white. She is associated with the pearl by her appearance and purity and by the fact that she is adorned with pearls. Whether or not this association implies an elegiac reading of the poem, it is clear that the maiden (and thus the pearl) represents the beauty, perfection, and eternity of the soul beyond the ravages of place and time. The maiden identifies herself as the bride of Christ, a traditional symbol for the righteous soul, derived from Revelation 19:7-9. Her status as bride and her position in Heaven will become the main focus of her debate with the dreamer.

The poem's third setting, the New Jerusalem, is described by the pearl maiden and only glimpsed by the dreamer. This setting is clearly beyond the reach of the dreamer as long as he lives, at least in this world. When he foolishly attempts to cross the river separating the earthly paradise where he stands from the New Jerusalem whence the pearl maiden speaks, he is startled from his dream and awakes to find himself in the very garden where he fell asleep. However, this third setting, along with the maiden's discussion of Christ's parable of the pearl of great price, provides yet another significance of the pearl—Heaven itself. The maiden's advice to the dreamer is to forsake the mad world and purchase Heaven, the spotless and matchless pearl. He is, she scolds, too concerned with his earthly jewel.

The close associations of the pearl with smoothness and with roundness, whiteness, and brightness are extended in the poem so that the pearl comes to symbolize perfection and purity. The traditional symbolic significance of the circle and sphere as representing the soul and eternity is also developed in the poem, both in its imagery and in its symmetrical structure, with each stanza linked by concatenation from beginning to end. This linking device has been compared to a chain and to a rosary. The poem's final line, furthermore, echoes its first, the 101 stanzas implying not only the completion of a full circle but also the beginning of another. The whole suggests eternity. The centrality of the number twelve, traditionally the apocalyptic number, is also appropriate; it appears repeatedly in the Book of Revelation. Thus, the image of the pearl, the vision of Heaven, and the poem itself merge into one. As Thorlac Turville-Petre concludes, "Heaven, the pearl and the poem are all constructed with the same flawless circularity, an idea which reflects the words at the beginning and the end of the Apocalypse: 'I am Alpha and Omega, the beginning and the end, saith the Lord.'"

Thematically the poem is also concerned with Heaven and its perfect nature, order, and ideals. Much of *Pearl* develops a debate between the pearl maiden and the obtuse earthbound dreamer. As in *Cleanness*, a parable of Christ is at the center of the poem's teaching. The parable of the workers in the vineyard is particularly suitable, because it represents sharply the distinction between humanity's sense of worth and reward based on reason and a general sense of fairness and God's loving gifts of mercy and grace tendered equally to all. Christ tells how the owner of the vineyard pays those workers who labored for only an hour the same amount as those who labored all day. This apparent unfairness elicits protests and grumbling from the latter, and the dreamer foolishly allies himself with them by similarly complaining to the pearl maiden. The earthly expectation is simply not met in Heaven. The parable makes the point cogently: The last will be first and the first last.

From the divine perspective, no human is worthy of Heaven. Salvation is a gift of God. This gift is an example, the pearl maiden argues, of God's courtesy. Thus, although the ideals of cleanness and truthfulness remain important in *Pearl*, the poet here concentrates on the ideal of courtesy as his basis for exploring the nature of Heaven. God is portrayed as a noble and courteous chieftain, and the Virgin Mary is known not only as the Queen of Heaven—her traditional title—but also Queen of Courtesy. All the righteous become, in fact, kings and queens, members of the chivalric court of equals because they are members of Christ's body through courtesy. The poem thus expands the traditionally social virtues of the chivalric ideal into a religious concept with a wide range of applications. In addition to the usual sense of the term to signify good breeding, proper speech, kind manners, and unhesitating generosity, in *Pearl*, courtesy connotes as well the freely given grace of God and the loving relationship between humanity and the divine lost on Earth through sin but available in Heaven.

### SIR GAWAIN AND THE GREEN KNIGHT

As a romance in the chivalric tradition dealing with knights of renown and beautiful courtly ladies, *Sir Gawain and the Green Knight* quite naturally also examines the ideal of courtesy. It is not discussed as a characteristic of Heaven, for the romance limits its focus to earthly heroes and events, although they may be superhuman and altogether marvelous. Courtesy is examined as a characteristic of the Arthurian court and especially of Gawain, the nephew of King Arthur, a favorite of the charming ladies of the court, and the epitome of chivalry. His character does, however, merge secular ideals with religious devotion. This merger is evident in his elaborate shield, described and explained at length by the poet. Decorated with a pentangle, the "endless knot" suggesting eternal ideals, the shield reflects not only Gawain's bravery, generosity, truthfulness, cleanness, and courtesy, but also his devotion to the five wounds of Christ and the five joys of the Virgin. However, through the mysterious challenge of the Green Knight, Gawain and the chivalric ideas he represents are both tested severely. When the requirements of courtesy come into conflict with truthfulness and cleanness, even the perfect knight may fail.

Although the poem is generally divided into four parts, the testing of the knight takes place as the hero moves through three locales. At first, Gawain is portrayed at the Arthurian court, feasting over Christmas and celebrating the New Year with King Arthur, the knights of the Round Table, and Queen Guinevere. Here he is tested in his duty as a knight when the reputation of Camelot is threatened. Acting courteously and bravely, he accepts the challenge of the Green Knight, whom he beheads—only to be told by the enchanted figure that Gawain's turn for the return blow will come

in a year and a day. As J. A. Burrow notes, this test of courage in combat is the easiest for Gawain to pass, for it involves an obvious knightly virtue—truthfulness to his word—in conflict with the desire for life, and brave knights often face such challenges successfully.

The hero's second locale is the court of Bertilak at Hautdesert, where a year later Gawain rests on his journey to meet the unknown Green Knight. Here, Gawain is welcomed in a chivalric court and undergoes a much more subtle test. At this court, the ideals of truthfulness and cleanness come into conflict with the demands of courtesy. Burrow sees Gawain here as "subjected to one of the most complex and elaborately contrived test situations in all medieval literature." After agreeing with Bertilak to exchange each evening whatever he gains during the day, Gawain is tempted by Bertilak's beautiful wife. She approaches him in bed for three mornings, calling on his reputation as a courtly lover. Gawain must overcome this threat to cleanness and loyalty to his host while remaining courteous to the lady. This he accomplishes through his great talent for gentle speech. Each morning, the lady settles for a kiss from Gawain, which he passes on to his host each evening. The host, who has spent his days hunting, similarly gives Gawain his winnings. On the third morning, however, apparently successful in turning back the lady's sexual advances, Gawain accepts a green girdle from her. That evening, he does not give it to Bertilak, ostensibly because he would be discourteous in revealing the lady's gift, but also because the green girdle's magical powers will protect him when he faces the Green Knight the following day. Thus, in one decision, Gawain fails the test of truthfulness by breaking his word to Bertilak, and the test of bravery by carrying an enchanted girdle to the Green Chapel.

Finally, Gawain journeys to the poem's third locale, the Green Chapel. Here he meets the Green Knight, who three times swings his axe over the bowed head of Gawain. The third time, he nicks the skin, symbolizing Gawain's failure at Hautdesert in his third temptation. The Green Knight now reveals himself as Bertilak and explains that he has known all along of his wife's morning rendezvous with Gawain. The whole adventure, Gawain discovers, has been instigated by the enchantress, Morgan le Fey, as a means of testing Arthur's court. Although Bertilak praises Gawain's performance under this test, the hero himself is humiliated and angry. He has failed the test of bravery and truthfulness and now, in an antifeminist harangue, he also reveals his lack of courtesy.

Like *Pearl*, *Sir Gawain and the Green Knight*, after 101 stanzas, ends where it begins. Recalling the introduction, the poem returns to Camelot. Gawain, however, has been changed by his experience, and although the knights and ladies of the Round Table—along with many modern readers—believe he has acted as honorably as can be expected of any mortal, Gawain takes his failure very seriously.

The poet has shown that earthly virtues alone, even those of the greatest knight, fail. Human values and societies are by definition sinful and subject to the ravages of time and weaknesses of the flesh. Thus, the poet introduces the Arthurian court with references to the fall of Troy, war, and betrayal. Furthermore, the ideal societies of Camelot and Hautdesert represent vulnerable and artificial islands of civilization surrounded by wild nature and affected by the changing seasons. By the end of the poem, the dominant symbol of Gawain's character has been changed. Instead of the pentangle, he is now associated with the green girdle, which he wears as a penitential reminder of his failure.

Gawain's marvelous adventure is narrated in the third person, but the point of view is generally limited to Gawain's perceptions of events. The result is a masterful story with suspense and awe in which the reader, surprised like the hero by the unfolding plot, sympathizes with the hero's bewilderment. As Larry Benson and other scholars have shown, the plot artistically combines several traditional romance and folklore motifs into a seamless whole. Like *Pearl*, it is symmetrically structured: It counterpositions the two courts, two feasts, two journeys of the knight, and his two symbols, and it balances the three temptations of Gawain with Bertilak's three hunting expeditions and the three blows of the axe at the Green Chapel. Also like *Pearl*, it includes descriptions of great natural beauty, and like *Patience*, it creates a character overwhelmed by the supernatural. Like *Cleanness*, *Sir Gawain and the Green Knight* relates a narrative of strange visitors and violent deeds in vigorous and forceful verse filled with realistic

details. It shares with the other poems of the Cotton Nero manuscript many stylistic and thematic features, and remains the greatest work of the Pearl-Poet.

BIBLIOGRAPHY

Andrew, Malcolm, and Ronald Waldron, eds. *The Poems of the Pearl Manuscript: "Pearl," "Cleanness," "Patience," and "Sir Gawain and the Green Knight."* Berkeley: University of California Press, 1979. Primarily a scholarly edition of the poems but includes a good bibliography and extensive introduction.

Blanch, Robert J., and Julian N. Wasserman. *From "Pearl" to "Gawain": Forme to Fynisment.* Gainesville: University Press of Florida, 1995. Presents the thesis that works within the Pearl manuscript not only share a common author but also are connected and intersect in fundamental ways. Explores interrelated themes such as language, covenants, miracles, and the role of the intrusive narrator. Includes bibliography and index.

Brewer, Derek, and Jonathan Gibson, eds. *A Companion to the Gawain-Poet.* Arthurian Studies 38. Rochester, N.Y.: Boydell & Brewer, 1999. A collection of original analysis by an international group of medievalists. Explores a range of topics including theories of authorship, the historical and social background to the poems, the role of chivalry, and the representation of women. Includes illustrations and maps, and bibliography and index.

Condren, Edward I. *The Numerical Universe of the Gawain-Pearl Poet: Beyond Phi.* Gainesville: University Press of Florida, 2002. Condren argues that the poems of the Pearl-Poet are linked by mathematical equations called the Divine Proportion in the Middle Ages and phi by modern mathematicians.

Gardner, John, ed. *The Complete Works of the Gawain-Poet.* Chicago: University of Chicago Press, 1965. Gardner's long introduction discusses what is known about the poet in question. Describes conventions and traditions in the poems, analyzes the poems themselves, and offers notes on versification and form. Gardner's own modern verse translations of the poet's works, including *Saint Erkenwald*, compose the body of this volume.

Howard, Donald R., and Christian Zacher, eds. *Critical Studies of Sir Gawain and the Green Knight*. Notre Dame, Ind.: University of Notre Dame Press, 1968. This collection of twenty-three essays includes two essays of introduction and background followed by discussions of critical issues, style and technique, characters and setting, and interpretations. Quotations are in Middle English with Middle English alphabet characters.

Moorman, Charles. *The Pearl-Poet*. New York: Twayne, 1968. This volume is an excellent introduction to the anonymous writer of *Pearl, Patience, Purity*, and *Sir Gawain and the Green Knight*. Biographical information is by necessity replaced by more general information about the fourteenth century. Includes a chapter that examines each poem in turn, a chronology, and an annotated bibliography.

Rhodes, Jim. *Poetry Does Theology: Chaucer, Grosseteste, and the Pearl-Poet*. Notre Dame, Ind.: University of Notre Dame Press, 2001. Contains a chapter looking at religion in the Pearl-Poet's works.

Spearing, A. C. *The Gawain-Poet: A Critical Study*. New York: Cambridge University Press, 1970. After a brief discussion of the Middle Ages, the alliterative tradition, and the question of authorship, this book devotes one chapter to each of the four poems attributed to the poet. The extensive quotations from the poetry have not been modernized, although only modern alphabet letters are used.

*Richard Kenneth Emmerson*

---

# HAROLD PINTER

**Born:** London, England; October 10, 1930
**Died:** London, England; December 24, 2008

PRINCIPAL POETRY

*Poems*, 1968, 1971 (edited by Alan Clodd)
*Poems and Prose, 1949-1977*, 1978, 1986 (revised as *Collected Poems and Prose*, 1991, 1996)
*I Know the Place*, 1979

*Ten Early Poems*, 1992
*Various Voices: Prose, Poetry, Politics, 1948-1998*, 1998
*Poems by Harold Pinter*, 2002
*War*, 2003
*Various Voices: Prose, Poetry, Politics, 1948-2005*, 2005
*Six Poems for "A,"* 2007
*Various Voices: Sixty Years of Prose, Poetry, Politics, 1948-2008*, 2009

OTHER LITERARY FORMS

Although Harold Pinter was primarily known as a dramatist, poetry was an essential element in his work. He published in various genres including plays and sketches, screenplays, a novel, and nonfiction, including essays, articles, and public speeches. Some of his best-known plays are *The Birthday Party* (pr. 1958), *The Caretaker* (pr., pb. 1960), *The Homecoming* (pr., pb. 1965), and *Betrayal* (pr., pb. 1978).

ACHIEVEMENTS

Harold Pinter received numerous accolades. He was named a Companion of Honour by Queen Elizabeth II in 2002. He was awarded the Nobel Prize in Literature in 2005 and the French Légion d'Honneur in 2007. His other awards include the David Cohen Prize (1995), the Lawrence Olivier Special Award (1996), Wilfred Owen Poetry Award for his antiwar poetry (2005), the Prague Franz Kafka Prize (2005), and the Europa Theatre Prize (2006). In the latter part of his life, Pinter became politically involved and was noted for his opposition to U.S. foreign policy. His works have been translated into many languages.

BIOGRAPHY

Harold Pinter was born to a Jewish family in London's East End. The son of a tailor, Pinter was an only child, morose, morbid, and lonely, with few friends. As a young boy, he was aware of the anti-Jewish fascist marches on the predominately Jewish East End, which were met with strong resistance. He grew up in a working-class area, surrounded by fascist threats and economic insecurity. Near his house was the Lee River, which Pinter fantasized as idyllic. Indeed, Pinter's out-

*Harold Pinter* (Hulton Archive/Getty Images)

put is permeated with the juxtaposition of beauty and squalor, security and insecurity.

Following the declaration of war in 1939, he was evacuated to a castle in Cornwall. He returned home during the Blitz and in September, 1942, gained a scholarship to the selective Grocer's Company High School, Hackney, where he stayed until July, 1948. Pinter associated his childhood with a lack of money and walking. Many years later, he recalled walking a long way to the home of his school and lifelong friend, Henry Woolf, to find only Woolf's parents at home. While waiting for his friend, he began to write a poem. Almost reverentially, Woolf's parents watched the young Pinter write his poem. Pinter first began to write at the age of thirteen because he was obsessed with a girl who tormented him.

Pinter formed lifelong friendships at school. They provided continuity and stability in an ever-changing world. He acted, wrote poetry, and read. He was greatly influenced by his English teacher Joseph Brearley, the

subject of one of Pinter's finest poems "Joseph Brearley 1909-1977" (reprinted in *Various Voices*). The poem is replete with references to the London landscape. Indeed, Pinter's drama is also full of specific place names in the capital and lists.

From 1949 to 1951, Pinter used his parents' home as a base to explore London, as well as to write and read. He discovered the work of the Scots poet W. S. Graham. In the early summer of 1951, Pinter got a job in a repertory company touring Ireland. After returning from Ireland, from 1953 until 1957, he wrote and attempted to earn a living by appearing in repertory companies. On September 14, 1956, he married the actress Viven Merchant (born Ada Thompson). They had one son. Pinter's big break came during the autumn of 1956, when Woolf managed to persuade Pinter to write a play, *The Room*, which Woolf performed at Bristol University Drama Department on May 15-16, 1957. The first performance of *The Birthday Party* took place on April 28, 1958. *The Caretaker*, first performed in 1960, brought Pinter success and financial security.

Based in London, Pinter continued to write in various genres. He became reacquainted with Lady Antonia Fraser in January, 1975, at a revival of *The Birthday Party*. They instantly fell in love. He left his wife and home on April 28, 1975. In October, 1980, Pinter and Fraser married. She brought to the marriage six children from her first marriage. Well-connected socially and politically committed on the Left, Fraser encouraged her husband's left-wing activism and his poetry.

Early in the twenty-first century, Pinter was diagnosed with cancer of the esophagus, and he gave up writing drama to devote his attention solely to writing poetry. These final years, he produced moving love poems addressed to Fraser.

### ANALYSIS

Poetry is a form that continually interested Harold Pinter. During sixty years of creativity, in addition to his plays and film scripts, he wrote innumerable poems, including nearly one hundred that were published. Some of his poems were initially published in now defunct journals such as *Poetry London* under pseudonyms such as "Harold Pinta." Some of these poems have been reprinted in anthologies of prose and poetry, in private-press publications (such as *Ten Early Poems* under the Greville Press imprint), and in various editions of his *Collected Poems and Prose* and *Various Voices*.

Pinter's first published work, including poems and prose pieces that appeared in his school magazine, belong to the period of the 1940's and early 1950's. "New Year in the Midlands" and "Chandeliers and Shadows" (from *Poems*) were published in *Poetry London* in the August, 1950, issue and the poem "One a Story, Two a Death" in the final issue. In the summer of 1951, Pinter's poem "I Shall Tear off My Terrible Cap" (from *Poems*) was published in the *Poetry Quarterly*. "Chandeliers and Shadows" expresses desperation, depicting scenes of decadence and sexual depravity with a sense of chaos throughout the universe. In this poem, the insane and a random deity rule over a room, and God has been transformed into a monster.

Pinter continued to write poetry during his stay in Ireland. "The Islands of Aran Seen from the Moher Cliffs" (1951; from *Poems*), in five verse quatrains, extols the magnificent coast and the myths related with that area of Ireland. The Hackney railings and landscape of childhood are transformed into the Irish coastal countryside. Loss, deprivation, isolation, alienation, betrayal, and love are frequent themes in Pinter's poems. "Episode" (1951; from *Poems*) is a poetic dialogue with a rejected main voice, an apparently successful rival, and a silent "she" over whom they feud. There are also poems of celebration. "Poem" (1953; from *Poems*), for example, focuses on love and stability: The final four words, which are repeated through the poem, conclude on a note of Pinteresque ambiguity amid the Irish coastal scenery.

Pinter used poetry to mark the key points in his life. For example, "Paris" (1975; reprinted in *Collected Poems and Prose*), with its two verses of four lines each, celebrates Pinter and Fraser's initial intimacy. The longer "Ghost" (1983; reprinted in *Collected Poems and Prose*), in two six-line verses, was written after the death of Pinter's first wife, Merchant, with whom so much of Pinter's early work was interwoven. It begins with a startling image of strangulation and concludes with the image of the physical touch of a dead body, an image echoed in Pinter's later poetic lament for his dead father, "Death."

### "REQUIEM FOR 1945"

"Requiem for 1945" (dated 1999; in *Various Voices*) is a poem of bleakness and political despair. Its language is relatively restrained, with a cumulative use in the poem of the definite article "the," which occurs six times in the second, third, and fourth lines. A further ambiguity lies in the final word of the poem, "desire": desire for life, for a different social order, and unfulfilled personal dreams are extinguished by death. The poem, unusual for Pinter, is a single verse of eight lines in length. Certainly it is a powerful poem of intense bitterness.

### WAR

The eight poems found in *War* are full of imagery of death, destruction, and anti-Americanism. With titles such as "God Bless America," "The Bombs," "Democracy," "Weather Forecast," "American Football: A Reflection Upon the Gulf War," "Death," and "The Special Relationship," these poems contain the violent, the vicious, and the visceral, along with expletives. They are overtly political, and they project hostility to the major international powers. "Democracy" consists of four separate, very short sentences; it is crude and representative of much of Pinter's poetry at this time, the exceptions being "Death" and "Cancer Cells." Dated August, 1991, "American Football" uses repetitive obscene language to express forceful disgust. It contains little subtlety but can be seen as an accurate image of the cruelty and violence of war.

"Death" (subtitled "Births and Deaths Registration Act of 1953" in *Various Voices* but not in this volume), one of Pinter's best poems, was written after the registration of his father's death. The poem, which marked a turning point in Pinter's life, contains representative Pinter markers: repetition, the language of interrogation, repetitive questions, and echoing pronoun usage. The first two lines of the third verse and the last verse are run on. The poem has seven verses, with the first, third, and fourth containing three lines. The second and fifth verses consist of interrogative questions. The sixth verse has four lines, each of which consists of a question. The last verse has five lines, each starting with the same words, and the lines are run on with punctuation left out, even at the end of the final word of the poem. With one exception, at the end of the penultimate line, the words are monosyllabic. In the last verse, the form and content intertwine powerfully in this poem of personal lament for a dead father.

### "CANCER CELLS" AND "TO MY WIFE"

"Cancer Cells," (2002; in *Various Voices*), is another poem reflecting a key turning point in Pinter's life, his cancer. Pinter's love for his wife is celebrated in "To My Wife," (2004; in *Six Poems for "A"* and *Various Voices*). These two poems reveal differing verse forms. In "Cancer Cells," two verses of two lines extend to a third. The subject of the poem, cancer cells extend into a fourth verse of seven lines and subside with treatment in the final verse of four lines.

"To My Wife" has five celebratory verses of two lines. The initial line starts with the pronoun "I." The first word of the remaining three verses is "You." In each verse, the personal pronouns effectively inter-

twine. The language is mainly monosyllabic with extensive repetition and tense interplay. The tender lyricism that is also present in plays such as *Landscape* (pb. 1968) and *Silence* (pr., pb. 1969) is found in Pinter's late love poems that have Fraser as their subject.

### "BODY"

"Body" (2006; appeared in the *Saturday Guardian*), an eight-line run on single-verse poem without punctuation, is obsessed with death and the distinction between the living and the dead. Repetition and very slight word changes are found in the opening two lines. A poem that begins positively is transformed by grotesque language in which Pinter's obsession with dead bodies is evident. The poem is reminiscent of the disturbed states of paranoia found in some of Pinter's earlier poems, "The Error of Alarm" and "Afternoon," both dating from the 1956-1957 period and reprinted in *Collected Poems and Prose*.

### OTHER MAJOR WORKS

LONG FICTION: *The Dwarfs*, 1990.

PLAYS: *The Room*, pr. 1957 (one act); *The Birthday Party*, pr. 1958; *The Dumb Waiter*, pr. 1959; *The Caretaker*, pr., pb. 1960; *The Collection*, pr. 1961; *A Slight Ache, and Other Plays*, 1961; *The Lover*, pr., pb. 1963; *The Homecoming*, pr., pb. 1965; *Tea Party*, pb. 1965; *The Basement*, pb. 1967; *Landscape*, pb. 1968; *Silence*, pr., pb. 1969 (one act); *Old Times*, pr., pb. 1971; *No Man's Land*, pr., pb. 1975; *Plays*, 1975-1981, revised 1991-1998 (4 volumes); *Betrayal*, pr., pb. 1978; *The Hothouse*, pr., pb. 1980 (wr. 1958); *Family Voices*, pr., pb. 1981; *Other Places: Three Plays*, 1982 (includes *Family Voices*, *Victoria Station*, and *A Kind of Alaska*; revised in 1984, includes *One for the Road* and deletes *Family Voices*); *Mountain Language*, pr., pb. 1988; *The New World Order*, pr. 1991; *Party Time*, pr., pb. 1991; *Moonlight*, pr., pb. 1993; *Ashes to Ashes*, pb. 1996; *The Dwarf and Nine Revue Sketches*, 1999; *Celebration*, pr., pb. 2000; *Remembrance of Things Past*, pr., pb. 2000 (with Di Trevis; adaptation of Marcel Proust's novel); *Press Conference*, pr., pb. 2002 (sketch).

SCREENPLAYS: *The Servant*, 1963; *The Guest*, 1964; *The Pumpkin Eater*, 1964; *The Quiller Memorandum*, 1966 (adaptation of Adam Hall's novel); *Accident*, 1967; *The Birthday Party*, 1968 (adaptation of his play); *The Go-between*, 1971; *The Homecoming*, 1971 (adaptation of his play); *The Last Tycoon*, 1976 (adaptation of F. Scott Fitzgerald's novel); *Proust: A Screenplay*, 1977; *The French Lieutenant's Woman*, 1981 (adaptation of John Fowles's novel); *Betrayal*, 1983 (adaptation of his play); *Turtle Diary*, 1985; *Reunion*, 1989; *The Handmaid's Tale*, 1990 (adaptation of Margaret Atwood's novel); *The Heat of the Day*, 1990 (adaptation of Elizabeth Bowen's novel); *Party Time*, 1991 (adaptation of his play); *The Remains of the Day*, 1991 (adaptation of Kazuo Ishiguro's novel); *The Trial*, 1992 (adaptation of Franz Kafka's novel); *Collected Screenplays*, 2000 (3 volumes).

NONFICTION: *Pinter at Sixty*, 1993; *Conversations with Pinter*, 1996; *Death, Etc.*, 2005.

EDITED TEXT: *One Hundred Poems by One Hundred Poets*, 1991 (with Geoffrey Godert and Anthony Astbury).

BIBLIOGRAPHY

Baker, William. *Harold Pinter*. New York: Continuum Press, 2008. A detailed assessment of Pinter's work, including analysis of his poetry.

Baker, William, and John C. Ross. *Harold Pinter: A Bibliographical History*. New Castle, Del.: Oak Knoll Press, 2005. Section C is devoted to a descriptive bibliography of Pinter's individual poems, as first published, beginning with "Dawn" in the *Hackney Downs School Magazine* in 1947 and concluding with "The Special Relationship" in the *Guardian* in 2004. Collections of Pinter's poems are covered in section 1, subsection 2.

Billington, Michael. *Harold Pinter*. Rev. ed. London: Faber and Faber, 2007. Places some of Pinter's poems in their biographical context.

Fraser, Antonia. *Must You Go? My Life with Harold Pinter*. London: Weidenfeld and Nicolson, 2010. Fraser discusses her relationship with Pinter, from its beginnings to his death.

Gussow, Mel, and Ben Brantley. "Harold Pinter, Whose Silences Redefined Drama, Dies at Seventy-eight." *The New York Times*, December 26, 2008, p. A1. Lengthy obituary covers Pinter's life and works. Touches on his poetry as well as his plays.

*William Baker*

---

# ALEXANDER POPE

**Born:** London, England; May 21, 1688
**Died:** Twickenham, England; May 30, 1744

PRINCIPAL POETRY

*Pastorals*, 1709
*An Essay on Criticism*, 1711
*The Rape of the Lock*, 1712, 1714
*Windsor Forest*, 1713
*The Works of Mr. Alexander Pope*, 1717 (first collected edition including "Elegy to the Memory of an Unfortunate Lady" and *Eloisa to Abelard*)
*Cytherea*, 1723
*The Dunciad*, 1728-1743
*Moral Essays*, 1731-1735
*An Essay on Man*, 1733-1734
*Imitations of Horace*, 1733-1737
*Epistle to Dr. Arbuthnot*, 1735
*Epilogue to the Satires*, 1738
*One Thousand Seven Hundred and Thirty-eight*, 1738
*The Twickenham Edition of the Poems of Alexander Pope*, 1939-1967 (11 volumes; John Butt, general editor)

OTHER LITERARY FORMS

Apart from original poetry, Alexander Pope's works include an edition of William Shakespeare, a translation (1715-1720) of Homer's *Iliad* (c. 750 B.C.E.) and (1725-1726) *Odyssey* (c. 725 B.C.E.), an edition of his personal correspondence, and a prose satire titled *Peri Bathos: Or, The Art of Sinking in Poetry* (1727). Pope's edition of Shakespeare is chiefly of interest for the response that it brought from Lewis Theobald, a rival editor of Shakespeare's plays. Although not always unjust in his criticisms, Theobald did overlook some of the genuine excellences of Pope's edition, especially Pope's penetrating introduction. (It must be admitted, however, that even this is vitiated at times by Pope's inability to appreciate Shakespeare's so-called deviations from the eighteenth century notion of "correctness.") The translations from Homer are not strictly literal, but are rather adaptations of Homer's genius to the conventions and expectations of Augustan sensibility. Still, they are regarded as the most readable and eloquent versions of Homer to come out of the eighteenth century, notwithstanding the numerous instances of periphrasis (the substitution of a phrase such as "finny prey" for "fish") that belie the vigor of the original.

Pope's edition of his own letters is among the most notorious of his publications. By allowing several of his letters to be published without his apparent permission, Pope was able to bring out an ostensibly "correct" version of his private correspondence, the chief purpose of which was to present him in a favorable light to posterity. Understandably, the letters are rather too self-conscious and artificial for modern tastes.

*Peri Bathos* is a hilarious instructional booklet detailing all the elements that are necessary to produce poetry that is vulgar, tautological, florid, and inane. One other composition of Pope surely deserves mention: an essay contributed to *The Guardian* on the aesthetics of gardening. Pope had a decisive influence on the development of eighteenth century taste in gardens. In opposition to the rigid formalities that characterized the landscaping of the period, Pope held that gardens should be arranged in a more natural manner.

## ACHIEVEMENTS

Alexander Pope's position in the history of English poetry has been, at times, a subject of acrimonious debate. In his own day, Pope's achievement was frequently obfuscated by the numerous political controversies that surrounded his name. Although he finally emerged, in the estimation of the eighteenth century, as the greatest English poet since John Milton, his reputation soon reached its lowest ebb, during the Romantic and Victorian periods; he was derided by Thomas De Quincey as an author of "moldy commonplaces" and demoted by Matthew Arnold to the position of being a "classic of [English] prose." Even in Edith Sitwell's generally favorable study (1930), Pope is appreciated for achieving, in certain poems, a richness of imagery "almost" as lush as that of John Keats. In short, it was not until recently that the balance was redressed. Pope is now recognized as one of the consummate craftspeople of the English language.

Responding to and expressing the fundamental aesthetic tenets of the Augustan Age, Pope cannot be fully appreciated or understood without some awareness of the neoclassical assumptions that undergird his compositions. Pope's audience was more homogeneous than Shakespeare's and less enthusiastic (in Samuel Johnson's meaning of that term) than Milton's. As a result, he eschews the dramatic intensity and colloquial richness of the former and bypasses the mythopoeic passion and religious afflatus of the latter. (It must be remembered, however, that the Miltonic allusions in, say, *The Rape of the Lock* are not intended to derogate Milton, but to expose, by sheer force of contrast, the small-mindedness of eighteenth century society.)

Sophisticated allusion, verbal brilliance, the promulgation of moral and aesthetic standards—these are the components of Pope's poetic art. The audience for which Pope wrote was small, urban, and keenly intelligent, capable of appreciating a high degree of technical virtuosity in its poets. These poets were not expected to indulge in lyrical effusions on the subject of their private griefs or to thrust forward their own personal speculations on the end and aim of human existence. On the contrary, their purpose was to crystallize in language conspicuous for its clarity, balance, and poise, the cultural standards, aesthetic ideals, and moral certitudes that they could presume to hold in common with a sensitive and educated audience. As Pope's career progressed, these ideals seemed increasingly remote from the political and literary arenas where he was forced to contend; hence, his later poetry—especially *The Dunciad*—reveals a growing rift between Pope and his public. On the whole, however, Pope's is a public voice which distills in witty and unforgettable couplets the values of self-control, civic virtue, uncorrupted taste, critical intelligence, and spiritual humility.

As a youth, Pope was exhorted by William Walsh, a former member of John Dryden's literary circle, to pursue "correctness" in his compositions. Pope's career as a poet witnesses to the assiduity with which he acted on Walsh's advice. No poet has brought to the rhyming couplet an equivalent degree of perfection or given to the form, distinguished by its technical difficulty, a greater suppleness and elasticity in the expression of various moods and situations. From the farcical brilliance of *The Rape of the Lock* and the passionate intensities of *Eloisa to Abelard* to the dignified discursiveness of *An Essay on Man* and the nervous energy of *The Dunciad*, Pope attains a perfect balance between thought and expression, between verbal wit and the felt rendering of experience.

BIOGRAPHY

The two most important elements in Alexander Pope's life were his being born a Catholic and his contracting, during his twelfth year, a severe tubercular infection from which he never fully recovered. Because of his Catholicism, Pope was compelled to live outside London and was not allowed to enroll in a formal university program. Because of his illness, Pope attained a height of only four and a half feet, suffered from migraine headaches, was obliged to wear several pairs of hose and an elaborate harness to compensate for the slightness of his legs and the curvature of his spine, and was subject to frequent and caustic ridicule by critics, such as John Dennis, who directed their rancor at his physical deformities as much as at his poetic efforts. Pope's physical ailments and the acrimony with which political and literary pundits attacked both his person and his work should never be forgotten in evaluating, say, the optimistic faith of *An Essay on Man* or the acidulous satire of *The Dunciad*. The affirmations of the former poem were not written out of ignorance of human suffering, and the vituperations of the latter poem cannot be understood apart from the contumely that Pope suffered at the hands of his adversaries—Lady Mary Wortley Montague, Lord Hervey, John Dennis, Joseph Addison, and Lewis Theobald, to name a few. Pope's reference in *Epistle to Dr. Arbuthnot* to "this long disease, my life," is no literary confabulation but an accurate description of his sufferings.

There were, however, compensations. In the library of his father, a wealthy linen merchant who retired to a vast estate at Binfield in 1700, Pope acquired a profound, if desultory, knowledge of English history and letters. In his youth, he was, moreover, the special favorite of William Wycherley, who encouraged the publication of Pope's *Pastorals* in Jacob Tonson's *Miscel-*

*Alexander Pope* (Library of Congress)

*lany* (1709). In 1713, Pope was to find companionship and support in "The Scriblerus Club," a Tory brotherhood that included among its principal members Jonathan Swift, John Gay, and John Arbuthnot. Together, they inveighed against the scientific rationalism and aggressive commercialism that, they believed, threatened the survival of humanistic values in the first half of the eighteenth century. It is important to remember that the political climate of Pope's day was such that poetic compositions were less frequently evaluated on their intrinsic merits than on the sponsorship that they were accorded by either Tory or Whig. Thus Pope's literary career was plagued at its inception by mean-spirited attacks from henchmen of the political and literary establishment.

Pope's masterful translation of the *Iliad* (first English translation, 1611), from which he earned £9,000, enabled him to retire in 1719 with his mother (for whom he scrupulously cared until the end of her life) to

Twickenham: a neoclassical villa designed in part by Pope himself, where he was able to indulge his love of gardening and to escape from the contumacious atmosphere of literary London. Here, in the companionship of Swift, Gay, Viscount Bolingbroke, and Arbuthnot, Pope was granted some respite from the venomous attacks upon his person and character, the history of which virtually makes up the rest of his recorded biography. Apart from a deep attachment to Martha Blount, a Catholic neighbor sympathetic to Pope's aspirations and literary ideals, his life was a constant endeavor to stem the materialistic current of his times by iterating in polished and penetrating couplets a theocentric humanism that espoused the virtues of self-discipline, the recognition of metaphysical values, and the need for standards of measure and restraint.

## ANALYSIS

Alexander Pope's poetry is an unmistakable challenge to the post-Romantic sensibilities of the twentieth century reader. John Stuart Mill's dictum that "eloquence is *heard*, poetry is overheard," seems entirely contradicted by the public and topical voice that characterizes the epistles, satires, and philosophic exordiums of Pope. The language of introspective reverie that poets, from the nineteenth century on, cultivate in lonely self-communion among the bowers of a refined aestheticism could not be further removed from the racy, tough, and contentious idiom of Pope. That is not to say that Pope's language is devoid of sculptured phrases or chiseled locutions; on the contrary, his compositions are exquisitely wrought and develop with an inevitability that makes Pope, after William Shakespeare, the most quoted poet in the English language. Following the translation of the *Iliad*, however, Pope's works became increasingly didactic and satirical in nature and engaged in topical assaults on the foibles, idiosyncrasies, and shortcomings that characterized the literary and political arena during the reigns of Anne and George II. The astonishing thing is that these topical satires of literary hacks long since forgotten and social customs consigned to oblivion, touch, time and again, upon that which is enduring and universal in the moral being of humanity. The literary battles and political machinations that gave occasion to Pope's vitriolic ut-

terances may be forgotten, but the integrity with which Pope affirmed the centrality of letters, the tempering spirit of humanism, the need for standards, and the cultivation of reverence as indispensable ingredients of a just and balanced society, retains its relevance in the broken world of the twentieth century.

Like Vergil, Pope began as a writer of pastorals; his first poems, composed when he was sixteen, are delicate evocations of an idyllic world of shepherds and shepherdesses poised among settings reminiscent of François Boucher and Jean Fragonard. These highly stylized exercises won for him the accolades of contemporary critics and gave him the confidence to essay the next task that tradition prescribed for the developing poet: the epic. Pope's translation of the *Iliad*, the first books of which appeared in 1715, was a watershed in his poetic career. Though Pope had already written poems that prefigure his later orientation as a satirist, it was the publication of the *Iliad* that triggered the wholly irrational and unexpected assault on Pope's life, family, writings, and physiognomy by his political enemies and rivals to poetic fame. These attacks diverted Pope from the musings of *Windsor Forest*, the perorations of *An Essay on Criticism*, and the witticisms of *The Rape of the Lock*, and obliged him, to paraphrase a Nobel laureate, "to grab his century by the throat." After 1719, Pope's career is notable for the increasing venom of his pen and the sustained brilliance of his polemic.

### AN ESSAY ON CRITICISM

Pope's first important utterance gives us direct access to the critical values of the Augustans and remains the best and most compendious statement of a poetic tradition that extends from Horace to Nicolas Boileau-Despréaux. Indeed, as a distillation of neoclassical attitudes, Pope's *An Essay on Criticism* is without a peer. The critical assumptions on which the poem is based could not be further removed from the splintered aesthetics and boneless relativism of the present: As a statement of poetic intention and practice, it provides a necessary corrective to the farrago of contradictions that characterize the contemporary critical scene. Pope vigorously attacks the notion that taste is a purely subjective matter, arguing that a deterioration in aesthetic values is both a symptom and a portent of a general disequilibrium in the moral being of the individual and the political fabric of society. The poem's controlling symbol is the sun—an emblem of universal reason and light whose rays are an expression of the original creative word, or *logos*. Individual taste is evaluated from the perspective of this light-giving word, which is identified in the poem as "Unerring Nature, still divinely bright,/ One clear, unchanged, and universal light." Though individual judgments may differ, they may and should be regulated—as watches by the sun—in accordance with objective standards of value and taste. Thus, the rules that govern the composition of poetry are not arbitrary inventions, but expressions of the natural law of measure and restraint: "Those Rules of old discovered, not devised/ Are nature still, but Nature methodized;/ Nature, like Liberty, is but restrained/ By the same laws which first herself ordained."

The first duty of a poet and a critic, then, is to recognize the law of human limit, and to balance individual judgments by constant and circumspect reference to a hierarchy of inherited values. Pope does not recommend the self-abnegation of the poet in the face of his predecessors, but rather his need to adapt to his own time those values that inform ancients and moderns alike and are of continued relevance because their source is eternal and their origin beyond the vagaries of individual taste. Still, Pope maintains that the success of a composition must be estimated by the value and significance of the poet's purpose and the artistic integrity with which that purpose is fulfilled, rather than by arbitrary and invidious comparisons between works of antithetical spirit and intention. In this regard, "Pegasus, a near way to take,/ May boldly deviate from the common track;/ From vulgar bounds with brave disorder part,/ And snatch a grace beyond the reach of art."

There is, however, one important qualification to this expansionist poetics. Namely, that although the poet's deviations may elude the letter of aesthetic law, they must not violate the spirit of that law: "Moderns, beware! or if you must offend/ Against the precept ne'er transgress its end." As Pope argues at the opening of Part 2 of *An Essay on Criticism*, the poet and the critic must never allow themselves to become victims of pride or to equate the spark of their peculiar talents or insights with the all-embracing splendors of the eternal

*logos*. Poets and critics of lesser rank, according to Pope, allow their obsession with the parts of a composition to take precedence over their comprehension of its total design. An efflorescence of decorative detail in a poet and a pedantic and small-minded preoccupation with minutiae in a critic are unmistakable indications of debilitated sensibility and false judgment: "But true Expression, like th' unchanging Sun,/ Clears and improves whate'er it shines upon." To value sound over sense, expression over content, nuance over theme, is to sacrifice instruction to delight and to worship the dead letter at the expense of the living spirit.

Furthermore, the prosody of a poetic composition should be judged by the following criteria: "'Tis not enough no harshness gives offence,/ The sound must seem an echo to the sense." Pope crystallizes this point in a series of couplets rich in verbal pyrotechnics. The lines sing, strain, limp, or lilt in accordance with the action described:

> Soft is the strain when Zephyr gently blows,
> And the smooth stream in smoother numbers flows:
> But when loud surges lash the sounding shore,
> The hoarse, rough verse should like the torrent roar:
> When Ajax strives some rock's vast weight to throw,
> The line too labours, and the words move slow;
> Not so, when swift Camilla scours the plain,
> Flies o'er th' unbending corn, and skims along the main.

Here, as so often, the restraint of the couplet inspires Pope to rhythmic feats that make a game of art and bear witness to his own adage: "The winged courser, like the generous horse/ Shows most true mettle when you check his force."

After attacking the patronage system and the proclivity of critics to celebrate poets of superior social rank while denigrating those genuine talents who arouse jealousy and spite, Pope goes on to affirm that, in their ultimate issues, literary, social, and moral values are mutually interdependent. A vacillating and fickle critic inconstant in his service to the muse is thus compared to a degenerate amorist who abandons the lawful embraces of his wife for the specious thrills of a strumpet. Constipated scribblers who "Strain out the last droppings of their sense/ And rhyme with all the rage of Impotence," and Restoration rakes who combine "Dulness with Obscenity . . ./ As shameful sure as Impotence in love," underscore Pope's sense that larger issues of decorum, decency, and health are involved in questions of literary tact. For Pope, the authentic poet and critic is honest and circumspect, capable of elasticity in his judgment but constrained by nature and common sense. He does not neglect the rigors of composition in a false straining for effect nor abandon moral and metaphysical principles to flatter public taste. Pope never deserted the values adduced in *An Essay on Criticism*, and the poem may be profitably used as a yardstick to measure the underlying integrity of Pope's poetic vision and the vigilance with which he applied it to the literary and cultural aberrations of his age.

*An Essay on Criticism* was followed by *Windsor Forest* and *The Rape of the Lock*; the former poem is an expression of unity in diversity in which the ecological balance of Windsor Forest is perceived as analogous to the balanced and harmonious development of the British realm following the Peace of Utrecht. Pope's perception of a concordant cosmic design maintained by the mutual subservience of antagonistic forces adumbrates the more compelling philosophic arguments of *An Essay on Man*.

### THE RAPE OF THE LOCK

Pope's most brilliant achievement in his early work is, of course, *The Rape of the Lock*. Its sophisticated humor and virtuoso technique are unsurpassed. In this genial spoof of a society abandoned to the pursuit of spurious values, Pope avoids the extreme indignation of his later satires. Instead, he takes an impish delight in the conventions and rituals that are the object of his gentle mockery. Though Belinda and the Baron may be self-regarding fools, the poet obviously relishes their behavior.

The poem itself derives from an actual quarrel between Arabella Fermour and her suitor, Lord Petre. At the request of his friend, John Caryll, Pope undertook the poem, hoping, through his raillery, to laugh the young beau and belle into common sense. Not surprisingly, the tempers of Miss Fermour and Lord Petre were not mollified when, in consequence of Pope's poem, their misadventures became the talk of the town.

Pope's principal strategy in this mock-epic is to stand the conventions of epic poetry on their heads. By counterpointing the dramatic situations and epic conventions of Homer, Vergil, and Milton with the fatuities of a vain coquette and a foppish lord, Pope exposes the pretensions and trivialities of the eighteenth century upper class. Hence, the battle for Troy, Latium, or Heaven becomes a bathetic war between the genders; the celestial powers of the *Iliad* or *Paradise Lost* (1667, 1674) are reduced to diminutive sylphs; and the ferocious appetites of the Homeric warrior are replaced by the pampered palates of a degenerate aristocracy. As in *An Essay on Criticism*, the controlling metaphor is the sun. Belinda's propensity to arrogate to herself the divine attributes of that celestial orb reflects the expansive self-conceit permeating her entire culture. As they are over and over in Belinda's world, the finite preoccupations of pleasure, seduction, flirtation, and gossip are accorded an infinite status. The worship of these things becomes, in consequence, obsessional and demoniac. Thus the sylphs who whisper in Belinda's ear on the eve of her molestation by the Baron recall the seductive whispers of Milton's Satan in the ear of the sleeping Eve. Moreover, as Belinda sits before her boudoir mirror and allows herself to be transformed by the ministrations of her attendant sylphs, the religious connotations of Pope's imagery underscore the debasement of true worship into self-worship through "the sacred rites of Pride." Still, Pope's condemnation of Belinda's world is not unequivocal: The radiance, iridescence, and bejeweled splendor of this perfumed society retain a vestige of that divine light that the society caricatures or distorts.

In the last analysis, however, Belinda's chastity is not a positive virtue but an expression of vanity. Her aloofness is a deliberate and insulting challenge to her suitors, whose numbers swell as she remains unfixed and flirtatious. Nowhere is this more apparent than in Belinda's outcry in canto 4, after the Baron has successfully clipped and stolen a lock of her hair: "Oh hadst thou, cruel! been content to seize/ Hairs less in sight, or any hairs but these!" Belinda is not consciously aware of the comic and lewd implications of her statement, but Pope's cruel joke is definitely intended at her expense. Belinda's unconscious preference for a private seduction over a public insult—that the Baron should have seized "hairs less in sight"—reveals how virtue and chastity remain for her largely a matter of appearance. With the exception of Clarissa, who councils Belinda to exercise restraint, humility, and humor, the moral spinelessness of this society—its appalling indifference to standards and its inability to discriminate between the trivial and the tragic—is epitomized in Pope's use of the couplet and in his juxtaposition of incongruous images. For example, Belinda's cries at the Baron's violation of her lock are described as follows: "Not louder shrieks to pitying heaven are cast,/ When husbands, or when lap dogs breathe their last;/ Or when rich China vessels fallen from high/ In glittering dust, and painted fragments lie!" The deaths of husbands and of lap dogs, the breaking of china, and the loss of virginity are reduced to the same level.

The poem ends in a mock apotheosis. In the midst of the fracas between Belinda and the Baron, the pilfered lock ascends comet-like to the starry heavens to assume its place among the other constellations. Pope concludes with a poignant reminder of mortality and an implicit plea for Belinda to attain fulfillment in marriage and love: "For, after all the murders of your eye,/ When after millions slain, yourself shall die;/ When those fair suns shall set, as set they must,/ And all those tresses shall be laid in dust,/ This Lock, the Muse shall consecrate to fame,/ And midst the stars inscribe Belinda's name."

### ELOISA TO ABELARD

Following *The Rape of the Lock*, Pope's efforts were directed toward a mode of composition with which he is not usually identified: the elegiac verses "Elegy to the Memory of an Unfortunate Lady" and the romantic psychodrama, *Eloisa to Abelard*. The "Elegy" is, perhaps, only partially successful; its chief interest lies in the poet's vacillation between a Christian and a Stoic understanding of the lady's death. *Eloisa to Abelard* is another matter altogether. G. Wilson Knight claims that it "is certainly Pope's greatest human poem and probably the greatest short love poem in our language"—a judgment from which few critics are likely to dissociate themselves.

In the form of an epistle to her beloved and banished Abelard, Pope's Eloisa dramatically expresses the psychological tensions that threaten her reason and divide her soul. Confined to a monastery (ironically founded by Abelard), she receives, at length, a letter from her former lover that reawakens her suppressed passion. The recrudescence of these feelings not only threatens her stability, but also, in her own estimation, endangers her soul; and her situation is rendered even more poignant by the fact that Abelard, having been castrated by henchmen in the employ of her outraged uncle, can neither respond to nor share in her struggles against the flesh. Here the couplet is used not only ironically to counterpose discordant images, as in *The Rape of the Lock*, but also to reflect, in balanced antitheses, the very struggles of Eloisa's soul. In the extravagance of her affliction, Eloisa takes on the attributes of a Shelleyan heroine, preferring damnation with Abelard to redemption without him: "In seas of flame my plunging soul is drowned,/ While altars blaze, and angels tremble round." Even as she submits to the decrees of Heaven and composes herself to meet her maker, she erotically mingles her love for Abelard with her struggle for salvation: "Thou Abelard! the last sad office pay,/ And smooth my passage to the realms of day,/ See my lips tremble, and my eyeballs roll,/ Suck my last breath, and catch my flying soul!" *Eloisa to Abelard* belies the notion that Pope was incapable of composing in the pathetic mode. As Lord Byron observed, "If you search for passion, where is it to be found stronger than in *Eloisa to Abelard*."

Between *Eloisa to Abelard* and *An Essay on Man*, Pope composed a preliminary version of *The Dunciad* (1728), but it was not until 1742 that the poem appeared in its final form.

### AN ESSAY ON MAN

Pope's principal achievements from 1731 to 1737 were *An Essay on Man* and associated ethical epistles. These moral essays encompass a variety of subjects: two addresses, to the earl of Burlington and Lord Bathurst, respectively, on the uses of riches; a study of the Ruling Passion in the development of individual character, addressed to Lord Cobham; and an epistle to Martha Blount on the hypocrisy of women in sophisticated society. The key to each of these studies of the foibles and idiosyncrasies of human character is provided by *An Essay on Man*—Pope's most celebrated poem during his own lifetime and the chief source of his international fame. The poem deserves close study. As a synthesis of eighteenth century apologetic thought on the nature of humankind, the existence of evil, and the harmony of the creation, it is unsurpassed. Apart from its creedal assertions—which are considerable and not to be dismissed as glib rationalizations or "moldy commonplaces," as Thomas De Quincey would have it—the poem's chief merit lies in Pope's ability to express in taut and pellucid couplets the fundamentals of a religion derived from natural law. In a word, it exemplifies Pope's dictum that "True Wit is Nature to advantage dress'd/ What oft was thought but ne'er so well expressed."

Although Pope's ontology is based on reason and observation as opposed to dogma or revelation, the poem does not deny metaphysical axioms. On the contrary, it continually approximates to "some sphere unknown." The recognition of this metaphysical "sphere" is elaborated in language that is purged of sectarian or denominational accretions, reflecting Pope's belief in a natural illumination or "way" vouchsafed to all men irrespective of particular creeds, forms of worship, or varieties of belief. In short, it is an eighteenth century Dao that reflects and transcends the thought and expression of the period. Pope's poem is intended to develop in readers a capacity to recognize the interdependencies of all things; to attune themselves in thought and action to the whole of creation; and to accept in humility and reverence an appointed place in the cosmic design.

The first epistle is chiefly concerned with demonstrating that the human place in the scheme of creation is providentially ordained. Pope claims that apparent human limitations are blessings in disguise: If people were possessed of prescience greater than that with which divine wisdom has endowed them, they would pose a threat to cosmic order—that "great chain, that draws all to agree"—and attempt to make themselves the center of the universe. This would be in direct opposition to ". . . the first Almighty Cause," that "Acts not by partial, but by general laws." Although human limitations tax people sorely and the apparent indifference of the universe offends their sense of justice, it is precisely those limitations that allow people to exist at all and permit them to develop, through interaction with others, conscious senses of identity. If natural laws

were suspended every time people were threatened by their operation, the world would turn topsy-turvy and the order of both the universe and human society would fall into chaos. Hence, "The general Order, since the whole began,/ Is kept in Nature, and is kept in Man." Furthermore, if human beings were granted access to the divine plan and made privy to the Creator's will, their stature as a being midway between the Infinite and nothing would be destroyed. Pope reasons: "If nature thundered in his opening ears,/ And stunned him with the music of the spheres,/ How would he wish that Heaven had left him still/ The whispering Zephyr and the purling rill?" To be sure, humans, through an act of faith, must develop the capacity to perceive the infinite in and through the finite, but to cherish the illusion that, in their present state, they are or should be equal to the "Mind of All" is to "invert the laws/ Of Order" and to sin "against th' Eternal Cause."

Pope cautions that humankind should not expect more from life than it is capable of providing and that people should look to death for the fulfillment of the hope that has been implanted in them as a sign of their transcendent destiny. Therefore, people should comport themselves authentically to the divine will: "Hope humbly then, with trembling pinions soar,/ Wait the greater teacher Death, and God adore./ What future bliss, he gives not thee to know/ But gives that Hope to be thy blessing now." In the last analysis, true happiness is a consequence of a person's adjustment to that "stupendous whole,/ Whose body Nature is, and God the soul." From this proceeds the recognition that "All nature is but art, unknown to thee,/ All Chance, Direction, which thou canst not see,/ All Discord, Harmony, not understood;/ All partial Evil, universal Good."

For Pope, as it is in great things, so it is in small. As a microcosm of the universe, humankind's internal being reflects those same polarities and tensions that, held in harmonious balance, sustain and animate the cosmic scheme. Just as nature may deviate from that balance in eruptions, earthquakes, and cosmic catastrophes, so human equilibrium may itself be usurped by the dominance of a particular passion or impulse. Pope argues, however, that the human mental constitution, despite its precarious balance, witnesses to the ingenuity of its Maker. Reason, by itself, is not enough to activate, kindle, and inspire people's existence. Without the promptings of passion, humanity would sink into a contemplative torpor. Thus, "Two Principles in human nature reign;/ Self-love, to urge, and Reason, to restrain." In the elaboration of these mental categories, Pope strikingly anticipates Sigmund Freud. Pope's "self-love" and "Reason" are roughly equivalent to Freud's "id" and "super-ego."

Like Freud, Pope recognizes that "Self-Love"—the id, or pleasure-principle—is the source of those instinctual urges that give vitality and movement to our lives. He also affirms that "Reason"—the superego, or reality-principle—is necessary to direct those urges into socially acceptable channels and to keep them from becoming self-destructive. To expunge these passions altogether would destroy the human organism and rob life of its daring and splendor. Thus, "Love, Hope, and Joy, fair pleasure's smiling train,/ Hate, Fear, and Grief, the family of pain,/ These mixed with art, and to due bounds confined,/ Make and maintain the balance of the mind." Moreover, each person possesses "One Master Passion" that gives life impetus and direction. Without that passion, people's lives would proceed without tremor, but their potential for virtue and creation would be severely diminished.

Like Freud, Pope here posits a theory of sublimation that recognizes that all virtues and achievements are transformations of subliminal and potentially destructive energies: "Nor Virtue, male or female, can we name,/ But what will grow on Pride, or grow on shame./ Thus Nature gives us (let it check our pride)/ The virtue nearest to our vice allied." Hence, lust, restrained and harmonized by Reason, becomes love: Spleen becomes honesty; envy, emulation; avarice, prudence; and idleness or sloth—as Friedrich Nietzsche himself observed—philosophy. Finally, "Even mean Self-love becomes, by force divine,/ The scale to measure others' wants by thine./ See, and confess, one comfort still must rise,/ 'Tis this, Though Man's a fool, yet God is wise."

After examining the internal economy of human nature in the second epistle, Pope next scrutinizes the relationship between the individual and society. Not surprisingly, Pope's perception of society as an association of countervailing forces parallels his remarks on human psychology and cosmic order. Just as virtue is a product of sublimated vice, so human institutions — families, religious organizations, political bodies—are a product of human weakness. If humans are born needy and deficient, that is not an argument against divine dispensation; on the contrary, it is precisely those deficiencies that necessitate the formation of a society based on mutual solicitude and love. In this way, self-love imperceptibly yields to social love—a love that is directly inspired by the human need for and reliance on one another. The image that Pope uses to characterize this movement from self-love to social love and, finally, to cosmic love, is that of a pebble dropped in a peaceful lake:

> Self-love but serves the virtuous mind to wake,
> As the small pebble stirs the peaceful lake;
> The center moved, a circle straight succeeds,
> Another still, and still another spreads;
> Friend, parent, neighbor, first it will embrace;
> His country next; and next all human race.

At length, these spreading circles and widening arcs of worship encompass the whole of Being and reflect, in miniature, the love of God for his creation. As Maynard Mack observes: "The controlling theme of *An Essay on Man* is the theme of constructive renunciation. By renouncing the exterior false paradises, man finds the true one within. By acknowledging his weakness, he learns his strengths. By subordinating himself to the whole, he finds his real importance in it."

Although it is important to estimate Pope's achievement in *An Essay on Man* in terms of his stated purpose, there is perhaps one legitimate criticism to which the poem gives rise: Pope's failure to recognize and express the intense spiritual struggle involved in accepting one's place in the divine plan. To be sure, Pope's response to those who would question God's justice is not dissimilar from the response accorded Job: "Where was thou when the foundations of the world were laid?" Unlike the Hebrew poet, however, Pope fails to dramatize the efforts of the individual to adhere to the divine will. Pope seems to regard all questionings of or disputations with Providence as manifestations of human pride. In this way, Pope vitiates the existential validity of his doctrines and devalues human beings' struggle to bring their will and intelligence into conformity with the Creator. As one critic remarks: "The wisdom that teaches us not to weep cannot dry our tears, still less can it draw them forth." In the final analysis, however, *An Essay on Man* is a compelling and thoughtful theodicy. As a poetry of statement, it comes as close as any statement or assertion can to justifying and explaining the cosmic order. If it leaves the existential dimension of that order out of account, it must be remembered that Pope's intention is to "vindicate the ways of God to Man" through argument and persuasion rather than to *justify* those ways through drama or personal testimony.

### EPISTLE TO DR. ARBUTHNOT

The next phase of Pope's career is characterized by rage and indignation at a literary and social milieu in which intellectual blankness and moral bankruptcy are the accepted standard. Pope's voice becomes increasingly apocalyptic as he contemplates, with derision and dismay, the opportunistic secularism of the Augustan Age. In the Horatian satires and epistles, Pope expresses his outrage at the moral breakdown in the court of George II and the brutalizing cynicism in the administration of Robert Walpole, where "Not to be corrupted is the shame."

From an aesthetic point of view, the most interesting of these Horatian diatribes is *Epistle to Dr. Arbuthnot*. Again Pope astonishes readers with the expressive capabilities of the rhyming couplet. By using enjambment and an almost syncopated rhythm to resist the couplet's natural tendency to fall into balanced antitheses with neatly placed caesuras in the middle of a line, Pope is able to capture the idiomatic flavor of a living conversation. One can hear Pope's labored breathing as he slams the door on those flatterers and careerists who have pursued him to the very threshold of Twickenham: "Shut, shut the door, good John!, fatigued I said,/ Tie up the Knocker, say I'm sick, I'm dead./ The Dog Star rages! nay 'tis past a doubt,/ All Bedlam, or Parnassus, is let out." The poem is not merely an attack on Pope's detractors—Atticus (Addison), Bufo (the earl of Halifax), and Sporus (Lord Hervey)—but a withering indictment of a literary establishment that pursues reputation, influence, fashion, and power to the neglect of truth.

### THE DUNCIAD

The ultimate expression of Pope's outrage at a world that ravages the principles of order adduced in *An Essay on Man* and subverts the disciplined training of the moral sensibility and character to curry favor is, of course, *The Dunciad*. Like *The Rape of the Lock*, *The Dunciad* is a mock-epic; but unlike its predecessor, the satire here is scathing to the last degree. In its first version, Pope's principal antagonist was Lewis Theobald, a humorless and dry-as-dust pedant who is chiefly remembered for having pilloried Pope's edition of Shakespeare. In the final version, Theobald is replaced by Colly Cibber, a negligible drudge who, according to Pope, achieved the position of poet laureate through flattery and the propitiation of Dullness. As the King of Dunces, Cibber presides over a factious following of dilettantes and poetasters. In book 4, the reign of Dullness shakes the very foundations of civilization as chaos supplants cosmos and moral order is overthrown. Educators, scientists, lawyers, politicians, pedants, and versifiers are all subjected to the withering scorn of Pope's pen. Each has allowed the allures of self-advertisement to compromise the disinterested search for value and truth. In short, *The Dunciad* is a vision of cultural fragmentation and breakdown in which the holistic vision of *An Essay on Man* deteriorates into the deconstructionism, the intellectual madness and lawlessness of those who only "See Nature in some partial narrow shape,/ And let the Author of the whole escape." The arts and sciences, perverted from their true function, become soulless self-reflections of man's skill: "Art after art goes out and All is Night,/ Lo! thy dread empire, CHAOS! is restored,/ Light dies before thy uncreating word./ Thy hand, great Anarch! lets the curtain fall;/ And universal Darkness buries All."

*The Dunciad* is a trenchant and corrosive probing of the moral, political, and cultural decay of a society controlled by self-important publicists, crass careerists, and opportunistic power-brokers. It is perhaps regrettable that Pope felt the need to encrust this poem with tedious and obscure references to the intellectual disloyalists of his day. Even so, the cumbersome and tortuous inventory of malodorous statesmen and maleficent critics is arguably at one with the poem's substance; the burden that they impose on the reader is a verbal equivalent to their stifling effect on a society from which every vestige of the spirit has been systematically expunged. Moreover, it is important to remember that these references are themselves a parody of "bookful blockheads ignorantly read/ With loads of learned lumber in their head." As Austin Warren observes apropos of Pope's dunces: "The context provides the categories which are permanent, while the proper names are annually replaceable."

Viewed as a whole, Pope's achievement is astonishing in its range and diversity. As the guardian and interpreter of a spiritual tradition distilled from the collective wisdom of Western culture, Pope articulates a "coherent romanticism," as it has been termed by G. Wilson Knight, which has as immediate a bearing on the fractured world of the twentieth century as it had on the refractory world of the Augustans. For those who believe that the preservation of humanistic letters and the survival of spiritual values are inextricably intertwined, Pope's poetry will continue to carry urgency and command attention.

OTHER MAJOR WORKS

NONFICTION: *Peri Bathos: Or, The Art of Sinking in Poetry*, 1727; *Mr. Pope's Literary Correspondence*, 1735-1737; *The Correspondence of Alexander Pope*, 1956 (5 volumes; G. Sherburn, editor); *The Literary Criticism of Alexander Pope*, 1965.

TRANSLATIONS: *The Iliad of Homer*, 1715-1720; *The Odyssey of Homer*, 1725-1726.

EDITED TEXT: *Works of Shakespeare*, 1723-1725 (6 volumes).

MISCELLANEOUS: *The Works of Mr. Alexander Pope*, 1717-1741.

BIBLIOGRAPHY

Baines, Paul. *The Complete Critical Guide to Alexander Pope*. New York: Routledge, 2000. This introduction offers basic information on the author's life, contexts, and works, and outlines the major critical issues surrounding Pope's works, from the time they were written to the present.

Curry, Neil. *Alexander Pope*. London: Greenwich Exchange, 2008. Curry examines Pope's writings in detail, concentrating on satirical verses.

Damrosch, Leopold, Jr. *The Imaginative World of Alexander Pope*. Berkeley: University of California Press, 1987. Highly recommended for its success in the "imaginative recovery" of Pope, his work, and his world. This is a full and rich treatment, covering a wide range of topics.

Erskine-Hill, Howard, ed. *Alexander Pope: World and Word*. New York: Oxford University Press, 1998. A collection of essays that take a fresh textual approach to Pope's achievement. The contributors focus on topics and issues important to Pope but rarely discussed, including nonsexual relations between men and women.

Goldsmith, Netta Murray. *Alexander Pope: The Evolution of a Poet*. Burlington, Vt.: Ashgate, 2002. This biography covers Pope's development as a poet and also examines his legacy.

Hammond, Brean S. *Pope*. Atlantic Highlands, N.J.: Humanities Press, 1986. Hammond's five chapters are thematically organized, dealing in turn with Pope's life, his politics, his ideology, his writing career, and his attitudes toward women. Includes bibliography.

Mack, Maynard. *Alexander Pope*. New York: W. W. Norton, 1985. This work has been called the definitive biography of Pope. Bringing to his task a lifetime of distinguished scholarship, Mack paints a complex, fully dimensioned portrait of Pope while providing an especially rich re-creation of English society during the period known as the age of Pope.

Rumbold, Valerie. *Women's Place in Pope's World*. New York: Cambridge University Press, 1989. Although Pope has long been celebrated for his sympathetic portraits of women, Rumbold's work is very successful at examining the social roles open to women in the generally oppressive, restricted world of eighteenth century England.

Warton, Joseph. *Alexander Pope and His Critics*. Edited and with an introduction by Adam Rounce. New York: Routledge, 2004. This three-volume set contains Warton's *An Essay on the Genius and Writings of Pope* and other critics' responses to Pope and also to Warton. Contains considerable discussion of the eighteenth century view of Pope.

Weinbrot, Howard. *Alexander Pope and the Traditions*

*of Formal Verse Satire*. Princeton, N.J.: Princeton University Press, 1982. Pope's greatest achievements as a poet were in the genre of satire. Weinbrot considers the satiric enterprise in early eighteenth century England.

*Stephen I. Gurney*

----

# E. J. PRATT

**Born:** Western Bay, Newfoundland, Canada;
   February 4, 1882
**Died:** Toronto, Ontario, Canada; April 26, 1964

PRINCIPAL POETRY

*Rachel: A Sea Story of Newfoundland in Verse*,
   1917
*Newfoundland Verse*, 1923
*The Witches' Brew*, 1925
*Titans*, 1926
*The Iron Door: An Ode*, 1927
*The Roosevelt and the Antinoe*, 1930
*Many Moods*, 1932
*The Titanic*, 1935
*The Fable of the Goats, and Other Poems*, 1937
*Brébeuf and His Brethren*, 1940
*Dunkirk*, 1941
*Still Life, and Other Verse*, 1943
*Collected Poems*, 1944
*They Are Returning*, 1945
*Behind the Log*, 1947
*Ten Selected Poems*, 1947
*Towards the Last Spike*, 1952
*Magic in Everything*, 1955
*The Collected Poems of E. J. Pratt*, 1958
*Here the Tides Flow*, 1962
*Selected Poems*, 2000

OTHER LITERARY FORMS

   E. J. Pratt's career as a poet began with an unpublished verse drama, *Clay*. The play is weak in many ways, but as a whole it shows Pratt's early interest in dramatic intensity, a characteristic of his later poetry.

*Clay* reveals the poet's increasing ability to control monologue and dialogue within a larger literary structure. Other literary efforts include two short stories ("'Hooked': A Rocky Mountain Experience," 1914, and "Golfomania," 1924), critical articles, reviews, and introductions to books (most notably, Herman Melville's 1929 edition of *Moby Dick*, and Thomas Hardy's 1937 edition of *Under the Greenwood Tree*). Two other works of significance are his published thesis, *Studies in Pauline Eschatology and Its Background* (1917) and his religious verses and hymns, included in Denzil D. Ridout's *United to Serve* (1927).

ACHIEVEMENTS

   To define E. J. Pratt's accomplishment is problematic: He is the best-known and most respected of all Canadian poets, yet he is an isolated and a solitary figure. His achievement is based on compelling and moving lyric and narrative verse, but his poetic masters cannot be easily traced and his poetic disciples cannot be found. Pratt avoided formulating a strict poetic creed, and he refused to follow the rules of any poetic school; thus he cannot be conveniently categorized or explained. Pratt's artistic vision is indisputably broad, warm, humanistic, and universal. Courage in the face of a hostile natural environment, fidelity to the values that cultivate and civilize, compassion for those not always able to endure the trials of simple existence—these compose the core of Pratt's preoccupation as a poet. His success in making these concerns concrete, particular, and forceful twice won him the Governor General's Award, Canada's most coveted prize for literature.

   Part of Pratt's success rests in his conviction that poetry is public writing, not private exposé or confession. By using plain language and traditional end-rhyme, as well as disarmingly simple plots or events (subtly enhancing all these through wit, irony, and contemporary themes), Pratt created a poetry that caught the attention and earned the admiration of both the general reader and the scholar. If anything, his career marks the culmination of the poetry and poetic craft that preceded him—that of Bliss Carman, Charles G. D. Roberts, F. R. Scott, and Archibald Lampman; it also led the way to the acceptance of modernism, though Pratt stops just short of being Canada's first indisputable modernist.

Pratt's most significant contributions to Canadian literature lie in the concreteness and precision of his "impersonal" lyrics and his fast-paced, economical, direct narratives. His lyrics resemble small sculptures; the visual and emotional impact of feeling arrested in words durable as stone attracts the reader's eye. The representative images of love, hope, loss, or fear captured in these poems are never clever, abstruse, academic, or strained. Pratt was the first Canadian poet to present an image and then refrain from commenting, explaining, moralizing, or philosophizing for the reader—tendencies that often characterized the poets who preceded him.

In the narratives, Pratt's contribution is even more significant. In poems such as *The Titanic* and *Brébeuf and His Brethren*, he gave shape to and refined the "documentary" narrative in verse, a form no longer popular. Pratt can be viewed as the last practitioner of direct narratives in Canadian writing. Second, Pratt was the last Canadian who did not fall under the spell of modernism *à la* T. S. Eliot or Ezra Pound. Pratt wrestled with a poetic form that he himself termed "extravaganza." The form is based on wit, comedy, hyperbole, and discontinuity, and the narratives of this type may represent the first literary form of significance created by a Canadian.

## BIOGRAPHY

Edwin John Pratt was born in Newfoundland, the son of John Pratt, a Methodist missionary from Yorkshire, and Fanny Knight, a sea-captain's daughter. Pratt spent his first twenty-three years in Newfoundland, and his early life in the outport villages marked him: The sea can be felt in his rhythms and the coastal shore perceived in his imagery. In 1901, he graduated from the Methodist College in St. John's. For nearly six years, Pratt was a probationer in the Methodist ministry who taught and preached in various villages. In 1907, he elected to go to Toronto to study philosophy at Victoria College. He soon earned his M.A. degree, then decided to complete a B.A. in divinity. In 1917, having again changed his field of study, he received his Ph.D. in psychology. Pratt married Viola Whitney in 1918; two

years later, she gave birth to their only child, Mildred Claire. Also in 1920, Pratt shifted careers again: This time he became a professor of English at Victoria College, a position he retained until his retirement in 1954, when the title professor emeritus was conferred on him. Pratt died ten years later. In academic terms, then, this poet's training was unusually long and varied; its effects can be seen in his poetry. Pratt's early life in Newfoundland taught him to love poetry that was as direct and immediate as a ballad of the sea, and his later years of education in philosophy, divinity, psychology, and literature supplied his characteristic themes. Pratt's language is clear and plain, not regional; his themes are universal, not private.

## ANALYSIS

The poetry of E. J. Pratt falls into three categories: the shorter lyrics, the documentary-like narratives, and the extravaganzas. The division in form, however, does not suggest a division in outlook. Pratt is almost always concerned with the clash between the human, as individual or group, and the amoral strength and power of the natural world. As a man, Pratt admired courage, civilization, and compassion; as a poet, he celebrated their purpose, function, and value. He saw people inhabiting a world where there are no answers about the rightness of values, but he also perceived that no person can live without them. Pratt did not preach or lecture his readers, nor did he argue with them; rather, he showed his readers the paradoxes and ironies that result when a morally sensitive being inhabits an essentially amoral world.

The theme is examined most easily in Pratt's lyrics. The short poems are often elusive and complex, rich in meaning and powerful in impact. Many of the poems, moreover, begin in Pratt's own experience, but by the time he has finished with them, they are purified of the narrowly private and personal. Once Pratt has finished with a lyric, it stands open for all readers of all ages.

### "EROSION"

A poem such as "Erosion" is typical of Pratt's artistry and technical mastery. When Pratt was a young boy in a Newfoundland fishing village, his father, a minister, would often, as the most trying of his duties, have to announce to a woman the death at sea of her husband or son. The shock recorded in the woman's face etched itself on the poet's mind immediately, but it took him nearly thirty years to record the experience properly in verse.

The final version of the poem is only eight lines long, and Pratt omits everything that would detract from his central idea—the impact of the sea's force on the woman's life. Pratt dismisses his father's presence, his own presence, and the announcement of death. In their place, the poet stresses the passage of time. The first stanza of the poem portrays the sea's unending effort to "trace" features into a cliff. The features in the stone, as all those who have walked along a shoreline know, have a disconcertingly "human" look. In Pratt's poem, then, the sea has, for more than a thousand years, attempted to humanize nature (the cliff) by giving it a face.

The second stanza of the poem stresses that the woman looking at the sea-carving changes dramatically in the mere hour of watching the power and strength of a storm at sea. Possibly her son or husband is in a ship caught in that storm, but the poet deliberately avoids commenting on that point. It is enough to know that the sea has failed to complete the face in the cliff, and that the woman's face, in an hour, has turned to granite. The result, the poem suggests, is that the face of the cliff and the face of the woman resemble each other. The complex response that the short poem elicits, then, is that the sea may be humanizing the cliff, but that it is dehumanizing the woman, for she takes on a more elemental, stonelike appearance.

The poem, then, records the irony of an amoral world that appears to humanize, but, in fact, dehumanizes. The poem, however, is multileveled. Throughout the eight lines, the sea is compared to an artist who traces and sculpts his forms with diligence and care. To attribute artistic qualities to the sea outlines its creative, rather than its destructive, power. The reader who puzzles over this positive feature is on the way to an understanding of Pratt's complexity, despite the seeming simplicity. A second reading of this elusive poem suggests that the woman may be merely overawed by the sea's power, magnificence, and force. Recalcitrant nature, insensitive to the movements and powers surrounding it, requires centuries to change; the woman is

transformed in her moment of insight. The rock passively undergoes its metamorphosis as the sea carves its pattern on it. The permanence, durability, and strength of the cliff rest on its impassive and insensible state.

The woman, in sharp contrast, observes the storm at sea and undergoes a metamorphosis springing from the inner source of being, the emotions. Unlike the cliff, which is acted on by an outside force, the woman actively responds to what she sees. Her sensibility, in other words, sets her apart from nature. Furthermore, her ability to feel is similar to that of the sea, yet stronger; what the sea can do in a thousand years, her emotions can do in an hour. At the same time, the sculpture of the cliff resembles the sculpture on her face, a parallelism that suggests the truly complex, ambiguous, and ironic tone of the poem. The essential quality that distinguishes a human being from nature (the ability to feel) is precisely the characteristic that underscores the resemblance to it, since both must suffer physical "erosion." Ironically, the inner ability to respond affirms that human sensitivity, perception, and insight are both magnificent and frightening—in a word, awesome. Loneliness, fear, isolation, and loss are felt by all humans, and Pratt points out the irony of all human experience—the very ability to feel emotions can both ennoble and destroy.

### "FROM STONE TO STEEL" AND "THE SHARK"

In numerous other poems, Pratt constantly reinvigorates his theme by illustrating how humans can be both elevated and demeaned by the qualities they cherish most. In "The Shark," a speaker sees this "tubular" creature as the symbol of the human need to inhabit a world filled by creatures wholly other than humans, for they are "cold-blooded." The very ability to perceive differences isolates humans and adds to their fear and loneliness. In "From Stone to Steel," Pratt sees the inherent human urge to offer sacrifices as the supreme example both of people's noblest virtue and of their most ignominious vice. On one hand, the sacrifice indicates a belief in something or someone higher than human beings, thereby leading humans to the grace of the temple. On the other hand, the urge to sacrifice may be abused, leading humans to tyranny and barbarism, for people can also force others to become sacrificed.

## DOCUMENTARY REALISM

In the lyrics, no emotion presented by Pratt is simple or clear-cut. In fact, he delights in tracing the complexities of emotions that all humans feel and experience but can never explain or understand. When readers turn to the longer narratives, they are again astounded by Pratt's mastery of a direct, clear story which, on careful reading, demands all their intelligence, sensibility, and emotion. The most notable of these narratives are "The Ice-Floes," *The Titanic*, *The Roosevelt and the Antinoe*, and *Brébeuf and His Brethren*. All the narratives listed here share the quality of "documentary" realism. Pratt carefully researched and studied the materials for these poems, and one of their features is historical accuracy. The poems are, however, profound studies of human emotion. In each work, furthermore, Pratt concentrates on the interest of a community in crisis.

"The Ice-Floes" centers on the Newfoundland seal hunt. A group of hunters form the focus, although the events are recorded through one spokesman. The narrative concentrates on the dangers undertaken by the men so that they may survive in a hostile environment. The very courage, determination, and relentlessness that they display, however, makes them the victims of the elements they are attempting to overcome. Staying too late and too long on the ice floes, wholly immersed in the challenge of their hunt, they become trapped by a sudden, violent storm. Like the seals they hunt, the men have become the victims of a force they cannot master. Their dogged endurance and determination has betrayed them.

## THE TITANIC AND THE ROOSEVELT AND THE ANTINOE

In *The Titanic* and *The Roosevelt and the Antinoe*, Pratt again explores the need for courage, fidelity, and compassion. In *The Titanic*, he ruthlessly documents the sleep of human reason. The ship's machinery is believed to be infallible. The illusion that humans can rival God by creating an unsinkable ship leads to hubris. The intelligence that can design the ocean liner fails to recognize that no human creation is perfect. The delusion holds to the end; humans have created the very force that takes them to death at sea. In *The Roosevelt and the Antinoe*, the form of presentation is reversed. The captain of the ship perceives that

success is based on the unpredictable toss of a wave and that no resource known to humanity can foretell the result. Without the courage to try, without the conviction that nature is fundamentally indifferent, Pratt's captain learns to understand, no human achievement is possible.

## BRÉBEUF AND HIS BRETHREN

The final poem of interest in Pratt's series of documentary narratives is *Brébeuf and His Brethren*. The poem is acknowledged as his masterpiece in this vein. It presents the lives of the martyrs who brought the Christian faith to Canada and who eventually died at the hands of the Indians. The climax of the poem is crucial to an understanding of the whole. Brébeuf is violently tortured by the Indians, who celebrate his murder with a mock baptism and communion. Dying, Brébeuf must endure the abuse of the very religious rites that he has taught the Indians. The rituals that are to cleanse, ennoble, and enlighten the spirit merely allow the Indians to indulge in barbarism and brutality, culminating in cannibalism. The poem, then, echoes the ambiguous sacrifices of "From Stone to Steel" and indicates Pratt's ever-increasing sense of irony in human experience and action.

In the atomic age, far removed from the pioneers and early settlers, an age wherein the products of intelligence have given humans reason to fear even the best in themselves, Pratt is not foreign or incomprehensible or old-fashioned. The documentary narratives may appear traditional, but their philosophical outlook has been considered extremely modern.

## EXTRAVAGANZAS

One further strand of Pratt's development should be discussed here, his extravaganzas: *The Witches' Brew*, *Titans* ("The Cachalot" and "The Great Feud"), *The Fable of the Goats*, and *Towards the Last Spike*. All these works are characterized by wit, irony, and humor. Each is based on some kind of trial, and by the end of every one of them, the readers' ability to master ambiguities, inconsistencies, and paradoxes is fully tested as well. In the extravaganzas, Pratt vigorously displays that no intuition or perception or theory about reality is adequate to explain the world that humans inhabit. In *The Witches' Brew*, a tour de force about an alcoholic orgy among sea creatures who are visited by an incongruous assemblage of theorizers about reality—from John Calvin to Immanuel Kant—no one, including the narrator, can explain the behavior of Tom, the rakish cat from Zanzibar. The cat is partly a creature of evolution and partly a creature derived from some magic spark, but once drunk he is brutal, callous, and dangerous. *The Witches' Brew* is a black comedy centering on humanity's inexplicable beginnings and its intrinsic irrationality. No one in the poem, least of all Tom, can understand why he does the things he does, and not one of the wise shades can provide an answer.

In many ways, the narrative is amusing, but it is equally terrifying, for Tom murders all his kin in the course of the poem. At each turn of events, moreover, the reader questions why the cat should be compelled to destroy every warm-blooded creature in sight. Pratt seems to be drawing on his eclectic education to dismiss theories of Christianity, science, philosophy, and evolution. The world, Pratt's extravaganzas insist, will not conform to the expectations, wishes, theories, or desires of humans or creatures.

Such a vision, however, should not be read as pessimism. For Pratt, the acknowledgment of human reason is central because the admission compels people to rely on compassion, understanding, and mercy, rather than on theory or abstraction. Alexander Pope once expressed this notion by declaring that "a little knowledge is a dangerous thing"; Pratt would modify the line this way: The illusion that the quantity of knowledge can replace its quality is even more dangerous than the knowing of nothing at all.

### TOWARDS THE LAST SPIKE

In *Towards the Last Spike*, Pratt's last major narrative, he redevelops his extravaganza by muting its outrageousness. He now blends extravaganza and narrative to examine the history of the Canadian transcontinental railway. The final product is Pratt's most daring experiment, and if it fails, it fails only in the sense that Pound's *Cantos* (1925-1972) dealing with John Adams may be said to have failed. The deliberate fragmentation, the mixture of history and invention, and the blend of the actual and the literary often tax the reader beyond endurance.

The poem is necessary, however, for a complete understanding of Pratt's aims as a poet. In *Towards the Last Spike*, Pratt wished to unify the various strands of his writing. The poem dramatizes what people can achieve with courage, compassion, and fidelity to the values that advance the ambitions of a culture. Pratt chooses for subject matter the forging of a railway line that, both metaphorically and literally, made a physical reality of a nation previously only dreamed of and talked about. It is, above all, a positive vision, although the poem is neither naïvely optimistic nor overly idealistic about human success in a world that is fundamentally other than sentient humans. The universe cannot be conquered, controlled, or explained in Pratt's poetic vision, but humans can be dignified by their actions. *Towards the Last Spike*, in a huge "Panorama," records Pratt's belief that humans do not simply exist in a monstrous world, but that they are beings burdened with the awesome task of using their vision, courage, and endurance to accomplish the dreams with which they are, for some inexplicable reason, born. This constant determination to face the test is, for E. J. Pratt, humanity's central claim to dignity.

### OTHER MAJOR WORKS

SHORT FICTION: "'Hooked': A Rocky Mountain Experience," 1914; "Golfomania," 1924.

NONFICTION: *Studies in Pauline Eschatology and Its Background*, 1917; "Introduction," in *Moby Dick*, 1929; "Introduction," in *Under the Greenwood Tree*, 1937.

### BIBLIOGRAPHY

Djwa, Sandra. *E. J. Pratt: The Evolutionary Vision*. Vancouver, B.C.: Copp Clark, 1974. An authoritative and insightful study of Pratt and a must for scholars of his work. Particularly noteworthy is how Djwa delineates Pratt's views on the roles of fate and free will in determining human action. Especially informative is the section on how Pratt adapts his many sources for *The Titanic*.

McAuliffe, Angela T. C. *Between the Temple and the Cave*. Ithaca, N.Y.: McGill-Queen's University Press, 2000. A critical study of Pratt's poetry with a focus on its religious aspects. Includes bibliographical references and index.

Pitt, David G. *E. J. Pratt: The Truant Years, 1882-1927.* Toronto, Ont.: University of Toronto Press, 1984. The first volume in a full-length biography of Pratt, highly recommended for Pratt scholars and general readers alike. It is meticulously researched and contains plenty of biographical details to enhance understanding of Pratt's poems.

_____. *E. J. Pratt: The Master Years, 1927-1964.* Toronto, Ont.: University of Toronto Press, 1987. The second volume in Pitt's biography, equally accessible to both scholar and general reader.

Pratt, E. J. *E. J. Pratt on His Life and Poetry.* Edited by Susan Gingell. Toronto, Ont.: University of Toronto Press, 1983. A valuable resource of Pratt's evaluation of his life and work from the mid-1920's to the 1950's. This volume provides much understanding about Pratt and his creative process. Included are two interviews Pratt gave on Canadian television in the 1950's. Gingell's introduction explores the nature of Pratt's commentaries on his work and appraises their value in terms of their literary and social context.

Vinson, James. *Great Writers of the English Language: Poets.* New York: St. Martin's Press, 1979. The entry on Pratt acknowledges that he is regarded as Canada's "pre-eminent narrative poet." Cites *Brébeuf and His Brethren* as his finest long narrative, an example of his ability to establish dramatic coherency in his verse. Notes also Pratt's preoccupation with primeval themes of conflict in his poems.

Wilson, Milton. *E. J. Pratt.* Toronto, Ont.: McClelland & Stewart, 1969. A concise but comprehensive literary criticism of Pratt's works, emphasizing his strength as a narrative poet. Discusses his shorter, more lyrical poems, his longer narratives, as well as the sea poems and *Brébeuf and His Brethren.*

*Ed Jewinski*

# F. T. PRINCE

**Born:** Kimberley, South Africa; September 13, 1912
**Died:** Southampton, England; August 7, 2003

PRINCIPAL POETRY

*Poems,* 1938
*Soldiers Bathing, and Other Poems,* 1954
*The Stolen Heart,* 1957
*The Doors of Stone: Poems, 1938-1962,* 1963
*Memoirs in Oxford,* 1970
*Drypoints of the Hasidim,* 1975
*Afterword on Rupert Brooke,* 1976
*Collected Poems,* 1979 (includes *A Last Attachment*)
*The Yüan Chên Variations,* 1981
*Later On,* 1983
*Walks in Rome,* 1987
*Collected Poems, 1935-1992,* 1993

OTHER LITERARY FORMS

F. T. Prince wrote widely in addition to his poetry. Among his more important publications are *The Italian Element in Milton's Verse* (1954), *William Shakespeare: The Poems* (1963), and *The Study of Form and the Renewal of Poetry* (1964).

ACHIEVEMENTS

Equally distinguished as poet and scholar, F. T. Prince brought to all his work a formidable and wide-ranging intellect, an informed compassion, and a remarkable eloquence. In addition, his poetry demonstrates that he had a perfect ear. Never involved in "movements" in the politics of literature, he sometimes seemed a lonely figure, yet other poets were always aware of his quality and importance, and his dedication to his craft was a signal influence on younger writers at times when contemporary work seemed to have lost its way. A consummate craftsperson, at home in free or fixed forms, he was almost unique in being able to place all his learning at the service of his poetry.

His work has been recognized by the award of honorary doctorates in literature from both the University of Southampton and New York University. In 1982, he won the E. M. Forster award from the American Academy and Institute of Arts and Letters.

BIOGRAPHY

Frank Templeton Prince was born in Kimberley, Cape Province, South Africa, where his father, Henry Prince, was a prosperous businessman in the diamond trade. His mother, Margaret Hetherington Prince, had been a teacher. Both parents were English. Prince was a sensitive and studious child. He already possessed keen powers of observation and an eye for detail that led to an early interest in painting. His mother's influence and the stories and poems she read to Prince and his sister encouraged the boy to write, and he was a poet from the age of fifteen.

After a short period in which he trained as an architect, Prince went to England in 1931 and entered Balliol College, Oxford. He earned a first-class honors degree in English in 1934. It is apparent that the move to Oxford was both important and inevitable, since the poet's sensibility and culture were, almost from the start, strongly European. He went up to Oxford already fluent in French and deeply read in French poetry. He supported this by reading Dante in Italian and by making several visits to Italy. He found the whole period of the Renaissance, and in particular its art, highly congenial.

A meeting with T. S. Eliot in 1934 probably led to the later inclusion of Prince's first collection, *Poems*, in the Faber and Faber poetry list in 1938. Eliot recognized Prince's ability as well by printing the younger poet's "An Epistle to a Patron" in the *Criterion*, which Eliot edited.

During 1934-1935, Prince was a visiting fellow at Princeton University, but he returned to London to work at the Royal Institute of International Affairs, an unlikely office for so apolitical a man. He was, however, writing, and a meeting with William Butler Yeats in 1937, when Prince traveled to Dublin to meet the great man, suggests that poetry held pride of place in his mind.

There is no acknowledgment in Prince's work at this point that Europe was on the point of war, but the poet was soon to be personally involved. He was commissioned into the Intelligence Corps of the British army in 1940 and sent to Bletchley Park. This was the Government Communications Centre, hardly a typical army environment. Men were allowed to wear civilian clothes, discipline was relaxed, and among the creative people involved there, many were not of the type to worry unduly about military correctness. The poet Vernon Watkins served there, as did the composer Daniel Jones, a friend of Dylan Thomas. Prince was at Bletchley Park until March, 1943, when he was posted to Cairo. Before leaving, he married Elizabeth Bush. There are two daughters from the marriage.

His time in Egypt, which lasted until 1944, gave Prince the experience that resulted in the writing of his best-known poem, "Soldiers Bathing." On his return, Prince spent several months as an interpreter in Italian prisoner-of-war camps in England before his demobilization.

In 1946, Prince began his academic career, being appointed lecturer in English at the University of Southampton, at that time a small university in an interesting city, which must have been a pleasant appointment for Prince. In any event, he stayed there for nearly thirty years, becoming eventually professor of English

*F. T. Prince*

and, between 1962 and 1965, dean of the faculty of arts. It was there, moreover, that he wrote the great bulk of his postwar poetry. He was a visiting fellow of All Souls College, Oxford, in 1968, and Clark Lecturer at Cambridge in 1972. From 1975 to 1978, he was a professor of English at the University of the West Indies, in Mona, Kingston, Jamaica. He then spent the next years as visiting professor at several institutions that included Amherst College, Washington University, and Sana'a University in North Yemen, Arab Republic.

He was writer-in-residence at Hollins College in Virginia in the spring of 1984 and spent two summers teaching at Dalhousie University, Halifax in the mid-1980's. During the 1980's, his American admirers, among them John Ashbery, showed their respect for his work and assisted in its dissemination. Until his death in August of 2003, Prince made his home in Southampton.

### ANALYSIS

The *Collected Poems* of 1979 brought together all the early work from *Poems* and *Soldiers Bathing, and Other Poems* that F. T. Prince wanted to retain. He also included the whole of *The Doors of Stone* and four long, late poems, *Memoirs in Oxford*, *Drypoints of the Hasidim*, *Afterword on Rupert Brooke*, and *A Last Attachment*. These poems may be safely considered the work by which Prince would wish to be judged.

### "TO A MAN ON HIS HORSE" AND "AN EPISTLE TO A PATRON"

The first poem is "An Epistle to a Patron," so admired by Eliot. When one recalls that the great young poet of the day was W. H. Auden and that the most admired poetry then was political and very aware of the contemporary world, Prince's lines are startling.

> My lord, hearing lately of your opulence in promise and your house
> Busy with parasites, of your hands full of favours, your statutes
> Admirable as music, and no fear of your arms not prospering, I have
> Considered how to serve you . . .

The reader is at once in Renaissance Italy, a period much favored by Prince and one in which he is at home.

Although the poem is written in the first person, it must not be assumed that the voice is Prince's voice. Rather, the poem is a dramatic monologue. It is not in the manner of Robert Browning either, although it moves in an area Browning sometimes occupied. Its splendid opulence, its sonorous and bewitching periods, are not like Browning. Nor do they hide the slyness, the mockery behind the flattery with which this postulant addresses his hoped-for patron. Ben Jonson could have written it, but it is a strange invention for the late 1930's. If Prince uses the first person voice, as he does often throughout his career, rarely does he speak as himself—then he is a more everyday speaker altogether—but rather as a real resident of those times and places into which his learning and his curiosity have led him. His manner is courtly and aristocratic. If he uses, as he does in the opening lines of "To a Man on His Horse," a poetic inversion, it is for the dance of the statement, because he wants the movement:

> Only the Arab stallion will I
> Envy you. Along the water
> You dance him with the morning on his flanks . . .

The early work is full of such lines, stately, strangely out of time, full, too, of references to painters such as Paolo Veronese or statesmen such as Edmund Burke. It is a paradox when one realizes that Prince's most famous poem, "Soldiers Bathing," is not at all like the rest of the early work, that it is written about ordinary men, poor, bare, forked animals of the twentieth century. It gave Prince an immediate fame and is known to many readers who know nothing else the poet has written.

### "SOLDIERS BATHING"

"Soldiers Bathing" is a poem of sixty-six lines, organized in six irregular verse paragraphs. The lines are not of regular length, and they rhyme in couplets. In it, the poet, an army officer, watches his men as, forgetting momentarily the stress and mire of war, they swim and play in the sea. It is often a clumsy poem, the longer second line of some of the couplets occasionally dragging along without grace, the structure and movement absurdly prosaic for a poet of Prince's skill, yet it is intensely moving. The extraordinary syntax of the last line of the first stanza, so written, surely, to accommodate the rhyme, has been noted by many critics, particularly by Vernon Scannell in *Not Without Glory*. "Their flesh worn by the trade of war, revives/ And my mind towards the meaning of it strives." It is also, however, full of marvelous compassion, as Prince, recalling Michelangelo's cartoon of soldiers bathing, is able to unite friend and foe, dead and living soldiers, through his insight into the continuing folly of wars. He does this through his knowledge of art, but his own comfort comes from his religion. Prince is a Catholic, and the reader's understanding of his poetry is incomplete without this knowledge. He arrives at a sad conclusion: "Because to love is frightening we prefer/ The freedom of our crimes." He began the poem under "a reddening sky"; he ends it "while in the west/ I watch a streak of blood that might have issued from Christ's breast." This is a typical movement in a poem by Prince, one in which the plain and dissimilar elements are united in an understanding brought about by the poet's belief.

The great popularity of that fine poem tended to overshadow a number of poems that might more surely have suggested the nature and direction of Prince's gift. There were, for example, some love poems of great beauty and passion. He was to develop this ability until, in July, 1963, an anonymous reviewer in *The Times Literary Supplement* could write of Prince that he is "one of the best love poets of the age, a lyricist of great charm and tenderness and emotion, counter-balanced by a subtlety of thought and metaphor which often reminds one of Donne. . . ." The reference to John Donne is felicitous, since there is an affinity in the work of these men, brought into even clearer focus by Prince's liking for and familiarity with the seventeenth century.

### THE DOORS OF STONE

*The Doors of Stone*, then, contains poems of all the categories noted so far: monologues such as "Campanella" and "Strafford," love poems such as the eighteen sections of "Strombotti," and poems suggested, like "Coeur de Lion," by history. They demonstrate once again the curious, elusive quality of Prince's poetry; it possesses dignity, honesty, even directness, yet the poet himself remains aloof, often behind masks.

### MEMOIRS IN OXFORD

Almost as a rebuff to that opinion, Prince's next book was a long autobiographical poem, *Memoirs in Oxford*. Written in a verse form suggested by the one Percy Bysshe Shelley used in *Peter Bell the Third* (1839), it is at once chatty, clever, and revealing. It is particularly helpful about the poet's early life. It is also a delightful and accomplished poem—and a very brave one. To write a long poem in these days is unusual; to abandon what seems to be one's natural gift for eloquence and adopt a different tone altogether in which to write a long poem might seem foolhardy. Yet it is a very successful poem, having the virtues of clarity, wit, and style as well as some of the attraction of a good novel.

### DRYPOINTS OF THE HASIDIM

Prince's father was of partly Jewish extraction, which might account for his interest in those "Dark hollow faces under caps/ In days and lands of exile . . . and among unlettered tribes" which figured so strongly in his next long poem, *Drypoints of the Hasidim*. Hasidism was a popular Jewish religious movement of the eighteenth and nineteenth centuries, and Prince's poem is a long meditation on the beliefs of this movement. Despite its learning, it is extremely clear, like all of Prince's poetry. Rarely can there have been a poet so scholarly and knowledgeable whose verse is so accessible.

As if to emphasize his virtuosity, Prince's next work is a verse reconstruction of the life and times of Rupert Brooke, the young and handsome poet whose early death in World War I assured him of fame. Using the information provided by Christopher Hassall in his biography of Brooke, Prince wrote from his own standpoint of "the damned successful poet" and also added, years after his own war, a commentary on youth and love and the ironies of war. The texture of these lines is far removed from the great splendors of the young Prince:

> But Bryn quite blatantly prefers
> Walking alone on Exmoor to the drawing-room
> With the Ranee, and she finds all the girls so odd . . .

It does, however, contain a real feeling of the times, despite occasional prosiness.

### A LAST ATTACHMENT

Prince had never been afraid of the long poem; even as a young man, he wrote pieces of unusual length for modern times. *A Last Attachment* is based on Laurence

Sterne's *Journal to Eliza* (1904). Shorter than the two poems previously noted, it once again considers the recurring problems that are central to Prince's preoccupations: love, the onset of age, an inability to settle and be content, jealousy, the triumphs and failures of the creative and artistic life—all great problems, glanced at, too, in *The Yüan Chên Variations*. They are problems that no doubt beset Prince himself, but he has chosen with dignity and objectivity to consider them most often through a series of characters taken from literature or history or art, rather than use direct personal experience. He has written of them all with elegance and seriousness and with great skill and honesty. His poetry is sometimes said to be unfashionable, and so it is if the word means that he belongs to no group, is determined to be his own man. He has always commanded the respect of his fellow poets, and that, very probably, is a guarantee of his importance and his growing stature.

### COLLECTED POEMS, 1935-1992

Prince converted to Catholicism in the 1930's. His poetry did not take on a doctrinal cast, even though the exotic aestheticism of his earliest poems cooled somewhat. The resulting seriousness and intensity benefits from this interesting mix of sensuous diction and moral gravity. For example, in "An Epistle to a Patron," the poet speaker addresses his "patron" as "A donor of laurel and of grapes, a font of profuse intoxicants." This kind of aesthetic paganism yields to the passionate religious feeling of "Soldiers Bathing":

> I feel a strange delight that fills me full
> Strange gratitude, as if evil itself, were beautiful
> And kiss the wound in thought, while in the west
> I watch a streak of red that might have issued from
>     Christ's breast.

Although the modern reader will detect touches of late Pre-Raphaelite sensual religiosity in these lines, a second look will also evoke the tragic joy of Gerard Manley Hopkins at his most intense. As evident in many of the poems in this collection, the opposites of sense and spirit never cease to dance their all-consuming rhythms in Prince's verse.

Opposites are a dialectical challenge for Prince. They do not deconstruct into a deferred meaning that is food only for skeptical detachment. The voice of the

Sibyl (from the myth involving Apollo and Sibyl of Cumae) is historicized in the monologue, "The Old Age of Michelangelo." The great artist speaks for Prince's own struggle with the opposites of desire and faith that have raged in unabated confrontation:

> And now I have grown old
> It is my own life, my long life I see
> As a combat against nature, nature that is our enemy
> Holding the soul a prisoner by the heel;
> And my whole anxious life I see
> As a combat with myself, that I do violence to myself
> To bruise and beat and batter
> And bring under
> My own being,
> Which is an infinite savage sea of love.

Prince also has his lighter vein and delights in the play of verse as well as its passion. In "The Doors of Stone," he experimented with an Italian stanza first introduced to English poetry by Sir Thomas Wyatt. These stanzas, "Strambotti," enable Prince to exercise his dialectical imagination in a poised, cerebral dance of witty argument and rhyme.

The collection also showcases Prince's cosmopolitan life, perhaps most impressively in *Drypoints of the Hasidim*, a later and long poem of more than four hundred lines. It is a measure of his devotion to religious experience that he, a devout Catholic, should have been drawn to the intense inwardness of Jewish mysticism.

OTHER MAJOR WORKS

NONFICTION: *The Italian Element in Milton's Verse*, 1954; *William Shakespeare: The Poems*, 1963; *The Study of Form and the Renewal of Poetry*, 1964.

TRANSLATION: *Sir Thomas Wyatt*, 1961 (of Sergio Baldi's biography).

BIBLIOGRAPHY

Davie, Donald. "Beyond the Here and Now." Review of *Collected Poems*. *The New York Times Book Review*, April 8, 1979, 13. In reviewing *Collected Poems*, Davie notes that Prince has done nothing as fine as "Soldiers Bathing," considered one of the best poems to come out of World War II. He criticizes Prince for not "giving us what we ask for," although he concedes that *Collected Poems* will be well liked.

Howell, Anthony. "Obituary: F. T. Prince—Poet Famed for Lyrical Images of 'Soldiers Bathing.'" *The Guardian*, August 8, 2003, p. 27. Describes the poet's relationship with fame, calls him one of the twentieth century's outstanding poets, and discusses his most famous poem.

Levi, Peter. "F. T. Prince." *Agenda* 15 (Summer/Autumn, 1977): 147-149. An appreciative review of Prince, commending him for his craftsmanship. Levi calls him a distinguished poet and scholar, one who is both intelligent and curious. Reviews *Drypoints of the Hasidim* and discusses the iambic pentameter verse and the allusive stories that form a complete sequence of the history of Hasidism.

Nigam, Alka. *F. T. Prince: A Study of His Poetry.* Salzburg: Institute for English and American Studies, 1983. In the foreword, Prince himself praises Nigam for her "careful and sensitive" study of his poetry. In this full-length study, Nigam analyzes Prince's art and vision, including a historical background of his poetry and its place in twentieth century verse. Contains solid literary criticism. A must for Prince scholars.

Poburko, Nicholas. "Poetry Past and Present: F. T. Prince's *Walks in Rome.*" *Renascence* 51, no. 2 (Winter, 1999): 144-165. An extended analysis of Prince's *Walks in Rome* that favorably compares Prince with other modern poets, gives a brief biography, and notes how Prince is revealed in the poem.

*Leslie Norris*

---

# MATTHEW PRIOR

**Born:** Wimborne, England; July 21, 1664
**Died:** Wimpole, England; September 18, 1721

### PRINCIPAL POETRY

*A Satyr on the Modern Translators*, 1685
*Satyr on the Poets: In Imitation of the Seventh Satyr of Juvenal*, 1687

*An English Ballad*, 1695
*Carmen Saeculare for the Year 1700—To the King*, 1700
*Poems on Several Occasions*, 1707, 1709
*Solomon on the Vanity of the World*, 1718
*Lyric Poems*, 1741

### OTHER LITERARY FORMS

Matthew Prior (PRI-ur) is primarily known for his poetry. His verse, however, ranges widely, from verse epistles and songs to prologues and epilogues for plays. Indeed, there is virtually no kind of poem that he did not attempt, with the exception of the epic. His age expected such versatility from a serious poet, and it regarded him as one of its best. Even if today's readers have relegated him to the second rank, they must acknowledge his virtuosity.

### ACHIEVEMENTS

Matthew Prior does not have the literary stature of his contemporaries Alexander Pope or John Dryden, but he is probably the foremost Augustan poet after them. Augustan poetry takes its name from the Rome of Caesar Augustus, patron of the arts, with whose values many English poets of the late seventeenth and eighteenth centuries felt a special kinship. One way for a poet to establish his ties with ancient Rome was to write the kinds of poetry that the Romans wrote; a hierarchy of such kinds or genres in art had existed since the Renaissance.

Prior wrote in all of them except epic poetry, which stood at the pinnacle of the hierarchy and was the form that Dryden and Pope so brilliantly exploited satirically. Prior's strength was in some of the lesser genres, including odes, pastorals, verse narratives, epigrams, satires, verse essays, elegies, and epitaphs. According to the British *Dictionary of National Biography*, Prior "is one of the neatest of English epigrammatists, and in occasional pieces and familiar verses has no rival in English." Samuel Johnson, the dominant literary figure of the later eighteenth century, wrote that Prior's "diligence has placed him amongst the most correct of the English poets; and he was one of the first that resolutely endeavored at correctness." Prior may not have possessed the force of Dryden or the penetrating vision of

Pope, but he achieved an elegance seldom matched by poets of any age.

BIOGRAPHY

Matthew Prior, born July 21, 1664, was himself aware of his limitations as a poet. In his "Essay on Learning," he observes: "I had two Accidents in Youth which hindred me from being quite possest with the Muse." One was the accident of his education. He had been singularly fortunate, as the son of a laborer, to have been assisting in his uncle's tavern one day when Lord Dorset found him reading Horace and asked him to turn an ode into English. Impressed with the result, Dorset undertook to provide for Prior's subsequent education. Advantageous as this sponsorship proved, Prior lamented that he was "bred in a Colledge where prose was more in fashion than Verse . . . so that Poetry which by the bent of my Mind might have become the business of my Life, was by the Happyness of my Education only the Amusement of it." The other accident of youth was, likewise, a form of success in activities other than writing poetry. As secretary to the newly appointed ambassador to The Hague for King William in 1691, Prior showed such political and business aptitude that he found himself serving in various diplomatic roles over the next twenty-two years, including negotiator for the Treaty of Utrecht in 1711-1712, a treaty that would become popularly known—especially among Queen Anne's Whig opposition—as "Matt's Peace."

When the queen died in 1714 and the Whigs assumed power, Prior found himself under house arrest. His friends came to his financial rescue after his release in 1716, and Lord Harley helped Prior purchase Down Hall, whose condition he joked about in one of his last poems: "Oh! now a low, ruined white shed I descern/ Until'd, and unglaz'd, I believe 'tis a barn." After some rebuilding under the direction of the architect James Gibbs, however, Prior was able to spend his last years, like Horace on his Sabine Farm, in rural retirement. Prior died while visiting Lord Harley in 1721, equally famous for his political career as for his poetic one. Even if he was not the foremost poet of his age, Prior is to be admired as a late Renaissance embodiment of the "universal man," a statesman and a poet.

ANALYSIS

Matthew Prior's political and poetical interests served each other well when special events called for panegyrical poems. Much of Prior's early poetry is of this kind. His first published poem was an ode, "On the Coronation of the Most August Monarch K. James II, and Queen Mary. The 23rd. of April, 1685." Prior writes that he cannot prevent his fancy from imagining the king, rowing up the Thames with his company, to be crowned. Prior compares the impending arrival with Jason's when he bore the golden fleece back to Greece, with the rising of the sun, with a Roman triumph, and with the first coming of Christ. The urge to draw such analogies was typical of Augustan poets, but to do so in praise of the king was to risk seeming self-serving, if not obsequious. Indeed, many writers of birthday odes to the king or queen

*Matthew Prior* (Hulton Archive/Getty Images)

were exactly that. Prior avoids the trap by framing his praise as a flight of fancy, as a prompting of his soul that he cannot restrain as he anticipates the event.

Prior's poems of praise do not always take the stricter poetic forms that the term "ode" may imply. His 565-line poem to the king, *Carmen Saeculare, for the Year 1700—To the King*, is in rhymed quatrains, or linked pairs of couplets. In 1695, he wrote a ballad to celebrate the English recapture of Namur from France, a poem that mocks a French "victory" poem of 1692, stanza by stanza.

Perhaps the best example of Prior's ability to carry off a difficult task with elegance is his poem "To a Child of Quality of Five Years Old: The Author suppos'd Forty." To write a poem praising the child of a nobleman (the earl of Jersey) is to risk sentimentality, if not fulsomeness. Prior amuses his readers by amusing himself with the idea that an age difference will always separate this girl from him. He can lament her indifference now, as if he were a Petrarchan lover, and at the same time describe the reality of seeing his verses used to curl her doll's hair. His regrets are not wholly contrived since, trapped by old age, Prior will indeed "be past making love,/ When she begins to comprehend it." Unlike the occasional poems, of little interest today, this lyrical ode reveals Prior's ability to bring freshness to a potentially tedious subject and to execute a difficult task with grace.

### CLOE POEMS

Prior wrote numerous love poems that in their use of artificial diction, their shepherds and shepherdesses, and their imaginary, timeless, deity-inhabited landscape of Arcadia, are pastoral. In the last of a sequence of poems about Cloe, his mistress in these poems, he calls their dispute a "Pastoral War"; she is no milkmaid, however, and Prior's pastorals are personal lyrics as well as exercises within this conventional genre. Prior implies his regard for Cloe in traditional ways: Cupid mistakes Venus for Cloe and shoots his mother, or Venus mistakes a picture of Cloe for one of herself. In "Cloe Hunting," Apollo mistakes her for his sister Cynthia, only to be chided by Cupid.

In later poems to Cloe, however, the pastoral setting becomes less important, while the relation between Prior and Cloe becomes less convention-bound and

more psychologically interesting. In "A Lover's Anger," Prior begins peevishly to chide Cloe for being two hours late. Cloe protests that a rosebud has fallen into her dress and invites him to look at the mark it has made on her breast. Prior looks and immediately forgets what he had been about to say, having been drawn from the world of watches and missed appointments into her innocent paradise, where one need worry only about love and, occasionally, a falling rosebud. Clearly, however, the pastoral condition is a temporary and imaginary refuge from the real world, which also exists in the poem.

In "Cloe Jealous," Prior's beloved is no longer content to believe in the "pastoral" world that idealized their relationship. Although at first Cloe pretends to weep for "Two poor stragling Sheep," she quickly reveals that she really worries that she is losing her beauty. Prior's "Answer to Cloe Jealous, in the same Stile. The Author sick" avoids her concerns as he describes himself as a dying shepherd, never more to torment her with jealousy. "A Better Answer," he decides, is to treat her as an equal, to flatter her into accepting his infidelities as mere "Art," whereas his "Nature" is to love Cloe best. "I court others in Verse; but I love Thee in Prose," he adds, neglecting to point out that this very answer is another set of verse fabrications. This is one of Prior's most delightful poems, and one that pushes the Cloe series of love lyrics beyond the ordinary limits of its convention; "A Better Answer" both assumes and undercuts the pastoral tradition, while, at the same time, the poem reasserts it.

### RIBALD TALES

Prior is perhaps less successful as a storyteller than he is as a lyricist. The best-told of his ribald tales is "Hans Carvel," the Rabelaisian story of a man who, "Impotent and Old,/ Married a Lass of LONDON Mould." Hans contracts with Satan (in the shape of a lawyer) to restrain his wife's social activities. In solving his problem, Hans finds that the devilish joke is on him, in an ending that Samuel Johnson accurately describes as "not over-decent." By contrast, "Henry and Emma: A Poem, Upon the Model of the Nut-brown Maid," is a moral tale. Most readers agree that the testing of Emma by Henry, who pretends to be leaving for a life of exile to see whether she will accompany him, makes both characters unsympathetic. The possibility exists that Prior meant the poem to be an ironic adaptation, a mocking of the fidelity endorsed in the original, but the evidence for this reading is thin. In either case, Johnson's charge that the dialogue is "dull and tedious" cannot be refuted.

### EPIGRAMS AND EPITAPHS

There can be little disputing Prior's excellence as a writer of epigrams, or short verses with a surprising turn or insight. His best known epigram he calls "A True Maid": "No, no; for my Virginity,/ When I lose that, says ROSE, I'll dye:/ Behind the Elmes, last night, cry'd DICK/ Rose, were You not extreamly Sick?" An epigram of unknown date pushes a philosophical commonplace to a very unphilosophical conclusion: "RISE not till Noon, if Life be but a Dream,/ As Greek and Roman Poets have Exprest:/ Add good Example to so grave a Theme,/ For he who Sleeps the longest lives the best." Epigrams have been described as having a sting in the tail, and Prior's sting is sharp enough to lead one to wonder whether he had a natural bent for satire that his political interests led him to restrict.

### SATIRES

Prior did write some satires on nonpolitical subjects. One of his earliest poems is *A Satyr on the Modern Translators*, on John Dryden in particular for his translation of Ovid's *Epistles* (1681-1683). In a letter, Prior objects: "Our Laureate might in good manners have left the version of Latin authors to those who had the happiness to understand them." Imitations of the Roman literati, on the other hand, were not an abuse of their work but rather an almost obligatory exercise. For example, Prior wrote *Satyr on the Poets*. Perhaps Prior's most original piece is "Alma: Or, The Progress of the Mind," which he wrote while under arrest in 1715-1716. Johnson found the poem in need of a design, while others have argued that Pyrrhonism unifies it. Satire, however, is traditionally loose in its structure, and "Alma" is surely a satire on intellectual systems. The poem's main speaker is Matt, a system-builder. The poem was inspired by *Hudibras* (1663, 1664, 1678), Prior says, and Matt's less learned companion, Dick, like Ralpho or Don Quixote's Sancho Panza, is not readily impressed by Matt's ethereal notions. The soul or mind, poetically termed "Alma," Matt explains, sits in judgment over the testimony of the senses. He

goes on to develop a theory that the mind enters the toes at birth, makes its way to the midsection by adulthood, and causes the enmity and senility of later age when it rises from the seat of action to the head, from which it escapes—ever upward—at death. Dick questions Matt, usually to be put in his place, but Dick does have the last say in the last stanza, where he rejects this sort of wisdom in favor of folly—and calls for a bottle of wine. When one considers the satire of Prior's friend Jonathan Swift in *The Mechanical Operation of the Spirit* (1710), one senses the limits of Prior's explorations as a satirist. Nevertheless, "Alma" is original enough to be of considerable historical interest.

### SOLOMON ON THE VANITY OF THE WORLD

The poem that Prior believed he would be remembered for is *Solomon on the Vanity of the World*, his longest poem, in which Solomon examines knowledge, pleasure, and power, in turn, as sources of human happiness. Not surprisingly, since texts from Ecclesiastes precede each section, Solomon concludes that all human endeavor is vain. Before he submits to the will of his Creator, however, Solomon reflects at length, and even at their best the reflections are disappointing. Book 2, for example, opens with the building of a palace and garden, as grand as wealth can provide. There is no ironic edge to the description, which might have made Solomon's folly more evident; instead, the expensive undertaking sounds very magnificent and Solomon's sudden change of attitude—"I came, beheld, admir'd, reflected, griev'd"—seems unmotivated. Everyone has experienced a sense of "the Work perfected, the Joy was past," but one hopes for more than commonplaces, or at least for more pleasure in the weaving of a fabric on which the commonplaces can be stitched, in a poem of 2,652 lines.

### "JINNY THE JUST"

Epitaphs are meant for tombstones, and Prior composed them throughout his career, from his "An Epitaph on True, her Majesty's Dog," in 1693, to a surprisingly long one for his own tomb in the Poets' Corner of Westminster Abbey. Elegies are about loss, and when they are about a specific death they become occasional poems. One of Prior's best poems is his verse portrait "Jinny the Just," about a recently deceased serving woman whom he describes as "the best Wench in the

Nation." She is "just" in that she is naturally moderate, "between the Coquette, and the Prude." In one stanza (of thirty-five), Prior seems to capture the essence of a lifetime: "While she read and accounted and pay'd and abated/ Eat and Drank, play'd and work't, laught and cry'd, lov'd and hated/ As answer'd the End of her being created." Jinny actually existed, though her identity has never been discovered. She is assumed to have been Prior's mistress for a time, and Prior's lifelong preference for women of the lower classes seemed evidence, to his friends, of Prior's own humble origins. Prior never married.

OTHER MAJOR WORKS

SHORT FICTION: *Dialogues of the Dead*, 1721.

MISCELLANEOUS: *The Literary Works of Matthew Prior*, 1959 (H. Bunker Wright and Monroe K. Spears, editors).

BIBLIOGRAPHY

Gildenhuys, Faith. "Convention and Consciousness in Prior's Love Lyrics." *Studies in English Literature, 1500-1900* 35, no. 3 (Summer, 1995): 437. The poetry of Prior was part of the growing eighteenth century interest in women as subjects rather than simply objects of male passion. The amorous lyrics of Prior and their popularity are examined.

Kline, Richard B. "Tory Prior and Whig Steele: A Measure of Success?" *Studies in English Literature* 9 (Summer, 1969): 427-437. Any evaluation of Prior's poetry must recognize the intensely active role that politics played in his life and work. By pairing Prior with the redoubtable Whig Sir Richard Steele, Kline provides a nice sense of the complex political climate of the late seventeenth and early eighteenth centuries.

Nelson, Nicholas H. "Narrative Transformations: Prior's Art of the Tale." *Studies in Philology* 90, no. 4 (Fall, 1993): 442. Discusses four verse tales written by Prior that Samuel Johnson found effective: "Hans Carvel," "The Ladle," "Protogenes and Apelles," and "Paolo Purgatani and His Wife: An Honest, but a Simple Pair."

Rippy, Frances Mayhew. *Matthew Prior*. New York: Twayne, 1986. An excellent assessment of Prior's life and work, and, given the paucity of critical materials, an invaluable sourcebook. Includes a chronology and a bibliography.

Sitter, John. "About Wit: Locke, Addison, Prior, and the Order of Things." In *Rhetorics of Order/Ordering of Rhetorics in English Neoclassical Literature*, edited by J. Douglas Canfield and J. Paul Hunter. Newark: University of Delaware Press, 1989. A very nice attempt to place Prior within the early neoclassical tradition—a tradition influenced as much by the empiricist philosophy of Locke as by the "classics."

Thorson, James L. "Matthew Prior's 'An Epitaph.'" *Explicator* 51, no. 2 (Winter, 1993): 84. Prior's "An Epitaph" is discussed. Prior's theme, that retiring to the country in not an ideal but, to a thoughtful person, a sentence of mental and moral death, is beautifully exemplified.

*James R. Aubrey*

# Q

## FRANCIS QUARLES

**Born:** Romford, Essex, England; 1592
**Died:** London, England; September 8, 1644

PRINCIPAL POETRY

*A Feast for Wormes Set Forth in a Poeme of the
    History of Jonah*, 1620
*Pentelogia: Or, The Quintessence of Meditation*,
    1620 (appended to *A Feast for Wormes*; 1626,
    published as a separate chapbook)
*Hadassa: Or, The History of Queene Ester*, 1621
*Job Militant, with Meditations Divine and Morall*,
    1624
*Sions Elegies, Wept by Jeremie the Prophet*, 1624
*Sions Sonets Sung by Solomon the King*, 1624
*An Alphabet of Elegies Upon the Much and Truly
    Lamented Death of . . . Doctor Ailmer*, 1625
*Argalus and Parthenia*, 1629
*The Historie of Samson*, 1631
*Divine Fancies: Digested into Epigrammes,
    Meditations, and Observations*, 1632 (in four
    books)
*Divine Poems*, 1633
*Emblemes: Divine and Moral*, 1635 (in five books)
*Hieroglyphikes of the Life of Man*, 1638
*Solomons Recantation, Entituled Ecclesiastes
    Paraphrased*, 1645
*The Shepheards Oracles: Delivered in Certain
    Eglogues*, 1646
*Hosanna: Or, Divine Poems on the Passion of
    Christ*, 1647

OTHER LITERARY FORMS

In later life, Francis Quarles (kwahrlz) published a
pious work in prose called *Enchiridion, Containing Institutions Divine and Moral* (1640). This very popular
collection of aphorisms on religious and ethical subjects was reissued in an expanded edition the year after
its original publication. It is notable for its stylish
phrasing and wordplay.

Always strongly royalist in his sympathies, Quarles
produced several prose works of a political nature toward the end of his life, as the struggle between king
and Commons became more pronounced. *Observations Concerning Princes and States upon Peace and
Warre* (1642) may perhaps be grouped with such
works; although it is essentially another collection of
pious meditations, it had obvious political implications
in such volatile times, similar to those of the poetry in
*The Shepheards Oracles*. More explicitly polemical is
*The Loyal Convert* (1644), a defense of the king's political and religious position. Of a like nature are *The
Whipper Whipt* (1644) and *The New Distemper* (c.
1644). The three royalist polemics were republished
under the collective title *The Protest Royalist in His
Quarrell with the Times* (1645) shortly after the author's death.

Among Quarles's other posthumous publications
are *Judgement and Mercy for Afflicted Soules: Or,
Meditations, Soliloquies, and Prayers* (1646; an unau-
thorized and inaccurate edition of part 2 of this work
had been published in 1644 under the title *Barnabas
and Boanerges: Or, Wine and Oyl for Afflicted Soules*).
*Judgement and Mercy for Afflicted Soules* is a book of
prose meditations which would today probably be classified as prose poems. Also among the posthumous
works, and somewhat surprisingly, is a play—or rather
an interlude or masque—called *The Virgin Widow: A
Comedie* (pb. 1649, written in 1641 or 1642). This
comedy in mixed prose and verse is less amusing than it
might have been, overwhelmed as it is by its strong didactic purpose and allegorical framework.

ACHIEVEMENTS

Nowhere in literary history is the fickleness of fashion more clearly illustrated than in the case of Francis
Quarles. As Horace Walpole, looking back on the earlier period from the vantage point of 1757, aptly observed in a letter to George Montagu, "Milton was
forced to wait till the world had done admiring
Quarles." In the century of William Shakespeare, John
Donne, Ben Jonson, Robert Herrick, George Herbert,
John Milton, Richard Crashaw, Andrew Marvell,

Henry Vaughan, and John Dryden, Quarles was by far the most popular poet.

The success of Quarles in his own day can be explained in relation to those very weaknesses that deny him an audience today and mark his productions as mere historical curiosities, for Quarles had a special genius for popularization. His objective throughout his career was to reach a wide audience with an uplifting message. In this objective—so unlike Milton's appeal to a "fit audience though few"—he succeeded as few authors have; yet his success is exactly analogous to the success of a twentieth century poet such as Rod McKuen. The difference is only that the seventeenth century was profoundly moved by religious and political emotions, whereas in contemporary society it is romantic love alone that can fire the imagination of the general public.

## BIOGRAPHY

Francis Quarles was a younger son of an old gentry family settled in Essex. He was born in 1592 at his father's manor of Stewards at Romford and baptized on

*Francis Quarles* (Archive Photos/Getty Images)

May 8 of the same year. One of his sisters became by marriage an aunt of the poet Dryden. Quarles attended Christ's College, Cambridge, receiving the degree of B.A. in 1608 while still in his teens. Afterward he spent some time at Lincoln's Inn studying law, although there is no indication that he ever pursued the law as a profession. In 1613, he embarked on what promised to be a career as a courtier with an appointment as cupbearer to Princess Elizabeth on her marriage to Frederick V, elector of the Palatinate. Quarles accompanied the couple to Germany, but he had returned to England before the terrible reversal of their fortunes in 1620, when the armies of the emperor expelled them from Bohemia, where Frederick had served briefly as elective king.

Back in England, Quarles married Ursula Woodgate on May 28, 1618. He and his wife had eighteen children. The eldest son, John, grew up to become a minor poet in his own right. It was shortly after his marriage that Quarles began publishing poetry, and numerous volumes of his biblical paraphrases and other religious poems issued from the press in rapid succession.

As a result of a reputation for piety that grew as each new volume was published, Quarles was offered the post of private secretary to James Ussher, then bishop of Meath, later Anglican archbishop of Armagh and primate of Ireland. Quarles and his whole family lived in Ussher's episcopal palace in Dublin. Ussher is remembered as the author of a biblical chronology cited by fundamentalists in their rejection of the theory of evolution, and he was helped in his historical researches by Quarles. Curiously, it was during this period that Quarles published his first secular work, *Argalus and Parthenia.*

Retiring to Essex, Quarles spent several years preparing his next work for publication. This was *Emblemes,* the volume which brought him his greatest fame. It was an immediate and enormous success, which Quarles followed up a few years later by issuing another volume in a similar vein, *Hieroglyphikes of the Life of Man.* This was the last book of his poetry published during his lifetime; during the remaining years of his life, however, he did publish occasional elegies as chapbooks.

In 1639, Quarles was appointed to succeed the playwright Thomas Middleton in the largely ceremonial office of chronologer to the city of London. Taking up his residence in London, Quarles thereafter devoted himself to prose composition. In addition to writing an extremely popular manual of piety, as the political situation worsened, he also began writing polemical tracts in defense of the king's policies. With these, he became politically suspect to the Parliamentarians despite the continued attraction his poetry had for the whole Puritan party. The Parliamentary army searched his library, and manuscripts are said to have been burned. If any of his manuscripts were destroyed at the time, they must have been of a political nature, since after his death in 1644, his widow published a number of works of various other sorts, including a play and religious works in both prose and verse.

## ANALYSIS

Francis Quarles was not an innovator. Most of his works are in genres that were already riding a wave of popularity when he wrote—in fact, genres that had just become popular. He had a special knack for seeing the basic principles governing such genres and for creating works that adhered to these aesthetic principles with stark simplicity and without deep-felt personal involvement of the sort that is now regarded as the hallmark of, for example, the Metaphysical poets, the poets among Quarles's fellows who have enjoyed the highest critical prestige among later generations. Of course, it is not to be doubted that Quarles had deeply felt religious and political beliefs, but the popular success he enjoyed in his own day was a direct consequence of his inability to express more than surface impressions and clichés—or, to put the most positive face on his achievement—of his willingness to circumscribe his literary compositions by those surface impressions and clichés that express the popular imagination. It was with considerable truth that in the second half of the seventeenth century an antiquary described Quarles as "the sometime darling of our plebeian judgment."

### EMBLEM BOOKS

Quarles's popularization of the emblem is of great historical interest. The enormous sales of emblem books in the seventeenth century are at first hard to understand. Certainly the special attraction of such works

for the Puritans was as an alternative to the images that their religious beliefs proscribed inside churches, and Quarles was phenomenally popular with this group despite his avowed royalism and his support of episcopacy. For other readers, emblems were expressions of the fashionable baroque sensibility.

Emblems are, indeed, more important to the history of poetry than the fleeting popularity of emblem books during the seventeenth century would suggest. The emblematic frame of mind was fundamental to the age, informing many of the works of its major poets, and especially those of such Metaphysicals as Herbert. In fact, to understand Metaphysical imagery it is necessary to know something of the emblem tradition. Quarles's abiding historical significance is as the exemplary writer of emblem books. It is, however, important to remember that the works of Quarles always illustrate and synthesize trends; they capitalize on rather than inaugurate fashions. Herbert wrote emblematically but not because he had read Quarles. It was Quarles who read—and in his way popularized—Herbert. Although Herbert was certainly influenced by emblem books, Quarles's own emblem books were not published until after Herbert's death.

The art of the emblem consists of the successful marshaling of three things: a motto or scriptural text, a picture, and a poem or epigram. Emblem books had been published in English before Quarles, but his were the first English emblem books to be based exclusively on biblical texts, even though similar Continental works had been circulating and their popularity with English audiences had, in fact, inspired Quarles to produce his works. The shift in popularity from secular to religious emblems at the end of the sixteenth century has been chronicled by Mario Praz.

The emblem poet chooses a motto; he commissions an engraving to provide a literalist illustration of the motto; but from the modern point of view, he creates only the epigram commenting on the significance of the motto and making use of the imagery of the picture. In the case of *Emblemes* and *Hieroglyphikes of the Life of Man*, Quarles's contribution was, in fact, somewhat less. According to Gordon S. Haight, all but ten of the mottoes and illustrations in *Emblemes*, for example, were derived from two Continental emblem books, although the illustrations were redrawn and newly engraved—in somewhat less than inspired fashion. Quarles's poems in *Emblemes* are not, however, mere translations of the anonymous *Typus mundi* (1627) and of Herman Hugo's *Pia Desideria* (1624; *Pia Desideria: Or, Divine Addresses, in Three Books*, 1686). As Rosemary Freeman points out, the similarities between Quarles's emblem poems and those of his sources are for the most part only such as inevitably occur when two authors treat the same subject.

In fact, Quarles's poems tend to overwhelm his illustrations and take on a life beyond the scope of true emblems. The poor quality of the engravings aside, Alexander Pope's jibe in *The Dunciad* (1728-1743) that "the pictures for the page atone," that "Quarles is sav'd by beauties not his own," is thus somewhat wide of the mark. Poetry so interrelated with illustration could not, of course, retain its popularity when fashions in the visual arts changed.

Quarles nevertheless achieved some critical respectability in the nineteenth century as a result of his skillful metrics. Since then, fashions in content have changed. Indeed, the bizarre imagery of Quarles's emblem illustrations is probably more in tune with contemporary taste than are his religious values. The chief recommendation of Quarles's emblem poetry today is its metrical control and variety. Although the diction is sometimes questionable and the subject matter is usually conventional, at least in these emblem poems Quarles did not hobble himself even further by restricting his verse to the couplet.

### MEDITATIONS

The poems of *Emblemes* chronicle the troubled relationship of Anima, the soul, and Divine Love, pictured throughout as the Infant Jesus. The poems of *Hieroglyphikes of the Life of Man*, a shorter volume utilizing a somewhat wider range of verse forms, belabor the image of a candle to illustrate the workings of God's grace.

The systematic practice of meditation was a popular pursuit in the seventeenth century, and works of devotion based on principles of meditation, as Helen C. White has shown, were popular reading matter in a way that transcended sectarian interests. In fact, the two standard guidebooks of meditative technique in Protestant England were by Roman Catholics. Quarles's works in the meditation genre are in the tradition of the *Ejercicios espirituales* (1548; *The Spiritual Exercises*, 1736) of Saint Ignatius of Loyola, which emphasize an initial composition of place (a descriptive setting of the scene), rather than in the tradition of Saint Francis de Sales, whose recommendation of sensuous immediacy was so influential with the Metaphysical poets.

Often described by Quarles simply as biblical paraphrases, his meditations typically deal with material from the historical books of the Old Testament. As a result, while the meditations of Donne and Thomas Traherne can still be appreciated for their powerful personal involvement with salvation and while the meditative poems of Crashaw can still overwhelm modern readers with their sensuousness, the meditations of Quarles now seem to be simply quaint—to be merely decorative distortions of the compelling simplicities of biblical chronicle. *A Feast for Wormes Set Forth in a Poeme of the History of Jonah, Hadassa, Job Militant, with Meditations Divine and Morall*, and *The Historie of Samson* are works in this vein. In *The Historie of Samson*, in particular, Quarles seems to miss the spiritual and even the dramatic point of the story (so effectively retold by Milton) when he devotes seven times as much space to the woman of Timnath as to the final destruction of the Philistines.

Leaving Old Testament material and turning to the Passion and death of Christ for material in *Pentelogia* and *Hosanna*, Quarles is no more successful. He tends to moralize a scene rather than to evoke it, and his work is at best uneven, showing lapses of taste and diction as, indeed, Alexander B. Grosart—Quarles's warmest appreciator—admits. The purely analytic and contemplative sections that follow the explicit paraphrases in all the works of this group, however, contribute to meditative objectives in a more consistent way. Quarles usually writes in couplets, and the analytic sections in particular occasionally achieve some of the grace and lucidity of Pope.

### DIVINE FANCIES

The best of Quarles's work ostensibly in the meditative genre is in the *Divine Fancies*, which uses meditative technique very impressionistically. In the *Divine Fancies*, Quarles moves into explicit epigram, a more congenial format for couplets since it is the nature of epigram to be pointed, biting, and limited. The epigrams of *Divine Fancies* are also essentially argumentative rather than devotional and thus really not meditative in tone. They frequently summarize in a few terse lines some point of catechism, but they have no poetic resonance. In fact, despite W. K. Jordan's description of Quarles as an early advocate of a kind of religious toleration, these epigrams reveal a considerable narrowness of spirit on points of sectarian dispute, especially those concerning church discipline.

### PASTORAL WORKS

Another popular form that Quarles adapted was the pastoral. Pastoral works are descriptions of the lives of shepherds by people who know a great deal about poetic technique but very little about sheep. The object is to create an idealized world beyond the distractions of this world. Secular pastoral does so chiefly to provide enjoyment; works in this genre are romances. Religious pastoral does so to promote understanding of spiritual realities. Quarles works in both genres.

*Argalus and Parthenia*, his secular pastoral, is a versification of Sir Philip Sidney's *Arcadia* (1590, 1593, 1598). While usefully circumscribing the wild richness of Sidney's interminable prose romance, Quarles unwisely chooses his favorite verse form, the couplet, for this work. Couplets easily become tedious in a long narrative work unless the constant rhymes can be given a satirical point, as in *The Rape of the Lock* (1712, 1714) by Pope or *Hudibras* (1663, 1664, 1678) by Samuel Butler, but even though Quarles substitutes a tone of cool detachment for Sidney's engaging gaiety, he fails to take the further step into satire.

Quarles's chief religious pastoral is in *The Shepheards Oracles*. The eclogues—or dialogues—in this work are textbook illustrations of how religious pastoral works. The pastoral poet begins by taking literally Christ's image of himself as the Good Shepherd. Indeed, it is from this image that the conventional term "pastor" for priest is derived. The dialogues of *The Shepheards Oracles* concern a wide variety of subjects from the Nativity to the wars of religion. Roman Catholics and Dissenters come in for considerable abuse.

Two works very hard to classify are *Sions Elegies, Wept by Jeremie the Prophet* and *Sions Sonets Sung by Solomon the King*. Each is in form no more than a free translation of a book of the bible. The lament of the Prophet Jeremiah for the lost Jerusalem that Quarles presents in *Sions Elegies, Wept by Jeremie the Prophet* has more in common with traditional works of religious pastoral than with the elegiac poems that Quarles wrote about his contemporaries. Through Jeremiah, Quarles is asking his readers to contemplate religious truths. *Sions Sonets Sung by Solomon the King* is a free rendering of the Song of Solomon. Quarles carefully includes marginal glosses so that the reader will not lose sight of the religious allegory and think he is reading love poems.

### ELEGIES

Quarles also wrote a number of elegies; his most famous work in the genre is his epitaph for the poet Michael Drayton (1631), which appears on Drayton's memorial in Westminster Abbey. Quarles's only substantial book of elegiac poetry is *An Alphabet of Elegies Upon the Much and Truly Lamented Death of . . . Doctor Ailmer*. These twenty-two short poems and an epitaph commemorate Dr. Aylmer (also Ailmer), archdeacon of London. The twelve-line verse form is a kind of truncated sonnet with a sprightliness at odds with—or perhaps redeeming—the lugubrious content.

Archbishop Ussher is commemorated in one of the poems in *Divine Fancies*, and included in *The Shepheards Oracles* is an elegy for the great Protestant hero Gustavus II Adolphus, king of Sweden. Published as individual chapbooks in Quarles's later years were elegies commemorating Sir Julius Caesar (1636); Jonathan Wheeler (1637); Dr. Wilson of the Rolles (1638); Mildred, Lady Luckyn (1638); Sir Robert Quarles, the poet's brother (1639); Sir John Wostenholme (1640); and the countess of Cleveland and her sister Cicily Killigrew (1640). Interesting for its verse forms but not included in Grosart's standard edition is a chapbook called *Threnodes on the Lady Marshall . . . and . . . William Cheyne* (c. 1641); and recently Karl Joseph Höltgen has identified both an epitaph for Sir Charles Caesar and the inscription on the D'Oyley monument at Hambleden as being by Quarles.

### OTHER MAJOR WORKS

PLAY: *The Virgin Widow: A Comedie*, pb. 1649 (masque).

NONFICTION: *Enchiridion, Containing Institutions Divine and Moral*, 1640; *Observations Concerning Princes and States upon Peace and Warre*, 1642; *The Loyal Convert*, 1644; *The New Distemper*, c. 1644; *The Whipper Whipt*, 1644; *The Protest Royalist in His Quarrell with the Times*, 1645; *Judgement and Mercy for Afflicted Soules: Or, Meditations, Soliloquies, and Prayers*, 1646.

BIBLIOGRAPHY

Diehl, Houston. "Into the Maze of Self: The Protestant Transformation of the Image of the Labyrinth." *Journal of Medieval and Renaissance Studies* 16 (Fall, 1986): 281-301. Examines how Quarles's poetry was a major factor in the change of meaning of the maze in literature. Quarles used the emblem of the maze to mean the soul, or the interior life of the individual.

Gillmeister, Heiner. "Early English Games in the Poetry of Francis Quarles." In *Proceedings of the XI HISPA International Congress*, edited by J. A. Mangan. Glasgow: Jordanhill College of Education, 1986. Gillmeister explores Quarles's use of British games played in the Middle Ages to add metaphorical meaning and structure to his poetry.

Grosse, Edmund. *The Jacobean Poets*. 1894. Reprint. Charleston, S.C.: BiblioBazaar, 2009. This classic work gives good comprehensive coverage of twelve poets from the late sixteenth and early seventeenth centuries. The chapter on Quarles provides a short biography and discusses his major works.

Hassan, Masoodul. *Francis Quarles: A Study of His Life and Poetry*. Aligarh, India: Aligarh Muslim University, 1966. This volume is one of the few modern books on Quarles, and so is valuable to any student of his work. As the title suggests, Hassan provides a comprehensive biography interwoven with an analysis of Quarles's major works. Includes a bibliography.

Leach, Elsie. "The Popularity of Quarles's Emblems: Images of Misogyny." *Studies in Iconography* 9 (1983): 83-97. Feminist critic Leach describes the moral and divine imagery used by Quarles in his poetry in terms of how it supported the status quo of male domination over women. An interesting and unusual study of the Jacobean era poet. Valuable for serious Quarles scholars.

Wilcher, Robert. "Quarles, Waller, Marvell, and the Instruments of State." *Notes and Queries* 41, no. 1 (March, 1994): 79. The influence that poets Quarles, Edmund Waller, and Andrew Marvell had on each other and exerted in the development of government is discussed.

*Edmund Miller*

# R

## SIR WALTER RALEGH

**Born:** Hayes Barton, Devon, England; c. 1552
**Died:** London, England; October 29, 1618
**Also known as:** Sir Walter Raleigh

PRINCIPAL POETRY

*The Poems of Sir Walter Raleigh Now First
    Collected, with a Biographical and Critical
    Introduction*, 1813
*The Poems of Sir Walter Raleigh*, 1962 (Agnes
    Latham, editor)

OTHER LITERARY FORMS

Almost immediately after his execution in 1618, the reputation of Sir Walter Ralegh (RAWL-ee) as a patriotic and courageous opponent to James I developed, and as opposition to James and Charles I increased, many prose works were attributed to Ralegh from about 1625 through the end of the seventeenth century. Of those certainly written by Ralegh, there are two pamphlets, *A Report of the Fight About the Iles of Açores* (1591) and *The Discoverie of the Large, Rich and Bewtiful Empyre of Guiana* (1596), which express the aggressive buoyancy of Elizabethan imperialist designs on South America and of the control of trade to the New World. Ralegh's major work outside his poetry is the monumental, unfinished *The History of the World* (1614), dedicated to and yet containing scarcely disguised criticism of King James, who had him imprisoned between 1603 and 1616, and who (after Ralegh's hopeless expedition to Guiana to find El Dorado) had him executed. *The History of the World* was part therapy, part histrionic pique and, like most of Ralegh's career, significant far beyond its surface ambiguities and chronological contradictions. Torn between being an account of the "unjointed and scattered frame of our English affairs" and a universal history, it is a tribute as well to the dead Queen Elizabeth, "Her

whom I must still honour in the dust," and an indictment of what Ralegh perceived as the corruption of the Jacobean court. For Ralegh, in *The History of the World* as much as in his poetry, the court was his stage, a place of "parts to play," in which survival depended on "fashioning of our selves according to the nature of the time wherein we live," and the power of which dominated his language and, in the most absolute sense, his life. Like his poems, *The History of the World* is a moving and (far beyond his knowledge) revealing document of the power of the court over the men and women who struggled within it.

ACHIEVEMENTS

Sir Walter Ralegh's importance belies the slimness of his poetic output. The author of perhaps two dozen extant poems and a number of brief verse translations, the latter appearing in his *The History of the World*, Ralegh is nevertheless one of the most important of the Elizabethan courtly makers, articulating with fearful clarity not merely the gaudy surface and fashions of the late Elizabethan age, but also much of the felt pressure of the court, his society's dominant social power, on the lives and sensibilities of those caught in it. Ralegh described himself toward the end of his life as "a seafaring man, a Souldior and a Courtier," and his poetry articulates much of what drove him to those vocations. He knew, deeply and bitterly, that, as he puts it in *The History of the World*, there is nothing more to "becoming a wise man" than "to retire himself from Court." However, the court was his stage, and it was, he wrote, the "token of a worldly wise man, not to warre or contend in vaine against the nature of the times wherein he lived." The achievement of his poetry is that it gives reverberating expression to the struggles of those who lived in and were controlled by the Elizabethan court. Most of his poems look, on the surface, like delicate, even trivial, songs, complaints, and compliments typical of Petrarchanism; but they are rich, if often confused, responses to the complex and powerful set of discourses, symbolic formations, and systems of representation that constituted the Elizabethan court. They offer a unique insight into the interplay between the social text of Elizabethan society (the events that made Ralegh's history) and the literary text (the poems that he made of those events). He is, in many ways, the quintessential court poet of the Elizabethan period inasmuch as his poems are haunted by, determined by, and finally silenced by, the power of the court.

## BIOGRAPHY

Although Ralegh is often spelled Raleigh, Walter Ralegh signed his name once as Rawleyghe, in 1587, then signed it Rauley until 1583, and more or less spelled it consistently as Ralegh from 1584 until his death in 1618. He was the quintessential *arriviste*: Born in Devon, educated at Oxford, he rapidly became a court favorite and was knighted in 1584, but fell into disgrace when, after a bitter rivalry with the up-and-coming younger earl of Essex, he was imprisoned for seducing one of the queen's maids-of-honor, Elizabeth Throckmorton, whom he later married. He was increasingly unpopular for, among other things, his flamboyant lifestyle. When James came to the throne, Ralegh

was sentenced to death for treason, although the sentence was reduced to imprisonment in the Tower of London. During his imprisonment, between 1603 and 1616, Ralegh became a close friend of the prince of Wales, wrote extensively, and became a center of influence and even of counterestablishment power. He was released by James in 1616 and sent on an ill-fated expedition to Guiana, and on his return, executed—his death bewailed by as many people in 1618 as had desired it fourteen years earlier.

## ANALYSIS

If readers take him at his face value (or at the value of one of his many faces), Sir Walter Ralegh epitomized, accepted, and chose to live out the daring expansiveness and buoyancy of the Elizabethan court. He conceived of his own life as a poem, as a flamboyant epic gesture, and his poems were the manifestations of his public role and his political ambitions. However disguised in the garment of Petrarchan plaint, mournful song, lament for lost love, carpe diem or *ubi sunt* motif, Ralegh's poems are the articulation of the ruthless and sometimes blatant struggle for power that created and held together the court of Elizabeth. "Then must I needes advaunce my self by skyll,/ And lyve to serve, in hope of your goodwyll" he (possibly) wrote—and advancing himself with skill meant using the court as an arena of self-assertion, or (in another of the metaphors that disseminate contradictions throughout his work) as a new world to be conquered.

Ralegh's career as a poet and a courtier (the two are almost inseparable, literary and social text repeatedly writing and rewriting each other throughout his life) should not be simply seen as the daring, willful assertion of the gentleman adventurer who strode into the queen's favor with a graceful and opportune sweep of his cloak. That would be to take too much for granted at least some of his poems and the power in which, through them, Ralegh hoped to participate. Ralegh's poetry is put into play both by and in power; it demonstrates, probably more clearly than that of any other Elizabethan poet, the unconscious workings of power on

*Sir Walter Ralegh* (Library of Congress)

discourse, specifically on the language which it controlled, selected, organized, and distributed through approved and determined procedures, delimiting as far as possible the emergence of opposition forces and experiences. The Elizabethan court used poetry and poets alike as the means of stabilizing and controlling its members. To confirm its residual values, it tried to restrict poet and poem as far as possible to the dominant discourses of a colorful, adventurous world, but only at the cost of a frustrating and, in Ralegh's case, despairing powerlessness.

### PETRARCHAN LYRICS

Much of Ralegh's poetry looks like typical Petrarchan love poetry—it can be, and no doubt was, to many members of its original audience, read as such. The surface of his verse presents the typical paraphernalia of the Petrarchan lyric—hope and despair, pleasure and fortune, fake love, frail beauty, fond shepherds, coy mistresses, and deceitful time. The magnificent "As you came from the holy land," which is possibly by Ralegh, can be read as a superbly melancholy affirmation of love, one of the most moving love lyrics of the language. "Nature that washt her hands in milke" takes the reader through a witty blazon of the perfect mistress's charms, her outside made of "snow and silke," her "inside . . . only of wantonesse and witt." Like all Petrarchan mistresses, she has "a heart of stone" and so the lover is poised, in frustration, before his ideal. Then in the second half of the poem, Ralegh ruthlessly tears down all the ideals he has built. What gives the poem its power is the unusually savage use of the Elizabethan commonplace of Time the destroyer, the thief—ravaging, lying, rusting, and annihilating. Time "turnes snow, and silke, and milke, to dust." What was to the lover the "food of joyes" is ceaselessly fed into the maw of death by time and remorselessly turned into excreta; the moistness of the mistress's wantonness rendered dry and repulsive. Likewise, the reply to Christopher Marlowe's "The Passionate Shepherd" is an impressively terse expression of the carpe diem principle, creating an impassioned stoical voice through the stylistic conventions of the plain Elizabethan voice. Typically, Ralegh has superb control of mood, movement, voice modulation, and an appropriately direct rhetoric.

### GIFTED AMATEUR

Ralegh's poems are those of the gifted amateur—seemingly casual compliment, occasional verse typically dropped, as the manuscript title of another poem has it, "into my Lady Laiton's pocket." Such a poem looks like one of the many erotic lyrics of the Renaissance which, as Michel Foucault has written, allowed men to overhear and will another to "speak the truth of" their sexuality. Ralegh's poetry, however, does more than introduce sexuality into discourse: Inevitably the language of erotic compliment and complaint is inseparable from the language of power. Despite their seemingly trivial, light, or occasional nature—epitaphs on Sir Philip Sidney's death, "A farewell to false love," dedicatory poems to works by George Gascoigne or Edmund Spenser, or poems directly or indirectly written to the queen—their significance reverberates far beyond their apparently replete surface configuration of stock metaphor and gracefully logical structure.

### RALEGH'S PUBLIC ROLES

Ralegh's predominant public roles were those of a man who consciously identified entirely with what he perceived as the dominant forces of his society—and, like his poetry, Ralegh's life is like a palimpsest, requiring not only reading but also interpretation and demystification in depth. As Stephen Greenblatt has suggestively argued, "Ralegh" is in a way a curiously hollow creation, the production of many roles in the theater of the court. Greenblatt has argued that Ralegh saw his life as a work of art, and the court as a "great theater" in which the boldest author would be the most successful. His career from the late 1570's might suggest that his multiplicity reflects an inner hollowness as he shifts back and forth among the roles of courtier, politician, explorer, freethinker, poet, philosopher, lover, and husband.

In Ralegh's public career, two dominant discourses clash and contradict—one seeing all human activity as an assertion of the adaptability of the actor, the other a pessimistic view of life as an empty, futile, and unreal theater. While Ralegh adapted to different roles as his ambitions shifted, his very restlessness bespeaks the power of the court. Unlike Sidney, who was a courtier by birth and privilege, Ralegh became one because his identity and survival depended on it. His place in a world that was dangerous and unpredictable was never stable, and even its apparently fixed center, the queen, was unpredictable and arbitrary.

### PROBLEMS OF ATTRIBUTION

Introducing Ralegh's role as a poet, it must be noted how the term "possibly" must be continually used to qualify assertions about the authorship of many of the poems attributed to him. Despite the confident assertions of some modern editors, Michael Rudick has shown that scholars do not in fact know whether many of the poems attributed to Ralegh in the manuscripts and miscellanies in which Elizabethan court poetry habitually circulated are in fact his; despite possessing more holograph material for Ralegh than for any other Elizabethan poets except Sir Thomas Wyatt and Robert Sidney, scholars can only speculate about the authorship of many of the best poems attributed to him. Even modern editors and biographers attribute poems to him on primarily sentimental grounds, but in one important sense, the lack of definitive attribution does not matter: Elizabethan court poetry often speaks with the voice of a collectivity, its authors *scriptors* or spokesmen for the values of a dominant class and its ideology. In short, the author's relationship to the languages that traverse him is much more complex than is allowed for by the sentimental nineteenth century biographical criticism that has held sway in Ralegh scholarship until very recently. In any court lyric, there is an illimitable series of pretexts, subtexts, and post-texts that call into question any concept of its "author" as a free, autonomous person. Ralegh's poems, like those of Sir Philip Sidney or Spenser, are sites of struggle, attempts by Ralegh (or whatever court poet may have "written" them) to write himself into the world. Hence there is a sense in which we should speak of "Ralegh" as the symptomatic court poet, rather than Ralegh the poet—or, perhaps, of "Ralegh" and "his" poems alike as texts, requiring always to be read against what they seem to articulate, often speaking out in their silences, in what they cannot or dare not say but nevertheless manage to express.

### COURT IDEOLOGY

Some of the poems are, however, very explicit about their ideological source, even verging on propagandist art. "Praisd be Dianas faire and harmles light" is a poem (again possibly by Ralegh) which reifies the ideals of the court in a hymn of celebration, demanding in ways that other Elizabethan lyrics rarely do, allegiance to the magical, timeless world of the Elizabethan court, in which no challenge to the replete atmosphere can be admitted and in which the readers are permitted to share only so long as they acknowledge the beauty of the goddess whom the poem celebrates. The poem's atmosphere is incantatory, its movement designed like court music to inculcate unquestioning reverence and subordination. Only the subhuman (presumably any reader foolish, or treasonous, enough to dissent from its vision) are excluded from the charm and power that it celebrates: "A knowledge pure it is hir worth to kno,/ With Circes let them dwell that thinke not so."

George Puttenham mentions Ralegh's poetry approvingly as "most lofty, insolent and passionate," and by the mid-1580's, when he expressed his view, Ralegh already had the reputation of being a fine craftsperson among the "crew of courtly makers, noblemen and gentlemen" of Elizabeth's court. In what another of Ralegh's contemporaries called the "*Terra infirma* of the Court," Ralegh used his verse as one of the many means of scrambling for position. His verse, in C. S. Lewis's words, is that of the quintessential adaptable courtly amateur, "blown this way and that (and sometimes lifted into real poetry)." He is the lover, poor in words but rich in affection; passions are likened to "floudes and streames"; the lover prays "in vayne" to "blinde fortune" but nevertheless resolves: "But love, farewell, thoughe fortune conquer thee,/ No fortune base nor frayle shall alter mee" ("In vayne my Eyes, in vayne yee waste your tears"). However apparently depoliticized these poems are, they are the product of the allurement and dominance of the court, their confidence less that of the poet himself than of the power of the structures in which he struggles to locate himself. His characteristic pose is that of the worshiper, devoted to the unapproachable mistress or, as the idealizing devotee with the queen as the unwavering star, the chaste goddess, the imperial embodiment of justice, the timeless principle around which the universe turns. In the way that Ben Jonson's masques were later to embody the ideology of the Jacobean court, so Ralegh's poems evoke the collective fantasy of the Elizabethan—a world that is harmonious and static, from which all change has been exorcized.

### HATFIELD POEMS

Aside from this miscellany (sometimes startlingly evocative, invariably competent and provoking), there are four closely connected and important poems, all undoubtedly Ralegh's, which were found in his own handwriting among the Cecil Papers in Hatfield House, north of London, the family home of Ralegh's great enemy Robert Cecil. They are "If Synthia be a Queene, a princes, and supreame," "My boddy in the walls captivated," "Sufficeth it to yow, my joyes interred"—which is headed "The 21th: and last booke of the Ocean to Scinthia"—and "The end of the bookes, of the Oceans love to Scinthia, and the beginninge of the 22 Boock, entreatinge of Sorrow." The existence of a poem, or poems, directly written to the queen and titled *Cynthia* seems to be mentioned by Spenser in *The Faerie Queene* (1590, 1596) and it is usually characterized as being parts of or related to the Hatfield poems. It is probably, however, that the third and fourth poems were written, or at least revised, during Ralegh's imprisonment in 1592.

### "THE 21TH: AND LAST BOOKE OF THE OCEAN TO SCINTHIA"

"The 21th: and last booke of the Ocean to Scinthia," the most important of the group, appears to be a scarcely revised draft of an appeal, if not to the queen herself, at least to that part of Ralegh's mind occupied by her power. It lacks narrative links; its four-line stanzas are often imperfect, with repetitions and gaps that presumably would have been revised later. Its unfinished state, however, makes it not only a fascinating revelation of Ralegh's personal and poetic anguish, but also perhaps the clearest example in Elizabethan court poetry of the way the dynamics and contradictions of power speak through a text. "The 21th: and last booke of the Ocean to Scinthia" repeatedly deconstructs the philosophy to which it gives allegiance: Its incoherences, gaps, uncertainties, and repetitions both affirm and negate Elizabethan mythology. What in Ralegh's other poems is expressed as complete ideological closure is undermined by the fractures and symptomatic maladjustments of the text. Nowhere in

Elizabethan poetry is a poem as obviously constitutive of ideological struggle.

The poem is addressed to a patently transparent Cynthia who has withdrawn her favor from the faithful lover. Ralegh projects himself as a despairing lover fearfully aware that his service has been swept into oblivion, simultaneously acknowledging that honors inevitably corrupt and that he cannot keep from pursuing them. The "love" that he has seemingly won includes favors that open doors not only to glory but also to ruin and death. However, even knowing this, it is as if he cannot help himself "seeke new worlds, for golde, for prayse, for glory," with the tragic result that "Twelve yeares intire I wasted in this warr." The result of his "twelve yeares" dedication has been imprisonment and disgrace, yet he is helpless before his own inability to abandon the glories of office. "Trew reason" shows power to be worthless, but even while he knows that "all droopes, all dyes, all troden under dust," he knows also that the only stability in the world of power is the necessity of instability and emulation.

The Petrarchan motifs with which the successful courtier has played so effectively, almost on demand—the helpless lover wooing the unapproachable mistress who is the unattainable goal of desire—have suddenly and savagely been literalized. The role that Ralegh has played has exploded his habitual adaptability. He cannot protest that the game of the despairing lover is only a game; it has now become real. In 1592, he wrote to Cecil: "My heart was never broken till this day, that I hear the queen goes away so far off—whom I have followed so many years with so great love and desire, in so many journeys, and am now left behind her in a great prison alone." The letter is an obvious echo of the lines from Ralegh's adaption of the Walsingham ballad, "As you came from the holy land." The contradictions of Ralegh's life which the poem now voices had been repressed and silenced during his imprisonment, but now they are revealed as terrifyingly real. By marrying, Ralegh himself has ceased to play Elizabeth's game; he has thus found that the role of masochistic victim in which he cast himself for political advantage has been taken literally and he has become an outcast. "The 21th: and last booke of the Ocean to Scinthia" expresses the agony of a man whose choices and commitments have been built on the myth of a changeless past in an ever-moving power struggle. The very unfinished quality of Ralegh's fragment is the perfect formal expression of the disruptiveness that has overwhelmed him.

### "THE LIE"

It is fortunate that another key poem in this period is among the Hatfield manuscripts. "The Lie" is a release of explicit rage, a struggle to find form for deep frustration and venom, finding no alternative to renunciation and repulsion. It is a statement of deeply felt impotence, probably written after Ralegh's release from prison in 1592, but before he was restored to favor. Ralegh's poem is seemingly total in its rejection of the ideology by which he has lived: Natural law, universal harmony, love, and court artifice are all rejected in a mood of total condemnation. However, Ralegh's poem is neither philosophically nihilistic nor politically radical: The force of his revulsion from the court does not allow for any alternative to it. What dies is the "I" of the poem, as he gives the lie to the world, and takes refuge in a savage *contemptus mundi*. "The Lie" is at once an explosion of frustration and beneath ideological confidence. In such poems, the ideology is betrayed by writing itself; the poem constantly releases an anxiety for realities that challenge the surface harmonies and struggle unsuccessfully to be heard against the dominant language of the court poetic mode. What readers start to recognize as Ralegh's characteristic melancholic formulation of the persistence of "woe" or pain as the very mark of human self-consciousness is the special telltale sign of his texts as sites of struggle and repression. "The life expires, the woe remains" is a refrain echoed by "Of all which past, the sorrow, only stays" ("Like truthless dreams") and by phrases in *The History of the World* such as "Of all our vain passions and affections past, the sorrow only abideth." Such recurring motifs impart more than a characteristic tone to Ralegh's verse. They point to the frustrated insurrection of subjugated experience struggling to find expression, knowing that there are no words permitted for it.

### LEGACY

Ralegh's poems, then, are haunted by what they try to exorcise: a fragility that arises from the repressed political uncertainties of court life in the 1580's and 1590's and that undermines his chosen role as the spokesperson of a replete court ideology. Despite its confident surface, all his verse is less a celebration of the queen's power than a conspiracy to remain within its protection. The Petrarchan clichés of "Like truthless dreams, so are my joys expired" and the Neoplatonic commonplaces of the "Walsingham" ballad become desperate pleas for favor, projections into lyric poems of political machinations. "Concept begotten by the eyes" also starts out as a stereotypical contrast between "desire" and "woe" and emerges as a poignant cry of radical insecurity and a powerless acknowledgment that the personality of the court poet and of Ralegh himself is a creation of the discourses he has uneasily inhabited and from which he now feels expelled. The Hatfield poems illustrate with wonderful clarity what all Elizabethan court poetry tries to repress: that however the poet asserts his autonomy, he is constituted through ideology, having no existence outside the social formation and the signifying practice legitimized by the power of the court. Ralegh, like every other poet who wrestled within the court, does not speak so much as he is spoken.

More than twenty years later, after a revival of fortunes under Elizabeth, arrest, imprisonment, release, and rearrest under James, Ralegh prematurely brought his history to an end. The work, written to justify God's providential control of time, articulates a view of history that radically undercuts its author's intentions. For Ralegh, history has no final eschatological goal, no ultimate consummation. It consists only of the continual vengeance of an angry God until "the long day of mankinde is drawing fast towards an evening, and the world's Tragedie and time neare at an end." A few years later, on the eve of his execution, Ralegh took up the last lines of the lyric written twenty-five years before on the ravages of time that he had felt all his life:

> Even such is tyme which takes in trust
> Our yowth, our Joyes, and all we have,
> And payes us butt with age and dust:
> When we have wandred all our wayes,
> Shutts up the storye of our dayes.

He appended to it, in two new lines, the only hope of which he could conceive, a deus ex machina to rescue him, in a way that neither queen nor king had, from the grip of time's power: "And from which earth and grave and dust/ The Lord shall raise me up I trust." It is a cry of desperation, not a transformation of "the consuming disease of time" as he puts it in *The History of the World*. What is finally triumphant over Ralegh is the power of the world in which he courageously yet blindly struggled and of which his handful of poems are an extraordinarily moving acknowledgment and testament.

OTHER MAJOR WORKS

NONFICTION: *A Report of the Fight About the Iles of Açores*, 1591; *The Discoverie of the Large, Rich, and Bewtiful Empyre of Guiana*, 1596; *The History of the World*, 1614.

MISCELLANEOUS: *Works of Sir Walter Ralegh*, 1829 (8 volumes; Thomas Birch and William Oldys, editors); *Selected Prose and Poetry*, 1965 (Agnes Latham, editor).

BIBLIOGRAPHY

Beer, Anna. *Bess: The Life of Lady Ralegh, Wife to Sir Walter*. London: Constable, 2004. Beer tells the story of Elizabeth Throckmorton, whose marriage to Ralegh provoked the queen.

Greenblatt, Stephen J. *Sir Walter Ralegh: The Renaissance Man and His Roles*. New Haven, Conn.: Yale University Press, 1973. Greenblatt discusses Ralegh's role-playing and theatrical nature as demonstrated in his court poetry and in *The History of the World*, both of which receive chapter-length treatments. He also provides the context for *The Discoverie of the Large, Rich, and Bewtiful Empyre of Guiana*, which he regards as reflecting Ralegh's personal sorrow and the national myths of his age.

Lacey, Robert. *Sir Walter Ralegh*. 1974. Reprint. London: Phoenix Press, 2000. Lacey's account reflects the multifaceted nature of his subject in the book's structure. There are some fifty chapters, divided into seven sections, each charting the ups and downs of Ralegh's checkered career. From country upstart to royal favorite, from privateer to traitor in the Tower, his life was never still.

Lyons, Mathew. *The Favourite: Ambition, Politics and Love—Sir Walter Ralegh in Elizabeth I's Court.* London: Constable, 2009. Examines Ralegh's relationship with Queen Elizabeth and how he fell out of favor.

Ralegh, Walter. *The Letters of Sir Walter Ralegh*. Edited by Agnes Latham and Joyce Youings. Exeter, England: University of Exeter Press, 1999. Brings together all that is known of Ralegh's correspondence, uncollected since 1868 and much expanded and refined. Students of history and literature will grasp at this book as it throws a beam across the life of one of the more attractive personalities of the late Tudor and early Jacobean periods.

Waller, Gary. *English Poetry of the Sixteenth Century*. 2d ed. New York: Longman, 1993. Waller deconstructs Ralegh's poetry, which he claims demonstrates how power works on language. For Waller, Ralegh's poetry simultaneously pays homage to and criticizes the courtly arena where he must play different roles. "As You Come from the Holy Land" and one of the "Scinthia" poems, thus, become poems of tension and value.

*Gary F. Waller*

----

# HENRY REED

**Born:** Birmingham, England; February 22, 1914
**Died:** London, England; December 8, 1986

PRINCIPAL POETRY

*A Map of Verona*, 1946
*Lessons of the War*, 1970
*Collected Poems*, 1991

OTHER LITERARY FORMS

Most of Henry Reed's work was in genres other than poetry. His first publication was a critical study, *The Novel Since 1939* (1946), and he also translated Paride Rombi's *Perdu and His Father* (1954) and Dino Buzzati's *Larger than Life* (1962).

Mainly, however, Reed was a prolific creator of drama, especially radio plays. In particular, he enjoyed a fruitful literary relationship with the Italian language and the Italian playwright Ugo Betti, a number of whose works Reed translated and adapted for radio broadcast in London and for stage production in London and New York. His adaptations of Betti include *The Queen and the Rebels*, *The Burnt Flower-Bed*, and *Summertime*, all produced in London in 1955 and published as *Three Plays* (1956). Other adaptations of Betti were *Island of Goats*, produced in New York in 1955 and published as *Crime on Goat Island* (1955), and *Corruption in the Palace of Justice*, produced in New York in 1958. He also adapted Natalia Ginzburg's play *The Advertisement* (1968) for production in London in 1968 and in New York in 1974. Reed's most fruitful relationship, however, was with the British Broadcasting Corporation, for which he wrote or adapted some forty to fifty radio plays, including the previously mentioned works by Betti. Reed's writing for radio began with *Moby Dick: A Play for Radio from Herman Melville's Novel* (1947), brief lyric sections of which form the last part of Reed's collection *A Map of Verona*.

### ACHIEVEMENTS

In Britain, Henry Reed was perhaps better known for his radio plays and his adaptations of Ugo Betti than for his poetry, whereas in the United States, he was known almost exclusively for his poetry—or, more specifically, for "Naming of Parts" and "Judging Distances," which originally appeared with a third poem ("Unarmed Combat") under the general title "Lessons of the War." Much anthologized for introductory literature courses, these two humorous lyrics emphasizing the futility of war have been read by possibly half the undergraduate population of the United States during the 1970's and 1980's. During the period of the Vietnam War especially, the two poems struck a responsive chord in the hearts of American college students. These two fine poems deserve the circulation they have achieved, but unfortunately the rest of Reed's poetry is little known in the United States. His other work is even less known, except possibly among scholars of drama and Italian.

For a first collection of poetry, *A Map of Verona* maintains a remarkably high quality throughout, though it does not entirely escape the unevenness typical of first collections. For the sake of completeness and perhaps for its greater explicitness, the less-inspired third

poem of the "Lessons of the War" group should be read. Among other poems that stand out and illustrate other aspects of Reed's poetic talent are "A Map of Verona," "The Door and the Window," "The Builders," a group titled "Tintagel" ("Tristram," "Iseult Blaunchesmains," "King Mark," and "Iseult la Belle"), and a group titled "Triptych" ("Chrysothemis," "Antigone," and "Philoctetes"). Finally, admirers of T. S. Eliot, as well as other readers, should not miss Reed's wicked little parody, "Chard Whitlow/(Mr. Eliot's Sunday Evening Postscript)."

Perhaps time will smooth out some of the imbalances in Reed's reputation, but as a poet he will likely remain known as someone who strangely produced only one early collection and who is best known for his gently humorous antiwar sentiments. No doubt Reed himself could well appreciate the irony of this situation, since one of his favorite poetic subjects is the person transfixed in time by a single defining (and somewhat immobilizing) act. Reed's act of poetic self-definition, however, is certainly not the whole story of his writing career. He will probably also be known as something of a media pioneer, a writer who could switch smoothly from print to performance to electronic medium. These smooth transitions were forecast in the nature of his poetry.

### BIOGRAPHY

Henry Reed was born and educated in Birmingham, a sprawling manufacturing center in the English Midlands. There is no evidence that this setting had much influence on his poetry, unless it encouraged a desire to travel to and write about sunnier climes. He attended the King Edward VI School in Birmingham and took an M.A. degree at the University of Birmingham.

The influence of his education is evident throughout Reed's poetry, which, like the poetry of so many young Britons from the universities, smacks somewhat of Survey of British Literature. For example, one can detect echoes of Andrew Marvell, Alfred, Lord Tennyson, Matthew Arnold, Joseph Conrad, and Eliot. In addition, many of Reed's subjects are literary in inspiration. Seemingly, the weight of the great tradition bore down heavily on Reed, and reaction to this weight could have contributed to his move from poetry to radio plays.

Certainly another influence on Reed's writing career was his experience of World War II, when he served in the Royal Army and with the Foreign Office. His military training provided inspiration for the poems in the "Lessons of the War" series. In addition, the war brought him to London, where he subsequently formed the association with the BBC that defined his career. He died on December 8, 1986, in London.

ANALYSIS

In "A Map of Verona," Henry Reed states that "maps are of place, not time," while in "Judging Distances" one reads that "maps are of time, not place." These two versions of reality are not as contradictory as they might appear, if one considers the source of each. The first version comes from Reed himself, while the second is the official army doctrine mechanically voiced by a training officer to a group of recruits. The first version acknowledges the inability of humanity's puny symbols to represent reality, while the second asserts the military's wishful thinking, its need to be in control, to pour reality into a uniform and make it stand up and salute. One cannot blame the military for trying, as indeed it must, but the futility of its efforts is laughable: In "Judging Distances," the military theory is demolished, appropriately enough, by a pair of lovers in the distance, who finish making love even as the training officer and woebegone recruits watch.

Like the military, though with somewhat more success, Reed in his poems is intent on creating maps of reality. In his poems, both place and time have important roles, as they intersect with human actions. Reed is interested in place for its own sake, but he is also interested in its effects on human actions. Even more, he is interested in how human actions reverberate in time—the anticipation of actions, how actions fade from memory, how the meaning of actions changes with time, how, on the other hand, actions define and transfix personalities. For Reed, reality is as fluid as the stream in his poem "Lives" that cannot be caged. To try as best he can to catch and bottle this reality, Reed concentrates on dramatic moments or their consequences, particularly their moral consequences. Supporting Reed's penchant for the dramatic is his gift of mimicry, for capturing the sound of the human voice, as amply demonstrated in his parodies of T. S. Eliot and of the training officer in the "Lessons of the War" poems. Thus, it should come as no surprise that, although Reed writes in a variety of forms, some of his best poems are dramatic monologues. It should also come as no surprise that he eventually changed to writing drama.

**"A MAP OF VERONA"**

Perhaps the most important poem for understanding Reed's ontology, and a good poem in its own right, is "A Map of Verona." At first, it seems no more than a pleasant travel advertisement: For "a whole long winter season," Reed's thoughts have dwelt on an open map of Verona. His intention to visit Verona reminds him of a stay in another Italian city, "My youthful Naples." Naples is associated in his mind with "a practice in sorrow," with "a sketch in tenderness, lust, and sudden parting." No doubt at the time this experience, despite its air of youthful experimentation, was deeply moving; now, however, he can barely recall its "underground whispers of music." Reed does recall, though, that he once studied an open map of Naples with the same expectation with which he now studies the map of Verona, and his map-studies then were totally "useless," since "maps are of place, not time." Still, studying the map of Verona and hearing other travelers relate their tourist impressions of the city help to "calm" Reed's "winter of expectations." The city of Verona does indeed exist, and "one day" Reed will go there: "in tomorrow's cave the music/ Trembles and forms inside the musician's mind." Meanwhile, echoing the poem's epigraph from Arthur Rimbaud, Reed can only wonder "in what hour of beauty" and "in what good arms" he will attain "those regions and that city." Finally, he wonders "what good Arms shall take them away again."

On both a literal and a symbolic level, "A Map of Verona" suggests the nature of experience. Among other things, Reed seems to say that, for the most part, people's lives are suspended between remembrance and expectation. Then, when a big moment comes, people are often too youthful to appreciate it or too experienced to believe that it will last. Still, even though remembrance fades and expectation is uncertain, both enrich one's life. Indeed, their enriching context makes it possible for a person to know a big moment when it arrives. Then there is always the potential for the big, fulfilling moment to come, in whatever "hour of beauty" or in whatever "good arms." In "A Map of Verona," the city of Verona, a jewel of Western civilization and the home of Romeo and Juliet, symbolizes this fulfillment.

### "LESSONS OF THE WAR"

Reading "A Map of Verona" is good preparation for reading the "Lessons of the War" poems. Though vastly different in subject, the poems are not as different in theme as might appear; they merely approach much the same theme from different directions. Despite the tenuous nature of experience and the way so much of life hangs between memory and expectations, "A Map of Verona" asserts the potential for human fulfillment. If there is one sure way of cutting off that potential, and typically at an early age, it is war. The incongruity—indeed, insanity—of war is suggested in the "Lessons of the War" poems by the way time and place conspire against the military training going on. While a training officer tries to hammer home his dull lessons, springtime is bursting out all over: Flowers are blooming, bees are "assaulting and fumbling the flowers," and lovers are making love. While nature moves full speed ahead toward the fulfillment of life, the soldiers train to eliminate life and in so doing put their own lives on the line. How such lessons go against the grain is also rendered dramatically in the person of Reed's recruit, who has trouble paying attention and through whose mind the reader hears the training officer's words and the recruit's spoken and unspoken responses. His rather obsessional notions demonstrate the difficulty, in springtime, of turning a young man's fancy to thoughts of war.

Although the theme of these poems is sober, their predominant tone is not. Their tone is established by the humorous dramatic situation, especially as this situation is reflected in the diction. Each of the poems begins with a parody of the training officer that reveals his routine mentality, his jargonistic but otherwise limited vocabulary, and his limited knowledge. All these provide marvelous openings for the clever young recruit, who responds to the officer's military litany by twisting it into poetic or profound—but always humorous—meanings. In "Naming of Parts," for example, the officer's breakdown on a rifle's parts gives the recruit a fertile field for sexual puns. This particular instance of contrasting diction, like the general contrast between the voice of the training officer and the voice of the recruit, reinforces the theme of the military's sterile, deadening influence.

### "TRIPTYCH" AND "TINTAGEL"

The "Lessons of the War" poems well illustrate Reed's talent for humor, but most of his poems are somber both in theme and tone. What does not change is Reed's eye for the dramatic situation. His sense of drama can be felt strongly in two groups of poems that consist mostly of dramatic monologues and that might be considered the peak of Reed's poetic achievement. These are the two groups titled "Tintagel" and "Triptych." "Tintagel" consists of four poems named after the principals in the Tristram story: "Tristram," "Iseult Blaunchesmains," "King Mark," and "Iseult la Belle." In a note, Reed indicates that these four characters "represent four aspects of a problem known (in one or more of these aspects) to most men and women." He depends on the reader's knowledge of the Tristram legend to fill in the details—that these characters represent four corners of a love quadrangle with one side missing: Iseult Blaunchesmains loves Tristram who loves Iseult la Belle who returns his love but is married to King Mark. Already the poems sound like the scenario of an Italian drama or opera, and as the four characters speak their loves and sorrows, either through their own voices or the voice of a sympathetic narrator, they sound more and more like Luigi Pirandello's six characters, doomed to repent their roles to eternity. They have, in effect, become archetypal characters transfixed in time by their self-defining actions. They are like some traumatized people in real life, locked into one searing emotional experience that repeats itself endlessly in their consciousness.

The three characters in "Triptych," all from Greek drama, have likewise defined their personalities for all time through their actions. Here, however, the characters are not equally condemned; indeed, Reed notes that the speakers in the three poems "represent a moral progression, culminating in a decision." The three poems are "Chrysothemis," "Antigone," and "Philoctetes." Chrysothemis and Philoctetes speak for themselves in dramatic monologues, but in the second poem two witnesses to Antigone's death react to it in a dialogue.

Chrysothemis, the sister of Electra and Orestes, represents the onlooker who will not get involved no matter how many atrocities she witnesses; after the house of Atreus has decimated itself, she stays behind to care for the remaining children and the decaying house. The house symbolizes her moral state, though she tries to believe she is playing a useful role. The main speaker in "Antigone" is a chance onlooker who, though not involved in the action, is sensitive to its moral consequences, in particular to the way Antigone acts unhesitatingly on what she knows is right. Finally, the ostracized Philoctetes represents the person who wants to get involved and is rejected, but who overcomes his bitter suffering and sense of personal wrong to act decisively when the time comes: Even after years of intense frustration, he goes as straight to his mark as do his blessed arrows. The traumatized person is not necessarily transfixed in time; rebirth is possible.

These two groups of poems involving serious drama verge closer and closer to drama itself. The last group of five poems in *A Map of Verona* comes from an actual drama, Reed's radio version of *Moby Dick* for the BBC. In a note, Reed refers to these poems as "lyric interludes." The transition from poet to dramatist is complete. Very likely Reed's friends mourned the transition, but very likely William Shakespeare's friends did the same.

## OTHER MAJOR WORKS

PLAYS: *The Burnt Flower-Bed*, pr. 1955 (adaptation of Ugo Betti); *Island of Goats*, pr. 1955 (adaptation of Betti; also known as *Crime on Goat Island*); *The Queen and the Rebels*, pr. 1955 (adaptation of Betti); *Summertime*, pr. 1955 (adaptation of Betti); *Three Plays*, 1956; *The Advertisement*, pr. 1968 (adaptation of Natalia Ginzburg); *Corruption in the Palace of Justice*, pr. 1958 (adaptation of Betti).

RADIO PLAYS: *Moby Dick: A Play for Radio from Herman Melville's Novel*, 1947; *Pytheas*, 1947; *A By-Election of the Nineties*, 1951; *The Dynasts*, 1951; *The Streets of Pompeii*, 1952; *A Very Great Man Indeed*, 1953; *The Auction Sale*, 1958; *The America Prize*, 1964; *Hilda Tablet and Others: Four Pieces for Radio*, 1971; *The Streets of Pompeii, and Other Plays for Radio*, 1971; *The Two Mrs. Morlis*, 1971.

NONFICTION: *The Novel Since 1939*, 1946.

TRANSLATIONS: *Perdu and His Father*, 1954 (of Paride Rombi's novel); *Larger than Life*, 1962 (of Dino Buzzati's novel).

## BIBLIOGRAPHY

Beggs, James S. *The Poetic Character of Henry Reed*. Hull, Yorkshire, England: University of Hull Press, 1999. The only full-length study devoted to Reed's life and works, this volume is enriched by information and insights Beggs obtained by interviewing two of Reed's colleagues. While emphasizing analysis of the poetry, the volume also offers discussion of the major radio plays and translations.

Cleverdon, Douglas. "Henry Reed." In *Poets of Great Britain and Ireland, 1945-1960*, edited by Vincent B. Sherry, Jr. Vol. 77 in *Dictionary of Literary Biography*. Detroit: Gale, 1984. A biographical and critical overview, emphasizing the technical qualities of the poetry and the verse dramas.

Drakakis, John, ed. *British Radio Drama*. New York: Cambridge University Press, 1981. Contains an excellent chapter by Roger Savage that, although ultimately concerned with Reed's radio plays, gives exceptional biographical information and makes numerous references to the poetry. It embraces Reed's career and acknowledges his work as a poet, critic, translator, and dramatist. This introductory essay includes notes with references that are reviews of Reed's work and some articles not necessarily concerning him directly.

Gunter, Liz, and Jim Linebarger. "Tone and Voice in Henry Reed's 'Judging Distances.'" *Notes on Contemporary Literature* 18 (March, 1988): 9-10. Provides an informative analysis of the structure and theme of Reed's poetry. Useful information on Reed's poetic and technical devices.

O'Toole, Michael. "Henry Reed, and What Follows the 'Naming of Parts.'" In *Functions of Style*, edited by David Birch and Michael O'Toole. London: Pinter, 1988. Examines the stylistics of modern English. Central to an appreciation and understanding of Reed's poetic works. Includes a foreword by M. A. K. Halliday.

Parini, Jay, ed. *British Writers: Supplement XV*. Detroit: Charles Scribner's Sons, 2009. This collection on the work of British writers contains an entry describing the life and works of Reed.

Scannell, Vernon. "Henry Reed and Others." In *Not Without Glory: Poets of the Second World War*, edited by Vernon Scannell. London: Woburn, 1976. Scannell gives a close reading of "Naming of Parts" and the other two poems in the "Lessons of the War" section of *A Map of Verona*, tracing their imagery, syntax, and other formal and thematic elements.

Taylor, John Russell. *Anger and After*. London: Methuen, 1962. Rev. ed. *The Angry Theatre: New British Drama*. New York: Hill & Wang, 1969. Although it focuses on British drama, Taylor's book places Reed in the cultural context of his time. A standard resource, important for students of twentieth century British arts and literature. Bibliography.

*Harold Branam*

---

# John Wilmot, earl of Rochester

**Born:** Ditchley Manor House, Oxfordshire, England; April 10, 1647

**Died:** Woodstock, Oxfordshire, England; July 26, 1680

## Principal poetry

"A Satire Against Mankind," 1675

*Poems on Several Occasions by the Right Honourable E. of R.*, 1680 (attribution questionable)

*Poems, &c. on Several Occasions: With "Valentinian," a Tragedy*, 1691

*A Satire Against Mankind, and Other Poems, by John Wilmot, Earl of Rochester*, 1942 (Harry Levin, editor)

*Poems*, 1953 (Vivian de Sola Pinto, editor)

*The Complete Poems of John Wilmot, Earl of Rochester*, 1968 (David M. Vieth, editor)

*The Poems of John Wilmot, Earl of Rochester*, 1984 (Keith Walker, editor)

## Other literary forms

The first complete, unexpurgated edition of John Wilmot, earl of Rochester's letters appeared in 1980 as *The Letters of John Wilmot, Earl of Rochester*, edited by Jeremy Treglown. It includes more than one hundred very readable letters to his wife, to his mistress, and to his close friend, the courtier Henry Savile. Rochester's most sustained prose work is the broadside "Alexander Bendo's Bill," which satirized mountebanks and compared them to politicians, the quacks of state affairs. One version of this piece appears in Vivian de Sola Pinto's *Enthusiast in Wit: A Portrait of John Wilmot Earl of Rochester 1647-1680* (1962). There is also proof of Rochester's interest in drama—a scene for Sir Robert Howard's unfinished play *The Conquest of China*, and in 1678 a lengthy adaptation of John Fletcher's tragedy *Valentinian*, called in manuscript *Lucina's Rape*. Rochester did not live to complete the alteration, but in February, 1684, his play was given a magnificent production at the King's Theatre in London.

## Achievements

John Wilmot, earl of Rochester, is the one major poet among the literary courtiers of the Restoration. His standing as a poet still suffers from his reputation as a heartless rake. This view can no longer be taken seriously, since even in those of his love songs that express intense passion and cheerful irresponsibility, there is also a powerful current of fidelity. Rochester's devotion to his friends was only exceeded by the sincere intensity of thought and sentiment of the lyrics that he addressed to his wife. He embodied the Restoration definition of wit, not only having the capacity for a clever turn of phrase but also possessing a fierce intelligence. In his satires, he becomes a poet of skepticism, morally indignant, drawn to heterodoxy and paradox, but continually searching for the eternal truths promised by religion and for the assurances of love, friendship, and power.

Although his importance must be decided on the basis of a rather small canon (about seventy-five poems, a hundred letters, and an adaptation of a play), he has maintained a vocal group of admirers. The poet Andrew Marvell thought him the "best English satyrist,"

Voltaire called him a "Man of Genius with a shining imagination," and Alfred, Lord Tennyson, respected the "almost terrible force" of his "A Satire Against Mankind." In the twentieth century, Rochester has been described as a traditional Augustan more akin to Jonathan Swift and Alexander Pope than to John Dryden, a destructive nihilist, and a Christian pilgrim journeying not toward a goal but in search of one. The diversity of these viewpoints is exceeded only by their relative narrowness or exaggeration.

The most plausible contemporary view finds Rochester a mature product of the Restoration; his work illuminates the cultural, literary, and intellectual climate of that period. The 1968 publication of David M. Vieth's critical edition of the complete poems initiated a Rochester revival. Numerous books and articles and a concordance to the poems followed, and in 1980, a major part of *Tennessee Studies in Literature* was dedicated to the poet. Rochester remains the finest lyrical poet of the Restoration, the last important Metaphysical poet, and an influential satiric poet who helped make possible the achievements of the Augustan satirists.

BIOGRAPHY

John Wilmot was born in Ditchley, Oxfordshire, England, on April 10, 1647. He was the son of Henry, Viscount Wilmot, a distinguished Cavalier general, who had fought for Charles I and was made earl of Rochester by him. Later his father would effect the escape of Charles II from England to exile in France. Anne St. John, his mother, was the daughter of Sir John St. John, a Wiltshire knight and prominent Puritan.

John Wilmot inherited the earldom of Rochester and Adderbury Manor at the age of eleven. A handsome and precocious youth, he entered Wadham College, Oxford, at thirteen, where he was exposed to the most advanced scientific and philosophical thinking of the time: "the real centre of the English Enlightenment." His earliest poetry was written there in celebration of Charles II on his return in May, 1660; these few lines reminded the king of his debt to Wilmot's father. He richly rewarded the son, conferring a master's degree on the boy, granting him a pension of five hundred pounds a year, and arranging for his Grand Tour complete with a learned Scottish physician and virtuoso as his tutor.

*John Wilmot, earl of Rochester* (Hulton Archive/Getty Images)

After touring France and Italy, he returned to England in the winter of 1664 and joined the court of Charles II, immediately gaining notoriety for wit, profanity, and debauchery. Soon Rochester became the informal leader of a fashionable group of literary wits known as the Merry Gang, which included the playwright Sir George Etherege; John Sheffield, earl of Mulgrave; Charles Sackville, earl of Dorset; the poet Sir Charles Sedley; and Rochester's closest friend, Henry Savile.

Influenced by the writings of Thomas Hobbes, Rochester interpreted his materialist philosophy as a defense of sensuality and began an active revolt against both Cavalier romanticism and Puritan idealism. Although critics now agree that his reputation as a frantic rake and libertine was largely undeserved, the early lyrics and songs of this period display a determined hedonism and thorough enjoyment of the high-spirited frolic of the Whitehall Palace. In *Royal Charles: Charles II and the Restoration* (1979), Lady Antonia Fraser describes the famous Cornelis Huysmans portrait of Rochester as "a young man of almost insolent sensuality, wide lips curling with devilment," but with "something of the Angel yet undefaced in him." This indiscriminate life of pleasure soon proved unsatisfactory, and thereafter Rochester pursued a less insecure style of living.

In 1665, he met the beautiful young heiress Elizabeth Malet, and with the encouragement of the king, he asked her to marry him. When she refused, he abducted her; he was subsequently caught and imprisoned in the Tower. Soon released, he joined the navy and fought in the Dutch War of 1665 and 1666. His valorous conduct in battle helped to restore him to the favor of the king, and in 1667, he continued his success by marrying Malet. More honors descended on the twenty-one-year-old Rochester: The king appointed him a Gentleman of the Bedchamber with a salary of one thousand pounds, commissioned him captain in the horse guards, and arranged his summons to a seat in the House of Lords.

By all accounts, Rochester and his wife enjoyed a happy marriage, and four children resulted. Monogamy, however, suffered numerous assaults; the custom of keeping a mistress was followed by most Restoration aristocrats, and Rochester was no different in this regard. Elizabeth Barry, who became the greatest actress of the age, bore a daughter in 1677 and regarded Rochester as the father both of her child and of her career.

The 1670's marks the real development of Rochester as a poet. Always an impressive conversationalist, he began writing realistic and energetic satires of court life. The outspoken quality of his criticism alienated many of its victims—especially the king, who had him banished from court more than once. This reaction did not deter him from writing more fierce lampoons and from actively supporting the theater. Dryden thanked Rochester for his help with the Epistle Dedicatory to *Marriage à la Mode* (pr. 1672). Within two years, however, Rochester attacked Dryden in his satire "An Allusion to Horace" (1675). This work served as a dividing line between the factions of Whig and Tory writers.

The last four years of Rochester's life were characteristically dramatic; the evidence delineates the final stages of his long syphilitic illness and a remarkable spiritual conversion only a few weeks before his death. In the winter of 1679 to 1680, he shocked friends by his sincere interest in meeting Gilbert Burnet, a Scottish clergyman, to discuss the principles of Christianity. Although Rochester had maintained a rigid skepticism throughout his life, these conversations, with the knowledge of imminent death, triggered a sensational repentance. Declaring that religion had brought him the sense of "felicity and glory" that he had missed pursuing worldly pleasures, Rochester died on July 26, 1680, at Woodstock. He was thirty-three, and his death would release a mass of contradictory comment from biographers proclaiming him either an edifying example of conversion or a debauched pornographer with, in Pope's phrase, "a very bad turn of mind." The one truth that can be acknowledged by the evidence is that he possessed "the greatest poetic gift of all the noble Wits."

ANALYSIS

The reputation of John Wilmot, earl of Rochester, as a poet has suffered from the overly dramatic legends about his life. Whatever past judgments have been made of his work seem unfairly colored by a considerable amount of untruthful scandal. Although modern biographers tend to rehabilitate such men completely and to give less perfidious definitions to the term "libertine," there is little to be gained here by denying the truth of his professed hedonism and his actual debauchery. Unwilling to allow his biography to overwhelm his work, two contemporary critics, Vieth and Dustin Griffin, have affirmed the undeniable wit and power of his verses. Appreciation of the value of the early satires, the songs, and "A Satire Against Mankind" develops from first agreeing that Rochester is a product of his own time. Although this work, particularly the late satires, was influential for the Augustans and even shared some of their values, one should view Rochester's poems as mirroring the Restoration milieu socially, intellectually, and stylistically.

The major themes of Rochester's poetry derive from his evaluation of love, friendship, and courtly life. In each of these areas, he weighs humanity's promise for achieving the ideal against his predilection for evil and folly. As a skeptic, he is not under the mystical spell of religion; his poems reveal a man in search of certainties in the face of an awareness that such serenity is, for him, remote and unrealizable.

As literature of the Restoration, the poems reveal aristocratic attitudes of the past under severe stress from the philosophies of the Enlightenment. Rochester's knowledge of René Descartes, Thomas Hobbes, and John Locke allows him to suspend an automatic acceptance of traditional value systems and instead to question, analyze, and debate issues concerning the human condition.

Griffin, in *Satires Against Man: The Poems of Rochester* (1973), finds that one constant motif of his work was a rational humanist morality. Rather than trusting society or religion to establish laws for the restraint of man, Rochester depends on pleasure and pain and on following "nature" as the way to govern conduct. His tendency toward skepticism causes him to doubt whether morals can guide humans to right conduct; in typical Restoration fashion, Rochester insists upon the immediacy of experience both with regard to sensual desires and in more abstract concerns: belief, conduct, and literary convention. Immediacy suggests security, a safe haven from the "ugly cheat" of life. If traditional moral and religious restraints are held in contempt, as they were at court, Rochester has only to rely on sensual contentment. Inevitably, his poems reflect his dissatisfaction with such experience; in fact, his constant theme is the disproportion between human desires and the means for satisfying them. While remaining a sensualist, he never reflects satisfaction in the poetry, because he never loses sight of the ultimate futility of the human condition. His poetry describes the suffering, anger, frustration, and failure of humanity, and does so with energy and clarity. In failing to achieve security, Rochester's analysis also reveals the zest of humans' restless, acquisitive, and competitive nature, while affirming the poet's admiration of personal goodness, of freedom from pretension and greed.

### TEXTUAL NOTES

During Rochester's lifetime, his lyrics, songs, lampoons, and satires were circulated in manuscript copies among the court of Charles II. A few of his writings were printed as broadsides or in miscellanies; his great "A Satire Against Mankind" was printed as a folio broadside in 1675. The textual issue of whether a reliable contemporary edition of his poetry exists is a complicated one. In the late summer of 1680, a book professing to be the *Poems on Several Occasions by the Right Honourable the E. of R.* was published under the ostensible imprint of a nonexistent Antwerp printer. In an effort to capitalize on his name and popular reputation as a wild courtier, sixty-one poems were offered, of which many were pornographic and more than a third were not even written by Rochester. Nevertheless, the book was extremely popular and numerous editions were produced to satisfy public demand. In his book *Attribution in Restoration Poetry: A Study of Rochester's "Poems" of 1680* (1963), Vieth explains that the earliest of these editions was based on a responsible manuscript miscellany copy text, and that despite the shortcomings of *Poems on Several Occasions*, it is the most important edition of Rochester published prior to the twentieth century. Since 1926, many editors have struggled with the Rochester text. The difficulties arose over an unusually problematical canon, the varying authority of texts from which the poems came down to readers, and the obscene nature of some of the genuine poems. In 1968, the definitive critical edition was published: Vieth's *The Complete Poems of John Wilmot, Earl of Rochester*. In solving the aforementioned difficulties, Vieth found seventy-five authentic poems, eight other poems possibly written by Rochester, and nearly two hundred spurious poems.

### "A SONG: MY DEAR MISTRESS HAS A HEART"

Rochester's poems fall into four chronological categories: prentice work (1665-1671), early maturity (1672-1673), tragic maturity (1674-1675), and disillusionment and death (1676-1680). Representative of Rochester's prentice work is the early poem "A Song: My dear Mistress has a heart" (exact date unknown), a self-consciously conventional poem incorporating characteristics of the courtly love tradition. As in many of his other songs, Rochester explores the complexities of human sexual nature while entertaining rather than instructing the reader. In two eight-line stanzas of ballad measures, the poet employs the familiar figures and concepts of Restoration lyrics—the enslaving mistress whose "resistless Art" has captured the poet's heart. While recognizing "her Constancy's weak," he is powerless to escape her "Killing pleasures and Wounding Blisses" and must only trust that this poem will convince her of his deepest regard. Without varying from the sophisticated pattern, Rochester writes a tender, graceful love lyric. What seems missing is the poet's individual voice, which would bring this artificial form to life with the sheer intensity of his wit.

### "FAIR CHLORIS IN A PIGSTY LAY"

Another early poem, "Fair Chloris in a pigsty lay" (exact date unknown), marks him as an authentic poetic voice with its sudden, often brutal, wit that shocks the reader, demanding his notice. Rochester's Chloris is not the conventional dreaming shepherdess of the pastoral; she is a swineherdess of the most lustful and crude sort. Surrounded by her murmuring pigs while she sleeps, Chloris dreams of a "love-convicted swain" who calls her to a cave to rescue a trapped pig, only to throw himself lustfully upon her. Instead of a self-abasing lover pleading with his mistress, Rochester reverses the persona as Chloris finds herself the object of a crude rape. The poem's final stanza undercuts the brutality yet retains the indecency, as Chloris wakes, realizing that it was only a dream. Her innocence is preserved, although she has enjoyed the secret pleasure of a fantasy lover. While maintaining a humorous and playful tone, Rochester adds a final unexpected twist of eroticism which lifts this song above the conventionality of the earlier one. Such a mocking tone foreshadows the poems of his mature period; the "innocent" Chloris becomes the voracious Corinna of "A Ramble in St. James's Park."

### "A RAMBLE IN ST. JAMES'S PARK"

The poems of 1672-1673, the period of Rochester's early maturity, reveal his accomplishment as a lyricist and his virtuosity as a satirist. Vieth believes that the satires of 1674 display the zenith of Rochester's achievement, but "A Ramble in St. James's Park" is a triumph. The poem is a comprehensive Juvenalian satire on sexual relations in the *beau monde*, displaying the speaker as one who ridicules the corruption in himself and in his fellow revelers. The speaker describes an after-dinner walk in the park in search of love. In the park, once a place of elegance and now a scene of dissipation, he unexpectedly "beheld Corinna pass," who is his mistress and should acknowledge him, but instead "proud disdain she cast on me." Watching further, he sees her leave in a coach with three "confounded asses." Bitterly disillusioned, not by her lust but by her

passive and treacherous submission to fools, he curses her for a "fall to so much infamy." The speaker, who had considered himself morally superior to his companions, now concludes with an ironic self-satire, an attack on the pastoral for idealizing such settings, and a lampoon against indiscriminate lust.

The villain is not the libertine speaker but Corinna, who offends all humanity by engaging in sex unfeelingly. Honest lustful passion remains a justifiable principle, while unfeeling sex with affected fools is a far worse sin than mere lust. Rochester shows his displeasure with Restoration men and women who respond to unnatural longings and reject those desires born of natural reason. The material is vigorous and often violent in tone, impatient with the sham of Cavalier and Restoration conventions in love poetry. The best of Rochester's bawdy satires, it is motivated not by its profane qualities but in part by a prejudice against the debasement of sex.

### TRAGIC MATURITY

In the period of his tragic maturity, Rochester found his vehicle as a poetic stylist by controlling the heroic couplet for formal verse satire. The influence of the Roman satirists Horace and Juvenal provided some impetus for Rochester; his best model, however, was Horace's disciple, Nicolas Boileau-Despréaux, the first major seventeenth century satirist to attempt a recreation of classical forms. "Timon" and "A Satire Against Mankind" transcend Boileau with their economy of phrase, skillful use of narrative and descriptive styles from one victim's portrait to another, and the command displayed between the realization of the speaker and the various dramatic scenes. John Harold Wilson, in *The Court Wits of the Restoration* (1948), argues that Rochester was roused in the 1670's "to a true misanthropy by the contrast between man's promise and his performance . . . he made war on mankind at large." In these poems, the complacency of humankind provokes an outrage unmatched at any other point in his career.

### "TIMON"

"Timon" has as its principal speaker a man named Timon, who resembles Rochester in character, interests, and social status. The reference to William Shakespeare's misanthropic Timon of Athens is obvious, although the name may also allude to his honesty in the face of a corrupted humanity. The account begins with an unwilling visit to a dinner party where an insistent host—a total stranger "who just my name had got"— promises that the other guests will be his friends Sedley, Savile, and Buckhurst. Not surprisingly, these assurances remain unfulfilled. Timon's company consists of four fools, "Halfwit and Huff, Kickum and Dingboy." The hostess appears, an ancient flirt, and presides over a tedious banquet complete with displays of corrupted taste in food and poetry. Inevitably, rough verbal antics culminate in bouts of plate hurling and Timon's own relieved escape into the night.

Rochester establishes the thematic unity of the poem by implying that Timon's social and intellectual standards have been violated by the attitudes and actions of the host, his wife, and the four "hectors." In the earlier model for the poem, the Horatian speaker was a paragon of good sense and propriety. Rochester's Timon flaunts a delighted malice before the rest of the human race and does so in the bawdiest terms. Detailing the physical characteristics of the hostess, Timon develops a vicious portrait; the entire description, however, includes the most damning evidence—the victim's conversation, which displays her foolishness, affectation, and crudity. The speaker's character also comes under scrutiny; his curious interest in the dinner conversation and his obsession with sex create a disturbing uncertainty in the poem. Rochester may have meant to mock Timon for having agreed to attend the dinner party; his skeptical nature should have warned him against finding true companions. Also, the speaker's sexual crudity, although strikingly overt, is at least without affectation. As in the earlier "A Ramble in St. James's Park," the rake admits his belief in sexual freedom, his appreciation for honest, generous lust. Ultimately he finds frustration and humiliation. The same theme which appeared in the earlier work is alluded to in "Timon"; sensual experience is ultimately a failure. Timon realizes the accuracy of this attitude in his comments on the host's wife: "Fit to give love . . . But age, beauty's incurable disease, had left her more desire than power to please." Timon's faults cannot be ignored, but in contrast to the affected hosts and boorish guests he gains the reader's trust.

## "A SATIRE AGAINST MANKIND"

Rochester's most impressive poem is his "A Satire Against Mankind." It is a discourse in which the speaker offers the paradoxical thesis that it is better to be an animal than a man; however, Rochester is more concerned with emphasizing the loathsomeness of being human than the virtues of being an animal. He attacks Reason itself, the pure rationality that he had formerly worshiped.

The poem reflects the skepticism of the age, and the recurrent motif in Rochester's work of a division between the actual and the ideal. The philosophy of cynicism goes back to classical sources, to Epicurus and the Skeptics. It seems that Rochester adopted their arguments in order to counter particular schools of rationalistic thought such as the vain and strident Christian rationalism of the Cambridge Platonists, the godlike reasoning eminence of the university Schoolmen, and the anti-Aristotelian rationalism of the Anglicans. The exaltation of humanity, the thesis that God is pure reason, the continual optimism about humanity's capacities for perceiving the meaning of the cosmos and God's laws through reason—all these notions were ridiculed by him.

Rochester's immediate, most influential source was Hobbes, whose materialist-sensationalist philosophy was the basis for his view of human motivation. Every person is an enemy to every other person in his or her desire for gain, for safety, and for glory. This continual desire for security, for certainty, is characteristic of the libertine, who disdains convention and orthodoxy as paths to power. The rake instead exploits other people's weaknesses, thus gaining mastery over their lives. Those conventional figures of the community who might censure him are hypocrites who have disavowed their true desires for gain and glory. All those virtues that humans profess to follow in the name of social order are merely rationalizations of their fear and desire for security, and Rochester improves on Hobbes, believing that humans only convert this fear into more "respectable" passions. Rochester exhibits a bitter, relentless cynicism about human possibility; even the rake's mastery proves to be a painful failure.

The poem is a formal verse satire in which the satirist contemplates a particular topic and anticipates the imaginary response of someone else to his thoughts. This structure of the satire has caused much debate among critics who believe that the poem is a philosophical discourse on epistemology and ethics. Other scholars make a good case for the view that the poem is a unified polemic against human pride: pride in reason, learning, and "accomplishment." Griffin accepts both viewpoints while offering his analysis of the work as primarily a four-part discourse, with a speaker presenting and defending the paradox that it is better to be an animal than a man.

The first part of the poem states the thesis, suggesting that all men are equally ridiculous, and proposes a distinction between wits and fools. This difference proves a false one. The second part raises the imagined objections of the satirist's opponent, who offers a distinction between wit and reason that only reveals the ambiguous, confused nature of the opponent's argument. The third part develops the satirist's response to these objections, analyzing first reason and then humankind's "wisdom" and "nature." He seems willing to accept the middle ground between pure instinct and pure reason "which distinguishes by sense." The paradoxical quality of the poem is again asserted as the satirist turns from this compromise to attack all humankind once more. Instinct, although preferable to right reason, remains unattainable since all people are "knaves." The fourth part functions as the epilogue in which the satirist recapitulates his argument and in so doing reformulates his paradox. Significantly, Rochester adds here that all people are slaves, as well as knaves, only some are worse in these respects than others. The final line—"Man differs more from man, than man from beast"—sharpens the total satiric effect of the poem. Animals, after this exacting analysis, still remain closer to the ideal of godlike humans ("meek humble man of honest sense") than the rabble (wits, fools, cowards, knaves, and the poet). The beasts are a better reflection of human moral ideals than are humans themselves.

"A Satire Against Mankind" remains an impressive effort and an example of the best Rochester was capable of during his mature period. Its effects are beautifully judged, as is its destructive critique of human pre-

tension; however, Rochester's own predicament as a man and as an artist persists with no real hope or secure possibility for a better world.

### "AN EPISTOLARY ESSAY FROM M. G. TO O. B. UPON THEIR MUTUAL POEMS"

The sixteen poems of Rochester's final period, the period of disillusionment and death, reflect a decline in the quantity and quality of his work. The most effective poem of this group is "An Epistolary Essay from M. G. to O. B. upon their Mutual Poems" (1679). Serving as a companion piece to "A Very Heroical Epistle in Answer to Ephelia" (1675), this informal critical essay expresses the views on love and poetry of a bold libertine persona, M. G. (John Sheffield, earl of Mulgrave). The speaker writes to a friend, O. B. (John Dryden), in praise of the latter's poems and in defense of his own violations of the traditional canons of good writing. Furthermore, after having lampooned in "A Satire Against Mankind" the idea that rational humans partake of the divine, Rochester here attacks the idea that poetry has a divine source. By employing this approach, he criticizes conventional wisdom, putting the burden of writing well on the poet's egotism instead of on divine will. The argument concludes with the notion that a poet is his own best critic and must rely on his own self-judgment. The arrogance of the piece marks Rochester's strength as a poet but his weakness as a man.

Confident about his own artistic strengths, he had nothing but contempt for the rabble of hacks and critics. His work possesses the poetic virtues of vigor and force; although often unconventional and strikingly obscene, his poems grow out of a literary tradition both classical and English. Although the spectacle of humankind provoked in him a Juvenalian outrage and profound disgust, he also revealed his admiration for personal goodness, for a man of Christlike humility and piety. The doubt that such a person existed would plague him his entire life; yet he continued the quest without abject despair. His complex emotional response to the literary, intellectual, and social milieu of the Restoration found an outlet in his poetry. Whether he projects rejection and nihilism or envisions an ideal which proves unreachable, Rochester remains one of the most original and notable poets of the age.

OTHER MAJOR WORKS

PLAY: *Valentinian*, pr., pb. 1685 (adaptation of John Fletcher's tragedy *Valentinian*).

NONFICTION: *The Letters of John Wilmot, Earl of Rochester*, 1980 (Jeremy Treglown, editor).

MISCELLANEOUS: *Collected Works of John Wilmot, Earl of Rochester*, 1926 (John Hayward, editor); *The Complete Works*, 1994 (Frank H. Ellis, editor).

BIBLIOGRAPHY

Burns, Edward, ed. *Reading Rochester*. New York: St. Martin's Press, 1995. A collection of eleven essays on Rochester's life and poetry. Sections focus on sexual politics, form and intellect, and Rochester and his literary contemporaries.

Combe, Kirk. *A Martyr for Sin: Rochester's Critique of Polity, Sexuality, and Society*. Newark: University of Delaware Press, 1998. Combe offers a way of looking at the poetry of Rochester that does not ignore his politics. Using the theories of Michel Foucault and others, the author analyzes Rochester's writings within their contemporary civil and cultural contexts.

Fisher, Nicholas, ed. *That Second Bottle: Essays on John Wilmot, Earl of Rochester*. New York: St. Martin's Press, 2000. Explores the full range and variety of the poet's work, including his treatment of themes of love and friendship, his influence on later poets and musicians, and his contribution to the Restoration theater.

Goldsworthy, Cephas. *The Satyr: An Account of the Life and Work, Death and Salvation of John Wilmot, Second Earl of Rochester*. London: Weidenfeld and Nicolson, 2001. A swashbuckling biography that considers Rochester's poetry in relation to his life.

Hammond, Paul. *Figuring Sex Between Men from Shakespeare to Rochester*. New York: Oxford University Press, 2002. A study of homosexual themes in seventeenth century British literature that emphasizes the homoerotic aspects of Rochester's poetry.

Johnson, James William. *A Profane Wit: The Life of John Wilmot, Earl of Rochester*. 2004. Reprint. Rochester, N.Y.: University of Rochester Press, 2009. This biography traces the life of Rochester and deals with the myths that surround him.

Pinto, Vivian de Sola. *Enthusiast in Wit: A Portrait of John Wilmot, Earl of Rochester*. Lincoln: University of Nebraska Press, 1962. An updated, expanded version of Pinto's *Rochester, Portrait of a Restoration Poet* (1935). Pinto offers a full biography of Rochester, with abundant detail on the poet's youth, riotous and colorful life in and out of exile at the court of Charles II, and dramatic deathbed conversion. The social, intellectual, and literary currents of Rochester's day are also treated in depth.

Thormählen, Marianne. *Rochester: The Poems in Context*. New York: Cambridge University Press, 1993. Emphasizes the references to contemporary life and politics in Rochester's poetry and his concern with literary craftsmanship beneath his rakish persona.

Vieth, David. *Attribution in Restoration Poetry: A Study of Rochester's "Poems" of 1680*. 1963. Reprint. New Haven, Conn.: Yale University Press, 1980. This extensive study, more than five hundred pages in length, considers early texts and ascriptions. Appendices list additional poems in the Yale manuscript. Bibliographical notes.

*Paul J. deGrategno*

---

# ISAAC ROSENBERG

**Born:** Bristol, England; November 25, 1890
**Died:** Near Arras, France; April 1, 1918

PRINCIPAL POETRY

*Night and Day*, 1912
*Youth*, 1915
*Moses*, 1916 (includes verse drama)
*Poems*, 1922 (Gordon Bottomley, editor)
*The Collected Poems*, 1949

OTHER LITERARY FORMS

Isaac Rosenberg's *Moses* combines poetry with verse drama. Rosenberg's prose, letters, and drawings can be found in two collections of his works, one edited by Gordon Bottomley and Denys Harding and published in 1937 and the other edited by Ian Parsons and published in 1979.

## ACHIEVEMENTS

Isaac Rosenberg was one of a group of young poets, including Rupert Brooke, Edward Thomas, and Wilfred Owen, whose lives were tragically cut short by World War I. Rosenberg's early poems were slight; it is as a war poet that his reputation was established, largely through the efforts of his mentor, Gordon Bottomley. What makes him unusual among British poets in general and war poets in particular is his Jewish perspective. That aspect coupled with his working-class background sets his poetry apart from the Georgian tones of Thomas or Brooke, or the upper-class tones of Siegfried Sassoon or Robert Graves.

## BIOGRAPHY

Isaac Rosenberg was the son of Barnett Rosenberg and Hacha Davidov. His father was a Lithuanian Jew whose impoverished family had emigrated from Russia to Bristol, England, shortly before Rosenberg's birth. Soon after, they moved to the East End of London, which was then the center of the Jewish immigrant community, a community that existed as a tightly knit group until the 1960's and from which emerged such Jewish writers as the dramatists Bernard Kops and Arnold Wesker.

His father opened his own butcher shop; when that failed, he became an itinerant peddler. The family lived in constant poverty, but it was cohesive, and Isaac Rosenberg grew up in a religious atmosphere. After an elementary school education, Rosenberg showed some artistic promise, and in 1907, he began attending evening classes at Birkbeck College, an affiliated college of the University of London, set up especially to help poor students. In 1908, he won the Mason Prize for his nude studies as well as several other awards. To earn a living, he became apprenticed to an engraver.

A few people noticed Rosenberg's talent and sponsored him at the Slade, London's most prestigious art school, which he entered in 1911. There he was influenced by such British artists as the Pre-Raphaelites, particularly Dante Gabriel Rossetti, and also by William Blake and the modernist Roger Fry. While continuing to study at the Slade, he struck out as an artist, setting up a studio in 1912 in Hampstead Road. He had also been writing poetry and sent some of it to Laurence

Binyon, an established Georgian poet who worked at the British Museum, and some to the *English Review*. He received encouragement from both the poet and the journal, and he decided to publish these poems at his own expense in a twenty-four-page pamphlet.

The next year, he met Edward Marsh, editor of *Georgian Poetry* and an influential literary figure in London. Marsh purchased some of his paintings and encouraged him to go on writing, introducing him to other poets such as the modernists T. E. Hulme and Ezra Pound. Rosenberg was still undecided as to whether he was better as a painter or as a poet.

At this point, Rosenberg's health deteriorated, and he sailed to South Africa to stay with one of his sisters. He remained there during 1914, returning to England in March, 1915. Marsh bought three more of his paintings, and Rosenberg published another volume of verse, again at his own expense. However, with the war on, the literary and artistic scene in London had broken up, and there were no immediate prospects or contacts for him. In the light of this, he decided, reluctantly, to enlist, though feeling no particular patriotism.

He was not in good health, rather underweight and undersized. Nevertheless, he was accepted by the army, joining the "Bantams" of the 12th Suffolk Regiment, later transferring to the King's Own Royal Lancasters. After initial training, he was dispatched to the Somme battle area of northern France in June, 1916. During this time, he wrote a play, *Moses*, and then several other dramatic pieces based loosely on Jewish mythology.

He continued to write poetry, now influenced by his experience of war. By 1916, there were few illusions left about the nature of modern warfare. Rosenberg was able to embrace what he saw and sought some positive response to it. Apart from ten days of leave in September, 1917, and a few short spells in the hospital, he served continuously on or just behind the front lines until his death. He was killed shortly before the end of the war while riding dispatches at night. His body was never recovered. His war poems were first collected and published in 1922 by Gordon Bottomley.

## ANALYSIS

Such is the lateness in poetic development in Isaac Rosenberg's short life that the majority of his output could be termed "early." His earliest dated poem is from 1905, but the so-called trench poems, on which his reputation solely depends, did not begin until 1916, when he enlisted and was posted to France. Thus the earlier poems span eleven years, with the best gathered into the 1912 and 1915 collections. The total number of poems gathered by his editors, including all the unpublished ones, is 154, of which only 10 percent represent the war poems.

Even though he did have friendships with several Imagist poets—Imagism being the first flowering of modern poetry—his early poetry, unlike his painting, seems typically Georgian. This movement, spanning the first fifteen years of the twentieth century, is best typified as Romantic in a suburban, restrained way, with the emphasis on nature as recreation and pretty images, being nostalgic in tone and with harmonious versification. Some critics have seen the influence of the Pre-Raphaelite painter-poet Dante Gabriel Rossetti, though the most obvious echoing is that of John Keats, another London city poet, whose poetry is full of woods, light, and shade and heightened sensory perceptions, with nature as an escape for the trapped urban spirit.

### "NIGHT AND DAY"

The long opening poem of the 1912 collection is titled "Night and Day" and apostrophizes the stars as he walks out of the city into the woods. The poet feels himself "set aside," seeking symbolic meaning in nature. Keats's "Sleep and Poetry" forms an obvious comparison. Echoes also sound of E. M. Forster's character Leonard Bast in his novel *Howards End* (1910). Other poems in the volume talk of "Desire" with an interesting religious reference; others show sympathy for the common people, a sympathy Rosenberg was to demonstrate later in his war poems.

### YOUTH

*Youth*, the 1915 volume, shows in some of its lyrics somewhat more focus and control, but the emotions stay at a very generalized level. "God Made Blind" is more like a poem by Thomas Hardy, England's most senior poet at the time. "The Dead Heroes" shows an entirely conventional view of patriotism at this stage.

### "ON RECEIVING NEWS OF THE WAR"

The uncollected "On Receiving News of the War," written from Cape Town, South Africa, shows a much less conventional and more genuine response. He writes, "God's blood is shed/ He mourns from His lone place/ His children dead." There is no heroism here, only divine pity. In 1915, he sent some of these poems to Lascelles Abercrombie, one of the most popular of the Georgians, whom Rosenberg considered "our best living poet." Abercrombie found the poems to possess a "vivid and original impulse," though he noted that Rosenberg had not yet found his true voice.

### MOSES

Rosenberg was also attracted to dramatic verse. In 1916, he had published *Moses*, which consisted of a small number of poems added to a fragment of what was presumably intended to be a larger dramatic work on the Israelite leader Moses. He took considerable license with the biblical story, placing Moses at the moment he was still a prince of Egypt, but just beginning to find his identity as a Hebrew. The speech rhythms and dramatic ideas show much more poetic talent than anything done before, but there is still too much verbiage to be truly dramatic.

Some of the other poems in the volume are much bolder in their conceptual range than anything before. "God" makes a defiant Promethean statement. "Chagrin" uses the image of Absalom hanging by his hair, linking this to Christ hanging on the cross, quite a new sort of poem. "Marching" is the first soldier poem, with taut strong rhythms. The language is much richer and more imagistic. In the volume as a whole, there is for the first time some awareness of modernism, as there had been for some time in his painting.

### THE LILITH THEME

While enlisted, Rosenberg also experimented with another Jewish myth, that of Lilith, mixing it strangely with unicorn myths and even a "Rape of the Sabine Women" theme. In his unpublished papers, there were a number of versions of this, titled variously "The Unicorn" or "The Amulet." As he works through various drafts, the blank verse becomes more dramatic, but his own imagination is revealed as mythic rather than dramatic, and there is no overall conceptual grasp of dramatic ideas or structure. Most of the verse consists of soliloquies or long monologues. Yet when it is considered that most of it was done under the most appalling physical conditions, it shows considerable commitment on the poet's part.

### TRENCH POEMS

Once under the pressure of fighting in France, Rosenberg's poetic talents crystallized quickly. Flowery sentiments and unfocused images, typical also of Keats's early style, were, as with Keats himself, left behind, and a genuine unsentimental human sympathy was revealed. "The Dying Soldier" sets the tone: it is lyrical, almost balladic, but it focuses on the pathos of the actual death, not the stark horrors of the overall scene. "In War" shows a great advance in poetic technique: The controlled stanza form displays a control of tone and emotion, taking the reader from an almost anaesthetized calm to a sudden panic of realizing it was his brother they were burying. This movement from something "out there" to "right here" becomes typical of these war poems.

Several themes and poetic ideas are revealed. One is the "titan." "Girl to a Soldier on Leave" uses this image for the infantry soldier: Romantic love cannot really be sustained in the face of trench experience. Some new mode of tragedy is being forged. In "Soldier: Twentieth Century," Rosenberg makes a political comment for the first time. The modern soldier is a "great new Titan." In the past, soldiers were fodder to keep tyrants in power. Now it is time that they wake up from sleeping "like Circe's swine" and rebel.

The second theme is a Jewish one: the burning of Solomon's Temple. "Destruction of Jerusalem by the Babylonian Hordes" is too anachronistic to be fully effective. The theme is reworked in "The Burning of the Temple." The poet asks if Solomon is angry at the burning of his glorious temple, to which the answer is, apparently not. If "God" is read for "Solomon" and the human body for the "Temple," then a powerful statement emerges: God's anger can be only ambiguously discerned.

The third theme is humorous. "The Immortals" is mock heroic, leading the reader to believe the soldier is fighting a heroic battle. In fact, he is fighting lice, which are immortal. Similarly, "Louse Hunting" depicts the real enemy in its "supreme littleness." In fact, Rosenberg has very little conception of the "enemy." For example, "Break of Day in the Trenches" shows a poet who strikes no poses, makes no gestures, and retains all his sensitivities after two years of continuous warfare. Others were driven insane. It is a gentle, sad, slightly ironic poem that shows Rosenberg as a human being rather than as a soldier. In fact, death on the battlefields is described as "murder," hardly a military perception.

The poem is an address to a rat, which like lice, were all too common in the trenches. However, the rat is not treated as vermin here. Rosenberg apostrophizes it for making no distinction between friend and foe, crossing indiscriminately between the two sides. The rat is "sardonic"; it "inwardly grins" as it sees fine young men from both sides being killed randomly and haphazardly, "sprawled in the bowels of the earth."

### "DEAD MAN'S DUMP"

Among the best war poems ever written are two by Rosenberg, "Returning We Hear the Larks," with its sense of precarious joy still possible for the human spirit, and "Dead Man's Dump." This poem is about the quintessential war dilemma: seeing individuals, living and worthy of life, even if on the point of dying, as against seeing the mass of impersonal lifeless corpses that are fit only for throwing into the ground and burying. Rosenberg seems to be on some sort of burial fatigue, jolting along in a mule-drawn cart somewhere in no-man's-land. All around "The air is loud with death," and corpses of friend and foe alike lie scattered around. Sometimes the cart jolts over them, crushing their bones. They approach a dying man who must have heard them coming, as he tried to cry aloud. However, by the time the cart gets to him, he is dead, and "our wheels grazed his dead face."

The poet writes as a human being: There is pity but no sentimentality. Rosenberg's visual imagination is most clearly seen in his images of the corpses, their former strength and spirit seen against their present contorted lifelessness, especially in relationship to the earth, which is sensed as a living entity, to whose embrace the living return in a haphazard, random way. His imagination is also engaged in motion and motionlessness. Verbs are particularly vivid: "lurched," "sprawled," "crunched," "huddled," "go crying," and "breaking," "crying," "torturing," "break," "broke," "quivering," "rushing" in the climactic ending. These verbs are so violent they push away the poet's natural inclination to pity: "The drowning soul was sunk too deep/ For human tenderness." He writes of a soldier whose "brains splattered on/A stretcher-bearer's face."

This is a much more sustained poem than many of the other war poems. It is in free verse, divided into irregular stanzas, twelve in all, with occasional rhymes and half-rhymes. It is modern in its versification, unlike that of fellow war poets Brooke, Owen, and Sassoon, who tried, not always successfully, to adapt forms of the gentle, restrained Georgian versification to the horrendous scenes and emotions they were describing. Rosenberg's images and rhythmic structures create drama and movement much more fluidly, and the climax of the poem is as powerful as anything else in World War I poetry. Clearly, Rosenberg could have become a great poet had he lived. The very control of the poem, written in conditions of chaos and horror, suggests the triumph of the human spirit.

OTHER MAJOR WORKS

MISCELLANEOUS: *The Collected Works of Isaac Rosenberg: Poetry, Prose, Letters, and Some Drawings*, 1937 (Gordon Bottomley and Denys Harding, editors); *The Collected Works of Isaac Rosenberg: Poetry, Prose, Letters, Paintings, and Drawings*, 1979 (Ian Parsons, editor); *The Poems and Plays of Isaac Rosenberg*, 2004 (Vivien Noakes, editor); *Poetry Out of My Head and Heart: Unpublished Letters and Poem Versions*, 2007.

BIBLIOGRAPHY

Bloom, Harold, ed. *Poets of WWI: Wilfred Owen and Isaac Rosenberg*. Broomall, Pa.: Chelsea House, 2002. A collection of essays about the war poets Wilfred Owen and Rosenberg. Contains a biography of Rosenberg and five essays on his works.

Cohen, Joseph. *Journey to the Trenches: The Life of Isaac Rosenberg, 1890-1918*. London: Robson, 1975. Three biographies of Rosenberg were published in 1975, their combined effect being to bring him to public notice as a significant war poet. Cohen's account is the most sympathetic to his Jewish roots and background.

Desmond, Graham. *The Truth of War: Owen, Blunden, Rosenberg*. Manchester, England: Carcanet Press, 1984. A thoughtful approach to three contrasting World War I poets. A good bibliography with good commentaries on all of Rosenberg's trench poems.

Giddings, Robert. *The War Poets: The Lives and Writings of the 1914-18 War Poets*. London: Bloomsbury, 1988. A popular biographical approach, enacting Rosenberg's life and experience in the context of his contemporaries.

Liddiard, Jean. *Isaac Rosenberg: The Half-Used Life*. London: Gollancz, 1975. The second of the 1975 biographies, and probably the most straightforward one. A good approach to the poems.

Maccoby, Deborah. *God Made Blind: Isaac Rosenberg, His Life and Poetry*. Chicago: Science Reviews, 1999. This biography and critical analysis examines how Rosenberg's Jewish faith played a role in his life and writings.

Quinn, Patrick, ed. *British Poets of the Great War: Brooke, Rosenberg, Thomas—A Documentary Volume*. Detroit: Gale Group, 2000. Looks at Rupert Brooke, Edward Thomas, and Rosenberg and compares and contrasts their work.

Roberts, David. *Essential Poetry of the First World War in Context*. Burgess Hill, England: Saxon, 1996. Several critical books have tried to bring a historicist approach to Rosenberg and the other war poets, trying to reconstruct the overall social and political context out of which the poetry was generated. Roberts deals more with the poetic material than some others. Full bibliography.

Wilson, Jean Moorcroft. *Isaac Rosenberg, Poet and Painter: A Biography*. London: Cecil Woolf, 1975. The third of the 1975 biographies, this time tracing the growth of Rosenberg's artistic ideas and the interplay between poetry and painting.

_____. *Isaac Rosenberg: The Making of a Great War Poet—A New Life*. Evanston, Ill.: Northwestern University Press, 2009. This biography of the war poet, whose brief life produced some memorable poems, expands on Wilson's earlier work.

*David Barratt*

# CHRISTINA ROSSETTI

**Born:** London, England; December 5, 1830
**Died:** London, England; December 29, 1894
**Also known as:** Ellen Alleyne

PRINCIPAL POETRY

*Verses*, 1847
*Goblin Market, and Other Poems*, 1862 (also pb. as *Poems*, 1866)
*The Prince's Progress, and Other Poems*, 1866
*Sing-Song*, 1872, 1893
*A Pageant, and Other Poems*, 1881
*Verses*, 1893
*New Poems*, 1896

OTHER LITERARY FORMS

*Commonplace, and Other Short Stories* (1870) suggests that Christina Rossetti (roh-ZEHT-ee) may have once had the notion of becoming a novelist. Unlike other female poets of the period, she wrote a great deal in prose, both secular and religious. "Commonplace," the title story, is not usually considered to be the best of these prose pieces. That honor is reserved for "The Lost Titian," the plot of which revolves around two friends' competitive praise for another friend's painting. In the end, all three discover one another's vanities. "Vanna's Twins" is a touching story of childhood and demonstrates Rossetti's power in delineating character among lower-middle-class Italians. *Speaking Likenesses* (1874), a series of stories told to some girls by their aunt as they pass the time sewing, stands in the shadows of Lewis Carroll's and Jean Ingelow's works of the same period.

*Annus Domini* (1874) is a devotional prose work, the first of several, which includes a prayer for each day of the year. These pieces were influenced by *The Book of Common Prayer*. Other devotional works include *Seek and Find*, 1879; *Called to Be Saints*, 1881; *Letter and Spirit*, 1882; *Time Flies*, 1885; *The Face of the Deep*, 1892; and *Maude*, 1897.

ACHIEVEMENTS

Soon after the publication of *Goblin Market, and Other Poems*, the *British Quarterly Review*, a highly respected literary journal of the day, commented that all the poems were "marked by beauty and tenderness. They are frequently quaint, and sometimes a little capricious." Christina Rossetti was praised in her time for the clarity and sweetness of her diction, for her realistic imagery, and for the purity of her faith. She was widely read in the nineteenth century but not often imitated. The latter is true perhaps because she did not introduce innovative techniques or subject matter. She is not read widely today, either, and is usually treated as a minor poet of the Victorian period, being eclipsed by her brother Dante Gabriel Rossetti and his fellow Pre-Raphaelite writers. Perhaps the simplicity of Christina Rossetti's faith seems remote and unrealistic to many contemporary readers, but this fact should not diminish her artistic contributions. Andrew Lang, in *The Cosmopolitan Magazine*, June, 1895, left this judgment: "For the quality of conscious art and for music and colour of words in regular composition, Miss Rossetti is unmatched."

BIOGRAPHY

Christina Georgina Rossetti was born on December 5, 1830, the youngest of four children. Her father, Gabriele, an Italian political refugee, was himself a poet and musician. Her mother, of half-Italian parentage, wrote a popular book on Dante, and her older brother, Dante Gabriel, became a noted poet and a leader of the Pre-Raphaelite Brotherhood.

Because of financial problems, the Rossettis moved from Portland Place to Mornington Crescent in 1851 so that Christina and her mother could open a small day school for children, thus providing a financial base for the family. By 1854, William Rossetti, Christina's brother, then a clerk in a revenue office, had rented a house on Albany Street, where the family lived together. After Christina's father died in that year, her mother and her siblings lived on there until 1867, and it was only because of William's marriage to Lucy Brown in 1874 that Christina and her mother moved to Torrington Square.

Christina was not a world traveler, but her few experiences abroad did affect her poetry. She went abroad but twice, once in 1861 and again in 1865, and it was the Italian journey that is reflected in so much of her writing. She wrote some poetry in Italian, but her love for Italy can be seen in much of her English work. One excellent example is "Vanna's Twins," the story of an Italian family living in England.

Her first book, published in 1847 when she was seventeen, was a collection of poems privately printed by her grandfather Gaetena Polidori, himself a writer. The volume titled *Verses* contained sixty-six pages of poems written by Rossetti between the ages of twelve and sixteen. The longest piece in the volume was "The Dead City," a poem that exhibits both immature technique and masterful poetic potential. Immersed in a Poe-like atmosphere, the motif is that of a traveler in a dark wood, having passed from a stage of light. She finds herself in a deserted city resplendent with an ornate palace. A sumptuous banquet is ready, but the guests have turned to stone. The poem anticipates Robert Browning, Matthew Arnold, and T. S. Eliot in its wasteland motif and echoes Keats's sensualism.

By 1850, Christina had become a tangential member of the Pre-Raphaelite Brotherhood, of which her brother Dante was the center, and she published various poems in the Brotherhood's magazine *The Germ*. Although Christina loved her brother dearly and respected the other members of the group, she felt that they were too concerned with morally questionable subjects for her to engage herself directly in the work. It was, ironically, through the Pre-Raphaelites that she met a young man named James Collison, to whom she was greatly attracted and whom, had it not been for his Catholicism, she might well have married.

In 1862, after having gained much attention through the poems in *The Germ*, Rossetti published a volume titled *Goblin Market, and Other Poems*. The work was greeted with general acclaim, her only critics being metric purists such as John Ruskin. She brought out another volume in 1866, *The Prince's Progress, and Other Poems*, which established her as England's greatest living woman poet, since Elizabeth Barrett Browning had died in 1861.

Although Christina was sickly in her youth,

it was in 1871 that she became seriously ill with Graves's disease, which brought many periods of depression and caused her to adopt the role of recluse. During these years of severe illness, she experienced several unpleasant events: Her sister Maria died of cancer in 1876; in 1877, she and her mother began the miserable nursing of Dante Gabriel through five years of psychotic depression; and in 1886, her mother died. In the midst of all this suffering, Rossetti continued to write. Her third volume of poetry, *A Pageant, and Other Poems*, was published in 1881 and praised highly by Algernon Swinburne, the only remaining member of the old Pre-Raphaelite coterie. She continued to enjoy the admiration of younger writers such as Theodore Watts-Dunton and Edmund Gosse. Between 1879 and 1892, she published five volumes of spiritual meditations.

*Christina Rossetti* (Hulton Archive/Getty Images)

In May, 1892, Christina was operated on for cancer; however, the cancer reappeared in a few months. After considerable suffering, she died on December 29, 1894.

## ANALYSIS

Christina Rossetti, often thought of as a religious poet, became the major woman poet of mid-Victorian England with the publication of *Goblin Market, and Other Poems* in 1862. Her only true "competitor," Elizabeth Barrett Browning, had died a few months earlier. "Goblin Market," the introductory poem of the volume, has remained her most famous work and illustrates her mastery of the lyric.

### "GOBLIN MARKET"

Because much of her lyric poetry is oriented toward children, "Goblin Market" is often classified as a children's poem. Even though the characters in the poem are young girls and goblins with fairy-tale associations, the poem is actually an allegory of temptation and redemption meant for adult reading. Rossetti's common theme of the need for renunciation is prevalent, though in the disguise of whimsical child's play. The poem produces a grotesque comic effect, supported by irregular meter and cumulative cataloging. The tempting fruit of the goblins, described in Rossetti's typical sensual manner as "sweet to tongue and sound to eye," causes Laura to succumb, desiring more, only to discover that her pleasure is terminated.

Lizzie acts as the savior. Like Christ, she goes into the grove of the men selling their wares and offers to buy some, only to discover that they really want her, not her penny. Although she suffers much physical abuse, the evil people are "worn out by her resistance," and she returns home jubilant with her penny in hand, able to comfort Laura with the assurance that one can find happiness without the temptations of pleasure. Later, when both girls have married, they are able to relate to their daughters in didactic fashion how one can avoid the pitfalls of the evil world.

Rossetti's strong visual imagination aligns her with the Pre-Raphaelites' interest in painting. Although she did not paint, Christina had a painter's eye: The love of colors, particularly gold, rose, violet, blue, and green, and the delight in decorative detail inform her lyrics. Her eye often sees unexpected analogies. In "Goblin Market," for example, she compares Laura's arched neck to a swan and a lily, both natural phenomena, but also to a vessel being launched, a rather startling comparison somewhat in the vein of the seventeenth century Metaphysical conceits. In fact, several critics have alluded to her love for seventeenth century poets, especially George Herbert and Henry Vaughan.

### "THE PRINCE'S PROGRESS"

In addition to her lyrics, Rossetti wrote a great deal of narrative verse, characteristically on the theme of lost or frustrated love. Most of these love-narratives are romantic and otherworldly; when Rossetti does attempt realism, especially in describing marital love, her images are pale and flat. One of the longer narratives, "The Prince's Progress," developed out of a lyric of 1861; Rossetti expanded it at her brother's suggestion to provide a title poem for her next volume of poetry. Much like the tale of Edmund Spenser's Red Cross Knight, this poem is the story of a princess waiting to be rescued by a prince.

The prince waits in his palace for a full month before leaving to meet his bride. When he finally hears the call, prompted by allegorical voices that represent fleeting time, he discovers that the journey will not be easy. It will be another Pilgrim's Progress. His first delay is the typical temptation of a beautiful maiden who keeps him as Dido detained Aeneas. Following his release, the prince finds himself in a nineteenth century wasteland with a blight lurking in the darkening air, "a land of neither life nor death." Here he discovers a cave with an old hermit who gives him the "Elixir of Life," but the elixir is insufficient. When he eventually leaves the cave, he is again diverted by self-indulgence, and when he finally arrives at his bride's door, he finds that she is dead, her body being prepared for burial. The poem is an interesting narrative in the vein of medieval romances, but it is obviously allegorical. The prince is admonished by the narrator, "You waited on the road too long, you trifled at the gate." The poem is permeated with ironies and allegorical symbolism proclaiming the vices of procrastination.

### "FROM HOUSE TO HOME"

"From House to Home" is another long narrative, allegorical in character, with lost love at the center. It tells of a variety of states of being. In the first of these states, the narrator is living in an earthly paradise: a castle of transparent glass set against a background of stately trees and pastures full of swift squirrels, singing birds, and leaping lambs. The young lady is called away by a male "angel." Day and night she seeks for him to no avail—he has vanished. Eventually she has a vision of a marvelously beautiful woman who is suffering the usual tribulations of a pilgrim on an allegorical journey. The martyred woman stands on ground with budding flowers, but every flower has a thorn and galls her feet. Cruel laughter and clapping hands remind the reader of the ways of danger and rebuke in life. The martyred one can be read here as both the archetypal man or woman in search of love and the Christian Church attempting to extend its love to others.

Two of the narratives reveal sides of Rossetti's personality that most of her poetry does not demonstrate. One of these, "A Royal Princess," suggests political interests. The poem is about an imagined political situation. A highborn heroine is sympathetic toward the suffering masses who threaten a revolt against the kingdom, and she determines to descend from her secluded, protected palace to help them.

### "THE LOWEST ROOM"

In "The Lowest Room" (a poem that Dante Gabriel Rossetti did not like) there is an evident implication that, bound by society's rules, women must be passive and must play given roles in life. Again, there are two sisters in the poem, but unlike those in other works, only the ideal sister is here rewarded with husband and child. The ideal one is described in feminine language; the other one, less attractive, dreams of Homer's soldiers. Masculine voluptuousness affects her. In projecting such a contrast, Rossetti implies that women in her society are told how to dress, how to act, and how to be successful. There is little room for individuality. The final acceptance of this less attractive female, the speaker of the poem, places her in the role of the typical passive woman waiting for her turn without being able to help in creating it.

### "MAIDEN SONG" AND "THE INIQUITY OF THE FATHERS, UPON THE CHILDREN"

Another narrative that takes a critical view of social conventions is "The Iniquity of the Fathers, upon the Children," in which an unmarried woman who has a

child is tormented by the community. The only justice, the narrator concludes, is that all are "equal in the grave." On the other hand, Rossetti's narrative style can show a fairy-tale naïveté, as in "Maiden Song," a tale of three sisters, Meggan, May, and Margaret, all of whom desire husbands. The first two take the first man who comes along, afraid they will be like Margaret sitting at home singing and spinning. Margaret's patience, however, is amply rewarded; she wins the king of the entire country for her husband.

### DEVOTIONAL POEMS

Rossetti's strong religious faith supported her during continuing illnesses, and she began to give most of her attention to writing devotional material. Her first poetry had shown her strong family affection and her religious feelings, particularly the sentiment of renunciation. The later poems (such as "A Novice," "A Martyr," and "I Have Fought a Good Fight") continue to focus on renunciation. The first is a flight from the world into the calm of the cloister; the latter two praise the eager laying down of life for the glory of God. Actually, religious ardor colors most of Rossetti's thoughts and results in much oversimplified verse echoing common platitudes about devotion. A poem such as "Whitsun Eve," however, illustrates poetic maturity, blending the love of God and the love of the beauty of creation. All that is pure in nature is pressed into the service of the one shining lamb.

### DUALISM

An interesting aspect of Rossetti's style is her use of the Victorian motif of two voices, so prominently associated with Alfred, Lord Tennyson's poetry. The Victorian world attempted to synthesize the Romantic values of the early nineteenth century with the classical theories of order and restraint more prominently displayed in the eighteenth century. From this attempt came a strong clash of values and great personal frustration. Adding to this problem was the growth of the industrial world and the increase in scientific knowledge. Rossetti's dualism establishes the concept of a universe based on a conflict of opposites, as in "Life and Death," "Twice," "Today and Tomorrow," and "Two Parted."

"Two Parted" deals with one true lover and one betrayer. Ironically, the betrayer in this case is the woman. "Today and Tomorrow" creates a dichotomy of living life to the fullest on the one hand and wishing to die on the other. "Life and Death" begins with a negative statement about life's bitterness, juxtaposing the good things of life with the unpleasant. "Twice" uses the counterpoint of the narrator's offering her heart while the man suggests that her heart is not ripe. In the narrative poems, this technique is carried out through the use of two opposing characters. Lizzie and Laura of "Goblin Market" illustrate the dualistic motif; in "Maiden Song" the conflict is between two plain sisters and the beautiful Margaret. This dualism is also apparent in Rossetti's religious poems, where there appears to be a confrontation between different views of salvation or different moral attitudes. A great number of traditional opposites are used here—time and eternity, earthly misery and heavenly bliss—demonstrating the torment of a trapped soul longing for escape. One such poem, "This near-at-hand," stresses the antithesis of Heaven and Earth.

The religious poems often describe a destructive end that results from the speaker's being torn between duty and desire. Sometimes the choice appears to have been made in error, and when it is, it seems to have arisen from weakness or beguilement. So choice itself becomes destructive; there is no solution; life is an absurdity. Even when the speaker is not caught in a personal dilemma, the poem repeats the impression that the world, as Matthew Arnold suggests in "Dover Beach," is a place of uncertainty, a virtual wasteland, a "darkling plain" where ignorant armies fight by night.

In the midst of all this dualism, the reader is left with the impression that Rossetti is earnestly searching for unity but cannot find it. In the secular love poems, she goes so far as to suggest that perhaps as ghosts, removed from the flesh, lovers could achieve such a unity. In the religious poems, her solution is, of course, union with God through Christ in death. Needless to say, much of her poetry reflects the struggle in her own life to find some solution to the paradox, irony, and bifurcation that life in general repeatedly offers. Rossetti's poetry reveals a dual personality: one side reflecting Pre-Raphaelite traits of fictional effects and sensual imagery, often set in a dream world; the other reflecting the assurances of her orthodox faith.

OTHER MAJOR WORKS

SHORT FICTION: *Commonplace, and Other Short Stories*, 1870; *Speaking Likenesses*, 1874.

NONFICTION: *Annus Domini*, 1874; *Seek and Find*, 1879; *Called to Be Saints*, 1881; *Letter and Spirit*, 1882; *Time Flies*, 1885; *The Face of the Deep*, 1892; *Maude*, 1897.

BIBLIOGRAPHY

Bloom, Harold, ed. *Christina Rossetti*. Philadelphia: Chelsea House, 2004. This collection contains essays on poetic fantasy, "Goblin Market," and the influence that Christina and Dante Rossetti had on each other.

Chapman, Alison. *The Afterlife of Christina Rossetti*. New York: St. Martin's Press, 2000. Analyzes Rossetti's work and considers the history of her reception.

Charles, Edna Kotin. *Christina Rossetti: Critical Perspectives, 1862-1982*. Selinsgrove, Pa.: Susquehanna University Press, 1985. Shows how literary criticism has changed in the last 120 years and how these changing attitudes have affected the way in which Rossetti's poems are perceived. Many nineteenth century reviewers concentrated on her religious poems, whereas modern critics focus on her works of fantasy.

Clifford, David, and Laurence Roussillon, eds. *Outsiders Looking In: The Rossettis Then and Now*. London: Anthem Press, 2004. Essays on the Rossettis, including Christina, that examine aspects of their lives and works.

Hassett, Constance W. *Christina Rossetti: The Patience of Style*. Charlottesville: University of Virginia Press, 2005. This analysis of the works of Rossetti examines questions of desire in "Goblin Market," and looks at her sonnets and *Verses* (1893).

Jones, Kathleen. *Learning Not to Be First: The Life of Christina Rossetti*. Moreton-in-Marsh, Gloucestershire, England: Windrush, 1991. An illuminating biography of Rossetti, both product and victim of the Victorian era's social and religious standards. Includes bibliography and index.

Marsh, Jan. *Christina Rossetti: A Writer's Life*. New

York: Viking Press, 1995. A biography that explains Rossetti's recurrent bouts of depression, traces her ties to London's literati, and discusses her place in the Pre-Raphaelite movement.

Mayberry, Katherine J. *Christina Rossetti and the Poetry of Discovery*. Baton Rouge: Louisiana State University Press, 1989. Mayberry maintains that Rossetti was a meticulous professional writer and not merely a talented amateur. She argues that Rossetti wrote about her role as a woman and therefore was an early feminist. Includes an index and a bibliography.

Roe, Dinah. *Christina Rossetti's Faithful Imagination: The Devotional Poetry and Prose*. New York: Palgrave Macmillan, 2006. An analysis of Rossetti's poetry that focuses on the devotional works, which are often ignored in critiques of her work.

Rosenblum, Dolores. *Christina Rossetti: The Poetry of Endurance*. Carbondale: Southern Illinois University Press, 1987. Rosenblum is the first to analyze thoroughly the text of Rossetti's poetry in the light of the new feminist criticism. She especially examines the significance of "Goblin Market," the themes of which are central to all Rossetti's works.

*John W. Crawford*

---

# DANTE GABRIEL ROSSETTI

**Born:** London, England; May 12, 1828
**Died:** Birchington, England; April 9, 1882

PRINCIPAL POETRY

*Poems*, 1870, 1881
*Ballads and Sonnets*, 1881
*Collected Works*, 1886
*The Works of Dante Gabriel Rossetti*, 1911
 (William Michael Rossetti, editor)

OTHER LITERARY FORMS

Dante Gabriel Rossetti (roh-ZEHT-ee) published the prose sketch "Hand and Soul" in *The Germ* (1850). In 1863, he completed the biography of William Blake left unfinished at the death of Alexander Gilchrist. Four volumes of Rossetti's letters, edited by J. R. Wahl and Oswald Doughty (1965-1967) have been published; his correspondence with Jane Morris was edited by John Bryson and Janet Camp Troxell and published in 1976.

ACHIEVEMENTS

Significant both as a poet and as a painter, Dante Gabriel Rossetti offers an opportunity to study the relationship between poetry and art. Among Victorian poets, Rossetti was excelled only by Alfred, Lord Tennyson, and Robert Browning, although, unlike other major poets of the period, he published relatively few poems. His work is chiefly concerned with the exploration of individual moments of experience. As a consequence, he worked best at the level of the short lyric or compressed narrative, in which his highly crafted style often achieves remarkable intensity.

BIOGRAPHY

Dante Gabriel Rossetti, christened Gabriel Charles Dante Rossetti, was born in London, May 12, 1828. His father, Gabriele Rossetti, was an Italian political exile with pretensions as a poet, who had published an eccentric commentary on Dante's *La divina commedia* (c. 1320, 3 volumes; *The Divine Comedy*, 1802) and supported himself teaching his native language. Rossetti's mother, Frances Polidori, although of Anglo-Italian background, was staunchly English in her severe moral standards and religious beliefs. The opposing views of life represented by his father and mother determined a conflict from which Rossetti was never able to free himself. Like his amiable, self-indulgent father in many ways, he was never able to exorcise the accusing voice of his mother's puritanism. He led the bohemian life of an artist, but felt guilty for doing so.

In 1845, Rossetti entered the Academy Schools of the Royal Academy of Art. There he associated himself with a group of young artists—notably, John Everett Millais and Holman Hunt—who were dissatisfied with the style and subject matter of Establishment painting, but eager to make names for themselves with the Establishment. Because the effects of light and naturalistic detail they sought were also to be found in late medi-

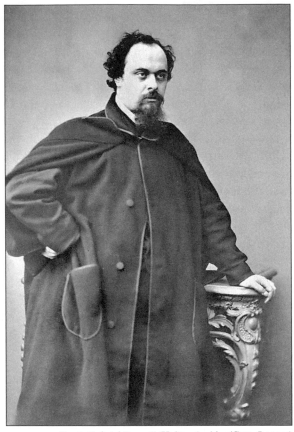

*Dante Gabriel Rossetti* (Hulton Archive/Getty Images)

eval art (prior to the painter Raphael), they called themselves the Pre-Raphaelite Brotherhood and began initialing their more daring paintings "P.R.B." In 1849-1850, the Brotherhood published a journal, *The Germ*, which included several poems by Rossetti, including "The Blessed Damozel" and the prose piece "Hand and Soul." Also in 1850, Rossetti publicly exhibited a painting for the first time, *Ecce Ancilla Domini!* Reviews of the painting—as well as of works exhibited simultaneously by Hunt and Millais—were hostile. Stunned, Rossetti determined never to exhibit his work again (a determination which, on the whole, he maintained). The art critic John Ruskin, however, defended the Pre-Raphaelites, first in a series of letters to *The Times*, then in a pamphlet "Pre-Raphaelitism," and subsequently became Rossetti's patron, although Rossetti's contempt for what he perceived as Ruskin's bourgeois dilettantism prevented them from ever becoming close friends.

In 1850, Rossetti met Elizabeth Siddal, a sixteen-year-old shopgirl who began serving as a model for members of the P.R.B. By 1852, Rossetti and Siddal were informally engaged. Despite her beauty and the limited artistic ability she developed under his influence, they were poorly matched. It is characteristic of Rossetti that he nevertheless married her in 1860. Their child was stillborn in 1861, and the next year Elizabeth committed suicide.

During the 1850's, while the Brotherhood itself was dwindling away, the reputation of its individual members had begun to grow. Rossetti never became a popular artist (as did Millais), but he began to receive commissions for his work and to attract a circle of younger admirers—two of whom, Edward Burne-Jones and William Morris, joined him in painting "frescoes" on the interior walls of the Oxford Union Society in 1857. There, Rossetti met Jane Burden, the woman he loved off and on for the rest of his life. Burden married William Morris in 1859 but seems to have become Rossetti's mistress in the late 1860's.

Fanny Cornforth was the third woman in Rossetti's life. They met sometime in the late 1850's, and after the death of Siddal, she became Rossetti's "housekeeper." Fanny was illiterate and lowborn, but with a striking voluptuous beauty very different from that of Elizabeth or Jane. Generally detested by Rossetti's friends, she was probably Rossetti's most loving companion.

Remorseful at the death of his wife, Rossetti had buried the manuscript of his poems with her and given up verse until at least 1866, when his relationship with Jane Morris prompted him to return to writing love poetry. In 1869, the manuscript of his earlier work was exhumed, and these poems, together with his later work, were published as *Poems* in 1870. By that time, Rossetti had a fairly steady income from his paintings. In 1862, he had leased Tudor House, 16 Cheyne Walk, the London home that was to become notorious for his eccentric hospitality and collection of exotic animals. However, his life during these years was not happy. He had become morbidly sensitive to criticism, and with the unfavorable reviews of his poetry (notably, Robert Buchanan's essay "The Fleshly School of Poetry" in 1871), he began to suspect a conspiracy against him. In 1872, he attempted suicide, and the last decade of his life was characterized by poor health, desultory work, and indulgence in the mixture of whiskey and chloral that became his favorite narcotic. A year after the publication of his second collection of poems, *Ballads and Sonnets* in 1881, he died at the seaside town of Birchington, where he had gone hoping to recover his health.

### ANALYSIS

Dante Gabriel Rossetti's poetry is conventionally divided into three periods. The first ends in 1850, with the publication of some of his best early poems in *The Germ* and the beginning of his relationship with Siddal. The second ends with her death in 1862; most of the poems from this period, however, were written between 1850 and 1854. The third and last group of poems date from 1868, when Rossetti began writing again after several years of relative inactivity, until his death in 1882. Again, however, most of the poems from this period were written during its first five years.

While these three periods can be differentiated, the actual placement of individual poems is often problematic. Since Rossetti did not publish a book of original verse until 1870 and habitually revised his poetry over the years, a particular work might in fact belong to more than one period. "The Blessed Damozel," for example, was written in 1847 and published first in *The Germ* in 1850; then in revised form in *The Oxford and Cambridge Magazine* (edited by William Morris) in 1856; next, with further revision, in the 1870 *Poems*; and finally, revised yet again, in the 1881 *Poems*.

This habit of lifetime reworking and revision, which extended to certain paintings as well, evidences two characteristics of Rossetti's work—a meticulous craftsmanship that defines the poem as a labored artifact rather than the spontaneous expression of feeling, and an intense personal identification with his own writing, that explains both his reluctance to publish and his extreme vulnerability to criticism. These two characteristics are contradictory if one assumes that personal identification with a text is a function of its truth to prior experience. Rossetti's case, however, argues that identification is not a function of mimesis, but of the act of writing. He identified with his poetry because he himself had written it. To acknowledge a poem "complete" was for him equivalent to acknowledging the end of

one of his own life processes. To bury the manuscript of his poems with the body of Siddal was not simply to bury his own past or sacrifice its achievement; it was, in a real sense, to bury a part of himself alive with her.

This is not to say that personal experience is not the subject matter of Rossetti's poetry—it often is—but that readers should expect to reach that experience only through the mediation of highly wrought style, the presence of which becomes, in his best poems, an index to the intensity of feeling it conceals. His concern with style makes Rossetti a difficult poet. It is difficult to naturalize his poetry—to reduce it to day-to-day familiarity. He offers no personality for the reader to admire—or hate. Indeed, this absence of self is a central concern of his creative effort. Rossetti's poems do not merely hide the self behind the artifice of verse making; they explore a fundamental opposition between language and feeling—the teasing ability of language almost to control reality and the disillusionment that necessarily follows from recognizing its failure to do so; the apparent communication embedded in a work of art turns out to be a denial of communication.

In its awareness of the limits of communication, Rossetti's poetry is contemporary. In its basic distrust of—and therefore fascination with—sexuality, it remains solidly Victorian. In its fondness for allegory and contrivance, it exemplifies the Pre-Raphaelite commitment to the Middle Ages. In its concern for the intense experience of the moment, it anticipates the poetics of the last years of the nineteenth century. Rossetti's numerous sonnets on paintings—a genre particularly successful in distancing the reader from the poet—echo similar poems by the French Symbolists. His ballad narratives link him to William Wordsworth and Samuel Taylor Coleridge; his concern for the self-sufficient consciousness, with Percy Bysshe Shelley. Rossetti can be said, therefore, to exemplify aspects of many periods but to be typical of none. He is typical only, perhaps, of himself, but it is a self carefully concealed behind, not expressed in, his writing. The study of Rossetti leads to an understanding not of his own personality or philosophy of life or of the age in which he lived, but of poetry itself—an understanding both of its strengths and of its liabilities. For this reason, his work remains a spur to the imagination.

### "THE BLESSED DAMOZEL"

"The Blessed Damozel," the most familiar of Rossetti's early poems, illustrates this pattern of imaginative effort and disillusionment. The "Damozel" leans out "From the gold bar of Heaven," looking down through space for her earthly lover. Space, however, is vast. The moon itself is no more than "a little feather/ Fluttering far down the gulf." Because she cannot see him, she speaks, imagining the reunion that will come "When round his head the aureole clings." Then "Will I ask of Christ the Lord . . . Only to live as once on earth/ With Love." Imagination proves an unsatisfactory substitute for real love; despite a Dantesque vision of angels in flight, she "laid her face between her hands./ And wept."

The poem turns on the old notion that lovers separated by death can take comfort in the hope of meeting again in the world to come. Rossetti, however, reverses the perspective. It is the lover in heaven who longs for earth; it is the spiritual world that is tormented by desire for the physical—and remains, for all its beatitude, "warm." Moreover, the consolation of hope is, it turns out, no consolation. It merely leads to an intense awareness of loss—not only on the part of the "Damozel" but for the speaker of the poem as well. For the "Damozel" is a fiction, and the parenthetical first-person interjections ground the poem in the fantasy of the earthly lover himself. He claims to "see" "her smile" and "hear" "her tears," but the protestation emphasizes the wishfulness of his dream. If her imagined reunion leads her to "tears," his imagined "Damozel" leads him to a heightened sense of separation from her. The "Damozel" is, as his attempt to visualize her suggests, unknowable. Her death is a barrier he cannot overcome by the language of the poem. The sensuousness of his conception—the "fleshliness" of which Rossetti was later accused—is not a radical characterization of the afterlife, but an implicit mark of the inadequacy of the earthly imagination.

"The Blessed Damozel" specifies the opposition between language and feeling as an opposition between poetry and eros. The poet's vision attempts to overcome the separation of lovers. His text is an act of desire that confronts him with the fact of desire—hence, of an unfulfilled and perhaps unfulfillable need. The world of Rossetti's poetry is thus one in which desire—generally sexual—defines itself by coming up against its own furthest limit—the verge of satisfaction. It asks the reader to experience the pain of near but never complete realization. It offers a nightmare world, in which all apparent realities are disclosed as expressions of the poet's desire.

The theme of frustrated eros is directly related to the tension between his father's bohemianism and his mother's puritanical morality. It enabled Rossetti to express his erotic sensibility while at the same time punishing himself for its existence. The inadequacy of poetic language is thus a function of the guilt that, in his own life, blocked Rossetti's personal happiness.

### "THE BRIDE'S PRELUDE"

"The Bride's Prelude," which was begun in 1848 and returned to later in the 1850's but never completed, illustrates the link between eros, guilt, and the failure of language. The poem, even in its fragmentary form, is Rossetti's longest narrative. It records the conversation between two sisters in an unspecified medieval setting: Aloÿse, the elder, whose wedding day it is, and Amelotte, the younger, who is helping her dress. Aloÿse is strangely silent; then, having knelt in prayer with her sister, she reveals the story of her past life. She had, years before, while her sister was being educated in a convent, fallen in love with a young man, a distant cousin who had yet to make a name for himself in the world, then staying with her powerful family. When her family lost a political struggle and was forced temporarily to flee its ancestral seat, the cousin had deserted them, leaving her with child. Discovering the situation, her father and brothers had reluctantly spared her life but, it would seem—the poem is deliberately vague— killed her illegitimate child. Now, circumstances have changed again; the family is back in power, the cousin has returned, and it is he—Urscelyn—whom she is about to marry. With this revelation, the poem ends. Rossetti wrote a prose summary of a missing conclusion, which his brother later published. Urscelyn, he explains, having become a skilled soldier of fortune and therefore of use to her family, wanting to ally himself with them once more, has offered to marry Aloÿse. Aloÿse, meanwhile, had fallen in love with and secretly betrothed herself to another man, whom Urscelyn, knowingly and treacherously, killed in a tournament. Thus, the enormity of marrying a man who had both betrayed her and murdered her lover is the message she wishes to convey to her sister. In conclusion, Rossetti states that "as the bridal procession appears, perhaps it might become apparent that the brothers mean to kill Urscelyn when he has married her."

The "perhaps" tells all. "The Bride's Prelude" is incomplete because Rossetti was unable to imagine an appropriate ending, and his prose summary is merely an evasion. The poem is also Aloÿse's story, and she, too, cannot bring her narrative to completion. Significantly, the text as it stands makes no mention of the second lover. Urscelyn's flight labels him a betrayer—but Aloÿse suggests that his motives were political and does not indicate that he knew she was pregnant. In other words, without Rossetti's prose summary, what seems to block Aloÿse's happiness is less the character of Urscelyn than her own sense of guilt. The conclusion that Rossetti claims he intended but could not bring himself to write would have radically altered the moral perspective of the poem. With it, Urscelyn is a clear-cut villain; Aloÿse, despite her youthful indiscretion, is a victim. Without the conclusion, "The Bride's Prelude" is a poem about Aloÿse's own reluctance to accept a happy ending to her years of suffering—to marry the man she had loved and from whom she has been separated by war and family pride. By telling her story to her sister, she confesses and thus overcomes the guilt that is the only obstacle to her happiness. Indeed, when in the closing line of the poem Aloÿse admits that her prayer has been to be able to "Show her what I hide," it appears that confession of the past, not complaint about the present, has been her leading motive. This purgation, however, is precisely what Rossetti does not grant her. She tells her story, but the poem breaks off before the consequences of the telling can be felt.

The ballad form of "The Bride's Prelude" is typical of Rossetti's narrative poetry. He was particularly fond of stanzaic patterns that include a slightly varying refrain. The mode was both satisfyingly medieval (and therefore Pre-Raphaelite) and conveniently disjunctive. Breaking narrative into a series of discrete, artificially defined units obviated the need for a coherent narrative personality. In poems such as "Sister Helen"

and "Eden Bower," the repetition of the verse form replaces development of the speaker's point of view as a unifying device. Even in "The Burden of Nineveh," an uncharacteristically ironic "modern" poem of social comment, patterns of repetition qualify the immediacy of the first-person speaker.

### "A LAST CONFESSION"

In Rossetti's two "modern" narratives, "A Last Confession" and "Jenny," he uses the more typically Victorian mode of dramatic monologue to achieve comparable distancing. Both are poems about erotic failure; in both, erotic failure is related to the failure of language to communicate.

"A Last Confession," which is given the setting "Regno Lombardo-Veneto, 1848," is unique in its treatment of the political issue—the Austrian occupation of Italy—with which Rossetti's father was identified. Its confessional mode is comparable to that of "The Bride's Prelude"; what it confesses, however, is not illicit passion but murder by a rejected lover. The speaker had adopted a little girl deserted by her parents, who, under the rigors of the Austrian regime, no longer had the bread with which to feed her. In time this foster fatherly love becomes sexual, but whether she responds in kind is uncertain. At length, they are separated and she appears to have taken up flirting with Austrians. On the way to meet with her for the last time, the speaker buys her the parting gift of a knife, such as "Our Lombard country-girls . . . Wear" to defend themselves against each other and the possibility of "a German lover." When she laughs at the gesture—another example of failed communication—he is enraged and plunges the knife into her heart. It is not certain that she is the "harlot" he believes she has become; the act of confession is a strategy aimed at exonerating the speaker, but since only his unreliable point of view is provided, his words can never fully realize their intention. The priest who listens to him is allowed no response. The reader is left with an uneasy feeling that the speaker's words, instead of unburdening his conscience, merely reiterate the crime.

### "JENNY"

The speaker of "Jenny" is a man who has gone home with a prostitute, who, instead of making love, falls asleep on his knee while he meditates on the meaning of her condition and consequently his own. Among the ironies of the poem is the fact that his audience is sleeping. His words, whatever their merit, go unheard. Moreover, Jenny, who might well have added a significant point of view to the discussion, is necessarily mute, so the speaker remains trapped in his own consciousness.

What the speaker thinks he has learned is easily summarized. He begins with an ironic assessment of "Lazy laughing languid Jenny,/ Fond of a kiss and fond of a guinea," and moves on to a more sympathetic recognition of the plight of a prostitute. She is, after all, not essentially different from other women; like them, she is a victim "of man's changeless sum/ Of lust": "Like a toad within a stone/ Seated while Time crumbles on;/ Which sits there since the earth was curs'd/ For Man's transgression at the first." Finally, he sees that even her love of money is merely a reflection of the economic forces at work throughout English society. Then, leaving a few gold coins in her hair, he kisses her sleeping form and departs in the morning light.

However, even in acknowledging that his own irony is a sign of being "Ashamed of my own shame," the speaker fails to achieve enlightenment. He remains ignorant of his own role in the situation and never gives credit to Jenny for being more than an attractive automaton. He does not blame himself for creating prostitution (although this is not his first such visit); he blames an abstract male "lust," and thus alienates himself from his own desire. The subject of the poem may be somewhat daring, but its inability to come to terms with female sexuality not only betrays Rossetti's participation in a Victorian stereotype, but also, and more significantly, betrays his tendency to treat women as counters in a process of masculine self-discovery. To acknowledge the full humanity of Jenny would legitimatize sexual relations with her: She would no longer be a victim, but a willing partner. She remains asleep, and the speaker's meditation has no practical consequences. The language of the poem, instead of effecting, across social and economic barriers, a relationship with Jenny, further insulates the speaker from significant behavior. He will return to his book-lined room—the books are emphasized in the poem—confident in decent feeling, incapable of decent action.

## "THE STREAM'S SECRET"

Rossetti's love poetry, in which the speaker is closely identified with or indistinguishable from the poet himself, contains his most painful accounts of the inadequacy of language. "The Stream's Secret," written in 1869, has been called at once his most revealing and his most concealing poem. Certainly it is a quintessential statement of the dilemma at the heart of his poetry. The speaker, who addresses the stream, exemplifies noncommunication. The stream's "secret" is, finally, that it can neither hear nor speak; that to confide in nature is to confide in a vacuum, not only denying oneself the possibility of a response, but also deluding oneself in the false hope that language is a medium of communication.

"The Stream's Secret" is also one of the most deliberately artful of Rossetti's poems, and its complex play with figures of speech makes it one of his most difficult. Rhetorical trope circles back on rhetorical trope, as in this typical stanza:

> Dark as thy blinded wave
> When brimming midnight floods the glen,—
> Bright as the laughter of thy runnels when
> The dawn yields all the light they crave;
> Even so these hours to wound and that to save
> Are sisters in Love's ken.

Midnight, compared metaphorically to the stream, is itself a means of characterizing the stream; with dawn, it provides a figurative characterization of the personified hours that are "sisters" to allegorized "Love." The reader is encompassed in a world defined by poetic devices. The speaker, in addressing the unanswering flow of water, attempts to anchor this continuum of language in concrete reality, but reality continues to elude him. The poet, who begins by asking when he and his love will be reunited and moves into an imaginary depiction of their reunion, is led, in the poem's final stanzas, to the recognition that Love, whom he first saw as a figure of passionate life, is synonymous with death, and that hope itself, as in "The Blessed Damozel," is a source of tears.

## THE HOUSE OF LIFE

The lesson of "The Stream's Secret" is borne out in Rossetti's major work, the collection of sonnets he called *The House of Life*. Originally published as a group of sixteen sonnets in 1869, extended into a group of fifty "Sonnets and Songs, toward a work to be called 'The House of Life'" in *Poems*; and finally published as a collection of 102 sonnets titled "The House of Life: A Sonnet-Sequence" in *Ballads and Sonnets*, the precise status of the work remains a problem. As ordered, the collection follows a general pattern of youth to age, love to loss, hope to disillusionment. Whether this ordering represents an organic sequence or is merely an adequate solution to the problem of arranging a large group of related but independent poems written over many years remains the object of critical debate.

The very existence of this critical debate argues that, if there is an organic sequence, it is not self-evident. Moreover, if there is no easy way to put the poems together, that difficulty may be an essential feature of Rossetti's conception. The untitled 1880 sonnet that introduces the collection suggests that the sonnets were written with deliberate reference to the limitations of their medium. "A Sonnet," Rossetti proclaims, "is a moment's monument,— Memorial . . . To one dead deathless hour." Such a poem is not a gesture of communication, but one of memorialization or arbitrary symbolism. Its message, explicit in the poem's leading similes, is akin to the carving on a tomb or the engraving on a coin. Verbal meaning is thus subservient to a role for which verbal meaning may in fact be irrelevant. The workmanship of the artifact increases its value, but one may appreciate the form of an inscription without in fact "reading" its message.

The introductory sonnet does not suggest that readers should look only at the form and not consider the expressive content of the sonnets that follow. Rather, it defines the limited role of the poet's art in the reader's experience of his poetry. Like the figures on John Keats's Grecian urn, the sonnets of *The House of Life* come into passionate being only insofar as the reader invests them with sympathy or understanding. The passion a reader can expect to experience in responding to the work of art will not be that of the poet/artificer who has provided its material cause, but his or her own. For, like a monument "in ivory or in ebony," the sonnet is not a recapturing of the past but

an acknowledgment of its loss, not the living voice of its maker but an obstacle between its maker and the reader of the poem; the poem is like a coin, not of real value, but the sign of goods and services in a potential act of human exchange.

The notion of "a moment's monument" also offers a rationale for the atomistic structure of the collection. Limited to the depiction of discrete events, the poet's format cannot link individual experiences into a total rendering of human life. The whole is inevitably less than the sum of its parts; the work in its entirety cannot overcome the poet's fragmented experience of love and love's loss. (In this respect, the form of *The House of Life* is comparable to the "Short swallow-flights" of Tennyson's *In Memoriam*, which deny the possibility of an integrated response to death, even when the ordering of the poem seems to provide one.)

"Silent Noon" (sonnet 19) exemplifies the notion of "a moment's monument" and thus typifies the collection. Two lovers pause in a summer landscape, the painterly details of which compose "visible silence, still as the hourglass." Recognizing the special nature of such moments, the poem ends by disrupting the landscape with the imperative cry, "Clasp we to our hearts, for deathless dower,/ This close-companioned inarticulate hour/ When twofold silence was the song of Love." The ultimate experience of love is silence—the postcoital oblivion of "Nuptial Sleep" (the sonnet singled out for its "fleshliness" by Buchanan and so deleted from the 1881 version of the collection). Language itself is therefore necessarily at odds with such states of being. The poet's description of landscape replaces the description of feeling denied here by the nature of feeling. The closing lines of the poem, in which he addresses his feelings, acknowledge their loss. Articulated self-consciousness implies that the "Inarticulate hour" has passed. Time, like the sand in the hourglass, only passes; it does not develop. Thus, the development of the poem—the formal demand of the sestet—disrupts the special experience of the time it seeks to "clasp."

To memorialize love as verse is thus to admit the loss of love—not only because there is no need to memorialize the living present, but also because language itself is a sign of loss. The laurel, as Rossetti admits, in a trope borrowed from Petrarch, is "Love's Last Gift" (sonnet 59), not the sign of continuing favor. If poetic language celebrates not the absent loved one but the poet's isolated self, why then write poetry? This question, which Rossetti poses implicitly in "The Stream's Secret," is central to *The House of Life*.

The four sonnets grouped under the heading "Willowwood" (49-52) suggest an answer when they identify erotic desire as a longing for submergence in self. The poet who leans over a well to kiss the image of Love which has become the image of his lover is a version of Narcissus, unable to resist the reflection of his own image. Fittingly, the imagery of the four sonnets is derived from the Wood of the Suicides (canto 13) in Dante's *Inferno* (in *La divina commedia*, c. 1320; *The Divine Comedy*, 1802). To dwell in the "Willowwood" of unfulfillable desire is to deny wholeness of self and cultivate in its place a self-destructive illusion of personal emptiness. Art, which once confronted humans with spiritual truths, has turned, as Rossetti argues in "St. Luke the Painter" (sonnet 74), "To soulless self-reflections of man's skill."

Thus, the earlier sonnets of sexual fulfillment and momentary happiness give way to poems of loss. Through memory, the poet attempts to idealize and thus recapture lost passion, but memory, as the introductory sonnet suggests, is itself a confirmation of hopelessness. At the same time, even this overreaching logic is impotent in the face of individual experiences. Moreover, the love poems of *The House of Life*, written with at least three very different women in mind, reflect a range of diverse experiences. No summary of the collection is adequate even as a summary.

Like Rossetti's poetic achievement as a whole, *The House of Life* is elusive and, largely for that reason, difficult. It offers a solipsistic world defined totally by the self, a world in which no external reality functions as a measure of the speaker's perceptions. For this very reason, however, it blocks the consciousness of the poet from the reader. The dreamer turns out to be the most elusive element in the dream.

## Other major works

NONFICTION: *Letters of Dante Gabriel Rossetti*, 1965-1967 (4 volumes; Oswald Doughty and J. R.

Wahl, editors); *Dante Gabriel Rossetti and Jane Morris: Their Correspondence*, 1976 (John Bryson and Janet Camp Troxell, editors); *Dear Mr. Rossetti: The Letters of Dante Gabriel Rossetti and Hall Caine, 1878-1881*, 2000 (Vivien Allen, editor); *The Correspondence of Dante Gabriel Rossetti*, 2002-2006 (6 volumes; William E. Fredeman, editor).

TRANSLATION: *The Early Italian Poets*, 1861 (revised as *Dante and His Circle*, 1874).

MISCELLANEOUS: *Collected Poetry and Prose*, 2003.

## Bibliography

Ash, Russell. *Dante Gabriel Rossetti*. 1995. Reprint. London: Pavilion, 1997. A beautifully illustrated book that analyzes the life and career of Rossetti as poet and painter. Includes bibliographical references.

Faxon, Alicia Craig. *Dante Gabriel Rossetti*. 1994. Reprint. New York: Abbeville Press, 2000. A biography of Rossetti that looks at his life as a poet and painter.

Helsinger, Elizabeth K. *Poetry and the Pre-Raphaelite Arts: Dante Gabriel Rossetti and William Morris*. New Haven, Conn.: Yale University Press, 2008. Examines Rossetti and Morris in regards to the Pre-Raphaelite brotherhood.

Holmes, John. *Dante Gabriel Rossetti and the Late Victorian Sonnet Sequence: Sexuality, Belief, and the Self*. Burlington, Vt.: Ashgate, 2005. Holmes analyzes the sonnets of Rossetti, focusing on *The House of Life*.

Keane, Robert N. *Dante Gabriel Rossetti: The Poet as Craftsman*. New York: Peter Lang, 2002. Keane provides literary analysis of each of the major poetic works of Rossetti.

McGann, Jerome J. *Dante Gabriel Rossetti and the Game That Must Be Lost*. New Haven, Conn.: Yale University Press, 2000. Reacting to sixty years of literary criticism that diminished and downplayed Rossetti's work, McGann asserts the enormity of Rossetti's accomplishment as a central artistic and intellectual figure of his generation.

Riede, David G., ed. *Critical Essays on Dante Gabriel Rossetti*. New York: G. K. Hall, 1992. Includes early responses and work done from the 1970's to 1991. The early essays provide the traditional assessment of Rossetti's work, and later essays indicate the directions that Rossetti criticism is likely to take in the coming years. Includes bibliographical references and index.

Waldman, Suzanne. *The Demon and the Damozel: Dynamics of Desire in the Works of Christina Rossetti and Dante Gabriel Rossetti*. Athens: Ohio University Press, 2008. Analyzes the works of the Rossettis in regard to the theme of desire. Dante Gabriel Rossetti's *The House of Life* is examined at length.

*Frederick Kirchhoff*

# S

## THOMAS SACKVILLE

**Born:** Buckhurst, England; 1536
**Died:** London, England; April 19, 1608
**Also known as:** Baron Buckhurst; First Earl of
Dorset

PRINCIPAL POETRY

"Complaint of Henry, Duke of Buckingham," in *A
Mirror for Magistrates*, 1563 (second edition)
"Induction," in *A Mirror for Magistrates*, 1563
(second edition)

OTHER LITERARY FORMS

Thomas Sackville's other contribution to English
literature was the play performed first before a select
audience at the Inner Temple (where Sackville was a
young student of the law) on January 6, 1561, and then
before Queen Elizabeth on January 18, "with grett
tryumphe" according to one observer. The title pages
of two of the three editions printed in the sixteenth century describe the drama as the joint work of two fellow
students, Sackville and Thomas Norton, yet the extent
of Norton's contribution is disputed. Because the play
was the first in England to use the elements of dramatic
blank verse, the regular form of tragedy, and a subject
from English chronicle history, its importance in literary history is assured. Moreover, the play is characteristic of the concerns of Sackville's two poems and of
his long public life: In language, structure, and theme, it
focuses on the political evils caused by an insecure succession. Both Norton and Sackville were involved in
parliamentary debate on the issue of Queen Elizabeth's
reluctance to marry, which was for the majority of the
years of her reign a topic of deep national concern.

One other work of Sackville is known, a prefatory
sonnet commending Thomas Hoby's *The Book of the
Courtier*, a 1561 translation of Baldassare Castiglione's
*Il libro del cortegiano* (1528). A recent survey of the
evidence (by Allan H. Orrick in *Notes and Queries*,
January, 1956) has concluded that there is no substance
to the tradition that Sackville wrote a number of sonnets
and other short poems now lost. Sackville had completed his few writings in belles letters by early 1561,
when he was twenty-five or twenty-six years old and
had already embarked on his entirely absorbing, important career. In addition to his literary writings, interesting letters and documents concerning public affairs
have survived.

ACHIEVEMENTS

Thomas Sackville's literary contemporaries, among
them Joshua Sylvester, Thomas Campion, and George
Turberville, praised his poetry highly. (Turberville
would not himself try, he claimed, to compete with
Sackville in the high style of epic.) In a dedicatory
sonnet to *The Faerie Queene* (1590, 1596), Edmund
Spenser acknowledged that Sackville was "much more
fit (were leasure to the same)" than he to write Elizabeth's praises. Again, among the portraits of the courtiers of his day in Spenser's *Colin Clouts Come Home
Againe* (1595), that of Aetion was probably meant to
represent Sackville: "A gentler shepherd may no where
be found:/ Whose *Muse* full of high thoughts invention,/ Doth like himselfe heroically sound." Certainly
Sackville's high birth and important career encouraged such commendations. As Spenser's lines suggest,
Sackville's contemporaries also recognized that his literary achievement mirrored that of his life.

*A Mirror for Magistrates*, a composite work which
records the fall from power of figures in English history, made an important statement on matters of national import, first bringing into prominence the great
Tudor investigation of issues of responsible government seen against a background of problems of recent
history, familiar to modern readers in the history plays
of William Shakespeare. Sackville's contribution has
been recognized as outstanding by readers from his day
to the present. Indeed, a false tradition soon developed,
making Sackville responsible for the planning and inception of the whole project. Sackville's "Complaint of
Henry, Duke of Buckingham" and especially the artful
"Induction" were recognized as first achieving a poetic
style appropriate for a national epic. Indeed, Sackville

was an important influence on Spenser in *The Faerie Queene*.

Sackville has thus held an honored if minor position in literary history. His reputation was enhanced by the view (until recently the common one) that between Geoffrey Chaucer and Spenser, English poetry experienced an uninspired, dull period—lightened only by Sackville himself. This judgment is now seen as exaggerated. Still, it points to Sackville's early, transitional achievement in approaching the "golden" style of the New Poetry of the high Elizabethan era.

### BIOGRAPHY

Sir Thomas Sackville, first earl of Dorset, was born in 1536 into a noble family. One ancestor had come to England with William the Conqueror, and a more recent ancestor was also a forebear of Queen Elizabeth. Sackville received, in all probability, a thorough and progressive education—for his father was a friend of the humanist educational reformer Roger Ascham, tutor to Queen Elizabeth and author of *The Scholemaster* (1570, which Ascham in fact wrote at Sackville's father's request for the poet's son). He attended Oxford University and then the Inner Temple, one of the Inns of Court, where, as a law student, he produced *Gorboduc* in 1561. Sometime between 1554 and 1559, when the first edition of *A Mirror for Magistrates* came out, Sackville had completed his two pieces for that work, although they were not included until the second edition, 1563. The poet's writings were encouraged by his humanistic studies in letters, complemented by an exposure at one of the Inns of Court to affairs and important personages. Sackville's travels to Rome and France (1563-1566), during which he was given the first of many diplomatic assignments by the Queen, then filled out the traditional education of an Elizabethan gentleman.

In his formal education and travels, as in his writings, Sackville always aimed at a public career. In 1558, he first sat as a member of parliament, at twenty-two years of age. On his father's death in 1566, he undertook the management of a vast estate, had already begun a family, and was well embarked on his long career as an ambassador, statesman, and government official. A member of the Privy Council, he sat as commis-

*Thomas Sackville* (Hulton Archive/Getty Images)

sioner in a number of trials of national importance. He was perhaps Queen Elizabeth's ambassador to Mary, Queen of Scots, bearing to her the news of her sentence of death; tradition reports that his diplomatic skill and gentle character served him well in this assignment. In 1589, he became a member of the Order of the Garter, and two years later was appointed chancellor of the University of Oxford. He succeeded Burleigh in 1599 as Lord High Treasurer of England, sat as Lord High Steward at the trial for treason of the earl of Essex, and was appointed Lord High Treasurer for life on the accession of James I in 1603. Aging and in progressively worsening health, Sackville remained in active service, dying suddenly at seventy-one or seventy-two years of age while sitting in session at the council table.

His life is not that of the prodigal Elizabethan courtier so much as of the dedicated and active man of public affairs. As the most recent commentator on the poet, Normand Berlin, points out, in Sackville "we have an interesting example of a man's life that imitated art." It is of great interest to the poet's youthful writings on the fall of princes that Sackville's subsequent career so often touched upon the fall of the great from political favor (and from life). He himself suffered an undeserved brief period of disfavor after failing to resolve an impossible political tangle associated with the earl of Leicester's governorship of the Netherlands in 1587. In all these affairs, Sackville showed depth of moral wisdom, devotion to his country, and an amiable but upright character. He fulfills to perfection the Renaissance humanistic dictum—indeed, it is the underlying thesis of Ascham's *The Scholemaster*—that practical training in letters and oratory would prepare a young "governor" for wise services to the realm.

## ANALYSIS

Thomas Sackville's contributions to *A Mirror for Magistrates* shows a typical Elizabethan compound of classical, medieval, and "native" elements: Renaissance English literature owes its characteristic variety and vigor to a mixing of sources and styles. Deriving from medieval traditions are the complaint form of tragedy (in which the ghost of a fallen "prince" tells his life story), an interest in the vicissitudes of Fortune, imitations from Dante Alighieri, and use of dream-vision conventions. At the same time, Sackville turns to the classics, notably to Vergil, for the descent into hell as well as for much imagery and many details, and he evokes an atmosphere of classical myth and ancient history through allusion and example. He also employs artful figures of rhetoric in a manner newly stylish in contemporary Tudor letters and uses such "native" elements as archaic diction and syntax to further the effect of synthesis among diverse literary elements. The result is a dignified and serious mixing of richly traditional elements.

In the sentiments and atmosphere of his two pieces, Sackville evokes the brooding, melancholic air of Elizabethan tragedy, anticipating later Elizabethan achievements in drama. (In his exaggerated expression of extreme emotionality, he works, however, in the earlier, mid-Tudor literary style.) He includes themes and images which become popular in Elizabethan drama and lyric, praising sleep, likening life to a play, and stressing that murder will not long remain hidden. Although such conceptions have roots in medieval and classical traditions, Sackville has gathered them into one poem

where they work together with cumulative effect. Finally, Sackville's evocation of an atmosphere of woe and lamentation goes beyond the mere presenting of misery to anticipate the great Elizabethan treatments of mutability, which culminated in the mature works of Spenser.

## A MIRROR FOR MAGISTRATES

*A Mirror for Magistrates* was planned as a continuation of John Lydgate's *Fall of Princes* (wr. 1431-1439, pb. 1494), which itself followed the model of Giovanni Boccaccio's *De casibus virorum illustrium* (1355-1374; *The Fall of Princes*, 1431-1438). Sometime after 1550, a group of collaborators headed by William Baldwin undertook to write a series of tragic episodes, selecting from the English historical chronicles those figures and episodes which would fit their design. A running prose commentary discusses each verse tragedy and links them together. Mentioning the authors of many of the pieces and here and there revealing the intentions of the compilers, this commentary evokes a real as well as literary world. The authors included well-known men respected as writers in their time, public figures who had survived the many political shifts of sixteenth century England—in a word, these were men who knew by experience the political reality of the tales they told. A first version was partly printed in 1555 but was suppressed by Queen Mary's chancellor Stephen Gardiner on suspicion of containing seditious references to contemporary conditions. Publication was made possible upon the accession of Elizabeth, in a first edition, in 1559, covering the period from Richard II to Edward IV and a second edition, 1563, presenting new tragedies primarily concerning Richard III.

Modern readers find *A Mirror for Magistrates* dull, didactic, and emotionally exaggerated. It was very popular in its time, however, going through a good number of editions and receiving successive versions and later imitations. Its analysis of recent political history brought to contemporary readers the latest thoughts on public issues; in addition, it provided some opportunity for the grim sport of seeking allusions to public controversies. The collection played a significant role in furthering the Tudor interpretation of history which has come to be called the Tudor Myth: A long period of destruction and disorder in the Wars of the Roses was England's punishment for violating the divinely sanctioned order when Henry IV deposed the rightful king, Richard II; a happy resolution was recently allowed in the accession of the great Tudor rulers.

Two central convictions underlie this reading of English history. First, the ruler of "magistrate" was believed to be the vice-regent of God, governing by divine right yet still accountable to God. Second, history was seen as a means of teaching political wisdom, presenting a "mirror" which shows (in Lily B. Campbell's words) "the pattern of conduct which had brought happiness or unhappiness to nations and to men in the past." In adopting these views, the authors of *A Mirror for Magistrates* played down the medieval vision of the capricious falseness of this world's glories, seeking instead to reveal the workings of divine justice in the affairs of men. Sackville thus presents his Duke of Buckingham as vulnerable to the uncertain charms of Fortune because of his own moral blindness and as being justly punished for his unscrupulous ambition.

The story of Sackville's contribution to *A Mirror for Magistrates* is obscure in many details, which were not entirely clarified with the discovery, by Marguerite Hearsey in 1929, of an early manuscript in the author's holograph. Generally, however, the introductory statements by Baldwin give a clear picture. When the first version was suppressed, Sackville proposed a more acceptable selection to which some new tragedies that he would write himself would be added, the whole to be prefaced by his "Induction" (introduction). This plan was not carried through, yet in the second edition (where it belonged chronologically), his "Complaint of Henry, Duke of Buckingham," was accompanied by the "Induction" because its literary excellence demanded inclusion.

### "INDUCTION"

Sackville chose the rime royal stanza of pentameter lines rhyming *ababbcc*, common in the late Middle Ages for serious verse, for both "Induction" and "Complaint of Henry, Duke of Buckingham." Although his strong iambics tend toward a thumping monotony, the effect is no more intrusive than in other mid-Tudor poets. Sackville also uses much alliteration; in Berlin's estimate, nine of ten lines use this device of repetition.

Although such old-fashioned poetic techniques have been criticized, they actually support Sackville's overall intentions in both poems by helping to create a verbal texture of strong, heavy strokes in which opposition or contrast predominate. His is not a poetry of subtle effects. When the narrator of "Induction" sorrows to see "The sturdy trees so shattered with the showers,/ The fieldes so fade that floorisht so before," a stark and fundamental contrast is asserted. The language and imagery highlight significant polarities—summer and winter, day and night, joy and sorrow. The meters, figures, and diction preferred by mid-Tudor writers here work together to evoke bold, contrastive meanings.

"Induction" sets an appropriate mood for tragedy in the opening description of a harsh winter scene. This seasonal description and the hellish personifications which follow are picturesque, in the sense of using detail and image to evoke a mood rather than to suggest a full allegory or to state meanings directly. The harsh setting and images present a pervasive context for tragedy. By the tenth stanza, the external details of winter are reflected in the narrator's inner thoughts about human failings; immediately such thoughts find externalization in trenchant personifications. First, the figure of Sorrow conducts the narrator to the porch of Hell, where, one by one, they meet figures such as Remorse of Conscience, Dread, Misery, Revenge, Age, and Death. Again, the detailed descriptions of each figure contribute to the poem's melancholic atmosphere, but in their cumulative import the visions suggest that unhappiness, deserved or undeserved, is inescapable in the human condition. Sackville keeps his narrator posed between revulsion and sympathy: He fears and yet feels pity for Famine, "how she her armes would teare/ And with her teeth gnashe on the bones in vayne." In such ways, the tragic visions impel emotional participation by the reader.

The portraits of Sleep and Old Age from this section of "Induction" have been much praised. Sackville's description of Old Age (lines 295-336) takes a detail or two from the mysterious old man of Chaucer's "Pardoner's Tale"; but it also borrows directly or indirectly from many classical and medieval sources. Typically, Sackville adapts and combines traditional materials, forming his own mixture and emphasis. In fact, the entire procession of figures in the middle section of the poem derives from a much briefer listing of personifications in book 6 of Vergil's *Aeneid* (c. 29-19 B.C.E.; English translation, 1553). Sackville has expanded Vergil's suggestive, brief jottings into full portraits by calling upon many traditional literary images and concepts.

Increasingly, the poem dwells on the presence of change and loss in human affairs. At the end of the procession of figures, the narrator and Sorrow meet Death and then War. The latter presents his shield, in which may be seen historical instances of the destruction of cities and realms, culminating in a vision of vanquished Troy (lines 435-476). The poem has progressed from a view of individual sorrows to the universal principle of mutability seen on the scale of the destruction of civilizations. Moving across Acheron into deepest Hell, Sorrow and the narrator enter a realm of intensified gloom and lamentation where the shades of the tragic dead, ghosts of "Prynces of renowne," tell their tales. In this way, "Induction" leads up to the tragic narrative told by the Duke of Buckingham.

Sackville's "Induction" is, in Berlin's words, "essentially a mood piece that is brilliant in its evocation of atmosphere, vivid in its imagery, concrete in its description, effective in its fusion of sense and sound, and unified in concept and performance." Generally, the personifications as well as the historical figures are presented as tragic victims of misfortune or of irresistible forces of change. In "Complaint of Henry, Duke of Buckingham," however, there occurs a significant shift to a focus on the individual's responsibility for his own sufferings.

### "Complaint of Henry, Duke of Buckingham"

As "Complaint of Henry, Duke of Buckingham" opens, the speaker Buckingham admits that his own choices led to his destruction, resulting from his opportunistic association with the villainous Richard of Gloucester. From the beginning, the poem establishes a didactic manner which seeks to analyze errors of judgment and excesses of ambition. Buckingham's story centers on the gigantic figure of Richard III, according to the Tudor interpretation an arch-villain whose fierce reign constituted the final purgation of a sick England

before God permitted the happy rule of the present Tudors. (Modern historians have shown that Richard III was much less evil and his opponents much less wholesome than in the Tudor Myth.)

In supporting Richard, the ambitious Buckingham takes advantage of "the state unstedfast howe it stood." He shares in murders, little thinking that blood will ask for "blud agayne." At this point, Sackville interrupts the narrative with the first of five interludes, each an interpolated didactic meditation on a theme befitting the stage reached in the narrative. These interludes help to slow the pace of the narrative, lending a dignity which Elizabethans thought proper to epic subjects; in addition, they help Sackville generalize from Buckingham's experiences to universal patterns. The first interlude discussed the folly of political murder, which is shown by many examples to lead to a chain of successive murders such as Shakespeare dramatizes in *Macbeth* (pr. 1606).

Buckingham resumes his narrative (line 169) to tell of a second wave of murders leading to Richard's coronation and of Buckingham becoming Richard's "chyefest Pyer." Hoping to ensure their final security, they kill Richard's two nephews (the notorious murder of the princes in the tower). With this act, the chain of murders takes on destructive force, both psychological and social. First, the conspirators experience the torments of inner fears, expounded upon in a brief second interlude (lines 211-238). When the narrative resumes, it reveals destructive external effects as well. Richard rules by fear, not love, violating the great Elizabethan commonplace that the people will lend assent to a benign rule: In the hearts of Richard's lieges there "lurkes aye/ A secrete hate that hopeth for a daye." The Tudor political theory of the divine right of kings stressed that kings are bound by morality and law. God allows rebellion against tyrants and brings them war, guilty fear, and untimely death. A third interlude expounds this theme with gruesome historical instances (lines 267-329).

Thus far, Buckingham has described his immorality and errors of judgment objectively, allowing Sackville to survey Tudor political ideas relating to power, ambition, and tyranny. This objective tone weakens as Buckingham now turns from Richard, who has become too cruel even for him and who, moreover, has clearly revealed that Buckingham is next in line for destruction. Although Richard III remains the exaggerated villain of Tudor tradition, Buckingham takes on a certain depth of interest and evokes increasing sympathy. From this point in the narrative, Sackville allows a gradual return to the rhetoric of lamentation so prevalent in "Induction." Buckingham now blames not his moral flaws but fatal errors of overconfidence. He trusts, first, in the strength of his assembled soldiers, who desert him. (In lines 421-494, a fourth interlude expounds upon the folly of trusting the "fyckle fayth" of the mob.) Then, Buckingham places his final confidence in a disloyal friend, Humfrey Banastair, who betrays him to Richard and to death.

Buckingham now breaks off his narration to fall into a faint from grief. His distress over the falsity of a trusted friend will seem less excessive if it is remembered that treason is the arch crime in Dante's *La divina commedia* (c. 1320; *The Divine Comedy*, 1802), punished in deepest hell. Although modern readers will find the concluding sections of the poem, which elaborate upon this theme, exaggerated in their emotional extremes, it is suggestive to note to what degree Sackville has transformed Buckingham into a mistreated and sympathetic figure for the readers' contemplation. The last of the interludes is spoken by Sackville's narrator, for Buckingham remains in a distressed faint, with one brief awakening, from lines 540 to 617. This interlude picks up again the descriptive imagery and lyric movement of "Induction," painting an often-praised picture of the calm of deepest midnight, where the "golden stars" whirl in correct cosmic order and each creature is "nestled in his restyng place." Against this orderly security is shown the despairing unrest of Buckingham, who becomes a figure of genuine terror, emphatically teaching the lesson of the end to which lives such as his will lead, as well as an object for pity. Capping off this impression of desperation, Buckingham concludes with his notorious curse against the progeny of Banastair.

Finally, shaking off his episode of crazed cursing, Buckingham returns to his former objective tone in the poem's concluding six stanzas. He offers himself as a direct mirror to kings, showing that he "who reckles rules, right soone may hap to rue."

In "Induction" and "Complaint of Henry, Duke of Buckingham," Sackville achieves two very different ends. The introductory poem evokes a poetic atmosphere for tragic narrative, creating myth through imagery and description. The story of Buckingham is, in contrast, historical and dramatic, presenting and then analyzing Buckingham's actions in a context of serious thought on political themes. The poems together show both the range and the potential of poetry in the mid-Tudor period of English literature. Although Sackville's techniques and themes are seldom subtle, they make up for this lack with a consistency of effect and a concentration on bold contrasts and strong moral certainties. Recent studies of Sackville have found him to be as much a poet of his own time as an innovator anticipating the coming triumphs of later Elizabethan verse. It remains true, however, that he realized, as did few of his contemporaries, what his medium could accomplish, treating important themes with dignity, consistency, and poetic interest.

OTHER MAJOR WORK

PLAY: *Gorboduc*, pr. 1561 (with Thomas Norton; authorized edition pb. 1570; also known as *The Tragedy of Ferrex and Porrex*).

BIBLIOGRAPHY

Berlin, Normand. *Thomas Sackville*. New York: Twayne, 1974. This study, part of Twayne's English Authors series, is among the most readable on Sackville's work and life and includes some fine criticism.

Campbell, Lily B., ed. *The Mirror for Magistrates*. New York: Barnes & Noble, 1960. An excellent text of the poems, with a lengthy and equally excellent introduction to the works.

Cauthen, Irby B., Jr., ed. Introduction to *Gorboduc: Or, Ferrex and Porrex*, by Thomas Sackville and Thomas Norton. Lincoln: University of Nebraska Press, 1970. Although brief, the introduction to the play offers approximately twenty pages describing the lives of the authors and the political atmosphere of the times, and provides textual criticism of the play.

Ruoff, James E., ed. *Crowell's Handbook of Elizabe-

*than and Stuart Literature*. New York: Thomas Y. Crowell, 1975. Listed under *Gorboduc* and *A Mirror for Magistrates*, one finds concise plot summary, critical synopses, and bibliography. The handbook still proves invaluable for students of Renaissance literature.

Swart, J. *Thomas Sackville: A Study in Sixteenth-Century Poetry*. Norwood, Pa.: Norwood Editions, 1977. Examines poetry in sixteenth century England and the place of Sackville in that tradition.

Zim, Rivakah. "Dialogue and Discretion: Thomas Sackville, Catherine de Medici, and the Anjou Marriage Proposal 1571." *Historical Journal* 40, no. 2 (June, 1997): 287-310. Sackville's previously unpublished letters of his secret interview with Catherine de Medici concerning the 1571 Anjou marriage proposal exploit the actuality of dramatic dialogue beyond the normal use of diplomatic correspondence.

_____. "Religion and the Political Counsellor: Thomas Sackville (1536-1608)." *English Historical Review* 122, no. 498 (September, 2007): 892-918. Although this article investigates the religious views of Sackville, it does deal with his writings and provides invaluable background information.

*Richard J. Panofsky*

# SIEGFRIED SASSOON

**Born:** Brenchley, Kent, England; September 8, 1886
**Died:** Heytesbury, England; September 1, 1967
**Also known as:** Saul Kain; Pinchbeck Lyre; Sigmund Sashun

PRINCIPAL POETRY

*The Daffodil Murderer*, 1913
*The Old Huntsman, and Other Poems*, 1917
*Counter-Attack, and Other Poems*, 1918
*War Poems*, 1919
*Picture Show*, 1920
*Recreations*, 1923
*Selected Poems*, 1925

*Satirical Poems*, 1926
*The Heart's Journey*, 1927
*Poems of Pinchbeck Lyre*, 1931
*The Road to Ruin*, 1933
*Vigils*, 1935
*Poems Newly Selected, 1916-1935*, 1940
*Rhymed Ruminations*, 1940
*Collected Poems*, 1947
*Common Chords*, 1950
*Emblems of Experience*, 1951
*The Tasking*, 1954
*Sequences*, 1956
*Lenten Illuminations and Sight Sufficient*, 1958
*The Path to Peace*, 1960
*Collected Poems, 1908-1956*, 1961
*An Octave*, 1966

OTHER LITERARY FORMS

Siegfried Sassoon (suh-SEWN) is nearly as well known for his prose works as for his poetry. From 1926 to 1945, he spent most of his time working on the two trilogies that form the bulk of his work in prose. The first of these was the three-volume fictionalized autobiography published in 1937 as *The Memoirs of George Sherston*. It begins in *Memoirs of a Fox-Hunting Man* (1928), by recounting the life of a well-to-do young country squire in Georgian England up to his first experiences as an officer in World War I. The second volume, *Memoirs of an Infantry Officer* (1930), and the third, *Sherston's Progress* (1936), describe the young man's war experiences. In the later trilogy, Sassoon discarded the thinly disguised fiction of the Sherston novels and wrote direct autobiography, with a nostalgic look back at his pleasant pastoral life in prewar England in *The Old Century and Seven More Years* (1938) and *The Weald of Youth* (1942). In *Siegfried's Journey, 1916-1920* (1945), Sassoon looks again at his own experiences during and immediately following the war. These autobiographical works are invaluable to the student of Sassoon's poetry because of the context they provide, particularly for the war poems.

Two other significant prose works should be mentioned. The first is Sassoon's *Lecture on Poetry*, delivered at the University of Bristol on March 16, 1939, in which Sassoon delineated what he considered to be the elements of good poetry. The second work is Sassoon's critical biography of the poet George Meredith, titled simply *Meredith* (1948), which also suggests some of Sassoon's views on poetry.

### ACHIEVEMENTS

According to Bernard Bergonzi, Siegfried Sassoon was the only soldier-poet to be widely read during the war itself. This gave Sassoon a unique opportunity to influence other war poets, which he did. Though his war poetry has been criticized for being mere description, for appealing to only the senses and not the imagination, and for being uncontrolled emotion without artistic restraint, there can be no doubt than Sassoon's poetry represented a complete break with the war poetry of the past in tone, technique, and subject matter. With uncompromising realism and scathing satire, Sassoon portrayed the sufferings of the front-line soldier and the incompetency of the staff for the express purposes of convincing his readers to protest continuation of the war. His *Counter-Attack, and Other Poems* was nearly suppressed because of poems such as "The General," which broke the prohibition against criticizing those in charge of the war effort.

Unquestionably, Sassoon's realistic subject matter and diction influenced other poets, most notably his friend Wilfred Owen, whose poetry was posthumously published by Sassoon in 1920; but Sassoon failed to influence later poetry because, as John Johnston notes, his war poetry was all negative—he provided no constructive replacement for the myths he had destroyed. Nor did Sassoon influence poetry in the 1930's because, according to Michael Thorpe, he was still a prisoner of war, and through his autobiographies he retreated from the political struggle of W. H. Auden and Stephen Spender and others into his own earlier years.

When in the 1950's Sassoon finally did have something positive to offer, no one was willing to listen. He was no longer well known or critically acknowledged. Certainly his future reputation will rest on the war poems; but in his religious poems of the 1950's, Sassoon did achieve a style of simple expression, compact brevity, and concrete imagery with a universally appealing theme, and this should be noted as a remarkable though largely unrecognized achievement.

### BIOGRAPHY

Siegfried Lorraine Sassoon was born in the Kentish weald in 1886, the second of three sons of Alfred Ezra Sassoon and Theresa Georgina Thornycroft. His father was descended from a long line of wealthy Jewish merchants and bankers who, after wandering through Spain, Persia, and India, had come to settle in England. The family was proud of its orthodoxy, and Siegfried's father was the first to marry outside the faith. Siegfried's mother, in contrast, was an artist, the close relative of three well-known sculptors, and a member of the landed gentry. The marriage was a failure, and Alfred Sassoon left when Siegfried was five, leaving the younger Sassoon to be reared by his mother as an Anglican.

Siegfried had no formal schooling as a child, though from the ages of nine to fourteen he learned from private tutors and a German governess. In 1902, he attended Marlborough, and in 1905, he entered Clare College, Cambridge. Sassoon's temperament was not disciplined enough for scholarly pursuits; he began by

*Siegfried Sassoon* (Hulton Archive/Getty Images)

reading law, switched to history, and ultimately left Cambridge without a degree. He returned to Kent, where, on an inherited income of five hundred pounds a year, he was able to devote his energies to foxhunting, racing, and writing poetry. Sassoon loved the pastoral beauty of the Kentish downs and attempted to portray it in a number of dreamy, sentimental lyrics. Between the ages of nineteen and twenty-six, Sassoon had nine volumes of poetry privately published, before he enjoyed a mild success with *The Daffodil Murderer* in 1913. The poem was chiefly intended as a parody of John Masefield's *The Everlasting Mercy*, but Sassoon's poem had a strong human appeal of its own. By this time, Sassoon had been befriended by Edward Marsh, the editor of *Georgian Poetry*. Marsh encouraged Sassoon's literary endeavors and persuaded him to come to London in May, 1914, where Sassoon began to move in the literary world and to meet such notable authors as Rupert Brooke. Sassoon, however, felt unhappy and lacked a sense of purpose, and when he enlisted in the army on August 3, 1914 (two days before England entered the war), it was to escape a sterile existence.

Sassoon's early life had been extremely sheltered, even pampered, and it was a very immature twenty-eight-year-old who went to war, totally unprepared for what he would find. After convalescence from injuries received in a fall during cavalry training, he accepted a commission and went through training as an infantry officer. Thus, he did not arrive in France until November, 1915, where he became transport officer for the First Battalion of the Royal Welch Fusiliers. Here he met and befriended the poet Robert Graves. In *Goodbye to All That* (1929), Graves describes his first meeting with Sassoon and relates how, when he showed Sassoon his first book of poems, *Over the Brazier* (1916), Sassoon, whose early war poems were idealistic, had frowned and said that war should not be written about in such a realistic way. Graves, who had been in France six months, remarked that Sassoon had not yet been in the trenches.

Graves already knew what Sassoon would soon discover, indeed what all the British troops in France were coming to feel: growing disillusionment at the frustration and the staggering casualties of trench warfare. There were 420,000 British casualties in the Somme of-

fensive beginning on July 1, 1916—an offensive that gained virtually nothing. The Somme was Sassoon's most bitter experience in the trenches; after it, he would never write the old kind of poetry again.

In spite of his pacifist leanings, Sassoon distinguished himself in the war. Called "Mad Jack" by his troops, Sassoon was awarded the Military Cross and recommended for the Distinguished Service Order for his exploits in battle: After a raid at Mametz, he took it upon himself to bring back the wounded; in the Somme in early July, he single-handedly occupied a whole section of an enemy trench, after which he was found in the trench, alone, reading a book of poetry. Ill with gastric fever in late July, he was sent home for three months, where he worked on poems to be included in *The Old Huntsman, and Other Poems*.

While in England, Sassoon met Lady Ottoline Morrell and her liberal husband, Philip, at whose home he spoke with such pacifists as Bertrand Russell, listened to open criticism of the war, and heard of Germany's peace overtures and the impure motives of members of parliament who wanted the war to continue.

Sassoon returned to active service in France in February, 1917, but in April, he was wounded in the Battle of Arras and sent home again. Haunted by nightmares of violence and by what the pacifists were saying, Sassoon resolved to protest the war on a grand scale. In July, in a remarkable move, risking public disgrace and military court-martial, Sassoon refused to return to active duty and wrote a formal declaration of protest to his commanding officer, which was reproduced in the press and which Russell arranged to have mentioned in the House of Commons. In his letter, Sassoon charged that the war was being deliberately prolonged by the politicians for ignoble purposes, even though there was a chance for a negotiated settlement with Germany, thus leading the men at the front line to be slaughtered needlessly. Sassoon hoped to be court-martialed, so that his protest would have propaganda value. To his dismay, however, the official reaction was largely to minimize the letter. In a moment of despair, Sassoon flung his Military Cross into the Mersey River and vowed to continue his protest.

At that point, Graves stepped in. Graves agreed with Sassoon's letter, but considered the gesture futile and feared for Sassoon's personal welfare. Graves arranged to have Sassoon appear before a medical board, and chiefly on Graves's testimony, Sassoon was found to be suffering from shell shock. The incident was closed, and Sassoon was sent to Craiglockhart hospital in Edinburgh, where physician W. H. R. Rivers became his counselor and friend, and where in August he met the brilliant young poet Wilfred Owen. Owen knew and idolized Sassoon as the author of *The Old Huntsman, and Other Poems* (which had appeared in May), and Sassoon's encouragement and insistence on realism had greatly influenced him. At Craiglockhart, during the autumn of 1917, Sassoon composed many of the poems of *Counter-Attack, and Other Poems*, which was published the following year.

Owen returned to active duty in November, and Sassoon, feeling that he was betraying his troops at the front by staying away in comfort, returned to duty a few weeks later. He went first to Ireland, then to Egypt, where he became a captain, then back to France in May. On July 15, 1918, Sassoon, returning from an attack on a German machine gun, was wounded in the head by one of his own sentries. He was sent to a London hospital, where he spent the rest of the war.

After the war, Sassoon retreated from the active life, becoming more and more contemplative (he had always been introspective and solitary) until he acquired a reputation as a virtual hermit. Immediately after the war, he joined the Labor Party and became editor of the literary pages of the *Daily Herald*, where he published satirical pieces with a socialist point of view. His satire of the 1920's, however, was uneasy and awkward, stemming from the fact that the issues of the day were not as clear-cut as the right and wrong about the war had been. Besides, he was not really sure of himself, feeling a need to explore his past life and find some meaning in it. Still, as the 1930's grew darker, Sassoon wrote poems warning of the horror of chemical and biological warfare. No one seemed to want to listen, however, and Sassoon, disillusioned, forsook "political" poetry completely. In part, the autobiographies that he worked on in those years were a rejection of the modern world and an idealization of the past. In part, too, they were an effort to look inside himself, and that same urge characterizes most of his later poetry, which is

concerned with his personal spiritual struggle and development.

Thus, the incidents of Sassoon's later life were nearly all spiritual. Only a few isolated events are of interest: In 1933, he finally married; he had a son, George, but Sassoon kept his personal relationships private, never mentioning them in his poetry. During World War II, Sassoon's home was requisitioned for evacuees, and later, fifteen hundred American troops were quartered on his large estate. After the war, Sassoon remained very solitary and appears to have cultivated his image as the "hermit of Heytesbury." When his volumes of poetry appeared in the 1950's, they were largely ignored by critics and public alike. The fiery war poet had outlived his reputation, but he had reached a great personal plateau: On August 14, 1957, Sassoon was received into the Catholic Church at Downside Abbey. His last poems, appearing in a privately published collection, *An Octave*, on his eightieth birthday (a year before his death), display a serene and quiet faith.

ANALYSIS

In 1939, Siegfried Sassoon delineated his views on poetry in a lecture given at Bristol College. While what he said was not profound or revolutionary, it did indicate the kind of poetry Sassoon liked and tried to write, at least at that time. First, Sassoon said, poetry should stem from inspiration, but that inspiration needs to be tempered by control and discipline—by art. Second, the best poetry is simple and direct—Sassoon disliked the tendency toward complexity initiated by T. S. Eliot and Ezra Pound. Third, Sassoon held the Romantic view that poetry should express true feeling and speak the language of the heart. Fourth, poetry should contain strong visual imagery, the best of which is drawn from nature. Finally, the subject matter of the best poetry is not political (again, he was reacting against the avowedly political poetry of Auden and his associates), but rather personal, and this examination of self led Sassoon to write spiritual poetry.

A review of Sassoon's poetry will reveal, however, that even in his best poems he did not always follow all these precepts, and that in his worst poems he seldom followed any. Sassoon's worst poems are most certainly his earliest ones. Sassoon's prewar lyric verses are lush and wordy, in weak imitation of Algernon Charles Swinburne and the Pre-Raphaelites, but full of anachronisms and redundancies. Some, such as "Haunted" and "Goblin Revel," are purely escapist; Lewis Thorpe suggests that Sassoon was looking for escape from his own too-comfortable world. The best thing about these early poems is their interest in nature—an interest that Sassoon never lost and that provided him with concrete images in later pieces. The best poems that Sassoon wrote before the war, *The Daffodil Murderer* and "The Old Huntsman," abandon the poetic diction for a colloquial style, and "The Old Huntsman" reveals a strong kinship with nature.

### THE WAR POETRY

Sassoon's early, idealistic war poetry is characterized by an abstract diction and generalized imagery. He was writing in the "happy warrior" style after the manner of Rupert Brooke's famous sonnet sequence and was even able to write of his brother's death early in the war as a "victory" and his ghost's head as "laureled." Perhaps the best example of these early poems is "Absolution," written before Sassoon had actually experienced the war. Sassoon romanticizes war, speaking of the glorious sacrifice of young comrades in arms who go off to battle as "the happy legion," asserting that "fighting for our freedom, we are free." The poem is full of such abstractions, but no concrete images. Its language is often archaic ("Time's but a golden wind"), and it is the sort of thing that Sassoon soon put behind him.

Edward Marsh, after reading some of Sassoon's earlier poetry, had told him to write with his eye directly on the object. As Sassoon began to experience the horrors of trench warfare, he did exactly that. His poems became increasingly concrete, visual, and realistic, his language became increasingly colloquial, and his tone became more and more bitter as the war went on. Early in 1916, he wrote "Golgotha," "The Redeemer," and "A Working Party," in which he tried to present realistically the sufferings of the common soldier. Such realistic depiction of the front lines characterized one of two main types of war poetry that Sassoon was to write in the next few years. The best example of sheer naturalistic description is "Counter-Attack," the title poem of Sassoon's most popular and most scathing volume of poetry. "Counter-Attack" begins with a description of the troops, who, having taken an enemy trench, begin to deepen it with shovels. They uncover a pile of dead bodies and rotting body parts—"naked sodden buttocks, mats of hair,/ Bulged, clotted heads."

### "REPRESSION OF WAR EXPERIENCE"

The horror of this description is without parallel, but where Sassoon really excels is in his realistic portrayal of the psychological effects of the war. Perhaps his best poem in this vein is "Repression of War Experience," from *Counter-Attack, and Other Poems*. The poem, in the form of an interior monologue, explores a mind verging on hysteria, trying to distract itself and maintain control while even the simplest, most serene events—a moth fluttering too close to a candle flame—bring nightmarish thoughts of violence into the persona's mind. In the garden, he hears ghosts, and as he sits in the silence, he can hear only the guns. In the end, his control breaks down; he wants to rush out "and screech at them to stop—I'm going crazy;/ I'm going stark, staring mad because of the guns."

### "THEY"

Sassoon was not merely presenting realistic details; he was being deliberately didactic, trying to use his poetry to incite a public outcry against the war. When home on leave, he had been appalled by the jingoistic ignorance and complacency on the home front. Sassoon's second main type of war poetry made a satirical attack on these civilians, on those who conducted the war, and on the irresponsible press that spread the lying propaganda. Justly the most famous of these poems is "They" (*The Old Huntsman, and Other Poems*), in which Sassoon demolishes the cherished civilian notion that the war was divinely ordained and that the British were fighting on God's side. Sassoon presents a pompous bishop declaring that, since the "boys" will have fought "Anti-Christ," none will return "the same" as he was. The irony of this statement is made clear when the "boys" return quite changed: blind, legless, and syphilitic. The bishop can only remark, "The ways of God are strange." "They" caused a great outcry in England by ruthlessly attacking the Church for forsaking the moral leadership it should have provided.

"They" also illustrates Sassoon's favorite technique

in satire: concentration of his ironic force in the last line of the poem. This kind of "knock-out punch" may be seen most vividly in the poem "The One-Legged Man" (*The Old Huntsman, and Other Poems*), which describes a soldier, discharged from the war, watching the natural beauty of the world in autumn and considering the bright, comfortable years ahead. The poem ends with the man's crushingly ironic thought, "Thank God they had to amputate!"

Certainly there are flaws in Sassoon's war poetry. Some of the verses are nothing more than bitter invectives designed merely to attack a part of his audience, such as "Glory of Women," "Blighters," and "Fight to the Finish." Even the best poems often lack the discipline and order that Sassoon himself later advanced as one main criterion of poetry. Further, Sassoon almost never got beyond his feelings about immediate experiences to form theoretical or profound notions about the broader aspects of the war. Sassoon himself realized this lack in 1920, when he brought out his slain friend Wilfred Owen's war poetry, which converted war experiences into something having universal meaning.

### "The Dug Out"

The war poetry, however, has a number of virtues as well. It uses simple, direct, and clear expression that comes, as Sassoon advocated, from the heart. Further, it uses vivid pictures to express the inexpressible horror of the trenches. "The Dug Out" (*Picture Show*) is an example of Sassoon's war poetry at its best. In its eight lines, Sassoon draws a clear picture of a youth sleeping in an awkward and unnatural position. The simple, colloquial language focuses on the emotional state of the speaker, and much is suggested by what is left unsaid. The speaker's nerves are such that he can no longer bear the sight of the young sleeper because, as he cries in the final lines, "You are too young to fall asleep for ever;/ And when you sleep you remind me of the dead." Arthur Lane compares such poems, in which the ironic effect is achieved through the dramatic situation more than through imagery, to those in the *Satires of Circumstance* (1914) of Sassoon's idol, Thomas Hardy, suggesting an influence at work.

### "Everyone Sang"

Perhaps the culmination of Sassoon's attempt to transcend his war experience is the much-admired lyric "Everyone Sang" (*Picture Show*). It is a joyous lyric expressing a mood of relief and exultation, through the imagery of song and of singing birds. Sassoon seems to have been expressing his own relief at having survived: "horror/ Drifted away." Lane calls these lines "pure poetry" of "visionary power," comparing them to poems of William Wordsworth and William Blake. He might have also mentioned Henry Vaughan, Sassoon's other idol, whose path toward poetry of a very personal spirituality Sassoon was soon to follow.

### "Lines Written in Anticipation . . ."

Unquestionably, it is for his war poetry that Sassoon is chiefly admired. Still, he lived for nearly fifty years after the armistice, and what he wrote in that time cannot be disregarded. He first flirted with socialism after the war; "Everyone Sang" may be intended to laud the coming utopian society. Then he attempted satiric poetry during the 1920's, which must be regarded as a failure. His targets varied from the upper classes to political corruption and newspapers, but the poetry is not from the heart; the satire is too loud and not really convincing. Michael Thorpe points out the wordiness of Sassoon's style in these satires, together with the length of his sentences. One blatant example is "Lines Written in Anticipation of a London Paper Attaining a Guaranteed Circulation of Ten Million Daily." Even the title is verbose, but note the wordy redundancy of the lines:

> Were it not wiser, were it not more candid,
> More courteous, more consistent with good sense,
> If I were to include all, all who are banded
> Together in achievement so immense?

### Religious searching and spirituality

Though he soon abandoned the satiric mode, Sassoon did maintain what Joseph Cohen calls the role of prophet that he had assumed in the war years, by continually warning, through *The Road to Ruin* and *Rhymed Ruminations*, of the coming disaster of World War II. His total despair for the modern world is expressed in "Litany of the Lost" (1945), wherein, with the ominous line "Deliver us from ourselves," Sassoon bid farewell to the poetry of social commentary. By now he was more interested in his spiritual quest.

Next to his war poems, Sassoon's poems of religious searching are his most effective. The quest begins with "The Traveller to His Soul" (1933), in which Sassoon asks, as the "problem which concerns me most," the question "Have I got a soul?" He spends over twenty years trying to answer the question. His work, beginning with *The Heart's Journey* and *Vigils*, is concerned with exploration of self and uncertainty about the self's place in the universe, with increasing questioning about what lies behind creation. With *Rhymed Ruminations*, Sassoon ends the 1930's on a note of uneasiness and uncertainty.

### SEQUENCES

The questions are answered in the three volumes *Common Chords*, *Emblems of Experience*, and *The Tasking*, which were combined to make the book *Sequences*. In the poem "Redemption" (*Common Chords*), Sassoon yearns for a vision of the eternal, which he recognizes as existing beyond his senses. Sassoon's lines recall Vaughan's mystical visions when he asks for "O but one ray/ from that all-hallowing and eternal day." In *The Tasking*, Sassoon reached what Thorpe calls a spiritual certainty, and his best poems in that volume succeed more clearly than the war poems in satisfying Sassoon's own poetic criteria as expressed in 1939. In "Another Spring," Sassoon speaks in simple, direct, and compact language about feelings of the heart—an old man's emotions on witnessing what may be his last spring. The natural imagery is concrete and visual as well as auditory, concentrating on "some crinkled primrose leaves" and "a noise of nesting rooks." Though the final three lines of the poem add a hint of didacticism, the poem succeeds by leaving much unsaid about the eternal rebirth of nature and its implications for the old man and the force behind the regenerative cycle of nature. It is a fine poem, like many in *The Tasking*, with a simple, packed style that makes these poems better as art, though doomed to be less familiar than the war poems.

### OTHER MAJOR WORKS

LONG FICTION: *The Memoirs of George Sherston*, 1937 (includes *Memoirs of a Fox-Hunting Man*, 1928; *Memoirs of an Infantry Officer*, 1930; and *Sherston's Progress*, 1936).

NONFICTION: *The Old Century and Seven More Years*, 1938; *Lecture on Poetry*, 1939; *The Weald of Youth*, 1942; *Siegfried's Journey, 1916-1920*, 1945; *Meredith*, 1948; *Siegfried Sassoon Diaries, 1920-1922*, 1981; *Siegfried Sassoon Diaries, 1915-1918*, 1983; *Siegfried Sassoon Diaries, 1923-1925*, 1985.

EDITED TEXT: *Poems by Wilfred Owen*, 1920.

### BIBLIOGRAPHY

Bloom, Harold, ed. *Poets of World War I: Rupert Brooke and Siegfried Sassoon*. Philadelphia: Chelsea House, 2003. Contains numerous essays on Sassoon, covering topics such as realism, satire, and spirituality in his poetry.

Caesar, Adrian. *Taking It Like a Man: Suffering, Sexuality, and the War Poets: Brooke, Sassoon, Owen, Graves*. New York: Manchester University Press, 1993. Caesar explores how four British poets reconciled their ideologies inherited from Christianity, imperialism, and Romanticism with their experiences of World War I.

Campbell, Patrick. *Siegfried Sassoon: A Study of the War Poetry*. Jefferson, N.C.: McFarland, 1999. Through primary documents and research, Campbell provides critical analyses of Sassoon's war poetry. Includes bibliographical references and an index.

Egremont, Max. *Siegfried Sassoon: A Life*. New York: Farrar, Straus and Giroux, 2005. This biography of Sassoon examines his life, including his relationship with Stephan Tennant, its breakup, and his subsequent marriage.

Fussell, Paul. *The Great War and Modern Memory*. 1975. Reprint. New York: Oxford University Press, 2000. This classic study of the literature arising from the experience of fighting in World War I pays special attention to Sassoon's fiction, autobiography, and poetry. Provides a useful context for Sassoon's work in comparison to other writers of the period.

Hipp, Daniel. *The Poetry of Shell Shock: Wartime Trauma and Healing in Wilfred Owen, Ivor Gurney, and Siegfried Sassoon*. Jefferson, N.C.: McFarland, 2005. Contains chapters examining the lives and works of three war poets: Sassoon, Wilfred Owen, and Ivory Gurney.

Lane, Arthur E. *An Adequate Response: The War Poetry*

of Wilfred Owen and Siegfried Sassoon. Detroit: Wayne State University Press, 1972. Lane highlights the use of satire and parody as he analyzes Sassoon's war verse. Contends that Sassoon and others, when faced with the horrors of trench warfare, were charged with creating a new mode of expression since the traditional modes proved inadequate.

Moeyes, Paul. *Siegfried Sassoon: Scorched Glory—A Critical Study*. New York: St. Martin's Press, 1997. Moeyes draws on Sassoon's edited diaries and letters to explore Sassoon's assertion that his poetry was his real autobiography. Includes bibliography and an index.

Wilson, Jean Moorcroft. *Siegfried Sassoon: The Journey from the Trenches—A Biography, 1918-1967*. London: Duckworth, 2003. Describes the later years of Sassoon's life, looking at his life after the war.

_____. *Siegfried Sassoon: The Making of a War Poet—A Biography*. New York: Routledge, 1999. Details Sassoon's early life, covering the years from his birth through 1918, and in doing so, closely examines his struggle to come to terms with being gay.

*Jay Ruud*

---

# SIR WALTER SCOTT

**Born:** Edinburgh, Scotland; August 15, 1771
**Died:** Abbotsford, Scotland; September 21, 1832
**Also known as:** First Baronet Scott

PRINCIPAL POETRY

*The Eve of Saint John: A Border Ballad*, 1800
*The Lay of the Last Minstrel*, 1805
*Ballads and Lyrical Pieces*, 1806
*Marmion: A Tale of Flodden Field*, 1808
*The Lady of the Lake*, 1810
*The Vision of Don Roderick*, 1811
*Rokeby*, 1813
*The Bridal of Triermain: Or, The Vale of St. John, in Three Cantos*, 1813
*The Ettrick Garland: Being Two Excellent New Songs*, 1815 (with James Hogg)

*The Field of Waterloo*, 1815
*The Lord of the Isles*, 1815
*Harold the Dauntless*, 1817

OTHER LITERARY FORMS

Sir Walter Scott's literary reputation rests firmly on his monumental collection of Waverley novels, the final revision of which was issued, in forty-eight volumes, between 1829 and 1833. The novelist produced those classics on a regular basis during the last eighteen years of his life—beginning with the three-volume *Waverley: Or, 'Tis Sixty Years Since* in 1814 and concluding, shortly before his death, with *Count Robert of Paris* and *Castle Dangerous* (under the collective title *Tales of My Landlord*, fourth series), both in 1831. In addition to the novels, Scott wrote numerous plays, including *Halidon Hill* (pb. 1822), *Macduff's Cross* (pb. 1823), *The House of Aspen* (pb. 1829), *Auchindrane: Or, The Ayrshire Tragedy* (pr., pb. 1830), and *The Doom of Devorgoil* (pb. 1830).

Scott's nonfiction prose includes *Religious Discourses by a Layman* (1828), *The History of Scotland* (1829-1830), and *Letters on Demonology and Witchcraft* (1830). He also produced three biographies of note: *The Life and Works of John Dryden*, first published in 1808 as part of his eighteen-volume edition of that poet's works, *The Memoirs of Jonathan Swift* (1826; originally included in the nineteen-volume *The Life of Jonathan Swift*, 1814); and *The Life of Napoleon Buonaparte: Emperor of the French, with a Preliminary View of the French Revolution* (1827, 9 volumes). In addition, as editor of *Ballantyne's Novelist's Library* 1821-1824 (10 volumes), Scott wrote biographical essays on each writer in the series (including Henry Fielding, Tobias Smollett, Samuel Richardson, Ann Radcliffe, Charlotte Smith, and Fanny Burney); he published those sketches separately in 1825 (2 volumes).

Finally, Scott expended considerable energy on a long list of editorial projects carried out between 1799 and 1831: In addition to the works of John Dryden and Jonathan Swift and the *Novelist's Library*, one may note *Minstrelsy of the Scottish Border* (1802-1803, 32 volumes), *A Collection of Scarce and Valuable Tracts* (1809-1815, 13 volumes), and *Chronological Notes of*

*Scottish Affairs from the Diary of Lord Fountainhall* (1822). Various editions of *The Journal of Sir Walter Scott* have appeared, beginning in 1890.

ACHIEVEMENTS

Sir Walter Scott's literary reputation rests on thirty novels. Few twentieth century readers and scholars have been interested in his poetry or have taken the time to examine the distinct stages of his literary career. With the publication of *Waverley* in 1814, Scott's literary life as a novelist began and his period of intense poetic production terminated. At the outset, then, one is tempted to view the poetry only in the context of its effect on the fiction—or, from another perspective, the effect of Scott the poet on Scott the novelist.

Ample reason exists, however, for studying the poetry on its own merits, for the imaginative power to be found in Scott's metrical romances, lyrics, and ballads. Some contemporary scholars support the claims of their Victorian predecessors, who argued that Scott, among all his "British" contemporaries, emerged as the first writer of the Romantic movement. Indeed, although literary historians correctly offer William Wordsworth's *Lyrical Ballads* (1798)—and its significant preface— as the key to understanding British Romanticism, Scott's *The Lay of the Last Minstrel*, published seven years later, reached a far wider audience (in both England and Scotland) than Wordsworth's collection and achieved a more noticeable impact among the poet's contemporaries than did the earlier work. In fact, no previous English poet had managed to produce a work that reaped such large financial rewards and achieved so much popular acclaim.

Interestingly enough, Scott's poetic achievements came in a form radically different from those qualities that marked the traditional "giants" of his age—Wordsworth, Samuel Taylor Coleridge, John Keats, Percy Bysshe Shelley, and Lord Byron. True, Scott considered, at a variety of levels, the prevalent Romantic themes: the rejection of scientific dogmatism, a return to the glamour of past ages, the discovery of happiness in primitivism rather than in modernity, the enjoyment of emotion, a basic belief in humanitarianism. He rejected, however, the radical sentiments of the Romantic movement. By nature and upbringing a conservative, Scott clung to Tory politics and to the established Church of England rather than rising up in actual or intellectual rebellion against such institutions. He had little or no interest in mysticism, overzealous passion, or the dark unconscious. Scott's poetry is distinguished by its considerable clarity and directness; it is the product of a gentlemanly and reasonably satisfied attitude toward promoting the values of his own social class. He did rush back into an imaginary past to seek out heroes and adventurers whom he found lacking in his own early nineteenth century cultural and artistic environment. Such escapes, however, never really detracted from his belief in the challenge of the present intellectual life and the present world, where, if everything else failed, courage would support the intellectually honest competitor.

Chronologically, Scott belongs with the early Romantics; culturally and intellectually, he occupies a middle ground between Scotland and England, and therein, perhaps, lies his ultimate contribution to poetry in English. He captured, first in the poems and later in his prose fiction, the essence of Scottish national pride; that pride he filtered through the physical image of Scotland, through its varied and conflicting scenery and its traditional romantic lore. The entire area— joined politically to Great Britain in 1707, but still culturally free and theologically independent during Scott's day (as it remains even to this day)—stimulated and intensified his creative genius and supplied the substance first for his poetry, then for his prose fiction. Nevertheless, Scott remained distinctly aware of England and receptive to the demands of the English public—his largest reading audience. For them he translated the picturesqueness of the Highlands and the Lowlands, the islands and the borders. While photographing (or "painting," as his contemporaries maintained), through his imagination, the language and the sentiment of Scotland, Scott gave to his English readers scenes and characters that could be observed as partly English. His poetry has a freshness, a frankness, a geniality, and a shrewdness peculiar to his own Scottish Lowlands. Still, as observers of that part of the world quickly appreciate, there is little difference between a southern Scotsman and a northern Englishman—which, in the end, may also be an apt commentary on Scott's poetry.

BIOGRAPHY

The fourth surviving son of Walter Scott and Anne Rutherford, Walter Scott was born on August 15, 1771, in a house in the College Wynd, Edinburgh. At the age of eighteen months, the infant contracted a fever while teething and, in the end, lost the use of his right leg. The circumstance became noteworthy not only for its effect on Scott's personality and his writing, but also as the first fully authenticated case of infantile paralysis in medical history. After the failure of various attempts to remedy the malady, Scott's father sent him to Sandy Knowe, near Kelso (Roxburgh), to live with his grandfather (Robert Scott) and his uncle (Thomas). Although the five years spent there contributed little or nothing toward curing the boy's lameness, they provided some experiences with lasting influence: subjection to republican and Jacobite prejudices; songs and legends taught to him by his grandmother (Barbara Haliburton); a trip to the spas at Bath, with a stopover at London on the way; sea-bathing at Prestonpans, near Edinburgh (and site of one of the key engagements of the Jacobite uprising of 1745), where he learned of the German wars from an old veteran of Invernahyle, one Captain Dalgetty.

In 1778, the boy returned to his father's house in George's Square, Edinburgh, and later that year entered the high school at Edinburgh. From his principal tutor, a strict Presbyterian named James Mitchell, Scott gained a knowledge of Scottish church history, while his mother encouraged him to read William Shakespeare. His health, however, continued to be a problem, so again the elder Scott sent his son off, this time to Kelso to live with an aunt, Jenny Scott. During his half-year's stay there, he met James Ballantyne and the blind poet Thomas Blacklock; there, also, he read James Macpherson's Ossianic poems, Edmund Spenser's *The Faerie Queene* (1590, 1596), and Thomas Percy's *Reliques of Ancient English Poetry* (1765). Most important, however, he began to collect ballads, a form and a tradition that would remain with him and influence his own literary and cultural directions. By November, 1783, Scott had prepared himself sufficiently to begin studies at Edinburgh University; he pursued only those disciplines, however, that aroused his interest (law, history, romantic legends, and literature). Further illness reduced his stamina, and his education was interrupted once more when he apprenticed himself to his father, copying legal documents. Eventually he did manage to earn a degree in law (1792) and gain admission to the Scottish bar.

Although Scott did indeed practice law and, after a reasonable period as a novice, did manage to earn a fair income from his labors, his interest focused more sharply than ever on literature, ballads, and Scottish folklore. Thus, between 1792 and 1799—first merely as a companion to the sheriff-substitute of Roxburghshire, then as sheriff-deputy of Selkirkshire—he engaged in his "border raids," exploring the country, collecting ballads and tales, and generally enjoying the hospitality of many and various true and traditional Scottish characters. To that activity, he added a deep interest in German literature; he learned the language (but not the formal grammar) well enough to read and to translate, publishing in 1799 an edition of Johann

*Sir Walter Scott* (Library of Congress)

Wolfgang von Goethe's *Goetz von Berlichingen* (1774), one of that writer's earliest heroic creations in which an old knight bows to the forces of decay about him. Scott did not emerge as a public figure, however, until about six years later, when he published *The Lay of the Last Minstrel*. In rather quick succession, he became a partner in and large contributor to James Ballantyne's publishing house, gained a permanent appointment (1806) as clerk of session at Edinburgh, and was a principal founder (along with John Murray the younger) of *Quarterly Review*, the Tory rival to *Edinburgh Review*. In 1813, he declined the honor of being named poet laureate of England in favor of Robert Southey. A year later, his first novel, *Waverley*, was published.

As sheriff of Selkirkshire, Scott went, in 1804, to live at Ashestiel, on the banks of the River Tweed (dividing England and Scotland); there he wrote, between 1805 and 1813, *The Lay of the Last Minstrel*, *Marmion*, *The Lady of the Lake*, *The Vision of Don Roderick*, *The Bridal of Triermain*, and *Rokeby*. In 1812, he had begun the construction of a baronial mansion at Abbotsford (near Melrose in Roxburghshire)—once known as the little farm of Cartleyhole belonging to the monks of Melrose. After taking up residence there he could, indeed, lay claim to the title of "gentleman." He continued to reap financial benefits from his writing, and in 1820, he received a baronetcy. He would, however, be denied the luxury of lasting contentment. Economic depression swept the British Isles in 1825; a year later, the firm of John Ballantyne and Company collapsed, and Scott found himself being left responsible (morally and actually) for most of the publishing house's debts. Rather than declaring bankruptcy, the poet-novelist pressed forward on a number of literary projects to pay his creditors. To compound the emotional strain and the problems of failing health, Scott's wife, Charlotte Carpentier, died in the same year.

Thus, the last several years of Scott's life were marked by struggle and overwork; he was kept afloat, so to speak, on the strength of his pride and personal integrity. By 1831, his health had declined seriously; an Admiralty frigate carried him on a sea voyage through the Mediterranean; he had been sent off from Abbotsford with a fresh sonnet by Wordsworth. While on board, he suffered a stroke of apoplexy resulting in pa-

ralysis and was forced to return to Abbotsford. There he lingered, from mid-July, 1832, until September 21, when he died quietly in the presence of all his children.

## ANALYSIS

Sir Walter Scott's poetry, unlike that of his Romantic contemporaries, is vigorous, high-spirited, and unreflective. Scott delighted in war and pageantry, in the rich traditions of antiquity. As a Scottish poet born among a people who sought action, he was drawn to his heritage, to his connections with the border chieftains and the House of Buccleuch. Thus, his narrative poems and ballads reflect the character of a strong and proud man who, though he was lame, dreamed of the ultimate masculine activities: of chivalry, adventure, the qualities of feudalism, and the military picturesqueness of another age.

### BALLADS

Any survey of Scott the poet must consider his interest in the popular ballad, an interest that came naturally because of the love for the old, harsh times. Scott saw in the popular Scottish ballad a contrast to the relative serenity of his own early nineteenth century. He relished the clannish loyalties, the bravery, the cruelty, the revenge, and the superstitions of the old ballads. Thus, he began with "The Chase" and "William and Helen" (1796)—two translations from the German lyric poet (and, coincidentally, lawyer) Gottfried August Burger (1747-1794); next came three strange, almost mystical ballads contributed to Matthew Gregory "Monk" Lewis's *Tales of Wonder* in 1801: "Glenfinlas," "The Eve of St. John," and "The Gray Brother." His interest in the ballad reached its height—a scholarly as well as a poetic pinnacle—with *The Minstrelsy of the Scottish Border*, wherein Scott the editor and poet gathered and polished the best examples of what will always be considered the true literature of Scotland.

The ballad, however, was not to be the end-all for Scott the poet, but rather a springboard to other forms and variations of ballad themes. He turned his poetic attention to a series of complex and ornamental romances wherein, instead of the harshness and rusticity of the border, lords, ladies, and even clerics came forth to expound lofty themes in elevated language. Still, the stuff from which the popular ballads sprang is there. In *The*

*Lay of the Last Minstrel*, for example, romantic love blends easily with magic, dwarfs, and goblins, while in *Marmion*, the early sixteenth century battle at Flodden Field in Northumberland, where the English, in 1513, defeated the Scots under James IV, allowed Scott to develop elaborate descriptions of conflict and chivalry, of the detailed instruments of warfare and the awesomeness of border castles. More important in terms of the ballad influence, *Marmion* draws considerable poetic life from its thoroughly romantic narrative—from intrigue, disguise, and unfaithfulness (both clerical and secular). *The Lady of the Lake* intensifies those actions, featuring Highland clans rushing to battle after being summoned by a fiery cross. Scott carried his readers on a tour of chieftain's lodge and king's court, setting the stage for James Fitz-James to reveal himself as King James and to restore the noble Ellen to her true love, Malcolm Graeme. Although the later poems—*The Vision of Don Roderick*, *Rokeby*, and *Harold the Dauntless*—reveal Scott as more than ready to abandon verse for prose fiction, the worlds of knighthood, sorcery, and the ancient bards and minstrels continued to fascinate him—no matter that the locales and circumstances seemed far removed from that wild terrain north of the River Tweed.

### HISTORY AND NARRATIVE

One must not too quickly assume that Scott's poetry contains little beyond historical or romantic re-creations. Although he himself readily admitted that his work did not rise to the levels of Wordsworth or Coleridge, he nevertheless remained a legitimate poet, not simply a compiler and reviser of historical verse tales. Scott fully realized the depth and complexity of human emotions; he chose, however, to portray the manifestations of those emotions within the context of his own historical knowledge and his own historical imagination. Thus, he could set forth value judgments and insights into history rather than simply displaying the past as mere background scenery. Scott knew only too well that he was living in the present—in a world marked by political and social revolution to which the romantic past must, for the sake of reason and order, subordinate itself. Nevertheless, history could continue to instruct the present; it could also amuse and it could momentarily ease the confusion within the minds of the poet's readers. History could help a restless and degenerate age to imagine the heroics of an older time.

With only a few exceptions, the poetry of Scott conveys action and excitement, for the poet had learned at an early age to master the conventions of narrative. But narration alone could not carry the essence of the poem. In *The Lady of the Lake*, he demonstrated the quality of painting lovely scenery, giving it dimension, and fusing it skillfully with the poetry of clan life. Scott opened the gates to the Scottish Highlands for his cultivated readers to the south. For the height of action and excitement, however, those same readers had to turn to *Marmion*, to the strong horse striding over green terrain in the fresh air, its shrill neighing and the sun's rays reverberating and reflecting from the shield and the lance of its rider. In fact, the poet stacked his details one upon the other in almost breathless fashion: "Green, sanguine, purple, red, and blue,/ Broad, narrow, swallow-tailed, and square,/ Scroll, pennon, pensil, brandrol."

### CHARACTERS

The major weakness of Scott as a poet is his inability to create believable characters. Margaret of Branksome Hall (in *The Lay of the Last Minstrel*) exudes considerable charm, but she does little beyond fulfilling her function as the typical "fair maid," even amid a fast-paced series of armed encounters and magical spells. Roderick Dhu, Malcolm Graeme, and Lord James Douglas (*The Lady of the Lake*) appear active enough, but they have little else to do aside from their obvious responsibilities as fierce Highland chieftains, outlawed lords, and young knights. Also acting according to form (and little else) are Roland de Vaux (*The Bridal of Triermain*), Philip of Montham (*Rokeby*), and Edith of Lorn and Lord Ronald (both from *The Lord of the Isles*)—although Edith's disguise as a mute page, as well as the dangers she encounters, allows her some room for depth and variety. There is little doubt that Scott's best poetic characters assume the forms not of romantic heroes but of heroic scoundrels, such as the stately forger Marmion and the pirate Bertram Risingham (*Rokeby*), whose evil nature contains some elements of good. Scott addressed this problem himself, stating that no matter how hard he had tried to do otherwise, his rogues emerged as heroes. More accurately, the rogues had more life and depth than did the heroes.

## NATURE

Scott's ballads and verse tales are not, however, anchored to the issues of characterization, to the conflicts between good and evil, or even to the differences between heroes and villains. Virtually obliterating the shallowness of those characters, the poet's almost passionate love for the beauties of nature infuses practically every poem. In that sense, and within the context of his abilities to communicate that love to a relatively large and varied reading audience, Scott may indeed be identified with the early Romantic poets. Traditionally, his sophisticated English readership perceived Scotland—especially the Highlands—as a physical and intellectual wilderness; at best, readers of that day recalled only the Gothic descriptions of James Macpherson's Ossianic poems or the Addisonian sketches of the essayist Henry Mackenzie. Then, with *The Lay of the Last Minstrel*, *Marmion*, and *The Lady of the Lake*, Scott revealed the culture of his native land, and "Cold diffidence, and age's frost,/ In the full tide of my song were lost." He carried his readers on his poetic back "Across the furzy hills of Braid," through "all the hill with yellow grain," and over "To eastern Lodon's fertile plain"; through Scott's lines, his readers far to the south undertook a vicarious trek into a land that had been virtually shut off from their imaginations.

In addition to satisfying the imaginative needs of his Romantic-age readers, Scott conscientiously guided them through an almost microscopic study of physical nature, as if he were conducting a tour: going over each scene, textbook in hand, noting the various species of plants and shrubs, stones and rocks, surveying "each naked precipice,/ Sable ravine, and dark abyss" to uncover "Some touch of Nature's genial glow." For example, in the description of Lake Coriskin (in *The Lord of the Isles*), the landscape portrait captures the warmth of nature and the poet's feeling for color: In addition to the genial glow of Nature, "green mosses grow" atop Benmore, while "health-bells bud in deep Glencoe"—all of which serves up a sharp contrast to the "Black waves, bare crags, and banks of stone" that constitute the "bleakest" side of the mountain. Again, in depicting Edinburgh and the camp in *Marmion*, the poet directs his audience to the "rose on breezes thin" that clash headlong with "Saint Giles's mingling din" as

he strives to document the specifics of the distance (topographical and imaginative) "from the summit to the plain."

## CRITICAL ASSESSMENTS

Critical response to Scott's poetry has ranged from kindness to indifference. Perhaps the fairest assessment of his poetry is Scott's own. He never aspired to equal Wordsworth or Coleridge or Byron; he wanted only to enjoy life and literature (indeed, even in that order), disclaiming everything beyond the love of Scotland and its traditions. That love obviously led him to poetry, as it did to prose fiction, to biography, to history, and to scholarly editing and collecting. When he finished with one of those aspects of the good, intellectual life, he simply went on to something else. Literary history must be prepared to accept Scott on his own terms and on that middle ground.

## OTHER MAJOR WORKS

LONG FICTION: *Waverley: Or, 'Tis Sixty Years Since*, 1814; *Guy Mannering*, 1815; *The Antiquary*, 1816; *The Black Dwarf*, 1816; *Old Mortality*, 1816; *Rob Roy*, 1817; *The Heart of Midlothian*, 1818; *The Bride of Lammermoor*, 1819; *Ivanhoe*, 1819; *A Legend of Montrose*, 1819; *The Abbot*, 1820; *The Monastery*, 1820; *Kenilworth*, 1821; *The Pirate*, 1821; *The Fortunes of Nigel*, 1822; *Peveril of the Peak*, 1823; *Quentin Durward*, 1823; *St. Ronan's Well*, 1823; *Redgauntlet*, 1824; *The Betrothed*, 1825; *The Talisman*, 1825; *Woodstock*, 1826; *The Fair Maid of Perth*, 1828; *Anne of Geierstein*, 1829; *Castle Dangerous*, 1831; *Count Robert of Paris*, 1831; *The Siege of Malta*, 1976.

SHORT FICTION: "Wandering Willie's Tale," 1824; *Chronicles of the Canongate*, 1827 (2 volumes); "Death of the Laird's Jock," 1828; "My Aunt Margaret's Mirror," 1828; "The Tapestried Chamber," 1828.

PLAYS: *Halidon Hill*, pb. 1822; *Macduff's Cross*, pb. 1823; *The House of Aspen*, pb. 1829; *Auchindrane: Or, The Ayrshire Tragedy*, pr., pb. 1830; *The Doom of Devorgoil*, pb. 1830.

NONFICTION: *The Life and Works of John Dryden*, 1808; *The Life of Jonathan Swift*, 1814; *Lives of the Novelists*, 1825; *The Life of Napoleon Buonaparte: Emperor of the French, with a Preliminary View of the French Revolution*, 1827; *Religious Discourses by a*

*Layman*, 1828; *Tales of a Grandfather*, 1828-1830 (12 volumes); *The History of Scotland*, 1829-1830; *Letters on Demonology and Witchcraft*, 1830; *The Journal of Sir Walter Scott*, 1890.

TRANSLATIONS: *"The Chase," and "William and Helen": Two Ballads from the German of Gottfried Augustus Bürger*, 1796; *Goetz of Berlichingen, with the Iron Hand*, 1799 (of Johann Wolfgang von Goethe).

EDITED TEXTS: *Minstrelsy of the Scottish Border*, 1802-1803 (3 volumes); *A Collection of Scarce and Valuable Tracts*, 1809-1815 (13 volumes); *Chronological Notes of Scottish Affairs from the Diary of Lord Fountainhall*, 1822.

## BIBLIOGRAPHY

Bold, Alan, ed. *Sir Walter Scott: The Long-Forgotten Melody*. London: Vision Press, 1983. Nine essays cover such subjects in Scott's works as the image of Scotland, politics, and folk tradition and draw on Scott's poetry for illustration. The essay by Iain Crichton Smith, "Poetry in Scott's Narrative Verse," shows appreciation for the art of the poetry. Includes endnotes and an index.

Crawford, Thomas. *Scott*. Rev. ed. Edinburgh: Scottish Academic Press, 1982. A revision and elaboration of Crawford's widely acclaimed study of Scott. Examines Scott's work as a poet, balladist, and novelist.

Goslee, Nancy Moore. *Scott the Rhymer*. Lexington: University Press of Kentucky, 1988. Aiming to restore Scott as a poet, this book analyzes in detail his major poems. A discussion of *The Lay of the Last Minstrel* is followed by examinations of the long poems from *Marmion* to *Harold the Dauntless*. These poems are affirmations of romance within self-reflexive frames of irony. Contains ample notes and an index.

Lauber, John. *Sir Walter Scott*. Boston: Twayne, 1989. A good starting point for a study of Scott. The first three chapters provide an overview of Scott's career; the rest provide discussions of the novels. Includes a chronology and a select bibliography.

Lincoln, Andrew. *Walter Scott and Modernity*. Edinburgh: Edinburgh University Press, 2007. Lincoln examines Scott's use of the past to explore issues in the modern world. He analyzes both widely read poems and Scott's better-known novels.

Mitchell, Jerome. *Scott, Chaucer, and Medieval Romance: A Study in Sir Walter Scott's Indebtedness to the Literature of the Middle Ages*. Lexington: University Press of Kentucky, 1987. Describes the influences of Geoffrey Chaucer and medieval romances at work in Scott's narrative poetry, early novels, middle novels written during his financial collapse, and novels of the darkly declining years. The style and structure of the novels are analyzed before a conclusion is drawn. Augmented by preface, notes, and an index.

Scott, Sir Walter. *The Journal of Sir Walter Scott*. Edited by W. E. K. Anderson. Edinburgh: Canongate, 1998. Scott's journals offer invaluable biographical insights into his life and work. Includes bibliographical references and index.

Sutherland, John. *The Life of Walter Scott*. Cambridge, Mass.: Blackwell, 1995. A narrative account that penetrates into the darker areas of Scott's life. The value of Scott's writing today as much as in his heyday is justified by Sutherland's account.

Todd, William B., and Ann Bowden. *Sir Walter Scott: A Bibliographical History, 1796-1832*. New Castle, Del.: Oak Knoll Press, 1998. Lists variant editions of the verse as well as the fiction, and casts light on Scott's occupations as advocate, sheriff, antiquarian, biographer, editor, historian, and reviewer.

Tulloch, Graham. *The Language of Walter Scott: A Study of His Scottish and Period Language*. London: Andre Deutsch, 1980. In eight chapters and two appendices, Tulloch examines Scott's use of Scotch-English in his poetry and fiction. The special features of the language are analyzed in terms of vocabulary, grammar, and spelling. Scott's reading is also examined as a source of his language materials. Includes a bibliography and an index.

*Samuel J. Rogal*

# SIR CHARLES SEDLEY

**Born:** Aylesford, Kent, England; March, 1639
**Died:** Hampstead, London, England; August 20, 1701

PRINCIPAL POETRY

"The Indifference: Thanks, fair *Vrania* to your
    Scorn," 1672
"Song: Love still has something of the Sea," 1672
"Song: Not *Celia* that I juster am," 1672
"To Cloris: *Cloris* I cannot say your Eyes," 1672
Prologue to *Epsom Wells*, 1673 (play by Thomas
    Shadwell)
"Advice to the Old Beaux: Scrape no more your
    harmless Chins," 1693
Prologue to *The Wary Widow or Sir Noisy Parrat*,
    1693 (play by Henry Higden)
"The Knotting Song: Hears not my *Phillis* how the
    Birds," 1694
*The Happy Pair*, 1702
*The Miscellaneous Works of the Honourable Sir
    Charles Sedley, Bart.*, 1702
"Song: *Phillis* is my only Joy," 1702
"Song: Smooth was the Water, calm the Air," 1702

OTHER LITERARY FORMS

Sir Charles Sedley (SEHD-lee) was also known for
his plays during his lifetime. His first theatrical venture
was translating an act of Pierre Corneille's *La Mort de
Pompée* (pr. 1643; *The Death of Pompey*, 1663) as a
joint project with Edmund Waller, Robert Filmer, Baron
Buckhurst, and Sidney Godolphin; it was performed in
1664 as *Pompey the Great*. Later plays include *The
Mulberry Garden* (pr., pb. 1668), *Antony and Cleopatra* (pr., pb. 1677), and *Bellamira: Or, The Mistress*
(pr., pb. 1687). Sedley's plays were treated with respect
during the Restoration and proved moderately successful at the box office, but they have not survived their era
in performance. They are available in Vivian de Sola
Pinto's 1928 edition of Sedley's works.

ACHIEVEMENTS

Sir Charles Sedley is remembered today as an important figure in a minor literary group: the Restoration

court poets, sometimes known as the court wits or the
merry gang of Charles II. The earl of Rochester is the
most prominent poet in this group; Sedley ranks immediately after him. In his own time, Sedley was known as
a man of taste and was as famous for his wit and conversation as for his writings. His judgment on a new play
or poem could help to establish or destroy a literary reputation. Today, Sedley is best known for his lyric love
poetry. The most immediately apparent elements in
his songs are a clever use of persuasion and an underlying Epicurean philosophy. In his biography of Sedley
(1927), Vivian de Sola Pinto has noted that as a group
the Restoration court poets represent "the triumph of
the intellectual and logical side of the Renaissance over
the imaginative and emotional elements." This gener-
alization surely applies to Sedley, who was a poet of
direct statement and controlled feeling rather than of
elaborate conceits and grand passion.

BIOGRAPHY

Sir Charles Sedley was born into a Cavalier family
and grew up during Oliver Cromwell's Protectorate. In
1656, he inherited his title on the death of his brother,
and in February, 1657, he married Katherine Savage. In
December, 1657, they had a daughter, Katherine, who
would become the mistress of James II. Sometime during the 1660's, Lady Sedley, suffering from the delusion that she was a queen, went permanently insane. In
1672, Sedley arranged for her to be removed to a convent in France, where she died in 1705, outliving her
husband by four years. After her departure, Sedley
formed a permanent relationship with Ann Ayscough,
with whom he had a son, Charles, in 1672.

Sedley was among the group of young gentlemen
who became the court favorites of Charles II upon his
restoration to the throne in 1660. He quickly established himself in the vanguard of the king's merry
gang, a group known for its riotous living and dangerous atheistic views. His most scandalous behavior occurred at the Cock Tavern in 1663. Sedley had been
drinking with several gentlemen when he appeared
nude on the balcony of the tavern before a crowd and
proceeded to deliver a mock sermon, which was offensive in both its content and mode of delivery. A trial followed, and for his indiscreet behavior, Sedley was

fined two thousand marks, half of which is believed to have been remitted by the king. Sedley's behavior during the 1660's was by all accounts fairly wild, but by the early 1670's, he had reformed, quite possibly as a result of the good influence of Ann Ayscough.

Despite his reputation for debauchery in the first decade of the Restoration, Sedley was not given solely to the pursuit of pleasure. Early in his life, he involved himself in public affairs. He was elected to Parliament in 1668 and was apparently sent to France in 1670 on an important diplomatic mission with the earl of Buckingham, Buckhurst, and Sir George Savile. He retained his seat in Parliament for most of his life, performing his most distinguished service during the reign of William III.

Sedley also pursued a second career in letters. He was not a prolific poet, but there is a consistent production of poems and plays from each decade of his life beginning with the 1660's. He may well have written more poems than have actually survived, for most of his verse was not written for publication. When his poems did appear in print, they were frequently anonymous. Since Sedley made no effort to collect his writings during his lifetime, undoubtedly much of his work was lost. The extant poems were intended to entertain a small group who belonged to the same class and knew one another personally. Poetry was a necessary accomplishment for a courtier, and poems were passed in manuscript within the court society.

Sedley's poems were remarkably consistent throughout his life, with the poems dating from the 1690's appearing to be cut from the same cloth as those written in the 1660's. Even though Sedley's world changed radically during his lifetime and most of his contemporaries had either died or stopped writing by the 1690's, these changes are not reflected in the substance or style of Sedley's poetry. In like manner, the changes in Sedley's personal life are not reflected in his poetry. At first glance, the poems appear to be graceful exercises on a variety of familiar literary themes, as noteworthy for the well-turned phrase as for any probing insights into the human experience, but they do reflect the spirit of an age. In *Restoration Carnival* (1954), Pinto notes that Sedley's poems "grew directly out of his life and are a natural product of the society in which he

*Sir Charles Sedley* (Archive Photos/Getty Images)

lived." Nowhere in his life or writings is there any indication that Sedley seriously challenged the values or customs of Restoration society. He lived his life in accordance with the rational skepticism of his class and era and is reported to have "died like a philosopher without fear or superstition." Thus, the consistency of his poetry may well be a reflection of the consistency of his life.

ANALYSIS

Most of Sir Charles Sedley's songs deal with familiar love themes. There are a number of ladies who are alternately encouraging or discouraging, and whose beauty is so striking that it has turned the poet's fancy. The poet is concerned not so much to praise the lady's charms as to persuade her to yield to the pressing demands of time and nature. Sedley was known in his day for the love invitation. Rochester, in "An Allusion to Horace," praises Sedley as a master of persuasion: "*Sidley*, has that prevailing, gentle Art,/ That can with a resistless Charm impart,/ The loosest wishes, to the chastest Heart." A number of Sedley's poems are obviously intended to encourage a lady to yield her virtue. Here, for example, is a short untitled piece on the way the poet passes lonely nights:

> Awake, my Eyes, at Night my Thought[s] pursue
> Your charming Shape; and find it ever new;
> If I my weary Eyes to Sleep resign,
> In gaudy Dreams your Love and Beauty shine;
> Dreams with such Extasies and Pleasures fill'd,
> As to those Joys they seem can only yield;
> Nor do they yield perhaps, wou'd you allow,
> Fair *Amidea*, that I once might know.

Rochester might have been thinking of this poem when he wrote his tribute to Sedley's art. The poem could be part of the sophisticated love games that were played in the comedies of the day, including Sedley's *The Mulberry Garden* and *Bellamira*. To create a feeling of longing within Amidea's heart, the poet employs an argument involving the lover's thwarted expectations of "Extasies," "Pleasures," and "joys," which are realized only in dreams. If one were to extend the argument beyond the poem, one would say that it goes against nature to thwart the fulfillment of such pleasures.

This argument is one more version of an important theme in most of Sedley's love lyrics: the pursuit and realization of pleasure. In a Sedley lyric, there are no metaphysical flights that take the reader into another country; the poet is concerned with securing his ease and pleasure in this world. In "An Essay on Satyr," John Sheffield, earl of Mulgrave, later duke of Buckinghamshire, notes that "little *Sid*" "Pleasure has always sought, but seldom found:/ Tho' Wine and Women are his only Care,/ Of both he takes a lamentable Share." Most of Mulgrave's portrait, which dates from 1679, involves a nasty attack on the reforms in Sedley's personal life. Nevertheless, for all its venom, it contains a basic truth about Sedley the poet: He always sought pleasure. This statement applies to the late as well as the early works.

### "To Liber" and "Out of Lycophron"

This strain of Epicureanism is more than only a ploy in the love game; it is a philosophical principle that was widely held in the Restoration. Sedley presents an Epicurean philosophy most explicitly in two translations

from the ancients: "Out of Lycophron" and "To Liber." Sedley's translation of Lycophron, an Alexandrian dramatist who lived in the third century B.C.E., stresses the limits of human understanding. Man does not know

> Whither he goes to Heaven or Hell;
> Or after a few moments dear,
> He disappear,
> And at last,
> Perish entirely like a Beast.

He should therefore not waste his time pondering what is unknowable; rather, he should give himself over to "Women, Wine and Mirth." The tone of this poem is complacent and urbane. There is none of the questioning and rage that one finds in Rochester when he confronts the possibilities of "Nothing." For Lycophron, life is reduced to "a few Moments dear." Even though man in death may be reduced to the status of a beast, Sedley's smooth verse takes the rough edges off this grim knowledge. He uses the possibility of nothing only as an argument to encourage man to secure his pleasure in this life. This Epicurean philosophy is even more emphatically stated in "To Liber," a translation of a Martial epigram. The speaker could be one Restoration gentleman giving another gentleman advice on how to spend his time most profitably. Thus, Liber should think "on charming Objects" and let "easie Beauty warm" his heart. The pursuit of pleasure and the easy satisfaction of appetite are sufficient as guiding principles.

### Pleasure and flirtation

The love lyrics fall into two main categories: those in which the speaker self-consciously considers his own pleasure and ease and how well they are served and those in which the speaker is an active participant in a flirtation, using his art and cleverness to secure the interest of a particular lady. Part of the charm of the poems in this second category is Sedley's obvious delight in the progress of a flirtation.

Two songs addressed to Phillis—"Phillis, let's shun the common Fate" and "*Phillis* is my only Joy"—fall into the first category. The speaker is as concerned with his own pleasure and ease as with the feelings or needs of Phillis. In the first song, the speaker states his theme in the opening lines: "*Phillis*, let's shun the common

Fate,/ And let our Love ne'r turn to Hate." The speaker defines the limits of love, the point at which love ceases to be a pleasure and becomes a burden. The only way to avoid love turning to hate is to leave off loving at the first signs of boredom or disinterest. Thus, the speaker will "dote no longer" than he can, and the couple will part when they begin "to want Discourse,/ And Kindness seems to taste of Force." The speaker envisions love in terms of mild, if delectable, pleasures: "A Smile of thine shall make my Bliss,/ I will enjoy thee in a Kiss." If Phillis should stop loving first, the speaker will "the Blame on Nature lay" and accept his fate without rancor but rather with pride "in Parting well." Love, then, is a kind of bargain. If one does not invest too much of himself in a love relationship, one will experience a fine pleasure and avoid needless pain and suffering.

In "*Phillis* is my only Joy," Sedley celebrates the pleasures that are secured at the price of self-deception. In the second line, the speaker announces that Phillis is as "Faithless as the Winds or Seas," but the rest of the first stanza is about the pleasure he receives from Phillis: She "never fails to please," and she makes him "Happier than before." In the second stanza, the speaker deals with the problems of Phillis's faithlessness, but he reduces it to a game, perhaps best suggested by the telling couplet, "She deceiving,/ I believing." The sense of balance in these two lines and elsewhere suggests that the speaker's self-deception is simply the price he knowingly and willingly pays to secure his own pleasure. When he asks in the final line, "What need Lovers wish for more?" the obvious answer is "Nothing."

In the second main category of Sedley love lyrics, the speaker is an active participant in a flirtation. In such poems, he does not analyze how well his ease and pleasure are served. Rather, his pleasure is revealed by his obvious delight in the business at hand. A number of these verses appear to be designed for real occasions. The most obvious example is "To Amaranta Whom He Fell in Love with at a Play-House." Pinto suggests that the occasion for this poem may have been an encounter between Sedley and a masked lady at the King's House in Drury Lane, which was reported by Samuel Pepys in his diary. The conversation between the two was so sparkling and entertaining that it proved more interest-

ing to Pepys than the performance of *The Maid's Tragedy* (pr. 1610-1611). The situation in the poem is dramatic. The speaker encounters a beauty at a playhouse; he soon finds himself experiencing the emotions of the "feigned Love" on the stage: "The Hopes and Fears, in every Scene exprest,/ Grew soon th' uneasie Motions of my Breast." The poet first engages in some idle banter; "And if I ventur'd on some slight Discourse,/ It should be such as could no Passion nurse." Soon he finds himself ensnared ("At last I play'd too near the Precipice"), and then love breaks through like a force—a cultivated force—of nature:

> Your Words fell on my Passion, like those Showers,
> Which paint and multiply the rising Flowers;
> Like *Cupid*'s self, a God, and yet a Child,
> Your Looks at once were awful, and yet mild.

Not all of Sedley's poems deal with such casual flirtations. Many pay direct compliments to a lady of virtue; some even declare an undying fidelity. Yet even in these poems there is frequently an underlying Epicureanism marking them as the work of Sedley. In one of Sedley's most famous songs, "Not *Celia*, that I juster am," the speaker declares his devotion to Celia. He "would change each Hour" like the rest of humankind, but such are the charms of Celia that he has no choice but to stay where his heart is "at rest." When he concludes that "'Tis easie to be true," it is clear that ease is the condition that permits him to be true.

The presence in the Sedley canon of this poem and several others declaring the speaker's faithfulness creates a minor problem. It is possible to read most of the poems simply as graceful exercises on a variety of common literary themes with no biographical relevance. After all, Sedley wrote lyrics into the 1690's that celebrate the pleasures of flirtation and inconstancy. Nevertheless, there are some poems that invite a more personal interpretation. For example, in *Restoration Carnival*, Pinto calls "Not *Celia*, that I juster am" Sedley's "one great love song" in which he sings of his "real ideal . . . the tranquility of a happy marriage of true minds." Such an assertion is not warranted by the poem itself. Why should the speaker in the Celia poem be closer to Sedley's own feelings than the speaker in one of the Phillis poems?

There are at least two ways to explain this phenomenon. First, all Sedley's poems may have a degree of personal relevance, the seeming contradiction between the speaker of different poems being more apparent than real. The courtiers of the Restoration considered libertinism and marriage to be two separate areas of their lives. Rochester, famous for his many sexual escapades, was by all accounts a devoted and affectionate husband and father. Heroes in Restoration comedies such as Dorimant in Sir George Etherege's *The Man of Mode: Or, Sir Fopling Flutter* (pr., pb. 1676) also display the same balance between the life of the libertine and the life of a husband. At the end of Etherege's play, Dorimant is not so much reforming as adding to his life by taking on a wife and engaging in a richer, fuller love relationship than he had experienced before. Second, the sentiments expressed in the Celia poem do appear to have a relevance to certain events in Sedley's life. He may have led the life of a libertine in the early years of his marriage, but when he found the right woman, he publicly declared his devotion to her and committed himself to her for life by going through a form of marriage in 1672 and treating her as his wife for the next thirty years. For Sedley, the concept of marriage was far more important than its legal definition.

### LOVE AND MARRIAGE

Some of Sedley's poems, such as "Constancy," deal with a "marriage of true minds" in which physical attraction is simply the beginning of a long-lasting relationship. This understanding of marriage is at the heart of "To Cloris: *Cloris*, I justly am betray'd," which Pinto sees as being addressed to Ann Ayscough. The poet begins by frankly admitting that he had laid a trap for Cloris, thinking "at first with a small Sum/ Of Love, thy Heap to overcome." The reverse happens, and the poet makes a full declaration of his love, even though he is prevented from marrying Cloris:

> My Hand, alas, is no more mine,
> Else it had long ago been thine;
> My Heart I give thee, and we call
> No Man unjust that parts with all.

So ends the poem in the 1702 edition. In the original 1672 publication of the poem there was an additional couplet: "What a priest says moves not the mind,/ Souls are by love, not words, combin'd." In this couplet, Sedley presents his basic view of marriage, which remained consistent throughout his life: Love, rather than social custom, determines a marriage. In *The Happy Pair*, a late poem written in the ratiocinative style of John Dryden's *Religio Laici* (1682), the poet dwells on the horrors of the marriage bed when love is not present:

> With feign'd Embrace they seem Love's Joys to crave,
>     But with their Bed, converted to a Grave:
> And whilst their backward Hearts like Load-stones meet,
>     They wish their Linnen were the Windingsheet.

The imagery is surprisingly vivid. Sedley is rarely as explicit about the joys of love as he is about the miseries of a mercenary marriage in these lines. His poem ends with a paean to the joys of a lowly marriage where both partners are poor but truly in love. Such a union may belong to a pastoral ideal, but in *The Happy Pair*, it is set against the distorted emotions and values of upper-class life, which destroy the chances for true love.

Sedley's views on marriage are consistent with his Epicureanism. If pleasure is the be-all and end-all of existence, love in marriage is the most satisfying pleasure. When love is missing, the marriage is a mockery. Presumably Sedley's unfortunate experience in marrying at a young age for the wrong reasons had taught him this lesson. In *The Restoration Court Poets* (1965), Pinto notes that the conclusion of *The Happy Pair* "with its praise of quiet domesticity shows that the wild gallant of the sixteen-sixties had by the end of the century developed into an Augustan 'man of feeling.'"

### LEGACY

Sedley, however, is not remembered today as a forerunner of eighteenth century sentimentalism. He was a poet of his times. To a certain extent, he lived the life that is portrayed so vividly in the world of Restoration comedies, where style, wit, and pleasure are important ends in themselves. This world may not have been quite as amoral as is sometimes thought. The pursuit of pleasure does not rule out the cultivation of sentiment and deep, lifelong attachments, but in the Restoration, it did rule out pomposity and sentimentality. Sedley's poetry exemplifies the grace and wit of an age that too often is remembered only as a time of license and immorality.

OTHER MAJOR WORKS

PLAYS: *Pompey the Great*, pb. 1664 (translation of an act with Edmund Waller, Robert Filmer, Baron Buckhurst, and Sidney Godolphin); *The Mulberry Garden*, pr., pb. 1668; *Antony and Cleopatra*, pr., pb. 1677; *Bellamira: Or, The Mistress*, pr., pb. 1687.

BIBLIOGRAPHY

Hopkins, P. A. "Aphra Behn and John Hoyle: A Contemporary Mention, and Sir Charles Sedley's Poem on His Death." *Notes and Queries* 41, no. 2 (June, 1994): 176. Discusses the death of Hoyle and his relationship with Aphra Behn and includes an anlysis of Sedley's poem on Hoyle's death, "A Ballad, to the Tune of Bateman."

Pinto, Vivian de Sola. *Restoration Carnivals, Five Courtier Poets: Rochester, Dorset, Sedley, Etherege, and Sheffield*. London: Folio Society, 1954. By the compiler of the 1928 edition of Sedley's plays, this is a thoroughly illuminating analysis that reveals much about the poets and their works. Offers a worthy overview of Sedley and his poetic achievements. Complemented by a bibliography.

_____. *The Restoration Court Poets: John Wilmot, Earl of Rochester; Charles Sackville, Earl of Dorset; Sir Charles Sedley; Sir George Etherege*. London: Longmans, Green, 1965. This volume compares and examines the critical and theoretical views of these four Restoration Court literary figures. The section on Sedley provides criticism helpful to an appreciation and understanding of Sedley's works.

_____. *Sir Charles Sedley, 1639-1701: A Study in the Life and Literature of the Restoration*. London: Longmans, Green, 1965. One of the few book-length works devoted to Sedley, by the well-known scholar of Restoration literature. Bibliography.

Vinson, James, ed. *Great Writers of the English Language: Poets*. Vol. 1. New York: St. Martin's Press, 1979. The entry by John H. Perry notes that Sedley, one of the chief poets of Charles II's reign, was primarily known for his love poems and songs. He claims that it was Sedley's satires, which betrayed the cynicism of the court, that made him less popular. Praises Sedley for his "perceptive eye and cutting pen."

Wilson, John Harold. *The Court Wits of the Restoration: An Introduction*. 1948. Reprint. New York: Octagon Books, 1967. Wilson provides a worthy overview and analysis of early modern English literature from 1500 to 1700 and offers a history and criticism of English wit and humor. He provides perspective on Sedley's life. Supplemented by a bibliography.

*Edward V. Geist*

---

# ROBERT W. SERVICE

**Born:** Preston, Lancashire, England; January 16, 1874

**Died:** Lancieux, France; September 11, 1958

PRINCIPAL POETRY

*Songs of a Sourdough*, 1907
*Ballads of a Cheechako*, 1909
*Rhymes of a Rolling Stone*, 1912
*The Rhymes of a Red Cross Man*, 1916
*The Shooting of Dan McGrew, and Other Verses*, 1920
*Ballads of a Bohemian*, 1921
*The Complete Poems*, 1933, enlarged 1938, enlarged 1942
*Twenty Bath-Tub Ballads*, 1939
*Bar-Room Ballads*, 1940
*Collected Poems*, 1940
*Songs of a Sun-Lover*, 1949
*Rhymes of a Roughneck*, 1950
*Lyrics of a Lowbrow*, 1951
*Rhymes of a Rebel*, 1952
*Songs for My Supper*, 1953
*Carols of an Old Codger*, 1954
*Rhymes for My Rags*, 1956
*Songs of the High North*, 1958
*Later Collected Verse*, 1965

OTHER LITERARY FORMS

Robert W. Service's novels never achieved any degree of literary significance or even popular acceptance; perhaps fiction simply allowed him some diversion from writing verse. The following titles, however, suggest the relationship between Service's poetry and his fiction: *The Trail of '98* (1910), *The Pretender: A Story of the Latin Quarter* (1914), *The Poisoned Paradise* (1922), *The Roughneck* (1923), *The Master of the Microbe* (1926), and *The House of Fear* (1927). Of greater value to the student are the three major autobiographical pieces, since each helps to cast some light upon both the poet and his work: *Why Not Grow Young? Or, Living for Longevity* (1928), *Ploughman of the Moon: An Adventure into Memory* (1945), and *Harper of Heaven: A Record of Radiant Living* (1948).

## Achievements

Perhaps the simplest way to come to grips with the poetry of Robert W. Service is to avoid the issue entirely and dismiss the man as little more than a terribly prolific balladeer, the writer of popular frontier verses that rhymed well enough to be memorized by schoolboys and sentimental adults but generally lacked poetic merit. A more reasonable approach would be to read the poetry in the light of Service's own intentions. Service saw himself as a grand combination of journalist and teller of tales (a twentieth century Scottish bard, if you will), whose medium was verse rather than the newspaper article or the short story. He preferred to roam certain parts of the world in search of characters whose stories had never really been told—or, at least, whose experiences had never reached a wide audience. In a sense, he listened to people who were themselves glad to come upon an eager listener; he transformed the details of those stories into rhythmic ballads for the benefit of still other listeners—his readers.

Apart from his poetry, he desired nothing more from life than to dream, to live as a recluse and a lover of liberty, to gaze in wonder at the beauty of the world, and to observe the complexities and the varieties of the human condition. At the same time, he was a practical man who realized early in life that freedom had to be bought with hard cash; thus, he wrote and worked for that freedom, and in the end he achieved it. His verse remained the natural outlet for his dreams, visions, and observations, the means by which he could share, with ordinary people, the mysteries and joys of human life.

As a poet, Service wanted to record, as quickly as possible, the actions and atmospheres of the moment; he did not waste time thinking—he simply saw and then he wrote. Thus, his readers were not required to approach his verse with any complex intellectual, cultural, or historical prerequisites; they needed only to read, to listen, and to imagine.

The achievement of Service may well be the triumph of a paradox, of a writer who wanted, essentially, to be left alone with himself and with his thoughts. Nevertheless, he knew that somehow he had to communicate with those around him and to convey to people the essence of myriad experiences (real and imagined) that otherwise they would never see or imagine. He would serve as the surrogate romantic for thousands of people inclined toward romanticism and independence yet rooted to practicality and convention. Service wrote easily, quickly, rhythmically—almost too simply. The boys whooping it up at the Malamute saloon, Sam McGee from Tennessee, the water where the silver salmon play, the great white silence of the wild, the absinthe drinkers of the Café de la Paix, the three grim and gory British Tommies, and the grimy men with picks and shovels—all came from the real world of his experience, but all belonged to the private world of his imagination as well.

Bret Harte and Eugene Field were Service's principal models. His poetry was strongly influenced by journalism; like the newspapermen who reported from Africa and the Far East, he sent poetic dispatches from the streets of Paris, the rough terrains of the Yukon, the Mackenzie basin, and the Arctic. Service's achievement was the triumph of verse as opposed to poetry; his poems appealed to the romantic young man in the tavern and to the equally romantic old spinster in the parlor. He thrust his heavily rhythmic songs into the hands of the schoolboy, who would recite them, and into the mind of the laborer, who would remember them. By his own admission, however, although he wrote for these people, he intended to please no one but himself.

## Biography

The eldest in a family of seven boys and three girls, Robert William Service was born in Preston, Lancashire, England, on January 16, 1874. His father, also

Robert Service, worked in a Scottish bank; his mother, Emily Parker, was the daughter of the English owner of a Lancashire cotton mill. From 1880 until 1895, young Service lived in Glasgow, where he received an education of some substance at the Hillhead High School. He also attended some classes at the university and engaged in a self-prescribed reading program at the public library and by way of Miss Bell's Circulating Library. The latter contributed significantly to his taste for literature and to his urge to travel abroad. Early realizing man's dependence upon money, Service worked at the Commercial Bank of Scotland. The drudgery of Glasgow, the bank, and schoolboy athletics, however, quickly gave way to romantic visions of Canada—of cowboys, gold prospectors, and beachcombers. The young man read pamphlets about Canada and set his sights on becoming a sturdy settler in a hard land—on raising grain, riding broncos, and roping steers. In 1895, he crossed the Atlantic aboard a tramp steamer, proceeded to British Columbia, and partook of the freedom of a backwoods ranch in the rough "wild west." From there, he made his way up and down the West Coast of the United States, enjoying still more freedom and learning about life on the road.

Despite his love for the vagabond life, Service had a strong practical streak, and in 1903, he determined that a steady job would allow him to save some money, which in turn would provide the necessary independence for writing, travel, and general leisure. After securing a position with the Canadian Bank of Commerce, he moved through its various branches: Victoria and Kamloops in British Columbia, and Dawson in the Yukon. This job was to provide him with more than a solid bank account. Between 1904 and 1912, Service witnessed as a bank clerk and recorded as a writer the decline of the Klondike gold rush that had begun three years after his arrival in Canada. Ironically, his own fortunes ran directly against the tide of the times; such poems as "The Shooting of Dan McGrew" and "The Cremation of Sam McGee" signaled the beginning of his own literary and financial strike.

"The Shooting of Dan McGrew" and "The Cremation of Sam McGee" were published in 1907, in Toronto, as parts of a larger collection titled *Songs of a Sourdough* (or, in New York, *The Spell of the Yukon,*

*Robert W. Service* (Hulton Archive/Getty Images)

*and Other Verses*). An insignificant novel, *The Trail of '98*, followed in 1910 and then a successful collection, *Rhymes of a Rolling Stone*, two years later. No longer in need of a banking career, Service left Canada in 1912 to cover, for the Toronto *Star*, the brief scuffle involving Turkey, Montenegro, Bulgaria, and Serbia known as the Balkan War. That experience introduced him to France and Paris. In 1913, he married Germaine Bourgoin, whose father owned a distillery outside Paris, and from that year, he maintained residences in France without renouncing his British citizenship. When World War I erupted, Service served first with an American ambulance unit and then with Canadian army intelligence, experiences recorded in *The Rhymes of a Red Cross Man*. After the war, he returned to the highways of the world: The circle began and ended at Paris, with intermediate stops in Hollywood and Tahiti.

Although his Hollywood experience encouraged him to write four additional pieces of pure melodrama between 1922 and 1927, those efforts did little to win

Service a reputation as a writer of serious fiction. Nevertheless, he continued to reap financial harvests from new verse collections and from complete editions of his poems. He determined to spend the remainder of his days in relative leisure, becoming a quiet and contented gentleman far different from the rough-and-tumble characters who roamed the lines of his ballads and autobiographical verse.

Between the wars, Service found time for two Russian journeys. Returning from the second one, he found himself cut off from his beloved France by World War II; he and his family spent the war years in Hollywood. In 1945, he returned once again to Brittany and Nice, purchased a villa at Monte Carlo, and published, between 1949 and 1956, seven separate volumes of verse and two volumes of his collected poetry. Service died of a heart attack on September 11, 1958—at the age of eighty-four—at his home (appropriately named Dream Haven) in Lancieux, Brittany.

ANALYSIS

The real difficulty in analyzing the poetic output of Robert W. Service is trying to separate the man from his work—if, indeed, such separation is possible or even necessary. No matter what the poem (for so many of them read as carbon copies of one another), there remains, at the end, the vision of the poet. The reader invariably sees the man of adventure and courage, the headstrong seeker of fame and fortune who, as a relatively young man, left Scotland and sailed for the American continent, there to see and to live with the last generation of pioneers, explorers, and true adventurers. Service detested any reference to himself as a "poet"; the word meant something higher than that to which he aspired or believed he could manage intellectually. To the last, he preferred to be known only as a verse writer, as one who had, since childhood, been talking and thinking in rhyme. In fact, he seemed more inclined toward the talking and the thinking than to expressing his observations and experiences on paper.

In many ways, Service's attitude and actions typified the wandering minstrel of another age, the vagabond strumming on the guitar, singing his own songs, talking about the old times, and telling of countless adventures (actual or imagined). Thus, from the pages of

his collected works echo the vigor and the harshness, the tragedy and the ribaldry of the fascinating northern wilderness of Canada. Service virtually immortalized a hundred treks of men and animals through snow and blizzard, privation and suffering, injury and death; yet he also captured in rhyme the sheer glamour and romance of a time when his distant readers equated money with gold dust, love and beauty with a heavily bespangled saloon girl, and art with a whiskey-reeking prospector banging away at an old barroom piano in the corner of a smoke-filled, noisy room. For Service, these were real people in the midst of real experiences—"comrades," he called them, persons with whom he had "tramped God's land together." The triteness and the clichés would come later, from the minds and pens of those who had never seen that about which they were to write and speak.

The "land God forgot" proved, however, to be merely a single stop on Service's personal poetic trek. France captured his heart and his rhythmic imagination, first during his bohemian days on the Left Bank, then while he served as a Red Cross ambulance driver during World War I. The songs written in the spring of 1914 reflect his bouts with poverty, when he had to write not for his living, but for his life. Nevertheless, the lines of those pieces are quick and happy attempts to shape the mood of one all too willing to spend his last sous not prudently on bread, but prodigally on beer. In "L'Escargot D'or," Service strolls down the Boul' Mich' in a lingering light that has all the exquisite tenderness of violet. The trees bow to him in their first translucent green; beneath, he sees lamps lit with the purest gold, while from the Little Luxembourg emanates a silver tingle of tiny voices. Boldly, he heads for the gay side of the street and enters the café, a place frequented at one time by Oscar Wilde and John Millington Synge, a place where one may "dream and drain,/ And drown despair." The strength of such poems lies in the reader's awareness that Service has no illusions about his mind or his art. Throughout the first part of *Ballads of a Bohemian*, he admits to not being fool enough to think of himself as a poet in the classical sense. Instead, he comes forth as one with a knack for rhyme and an intense love for making verse—or, from another point of view, for "tootling, tin-whistle music."

He asks only that his muse bring him bread and butter; if rhyme has been his ruin, he wants only to rhyme until the bitter end—to go down with what he wants to do, rather than be tied to what he has to do.

### WORLD WAR I

In August, 1914, however, the happy-go-lucky Bohemian from Glasgow saw the beginning of a world war. At forty, Service felt obliged to pack his happiness away in storage and apply his rhyme to a far different strain. Until that time, he later confessed, his verse had come from a land of his own making—a composite ground of hope, faith, and enthusiasm, of struggle, failure, and eventual triumph. With the coming of war, he believed he saw the end of what he termed "the exultant sunshine [of] our spirits" and the approach of "a deepening shadow of horror and calamity." While the poems of the Yukon carry a noisy, devil-may-care attitude ("there's 'hootch' in the bottle still"), the noise from France on the eve of World War I rings of frustration and fear and uneasiness, emanating from "nightmares of the past." In France, Service saw the shaping of minds in preparation for the battle; he comprehended the heredity and the discipline that sent village men out of their homes to seek barracks and battlefields and, eventually, death. His poems thus bemoan the docility with which farmers and tradesmen don baggy red trousers so as to let "some muddle-headed General" hurl them to destruction for some unknown cause or gain. To be shot in a saloon brawl in Dawson—"pitched on his head, and pumped full of lead"—is one thing; to be a father, a provider, and "fodder for cannon" is quite another matter.

### SONGS OF A SOURDOUGH

Rudyard Kipling's influence on Service (who at times seems to have committed the former's 1892 *Barrack-Room Ballads, and Other Verses* to memory) is quite apparent. Generally, Service favored vigorous description and narrative in long, swinging lines. In his first collection, *Songs of a Sourdough*, he illustrated fully the landscape of northern Canada, while at the same time capturing the fresh atmosphere of an almost unknown land. He wrote of lonely sunsets flaring forlornly down dreary and desolate valleys; of lordly mountains soaring scornfully, as still as death and as stern as fate; of the flames of lonely sunsets and giant valleys that consumed the night (except that his verb is "gulp"); of monster mountains scraping the sky; of an outcast, leper land that only the cry of the wolf can express, the lonely, "fell archspirit of the Wild." The poems of that place and of that period almost mirror one another ("Great White Silence," "The Call of the Wild," "The Spell of the Yukon," "The Law of the Yukon"), and the reader should notice particularly the violence of Service's adjectives, the crude satire in reference to men of a more normal and formal mode of existence, and the strong visual images of the naked grandeur of the land that the poet loved—even though God had forgotten it.

This land to which Service committed the early part of his adulthood made him a popular poet—and thus made him a wealthy man. However, he was able to extend his verse beyond the obvious level of "local color." Such poems as "The Shooting of Dan McGrew," "The Cremation of Sam McGee," and "The Ballad of the Black Fox Skin" became popular not only for the entertainment of their stories but also because the poet captured them in sound and rhythm. No doubt Service's yarns would have made first-rate short stories *à la* Bret Harte, Ambrose Bierce, or even Mark Twain. He chose, however, to condense and to versify those tales, giving them the force of brevity and rhyme, and wrapping them in neat packages of his own grim humor and quick command of alliterative phrasing.

Service is sometimes criticized for his failure to provide an accurate reflection of Canadian life. The error rests not with the poet, but with his audience. Service never sought to represent all aspects of Canadian existence. Instead, he chose to depict isolated conditions that prevailed at certain moments in the history of a remote section of the world; he captured with splendid specificity and rhyme the popular conception of the Canadian north.

Service the incurable romantic, the agent of free spirits everywhere, transported his fairly staid audience to the places where they could exercise their suppressed passions, their subconscious enthusiasm for the dangerous and the exciting. He carried to tens of thousands, in clear language and quick meter, the extreme Canadian north, the streets of Paris, the trenches of Flanders. Service possessed a limited but very practical poetic vision. Theories concerning poetry did not interest him. He sought only verse, and seemed quite content to follow the likes of Thomas Hood and Bret Harte, the real fashions of his day. He wanted, simply, to spend his days in the relative calm of his own privacy, testifying to "the rhapsody of existence," where youth and age might affirm "the ecstasy of being."

OTHER MAJOR WORKS

LONG FICTION: *The Trail of '98*, 1910; *The Pretender: A Story of the Latin Quarter*, 1914; *The Poisoned Paradise*, 1922; *The Roughneck*, 1923; *The Master of the Microbe*, 1926; *The House of Fear*, 1927.

NONFICTION: *Why Not Grow Young? Or, Living for Longevity*, 1928; *Ploughman of the Moon: An Adventure into Memory*, 1945; *Harper of Heaven: A Record of Radiant Living*, 1948.

BIBLIOGRAPHY

Athern, Stanley S. "The Klondike Muse." *Canadian Literature* 47 (Winter, 1971): 67-72. Athern encourages critics to examine the Klondike works of Service as a pioneering attempt to mythologize the Canadian gold rush as early environmental history. While not speaking highly of Service's talents, Athern gives valuable insight into Service's initial publications.

Berton, Pierre. *Prisoners of the North*. New York: Carroll & Graf, 2004. Historian Berton looks at some of Canada's most famous characters, including Service, who earned the money he desired but was saddled with the fame he sought to avoid.

Bucco, Martin. "Folk Poetry of Robert W. Service." *Alaska Review* 2 (Fall, 1965): 16-26. Bucco analyzes Service's Yukon poetry from the viewpoint that it used the search for gold as a metaphor for the quest for self. With this as his overriding theme, Bucco shows how Service created a vivid sense of tradition for the men who sought out the elusive riches buried in the forbidding North.

Burness, Edwina. "The Influence of Burns and Fergusson on the War Poetry of Robert Service." *Studies in Scottish Literature* 12 (1986): 135-146. Concentrates only on Service's war poetry and explores the influences that Robert Burns and Robert Fergusson had on Service. Burness draws interesting parallels between the men as she details the effects of realism, humor, and symbolism on the "universal" Scottish mind.

Hirsch, Edward. "A Structural Analysis of Robert Service's Yukon Ballads." *Southern Folklore Quarterly* 40 (March-June, 1976): 125-140. Hirsch suggests that Service's poetry should be judged by the aesthetics of oral traditions and not as literary artifacts. He analyzes some of Service's Yukon ballads as monologue compositions.

Klinck, Carl F. *Robert Service: A Biography*. New York: Dodd, Mead, 1976. Klinck's biography is invaluable in studying the life of this amazing poet. Drawing heavily on Service's two-volume autobiography, Klinck follows the poet's career, commenting on the influences that led to such a variance in the subject matter of Service's works.

Lockhart, G. W. *On the Trail of Robert Service*. Edinburgh: Luath Press, 1999. A short biography of Service and a narrative of his travels.

Mackay, James A. *Vagabond of Verse: Robert Service*. Edinburgh: Mainstream, 1995. An in-depth biography of Service. Includes bibliographical references and index.

Mallory, Enid. *Robert Service: Under the Spell of the Yukon*. Victoria, B.C.: Heritage House, 2006. This biography of Service focuses on his years in the Yukon and his Yukon poems. Contains a chapter on his parents.

Mitham, Peter J. *Robert W. Service: A Bibliography*. New Castle, Del.: Oak Knoll Press, 2000. This bibliography lists the works of Service, including his poetry.

*Richard E. Rogal*

# WILLIAM SHAKESPEARE

**Born:** Stratford-upon-Avon, Warwickshire, England;
    April 23, 1564
**Died:** Stratford-upon-Avon, Warwickshire, England;
    April 23, 1616

PRINCIPAL POETRY

*Venus and Adonis*, 1593
*The Rape of Lucrece*, 1594
*The Passionate Pilgrim*, 1599 (miscellany with
    poems by Shakespeare and others)
*The Phoenix and the Turtle*, 1601
*A Lover's Complaint*, 1609
*Sonnets*, 1609

OTHER LITERARY FORMS

William Shakespeare is perhaps the world's greatest dramatist—certainly, at the very least, the greatest to write in English. Of his thirty-seven plays, written over a career in the theater that spanned, roughly, 1588 to 1613, the most important are *Romeo and Juliet* (pr. c. 1595-1596); *Henry IV, Parts I* and *II* (pr. c. 1597-1598; 1598); *Hamlet, Prince of Denmark* (pr. c. 1600-1601); *Othello, The Moor of Venice* (pr. 1604); *Measure for Measure* (pr. 1604); *King Lear* (pr. c. 1605-1606); *Macbeth* (pr. 1606); *Antony and Cleopatra* (pr. c. 1606-1607); *The Winter's Tale* (pr. c. 1610-1611); and *The Tempest* (pr. 1611).

ACHIEVEMENTS

William Shakespeare also wrote some of the greatest love poems in English. His short erotic narratives, *Venus and Adonis* and *The Rape of Lucrece*, were typical examples of fashionable literary genres. Other minor poems include contributions to the miscellany *The Passionate Pilgrim* and *The Phoenix and the Turtle*, written for a collection of poems appended to *Love's Martyr* (1601), an allegorical treatment of love by Robert Chester. All these pale alongside the sonnets, which, in an age of outstanding love poetry, attain a depth, suggestiveness, and power rarely duplicated in the history of humankind's passionate struggle to match desire with words.

BIOGRAPHY

William Shakespeare was born in the provincial town of Stratford-upon-Avon in 1564 and died there in 1616. He spent most of his adult life in the London theaters and quickly attained a reputation as a dramatist, actor, and poet. Shakespeare's company prospered under the reign of James I, and by the time of his retirement from playwrighting about 1612, Shakespeare had acquired a respectable fortune. His career as a poet, distinct from his more public career as a dramatist, was probably confined to perhaps a decade, between 1591 and 1601, although the sonnets were later collected and published (perhaps without his permission) in 1609. Because of the absurd controversies that grew, mainly in the nineteenth century, about whether Shakespeare actually existed, it is worthwhile pointing out that there are many official records (christening record, marriage license, legal documents, correspondence, and so on) which may be consulted by the skeptical.

ANALYSIS

One of William Shakespeare's great advantages as a writer was that, as a dramatist working in the public theater, he was afforded a degree of autonomy from the cultural dominance of the court, his age's most powerful institution. All over Europe, even if belatedly in England, the courts of the Renaissance nation-states conducted an intense campaign to use the arts to further their power. The theater, despite its partial dependency on court favor, achieved through its material products (the script and the performance) a relative autonomy in comparison with the central court arts of poetry, prose fiction, and the propagandistic masque. When Shakespeare briefly turned to Ovidian romance in the 1590's and, belatedly, probably also in the 1590's, to the fashion for sonnets, he moved closer to the cultural and literary dominance of the court's taste—to the fashionable modes of Ovid, Petrarch, and Neoplatonism—and to the need for patronage. Although the power of the sonnets goes far beyond their sociocultural roots, Shakespeare nevertheless adopts the culturally inferior role of the petitioner for favor, and there is an undercurrent of social and economic powerlessness in the sonnets, especially when a rival poet seems likely to sup-

*William Shakespeare* (Library of Congress)

plant the poet. In short, Shakespeare's nondramatic poems grow out of and articulate the strains of the 1590's, when, like many ambitious writers and intellectuals on the fringe of the court, Shakespeare clearly needed to find a language in which to speak—and that was, necessarily, given to him by the court. What he achieved within this shared framework, however, goes far beyond any other collection of poems in the age. Shakespeare's occasional poems are unquestionably minor, interesting primarily because he wrote them; his sonnets, on the other hand, constitute perhaps the language's greatest collection of lyrics. They are love lyrics, and clearly grow from the social, erotic, and literary contexts of his age. Part of their greatness, however, lies in their power to be read again and again in later ages, and to raise compellingly, even unanswerably, more than merely literary questions.

### VENUS AND ADONIS

In his first venture into public poetry, Shakespeare chose to work within the generic constraints of the fashionable Ovidian verse romance. *Venus and Adonis* appealed to the taste of young aristocrats such as the earl of Southampton to whom it was dedicated. It is a narrative poem in six-line stanzas, mixing classical mythology with surprisingly (and incongruously) detailed descriptions of country life, designed to illustrate the story of the seduction of the beautiful youth Adonis by the comically desperate aging goddess Venus. It is relatively static, with too much argument to make it inherently pleasurable reading. Its treatment of love relies on Neoplatonic and Ovidian commonplaces, and it verges (unlike Christopher Marlowe's *Hero and Leander*, 1598, to which Shakespeare's poem is a fair but decidedly inferior fellow) on moralizing allegory, with Venus as flesh, Adonis as spiritual longing. The poem's articulation of the nature of the love that separates them is abstract and often unintentionally comic—although Shakespeare's characterization of Venus as a garrulous plump matron brings something of his theatrical power to enliven the poem. The poem was certainly popular at the time, going through ten editions in as many years, possibly because its early readers thought it fashionably sensual.

### THE RAPE OF LUCRECE

*The Rape of Lucrece* is the "graver labor" that Shakespeare promised to Southampton in the preface to *Venus and Adonis*. Again, he combines a current poetical fashion—the complaint—with a number of moral commonplaces, and writes a novelette in verse: a melodrama celebrating the prototype of matronly chastity, the Roman lady Lucrece, and her suicide after she was raped. The central moral issue—that of honor—at times almost becomes a serious treatment of the psychology of self-revulsion; but the decorative and moralistic conventions of the complaint certainly do not afford Shakespeare the scope of a stage play. There are some fine local atmospheric effects that, in their declamatory power, occasionally bring the directness and power of the stage into the verse.

### THE PHOENIX AND THE TURTLE

*The Phoenix and the Turtle* is an allegorical, highly technical celebration of an ideal love union: It consists of a funeral procession of mourners, a funeral anthem, and a final lament for the dead. It is strangely evocative, dignified, abstract, and solemn. Readers have fretted, without success, over the exact identifications of its characters. Its power lies in its mysterious, eerie evocation of the mystery of unity in love.

## SONNETS

Probably more human ingenuity has been spent on Shakespeare's sonnets than on any other work of English literature. In *Shakespeare's Sonnets* (1978), Stephen Booth briefly summarizes the few facts that have led to a plethora of speculation on such matters as text, authenticity, date, arrangement, and, especially, biographical implications. The sonnets were first published in 1609, although numbers 138 and 144 had appeared in *The Passionate Pilgrim* a decade before. Attempts to reorder the sonnets have been both varied and creative, but none represents the "correct" order. Such attempts simply fulfill an understandable anxiety on the part of some readers to see narrative continuity rather than variations and repetition in the sonnets. The "story behind" the sonnets has, as Booth puts it, "evoked some notoriously creative scholarship": speculation on the identity of the young man mentioned in many of the first 126 sonnets, of Mr. W. H., to whom the sequence is dedicated by the printer, of the "Dark Lady" of sonnets 127-152, and of the rival poet of some of the earlier sonnets—all these matters have filled many library shelves.

Such speculations—which reached their peak in critics and readers wedded to the sentimental Romantic insistence on an intimate tie between literary and historical "events"—are in one sense a tribute to the power of the sonnets. They are arguably the greatest collection of love poems in the language, and they provide a crucial test for the adequacy of both the love of poetry and the sense of the fascinating confusion that makes up human love. In a sense, the sonnets are as "dramatic" as any of Shakespeare's plays inasmuch as their art is that of meditations on love, beauty, time, betrayal, insecurity, and joy. Each sonnet is like a little script, with (often powerful) directions for reading and enactment, with textual meanings that are not given but made anew in every performance, by different readers within their individual and social lives. What Sonnet 87 terms "misprision" may stand as the necessary process by which each sonnet is produced by each reader.

It is conventional to divide the sonnets into two groups—1-126, purportedly addressed or related to a young man, and 127-152, to the "Dark Lady." Such a division is arbitrary at best—within each group there

are detachable subgroups, and without the weight of the conventional arrangement, many sonnets would not seem to have a natural place in either group. Sonnets 1-17 (and perhaps 18) are ostensibly concerned with a plea for a young man to marry; but even in this group, which many readers have seen to be the most conventional and unified, there are disruptive suggestions that go far beyond the commonplace context.

What may strike contemporary readers, and not merely after an initial acquaintance with the sonnets, is the apparently unjustified level of idealization voiced by many of the sonnets—an adulatory treatment of noble love that, to a post-Freudian world, might seem archaic, no matter how comforting. The continual self-effacement of the anguished lover, the worship of the "God in love, to whom I am confined" (110), the poet's claim to immortalizing "his beautie . . . in these blacke lines" (63), are all idealizations born out of a world of serene affirmation. Some of the most celebrated sonnets, such as "Shall I compare thee to a summer's day" (18) or "Let me not to the marriage of true minds" (116), may even seem cloyingly affirmative, their texts seemingly replete, rejecting any subtextual challenges to their idealism.

In the two hundred years since Petrarch, the sonnet had developed into an instrument of logic and rhetoric. The Shakespearian sonnet, on the other hand, with its three quatrains and a concluding couplet, allows especially for the concentration on a single mood; it is held together less by the apparent logic of many of the sonnets (for example, the "when . . . then" pattern) than by the invitation to enter into the dramatization of a brooding, sensitive mind. The focus is on emotional richness, on evoking the immediacy of felt experience. Shakespeare uses many deliberately generalized epithets, indeterminate signifiers and floating referents that provoke meaning from their readers rather than providing it. Each line contains contradictions, echoes, and suggestions that require an extraordinary degree of emotional activity on the part of the reader. The couplets frequently offer a reader indeterminate statements, inevitably breaking down any attempt at a limited formalist reading. The greatest of the sonnets—60, 64, 129, as well as many others—have such an extraordinary combination of general, even abstract, words and unspecified emotional power that the reader may take it as the major rhetorical characteristic of the collection.

In particular lines, too, these poems achieve amazing power by their lack of logical specificity and emotional open-endedness. As Booth points out, many lines show "a constructive vagueness" by which a word or phrase is made to do multiple duty—by placing it "in a context to which it pertains but which it does not quite fit idiomatically" or by using phrases that are simultaneously illogical and amazingly charged with meaning. He instances "separable spite" in Sonnet 36 as a phrase rich with suggestion; another example is the way in which the bewilderingly ordinary yet suggestive epithets sit uneasily in the opening lines of Sonnet 64. Often a reader is swept on through the poem by a syntactical movement that is modified or contradicted by associations set up by words and phrases. There is usually a syntactical or logical framework in the sonnet, but so powerful are the contradictory, random, and disruptive effects occurring incidentally as the syntax unfolds that to reduce the sonnet to its seemingly replete logical framework is to miss the most amazing effects of these extraordinary poems.

Shakespeare is writing at the end of a very long tradition of using lyric poems to examine the nature of human love, and there is a weight of insight as well as of rhetorical power behind his collection. Nowhere in the Petrarchan tradition are the extremes of erotic revelation offered in such rawness and complexity. Northrop Frye once characterized the sonnets as a kind of "creative yoga," an imaginative discipline meant to articulate the feelings that swirl around sexuality. Most of the conventional topoi of traditional poetry are the starting points for the sonnets—the unity of lovers (36-40), the power of poetry to immortalize the beloved (18, 19, 55), contests between eye and heart, beauty and virtue (46, 141), and shadow and substance (53, 98, 101). As with Petrarch's *Rerum vulgarium fragmenta* (1470, also known as *Canzoniere*; *Rhymes*, 1976) or Sir Philip Sidney's *Astrophel and Stella* (1591), it would be possible to create a schematic account of commonplace Renaissance thinking about love from the sonnets. To do so, however, would be to nullify their extraordinary power of creation, the way they force ejaculations of recognition, horror, or joy from their readers.

After half a century of existentialism, readers in the late twentieth century understood that one of the most urgent subjects of the sonnets is not the commonplaces of Renaissance thinking about love, nor even the powerful concern with the power of art, but what Sonnet 16 calls people's "war upon this bloody tyrant Time." It is no accident that the "discovery" of the sonnets' concern with time and mutability dates from the 1930's, when the impact of Søren Kierkegaard, Friedrich Nietzsche, and the existentialists, including Martin Heidegger, was starting to be widely felt in England and the United States. The sonnets' invitation to see humans' temporality not merely as an abstract problem but as part of their inherent nature—what Heidegger terms humans' "thrownness," their sense of being thrown into the world—seems central to a perception of the sonnets' power. Unpredictability and change are at the heart of the sonnets—but it is a continually shifting heart, and one that conceives of human love as definable only in terms of such change and finitude. The sonnets avoid the transcendentalism of Geoffrey Chaucer beseeching his young lovers to turn from the world, or of Edmund Spenser rejecting change for the reassurance of God's eternity and his providential guidance of time to a foreknown, if mysterious, end. Shakespeare's sonnets rather overwhelm readers with questions and contradictions. In Sonnet 60, for example, time is not an impartial or abstract background. Even where it is glanced at as a pattern observable in nature or humanity, it is evoked as a disruptive, disturbing experience that cannot be dealt with as a philosophical problem. Some sonnets portray time as a sinister impersonal determinant; some thrust time at the reader as an equally unmanageable force of unforeseeable chances and changes, what Sonnet 115 calls humanity's "million'd accidents."

In Sonnet 15, it may be possible to enter into an understandable protest against time destroying its own creations (a commonplace enough Renaissance sentiment), and to accede to a sense of helplessness before a malignant force greater than the individual human being. When the sonnet tries, however, by virtue of its formally structured argument, to create a consciousness that seeks to understand and so to control this awareness, the reader encounters lines or individual words that may undermine even the temporary satisfaction of the aesthetic form. Such, for example is the force of the appalling awareness that "everything that grows/ Holds in perfection but a little moment." What is the application of "everything" or the emotional effect of the way the second line builds to a seemingly replete climax in "perfection" and then tumbles into oblivion in "but a little moment"? The sonnet does not and need not answer such questions. In a very real sense, it cannot answer them, for readers can only acknowledge time's power in their own contingent lives. What is shocking is not merely the commonplace that "never-resting time leads summer on/ To hideous winter, and confounds him there" (5) but that each reading fights against and so disrupts the logical and aesthetic coherence of the reader's own sense of change and betrayal.

To attempt criticism of the sonnets is, to an unusual extent, to be challenged to make oneself vulnerable, to undergo a kind of creative therapy, as one goes back and forth from such textual gaps and indeterminacies to the shifting, vulnerable self, making the reader aware of the inadequacy and betrayal of words, as well as of their amazing seductiveness. Consider, for example, Sonnet 138. When one falls in love with a much younger person, does one inevitably feel the insecurity of a generation gap? What is more important in such a reading of the sonnets is the insistence that age or youthfulness are not important in themselves: It is the insistence itself that is important, not the mere fact of age—just as it is the anxiety with which a man or woman watches the wrinkles beneath the eyes that is important, not the wrinkles themselves. The note of insistence, in other words, is not attached merely to the speaker's age: It stands for an invitation to participate in some wider psychological revelation, to confess the vulnerability that people encounter in themselves in any relationship that is real and growing, and therefore necessarily unpredictable and risky.

Without vulnerability and contingency, without the sense of being thrown into the world, there can be no growth. Hence the poet invites the reader to accept ruefully what the fact of his age evokes—an openness to ridicule or rejection. The sonnet's insistence on being open to the insecurity represented by the narrator's age points not merely to a contrast between the speaker and his two lovers but rather to a radical self-division. This is especially so in the Dark Lady sonnets, where there is a savage laceration of self, particularly in the fearful exhaustion of Sonnet 129, in which vulnerability is evoked as paralysis. At once logically relentless and emotionally centrifugal, Sonnet 129 generates fears or vulnerability and self-disgust. Nothing is specified: The strategies of the poem work to make the reader reveal or recognize his or her own compulsions and revulsions. The poem's physical, psychological, and cultural basis forces the reader to become aware of his or her awful drive to repress words because they are potentially so destructive.

Even in the seemingly most serene sonnets, there are inevitably dark shadows of insecurity and anxiety. In Sonnet 116, for example, the argument is that a love that alters with time and circumstance is not a true, but a self-regarding love.

The poem purports to define true love by negatives, but if those negatives are deliberately negated, the poem that emerges may be seen as the dark, repressed underside of the apparently unassailable affirmation of a mature, self-giving, other-directed love. If lovers admit impediments, and play with the idea that love is indeed love which "alters when it alteration finds," that it is an "ever-fixed mark" and, most especially, that love is indeed "time's fool," then the poem connects strikingly and powerfully with the strain of insecurity about the nature of change in human love that echoes throughout the whole collection. Such apparent affirmations may be acts of repression, an attempt to regiment the unrelenting unexpectedness and challenge of love. There are poems in the collection that, although less assertive, show a willingness to be vulnerable, to reevaluate constantly, to swear permanence within, not despite, transience—to be, in the words of Saint Paul, deceivers yet true. Elsewhere, part of the torture of the Dark Lady sonnets is that such a consolation does not emerge through the pain.

In short, what Sonnet 116 represses is the acknowledgment that the only fulfillment worth having is one that is struggled for and that is independent of law or compulsion. The kind of creative fragility that it tries to marginalize is that evoked in the conclusion to Sonnet 49 when the poet admits his vulnerability: "To leave poor me thou hast the strength of laws,/ Since, why to love, I can allege no cause." This is an affirmation of a different order—or rather an acknowledgment that love must not be defined by repression and exclusion. Lovers can affirm the authenticity of the erotic only by admitting the possibility that it is not absolute. Love has no absolute legal, moral, or causal claims; nor, in the final analysis, can love acknowledge the bonds of law, family, or state—or if finally they are acknowledged, it is because they grow from love itself. Love moves by its own internal dynamic; it is not motivated by a series of external compulsions. Ultimately it asks from the lover the *nolo contendere* of commitment: Do with me what you will. A real, that is to say, an altering, bending, never fixed and unpredictable love is always surrounded by, and at times seems to live by, battles, plots, subterfuges, quarrels, and irony. At the root is the acknowledgment that any affirmation is made because of, not despite, time and human mortality. As Sonnet 12 puts it, having surveyed the fearful unpredictability of all life, lovers must realize that it is even "thy beauty" that must be questioned. At times this thought "is as a death" (64), a "fearful meditation" (65)—that even the most precious of all human creations will age, wrinkle, fade, and die. Just how can one affirm in the face of that degree of reality?

Under the pressure of such questioning, the affirmation of Sonnet 116 can therefore be seen as a kind of bad faith, a false dread—false, because it freezes lovers in inactivity when they should, on the contrary, accept their finitude as possibility. Frozen in the fear of contingency, which Sonnet 116 so ruthlessly represses in its insistent negatives, readers may miss Shakespeare's essential insight that it is in fact the very fragility of beauty, love, poetry, fair youth, and dark lady alike that enhances their desirability. Paradoxically, it is precisely because they are indeed among the wastes of time that they are beautiful; they are not desirable because they are immortal but because they are irrevocably time-bound. One of the most profound truths is expressed in Sonnet 64: "Ruin hath taught me thus to ruminate/ That Time will come and take my love away./ This thought is as a death, which cannot choose/ But weep to have that which it fears to lose." The power of such lines goes far beyond the serene platitudes of Sonnet 116. At their most courageous, humans do not merely affirm, despite the forces of change and unpredictability that provide the ever-shifting centers of their lives; on the contrary, they discover their greatest strengths because of and within their own contingency. To accept rather than to deny time is to prove that humanity's deepest life ultimately does not recognize stasis but always craves growth, and that fulfillment is built not on the need for finality, for being "ever fixed," but on the need to violate apparent limits, to push forward or die.

Against a sonnet such as 116, some sonnets depict love not as a serene continuation of life but rather as a radical reorientation. Readers are asked not to dismiss, but to affirm fears of limitation. It is in the midst of contingency, when meditations are overwhelmed by the betrayals of the past, while "I sigh the lack of many a thing I sought,/ And with old woes new wail my dear Time's waste" (Sonnet 30), that love may open up the future as possibility, not as completion—so long as one accepts that it is time itself that offers such possibility, not any attempt to escape from it.

The typical Renaissance attitude to time and mutability was one of fear or resignation unless, as in Spenser, the traditional Christian context could be evoked as compensation; but for Shakespeare the enormous energies released by the Renaissance are wasted in trying to escape the burden of temporality. The drive to stasis, to repress experiences and meanings, is a desire to escape the burden of realizing that there are some transformations which love cannot effect. Ultimately, it is impossible to get inside a lover's soul no matter how much the flesh is seized and penetrated. The drive to possess and so to annihilate is a desire derived from the old Platonic ideal of original oneness, which only Shakespeare among the Renaissance poets seems to have seen as a clear and fearful perversion—it certainly haunts the lover of the Dark Lady sonnets and readers are invited to stand and shudder at the speaker's Augustinian self-lacerations. In Sonnet 144, the two loves "of comfort and despair,/ Which like two spirits do suggest me still" are not just a "man right fair" and a "woman, colour'd ill": They are also aspects of each lover's self, the two loves that a dualistic mind cannot affirm and by which people may be paralyzed.

Throughout this discussion of the sonnets, what has been stressed is that their power rests on the seemingly fragile basis not of Shakespeare's but of their readers' shifting and unpredictable experiences. They are offered not in certainty, but in hope. They invite affirmation while insisting that pain is the dark visceral element in which humans must live and struggle. Many of the Dark Lady sonnets are grim precisely because the lover can see no way to break through such pain. What they lack, fundamentally, is hope. By accepting that, for a time, "my grief lies onward and my joy behind" (Sonnet 50), the lover may be able, however temporarily, to make some commitment. Sonnet 124 is particularly suggestive, categorizing love as "dear," costly, not only because it is "fond," beloved, but also because it is affirmed in the knowledge of the world. Moreover, while it "fears not Policy" it is nevertheless "hugely politic." It is as if love must be adaptable, cunning, even deceptive, aware of the untrustworthiness of the world from which it can never be abstracted: "it nor grows with heat, nor drowns with showers." Finally, the poet affirms with a strong and yet strangely ironic twist: "To this I witness call the fools of Time,/ Which die for goodness, who have liv'd for crime."

As Stephen Booth notes, Sonnet 124 "is the most extreme example of Shakespeare's constructive vagueness," its key the word "it," which, "like all pronouns, is specific, hard, concrete, and yet imprecise and general—able to include anything or nothing." "It" occurs five times, each time becoming more indeterminate, surrounded by subjectives and negatives: In this sonnet "composed of precisely evocative words in apparently communicative syntaxes which come to nothing and give a sense of summing up everything, the word *it* stands sure, constant, forthright, simple and blank." The blankness to which Booth points has been filled very specifically by generations of readers to force the poem into a repressive argument like that of Sonnet 116. For example, the key phrase "the fools of time" is usually glossed as local, historical examples of political or religious timeservers—but the phrase contains mysterious reverberations back upon the lovers themselves. There is a sense in which men are all fools of time. When Sonnet 116 affirms that "Love's not Time's fool," it betrays a deliberate and fearful repression; an

unwillingness to acknowledge that Love is not able to overcome Time; time is something that can be fulfilled only as it presents opportunity and possibility to humans. People rightly become fools—jesters, dancers in attendance on Time, holy fools before the creative challenge of humanity's finitude—and people die, are fulfilled sexually, existentially, only if they submit themselves, "hugely politic," to the inevitable compromises, violence, and disruption which is life. People "die for goodness" because in a sense they have all "lived for crime." People are deceivers yet true; the truest acts, like the truest poetry, are the most feigning.

The twelve-line Sonnet 126 is conventionally regarded as the culmination of the first part of the sequence. Its serenity is very unlike that of 116. It acknowledges that, even if the fair youth is indeed Nature's "minion," even he must eventually be "rendered." Such realism does not detract from the Youth's beauty or desirability; it in fact constitutes its power.

Whether one considers the Fair Youth or the Dark Lady sonnets, or whether one attempts to see a "hidden" order in the sonnets, or even if one wishes to see a story or some kind of biographical origin "within" them, perhaps their greatness rests on their refusal to offer even the possibility of "solutions" to the "problems" they raise. They disturb, provoke, and ask more than merely "aesthetic" questions; read singly or together, they make readers face (or hide from) and question the most fundamental elements of poetry, love, time, and death.

OTHER MAJOR WORKS

PLAYS: *Edward III*, pr. c. 1589-1595 (attributed to Shakespeare); *Henry VI, Part II*, pr. c. 1590-1591; *Henry VI, Part III*, pr. c. 1590-1591; *Henry VI, Part I*, pr. 1592 (wr. 1589-1590); *Richard III*, pr. c. 1592-1593 (revised 1623); *The Comedy of Errors*, pr. c. 1592-1594; *The Taming of the Shrew*, pr. c. 1593-1594; *Titus Andronicus*, pr., pb. 1594; *Love's Labour's Lost*, pr. c. 1594-1595 (revised 1597 for court performance); *The Two Gentlemen of Verona*, pr. c. 1594-1595; *A Midsummer Night's Dream*, pr. c. 1595-1596; *Richard II*, pr. c. 1595-1596; *Romeo and Juliet*, pr. c. 1595-1596; *King John*, pr. c. 1596-1597; *The Merchant of Venice*, pr. c. 1596-1597; *The Merry Wives of Windsor*, pr.

1597 (revised c. 1600-1601); *Henry IV, Part I*, pr. c. 1597-1598; *Henry IV, Part II*, pr. 1598; *Henry V*, pr. c. 1598-1599; *Much Ado About Nothing*, pr. c. 1598-1599; *As You Like It*, pr. c. 1599-1600; *Julius Caesar*, pr. c. 1599-1600; *Hamlet, Prince of Denmark*, pr. c. 1600-1601; *Twelfth Night: Or, What You Will*, pr. c. 1600-1602; *Troilus and Cressida*, pr. c. 1601-1602; *All's Well That Ends Well*, pr. c. 1602-1603; *Measure for Measure*, pr. 1604; *Othello, the Moor of Venice*, pr. 1604 (revised 1623); *King Lear*, pr. c. 1605-1606; *Macbeth*, pr. 1606; *Antony and Cleopatra*, pr. c. 1606-1607; *Coriolanus*, pr. c. 1607-1608; *Pericles, Prince of Tyre*, pr. c. 1607-1608; *Timon of Athens*, pr. c. 1607-1608; *Cymbeline*, pr. c. 1609-1610; *The Winter's Tale*, pr. c. 1610-1611; *The Tempest*, pr. 1611; *The Two Noble Kinsmen*, pr. c. 1612-1613 (with John Fletcher); *Henry VIII*, pr. 1613 (with Fletcher).

BIBLIOGRAPHY

Ackroyd, Peter. *Shakespeare: The Biography*. New York: Nan A. Talese, 2005. An examination of the life and works of Shakespeare, including his poetry.

Bate, Jonathan. *Soul of the Age: A Biography of the Mind of William Shakespeare*. New York: Random House, 2009. A biography of Shakespeare that attempts to look at his life and writings as they relate to the times in which he lived.

Bloom, Harold, ed. *The Sonnets*. New York: Bloom's Literary Criticism, 2008. A collection of essays that examine Shakespeare's sonnets, perhaps his best poetry.

Cheney, Patrick. *The Cambridge Companion to Shakespeare's Poetry*. New York: Cambridge University Press, 2007. A collection of essays offering literary, historical, and cultural information on Shakespeare's poetry. Bibliographies and suggestions for further reading make this an invaluable source for those interested in Shakespeare.

De Grazia, Margreta, and Stanley Wells, eds. *The Cambridge Companion to Shakespeare*. New York: Cambridge University Press, 2001. This work provides an extensive guide to Shakespeare's life and works.

Dobson, Michael, and Stanley Wells, eds. *The Oxford Companion to Shakespeare*. New York: Oxford University Press, 2001. An encyclopedic treatment of the life and works of Shakespeare.

Hart, Jonathan. *Shakespeare: Poetry, Culture, and History*. New York: Palgrave Macmillan, 2009. Hart looks at the poetry of Shakespeare and examines how culture and history influenced it and were influenced by it.

Heylin, Clinton. *So Long as Men Can Breathe: The Untold Story of Shakespeare's Sonnets*. Philadelphia: Da Capo Press, 2009. Heylin examines the history of the sonnets' publication and researches the possibility that Shakespeare never intended them to be published.

Hope, Warren, and Kim Holston. *The Shakespeare Controversy: An Analysis of the Authorship Theories*. 2d ed. Jefferson, N.C.: McFarland, 2009. The authors examines the various authorship controversies and theories surrounding Shakespeare's work. Although much of the discussion involves plays, it sheds light on the author himself.

Matz, Robert. *The World of Shakespeare's Sonnets: An Introduction*. Jefferson, N.C.: McFarland, 2008. Matz examines the sonnets in terms of the customs and beliefs that shaped them and with reference to Shakespeare's world.

*Gary F. Waller*

---

# PERCY BYSSHE SHELLEY

**Born:** Field Place, near Horsham, Sussex, England; August 4, 1792
**Died:** At sea off Viareggio, Lucca (now in Italy); July 8, 1822

PRINCIPAL POETRY

*Original Poetry by Victor and Cazire*, 1810 (with Elizabeth Shelley)
*Posthumous Fragments of Margaret Nicholson*, 1810
*Queen Mab: A Philosophical Poem*, 1813, 1816 (as *The Daemon of the World*)

*Alastor: Or, The Spirit of Solitude, and Other Poems*, 1816

*Mont Blanc*, 1817

*The Revolt of Islam*, 1818

*Rosalind and Helen: A Modern Eclogue, with Other Poems*, 1819

*Letter to Maria Gisborne*, 1820

*Adonais: An Elegy on the Death of John Keats*, 1821

*Epipsychidion*, 1821

*Posthumous Poems of Percy Bysshe Shelley*, 1824 (includes *Prince Athanase, Julian and Maddalo: A Conversation, The Witch of Atlas, The Triumph of Life, The Cyclops*, and *Charles the First*)

*The Mask of Anarchy*, 1832

*Peter Bell the Third*, 1839

*The Poetical Works of Percy Bysshe Shelley*, 1839

*The Wandering Jew*, 1887

*The Complete Poetical Works of Shelley*, 1904 (Thomas Hutchinson, editor)

*The Esdaile Notebook: A Volume of Early Poems*, 1964 (K. N. Cameron, editor)

OTHER LITERARY FORMS

Except for *A Defence of Poetry* (1840), Percy Bysshe Shelley's essays are not classics of English prose, but they have influenced writers as diverse as George Bernard Shaw, H. G. Wells, and Bertrand Russell, and they are very useful as glosses on the poetry. "On Love," for example, introduces Shelley's concept of the "antitype," the perfect mate, uniquely suited to one's intellect, imagination, and sensory needs, a "soul within our soul," but purged of all one finds unsatisfactory within oneself. Love is defined as the attraction to the antitype. Shelley movingly describes this longing for a mirror image of perfection:

> If we reason, we would be understood; if we imagine, we would that the airy children of our brain were born anew within another's; if we feel, we would that another's nerves should vibrate to our own, that the beams of their eyes should kindle at once and mix and melt into our own, that lips of motionless ice should not reply to lips quivering and burning with the heart's best blood. This is Love.

Love, as the attraction toward refined idealism, figures as well in Shelley's theory of the formative power of poetry.

In *A Defence of Poetry*, he argues that "the great secret of morals is Love." Through identification with the "beautiful which exists in thought, action, or person, not our own," one becomes moral through the process of empathizing. Love is thus an act of the sympathetic imagination. Because poetry, and literature in general, enhances and exercises the ability to empathize, it is an agent of tremendous potential for the moral regeneration of humankind. It goes without saying that the poet thus has a high office in the government of morality; he is Shelley's "unacknowledged legislator." By this phrase, Shelley did not primarily mean that poets are unacknowledged for the good they do, but rather that they themselves were not and could not be aware of the power of their beauty. Shelley's poet is not in control of his power, for, in the language of his great metaphor of the creative process,

> the mind in creation is as a fading coal which some invisible influence, like an inconstant wind, awakens to transitory brightness: this power arises from within, like the colour of a flower which fades and changes as it is developed, and the conscious portions of our natures are unprophetic either of its approach or its departure.

Hence, poets do not control their inspiration—in fact, when writing begins, the most intense phase of inspiration has already passed; they express more than they understand; they feel less than they inspire; they are "the influence which is moved not, but moves. Poets are the unacknowledged legislators of the World."

ACHIEVEMENTS

One of the six greatest English Romantic poets, Percy Bysshe Shelley is arguably the most versatile stylist among all English poets. His genius for versification enabled him to employ an astonishing variety of stanzaic patterns and poetic forms with equal facility. He has two basic styles, however—the sublime or rhapsodic, heard in such poems as *Alastor*, "Hymn to Intellectual Beauty," *Prometheus Unbound: A Lyrical Drama in Four Acts* (pb. 1820), and *Adonais*; and the urbane or conversational style, found in poems such as

*Julian and Maddalo*, *Letter to Maria Gisborne*, and *Epipsychidion*. In this latter mode, especially in the standard pentameter line with couplets, Shelley grew increasingly conservative prosodically, achieving a control almost neoclassical in balance and poise. Lyrical, unremitting intensity, however, is the defining quality of Shelley's verse.

BIOGRAPHY

In *Great Expectations* (1860-1861), Charles Dickens has the convict Magwitch put his life's story, as he says, into a mouthful of English—in and out of jail, in and out of jail, in and out of jail. Percy Bysshe Shelley's life falls into a similar pattern—in and out of love, in and out of love, in and out of love. Shelley admitted as much in a letter to John Gisborne, written the year he was to drown in a boating accident, and expressive of a truth he discovered too late: "I think one is always in love with something or other; the error, and I confess it is not easy for spirits cased in flesh and blood to avoid it, consists in seeking in a mortal image the likeness of what is perhaps eternal." At the age of twenty-nine,

*Percy Bysshe Shelley* (Library of Congress)

Shelley was still looking for his antitype; he believed he had found her, at last, in a nineteen-year-old Italian girl imprisoned in a nunnery, and had written one of his greatest poems, *Epipsychidion*, in celebration, typically disregarding the impact the poem would have on his wife Mary. Mary, however, had been party to a similar emotional event five years earlier when Shelley had abandoned his first wife, Harriet Westbrook Shelley, then pregnant with his second child, to elope with Mary. Both times Shelley speculated that the women could live with him, together, in harmony—the first combination, wife Harriet as sister, lover Mary as wife; the second combination, as stated metaphorically in *Epipsychidion*, wife Mary as Moon, Teresa Viviani as Sun to Shelley's Earth, with a comet, Claire Claremont, Mary's half-sister, zooming into their "azure heaven" as she willed.

One of Shelley's great biographers, Kenneth Neill Cameron, says that Shelley was rather ahead of his time, at least ahead of today's liberal divorce laws, but most readers still find the facts of Shelley's love-life disturbing. His vision of love is wonderful; his idealism

> that sought to change the world through love and poetry is wonderful; the reality of that vision and idealism translated into life was a disaster. Shelley knew it and this awareness caused him to seek self-destruction.

> His intense fits of love aside, Shelley could be the most thoughtful and loving of men. He was selfless, generous to a fault, a brilliant radical devoted to saving the world and just as passionately devoted to the pursuit of metaphysical truth. Edward John Trelawny provides a description of Shelley in his study, German folio open, dictionary in hand (Shelley always read literature in the original—Greek, Latin, Spanish, Italian, German—so that he could be sensitive to the style and linguistic nuances of the art), at 10 A.M., and the identical picture at 6 P.M., Shelley having hardly moved, forgetting he had not eaten, looking tired and pale. "Well," Trelawny said, "have you found it?," referring to some truth Shelley sought. "Shutting the book and going to the window," Shelley replied, "'No, I have lost it': with a deep sigh: 'I have lost a day.'"

Shelley was born into a family of landed gentry. His father, Timothy, was a member of Parliament and his grandfather Bysshe Shelley was a very wealthy landowner. Shelley studied at Eton, where he rebelled against the hazing system; fell madly in love with a cousin, Harriet Grove; attended Oxford, briefly, until his expulsion for printing a pamphlet defending atheism; and completed his teenage years by eloping with sixteen-year-old Harriet Westbrook, the daughter of a wealthy merchant. Harriet and Shelley had two children, Ianthe and Charles, the latter born after Shelley had left Harriet to elope with Mary Godwin, the sixteen-year-old child of Mary Wollstonecraft, author of *A Vindication of the Rights of Woman* (1792), and William Godwin, author of *The Inquiry Concerning Political Justice and Its Influence on General Virtue and Happiness* (1793). After Harriet committed suicide by drowning, probably because of her pregnancy with another man's child, Shelley married Mary. The couple lived in England for a while, but left for Italy to protect Shelley's health and to escape the group of friends, including William Godwin, who had come to depend on Shelley for financial support.

In Italy, they settled near Lord Byron, who had fled England for his own personal reasons—a divorce and a child allegedly by his half-sister. Mary and Shelley had two children, Clara and William. When Clara died from an illness exacerbated by the traveling that Shelley forced on his family in Italy, the love-light seemed to wane in the Shelleys' marriage. The following year, 1819, Shelley's son died, and even greater despondency descended on them. Shelley was also disheartened by his ineffectiveness as a poet—no popularity, no audience, no hope of saving the world through his poetry. In *Adonais*, his eulogy for John Keats, Shelley tempts himself to put the things of this world aside, to die. On July 8, 1822, Shelley and Edward Williams set sail from Leghorn, too late in the afternoon considering their destination and with a storm pending. They drowned in the brief tempest. Several weeks later, the two bodies were discovered on separate lonely beaches. In Shelley's pockets were a book of Sophocles and Keats's latest volume of poems, opened as if he had been reading. Byron, Trelawny, Leigh Hunt, and some Italian health officials cremated the bodies, Hellenic style, on the beach. Trelawny claims that Shelley's heart would not burn, or at least did not burn, and that he salvaged it from the ashes. Shelley, who likened the poet to fire and who prominently used the image of releasing one's fate to the stream, thus lived and died the myth of his poetry.

## ANALYSIS

Percy Bysshe Shelley mutedly noted in his preface to *Prometheus Unbound* that he had "what a Scotch philosopher terms, 'a passion for reforming the world.'" One might think that this would have endeared his work at least to the reading public left of center and to later readers who value the reforming spirit in humankind. Yet Shelley was almost able to name his readers, they were so few, and today, of the six major poets who dominate the canon of British Romanticism—William Blake, William Wordsworth, Samuel Taylor Coleridge, Byron, Keats, and Shelley—it is still Shelley who remains the least popular. For one reason or another, and though Shelley will always have a cadre of eloquent apologists, dedicated scholars, and brilliant explicators, he is usually out of favor with a significant group of readers. He has been criticized for bad thinking, for bad writing, and for bad living. Devaluations of his thought and poetry have largely been overcome, but this last—especially when made by sensitive feminist readers who find his narcissistic theory of love stupidly, if not heartlessly, destructive to the women in his life—is difficult to refute, if one grants its relevance to his art.

Shelley's theme of self-destructiveness leads to his poetry's most brilliant moments, but perhaps the weakness in Shelley's use of the antitype motif is that it fails to recognize even the possibility that the mate—the woman—exists in her own right, and that her likeness to the fiction of the poet's imagination might not be the best or safest evidence of her worth. In Lord Byron's *Manfred* (1817), the concept of the antitype is also used, but Byron is critical of the theme from the woman's point of view—Manfred has destroyed his lover, Astarte, with this dangerously egotistical love and madly strives to win her forgiveness. Shelley seems incapable of such a critique of his most important theme; therein may lie the weakness in his work. Except in this respect, Shelley was not in the least simpleminded concerning the problem of reforming the world according to his standards. Shelley desired more than the world could ever offer; he knew it, but he could not stop trying to close the gap between the ideal and the real, the vision and the fact. So powerful is his honesty that tension pervades his poetry, idealism playing against skepticism, irony hedging assertion. He ardently believed that humans were perfectible, if they would only will it. At its most optimistic, his poetry seeks to arouse the reader's will to strive for perfection; at its most pessimistic, it is the poet's private struggle with the desire to escape through death.

### JULIAN AND MADDALO

One might take a poem of balanced opposites as a synecdochic introduction to Shelley's thought and art. *Julian and Maddalo* presents the issues, the imagery that typically embodies them, and the quest to dissolve division in nature, society, and personal life. The conversants in this urbane, sophisticated debate are Julian, a thin disguise for Shelley, and Maddalo, or Lord Byron. Julian, the preface suggests, is the idealist, "passionately attached to those philosophical notions which assert the power of man over his own mind, and the immense improvements of which, by the extinction of certain moral superstitions, human society may be yet susceptible." Maddalo is the card-carrying cynic, and the tragedy from Julian's point of view is that Maddalo is one of the few who might be capable of changing the world, if he would only will it. It is Maddalo's weakness to be proud; he does not think the world worth the effort. A maniac also enters the poem as a character who was destroyed through unrequited love. Finally, Maddalo's little daughter is the ever-present, romantic image of humankind's potential.

The poem opens with a vision of harmony. Julian and Maddalo have been riding along the Lido of Venice, a waste of a beach, at sundown, and Julian responds to the correspondence he senses between the inner and outer worlds:

> I love all waste
> And solitary places; where we taste
> The pleasure of believing what we see
> Is boundless, as we wish our souls to be:
> And such was this wide ocean, and this shore
> More barren than its billows.

Not much later, Maddalo will offer a constricted image of the soul, but for now, Shelley allows his better half to continue. Disagreeing with earlier Romantic work of Wordsworth and Coleridge, which argued for the sufficiency of humankind's relationship with nature, Julian/Shelley adds a companion to the landscape experience: "and yet more/ Than all, with a remembered friend I love/ To ride as then I rode." The friends are in perfect accord with each other as well as with nature. As they gallop along the beach, the wind brings the "living spray" into their faces, the blue heavens open, "stripped to their depths," and the waves send forth a "sound like delight . . ./ Harmonizing with solitude," carrying into their hearts "aereal merriment." The personal relationship is as perfect: "the swift thought,/ Winging itself with laughter, lingered not,/ But flew from brain to brain." As they turn homeward, however, division slowly enters the poem, beginning with a discussion on "God, freewill and destiny:/ Of all that earth has been or yet may be." Julian takes the brighter side, Maddalo, the darker. Shelley represents the argument metaphorically as two perceptions of landscape. Julian first offers a perception of the dissolution of the landscape's natural boundaries created by the light of the setting sun; Maddalo then counters with a brilliant image of the constricted soul and the madding passions, the bell of the insane asylum.

Julian first calls attention to the division between East and West, earth and sky. The Alps are a "heaven-sustaining bulwark reared/ Between the East and West"; only "half the sky/ Was roofed with clouds of rich emblazonry"; the sun pauses in a "rent" between the clouds; the hills are separate like a "clump of peaked isles." Then quite dramatically light begins to do its work of transformation:

> as if the Earth and Sea had been
> Dissolved into one lake of fire were seen
> Those mountains towering as from waves of flame
> Around the vaporous sun, from where there came
> The inmost purple spirit of light, and made
> Their very peaks transparent.

This diffusion of water with fire, earth with air, air with fire, and water with earth, completed in the fleeting intensity of the Sun's pause, becomes a vision of hope for human reconciliation through love. The Sun's light is love and just as it can dissolve the perception of landscape boundaries so can the emotion dissolve boundaries in personal life and society. Nature teaches a lesson; even the city becomes a divine illusion, "Its temples and its palaces did seem/ Like fabrics of enchantment piled to Heaven."

Maddalo, however, is not taken by the vision. He insists on observing the sunset from a "better station." Between them and the Sun is now imagined the madhouse, "A windowless, deformed and dreary pile," its bell tolling "In strong and black relief" for the maniacs to begin their evening prayers. Looking at his image of the bell and the asylum, Maddalo interprets:

> And such . . . is our mortality
> And this must be the emblem and the sign
> Of what should be eternal and divine—
> And like that black and dreary bell, the soul,
> Hung in a heaven-illumined tower, must toll
> Our thoughts and our desires to meet below
> Round the rent heart and pray—as madmen do
> For what? they know not,—till the night of death
> As sunset that strange vision, severeth
> Our memory from itself, and us from all
> We sought and yet were baffled!

If Byron literally spoke these lines, they are among the best lines of poetry he ever composed. The soul is no beach stretching to the horizon; it is finite, and dreary, and obfuscating. It provokes the heart with its spirituality to strive for the infinite in complete bewilderment, till death closes the quest. There is nothing eternal and divine; it is simply mortality at odds with itself. In the twilight, the "black bell became invisible" and the enchanted city "huddled in gloom," its ships, towers, palaces—emblems of commerce, church, and government—faded into the absurdity of night.

The following day, Julian argues that

> it is our will
> That . . . enchains us to permitted ill—
> We might be otherwise—we might be all
> We dream of . . .
> Where is the love, beauty and truth we seek
> But in our mind? and if we were not weak
> Should we be less in deed than in desire?

Maddalo counters that such human weakness is incurable, that no matter how strong an argument Julian can make to prove the perfectibility of humankind, empirical evidence and experience will undermine it. Maddalo adduces as evidence the case of a maniac, who was like Julian an idealist but has been destroyed by unrequited love. Their visit to the maniac's cell in the asylum whose bell they had heard the preceding night reveals a man of rent heart, musing disjointedly and pathetically on his suffering. Still in love, he refuses to commit suicide because he does not want his former lover to feel responsible for his death. Julian feels that if he had the opportunity to befriend the man, he might save him, but the strength of Maddalo's argument has been felt. After many years, Julian returns to Maddalo's castle and learns from his grown daughter that the maniac's lover returned and he recovered; then, however, they separated once more. At Julian's entreaty, she reveals the whole story, but out of bitterness toward the world he refuses to disclose the resolution (as Shelley refuses to disclose it to his readers): "the cold world shall not know," concludes the poem. The debate has not resolved the issue. The maniac's recovery, although temporary, indicates that love is indeed the force that Julian has maintained, if one can sustain the will to love. Thus the poem returns to its starting point: Clearly one can will to love, or, at least, act as if one loved, but constancy is the problem, as the maniac's lover indicates.

## ALASTOR

The same tensions that animate *Julian and Maddalo* inform Shelley's first major poem, *Alastor*. The poet-persona of *Alastor* begins as a happy youth. He seeks knowledge and truth from philosophy, nature, history, and travel, and experiences moments of high inspiration, as when, standing amidst the ruins of the cradle of civilization, "meaning on his vacant mind/ Flashed like strong inspiration, and he saw/ The thrilling secrets of the birth of time." On his quest, he has been cared for by an Arab maiden, who brings food to him from her own plate and watches him dream innocently throughout the night, till to her father's tent she creeps "Wildered, and wan, and panting," but he does not recognize her love for him. Then, one night after leaving her locale, he has "a dream of hopes that never yet/ Had flushed his cheek." He dreams of his antitype, the perfect female of intellect, imagination, and sense to match his own. She speaks in low solemn tones of knowledge, truth, virtue, liberty; she next breathes the "permeating fire" of her pure mind in a song of passionate poetry; then, in the most erotic passage one will find in the Romantic canon, they join in sexual climax. She arises and the dreamer sees

> by the warm light of their own life
> Her glowing limbs beneath the sinuous veil
> Of woven wind, her outspread arms now bare,
> Her dark locks floating in the breath of night,
> Her beamy bending eyes, her parted lips
> Outstretched, and pale, and quivering eagerly.

He receives her, "yielding to the irresistible joy,/ With frantic gesture and short breathless cry," folding his frame in "her dissolving arms." At the moment of climax, "blackness veiled his dizzy eyes, and night/ Involved and swallowed up the vision; sleep,/ Like a dark flood suspended in its course,/ Rolled back its impulse on his vacant brain."

One would wish to sleep forever to have such dreams, for how can such a dream be fulfilled? The world, which was once so beautiful to the poet, now appears vacant when he awakens. Cryptically, the narrator tells us that "The spirit of sweet human love has sent/ A vision to the sleep of him who spurned/ Her choicest gifts." Was the Arab maiden one of those gifts, or was she merely the catalyst of an awakening sexuality? Regardless, he now "eagerly pursues/ Beyond the realms of dream that fleeting shade," knowing that the realm beyond dream is most likely death. He moves madly through society and nature more to burn out than to seek a likeness of the veiled maid. When he tires or seeks infrequent nourishment, an image of the maid's eyes forces him on. In a passage that underscores the narcissism of his quest, the reflection of his own eyes in a fountain where he drinks provokes her shadowy presence.

He moves on, following a stream to its unknown source, for he has dimly perceived an analogue between "What oozy cavern or what wandering cloud" contain its waters and what mysterious source his own thoughts and visions may have. He finally stops in a

virginal nook above the perilous mountain landscape and prepares to die. He is "at peace, and faintly smiling" as the crescent moon sets on his life: "His last sight/ Was the great moon," which as it declines finally shows only the tips of its crescent:

> the alternate gasp
> Of his faint respiration scarce did stir
> The stagnate night:—till the minutest ray
> Was quenched, the pulse yet lingered in his heart.
> It paused—it fluttered.

The moon sets, and he dies. Why does his heart pause and flutter? Is he duped by the moon's tips appearing to be eyes, or does he smile faintly because he is aware of the irony? Or does he move from irony to the excitement of belief at the moment before final truth? The reader cannot know, but the poem's narrator finds little hope for the world when "some surpassing Spirit,/ Whose light adorned the world around it" dies an untimely death not with "sobs or groans,/ The passionate tumult of a clinging hope;/ But pale despair and cold tranquillity."

As he moved like a phantom through the landscape, the poet of *Alastor* recognized that nature provided a condition like love for its animate and inanimate beings—swans floating in pairs, "Ivy clasp[ing]/ The fissured stones with its entwining arms"—but that he belonged outside the circle. Shelley could not maintain the romantic myth that, as Coleridge wrote in "This Limetree Bower My Prison," "Nature ne'er deserts the wise and pure," or, as Wordsworth wrote in "Lines Composed a Few Miles Above Tintern Abbey," "In nature and the language of the sense,/ [is] the anchor of my purest thoughts, the nurse,/ The guide, the guardian of my heart, and soul/ Of all my moral being." Shelley did write in his essay "On Love" that one seeks correspondence with nature when one is denied human love; he paraphrased an unknown source to the effect that, if one were in a desert, "he would love some cypress." As is evident in *Julian and Maddalo* and *Alastor*, Shelley preferred human companionship, because there is a force impelling the physical world that is antithetical to love. Shelley called this force Necessity, or physical determinism. *Mont Blanc* provides its principal image.

## MONT BLANC

In what becomes a showdown of sorts between mind and matter, imagination and necessity, Shelley begins *Mont Blanc* by recognizing that mind shares with matter a significant feature. The sense impressions that flow through the mind's stream of thought are impelled by a force as mysterious as that which drives the river from its home in the clouds down the mountain's ravine. Is it the same force? Critics have struggled with this problem, for Shelley did not make the matter very clear, or perhaps it is as clear as possible without being reductive of a difficult metaphysical question. On one hand, Shelley imagines the Power as residing above the world of mutability, "Remote, serene, and inaccessible," but not without profound effect on the world below. The Power's image is the mountain's summit, which none can see but which all can feel in the form of the forces it releases that destroy and preserve, its glaciers and its rivers. Its position is amoral, perfectly nonanthropomorphic. The glaciers wreak their havoc, "The dwelling-place/ Of insects, beasts, and birds" their spoil. "The race of man," too, "flies far in dread; his work and dwelling/ Vanished, like smoke before the tempest's stream." On the other hand, majestic rivers, such as the Arve of Mont Blanc, derive from the same source and are "The breath and blood of distant lands." Can the mind of humankind be a manifestation of such a power? This is the question to which the poem leads, but just as Shelley offers the answer in the final stanza, he undermines it.

Addressing the mountain he says, "The secret strength of things/ Which governs thought, and to the infinite dome/ of heaven is as a law, inhabits thee!" While thought may be governed by a psychological determinism, Shelley seems to imply a distinction between causally determined thought and the products of imagination—poetry and value. He stresses that "Mont Blanc yet gleams on high," above the vicissitudes of our world, where "In the calm darkness of the moonless nights,/ In the lone glare of day, the snows descend/ Upon that Mountain, none beholds them there," and without fanfare he begins describing, valuing, and symbolizing what he has just indicated none behold:

Winds contend
Silently there, and heap the snow with breath
Rapid and strong, but silently! Its home
The voiceless lightning in these solitudes
Keeps innocently, and like vapour broods
Over the snow.

The winds pile the snow for the coming glacier with the quality of "breath," because, while the glacier will bring death, its next state of being as river will bring life—"The breath and blood of distant lands." Likewise emphasizing the absent force of mind that now interprets and values the cold causality of the mountain's secret summit is the acknowledgment that all this is happening "Silently . . ./ . . . but silently!" No ears, no sound; no perceiver, no value. The poem concludes: "And what were thou, and earth, and stars, and sea,/ If to the human mind's imaginings/ Silence and solitude were vacancy?"

Something in the human mind renders value, recognizes or makes meaning for this universe, or decides there is no meaning. These are acts of ultimate power; the rest is a "dull round," as the human mind itself may enact when it refuses to transcend the path of association with its power to create, to vision, and to will. Shelley does not make this case as forcefully as it is presented here, however; he concludes with a question, not the strong declarative the reader might wish. The imagining undermines the assertion of "The secret strength of things"; the surmise of the conclusion undermines the imagining. This ambivalence does not derive from some precious sense of caution, but from Shelley's genuine uncertainty.

## PROMETHEUS UNBOUND

Shelley's belief in the power of love was unequivocal, however, and *Prometheus Unbound* reveals on a mythic scale the transformation that will occur when love rather than fear and hatred binds relationships among nations and humankind. *Prometheus Unbound* is a psychological drama that, along with other works of the Romantic period, asserts the power of mind in transforming the world. The French Revolution having failed to rid France of despotism, British writers sought to fulfill by individual transformation the apocalyptic hopes it had aroused. The logic was simple: If the mind and heart of the reader could be changed, the world would be changed. Thus Wordsworth, the major poet of the period, writes at the height of his optimism: "Paradise, and groves/ Elysian, . . ./ . . . why should they be/ A history only of departed things" (Prospectus to *The Recluse*). The hope of the Romantics was not naïve, but rather a variation of an eternal hope to improve the world.

Shelley's promise was that if humanity could just will to love, everything wonderful would follow. Thus, Prometheus, the mythic champion of humankind, chained to a rock in the Indian Caucasus for three thousand sleepless years, finds that he no longer hates the tyrant, Jupiter, and as a consequence, the universe swells with the love, the growth, and the energy of springtime.

Ironically, Prometheus's transformation begins, not more than fifty-five lines into the first act, as he dwells on the satisfaction he will feel when Jupiter is dethroned and made to kiss "the blood/ From [Prometheus's] pale feet," which could then trample him, except that he would disdain Jupiter too much to do so. Then he says: "Disdain? Ah no! I pity thee," for the suffering Jupiter will endure at his demise, and his pity leads to grief: "I speak in grief,/ Not exultation, for I hate no more,/ As then, ere misery made me wise." There is a significant relationship between Jupiter's power and Prometheus's hatred, Jupiter's demise and Prometheus's love: Though he has been the hero of humankind, Prometheus has been responsible for the tyranny of the universe, because he empowered Jupiter with his hate—in fact, willed the inflictions of Jupiter on humankind. When he transcends his hatred to love, Jupiter inevitably falls. It is the dialectic of the master and the slave; the slave's willed obeisance gives the master his power. Prometheus recalls his curse, which began the reign of Jupiter, and the reader begins to understand one half of the dialectic.

On a literal level, perhaps it appears foolish that the sufferer could hold power over the oppressor, as Prometheus claims, but, if one considers the action on the psychological level, where Shelley intended the battle to be fought and won, one can understand that a mind indulging in hatred blights the potential joy of life. At some level, Prometheus understands this, and retracts his curse, yet he must still undergo a test from the furies

(perhaps representing his historical consciousness), which brings to his sight the truth of humankind's condition. The Reign of Terror of the French Revolution, the rejection and murder of Christ, the general wave of personal violence and horror, are all summoned to reveal this darkest truth: "those who endure/ Deep wrongs for man, and scorn and chains, but heap/ Thousand-fold torment on themselves and him." The plight of humankind is absurdly tragic: "The good want power, but to weep barren tears./ The powerful goodness want: worse need for them./ The wise want love, and those who love want wisdom;/ And all best things are thus confused to ill."

Prometheus's response to this futility is: "Thy words are like a cloud of winged snakes/ And yet, I pity those they torture not." "Thou pitiest them?" the fury cries: "I speak no more," and vanishes defeated. Prometheus's love has endured. From this moment on, the action of the play moves forward, as if on its own pattern of necessity, to overthrow Jupiter and rejuvenate humankind. As love trickles down through the universe and the society of humankind, there are "thrones . . . kingless," men walking together without fawning or trampling, all "Scepterless, free, uncircumscribed." Though still subject to chance, death, and mutability, ruling over them like slaves, man is free, liberated consciousness, "The King/ Over himself." The "mind-forg'd manacles," to quote William Blake's "London," are sundered. The mind of man is now "an Ocean/ Of clear emotion/ A heaven of serene and mighty motion."

Yet, as wildly joyous and supremely optimistic as *Prometheus Unbound* is, the reader is warned at the close that even this mythic bliss cannot remain unguarded. Should the world fall again into its tyranny, the morality that will reincarnate her beauty, freedom, and joy again must be this:

> To suffer woes which Hope thinks infinite;
> To forgive wrongs darker than Death or Night;
> To defy Power which seems Omnipotent;
> To love, and bear; to hope, till Hope creates
> From its own wreck the thing it contemplates;
> Neither to change nor falter nor repent:
> This . . . is to be
> Good, great and joyous, beautiful and free;
> This is alone Life, Joy, Empire and Victory.

*Prometheus Unbound* is a difficult reading experience, a highly pitched lyric extended over four acts, without tonal relief, but it is essential reading for the student of Shelley and the Romantic period.

Part of Shelley's vision in *Prometheus Unbound* is that man would be passionate, "yet free from guilt or pain/ Which were, for his will made, or suffered them," and that women would be

> gentle, radiant forms
> From custom's evil taint exempt and pure;
> Speaking the wisdom once they could not think,
> Looking emotions once they feared to feel
> And changed to all which once they dared not be.

### EPIPSYCHIDION

Many might find Shelley a prophet of modern morality, or immorality, depending on point of view, but it is certain that even the most liberal in the nineteenth century could not quite live this ideal, not even Shelley's handpicked women. In *Epipsychidion*, however, he allows himself a pure fantasy of relational perfection that celebrates his discovery, at last, of his antitype. The chief skepticism of the poem is not that he might be excessive in his rapture, but rather that language is not capable of adequately expressing his rapture, its object being perfection. The poem opens with a rhapsodic invocation without parallel in English literature, and struggles throughout with its diction to aggregate images and symbols that might invoke a rhetoric of infinity. Shelley has found the veiled maid of *Alastor*: "I never thought before my death to see/ Youth's vision thus made perfect. Emily,/ I love thee; . . . Ah me!/ I am not thine: I am a part of *thee*."

This perfect woman was Teresa Viviani, the teenage daughter of the governor of Pisa, who had confined her in a nunnery. The Shelleys became interested in her plight and this lovely victim of paternal tyranny inflamed Shelley's soul. He imagines how perfect it would be if Emily/Teresa could join him and Mary in a ménage à trois, for he has never been one of the "great sect,/ Whose doctrine is, that each one should select/ Out of the crowd a mistress or a friend,/ And all the rest, though fair and wise, commend/ To cold oblivion," though the moral code might demand such behavior. "True Love in this differs from gold and clay,/ That to

divide is not to take away." Thus, if Mary would be the Moon—"The cold chaste Moon . . ./ Who makes all beautiful on which she smiles,/ . . ./ And warms not but illumines"—Emily would be the Sun and together they would form those spheres of influence "who rule this passive Earth,/ This world of love, this *me*." Finally, however, he and Emily both fly out of orbit, leaving the moon behind, to dwell in a paradisal isle.

Language cannot deal with the infinite limits of this vision: "The winged words on which my soul would pierce/ Into the height of love's rare Universe,/ Are chains of lead around its flight of fire.—/ I pant, I sink, I tremble, I expire!" Sympathetic readers of Shelley wince at these moments; his detractors triumph. Even Shelley was a bit embarrassed by the emotion of this poem, because the woman it celebrated finally married a boor. Shelley wrote to John Gisborne: "The 'Epipsychidion' I cannot look at." Mary Shelley also had a difficult time looking at it; *Epipsychidion* is the only poem in her excellent edition of Shelley's poems on which she does not comment.

### "HYMN TO INTELLECTUAL BEAUTY"

Shelley often wore his heart on his sleeve for daws to peck at, to paraphrase William Shakespeare's Iago, especially in the great series of poems representing himself as the *poète maudit*, the suffering poet vainly striving to save those who reject him. "Hymn to Intellectual Beauty," "Ode to the West Wind," and *Adonais* constitute the constellation and farthest reaches of this personal myth. Of course there is a great deal of vanity involved. One perceives that the world is not perfect; one attempts to save it and fails, thereby proving that the world really is bad, even worse than one thought. One then strives harder, becoming more assured that one is needed and that one's work is essential, rejection feeding vanity in a wicked, self-defeating cycle. Throughout, one retains one's heroic self-image.

In "Hymn to Intellectual Beauty," Shelley describes the dynamics of his dedication to poetry. While on a youthful search for truth, in much the manner of the poet of *Alastor*, he calls on the "poisonous names with which our youth is fed," God, ghosts and heaven, without success; he sees nothing, he hears nothing that responds to his Metaphysical anxieties in a direct way. He experiences something, however, that profoundly moves him. As he muses deeply "on the lot/ Of life" within the context of nature's springtime regeneration, "Sudden, thy shadow fell on me;/ I shrieked, and clasped my hands in ecstasy." The shadow is that of the spirit of beauty, an inexpressible something that transiently brings value to life—life's only value—by evoking in the receiver, its guest, a pulse of spiritual joy. If it could be a permanent experience, "Man were immortal, and omnipotent." The poet says that his life has been dedicated to creating a medium for evoking this spiritual condition. He vows that he will dedicate his "powers/ To thee and thine—have I not kept the vow?" he asks the spirit. His hope has been that if others could be given the experience of spiritual ecstasy, the world would be reborn. The time he has spent in reading, thinking, writing—those hours know, he says, that joy never

> illumed my brow
> Unlinked with hope that thou wouldst free
> This world from its dark slavery,
> That thou—O awful Loveliness,
> Wouldst give whate'er these words cannot express.

In seeking to suggest this evanescent condition, Shelley creates several of the most alluring similes in English, such as, in the fourth stanza: "Thou—that to human thought art nourishment,/ Like darkness to a dying flame!" As the mind is a fading coal, so the darkness intensified makes thought appear brighter, thereby nourishing its waning condition so that it does not appear to be waning at all. The loveliness of verse makes the mind seem as full of beauty and intensity as the moment of inspiration had promised. The poem's opening lines, however, are the ultimate of Shelleyan perfection: "The awful shadow of some unseen Power/ Floats though unseen amongst us!" It is "Like clouds in starlight widely spread,—/ Like memory of music fled,—/ Like aught that for its grace may be/ Dear, and yet dearer for its mystery." These lines are Shelley in his power, for no other poet has so effectively failed to express the inexpressible and thereby succeeded in his attempt to evoke it. While Shelley was curiously winning the battle of expression, however, he was losing the war.

## "ODE TO THE WEST WIND"

Unlike the modern age, which conceded, in the words of W. H. Auden, that "poetry makes nothing happen," the Romantic and Victorian periods permitted their artists to believe that they could and ought to be effectual. Several seemed to be: Wordsworth, Charles Dickens, Alfred, Lord Tennyson, and Robert Browning had enormous moral influence. Shelley did not; in fact, Matthew Arnold, the great social and literary critic of Victorian England, likened Shelley to an "ineffectual angel, beating in the void his luminous wings in vain." In 1819, at the age of twenty-seven, Shelley wrote his most perfect poem on his ineffectuality. "Ode to the West Wind" is a prayer for power to further the vision of *Prometheus Unbound* in nineteenth century England and Europe, by a poet who has been battered with failure.

In its five terza rima sonnet stanzas, which describe the autumn of earth, sky, sea, and poet—the elements of earth, air, water, and fire—Shelley's impassioned ode takes the literal cycle of the seasons through metaphorical transformations to approach an answer to the question: "If rebirth happens in nature, can it happen in society, with my verse, like the west wind, as the catalyst of the transition from near death to new life?" The first and last stanzas are illustrative of the metaphorical union the poet seeks with the regenerative wind. Stanza 1 presents the west wind in its dual function of destroying and preserving, driving dead leaves "like ghosts from an enchanter fleeing," and blowing seeds to "their dark wintry bed" where they will "lie cold and low,/ Each like a corpse within its grave, until/ [the wind of spring] shall blow/ Her clarion o'er the dreaming earth" to awaken the seeds to life. Of course, the dead leaves have the function of preserving the seed beds.

In the final stanza, the poet prays that his "dead thoughts" might be driven "over the universe/ Like withered leaves to quicken a new birth!" His seeds are his words, and because he is the equivalent of fire, his words are likened to ashes and sparks—some merely functional, some inspirational—that are now dormant in the waning hearth that is his life. Thus, if his verse could be sufficiently empowered by spirit, like a wind, he might produce a conflagration through the blowing about of ashes and sparks. As the spring of stanza 1 had her clarion, his verse will be "to unawakened Earth/ The trumpet of a prophecy." "O Wind," he closes, "If Winter comes, can Spring be far behind?" Clearly, if those leaves of stanza 1—"Yellow, and black, and pale, and hectic red,/ Pestilence-stricken multitudes"— which have been accurately interpreted as the suffering races of humankind, and those leaves of stanza 5—the poet's "dead thoughts"—can both be set afire by the spark of the poet's verse, both may rise from the ashes to new life. The final question, however, is threatening to the dream, for though it is certain that spring follows winter in nature, it is not at all certain that if total spiritual darkness covers humankind, a springtime of recovery will follow.

In stanza 4 of "Ode to the West Wind," Shelley represents himself as praying to the wind "in my sore need": "Oh! lift me as a wave, a leaf, a cloud!/ I fall upon the thorns of life! I bleed!/ A heavy weight of hours has chained and bowed/ One too like thee: tameless, and swift, and proud." He finally shed the weight of hours to join, not the wind, for that is to be bound still in the world of process, change, and dying hopes, but a poet of his generation who preceded him into the realm "where the eternal are." His elegy for John Keats, *Adonais*, signaled the final shift of his quest from social and personal visions of resurrected worlds and discovered antitypes to transcendence of human life and care.

### ADONAIS

Shelley believed that Keats had been mortally wounded by a scurrilous review of his early work, *Endymion: A Poetic Romance* (1818). "The savage criticism," he says in his Preface to *Adonais*, "produced the most violent effect on his susceptible mind; the agitation thus originated ended in the rupture of a blood-vessel in the lungs; a rapid consumption ensued, and the succeeding acknowledgments . . . of the true greatness of his powers, were ineffectual to heal the wound thus wantonly inflicted." This is not casebook medicine, but it does say something about the doctor who provides such an empathic diagnosis. Shelley self-consciously identified with Keats's early rejection and sought as well to identify with his early death.

Through the first thirty-seven stanzas of the poem, Shelley's narrator mourns Adonais's untimely death,

culminating with the fancy of Shelley's image visiting the tomb in homage to a dead fellow poet. The group of mourning poets stands aside to smile "through their tears" at this maudlin creature "Who in another's fate now wept his own." The muse, Urania, among the mourners for one of her most gifted, asks him his name; his response is to make "bare his branded and ensanguined brow,/ Which was like Cain's or Christ's." Then, in a moment of intense self-consciousness, Shelley disrupts this indulgent self-projection to criticize with truth—"Oh! that it should be so!" He is no important, mythical sufferer; though it has been his dream to be one, the comparison will not hold. Shortly, the poem moves to the second phase of its development, the realization that the living must not mourn for Adonais, who has "awakened from the dream of life," but for themselves: "*We* decay/ Like corpses in a charnel; fear and grief/ Convulse us and consume us day by day,/ And cold hopes swarm like worms within our living clay."

The second movement concludes with a pivotal question: "What Adonais is, why fear we to become?" The poem's third movement, stanzas 52-55, becomes darkly suicidal, but triumphant in its grasping of a new direction, a new vision. Life is imaged as a "dome of many-coloured glass" which "Stains the white radiance of Eternity,/ Until Death tramples it to fragments." Beyond Life is the Platonic "One," the blinding light of truth which humankind knows only from its shadows manifested in material form. "Die," the poet challenges, "If thou wouldst be with that which thou dost seek!" The beauties of natural, human, and aesthetic forms are "weak/ The glory they transfuse with fitting truth to speak." The challenge then becomes personalized as the poet addresses his heart, the image of his mortality and emotional life: "Why linger, why turn back, why shrink, my Heart?" Its hopes are gone, its love is gone, "what still is dear/ Attracts to crush, repels to make thee wither." The sky smiles, the wind whispers the invitation of Adonais: "oh, hasten thither,/ No more let Life divide what Death can join together." He feels the source of the fire he has represented as a poet, beaming, "Consuming the last clouds of cold mortality." Finally, the poem's concluding stanza aggregates the principal imagery of Shelley's major poetry to illustrate that throughout his work an undercurrent has been moving to this moment of poetic self-annihilation: The West Wind descends to blow; as in *Alastor*, the "spirit's bark is driven,/ . . . far from the trembling throng/ Whose sails were never to the tempest given"; the earth and skies, in contrast with the vision of *Julian and Maddalo*, are "riven" to accept the poet, rather than fused to involve him with a romantic vision of earth; he is now "borne darkly, fearfully, afar:/ Whilst burning through the inmost veil of Heaven,/ The soul of Adonais, like a star,/ Beacons from the abode where the Eternal are." The vision was sortly to descend to fact with Shelley's death by drowning.

Shelley admitted to a "passion for reforming the world." He sought an aesthetic medium that would inspire the will of man to close the gap between vision and reality. Shelley's art and thought are unique in the extremes that they bring to English literature; indeed, their fragile loveliness represents the hope and despondency possible only in an age that fervently believed in the infinite potential of man. He was a child of his age, and succeeding generations and imaginations will always need to be challenged by his visions.

## OTHER MAJOR WORKS

LONG FICTION: *St. Irvyne: Or, The Rosicrucian*, 1810; *Zastrozzi: A Romance*, 1810.

PLAYS: *The Cenci: A Tragedy in Five Acts*, pb. 1819; *Oedipus Tyrannus: Or, Swellfoot the Tyrant*, pb. 1820; *Prometheus Unbound: A Lyrical Drama in Four Acts*, pb. 1820; *Hellas: A Lyrical Drama*, pb. 1822; *Charles the First*, pb. 1824 (fragment).

NONFICTION: *The Necessity of Atheism*, 1811 (with Thomas Jefferson Hogg); *A Letter to Lord Ellenborough*, 1812; *An Address to the Irish People*, 1812; *Declaration of Rights*, 1812; *Proposals for an Association of . . . Philanthropists*, 1812; *A Refutation of Deism, in a Dialogue*, 1814; *A Proposal for Putting Reform to the Vote Throughout the Kingdom*, 1817; *History of a Six Weeks' Tour Through a Part of France, Switzerland, Germany, and Holland*, 1817 (with Mary Shelley); *An Address to the People on the Death of the Princess Charlotte*, 1817?; *A Defence of Poetry*, 1840; *Essays, Letters from Abroad, Translations, and Fragments*, 1840; *Shelley Memorials*, 1859; *Shelley's Prose in the Bodleian Manuscripts*, 1910; *Note Books of Shelley*, 1911; *A Philosophical View of Reform*, 1920; *The Letters of Percy Bysshe Shelley*, 1964 (2 volumes; Frederick L. Jones, editor).

TRANSLATIONS: *The Cyclops*, 1824 (of Euripides' play); *Ion*, 1840 (of Plato's dialogue); "The Banquet Translated from Plato," 1931 (of Plato's dialogue *Symposium*).

MISCELLANEOUS: *The Complete Works of Percy Bysshe Shelley*, 1926-1930 (10 volumes; Roger Ingpen and Walter E. Peck, editors); *Shelley's Poetry and Prose: Authoritative Texts and Criticism*, 1977 (Donald H. Reiman and Sharon B. Powers, editors).

## BIBLIOGRAPHY

Bieri, James. *Percy Bysshe Shelley: A Biography*. 2 vols. Newark: University of Delaware Press, 2004-2005. A well-reviewed valuable addition to Shelley scholarship. Examines the poet's life through analysis of his cultural, literary, personal and romantic contexts. Includes bibliography and index.

Bloom, Harold, ed. *Percy Bysshe Shelley*. New York: Chelsea House, 1985. An excellent selection of some of the most important works on Shelley published since 1950. Bloom's introduction, an overview of Shelley's poetry, is highly recommended.

Blumberg, Jane. *Byron and the Shelleys: The Story of a Friendship*. London: Collins & Brown, 1992. Blumberg describes the friendship among Lord Byron and the Shelleys. Bibliography and index.

Cronin, Richard. *Shelley's Poetic Thoughts*. New York: St. Martin's Press, 1981. An incisive study of Shelley's thought within his poems and his manner of handling language. Cronin scrutinizes poetic forms as they manage realism and fantasy, elegy and dream. Contains notes and an index.

Duff, David. *Romance and Revolution: Shelley and the Politics of a Genre*. New York: Cambridge University Press, 1994. Duff examines Romanticism and politics in the work of Shelley. Bibliography and index.

Everest, Kelvin, ed. *Percy Bysshe Shelley: Bicentenary Essays*. Cambridge, England: D. S. Brewer, 1992. A collection of biographical and critical essays on the life and works of Shelley. Includes bibliographical references.

Frosch, Thomas R. *Shelley and the Romantic Imagination: A Psychological Study*. Newark: University of Delaware Press, 2007. This volume offers detailed analysis of a few of Shelley's major works. Readers are given insight into the possible meaning behind his themes and characterizations and the personal reasons that Shelley's may have had for using them.

Hamilton, Paul. *Percy Bysshe Shelley*. Tavistock, England: Northcote House/British Council, 2000. Hamilton's biography provides the story of Shelley's life and criticism and interpretation of his works.

Höhne, Horst. *In Pursuit of Love: The Short and Troublesome Life and Work of Percy Bysshe Shelley*. New York: Peter Lang, 2000. A biography of Shelley offering insights into his life and work. Includes bibliographical references and index.

Holmes, Richard. *Shelley: The Pursuit*. New York: E. P. Dutton, 1975. This major biography presents Shelley as a sinister and sometimes cruel artist of immense talent. Holmes claims new answers to questions about Shelley's Welsh experiences and about his paternity of a child born in Naples. Critical readings of Shelley's writings are less valuable than their biographical context. Contains illustrations, bibliography, notes, and an index.

Lewis, Linda M. *The Promethean Politics of Milton, Blake, and Shelley*. Columbia: University of Missouri Press, 1992. Lewis examines the Greek myth of Prometheus in Shelley's *Prometheus Unbound*, John Milton's *Paradise Lost*, and the works of William Blake. Bibliography and index.

Morton, Timothy, ed. *The Cambridge Companion to Shelley*. New York: Cambridge University Press, 2006. This collection of essays by international scholars examines Shelley, lending much of its attention to lesser-known areas of his writing, including drama, prose, and translations. The essays are organized thematically and are divided into three sections, focusing on his life, his writing, and the role he played in the culture and politics of his time.

All the essays are previously unpublished and offer new perspectives on Shelley's writing and his role in the literary canon.

Simpson, Michael. *Closet Performances: Political Exhibition and Prohibition in the Dramas of Byron and Shelley*. Stanford, Calif.: Stanford University Press, 1998. Simpson examines the role of politics and censorship in the plays of Lord Byron and Shelley. Bibliography and index.

Sperry, Stuart M. *Shelley's Major Verse: The Narrative and Dramatic Poetry*. Cambridge, Mass.: Harvard University Press, 1988. This excellent study of *Queen Mab*, *Alastor*, *The Revolt of Islam*, *Prometheus Unbound*, *The Cenci*, *The Witch of Atlas*, *Epipsychidion*, and *The Triumph of Life* attempts to synthesize philosophical, psychological, and biographical approaches to Shelley.

Wasserman, Earl R. *Shelley: A Critical Reading*. Baltimore: The Johns Hopkins University Press, 1971. Wasserman's massive, detailed readings of virtually all Shelley's major poems have been extremely influential. Wasserman emphasizes Shelley's metaphysical skepticism and discusses his conceptions of existence, selfhood, reality, causation, and their relation to transcendence. Some of the readings are very dense and may be intimidating for the beginning student, but no serious student of Shelley can ignore them.

Wheatley, Kim. *Shelley and His Readers: Beyond Paranoid Politics*. Columbia: University of Missouri Press, 1999. Examines Shelley's reception in major British periodicals and the poet's idealistic passion for reforming the world.

Wroe, Ann. *Being Shelley*. Bloomington: Indiana University Press, 2007. This biography focuses on the themes and images that were present throughout Shelley's life and works. Wroe examines his poetry, notes, books, and letters to reveal the links between his life and writing.

*Richard E. Matlak*

# SIR PHILIP SIDNEY

**Born:** Penshurst, Kent, England; November 30, 1554
**Died:** Arnhem, the Netherlands; October 17, 1586

PRINCIPAL POETRY

*Astrophel and Stella*, 1591 (pirated edition printed
 by Thomas Newman; 1598, first authorized
 edition)
*Certaine Sonnets*, 1598
*The Psalmes of David, Translated into Divers and
 Sundry Kindes of Verse*, 1823 (with Mary
 Sidney Herbert, Countess of Pembroke)
*The Complete Poems of Sir Philip Sidney*, 1873 (2
 volumes)
*The Poems of Sir Philip Sidney*, 1962 (William A.
 Ringler, Jr., editor)
*The Psalms of Sir Philip Sidney and the Countess of
 Pembroke*, 1963 (J. C. A. Rathmell, editor)

OTHER LITERARY FORMS

Although Sir Philip Sidney's best-known work is
*Astrophel and Stella*, his major work and the one to
which he devoted most of his literary energy and much
of his political frustration was *Arcadia* (originally titled
*The Countess of Pembroke's Arcadia*). This long, much-
revised epic prose romance was written and revised
between 1578 and 1586; it was first published in an unfinished version in 1590, then in 1593 in a revised and
imperfect version, again in 1598, and repeatedly in
many editions for more than a century. The equivalent
in prose of Edmund Spenser's *The Faerie Queene*
(1590, 1596), it is an encyclopedic romance of love,
politics, and adventure, incorporating many stories and
discussions of philosophical, theological, erotic, and
psychological issues. Almost as important is Sidney's
critical treatise, *Defence of Poesie* (1595; published in
another edition as *An Apologie for Poetry*), written
about 1580, and setting forth in a seductive, if never
quite logically coherent argument, a celebration of the
nature and power of poetry, along with some prescrip-
tive (and perceptive) comments on the current malaise
of English poetry, drama, and the literary scene generally. Other works Sidney wrote include *The Lady of
May* (pr. 1578), a pastoral entertainment; the first forty-
four poems in a translation of the Psalms, later revised
and completed by his sister Mary; and a number of
other miscellaneous poems, prose treatises, and translations, mainly designed to further the cause of the
Protestant faction in Elizabeth's court.

ACHIEVEMENTS

"Our English *Petrarke Sir Philip Sidney* . . . often
comforteth him selfe in his sonnets of Stella, though
dispairing to attaine his desire. . . ." Thus Sir John
Harington in 1591, and generations of readers have
similarly sighed and sympathized with Astrophel's
tragicomic enactment of "poore Petrarch's long deceased woes." In literary history, *Astrophel and Stella*
marks a poetical revolution no less than William
Wordsworth's *Lyrical Ballads* (1798) or T. S. Eliot's
*The Waste Land* (1922); the poem is the product of a
young, ambitious poet, acting on his impatience with
the poetry he criticized in his manifesto, *Defence of
Poesie*. "Poetry almost have we none," he wrote, "but
that lyrical kind of songs and sonets," which "if I were a
mistresse would never persuade mee they were in
love." Sir Philip Sidney has also had a special place in
England's broader cultural history. Part of his fascination has been the ways succeeding ages have appropriated him: as a lost leader of the golden Elizabethan age,
Victorian gentleman, anguished Edwardian, committed existentialist, apolitical quietist, even a member of
the Moral Majority. Like all great writers, Sidney and
his works have been continually reinterpreted by successive ages, his poems and his life alike inscribed into
different literary, political, and cultural discourses. As
contemporary scholars have become more attuned to
both the linguistic and ideological complexity of Renaissance literature generally and to the new possibilities of contemporary critical methods, Sidney's writing
has been seen, both in its seemingly replete presence
and its symptomatic gaps and absences, as central to an
understanding of Elizabethan poetry and culture.

None of Sidney's poetry was published in his lifetime, and yet along with his other writings it circulated
among a small coterie of family and court acquaintances during the 1580's. Sidney's vocations were
those of courtier, statesman, Protestant aristocrat, and

patriot before that of a poet, and his poetry encourages the piecing together of a more problematic Sidney than that afforded by conventional hagiography. Sidney's writings often served, as A. C. Hamilton argues, "as a kind of outlet for political interests, compensating for the frustrations and failures" of his life: "problems that prove insurmountable in his career" were transposed and wrestled with in his fictions.

Sidney's major poetic work, *Astrophel and Stella*, in particular marks the triumphant maturity of Elizabethan court poetry, the belated but spectacular adaption of Petrarchanism to English aristocratic culture. It remains one of the most moving, delightful, and provocative collections of love poems in the language, all the more powerful in its impact because of the variety of needs that strain within it for expression—erotic, poetic, political, religious, cultural. One may read it, as Harington did, as the expression of thwarted, obsessive love, but it opens itself, like its author, to much richer readings, which reinforce Sidney's position as the central literary and cultural figure in the English Renaissance before William Shakespeare.

*Sir Philip Sidney* (Library of Congress)

BIOGRAPHY

Sir Philip Sidney was born into one of England's leading aristocratic families. His father was one of Elizabeth I's most loyal civil servants, serving as Lord President of Wales and Lord Deputy of Ireland. On his mother's side, Sidney was related to the influential Leicester family, one of the major Protestant powers in the country. He was educated under the stern Calvinist Thomas Ashton at Shrewsbury School, along with his lifetime friend and biographer Fulke Greville; in 1568, he went to Oxford, but he left without a degree in 1571. In 1572, he went on a Grand Tour through Europe, where he was introduced to and widely admired by major European scholars and statesmen, especially by leading Huguenot and German Protestants. In 1575, he returned to England and joined Elizabeth's court. He contributed a masque, *The Lady of May*, to one of the royal entertainments in 1578 and was employed by the

queen in a number of minor matters. Unfortunately, he alienated Elizabeth, partly because he was so forthright in his support of European and English Protestant ideals and partly because of his own personal charisma. In a stormy career at court, he alternated between periods of willing service and periods of retirement to his sister's house at Wilton, near Salisbury, where an increasing number of Elizabethan poets, intellectuals, and thinkers were gathering—almost as an alternative to the queen's court. In 1580, he quarreled with the earl of Oxford over whether the queen should consider marrying the French Catholic duke of Anjou. His advice on the matter was ignored, or played down, and he contemplated going illegally to the New World. Elizabeth's attitude to the man the English court so much admired (almost as much as many Europeans) was an ambivalent one: Sidney was probably too much a man of outspoken principle to be of use to her in her devious political dealings.

Sidney's literary career therefore developed in part out of the frustrations of his political career. Most of his works were written in his periods of chosen, or enforced, retirement to Wilton, and often grew out of discussions with friends such as Fulke Greville and Edward Dyer and his sister, Mary. He looked at the poetry being written in England, contrasted it most unfavorably with that of European courts, and so set out deliberately, by precept and example, to improve it. The result was an outburst of writing that marked a literary revolution: *Defence of Poesie*, probably started by 1578, was a sophisticated, chatty, and persuasive theoretical treatment. *Astrophel and Stella*, written in 1581-1582, is the first major Petrarchan sonnet collection written in English; the continually revised romance *Arcadia*, dedicated to his sister, was started in 1578, and was still being revised shortly before his tragic death in the Battle of Zutphen in 1586. Sidney was given a hero's funeral in London. Monarchs, statesmen, soldiers, and poets from all over Europe sent condolences, wrote memorials, and for the next sixty years or so, Sidney's person, prestige, and power hung over the English court and culture as a reminder of how the Renaissance ideal of the courtier could be combined with Protestant piety.

ANALYSIS

Sir Philip Sidney was educated to embrace an unusual degree of political, religious, and cultural responsibility, yet it is clear from his comments in *Defence of Poesie* that he took his literary role as seriously. Both this critical treatise and *Astrophel and Stella* are manifestos—not only of poetic but also of broader cultural practice. Both look forward to a long-needed renaissance of poetry and culture generally. For Sidney, poetry and its broader social uses were inseparable. Indeed, it is only with distortion that one can separate a "literary" from a "social" text, even with a Petrarchan love sequence such as *Astrophel and Stella*. Like other Elizabethan court poets, Sidney wrote his poetry within a structure of power and tried to carve out a discursive space under ideological pressures that attempted to control and direct the languages by which the court operated.

THE ELIZABETHAN COURT

The court was more than a visible institution for Sidney and his contemporaries: It was a felt pressure

that attempted to fix and determine all that came within its reach. Sidney's life and poetry are especially interesting examples of how the Elizabethan court's power operated on poetry. The court poets—for example, Sir Walter Ralegh and the earl of Oxford—acted as spokespeople for the court's values, yet inevitably the strains and tensions of their roles show through in their poetry. Poetry was both an expression of the power of the court and a means of participating in that power. Where a poem like Ralegh's "Praised be Diana's Fair and Harmles Light" shows the court contemplating its own idealized image, Sidney's poetry has a more uneasy relation to the court's power. Although on the surface his writing appears to embody, in Terry Eagleton's words, a "moment of ideological buoyancy, an achieved synthesis" of courtly values, Sidney's own position in the court makes his poetry an especially revealing instance of the struggles and tensions beneath the seemingly replete surface of the court and court poetry alike.

More than any of his contemporaries before John Donne and Shakespeare, Sidney in his poetry evokes a felt world of bustling activity, psychosocial pressure, cultural demand—in short, the workings of power on literary and historical discourse. The institutions that shape the poetry—the court, its household arrangements, its religious and political controversies—are evoked in the tournaments (41), the gossip of "curious wits" (23) and "courtly nymphs" (54), and make up an atmosphere of energetic worldliness. What distinguishes Sidney's poetry is the forceful way that something more than the glittering surface of the court energizes it. Despite his posthumous reputation as the perfect Renaissance courtier, Sidney's public career was one of political disappointment and humiliation; he seems to have been increasingly torn between public duty and private desire, much in the way the hero of his sonnet sequence is.

All of Sidney's works are permeated with the problem of authority and submission. Like himself, all of his heroes (including Astrophel) are young, noble, well educated, and well intentioned, but as they become aware of the complexities and ambiguities of the world, they become diverted or confused, and Sidney finds himself caught between compassion and condemnation of their activities. In *Arcadia*, Sidney attempted to solve in fiction many of the tensions that beset his life, and *Astrophel and Stella* similarly served as an outlet for political and social frustration. In the prose romance, Sidney's narrative irresolution and (in an early version) premature and repressive closure reveal deep and unsettling doubts; similarly, the ambivalences and hesitations, the shifting distance between poet and character, and the divided responses to intellectual and emotional demands in *Astrophel and Stella* articulate Sidney's ambivalent roles within the court.

### PROTESTANTISM

One of the fundamental influences giving Sidney's life and poetry their particular cast is Protestantism. Indeed, perhaps the most potent factor disrupting the repleteness of the court poetic was Sidney's piety and his struggle with creating a Protestant poetic. In A. C. Hamilton's phrase, Sidney was "a Protestant English Petrarch." Unlike his close friend Fulke Greville, for whom a radical Augustinian suspicion of metaphor and writing itself consistently undermined poetry's value, Sidney tried to hold together what in *Defence of Poesie* he terms humanity's "erected wit" and its "infected will." Indeed, what Sidney perhaps uniquely brought to the Petrarchan lyric was a self-conscious anxiety about the tension between courtly celebration and Protestant inwardness, between the persuasiveness and rhetoric and the self-doubt of sinful humankind, between the insecurity of people's word and the absolute claims of God's.

The tension in Sidney's writing between the courtly and the pious, John Calvin and Baldassare Castiglione, disrupts *Astrophel and Stella* most interestingly. Sidney's own theory sees poetry focusing on the reformation of will and behavior, and it is possible to read his own sequence as an exemplum of the perils of erotic love, or, in Alan Sinfield's words, "the errors of unregulated passion." Sidney displays Astrophel deliberately rejecting virtue, treating Stella as a deity in a "direct challenge to Christianity" and to right reason. His cleverness is displayed in trying to avoid or repel the claims of reason and virtue, and the outcome of the sequence is the inevitable end of self-deception. The inwardness of *Astrophel and Stella*—not necessarily, it

should be noted, its supposed autobiographical dimension, but its concern with the persona's self-consciousness, even self-centeredness, as lover, poet, courtier—is thus a fascinating blend of Petrarchan convention and Protestant self-concentration, and one that points to a distinctive late sixteenth century strain within the inherited vocabulary and rhetoric of the poet in his role in the court.

### THE COURT POET

When Sidney returned from his Grand Tour, he looked back across the Channel to the sophisticated academies and court circles that were encouraging writers, scholars, and musicians, and that were united by a synthesis of Christian, usually Protestant, piety and high Neoplatonism. The French academies, in particular, displayed a self-consciousness that distinguished them very strongly from the medieval courts. Shortly after Sidney's return, his sister Mary became the countess of Pembroke and established at Wilton what one of her followers was to term a "little Court," dedicated, both before and after his death, to continuing the renaissance of English courtly culture. Sidney's whole literary career became a frustrated attempt to realize a new role for the court poet, one based on the integrity and responsibility of values that he was unable to embody in his public life, and that more and more he poured into his writing. His remark to the earl of Leicester that he was kept "from the courte since my only service is speeche and that is stopped" has wider application than to its occasion, the French marriage crisis. It articulates a frustration toward the traditional subservience of a poet to the court, a stubborn insistence on forging a distinctive role for the poet.

Part of the fascination Sidney has traditionally evoked is what is often perceived as his ability to balance opposite ideological, rhetorical, or vocational demands on him. Certainly in *Defence of Poesie* and *Astrophel and Stella*, the elements of such a dialectic can be found. The promise of divinity that Astrophel perceives in Stella's eyes is, in Sidney's sympathetic comedy, wittily undermined by his self-consciousness, bashfulness, physical overeagerness, and human imperfection. In *Defence of Poesie*, Sidney describes poetry as a fervent reaching for the sublime, veiling truth to draw its reader toward it, and asserts that the power to move and so to bring about an enactment of poetry's transforming powers certainly lies within humankind's godlike nature. Yet for Sidney there was the seemingly inseparable problem of humanity's "infected will," and the reformed emphasis on human depravity and the untrustworthiness of the mind seems to have posed crucial problems for him and for the possibility of creating a Protestant poetic. Although elements of an opposition between rhetoric and truth, humanism and piety, Calvin and Castiglione, can be isolated, despite his most anxious intentions, Sidney does not manage to hold them together satisfactorily. In fact, his very fascination for later ages and his centrality for understanding sixteenth century poetry are grounded in such contradictions. "Unresolved and continuing conflict," in Stephen Greenblatt's phrase, is a distinctive mark of Renaissance culture, and Sidney's is a central place in that culture.

### The Psalmes of David

The versification of the Psalms, started by Sidney about 1579 and revised and completed by his sister, the countess of Pembroke, after his death, comprises the first post-Reformation religious lyrics that combine the rich emotional and spiritual life of Protestantism with the new rhetorical riches of the secular lyric. There are distinctive Protestant notes—a strong stress on election in Psalm 43, echoing Théodore Bèze's and Calvin's glosses rather than the original text, for example—and other psalms, where a strain of courtly Neoplatonism is highlighted, notably in Psalm 8, which (like Pico della Mirandola rather than Calvin) presents humanity as a privileged, glorious creation "attended" by God, an "owner" of regal and "crowning honour." Humans emerges as free and wondrous beings, like their creator, "freely raunging within the Zodiack of his owne wit," as Sidney put it in *Defence of Poesie*. Here Sidney juxtaposes, without integrating them, the great contraries of his age.

It is now generally believed that the psalms were originally drafted by Sidney early in his career, perhaps about 1579. Also written in this early period are a number of miscellaneous poems, including the so-called Certain Sonnets and many of the poems inserted into *Arcadia*. These are mainly of interest for showing Sid-

ney's eager experimentation—with quantitative verse, pastoral dialogue, song, metrical and stanzaic patterns, and above all the appeal to the feelings of the reader, notably in "Leave me ô Love, which reachest but to dust" and the magnificent double sestina from *Arcadia*, "Yee Gote-heard Gods."

### Astrophel and Stella

Sidney's most sustained and most celebrated work is his sonnet sequence *Astrophel and Stella*, probably written in 1582, which dramatizes a frustrated love affair between a courtier and an admired lady. As Germaine Warkentin has shown, Sidney may have been tinkering with his "Certain Sonnets" during 1581-1582, abandoning them the next summer "to compose one of the three most distinguished sonnet sequences of the English Renaissance." Certainly *Astrophel and Stella* conveys an intensity that suggests a short burst of concentrated writing.

This sequence of 108 sonnets and eleven songs anatomizes the love of a young, restless, self-conscious courtier, Astrophel, for a lady, Stella, his star. His purpose is set out in the opening sonnet, in which he claims, "I sought fit words to paint the blackest face of woe/ Studying inventions fine, her wits to entertaine." The reader is taken into the familiar world of Petrarchan convention and cliché: Astrophel the doubting, self-conscious, aggressive lover; Stella, the golden-haired, black-eyed, chaste and (usually) distant and (finally) unobtainable lady. The figures are equally familiar—debates between Hope and Absence, denials of loving at first sight, the frustrated desire alleviated by writing, the beautiful woman with the icy heart who pitilessly resists siege, and the final misery of the lover who ends his plaints in anguish, swearing in the end by all he has left, her "absent presence." Like the best *Petrarchisti*, Sidney makes the traditional motifs intensely dramatic. For the first time in English poetry since Geoffrey Chaucer, C. S. Lewis suggests, "a situation is not merely written about: it is created, presented, so as to compel our imaginations." Earlier Petrarchan poets such as Sir Thomas Wyatt had conveyed urgency and conversational informality, but, read as a whole, English poetry had not, since Chaucer, been distinguished by such continual, even restless, conflict and energy.

### USES OF RHETORIC

Modern critics, reacting against earlier impression-istic, Romantic criticism, have shown how the energy and variety of Sidney's poetry rests on a thorough exploitation of the riches of Renaissance rhetoric—through his use of apostrophe, dialogue, irony, shifts in decorum, and modulations of voice. As Ringler points out, perhaps "the most valuable product of his studies and disputations in Oxford was the thorough training he received in logic and formal classical rhetoric"; to these he added intense study and practice in ways of loosening the rhythmic movement of English line and working within the formal demands of stanzaic and metrical form. By a thorough familiarity with the conventional techniques of Renaissance love verse—which he parodies in 6, 9, and 15, for example—Sidney works within the eloquent courtly poetic, mocking and adapting it where necessary. Sidney uses his poems as workshops, experimenting with a great variety of stanzaic patterns and with devices such as inversion and feminine rhyme. Above all, he tries continually to juxtapose the movement of formal verse with an immediacy of idiom and logical development to involve his reader in the often tortuous movements of his character's broodings, arguments, and self-deceptions. Especially notable is the lightness and wit with which even Astrophel's most tortured self-examination is presented. Parody, the exaggerated use of erotic or literary clichés and puns, are all obvious enough, but the whole sequence is characterized by a sophisticated playfulness—the outrageous puns on "touch" in 9 leading to the self-pity (Astrophel's, not Sidney's) of the last line, the tongue-in-cheek anguish of the sonnets on Cupid, and the uproariousness of some of the erotic sonnets. Above all, the humor of the poet, indulging in his own mastery of language and able to dramatize his character, invites his readers to share his enjoyment at the varied follies and complexities of human love.

### PETRARCHANISM

If the Petrarchan tradition and the resources of Elizabethan rhetoric afforded Sidney a wonderfully flexible and rich poetic vehicle, there is nevertheless something limiting, even disturbing, about the literary mode in which he is working. Petrarchanism purports to be about love, and specifically about the obsession of a lover for a lady before whom he feels inferior, humble, and yet ennobled. Paradoxically, the sonnets become a weapon in an attempted mastery of the woman and their focus is exclusively on the anguish and achievements of the male lover. The conventions of Petrarchanism are those of a male-dominated society and its rhetorical strategies serve to elevate the woman only to subjugate her.

As Ann Jones and Peter Stallybrass have argued, "to Stella, Astrophel may speak of love as service," but outside his devotion to friends, "he can suggest a subtext of masculine domination." Within the struggle for mastery, rhetoric and erotic convention alike become means of domination. Stella herself is, like other Petrarchan mistresses, reduced to a disconnected set of characteristics, acknowledged only as they are manipulable or impinge on her lover's consciousness. She is entirely the product of her poet-lover's desires. *Astrophel and Stella* is a theater of desire in which the man has all the active roles, and in which she is silent or merely iconic, most present when she refuses him or is absent. Astrophel does not want—although it is arguable that Sidney might—to call into question the power of his anguish or the centrality of his struggles of conscience, yet it seems legitimate to ask what Stella might reply to Astrophel's earnest self-regarding pleas for favor. Even if her replies are not "in" most of the poems (and where they are, as in Song 8, they are reported through Astrophel), what might she say? Is her silence the repression of the character or of Sidney? Does her silence reflect a whole cultural blindness that fixes women as objects of gaze and analysis within a society they did not invent and could not control? When one considers in these ways how the dynamics of Sidney's text function, once again one finds "literary" and "cultural" texts interacting.

### BIOGRAPHICAL ELEMENTS

An older criticism faced (or perhaps avoided) these issues by focusing on the biographical "origins" of the sequence. In part an outcome of the Romantic valorization of poetry as the overflow of sincerity or genuine experience, criticism sentimentalized the obvious connections between Sidney's life and the fiction of Astrophel and Stella into a poetic roman à clef. Undoubtedly, Sidney plays with his reader's curiosity about some kind of identification between himself and Astrophel and between Stella and Lady Penelope Rich (née Devereux), to whom as a youth Sidney's family nearly arranged a betrothal and in whom he may possibly (though there is no firm evidence either way) have had more than a literary interest. Sidney certainly builds into his sequence references to his career, to his father, to contemporary politics, to his friends, and—of most interest to the curious—to Lady Rich's name in two sonnets (24, 37) that were omitted from the first publication of the collection, perhaps for fear of embarrassing repercussions. Even so, the relationship between Sidney and his characters and between the events of his life and those seemingly within his poems should not be simplified. Just as Sidney manages simultaneously to have much in common with Astrophel, be sympathetic with him, and yet to criticize or laugh at him, so the gap between Stella and the historical Lady Rich is even wider—at best one can regard some of the references to Stella as sly or wistful fantasies. As to whether Sidney and Lady Rich were sexually involved, *Astrophel and Stella* gives no firm evidence.

### LOVE AND COURTLY BEHAVIOR

A more rewarding approach is to try to trace the way the poems are traversed by a variety of overlapping and in many cases contradictory influences, including court politics, the psychology of love, poetry, rhetoric, and Christianity. Within its confusions, tensions, and contradictions, *Astrophel and Stella* highlights the diverse and often contradictory pressures and possibilities that constitute the situation of an Elizabethan poet and lover. One of the distinctive possibilities of Petrarchanism was to set the traditional medieval debate on the nature of love in terms of the lover's psychology and within the demands of the codes of courtly behavior. Part of the fascination Petrarch had for English poets in the late sixteenth century was their puzzlement about how the Petrarchist conventions might fit their experiences. The prestige and suggestiveness of Petrarchanism allowed poets to examine not only the relationship between love and poetry, but also the way its worldview, its rich schematization of human experience, and their own changing social and individual realities intersected.

### EROTIC LOVE

One of the dominant concerns of the sequence is undoubtedly that of the problems and difficulties of erotic experience—although depicted entirely from the male viewpoint. *Astrophel and Stella* typically focuses on the "thrownness" of love—on the lover finding himself within a preexisting structuring of experience, a "race" that "hath neither stop nor start" (23), but which continually disrupts his sense of a preexistent self. Sexuality becomes an object to be examined, supervised, confessed, and transformed into poetry. It should be noted, however, that the "self" that is put into question in *Astrophel and Stella* is not, or not primarily, that of Sidney. The poet offers his poems to an audience of sympathetic listeners as a mirror less of his experiences than of theirs. The intellectual tensions observable in *Astrophel and Stella* are dramatized as paradigms, the effect of which is to highlight the readers' or hearers' awareness of their own experiences. Sidney's poems work on their readers, suggesting and manipulating although never compelling into meaning. At times he refers to quite specific members of his audience—to other lover-poets in 6, in which Astrophel distinguishes his own "trembling voice" and the sincerity of his love from those of other lovers and so provokes them to respond by praising their own mistresses or talents. At times his suffering hero will ostensibly address a rather special audience—"I Stella's ears assayl, invade her ears," he says in Sonnet 61; or he (or Sidney) will address a friend (as in Sonnet 14), and even occasionally himself (as in 30). Yet the most important audience is unnamed: the readers who, through the poem's history, will read them, meditate on, and act out their drama.

### CRITICAL RESPONSE

Surveying the history of Sidney criticism, especially that of the modern era, one discovers a curious anxiety to find a coherent, sequential organization not merely made possible by the poems, but as a required means of reading them. *Astrophel and Stella* is thus often read as if it were a poetic novel. C. S. Lewis cautions against treating the Petrarchan sequence as if it were "a way of telling a story"; *Astrophel and Stella* is, he says, "not a love story but an anatomy of love," while Max Putzel speaks of the poems' "careful disorder." On the other hand, A. C. Hamilton argues that "the sonnets are organized into a sequence with a unifying structure," and other critics have written of what they see as careful structure and sequence. In Hamilton's scheme, sonnets 1-12 form an introduction, 13-30 concentrate on Astrophel's isolation, with 41-68 concerned with his moral rebellion, 71-85 with his attempt at seduction, and the remainder with his failure. Such divisions differ radically among the proponents of a narrative structure; in short, if a reader wishes to find a narrative development and final irresolution rather than an exercise in love's variety, then *Astrophel and Stella* is open to such a reading. Perhaps the most satisfying sequential reading of the collection is that by Ann Rosalind Jones, who stresses that although it is possible (and peculiarly satisfying) to see Astrophel as undergoing a gradual disintegration and loss of control, Sidney's sequence does not use the linking devices of other poets, such as Dante or Maurice Scève, which might strongly encourage a reading of the sequence as a growth in self-knowledge. Even when one constructs a sequence, it is primarily characterized by an unstable, eddying movement, "dramatically *dis*ordered," as Jones argues. "Even at the end of his experience," Astrophel can "predict the course of his writing no better than the course of his love" and so each sonnet becomes a new starting place. In short, while *Astrophel and Stella* allows for a linear development, it does not force one on a reader, encouraging the reader just as readily to view Astrophel's experience as unpredictable, random, and even as an exemplum of failure.

One recurring pattern is a tension between the demands of the public world of politics and responsibility and the private world of erotic desire. In many sonnets, Astrophel presents love in terms of a debate between traditional abstractions such as desire and reason, love and duty. Part of the reader's enjoyment lies in watching him, through Sidney's fond but penetrating perspective, indulging himself in false logic (52) or in seeing his dutifully constructed arguments against love undermined by the simple appearance of his beloved, as in 5, 10, or in the amusing self-contradictions of 47. Astrophel tries in vain to keep his two worlds and their demands separate. He claims that love gives him a private place, a sense of self from which the demands of courtly responsibility are shown to be trivial, but

caught between conflicting worlds of self-indulgence and political responsibility, he ends by succeeding in neither. The reader watches him corrupting his avowedly pure love into sensuality by the deviousness of political rhetoric. In Sonnet 23, he appears to reject the world, but in Sonnet 69, he expresses Stella's conditional encouragement of his advances in terms of the court's own language. Since, he argues, she has "of her high heart giv'n" him "the monarchie," as a king, he too can take some advantage from that power.

At the root of Astrophel's self-deception is the structure of Petrarchanism itself, which, as John Stevens and others have pointed out, was at once a literary convention and a very serious courtly game, one "in which three powerful discourses meet and join hands: love, religion, and politics." *Astrophel and Stella* is based on a formula by which the man is subjected to his lady while, at the same time, the situation enables him to pour fourth his eloquence in an attempt to influence her. The relationship is parallel to the relationship between courtier and monarch—built on absolute loyalty and subjection, frustration and rejection—interlaced with devious manipulation for the favors of the capricious, distant beloved. Thus while Astrophel speaks of the "joy" inspired by Stella and of his own "noble fire," he is attempting to manipulate Stella's vulnerability, seeking power over her in the way the devious courtier seeks hidden but real power over the monarch. In terms of sexual politics of the Renaissance court, Astrophel's world is one shared primarily by other male courtiers, using language as a means of domination and treating women as subject to their desire, much in the way courtiers themselves were at the mercy of the monarch.

Thus the reader watches Astrophel indulging himself in small subtle ways—playing on grammar in 63, twisting Stella's words, speaking openly to her in a kind of "manic playfulness," and allowing (or being unable to prevent) the emergence of the underlying physicality of his desires in a series of fantasies of seduction (71, 72, 74, 79, 80, 81). The songs serve especially well to highlight the wish-fulfillment of Astrophel's frustrations—especially the dramatization in Song 5 of Astrophel's self-involvement, and the graceful fantasy of Song 8, viewed wistfully by the narrator from a distance and culminating in Sidney's clever and moving breaking down of the distance between narrator and character in the final line, where he confesses that "my" song is broken.

As the sequence draws to its inevitably inconclusive end, Astrophel's fantasies become less and less realizable. He indulges in self-pity and then more realistically accepts the end of the relationship, vacillating between joy and grief, optimism and despair, dedication and unfaithfulness. As Hamilton points out, the mutability of human love which haunts so many Elizabethan sonnet sequences, especially Shakespeare's, enters Sidney's only indirectly, but where he immerses himself in the intensity of the living moment, as the sequence ends, he realizes he is "forever subject to love's tyranny, a victim of *chronos* forever caught in time's endless linear succession."

Readings of *Astrophel and Stella* inevitably point to it as a quintessential ideological and literary struggle, where a variety of impulses struggle for mastery. Like the best love poems, it asks its readers to look at themselves. Stella herself, the guiding metaphor of the sequence, is distinguished by her nature, behavior, influence, and power, always requiring, like a text, interpretation. Astrophel, like the reader of his creator's sequence, is an exegete of love. "What blushing notes doest thou in margin see," he asks, and goes on, as all readers do with the whole sequence, to choose his own convenient misunderstanding of Stella. Astrophel may state that all his "deed" is to "copy" what in Stella "Nature writes" (3) or assert that "Stella" is, literally, the principle of love in the cosmos (28), and that the words he utters "do well set forth my mind" (44), but Sidney knows, as his readers do, that love and its significance and its expression in language are far more complex matters.

*Astrophel and Stella* is what Roland Barthes terms a "playful" text, one that depends strongly on its audience, inviting participation both to reproduce the process, intellectual and emotional, by which the poem's struggles came to be verbalized and to go beyond them, adding one's own preoccupations. *Astrophel and Stella* has a capacity to invade its readers, to direct and inform their responses, but as well, to open them to an awareness that it functions only through a process of deliberate reciprocity. It is this joyful welcome to its readers that makes it such a landmark in English poetry.

OTHER MAJOR WORKS

LONG FICTION: *Arcadia*, 1590, 1593, 1598 (originally entitled *The Countess of Pembroke's Arcadia*).

PLAYS: *The Lady of May*, pr. 1578 (masque); *Fortress of Perfect Beauty*, pr. 1581 (with Fulke Greville, Lord Brooke; Phillip Howard, the earl of Arundel; and Baron Windsor of Stanwell).

NONFICTION: *Defence of Poesie*, 1595 (also as *An Apologie for Poetry*).

MISCELLANEOUS: *Miscellaneous Prose of Sir Philip Sidney*, 1973.

BIBLIOGRAPHY

Alexander, Gavin. *Writing After Sidney: The Literary Response to Sir Philip Sidney, 1586-1640*. New York: Oxford University Press, 2006. Alexander looks at the legacy of one of the most important Elizabethan writers by examining first his sister Mary Sidney, his brother Robert Sidney, his friend Fulke Greville, and his niece Mary Wroth, then examining poets and writers who were influenced by him.

Berry, Edward I. *The Making of Sir Philip Sidney*. Toronto, Ont.: University of Toronto Press, 1998. Explores how Sidney created himself as a poet by making representations of himself in the roles of some of his most literary creations, including *Astrophel and Stella* and the intrusive persona of *Defence of Poesie*.

Connell, Dorothy. *Sir Philip Sidney: The Maker's Mind*. Oxford, England: Clarendon Press, 1977. Considers Sidney's life and art in a biographical and historical context. Connell discusses in detail important historical influences on Sidney. Includes maps, a bibliography, and an index.

Duncan-Jones, Katherine. *Sir Philip Sidney: Courtier Poet*. New Haven, Conn.: Yale University Press, 1991. This useful biography links the details of Sidney's life at court to his poetic works.

Garrett, Martin, ed. *Sidney: The Critical Heritage*. New York: Routledge, 1996. A collection of essays that gather a large body of critical sources on Sidney. Includes bibliographical references and index.

Hamilton, A. C. *Sir Philip Sidney: A Study of His Life and Works*. New York: Cambridge University Press, 1977. A study of Sidney's life, poetics, and selected works. General survey places his work in a biographical context. Includes an appendix, notes, a bibliography, and an index.

Kay, Dennis, ed. *Sir Philip Sidney: An Anthology of Modern Criticism*. Oxford, England: Clarendon Press, 1987. A collection of scholarly criticism. Kay's introduction places Sidney in a cultural heritage and surveys the changes that have occurred in the critical approaches to Sidney's work. Includes a chronology, a bibliography, an index, and a list of early editions.

Kinney, Arthur F., ed. *Essential Articles for the Study of Sir Philip Sidney*. Hamden, Conn.: Archon Books, 1986. A collection of twenty-five articles with a wide range of critical approaches. Topics include Sidney's biography, *The Lady of May*, *Defence of Poesie*, *Astrophel and Stella*, and *Arcadia*. Includes bibliography.

Sidney, Philip, Sir. *Sir Philip Sidney: Selected Prose and Poetry*. Edited by Robert Kimbrough. Madison: University of Wisconsin Press, 1983. Kimbrough gives detailed attention to *Defence of Poesie*, *Astrophel and Stella*, and *Arcadia*. Also surveys the critical approaches to Sidney. Contains a chronology and a select bibliography.

Stillman, Robert E. *Philip Sidney and the Poetics of Renaissance Cosmopolitanism*. Burlington, Vt.: Ashgate, 2008. Stillman examines the poetry of Sidney, looking at topics such as the influence of his political views and the general culture. Also examines *Defence of Poesie*.

*Gary F. Waller*

# SIR ROBERT SIDNEY

**Born:** Penshurst Place, Kent, England; November 19, 1563
**Died:** Penshurst Place, Kent, England; July 13, 1626

### PRINCIPAL POETRY

*The Poems of Robert Sidney*, 1984 (the poems went unpublished during his lifetime; P. J. Croft, editor)

### OTHER LITERARY FORMS

Unlike his more famous brother Philip and his sister Mary, Sir Robert Sidney was not a prolific writer. Indeed, his career as a poet was probably confined to a few years, possibly as few as two. There are many letters by him in the Sir Robert Sidney papers, but he published no literary work in his lifetime. Likewise, his poetry remained in manuscript, probably at Penshurst, until the early nineteenth century, when it found its way into the Warwick Castle Library. The manuscript was first positively identified by P. J. Croft in 1973 and purchased by the British Library in 1974. It was subsequently printed in a modern-spelling version by Katherine Duncan-Jones, published as *The Poems of Robert Sidney* in 1984 by Oxford University Press.

### ACHIEVEMENTS

The discovery of the manuscript of Sir Robert Sidney's poetry in the 1970's added a distinctive voice to the courtier poets of the late sixteenth century. In his manuscript's ninety pages of nervous, often corrected handwriting are the works of a new Elizabethan poet of outstanding interest. Sidney does not quite possess Philip's variety or intimate control of tone and mood within a poem (the emotions of his verse are expressed in broader sweeps) but his ear is highly sensitive, and his poems reverberate with the great commonplaces of Elizabethan life and literature—time, absence, grief, and deprivation. Like his contemporary Sir Walter Ralegh, Robert Sidney turned to poetry only occasionally, yet he found in it a commitment that went beyond emotional solace, Like Ralegh's verse, Sidney's reveals the ideological power of the Elizabethan court over those who struggled for articulation within its frantic center or (in Robert's case) on its anxious margins.

### BIOGRAPHY

During his life and after, Sir Robert Sidney was overshadowed by the brilliance of his elder brother Philip. He was a dutiful son of a family that was ambitious but relatively new to the power struggles of the Elizabethan aristocracy. In his early life, Robert had none of the prestige or flamboyance of Philip. He dutifully went on his Grand Tour of Europe, pursued by letters of advice from his brother as to his reading, chivalric bearing, acquaintances, and finances. In 1585, he accompanied Philip, who had been appointed governor of Flushing, to the Low Countries, and was present at the Battle of Zutphen, where Philip was mortally wounded. Philip's death seemed to represent the death of an entire age. From the late 1580's, Elizabethans became increasingly bewildered and disillusioned, as the Armada victory turned sour, court infighting grew more and more frenetic, and the queen cultivated the trappings of high Neoplatonism to hold in check the corruption and confusion beneath the surface of the court.

In the shadow of his brother, Robert had undergone the usual initiation of the Elizabethan courtier. In 1584, he married Barbara Gamage, a young Welsh heiress—after some rather sordid negotiations. Their letters later show them to have grown into a most loving couple. He constantly addresses her as "sweet heart" or "dear heart," and the letters are full of sadness at his absence from her. In 1594, he wrote that "there is no desyre in me so dear as the love I bear you and our children . . . you are married, my dear Barbara, to a husband that is now drawn so into the world and the actions of yt as there is no way to retire myself without trying fortune further."

The intense strain of being an honest courtier during the 1590's is evident throughout his letters. Indeed, it might be said that Philip had the good fortune to die in 1586; Robert had to live on. In 1587, he was his brother's chief mourner, and like his sister Mary, he may have turned to poetry at this time partly in order to continue his brother's literary ideals. In 1588, he was appointed to Philip's old position of governor of Flushing, and with only a few brief breaks, usually to carry out some unpalatable diplomatic task imposed by Elizabeth, he spent most of the next decade in the Low Countries, his chief interest being to return home. Constantly exhorted to live up to his brother's standard, he seems to have been regarded by the queen as a convenient workhorse.

After years of frustration, Robert Sidney's fortunes improved under James's reign. Life at Penshurst in the early seventeenth century was celebrated in that most harmonious of poems by Ben Jonson, "To Penshurst,"

in which he praised what appeared to its aristocratic proprietors to be the rich, cooperative life of an organic and humane community. Incidentally, Jonson does not here explicitly mention Sidney as a poet—although this would not have been entirely unusual, as outside his immediate circle even Philip's reputation as a poet had hardly been mentioned before his death. In 1605, Sidney was created viscount de Lisle, and in 1618, earl of Leicester. He died in 1626, at age sixty-two, having survived his elder brother by forty years and his elder sister by five.

## Analysis

The retrieval of the manuscript poems written by Sir Robert Sidney was one of the most important Renaissance discoveries of the past one hundred years. The Sidney manuscript is the only extant substantial body of verse by an Elizabethan poet in his own handwriting and incorporating the poet's own revisions. In addition to their intrinsic interest, these poems dramatically change the present view of the literary activities of the Sidney circle—that unique, closely connected family group inspired by the genius and person of Sir Philip Sidney, Robert's brother.

Although references to the literary interests of all the Sidneys, including Robert, are found in many dedications, letters, and prefaces of the period, there are few references to him as a poet. George Chapman wrote of him in 1609 as "the most Learned and Noble Concluder of the Warres Art, and the Muses." There is a tradition that he wrote the lyrics for his godson Robert Dowland's *Musicall Banquet*, and he may have written verses in honor of his daughter's marriage. Certainly, like the rest of his family, Sidney was widely praised as a generous patron of literature. It is significant that the distinctive note of the encouragement of poets by the other members of the Sidney family was that they were poets themselves. "Gentle *Sir Philip Sidney*," wrote Thomas Nashe, "thou knewest what belonged to a schollar, thou knewest what paines, what toyle, what travel, conduct to perfection."

### Mary Sidney

Like that of his sister Mary, Sidney's poetic career may have started seriously only after his brother's death. It is clear that she did not begin to write seriously until after 1586, when she took upon herself the vocation to continue his work in forwarding the Elizabethan poetic Renaissance. The bulk of her work, an impressive body of poetry and prose, grows directly out of Philip's inspiration: She edited his manuscripts, completed his versifying of the psalms, and wrote or translated a number of works directly influenced by his critical theories or dedicated to his memory. It may be that Robert also wrote his verse as a similar, although less public, attempt to continue his brother's poetic intentions. He may have decided that Mary, more permanently settled at Wilton in the 1580's with the increasing comings and goings of Fulke Greville, Edmund Spenser, Samuel Daniel, and other poets, was better placed to forward the literary revolution of the Sidneys. It was to her that he sent the one extant copy of his manuscript, possibly during one of his much-desired but infrequent visits to England.

### SONNETS AND SONGS

The obvious comparisons are, then, between Sidney's poetry and that written by Philip and Mary. Like his brother's, Sidney's poems are in the form of a Petrarchan miscellany of sonnets and songs, although they show a greater variety of metrical and stanzaic patterns than the normal sonnet sequence of the 1580's and 1590's, a characteristic he may have derived from Mary, whose psalms are the most impressive formal experimentation in English verse before Gerard Manley Hopkins. In the countess's 165 psalms, there are 164 distinct stanzaic and metrical patterns, some of them being remarkably complex and subtle.

Robert's are technically less ambitious, although they certainly reflect a similar interest in working with complex patterns of verse—as evidenced by the three unusual thirteen-line stanzas of "Upon a wretch that wastes away/ Consumed with wants." Here the complex rhyme scheme (*aab cccb ddeeb*) and the varying line length (886886-33666 syllables) are reminiscent of the countess's experiments, as indeed are many of Sidney's pastorals and songs. None of the patterns exactly matches those of Mary and the diction is naturally closer to the typical love poetry of the era (such as in *England's Helicon*, 1600) than to her psalms, but they arise from the same fascination with formal experimentation: Just as in Mary's psalms only once is the

stanzaic pattern repeated, so in Sidney's twenty-four songs he never repeats a pattern, and within particular poems, too, he displays a technical virtuosity comparable to that of his brother and sister.

Song 1, "O eyes, a lights devine," for example, skillfully mixes lines of varied length, with a predominantly iambic beat. Like both Philip and Mary, he uses feminine rhyme very skillfully in the songs (as in Song 10, "You whoe fauor doe enioy"), and his technical skill is seen in such sophisticated mixtures as blending of rhyming anapests with the regular iambics in Song 4 ("My soule is purest fine/ doth not aspyre"). Like Mary, Sidney shows an excellent control of movement and balance within single lines, as, for example, in the final lines of Sonnet 21: "Or if on mee from my fayre heauen are seen/ Some scattred beames: Know sutch heate giues theyre light/ as frosty mornings Sun: as Moonshyne night."

### PHILIP'S INFLUENCE

If Sidney shares something of Mary's technical daring, the most important influence is nevertheless that of his brother. Sidney's sequence is clearly modeled on *Astrophel and Stella* (1591): It mingles sonnets with longer, more emotionally diffuse songs, and like Philip's sequence, Sidney's contains an interesting transformation of biographical reference into a devious fiction. The whole sequence is characterized by an opaque melancholy, a mood of disturbance and brooding, which, while endemic to Petrarchan sonnets in general, nevertheless takes as its subject Sidney's reading of his own political and personal career. While the collection is a typical Petrarchan miscellany, it is united even less than *Astrophel and Stella* by narrative or personas and is held together, more explicitly than in any other collection of late Elizabethan lyrics, by that most powerful of institutions and ideological forces, the Elizabethan court.

### WRITING FROM THE LOW COUNTRIES

Robert's poetry was probably written during his long, frustrating tour of duty in the Low Countries, perhaps begun (like Mary's) in the late 1580's but (at least in the one extant copy) copied probably at some time between 1596 and 1598. Perhaps Sidney's poetry was a reaction not only to his depressing exile from England but also to the melancholy duty of occupying his brother's old post. Much of Sidney's verse could be read as a moving expression of a frustrated politician's world of escape, yearning for his wife and children and home at Penshurst.

Sonnet 7, "The hardy Captein vnusde to retyre," speaks directly of his turning from the Low Countries "to the West" where "loue fast holds his hart" (Song 6). The sixth song of the collection is an especially revealing piece—as well as being the most impressive poetically. Like Ralegh's famous and haunting "As you Came to the Holy Land," it is based on the traditional lost ballad of a pilgrim traveling to Walsingham. Sidney's version is a 136-line poem, hauntingly evocative in its use of the ballad with its traditional dialogue, here occurring between a pilgrim and a lady who presumably represents Sidney's wife. Certainly, "the knight that loves me best," who "greefs liuerie weares," who "to the west . . . turns his eyes," to whom she refers is Sidney's wistful projection of his own exiled self held by duty to the Low Countries away from what later in the poem he terms: "the lady that doth rest near Medwayes sandy bed." Penshurst Place, the Sidney home, stands on the Medway River just outside Tonbridge and almost due west of Flushing. Interestingly enough, Sidney revised this particular line to read "near ritch Tons sandy bed," which of course refers to Tonbridge.

### PETRARCHANISM

Song 6 is the most clearly autobiographical poem in the sequence, projecting a partly calculated, partly wistful view of Sidney's frustrated personal and political career. The bulk of the collection, in traditional Petrarchan fashion, is ostensibly concerned with love and is similar to a host of sequences written in the 1590's, such as Daniel's *Delia* (1592) or Michael Drayton's *Ideas Mirrour* (1594), although no poem mentions any identifiable or even coherently fictional mistress. The diction is typical of the English *petrarchisti*. The lovers "sowle" exists "in purest fyre" (Song 4); he accepts both the joys and griefs of love, in his "bands of service without end" (Sonnet 13). Readers encounter the familiar world of Petrarchan paradox: On one hand, there is the high idealism of the lover who affirms the beauty of "those fayre eyes" which "shyne in theyr former light" (Song 12); on the other hand,

there are the "paines which I vncessantly susteine" (Sonnet 2). The lady's beauties are "born of the heauens, my sowles delight" (Sonnet 3), while the lover's passions are "purest flames kindled by beauties rare" (Sonnet 4), as he contemplates in pleasurable agony how she takes "pleasure" in his "cruelty" (Sonnet 25), asking her why she "nowrishes" poisonous weeds of cold despair in love's garden instead of the plants and trees of love's true faith and zeal (Song 22).

This basic Petrarchan situation of frustration, contradiction, and paradox is decked out in familiar Neoplatonic garb. The world is a dark cave where love's lights never shine except through the beloved's eyes, the "purest stars, whose neuer diying fyres" (Sonnet 1) constantly burn a path between the heavens and the lover's soul. Sexual desire is rarely explicitly mentioned: the dominant mood is that of melancholy, the recurring emphasis on the lover's self-torturing helplessness, and to an unusual degree, on torture, disease, and violence. The lover is a continually lashed slave, flung from rocks, a leper, racked by gangrene, or in violent wars.

Even with the marked emphasis on violence, this is a world familiar to readers of Renaissance lyrics. Sidney's work is less versatile, metrically and metaphorically, than Philip's, with no double sestinas or quantitative verse and little of Philip's sly humor. What distinguishes Sidney's poems from the mass by second-rate poets such as Thomas Watson and Henry Constable and from the anonymous verse of a miscellany like *England's Helicon* is his remarkable control of form and tone, and his frequent use of a cryptic and direct address, not unlike the aphoristic tone of some of Greville's poems. Typical is the brief, pessimistic Song 17, which seems to reflect on deeply tragic events in the poet's experience.

### WELL-CRAFTED LINES

Robert's poetry, like the work of Philip and Mary, shows a deep commitment to the craft of poetry as well as to its inspiring or calculated consolations of erotic or political favor. It is more than conventional Petrarchan regret when he asserts that even "the most perfect stile cannot attaine" the expression of the mistress's beauties or the pangs of love. The poems are the work of a poet with a highly sensitive ear, and a range of tone that, while not broad, is deeply resonant, especially receptive to the way emotions may be attached to metaphors of absence and loss. In his *Caelica*, Greville often takes up the conventional assertion that, when apart, true lovers are paradoxically closer because of the spiritual nature of their love; but he places the motif in a grimly realistic context, affirming instead that "absence is pain." Similarly, Sidney's brooding over absence, delay, and loneliness have more than a conventional "feel" to them. Over and over again, the poet suffers from "greefs sent from her whom in my sowle I bless" (Song 23); constantly he feels that "delaies are death" (Song 18), as he waits "on unknown shore, with weather hard destrest" (Song 22). Such common Petrarchan motifs are made peculiarly effective especially through the grave, deliberate melancholic movement of the lines, which convey the passion, the hopelessness, and yet the continuing devotion of the lover.

### NEOPLATONISM AND CALVINISM

Intellectually, Sidney's verse is as rich a revelation of the peculiar strains and repressions of the Elizabethan aristocracy as that of Philip or Mary. His poetry, however, seems more detached from their particular religious interests. One of the most revealing notes of the literature of the Sidney circle is its continual attempt to balance the idealism of high Neoplatonism, and its emphasis on the autonomy of the human will and humans' desire for perfection, with the psychological and political demands of a strong Calvinistic piety, emphasizing God's transcendence of humanity and the corruption and worthlessness of human aspirations. It is interesting that Sidney seems relatively indifferent to this great intellectual debate; nor is there any sense that he was especially interested in the more extreme varieties of Neoplatonic or magical philosophy associated with John Dee or Giordano Bruno, which were current in the 1580's. Perhaps living isolated from the mainstream of English philosophical developments in the 1580's and 1590's, he was untouched by such speculation; altogether, Sidney's character and interests were more pragmatic and less speculative. His poetry had more immediate ends in view. A typically aspiring courtier, directing his poems at particular (never, of course, stated) ends, the intellectual tensions of his verse remain the stock-in-trade of the Petrarchan poet; his sequence is poetically but not intellectually sophisticated.

### THE ELIZABETHAN COURT

The particular feature of Sidney's poetry that makes his work important to readers of the ideologically opaque power struggles of the Elizabethan aristocracy is the intense way it articulates the silent power of the dominant institution of the age, the court. The basis of the Petrarchan sonnet collections of the late sixteenth century is not primarily erotic, despite their Petrarchan apparatus. Sexual desire is used—by Sidney's brother, as well as by Spenser, Daniel, Ralegh, and others—as a metaphor for political desire and frustration. Most of Sidney's poems do not evoke the frustrated sexual passion of a lover; they use that basic Petrarchan situation as a metaphor for political powerlessness and aspiration. The "lights divine" from which the lover is "exiled," "the only cause for which I care to see," and "these purest flames kindled by beauties rare," may be read as conventional Neoplatonic compliments of a beloved only if the realities of Elizabethan politics and the court's control of the discursive structures of both politics and poetry are ignored.

No less than Ralegh's "Cynthia" or "Praised be Diana's Fair and Harmless Light," Sidney's sonnets articulate the ideological dominance of the Elizabethan court; unlike Ralegh's—except in their intense anxiousness and their overly insistent protest of absolute devotion—they do not articulate any opposition to that hegemonic discourse. As his brother Philip's *Astrophel and Stella* so triumphantly shows, one of the distinctive features of the Petrarchan sequence is its encouragement to readers to decode it in a variety of ways—as erotic self-evaluation, philosophical meditation, or moral debate. Sidney's poems can be read as intense, extreme Neoplatonic poems of compliment and frustration, but they acquire an urgency and become rooted in the material life of late Elizabethan society when they are read as compensations for political powerlessness.

Not all of Sidney's poems can be read so directly in this way—there are a variety of translations, songs, and other miscellaneous pieces that may be seen as typical "workshop" exercises designed to show or practice his skills—but through the whole collection, one senses the enormous power of the Elizabethan court, creating and controlling its subjects by exerting power over their language, over their metaphors of political as well as poetical expression. The political world in which Sidney had, between 1586 and 1598, a marginal part, can be read from his poetical text: Finally the poetical text (the poems extant in his slim notebook) and the social text (the events which constitute the milieu in which he wrote) are indistinguishable, each flowing into the other to articulate the material and metaphorical dominance of the Elizabethan court.

### A TRUE SIDNEY

It is fascinating to see the emergence into literary and critical consciousness of such an interesting poet almost four hundred years after he wrote. When it was written, Sidney's poetry aimed to demonstrate his fitness to take part in the power of the court, but it demonstrated as well that he was a Sidney in another way—in his devotion to the craft and the importance of poetry. A decade or more after he wrote these poems, Sidney was praised by Jonson as a man of generosity, responsibility, and piety. Jonson speaks of how his children might "Reade, in their vertuous parents noble parts,/ The mysteries of manners, armes, and arts." Sidney's distinction in "armes and manners" was no mystery; he was a Sidney, a name which, as Jonson put it, was in "the impresse of the great." Until the rediscovery of his manuscript, however, Sidney's "arts" were indeed unknown. Perhaps by the time Jonson wrote "To Penshurst," Sidney himself had all but forgotten his youthful poetry. He had, after all, achieved his comfortable if minor place in the Jacobean aristocracy. One can only be glad that the longer span of history sometimes uncovers what the short time of individual men happens to bury.

### OTHER MAJOR WORK

NONFICTION: *Domestic Politics and Family Absence: The Correspondence (1588-1621) of Robert Sidney, First Earl of Leicester, and Barbara Gamage Sidney, Countess of Leicester*, 2005.

### BIBLIOGRAPHY

Croft, P. J., ed. *Autograph Poetry in the English Language: Facsimiles of Original Manuscripts from the Fourteenth to the Twentieth Century*. 2 vols. New York: McGraw-Hill, 1973. Includes Croft's introduction, commentary, and transcripts.

_____. *The Poems of Robert Sidney*. New York: Oxford University Press, 1984. This volume is edited from the poet's autograph notebook, found by Croft in 1973. It is the largest single collection of original Tudor poetry in existence. Includes an introduction and commentary by Croft.

Hay, Millicent V. *The Life of Robert Sidney, Earl of Leicester (1563-1626)*. London: Associated University Presses, 1984. Hay's biography of the poet includes genealogical tables, a bibliography, index, and an interesting account of Sidney's life as poet and politician.

Jonson, Ben. "To Penhurst." In *The Complete Poems*, by Ben Jonson. Edited by George Parfitt. New York: Penguin Books, 1996. In this tribute, Jonson acknowledges Sidney's contribution as poet and patron of the arts through an examination of Penshurst Place. This form of tribute based on a physical place went on to become a popular literary form.

Kelliher, W. Hilton, and Katherine Duncan-Jones. "A Manuscript of Poems by Robert Sidney: Some Early Impressions." *British Library Journal* 1 (1975): 107-144. A textual and bibliographic analysis of the find made by Croft.

Mazzola, Elizabeth. *Favorite Sons: The Politics and Poetics of the Sidney Family*. New York: Palgrave Macmillan, 2003. While this book focuses on Sir Philip Sidney, it contains much information on his sister and brother, although not always favorably inclined toward them

Parker, Tom W. N. *Proportional Form in the Sonnets of the Sidney Circle: Loving in Truth*. Oxford, England: Clarendon Press, 1998. Parker traces the relationship of poetic form to contemporary thinking about astrological matters in the love poetry of Robert and Philip Sidney as well as in the works of several of their contemporaries.

Sidney, Robert, and Barbara Gamage Sidney. *Domestic Politics and Family Absence: The Correspondence (1588-1621) of Robert Sidney, First Earl of Leicester, and Barbara Gamage Sidney*. Edited by Margaret P. Hannay, Noel J. Kinnamon, and Michael G. Brennan. Burlington, Vt.: Ashgate, 2005. Contains 332 letters between Robert Sidney and his wife that provide insight into their lives. A lengthy introduction to the work also provides biographical details and insight.

Warkentin, Germaine. "Robert Sidney's 'Darcke Offrings': The Making of a Late Tudor Manuscript *Canzoniere*." *Spenser Studies* 12 (1992): 37-73. An aesthetic appreciation of the work of Sidney that argues against the characterization of the poems as "Darcke Offrings" and for their consideration alongside the works of his famous brother.

*Gary F. Waller*

# JON SILKIN

**Born:** London, England; December 2, 1930
**Died:** Newcastle upon Tyne, England; November 25, 1997

PRINCIPAL POETRY

*The Peaceable Kingdom*, 1954
*The Two Freedoms*, 1958
*The Re-ordering of the Stones*, 1961
*Nature with Man*, 1965
*Poems, New and Selected*, 1966
*Amana Grass*, 1971
*The Principle of Water*, 1974
*The Little Time-Keeper*, 1976
*The Psalms with Their Spoils*, 1980
*Selected Poems*, 1980, 1988, 1993
*The Ship's Pasture: Poems*, 1986
*The Lens-Breakers*, 1992
*Watersmeet*, 1994
*Making a Republic*, 2002

OTHER LITERARY FORMS

In addition to being a noted poet, Jon Silkin (SIHL-kihn) was also an important literary critic, authoring a study of English poetry from World War I, *Out of Battle: The Poetry of the Great War* (1972, 1987), and a study of modern twentieth century poetry, *The Life of Metrical and Free Verse in Twentieth-Century Poetry* (1997). Related to his criticism was his editing of the significant collections *The Penguin Book of First World War Poetry* (1979, 1981), *Wilfred Owen: The Poems* (1985), *The Penguin Book of First World War Prose* (coeditor with Jon Glover; 1989), and *The War Poems of Wilfred Owen* (1994). Silkin also wrote one play, *Gurney*, published in 1985 and produced in London, as *Black Notes*, in 1986.

ACHIEVEMENTS

Jon Silkin was honored with the Geoffrey Faber Memorial Prize (1965) for *Nature with Man* and a C. Day Lewis Fellowship (1976-1977), and he was made a Fellow of the Royal Society of Literature (1986). Just as important is Jon Silkin's inclusion in such prestigious anthologies as *New Poets of England and America* (1957, 1962), *The New Poetry* (2d ed., 1966), *Poems of Our Moment* (1968), *British Poetry Since 1945* (1970), *The Norton Anthology of Modern Poetry* (1973), *The Oxford Book of Twentieth-Century English Verse* (1973), *The Hutchinson Book of Post-War British Poets* (1989), and *Anthology of Twentieth-Century British and Irish Poetry* (2001). His role as founder and continuing editor of the magazine *Stand*—devoted first to publishing modern poetry and its criticism, and later including modern fiction—also ensures Silkin a lasting place in the history of modern British literature.

BIOGRAPHY

Jon Silkin was the son of Jewish parents, Joseph Silkin, a lawyer, and Dora Rubenstein Silkin. War made a deep impression on Silkin as a child; as a youngster, one of Silkin's most vivid memories, referred to in his poetry, was of being evacuated from London to the countryside during the German bombing during World War II. After National Service in the Education Corps (1948-1950), during which he reached the rank of sergeant, Silkin spent the years between 1950 and 1956 as a manual laborer in London, an experience partly reflected in his first-person poems about cemetery groundskeeping and about workingmen. During this period, he founded the literary periodical *Stand* in 1952 and published his first major poetry collection in 1954.

After working as an English teacher to foreign students in 1956-1958, Silkin was appointed Gregory Fellow in Poetry at the University of Leeds, a position he held from 1958 to 1960. He came relatively late to a formal college education, earning his B.A. from the University of Leeds as a mature student. The degree, awarded in 1962, took him only two years to complete. In 1964, he became founding coeditor of Northern House Publishers in Newcastle upon Tyne and subsequently, as reflected in the locales of his poetry, held a variety of teaching, visiting instructor, and visiting writer-in-residence posts at universities and colleges in England, the United States (in Ohio, Iowa, Idaho, Kentucky, and Washington, D.C.), Australia, Israel, Japan, and Korea.

Married to the writer Lorna Tracy in 1974 and divorced in 1995, Silkin had four children; the death of the first, Adam, and birth of the second, David, had profound impacts on Silkin, manifested in his poetry, which likewise indicates how important love, marriage, children, and parenting remained throughout his life. He died in 1997.

*Jon Silkin*

## ANALYSIS

A third or more of Jon Silkin's approximately 350 poems deal with or touch on the subject of the natural world and humanity's relation with it, through concord, discord, or symbolic parallels. Animals, such as the persecuted fox of Silkin's antihunting poems, or various caged or free birds; insects, such as the bees, butterflies, moths, ants, and flies, with their interesting symbolism applicable to nature and humanity; plants, such as the various flowers of Silkin's distinctive flower poems; and inanimate nature, especially stones, river, sea, sky, and stars—all pervade Silkin's poetry both as subjects and repositories of imagery and symbolism. The poems most often anthologized have been selections from the fifteen flower poems (so named by Silkin himself) in *Nature with Man*: "A Bluebell," "Crowfoot (in Water)," "A Daisy," "Dandelion," "Goat's Beard and Daisy," "Harebell," "Iris," "Lilies of the Valley," "Milkmaids (Lady's Smock)," "Moss," "Peonies," "Small Celandine," "The Strawberry Plant," "The Violet," and "White Geranium." As Silkin himself explains in "Note on 'Flower' Poems" in *Nature with Man*, the flowers are either wild or cultivated, suggesting certain relationships with humanity, and the garden is "a kind of human bestiary, containing in the several plants earlier developed and anticipatory examples of human types and situations." Silkin goes on in his note to discuss almost every flower poem, explaining for example that "'Dandelion' . . . sees its subject as a seizer of space, and asks for political parallels to be made," including the idea of "nature being a 'preying upon.'" While Silkin's analyses of his own flower poems are perceptive (not always true of writers about their own work), they are not exhaustive: for example, lurking in the background of "Dandelion" is the etymology of the flower's name, from "lion's tooth."

As meritorious as these flower poems but not as well known are the ones from Silkin's later books: "Snow Drop" (from *Poems, New and Selected*), which suggests the paradoxes of a flower having insect-like qualities and appearing in sunshine, despite its name; "Ajuga" (from *The Ship's Pasture*), which explores the flower's intercontinental intermixture, the paradox of a mineral appearance of a plant, and the powerful psychological effects on the viewer; and "Inside the Gentian" (from *The Lens-Breakers*), which examines the flower's combination of visual art, mystery, magic, violence, and communicativeness.

### HUMAN RELATIONSHIPS

A third or more of Silkin's poems deal with romantic love, including marriage and the parent-child relationship, and an even larger proportion of his poems deal with all the varied relationships between human beings individually and in groups, societies, or nations. Romantic love, frequently with marriage implied, is celebrated in physical terms, sometimes quite sexually explicit, in poems such as "Community" and "Processes" (both from *Nature with Man*); "Opened" and "Our Selves" (both from *Amana Grass*); "Untitled Poem: 'The Perfume on Your Body'" (from *The Little Time-Keeper*); "Acids," "Going On," and "Water" (all from *The Psalms with Their Spoils*); "Given a Flower" and "The Lamps of Home" (both from *The Ship's Pasture*); and "Beings," "The Hand's Black Hymns," "Juniper and Forgiveness," and "Psalmists" (all from *The Lens-Breakers*). Such love may sometimes emphasize a triumph of life over death, or reach to the spiritual beyond the physical, an issue that is recurrent in Silkin's poetry, as are the words "flesh," "mind," and "spirit." Such physical love gone wrong is shown in one of Silkin's poetic sequences, "Poems Concerning Salome and Herod" (from *The Ship's Pasture*). Another difficult issue in romantic love includes separation, as in "Absence and Light" and "A Hand" (both from *The Ship's Pasture*) and "A Psalm Concerning Absence" (from *The Lens-Breakers*). Recurrent words in Silkin's poetry are "absence" and "space," which refer to lovers' separation as well as death. Also problematic in love may be constancy or fidelity, as in "Fidelities" (from *The Lens-Breakers*).

For many couples, with love and marriage come children, and Silkin's responses to them range from elegy on their tragically premature death, as in "Death of a Son: Who Died in a Mental Hospital Aged One," to wonder and celebration at their birth, as in "For David Emanuel"—both autobiographical poems from *The Peaceable Kingdom*. "Death of a Son," based on the death of Silkin's son and possibly his best-known poem, ends with these memorable lines:

He turned over as if he could be sorry for this
And out of his eyes two great tears rolled, like stones,
And he died.

A link between children and social criticism is shown in the poetic sequence "The People" (from *The Principle of Water*), in which a couple have difficulties with obtuse governmental authorities about the institutionalization and treatment of their disabled child in a case resembling that in "Death of a Son" and "For a Child: On His Being Pronounced Mentally Defective by a Committee of the LLC" (from *The Re-ordering of the Stones*). Lastly, the other side of the relationship—child to parent, rather than parent to child—is explored in "Fathers" (from *The Lens-Breakers*), in which the speaker deals with his father's death and cremation.

Unlike the passionless poet-critics he censures in "Three Critics" (from *The Re-ordering of the Stones*), Silkin is emotionally and socially engaged, writing poetry with social criticism of a government's or a society's mistreatment of parents and children, as in "For a Child"; of the working poor, as in "And I Turned from the Inner Heart," "Bowl," and "Furnished Lives" (all from *The Two Freedoms*), "Savings" (from *The Re-ordering of the Stones*), and "Killhope Wheel, 1860, County Durham" (from *The Principle of Water*); of whole groups of people, as in "Cherokee" (from *The Lens-Breakers*); or of pollution of the environment, as in "Crossing a River" (from *The Ship's Pasture*) or "The Levels" (from *The Lens-Breakers*). Worst of all, perhaps, is the failure of societies and nations to stop wars, spanning history from ancient times to the future nuclear war complacently lectured about by a government bureaucrat in "Defence" (from *Nature with Man*). The epigraph to *The Peaceable Kingdom*, drawn from the Biblical book of Isaiah about the wolf dwelling with the lamb, and the poem "Isaiah's Thread" (from *The Principle of Water*) show Silkin's continual awareness and criticism of the injuries inflicted in war throughout history: the Romans' war against the Jews in "Footsteps on the Downcast Path" (from *The Ship's Pasture*); the wars of the English against the Irish or Scots, in "Famine" (from *The Lens-Breakers*), "What Can We Mean?" (from *The Principle of Water*), and "Poem: 'At Laggan'" (from *Amana Grass*); the American Civil War, in "Paying for Forgiveness" and "Civil War Grave, Richmond" (both from *The Lens-Breakers*); World War I, in "Mr. Lloyd's Life" (from *The Lens-Breakers*); and World War II, in "We Stock the Deer-Park" (from *The Ship's Pasture*) and numerous poems about the Holocaust.

### JEWISH HERITAGE AND HISTORY

Related to Silkin's Jewish heritage are nearly fifty poems referring to the history and culture of the Jewish people from ancient to modern times, scattered throughout all of Silkin's works. In "First It Was Singing" (from *The Peaceable Kingdom*), Silkin equates the outcries of hunted animals and persecuted Jews, which motivate the "singing" of the animals and the Jewish poet. The suffering of Jews and the guilt of Christian societies involved in their massacre and oppression in medieval England is the subject of "Astringencies No. 1: The Coldness" (from *The Re-ordering of the Stones*), "The Malabestia" (from *The Principle of Water*), and "Resting Place" (from *The Psalms with Their Spoils*). The Holocaust of World War II is a focus of "Culpabilities" (from *The Re-ordering of the Stones*), "Jaffa, and Other Places" (from *Amana Grass*), "The People," "The Plum-Tree" (from *The Little Time-Keeper*), "Footsteps on the Downcast Path," and "Fidelities" and "Trying to Hide Treblinka" (both from *The Lens-Breakers*). An eight-poem section of *Amana Grass* ("A Word About Freedom and Identity in Tel-Aviv," "Reclaimed Area," "Jaffa, and Other Places," "What are the lights, in dark," "Conditions," "Ayalon," "Bull-God," "Divisions") is devoted to Israel, and in these poems, as well as "Communal" and "Climbing to Jerusalem" (both from *The Ship's Pasture*) and "Jews Without Arabs" (from *The Lens-Breakers*), Silkin considers how, from ancient through modern times, Jews have confronted the issues of struggling with the natural world to make the land more habitable or living in harmony with non-Jewish fellow inhabitants.

### METAPOETICS, LANGUAGE, AND COMMUNICATION

More than fifty of Silkin's poems deal with the topics of metapoetics (poetry about the nature, effects, or creation of literature or art), language, and communication. In *The Peaceable Kingdom*, Silkin suggests that the suffering and persecution of animals and Jews create their "singing." In "Prologue" and "Epilogue," the poems that open and close the book, he says that his poetry may function as a kind of Noah's ark to save the animals from injury by human beings as well as, perhaps, to unite all in enlightened, considered, and considerate harmony. In "From . . . the Animal Dark" (from *The Two Freedoms*), each of whose two sections is a partly disguised sonnet, appropriate to love poetry, the poet-speaker suggests that language charged by the poem may help create light, enlightenment, and the reunion of lovers. Likewise, in "Amber" (from *The Lens-Breakers*), the poem is equated to an amber pendant, a combination of art, nature, and preserver, whose beauty, warmth, electrical charge, and electrical attraction may touch the beloved both literally and metaphorically.

In contrast with the power of literature and language to enrich or unite, or to communicate with the divine, are the thwarting of this potential in sterility and divisiveness. "Three Critics," with implied ironic tautology, criticizes poet-critics who, following theory and social class, separate intellect from feeling and thus drain their verse of emotion, warmth, and conviction. "The Uses of Man and the Uses of Poetry" (from *The Psalms with Their Spoils*), with similar social criticism, laments the prison inmate who learns lyric and then satiric poetry but is rewarded with beating by the "warders" (guards). In "Crowfoot (in Water)," one of Silkin's celebrated flower poems, details suggest that the flower is "articulate" and has a capacity for communication, but this communication is "smutched" in the mouths and throats of hungry cattle that devour it. Also, in "Douglas of Sorbie and the Adder" (from *The Lens-Breakers*), based on a folktale, a mother is horrified by the realization that her young son and an adder are not only sharing food but also communicating. She orders the farm's day laborers to kill the snake, hoping for the child's success in Georgian London, but in an example of Silkin's ironic social criticism, she causes the death of her son through his grief over the death of the snake.

### OTHER MAJOR WORKS

PLAY: *Gurney*, pb. 1985 (pr. 1986 as *Black Notes*).

NONFICTION: *Out of Battle: The Poetry of the Great War*, 1972, 1987; *The Life of Metrical and Free Verse in Twentieth-Century Poetry*, 1997.

TRANSLATION: *Against Parting*, 1968 (of Nathan Zach).

EDITED TEXTS: *Poetry of the Committed Individual: A "Stand" Anthology of Poetry*, 1973; *The Penguin Book of First World War Poetry*, 1979, 1981; *Wilfred Owen: The Poems*, 1985; *The Penguin Book of First World War Prose*, 1989 (with Jon Glover); *The War Poems of Wilfred Owen*, 1994.

## BIBLIOGRAPHY

Bell, Arthur, Donald Heiney, and Lenthiel Downs. *English Literature: 1900 to the Present*. 2d ed. New York: Barron's, 1994. A section in chapter 12, "Varieties of Experimental Verse," gives a brief overview of Silkin's career through 1986, with comments on "Death of a Son" and the flower poems.

Brown, Merle. *Double Lyric: Divisiveness and Communal Creativity in Recent English Poetry*. New York: Columbia University Press, 1980. Chapter 6, "Stress in Silkin's Poetry and the Healing Emptiness of America," is a thirty-three-page survey of Silkin's work up to 1979 from the perspective of the "stress between imaginative realization and ideological commitment" by Silkin's most appreciative critic. Brown's brief "Afterword" is included in the 1975 edition of *The Peaceable Kingdom*, indicating themes of that book. Silkin composed an elegiac poem about Brown, "Wildness Makes a Form: In Memoriam the Critic Merle Brown."

Cluysenaar, Anne. "Alone in a Mine of Reality: A Matrix in the Poetry of Jon Silkin." In *British Poetry Since 1960*, edited by Michael Schmidt and Grevel Lindop. Oxford, England: Carcanet Press, 1972. A seven-page survey of Silkin's poetry books from 1954 to 1971 stresses Silkin's awareness in his poetry of the interconnectedness of things.

Forbes, Peter, ed. *Scanning the Century: The Penguin Book of the Twentieth Century in Poetry*. New York: Penguin, 2000. This anthology covering the poets of the twentieth century chronologically and by theme contains poems by Silkin in its "Lost Tribes" section. Some analysis included.

Huk, Romana. "Poetry of the Committed Individual: Jon Silkin, Tony Harrison, Geoffrey Hill, and the Poets of Postwar Leeds." In *Contemporary British*

*Poetry: Essays in Theory and Criticism*, edited by James Acheson and Romana Huk. Albany: State University of New York Press, 1996. Taking her title from the title of Silkin's anthology from *Stand* magazine, Huk analyzes the poetry from the perspective of political engagement.

Schmidt, Michael. *An Introduction to Fifty Modern Poets*. 1979. London: Pan Books, 1982. A five-page survey of Silkin's poetry books from 1954 to 1974 stresses the progression from book to book, as well as the worth of the poetry because of what it attempts despite the "unfinished" quality of individual poems.

Wheatley, David. "Grief and Women." Review of *Making a Republic*. *Irish Times*, August 31, 2002, p. 59. Wheatley notes that although this book is about Silkin's finding love late in life, instead of being celebratory, it is filled with the theme of British Jewish inheritance.

*Norman Prinsky*

---

# EDITH SITWELL

**Born:** Scarborough, England; September 7, 1887
**Died:** London, England; December 9, 1964

PRINCIPAL POETRY

*The Mother, and Other Poems*, 1915
*Twentieth Century Harlequinade, and Other Poems*, 1916 (with Osbert Sitwell)
*Clown's Houses*, 1918
*The Wooden Pegasus*, 1920
*Façade*, 1922
*Bucolic Comedies*, 1923
*The Sleeping Beauty*, 1924
*Poor Young People*, 1925 (with Osbert Sitwell and Sacheverell Sitwell)
*Troy Park*, 1925
*Elegy on Dead Fashion*, 1926
*Rustic Elegies*, 1927
*Five Poems*, 1928
*Popular Song*, 1928
*Gold Coast Customs*, 1929

*Collected Poems*, 1930

*Epithalamium*, 1931

*In Spring*, 1931

*Five Variations on a Theme*, 1933

*Selected Poems*, 1936

*Poems New and Old*, 1940

*Street Songs*, 1942

*Green Song, and Other Poems*, 1944

*The Song of the Cold*, 1945

*The Weeping Babe*, 1945

*The Shadow of Cain*, 1947

*The Canticle of the Rose*, 1949

*Façade, and Other Poems*, 1950

*Gardeners and Astronomers*, 1953

*Collected Poems*, 1954

*The Outcasts*, 1962

*Music and Ceremonies*, 1963

*Selected Poems*, 1965

*The Early Unpublished Poems of Edith Sitwell*, 1994

### OTHER LITERARY FORMS

In addition to her many collections of poetry, Edith Sitwell wrote several volumes of critical essays, biography, autobiography, social history, and fiction. Foremost among her critical studies are *Poetry and Criticism* (1925), *Aspects of Modern Poetry* (1934), and *A Poet's Notebook* (1943). Her critical biography *Alexander Pope* (1930) was meant to serve as a vindication of the man and poet. Having as much of an affinity for Queen Elizabeth as for Alexander Pope, she wrote of England's controversial monarch in *Fanfare for Elizabeth* (1946) and *The Queens and the Hive* (1962). *Bath* (1932) is a work of social history. *I Live Under a Black Sun* (1937) is a fictionalized biography of Jonathan Swift. She also edited several anthologies, of which *The Pleasures of Poetry* (1930-1932, 1934), *The American Genius* (1951), and *The Atlantic Book of British and American Poetry* (1958) are the best known. Her rather acerbic autobiography, which was posthumously published, is titled *Taken Care Of* (1965).

### ACHIEVEMENTS

In 1933, Edith Sitwell was awarded a medal by the Royal Society of Literature. Honorary degrees from Oxford, Leeds, Durham, and Sheffield universities followed, and she was made an associate of the American National Institute of Arts and Letters.

The best compliment ever paid to Sitwell was Evelyn Waugh's statement that she took the dullness out of poetry. Never boring or tiresome, the worst her adverse critics could say about her was that she was eccentric and exhibitionistic and her poetry too experimental. A few of her literary enemies—and at one time they were almost as numerous as her friends—did go a step further, however, and labeled her early poetry pretentious, rambling, and vacuous. Geoffrey Grigson, Julian Symons, and F. R. Leavis are only a few of the critics who thought her a dreadful poet, but William Butler Yeats, Cyril Connolly, Stephen Spender, Dylan Thomas, and T. S. Eliot believed she was one of the most creative artists of the twentieth century. Allen Tate summarized Sitwell best when, shortly after her death, he commented that she was "one of the great poets of the twentieth century . . . a remarkable and independent personality."

### BIOGRAPHY

Edith Louisa Sitwell, daughter of Sir George and Lady Ida Sitwell and sister of the two writers Osbert and Sacheverell, was born at Scarborough, England, in 1887. Though she was reared in an atmosphere of wealth and culture, her early years, as her brother Osbert wrote in his *Left Hand, Right Hand* (1944), were emotionally trying. An unwanted child, she suffered considerable physical and nervous anguish in being reared by a tyrannical father, who, among other things, made his only daughter wear a painful device to improve the shape of her aquiline nose. At an early age, she announced her intention of becoming a genius, and soon after she learned to write, she tried her hand at poetry. Physically, she grew to be a tall, pale, distinguished-looking young woman with heavy-lidded eyes and a Plantagenet presence.

Early in the 1920's, Edith, Osbert, and Sacheverell emerged as a literary cult of three. Their circle was graced by such figures as Yeats, Virginia Woolf, Aldous Huxley, and Eliot. The most prolific of the three Sitwells, Edith produced volume after volume of poetry, and she took to reading her work to literary groups. *Wheels,* an iconoclastic annual publication that she founded and edited, outraged many. Critics and philistines not appreciative of her efforts often felt the sting of her tongue.

Between 1914 and 1929, in what might be called her initial period, she reacted strongly against the "banal bucolics" of the Georgian poets and wrote a great deal of nonrepresentational verse, which to some extent parallels the paintings of Pablo Picasso and the cubists. During her middle period, which extended from 1930 to 1940, she abandoned her dream world of sensuous mood and tonal patterns, her "pure poetry," to write poems that, like Eliot's *The Waste Land* (1922) denounced the barbarism, the hypocrisy, the misdirection of modern society. At the time, she regarded poetry as akin to moral wisdom, and she delighted to play the role of a Sibyl or Cassandra. To accentuate her six-foot frame, she dressed in long flowing gowns, sometimes of startling Chinese red, sometimes of intricate brocade, and she swathed her head with tall turbans. To make herself even more notoriously recognizable, she wore heavy jewelry and gold amulets. She painted her long nails with bright silver polish and adorned her thin fingers with marble sized rings. All this was done, she said, as a gesture of defiance of her upbringing and as an act of faith in herself. For the sake of variety, however, she would often dress simply and entirely in black. One day, when asked for whom she was mourning, she responded: "For the entire world."

An eccentric but fascinating woman, Sitwell attracted the attention of many major celebrities and moved among them. Her famous friends and foes were legion. She was especially fond of such diverse personalities as Pavel Tchelitchew, Cecil Beaton, Gertrude Stein, Jacob Epstein, Alec Guinness, and Marilyn Monroe. She had little use for D. H. Lawrence, Lytton Strachey, H. G. Wells, George Moore, and John Galsworthy. It took her almost forty years to forgive Noël Coward for a devastating spoof, *London Calling* (1923), of her and her brothers. Friendships, rivalries, and public spats made her life interesting, but the central theme of her life remained poetry.

*Edith Sitwell* (AP/Wide World Photos)

In 1941, she entered her final period and turned, like Eliot, to traditional values, spiritual matters, and orthodox Christianity. Thirteen years later, she was made a Dame Commander of the Order of the British Empire. The following year, Dame Edith Sitwell was received into the Roman Catholic Church. Evelyn Waugh, who served as her godfather, cautioned her at the time that all too many Catholics were bores and prigs, crooks and cads, and that he himself was really pretty awful; but he added, mainly for Dame Edith's edification, how much worse he should be without the faith. She took Waugh's words to heart, and shortly after her reception, when questioned what meant most to her, with the zeal of a convert she replied: "The love of God, the love of mankind, and the future of humanity."

With such ideals uppermost in mind, she spent her final years in London, devoting herself even more zealously to literature. She continued to create and to encourage fledgling writers to do likewise, often writing warm introductions to their books. She died on December 9, 1964, after several months of illness.

## ANALYSIS

Edith Sitwell's early poems produced a series of shocks. To some, her verse was artificial; others could see that she purposefully created an artificial world. Her teeming imagination fashioned a luscious, semimechanical microcosm, one having "furry light" from "a reynard-coloured sun," trees that "hissed like green geese" with leaves as "hoarse as a dog's bark," a domain populated by "poor flaxen foundlings . . . upon a darkened stair." The world she wrote about in her poetry was, as she put it, "like a bare egg laid by the feathered air."

Of her seriousness as an artist, there is no doubt. A childless woman, she actually lay in her bed and labored for as long as six hours a day for more than forty years to bring forth reams of poetry. A few of her creations may be idiot brainchildren afflicted with echolalia; more are precocious offspring of her metaphysical imagination; most are somewhere between these extremes. In short, though she was wildly eccentric in all she did and wrote, she was still a poet of emotional depth and sincere human concerns. What she wrote was hardly for the common man, but she often maintained that the public enjoys poetry, "unless it is lethally boring or they are frightened out of doing so by bad critics." The matter, the form, and the method employed by so many of her contemporaries aroused her ire. Like an electric eel in a pond full of catfish, she attacked such poets for their lack of tactile and visual sensibility and their inability to please those sensibilities by means of the written word.

Most admirers of her work rank the poems of her last years higher than the verbal legerdemain of her experimental period. Louise Bogan is one of the few who prefers Sitwell's earlier efforts to her later brooding reflections on the world's evils. In many of her early poems, Sitwell was more concerned with evoking beauty and producing sonorous effects than with communicating ideas; however, in her later work she manifested a somberness and intensity, an almost grieving understanding of, and compassion for, the sufferings of humanity.

## THE MOTHER, AND OTHER POEMS

The pattern for much of Sitwell's early verse can be found in her first published work, *The Mother, and Other Poems*, wherein she deals with a prissy, dollhouse world full of such exotic objects as tambourines, mandolins, parakeets, nutmeg trees, and chinoiserie. Technically, the third poem in the collection, "Serenade," is one of the best. In its music of evening, the primacy of darkness is established in the opening lines: "The tremulous gold of stars within your hair/ Are yellow bees flown from the hive of night." In attributing the sun's color to the stars, she suggests a causal relationship between darkness and light, night and day. The yellow bees, born from the mothering hive of night to experience the darkness of the evening world, find the blossoms of the eyes of the beloved more fair "Than all the pale flowers folded from the light." Finally, "Serenade" pleads that the loved one open dreaming eyes "Ere those bright bees have flown and darkness dies."

## BUCOLIC COMEDIES

Most of the poems in *Clown's Houses* and *The Wooden Pegasus* are similar to those in *The Mother, and Other Poems*, but the poems making up *Bucolic Comedies* deal less with rhythm and exotica and more with what Sitwell labeled "sense transfusions." Though at first glance most of these poems may seem comedic nonsense, a careful reading indicates that even their oddest images have a purpose.

In "Aubade," for example, Sitwell depicts the sad stupidity of a servant girl on a country farm coming down to light a morning fire: "Jane, Jane,/ Tall as a crane,/ The morning-light creaks down again." The dawn "creaks" about Jane because early light does not run smoothly. It is raining and Jane imagines each drop of moisture hardening into a "dull blunt wooden stalactite." Facing daily chores of weeding "eternities of kitchen garden," she senses flowers that cluck and mock her. (The flowers "cluck" for they are cockscombs.) The flames of the fire remind her of the carrots and turnips she has to clean and cook continually. Her spirits hang limp as "the milk's weak mind." Like so many of Sitwell's early poems, "Aubade" contains recollections of her own childhood. Thinking of the servant, Jane, brings to the poet's mind "The shivering movement of a certain cold dawn light upon the floor suggestive of high animal whining or whimpering, a half-frightened and subservient urge to something outside our consciousness."

### FAÇADE

Sitwell's early volumes caught the attention of only a limited number of readers, but on June 12, 1923, after reciting her *Façade* at London's Aeolian Hall, she achieved instant notoriety. Everything about her performance provoked controversy. She sat with her back to the audience, barely visible behind a transparent curtain adorned with a crudely painted moon face. The ostensible purpose of the curtain was to allow the audience to concentrate chiefly on the auditory qualities of the poems. The moon face was in keeping with the dreamlike world of apes, ducks, grotesque lords and ladies, clowns, peasants, and servant girls she had written about. Rumors of the nature of *Façade* had reached the literary world after one or two private recitations, and on opening night a large and curious audience was present.

Sitwell chanted her poems through an instrument called a Sengerphone (named after its inventor, George Senger). Out of the Sengerphone, which was made of compressed grasses meant to retain the purity of magnified tonal quality, came such baffling words as "The sound of the onycha/ When the phoca has the pica/ In the palace of the Queen Chinee!" Music may have the power to soothe the savage breast—and there was little adverse reaction to William Walton's orchestration—but the response to Sitwell's poetry bordered on the primitive. After the performance the audience became so threatening that the poet had to remain on stage behind the curtain. Someone whispered to Sitwell that an old lady was waiting to hit her with an umbrella. Disgruntled spectators complained loudly that they were victims of an enormous hoax. They had come to *Façade* expecting to enjoy Walton's music and hear some edifying verse. What they heard sounded like gibberish. Had they listened more attentively they might have found subtle criticisms of modern life, innuendoes of decay, death, nothingness.

Never had more brickbats been hurled at a poet. In her defense, when Sitwell wrote *Façade*, she believed a change in the direction, imagery, and rhythms of poetry had become necessary, owing, as she expressed it, "to

the rhythmical flaccidity, the verbal deadness, the dull and expected patterns" of modern poetry. The poems in *Façade*, consequently, are in most cases virtuoso exercises in verbalizing, studies in rhythmical techniques. "Fox Trot," "Assface," "Sir Beelzebub," "Waltz," and "Hornpipe" are excellent examples of her rhythmical techniques; these poems, in particular, consist of experiments concerning the effect that sound has on meaning.

One trisyllabic word, Sitwell discovered, had greater rapidity than three monosyllabic words. Two rhymes placed immediately together at the end of each of two lines, furthermore, would be like "leaps in the air." In "Fox Trot," for example, she wrote: "'Sally, Mary, Mattie, what's the matter, why cry?'/ The huntsman and the reynard-coloured sun and I sigh." Other experiments were made to discover the influence of rhythm on the thickening and thinning, sharpening and softening, of consonants, as in certain lines of "Waltz": "The stars in their apiaries,/ Sylphs in their aviaries. . . ." These lines in turn are followed by others that end at times with a dissonance, at other times with a rhyme. To produce a waltz rhythm, she used disyllabic rhymes to begin as well as to end lines, "Daisy and Lily,/ Lazy and silly," followed by two long lines with assonance: "Walk by the shore of the wan grassy sea—/ Talking once more 'neath a swan-bosomed tree."

When Sitwell published *Façade*, she attempted in a long and complicated preface to rebut the protests and complaints of her critics. Those willing to accept her prosodic theories were still troubled by her startling imagery. Such conceits as "wan grassy sea," "swan-bosomed tree," "foam-bell of ermine," and "asses' milk of the stars," she maintained, were partly the result of condensations where the language of one sense was insufficient to cover meaning or sensation. The use of such imagery, she hoped, would "pierce down to the essence of the thing seen," revealing attributes that at first might appear alien to a tired eye or unresponsive ear. Perhaps the chief reason why *Façade* was so widely misunderstood was that Sitwell experimented with abstract patterns. Then, too, the apparent vacuity of some of the poems caused them to be suspect. Although the poems were useless, they were butterflies—and butterflies, she protested, can adorn the world and delight the beholder.

No two poems in *Façade* are alike; indeed, they differ radically from one another. "Hornpipe" is a jaunty piece set to nautical music. "Trio for Two Cats" has more than an amusing title; its fast rhythm creates an eerie mood accentuated with castanets. "I Like to Do Beside the Seaside" is set to a tango rhythm. "Scotch Rhapsody" begins with "Do not take a bath in Jordan, Gordan," and a heavy drumbeat sounds throughout. "By the Lake" has a slow pace and its cold imagery depicts a lonely winter night with two estranged lovers recalling a happy past. "Polka" has such clever running rhymes as "Robinson Crusoe rues so" and the "poxy, doxy dear." "Popular Song" is a joyful and carefree lyric about "Lily O'Grady,/ Silly and Shady,/ Longing to be/ A lazy lady." "Sir Beelzebub," who calls for "his syllabub in the hotel in Hell/ Where Prosperine first fell," is meant to mock the Victorians and their poet laureate, "Alfred Lord Tennyson crossing the bar."

In "The Drum," the verse conveys a sense of menace, of deepening darkness, through the use of subtle dissonances. It opens: "In his tall senatorial,/ Black and manorial/ House where decoy-duck/ Dust doth clack—/ Clatter and quack/ To a shadow black." The words "black," "duck," "clatter," and "quack" with their hard consonants and dead vowels, Sitwell explained, are "dry as dust, and the deadness of dust is conveyed thus, and, as well, by the dulled dissonance of the 'a's,' of the 'u' in 'duck' followed by the crumbling assonance of 'dust.'" A duck's quacking, she obligingly added, was for her one of the driest of sounds: "It has a peculiar deadness." In such Sitwellian fashion she explained other aural qualities of "The Drum." As for its essential meaning, she noted that it sprung from a story about witches and witchcraft told by the seventeenth century Neoplatonist Joseph Glanvill:

> Black as Hecate howls a star
> Wolfishly, and whine
> The wind from very far . . .
> Out go the candles one by one,
> Hearing the rolling of a drum. . . .
> Where the drum rolls up the stair, nor tarries.

Sitwell's verse was so radical that she often had to supply instructive analyses of individual poems. "Said King Pompey," she was kind enough to explain, is built upon "a scheme of *R*'s . . . to produce a faint fluttering sound, like dust fluttering from the ground, or the beat of a dying heart." There are obvious *r* sounds in the opening lines of the poem, but to what extent, it is reasonable to ask, do the *r*'s suggest "dust fluttering from the ground"? Sitwell would respond by expatiating on affective language and synesthetic exchange. A reader willing to consider the poem with an open mind is likely to fathom her technical experimentation with synesthesia, but whether the reader will affirm her theories about echo and meaning is another matter.

As soon as a reader is willing to accept her theory of *r* sounds, he or she is then asked to consider other aural impressions. Certain words ending in *ck*, she goes on, "cast little imperceptible shadows." In "The Bat," she plays on such words as "black," "quack," "duck," and "clack," in order, she says, to contrast shadows "so small yet so menacing, with . . . flat and shadeless words that end with 't' and with 'd.'" Some of the *a*'s, she contends, have neither depth nor body, are flat and death-rotten, though at times the words in which they occur cast a small menacing shadow because of the *ck* ending, and frequently these shadows are followed almost immediately by flatter, deader, more shadeless words.

### METAMORPHOSIS

A few years after *Façade*, Sitwell turned from phonological hypothesizing to conceptualizations of time. Between 1924 and 1928, she devoted three long poems to finite time—*The Sleeping Beauty, Elegy on Dead Fashion*, and *Metamorphosis*. Each of these works has a richness that deserves critical attention; but, more important, she slowly overcame an agonized preoccupation with the destructiveness of time. Of the three poems, *Metamorphosis* is the most important. Time initiates the metamorphosis of the poem's title, and in her verse, Sitwell searches for a solution to the infernal behavior of contemporary humans. Her hope at the end of the poem lies in the generative power of the sun, and she writes: "To rouse my carrion to life and move/ The polar night, the boulder that rolled this,/ My heart, my Sisyphus, in the abyss." The writing of *Metamorphosis*, however, left Sitwell in an even deeper spiritual abyss.

## GOLD COAST CUSTOMS

Sitwell followed *Metamorphosis* with one of the strongest poems of her early period, *Gold Coast Customs*. Admirers of her poetry thought it a sensation. William York Tindall labeled it "her *Waste Land*, footnotes and all." Yeats wrote that it was ennobled by the "intensity . . . endurance . . . wisdom" missing from much of contemporary poetry, the "something absent from . . . literature being back again." What Yeats especially liked about *Gold Coast Customs* was its concentration on the sterility of modern life. Relying on Georg Wilhelm Friedrich Hegel's *The Philosophy of History* (1932) and anthropological findings as sources, Sitwell began *Gold Coast Customs* by drawing parallels between an African tribe of cannibals and a Lady Bamburgher, a metaphorical goddess of materialism overly concerned with social rites. Convulsive rhythms suggest a *danse macabre*.

At the close of the poem, there is an intimation of the sacred, a quest for belief, some resolution of the futility of contemporary life. Sitwell's direction, broadly hinted at in the conclusion, was toward Christianity. Her lines allow the inference that she had become fully cognizant of the evil continuously erupting in the hearts of human beings. Convinced that there must be a greater design for life, that all moves toward a Day of Resurrection, she ends *Gold Coast Customs* with the words:

Yet the time will come
To the heart's dark slum
When the Rich man's gold and the rich man's wheat
Will grow in the street, that the starved may eat—
And the sea of the rich will give up its dead—
And the last blood and fire from my side will be shed.
For the fires of God go marching on.

## RELIGIOUS IMAGERY

During the time that Sitwell wrote *Gold Coast Customs*, she began to reflect on the sufferings of Christ, "the Starved Man hung upon the Cross, the God . . . who bears in his heart all wounds." Suffering became a dominant theme in several of her poems. In "Still Falls the Rain," she wrote of the bombing of London during World War II. A red flare dripping from the sky to the earth symbolizes blood—blood that stains the sky. On earth, where the bombs find their mark, actual blood-

shed takes place, a slaughter comparable to the crucifixion of Christ. The rain of Nazi bombs falls on guilty and innocent alike, on Dives and Lazarus. Despite humanity's horrendous deeds, its shedding of blood, Christ stands willing to forgive: "'Still do I love, still shed my innocent light, my Blood for thee.'"

"The Shadow of Cain," as its title indicates, is about modern fratricide. Its narrative concerns the second Fall of Man, symbolized by the dropping of the first atomic bomb on Hiroshima. The poem had its origin on September 10, 1945, when Edith and her brother Osbert were on a train going to Brighton, where they were to give a reading. Osbert pointed out a paragraph in the London *Times*, a description by an eyewitness of the actual dropping of the bomb. What most impressed the witness was "a totem pole of dust that arose to the sun as testimony to the murder of mankind. . . . A totem pole, the symbol of creation, the symbol of generation." Although most of the poem came into Edith's head as Osbert read the *Times* report, she did not write it down for several months. She continually revised it in her mind, and the poem passed through several stages. When she finally put pen to paper, she wrote how, after "that epoch of the Cold," the victims of the immolation reached an open door. All that was left to them were primal realities:

The Fate said, "My feet ache."
The wanderers said, "Our hearts ache."
There was great lightening
In flashes coming to us over the floor:
The Whiteness of Bread
The Whiteness of the Dead
The Whiteness of the Claw—
All this coming to us in flashes through the open door.

The foregoing lines, Sitwell claims, came to her in a dream. The three flashes of lightning she explains as three primal realities of preservation, death, and struggle. Beyond the open door she saw spring returning; for there was still the grandeur of the sun and Christ returning with the life-giving wheat of harvest. Then came the horror, the symbol of which was seen by the eyewitness at Hiroshima. A gulf was torn across the world, stretching its jaws from one end of the earth to the other. Loud were the cries in the hollow from those who once were men, and yet "those ashes that were men/ Will rise again."

The horror of Hiroshima affected Sitwell deeply. Did God in some mysterious way declare himself through such suffering? She began to incorporate into her work the re-creating energy of divine love. Her interest in prosodic experimentation was over. No longer would she tinker with sound effects, with the mechanics of rhyme. She encapsulated all her principles of versification into one central dictum: "Poetry should always be running on pleasant feet, sometimes swift, sometimes slow."

As a poet she now wanted to vent the depths of her heart in sonorous, free-flowing lines that would touch the hearts of others. To express truths about human beings and the universe, to point them in the direction of salvation, became her purpose. In her final period, her poems were hymns to the glory of life.

OTHER MAJOR WORKS

LONG FICTION: *I Live Under a Black Sun*, 1937.

NONFICTION: *Poetry and Criticism*, 1925; *Alexander Pope*, 1930; *Bath*, 1932; *The English Eccentrics*, 1933; *Aspects of Modern Poetry*, 1934; *Victoria of England*, 1936; *Trio*, 1938 (with Osbert Sitwell and Sacheverell Sitwell); *A Poet's Notebook*, 1943; *Fanfare for Elizabeth*, 1946; *A Notebook on William Shakespeare*, 1948; *The Queens and the Hive*, 1962; *Taken Care Of*, 1965; *Selected Letters of Edith Sitwell*, 1997 (Richard Greene, editor).

EDITED TEXTS: *Wheels*, 1916-1921; *The Pleasures of Poetry*, 1930-1932, 1934; *Planet and Glow Worm*, 1944; *A Book of Winter*, 1950; *The American Genius*, 1951; *A Book of Flowers*, 1952; *The Atlantic Book of British and American Poetry*, 1958.

BIBLIOGRAPHY

Brophy, James D. *Edith Sitwell: The Symbolist Order.* Carbondale: Southern Illinois University Press, 1968. Brophy examines the themes and techniques of Sitwell's admittedly difficult poetry. He finds in her work a coherent use of modernist Symbolism. A valuable study for close analysis of her poems and critical views. Supplemented by a select bibliography and an index.

Cevasco, G. A. *The Sitwells: Edith, Osbert, and Sacheverell.* Boston: Twayne, 1987. Edith and her younger brothers, all writers and famous personalities, are brought together in an excellent, compact survey of their writings and family life. Their texts are shown to respond to the major events that shaped the twentieth century: two world wars, an economic depression, and the opening of the atomic age. Contains a chronology, notes, a select bibliography, and an index.

Elborn, Geoffrey. *Edith Sitwell: A Biography.* London: Sheldon Press, 1981. Traces Sitwell's life, from her birth as an unwanted female to her solitary death (by her own command). Includes photographs that illustrate her life, twelve half-plates, two plates, notes, a bibliography, and an index.

Glendinning, Victoria. *Edith Sitwell: A Unicorn Among Lions.* London: Phoenix, 1993. Revisionary appraisal separates the myths from the newer status of Sitwell's work. Glendinning discusses Sitwell's poetry, her criticism, and her literary relationships. Includes six plates, seventeen half-plates, notes, and an index.

Pearson, John. *Facades: Edith, Osbert, and Sacheverell Sitwell.* London: Macmillan, 1978. A detailed, year-by-year account of the literary activities, travels, and relationships of the famous sister and her brothers, which places Sitwell in her literary environment. Photographs are placed throughout the text. Contains seventeen plates, notes, and an index.

Salter, Elizabeth. *The Last Years of a Rebel: A Memoir of Edith Sitwell.* London: Bodley Head, 1967. Salter was secretary to the poet from the time Sitwell was sixty-nine until her death. The author brings out Sitwell's humor, her loyalty, and her creative power. Salter has also published a companion book of extraordinary photographs and drawings. Presents an inside view from a devoted friend. Includes five plates, and six half-plates.

Sitwell, Edith. *Selected Letters of Edith Sitwell.* Edited by Richard Greene. Rev. ed. London: Virago, 1998. A collection including previously unpublished letters to a remarkable array of notables, including Bertrand Russell, Gertrude Stein, Cecil Beaton, Kingsley Amis, T. S. Eliot, and Virginia Woolf.

Van Durme, Debora. "Edith Sitwell's Carnivalesque Song: The Hybrid Music of *Façade*." *Mosaic: A Journal for the Interdisciplinary Study of Literature* 41, no. 2 (June, 2008): 93-111. An in-depth look at *Façade*, Sitwell's work as it was performed to music. The author looks at the musicality of Sitwell's work and examines in what respects it was a "musical entertainment," as it was billed to be.

G. A. Cevasco

# JOHN SKELTON

**Born:** Northern England, possibly Yorkshire; c. 1460
**Died:** London, England; June 21, 1529
**Also known as:** John Shelton

PRINCIPAL POETRY

*The Bowge of Court*, 1499
*Phyllyp Sparowe*, c. 1508
*The Tunnyng of Elynour Rummyng*, 1508
*Ware the Hawk*, c. 1508
*Speke, Parrot*, 1521
*Collyn Clout*, 1522
*Why Come Ye Nat to Courte*, 1522
*The Garlande of Laurell*, 1523
*Pithy, Pleasaunt, and Profitable Workes of Maister Skelton, Poete Laureate*, 1568
*The Complete Poems of John Skelton, Laureate*, 1931 (Philip Henderson, editor)
*Selected Poems*, 2003

OTHER LITERARY FORMS

In addition to the poems listed above, John Skelton wrote a play, or, more properly, an interlude (a short allegorical morality play), called *Magnyfycence* (1516), which counsels monarchs against excessive liberality. Skelton also participated in a popular form of court entertainment called "flyting," in which two courtiers trade insults before an audience of their peers. In particular, Skelton flyted one Christopher Garnish, and some of his "insults" persist in the *Poems Against Garnish* (1513-1514).

Finally, Skelton translated a significant number of works and had a reputation as an excellent Latinist. His translations apparently included the works of Diodorus Siculus, Cicero's *Ad familiares* (62-43 B.C.E.; *The Familiar Epistles*, 1620) and Guillaume Deguilleville's *La Pélerinage de la vie humaine*. The latter two works, mentioned in *The Garlande of Laurell*, do not survive. Skelton also composed a moral guidebook: *Speculum Principis* (1501, also known as *A Mirror for Princes*).

ACHIEVEMENTS

Modern readers find John Skelton's work hard to understand and appreciate. He lived and wrote just as the literary Renaissance and political Reformation began to reshape England. Skelton reveals in *The Garlande of Laurell* that he perceived himself to be the heir of the medieval poets Geoffrey Chaucer, John Gower, and John Lydgate. His language resembles the Middle English of these three forebears, but like the English of his contemporary Sir Thomas Malory, borders on what is now termed Modern English (the conventional boundary date between Middle and Modern English is 1500). The difficulty in reading Skelton, then, comes not from the archaic quality of his language but from its deliberate, often playful, polyglot tendencies and its unusual metrical properties. Skelton intermingles French and Latin words and phrases in many of his poems, often producing the kind of interlingual mix known as macaronic verse. He also loads his poems with allusions to the Bible and to contemporary political events. Metrically, Skelton's poetry surprises readers used to the iambic pentameter line that became the norm for English poetry after William Shakespeare. In many poems, Skelton uses trimeter (six-syllable) couplets with irregular rhythm. This meter is so characteristic of his poetry that it has become known as Skeltonic.

In his lifetime, Skelton was well rewarded and admired, although perhaps not as completely, or as consistently, as he might have liked. He is thought of today as the first poet laureate of England: That honor, however, was conferred on him not by the king but by the University of Oxford (1488) and later by the University of Louvain (1493) and the University of Cambridge (1493). The laureateship, which today implies particular patronage of the king or queen and entails the re-sponsibility of writing public occasional verse, titled Skelton to be recognized as a graduate with a degree in rhetoric. Although the implications of laureateship were not the same for Skelton as for a poet such as Alfred, Lord Tennyson (laureate to Queen Victoria), the honor was nevertheless great, and Skelton doted on the accomplishment for the rest of his life. Indeed, he named his last major work, which sums up his poetic career, *The Garlande of Laurell*. Skelton did enjoy the special attention of Henry VII, by whose grace he wore a robe of green and white, the Tudor colors, embroidered "Calliope," for the muse of epic poetry.

The first collected poems of Skelton appeared in 1568, were edited by Thomas Marshe, and were reissued in 1736. A two-volume edition, produced by the Reverend Alexander Dyce (1843), bridged the gap between the Renaissance and the current editions, notably *The Complete Poems of John Skelton, Laureate* (1931), edited by Philip Henderson.

## BIOGRAPHY

John Skelton's life and poetry are closely bound up with the world of the Tudor court under Henry VII and Henry VIII. The first sure facts about his life have to do with the laureate degrees he received. Two years after the award from Oxford, Skelton received glowing praise in William Caxton's preface to *The Boke of Eneydos* (1490). Caxton made clear his admiration for Skelton's immense knowledge of Latin, his translations, and his ability to write in English. Thus, by about the age of thirty, Skelton was known as a scholar and poet. At about this time, he became officially connected with the court of Henry VII, writing occasional state poems and eventually becoming official tutor to Prince Henry, who was intended to become a priest. Skelton himself took holy orders in 1498.

In 1502, Henry's older brother Arthur, the heir to the throne, died. Young Henry, now the next in line for the throne, no longer needed quite the same kind of instruction, and Skelton was sent from the court to be the rector of Diss, an area on the borders of Suffolk and Norfolk, ninety miles from London. It is uncertain how Skelton took this "exile." On one hand, he clearly enjoyed the prestige of his royal connection. On the other,

his first major poem, *The Bowge of Court*, written before his removal to Diss, established his recognition of the traditional problems of a courtier's life, including battles with hypocrisy, deceit, flattery, and despair.

At Diss, Skelton continued to write satirical poems as well as perform his clerical duties with apparent gusto. Skelton's life at Diss has been immortalized in a collection of stories by an anonymous author or authors, *The Merie Tales of Skelton* (1567). It is difficult to say how much truth is contained in this group of stories, which show Skelton teasing his puritanical bishop and flaunting his wife and child before his parish. In general, Skelton emerges in these tales as lusty, witty, and mischievous. If the tales are not true in fact, many biographers have assumed that they are true in spirit.

In 1509, Henry VIII became king, and Skelton initiated a campaign of compliments and requests designed to bring him back to court. In 1512, he returned to London officially titled *Orator Regius*—orator to the king. From that time on, Skelton lived in London and flourished as a satirist, attacking the evils of court life, particularly the abuse of power by figures such as Thomas Wolsey, whose rise to power apparently made Skelton jealous and certainly angered him. In 1521 and 1522, he wrote three satires directed at Wolsey: *Speke, Parrot*, *Collyn Clout*, and *Why Come Ye Nat to Courte*. Despite the bitterness of these poems, Skelton's wrath toward Wolsey seems later to have abated—or, at least, he lost his willingness to embarrass publicly the powerful man. His last known work, a part-prose, part-Skeltonic critique of Lutheranism, includes a dedication praising Wolsey. Skelton died on June 21, 1529, and was buried at St. Margaret's Church in Westminster.

## ANALYSIS

In 1490, William Caxton described John Skelton in glowing terms. He apparently viewed Skelton as a perfect example of a rising court scholar and poet, one worth praising in print. Desiderius Erasmus, who epitomizes the early Renaissance humanist, met Skelton in 1499 and admired him. However, the poet fell rapidly into obscurity after his death, surfacing in literary surveys only to be described as "beastly" or "scurrilous." These contradictions are easier to explain than might be supposed. First, Skelton's literary career underwent a marked shift beginning with the publication of *The Bowge of Court* in 1499. Until that time, Skelton's work had been what Caxton's remarks suggest: scholarly, patriotic, and sagacious. As he began to criticize political and religious changes in England, a new persona emerged. Subtly in *The Bowge of Court*, more fully in *Ware the Hawk*, and full blast in *Speke, Parrot*, Skelton reveals a sensibility by turns bitter, vitriolic, ribald, self-righteous, and intolerant.

Second, Skelton's reputation changed because his fundamental values were misperceived by later generations. Since he wrote in an unusually diffuse, free-spoken, irreverent manner, readers, especially in the nineteenth century, lost sight of the essentially conservative values that underlie his work. Skelton became accustomed, while relatively young, to certain habits of life. He associated himself with the Tudor court, he was devoutly religious, and he was committed to a certain kind of learning and literature that emphasized knowledge of Latin. When his stability was challenged by changes in government, church, and education, his poetry changed drastically. All his major work treats the theme of personal instability in a shifting world.

### THE BOWGE OF COURT

Thus, in *The Bowge of Court*, the condition of a courtier is revealed as "Dread"; in *Phyllyp Sparowe*, language and convention are twisted to reveal new, ironic possibilities of expression; in *Ware the Hawk*, the sanctity of the church is defended with a kind of comic hysteria. *Speke, Parrot* is the culmination of his stylistic experimentation; for many students today, this poem is unreadable, an impenetrable jungle of Latin, French, random allusion and odd statement. Skelton's poems after *Speke, Parrot* retain some of these macaronic devices but are not quite as difficult, and in *The Garlande of Laurell*, he returns to the relatively straightforward form of the dream vision.

*The Bowge of Court*, Skelton's first long poem, is an allegorical dream vision in the tradition of Chaucer's *House of Fame* (1372-1380). The title might be translated as "Patronage of Court" since "bouge" means free rations or board, as in the kind of stipend given to courtiers. The pattern of the poem resembles the Chaucerian dream vision as it was imitated in fifteenth century works such as *The King's Quair* and *The Court of Love*.

*John Skelton* (Archive Photos/Getty Images)

The poem's prologue introduces the speaker as a poet who is having trouble writing. When he falls asleep, he dreams of a stately ship, the *Bowge of Court*, carrying a cargo of Favor. The dreamer meets a lady-in-waiting to the owner of the ship; he tells her his name is Dread. The allegorical situation becomes apparent. The main character, Dread, represents anxiety: Like the poet-narrator, he cannot gain a firm foothold in life, and he seeks aid or reassurance from outside himself. Dread, unfortunately, has come to a very bad place for stability. Not only is the *Bowge of Court* a ship, but also its favors are dispensed only for money and only at the command of the ship's pilot, Fortune.

Dread's very nature—his fearfulness—makes him the target of attack by his fellow passengers on the ship. Almost immediately, he is caught up in a network of intrigue involving Favell (Flattery) and Suspect. Similarly, five other characters (ranging from the pickpocket Harvy Hafter to Deceit) increase Dread's anxiety, until he jumps overboard to escape them. At this point the dreamer awakens, and the poem ends.

*The Bowge of Court* differs significantly from dream visions by earlier writers, which usually provide a "psychopaunt," or dream guide, for the narrator. Dread is alone, and no one helps him draw a moral from his experience. *The Bowge of Court* criticizes court folly in the typical fashion of satire, but it also, perhaps more significantly, provides an analysis of Dread as a state of mind, and throws an emphasis on the speaker's insecurities.

### PHYLLYP SPAROWE

While Skelton was rector of Diss, he composed ironic elegies for two of his parishioners. Witty as these are, they are surpassed in whimsicality by the long, unusual poem *Phyllyp Sparowe*, in which Skelton eulogizes the pet bird of Jane Scrope, a young neighbor. The poem, written in Skeltonic trimeter, has been said to imitate the quick jerky movement of a sparrow.

The poem begins with a version of the Catholic burial mass, lamenting the death of the pet bird. Much of the poem is filtered through the mind of Jane, who both laments Philip lavishly and remembers with pleasure his charming habits in life. She imagines all the birds holding a mass in his honor, and she searches her memory for books that might provide him with an epitaph. In this section of the poem, Skelton relies on the reader's knowledge that parodies of the mass are traditional; he also assimilates Philip into the tradition in which Ovid and Catullus exploit the sexual implications of a sparrow who hops around in his mistress's lap and tries to get under the covers of her bed.

Furthermore, the poem contains a section headed "Commendations"; here Skelton, abandoning Philip, praises Jane herself. In all sections of the poem, Skelton freely adds snippets of Latin or French. *Phyllyp Sparowe* ends with an epilogue, clearly written after the rest of the poem had circulated, defending what had apparently struck many critics as blasphemous or inappropriate. Although Skelton does not offer a detailed defense of his own work, he might well have argued for its essential conservatism in religious matters. Skelton does not burlesque the burial mass or use it for vulgar purposes; he simply includes it among the devices by which he pokes fun at Jane's excessive mourning. Ultimately, the poem encourages a turning away from bathetic grief either to a happy contemplation of the past or to the celebration of Jane herself, who is young, alive, and human. Thus the poem's values and moral lesson are quite conservative; only the poem's exterior form is new and "shocking."

### WARE THE HAWK

*Ware the Hawk* shows Skelton, in his role as rector of Diss, calling down God's wrath on another parson who brought his hawk into Skelton's church and allowed it to defecate on the altar. The poem is simultaneously scathing and funny, although the humor is of a distinctly learned kind; for example, Skelton puns on "hawk" and the Latin word *hoc*. He invokes a catalog of the great tyrants of history in order to convey the enormity of his scorn for the offending parson and his hawk. The incident, whether real or fictional, gave Skelton an excuse to list what he considered various licenses taken by the parish priests. His wrath grows out of all proportion to the comic absurdity of the particular offense. Skelton seems to criticize both the speaker, who rants so futilely, and the man who allows his hawk to defile the sacred altar of God. Skelton puts his understandable sentiments into the mouth of a near-lunatic, again demonstrating the typical split in his work between conservative subject and unorthodox method.

### SPEKE, PARROT

Fourteen years after writing *Ware the Hawk* and *Phyllyp Sparowe*, Skelton produced his series of political poems attacking Cardinal Thomas Wolsey, who symbolized for Skelton the corruption of power in both church and state. In Wolsey, Skelton saw the decline of the old political and religious order he respected. Moreover, Skelton disliked the changing attitude toward education in the 1520's (in particular he lamented the decline of Latin studies in favor of Greek, and Wolsey himself established in 1520 a professorship of Greek at Oxford). Skelton thus had moral, political, and literary grudges against Wolsey, and they all came spilling out in *Speke, Parrot*, a macaronic mélange of history, biblical allusion, and moral reflection.

The speaker is Parrot, a natural mimic, who stands for the poet himself. The parrot is traditionally both poet and pet, and these dual identities suggest the duplicity of living at court while satirizing the court. The flexible pose allows Skelton to shift between scathing critical statements and sycophantic requests for food and treats. Description cannot do justice to the baffling effect of reading this poem, created by the mix of riddle, proverb, lyric, oath, and allusion. Throughout the poem, Parrot praises himself and indirectly criticizes Wolsey without naming him. He veils his criticism by using biblical names to stand for Henry and Wolsey.

*Speke, Parrot* attacks more than Wolsey alone. It attacks the world at present, the instability of fortune, the vanity of human wishes, and the inadequacy of eloquence. Parrot touches bitterly on all these pitfalls of the human condition. Insofar as Parrot offers Skelton's views, the poem again shows him using a radically new—nearly opaque—poetic technique to defend the ideas and systems to which he has become accustomed.

## COLLYN CLOUT

After the exuberant chaos of *Speke, Parrot, Collyn Clout* appears as a plain-spoken, modest attempt to assert much the same values. Like Dread and Parrot, the heroes of Skelton's earlier poems, Colin Clout knows that the world is in trouble; unlike them, he knows that he is part of the world. Since Colin is himself a minor cleric, he is implicated in the current problems he perceives in the Church. He seems to hold two positions at once (much like Parrot as poet and pet), both reporting overheard evil tidings about clerical abuses and pointing out that these rumors may be false. Although his manner of doing so is new, he resembles Parrot in his tendency to back away from criticism to the safe pose of naïveté.

The poem depicts a world gone awry. The higher-placed clergy are corrupt, and the lower ones (such as Colin), who may themselves be good, are afraid to speak out. The aristocrats, unwilling to assert their power, give themselves over to leisure. The poem focuses criticism on the bishops and on one bishop in particular, who, Colin prophesies, is headed for a fall despite his present power. It becomes certain that this man is Wolsey when Colin describes both his typically elaborate clothing and the tapestries that adorn the walls of his home, Hampton Court.

The specific abuses that Colin laments are predictable: He claims that the clergy are greedy, ignorant, lascivious. The bishops live in luxury while the common people suffer. On the other hand, it is clear that Colin respects the sincere clergy, and he particularly laments

that the nuns and monks have been turned out of their cloisters under Wolsey's regime.

After Colin has gone on for more than a thousand lines, the opposition is given a chance to speak for itself. Rather than offering a defense, however, Colin's respondent simply acknowledges the criticism and threatens to punish and condemn the critics. Colin's only possible escape at this point is to commit himself to Christ, stop writing, and disappear from view. As did Dread, he finally gives up and escapes, leaving behind his poem as a record of experience. Not resigned to the world's decay, he is nevertheless powerless to stop it.

## WHY COME YE NAT TO COURTE

The third of Skelton's attacks on Wolsey concentrates on the cardinal's political abuses. *Why Come Ye Nat to Courte* has neither the plain-speaking voice of Colin Clout nor the wise folly of Parrot. Instead, the poem seems to be a pastiche of satirical ballads unified only in their criticism of Wolsey. Among other things, Skelton blames Wolsey for misusing the Star Chamber (Henry's advisory council) and for inciting the war with France that began in 1522 and resulted in unpopular new taxes.

Whereas *Collyn Clout* and *Speke, Parrot* juxtapose the attitudes of a self-righteous speaker against the ill-doings of Wolsey as a symbolic monster, *Why Come Ye Nat to Courte* resembles a flyting, or insult match, in which both parties swing wildly at each other and everything; even Wolsey's physical deformity is fair game for attack. To the reader familiar with the other anti-Wolsey poems, little in this one seems new, and the very length of the poem (some twelve hundred lines) underscores its lack of structure. This lack is, arguably, in itself a key to the poem's meaning: Enraged and baffled by Wolsey's complete moral corruption, which seems responsible even for the cardinal's diseased eye, the speaker has lost the capacity both for objective judgment and calm reportage. Like the cardinal, the poet has developed limited vision, and only by a deliberate widening of perspective is he able to go on to write *The Garlande of Laurell*.

## THE GARLANDE OF LAURELL

As the title suggests, Skelton here forcefully reminds the reader of his own claim to wear the garland of laurel, symbol of the poetic vocation as handed down by Apollo. Unlike Chaucer and other medieval poets who dismiss their own claims to greatness and affect a modesty about their work, Skelton heralds himself as the new Homer of England. Like Dante in the fourth canto of the *Inferno* (c. 1320) joining the band of great classical poets, Skelton depicts himself as being welcomed into the Court of Fame by his great English predecessors Chaucer, Gower, and Lydgate, none of whom, he carefully points out, officially earned the right to wear the laurel.

Despite Skelton's ultimate inclusion in the Court of Fame, he acknowledges that some might carp at his being so honored. The poem takes the form of a dream vision in which Skelton's candidacy for Fame is assessed at the recommendation of Pallas. The Queen of Fame, however, disapproves of him because of his stylistic experimentation: He has not written in the ornate aureate style of which she approves. He partially assuages her by actually introducing, in this poem, a series of lyrics in honor of the countess of Surrey and other noble ladies.

Later, Skelton's accomplishments as a poet are reviewed, after which he is so cheered by the crowd (whose fickle favor he scorns) that he ascends to Fame without a formal judgment. *The Garlande of Laurell* also presents a loftier vision of poetry than that which pleases the fickle Queen of Fame and the rabble who crowd about her gates. For part of the poem, Skelton walks with Occupation (who represents his calling as a poet) through a paradisiacal landscape where he sees Apollo himself playing the harp. Compared with this serenity, the ironically intoned list of Skelton's works, in which *Speke, Parrot*, for example, is described as a commendation of ladies (which it is not), seems beside the point. In fact, it is surprising that Skelton, whose later poetry was so caught up in the incidental events of his day, saw his vocation as originating in a divinely ruled pastoral grove. Even more surprising, the poem offers itself, at the end, to the correction of Cardinal Wolsey, as if Skelton were pulling back somewhat from his recent harsh criticism.

Skelton's identification with Apollo and the great poetic tradition of England confirms that he is a literary, as well as a political and religious, conservative. In stressing the importance of the poet as visionary seer, he gives even more power to the predictions and complaints made in his earlier works. Unlike Dread in *The Bowge of Court*, Skelton is a dreamer with a guide and mentor—not only Occupation but also Pallas, goddess of wisdom.

OTHER MAJOR WORKS

PLAY: *Magnyfycence*, pb. 1516.

NONFICTION: *Speculum Principis*, 1501 (also known as *A Mirror for Princes*).

BIBLIOGRAPHY

Carlson, David R. *John Skelton and Early Modern Culture: Papers Honoring Robert S. Kinsman*. Tempe: Arizona Center for Medieval and Renaissance Studies, 2008. A collection of essays on Skelton that analyze his writings in terms of the time in which he lived.

Carpenter, Nan Cooke. *John Skelton*. New York: Twayne, 1968. This overview contains a preface, a chronology, and an outline of Skelton's life. Carpenter discusses all his important poetic works and highlights the poet's intimate technical knowledge of music, dance songs, and popular song tags. Skelton's reputation and influence is also discussed. Includes notes and references.

Griffiths, Jane. *John Skelton and Poetic Authority: Defining the Liberty to Speak*. New York: Oxford University Press, 2006. This work reassesses Skelton's place in English literature and links his work as a translator and writer to his poetic theory.

Kinney, Arthur F. *John Skelton, Priest as Poet: Seasons of Discovery*. Chapel Hill: University of North Carolina Press, 1987. Maintaining that Skelton's primary vocation, the priesthood, was fundamental to his literary work, Kinney attempts to give a comprehensive evaluation of his poetry. Includes notes and an index.

Richardson, J. A. *Falling Towers: The Trojan Imagination in "The Waste Land," "The Dunciad," and "Speke parott."* Newark: University of Delaware Press, 1992. Examines Skelton's *Speke, Parrot* and compares and contrasts it with T. S. Eliot's *The Waste Land* (1922) and Alexander Pope's *The Dunciad* (1728-1743).

Scattergood, V. J. *Reading the Past: Essays on Medieval and Renaissance Literature*. Portland, Oreg.: Four Courts Press, 1996. Includes a critical essay on the works of Skelton, bibliographical references, and an index.

Walker, Greg. *John Skelton and the Politics of the 1520's*. New York: Cambridge University Press, 1988. Discusses the political and social views of Skelton and gives a history of English political satire as well as a view of the politics and government in England during the first half of the sixteenth century.

*Diane M. Ross*

---

# CHRISTOPHER SMART

**Born:** Shipbourne, Kent, England; April 11, 1722
**Died:** King's Bench Prison, London, England; May 2, 1771
**Also known as:** Mary Midnight

## PRINCIPAL POETRY

*On the Eternity of the Supreme Being*, 1750
*On the Immensity of the Supreme Being*, 1751
*On the Omniscience of the Supreme Being*, 1752
*Poems on Several Occasions*, 1752
*The Hilliad*, 1753
*On the Power of the Supreme Being*, 1754
*On the Goodness of the Supreme Being*, 1755
*Hymn to the Supreme Being, on Recovery from a Dangerous Fit of Illness*, 1756
*Poems*, 1763
*A Song to David*, 1763
*Ode to the Earl of Northumberland*, 1764
*Hymns for the Amusement of Children*, 1772
*Jubilate Agno*, 1939 (as *Rejoice in the Lamb*, 1954)
*Collected Poems*, 1950 (2 volumes; Norman Callan, editor)

## OTHER LITERARY FORMS

In London, Christopher Smart did hackwork for booksellers, wrote songs for Vauxhall Gardens entertainment, and edited the magazine *Midwife: Or, Old Woman's Magazine* from 1749 to about 1750. *The Works of Horace, Translated Literally into English* (1756) is a prose translation of the poems from the Latin; *A Translation of the Psalms of David Attempted in the Spirit of Christianity* (1765) was rendered from the Hebrew in poetic form; another translation, *The Works of Horace Translated into Verse*, came out in 1767.

## ACHIEVEMENTS

Christopher Smart became a fellow of Pembroke Hall, the University of Cambridge, in 1745, and attained college office after receiving his master's degree in 1747. He won the Seaton Prize for poetry every year from 1750 to 1755, with the exception of 1754, when he did not enter.

## BIOGRAPHY

Christopher Smart was born in Shipbourne, Kent, where his father served as steward to William, Viscount Vane. His earliest love was Lord Vane's daughter Anne, but the two were forced apart. A precocious student, he was sponsored by the duchess of Cleveland for enrollment at Pembroke Hall, Cambridge. Her forty-pound annuity allowed him to concentrate on both scholarship and social life in college, where he gained a reputation as a hard drinker and incurred heavy debts. He received his bachelor's degree in 1742, followed by a master's in 1747, with election to college office the same year. He also married Anna Marie Carnan; the marriage was kept secret until its discovery forced him to give up his position. However, Smart was allowed to keep his connection in order to compete for the Seaton Poetry Prize each year. He won the prize in 1750, 1751, and 1753; after skipping a year of the competition in 1754, he came back to win again in 1755. The Seatonian odes are not considered successful, but they show the religious attitudes for which Smart was noted as well as his practice of the cataloging technique as a strategy.

Smart had left Cambridge for London in 1749 to make a living as a writer, taking various hack assignments in a variety of forms. On jobs for booksellers, mostly for his wife's stepfather John Newbery, he wrote humor, fables, lyric verses, and epitaphs. As a periodical writer, he remained poor and undistinguished, even as editor of *Midwife*.

*Christopher Smart* (Hulton Archive/Getty Images)

Smart was befriended by such noted figures as Samuel Johnson, Oliver Goldsmith, Thomas Gray, and David Garrick, who helped him during his periods of alcoholism and madness. Johnson supposedly did some of Smart's periodical writing, and Garrick performed in 1759 to raise money for him. Even with help from friends, however, Smart's family fell apart; his wife and two daughters moved to Ireland and remained there with his sister.

The study of Smart's life and his works has customarily revolved around his madness, which seems to have begun around 1756. He was confined several times for madness and for debts. Though there is no agreement on the causes or the exact label for his madness, it is generally considered to have been a religious form of monomania. *Hymn to the Supreme Being, on Recovery from a Dangerous Fit of Illness* is considered evidence of the techniques that would make his later works worthy of note. This poem receives notice as pivotal in his literary development from religious and technical perspectives.

Smart's compulsiveness and his fixation seem to have a shared religious root, resulting in what was con-

sidered his most bizarre public behavior: praying aloud whenever and wherever the inclination struck him. He said once, "I blessed God in St. James's Park until I routed all the company." Such behavior was categorized as enthusiasm in the eighteenth century, and the adjective "enthusiastic" was applied to many Dissenters seized by religious fervor.

Although his friends did not agree on the necessity for Smart's confinement, he was kept in St. Luke's Hospital from 1757 through part of 1758. When released that year, he seemed to grow worse, and mental problems caused him to be placed in a mental asylum from 1759 to 1763. Under these circumstances, he seemed to behave quietly and occupy himself with religious activities, with his writing, and with domestic chores. Among his friends who visited, Johnson said, "I did not think he ought to be shut up. . . . His infirmities were not noxious to society. He insisted on people praying with him; and I'd as lief pray with Kit Smart as anyone else." During this second confinement, he wrote his major works, *Jubilate Agno* (begun in 1759), which remained unfinished and unpublished during his lifetime, and *A Song to David*, his most important work.

After returning to society, having lost all contact with his family, Smart became involved in a series of bitter conflicts with other journalists, in which he revealed an indignation or self-righteousness that has been frowned on since that time.

Smart continued to deteriorate physically and behaviorally after he returned to London life, but he concentrated more and more on the writing of poetry and focused to an even greater extent on religious subjects. He published *A Translation of the Psalms of David Attempted in the Spirit of Christianity* in 1765 and his verse translation of Horace in 1767, several years before his final incarceration, which began in 1769. A number of biographical questions exist relating to the actual composition of his religious poems, with some critics interested in whether several were written simultaneously. Smart seems to have hoped that some of his works would be adopted by the Church of England for its liturgy, since his psalms and their arrangement not only imitate the Hebrew and the Anglican prayer book of his day but also follow the sequence of the Christian year.

Because Smart was not only a literary scholar and

linguist but also a student of natural phenomena, he drew these interests into his poetry. Much of what he knew about science came from books and reading, but he insisted on studying God's works in nature so that he could celebrate all creation.

The year 1769 brought further debt and lack of control, resulting in a final incarceration in King's Bench prison for debtors. During this year, Smart wrote *Hymns for the Amusement of Children*, a book of verses sharing his knowledge of nature and his love of God. It was in this prison that he died, remaining outwardly optimistic and happy regardless of his problems. He seems to have been absolutely sure of his salvation; at least he asserted his certainty flamboyantly and repeatedly, often to the discomfort and irritation of others.

ANALYSIS

Christopher Smart's masterpiece, *A Song to David*, is the primary reason for his reputation as a writer and the work on which his reputation as a poet rests to this day. *A Song to David* was first published in 1763, the year Smart was released from his second period of confinement. Such timing must have had more than a little to do with the speculation about the connection between madness and poetry that has remained a constant in criticism of Smart's literary productions. James Boswell, Johnson's famous biographer, seems to have begun the discussion that occupied Smart's contemporaries even when they were admiring of the work, as Boswell was. The Romantic poets William Wordsworth and Leigh Hunt were among the first to consider *A Song to David* a great lyric. Generally the Romantics were appreciative of Smart, but the Victorian Robert Browning is credited with reviving interest in his works. There is widespread agreement about the high quality of *A Song to David*, even though critical appreciation of Smart's other work waxes and wanes as tastes change.

**A SONG TO DAVID**

Writing a song of praise to the great Hebrew psalmist—*A Song to David*—appears to have been a deliberate act of emulation on the neoclassical poet's part. Although Smart suggested that good poetry was inspired by God rather than the muse, it is known from his translations of Horace into both poetry and prose that he learned how to apply the theory and advice gained from

his reading of the Roman poet. Typical of his era, however, he did not hesitate to combine classicism with Old Testament techniques and New Testament concepts. The trend toward imitation of Hebrew poetry seems to have been initiated by Bishop Robert Lowth's *Praelectiones de Sacra Poesi Hebraerorum* (1753, lectures on the sacred poetry of the Hebrews), published ten years earlier than *A Song to David*. This work attracted attention in scholarly and literary circles and even stimulated popular interest with its analysis of Hebrew poetics and the technical devices of Old Testament poetry.

*A Song to David* does more, however, than follow a trend. It is in some ways unique, and it expresses a personal exhilaration that illustrates the neoclassical concept of the sublime. This sublime, or grand and exalted effect, is never grandiose or bombastic. A look at the formal properties of the poem reveals that Smart was certainly in control, rather than insane, when he wrote this tribute to his hero and model, King David.

The poem is made up of eighty-six stanzas, each of which follows the same basic pattern: two lines of iambic tetrameter followed by an iambic trimeter line and then a repetition of this sequence, making a six-line unit. The rhyme scheme is *aabccb*, with all the end rhymes masculine. An outline of the poem's structure, made by Smart himself and labeled "Contents," is placed between the quotation from 2 Samuel 23:1-2 and the opening stanza.

The quotation introduces David as the subject capsules his life, from his ancestry to his anointing by Samuel and his sacred gift of poetry and song. Traditional interpreters of Hebrew Scripture will find in this passage allusions to the various subtopics addressed within the poem proper: David's ancestry, his monarchy, his sacred gift of poetry and song. David's lineage from the family of Jesse is essential to Smart's establishment of the connection between his Old Testament subject and Jesus Christ. Christian theology teaches that God became human in the form of Jesus of Nazareth, a descendant of the house of David, son of Jesse.

David was anointed king of Israel by Samuel, the same prophet who had anointed the first king, Saul. David, who was close friends with Jonathan, Saul's son, not only was the warrior who slew the Philistine giant Goliath but also served Saul's court as harpist, singer, and poet. The Book of Psalms in the Old Testament is traditionally considered the work of David. David was also the mastermind behind the design of the temple, which was built by his son Solomon (1 Chronicles 28). In the poem proper, Smart goes into more detail, establishing traditional biblical grounds for his treatment of David.

Identifying Smart's concept of David as well as the biblical allusions permeating the stanzas is essential in reading the poem. The David of this poem is not simply the David of the Old Testament and of Jewish history. The David addressed at the beginning of the poem combines the king, the harpist, and the Old Testament type (symbol) of Christ. Evidence from this poem and others, including translations of the Psalms, reveals that Smart incorporates into his David figure the Orpheus of classical mythology, the symbol of the poet as maker, who duplicates on the earthly plane God's act of creation. This creative power provides the thematic basis for the catalog of natural creation that dominates certain prominent sections of the poem. The singer-king is developed thus as the model for the way to praise God and the leader of Christendom in the various acts of praise, just as the psalmist or song leader might direct the congregation in communal praise. As a preliminary way of getting into a celebratory posture, Smart also praises David himself.

Stanza 5 begins the section on David's life, with each stanza from 5 through 16 developing details to support an adjective applied to David in the fourth stanza: "Great, valiant, pious, good, and clean,/ Sublime, contemplative, serene,/ Strong, constant, pleasant, wise!" The history and folklore traditionally associated with the hero are deftly introduced in this passage, with references to well-known characters and minor ones who were a part of David's rise to glory. The close friendship with Jonathan and the feats of the young hero are given more attention than the illicit love affair with Bathsheba, which Smart touches on very briefly. The colorful story of sex, murder, and repentance from 2 Samuel 11 and 12 is mentioned only as "his fall" and is presented as an example of how David "rose [to] his eminence o'er all" by learning from his sin. David's first wife, Michal, and the young girl Abishag, who was supposed to be a comfort to his old age, are mentioned in stanza 17 as means to show the superior importance of his muse, whose influence was greater than that of any of David's women.

The subjects inspired by his muse are then treated generally in a succession of three stanzas: God, angels, humans, and the world. Then he begins a catalog of Creation, which he turns into his own hymn of praise, making vivid word pictures, especially in the lines describing precious stones. The power of this inspired musicianship to overcome not only human foes but also spiritual and demonic ones is the subject of the next three stanzas.

The next section of the poem, introduced by the thirtieth stanza's focus on seven "pillars of the Lord," refers to another creation of David, an architectural act of praise known as Solomon's temple. Allusions are made to the seven pillars of wisdom from the ninth chapter of Proverbs, the seven days of creation as recounted in the first chapter of Genesis, and the decorative pillars of the temple as described in 1 Kings 5-8. The majority of critics, however, see this passage as built on the rites and symbolic system of Freemasonry, which is traditionally associated with the builders of the temple. Each stanza begins with the name of a letter of the Greek alphabet, with vowels and consonants alternating.

Two stanzas complimenting David's knowledge introduce what Smart calls "an exercise upon the decalogue," referring to the Ten Commandments received by Moses. Ever intent on bringing the Hebrew vision of God and the Christian together, Smart reminds his reader to follow the advice of Saint Paul and "turn from old Adam [from the Book of Genesis] to the New [Jesus Christ]." A profusion of images forms the next catalog, which makes a glorious presentation of God's creatures participating in the grand impulse of nature to praise the Creator. This call to celebration and participation is developed under the heading of adoration, with David the singer as its leader. The word "ADORATION" is artfully placed in a different line within each stanza, so that it is given strategic emphasis. Certain of these stanzas reveal Smart's paraphrasing of psalms, including myriad details in the passages he had earlier labeled exercises on "right use" of the seasons and "how to subdue" the senses. The abundance of creation, with its systematic and plenary chain of being, is suggested, creating a joyous and effervescent tone of love and unity.

Stanza 72 begins the crescendo that develops to the finale, which was described earlier in Smart's outline as "an amplification in five degrees," once again suggesting the Masonic Order. Repetition of a series of adjectives, much like the repetition of "ADORATION," precedes the nature imagery used to define and illustrate the individual words: "sweet," "strong," "beauteous," "precious," and "glorious." Each adjective is taken through its own degrees of comparison, with sentences built around its meaning.

The last stanza of the poem is also the final one in the adjectival series, with its focus on the meanings of "glorious" as summed up in the person of Christ the King, who took on human form. Having brought together the creation, the incarnation, and the resurrection, which are the foundation of traditional Judeo-Christian belief, Smart ends on a note of triumph that seems as much a personal declaration as a thematic one: "DETERMINED, DARED, and DONE."

OTHER MAJOR WORKS

PLAYS: *Hannah: An Oratorio*, 1764 (libretto); *Abimelech: An Oratorio*, 1768 (libretto); *Providence: An Oratorio*, 1777 (libretto).

NONFICTION: *Mother Midnight's Miscellany*, 1751 (as Mary Midnight); *The Nonpareil: Or, The Quintessence of Wit and Humor*, 1757 (as Midnight).

TRANSLATIONS: *The Works of Horace, Translated Literally into English*, 1756; *A Poetical Translation of the Fables of Phaedrus*, 1765; *A Translation of the Psalms of David Attempted in the Spirit of Christianity*, 1765; *The Works of Horace Translated into Verse*, 1767.

BIBLIOGRAPHY

Curry, Neil. *Christopher Smart*. Tavistock, England: Northcote House/British Council, 2005. A biography of Smart that also examines his writings.

Dillingham, Thomas F. "'Blest Light': Christopher Smart's Myth of David." In *The David Myth in Western Literature*, edited by Raymond-Jean Frontain and Jan Wojick. West Lafayette, Ind.: Purdue University Press, 1980. The biblical David is central to Smart's highest poetic achievements, says Dillingham, whether used as subject, as in *A Song to David*, or as a model for imitation, as in the translations and biblical paraphrases. Smart combines the Old Testament figure with the Greek Orpheus and Christian theology in seeking a unified vision for his faith.

Hawes, Clement, ed. *Christopher Smart and the Enlightenment*. New York: St. Martin's Press, 1999. A reappraisal of Smart's legacy and his remarkable impact on twentieth century poetry. Analyzes the generative impact of Smart on modern poetry and music, demonstrating the reach of his contemporary resonance.

Jason, Philip K., ed. *Masterplots II: Poetry Series*. Rev. ed. Pasadena, Calif.: Salem Press, 2002. Contains an analysis of Smart's "My Cat, Jeoffry." Summary, forms and devices, and themes and meanings are discussed.

Mounsey, Chris. *Christopher Smart: Clown of God*. Cranbury, N.J.: Associated University Presses, 2001. A biography of the poet, detailing his confinement for mental illness. Includes bibliographical references and index.

Spacks, Patricia Ann Meyer. *Reading Eighteenth-Century Poetry*. Malden, Mass.: Wiley-Blackwell, 2009. In one chapter, Spacks examines the poetry of Smart and Mary Leapor, a kitchen maid who died of measles at the age of twenty-three. She sees both of them as outliers who were nonetheless able to achieve some popularity in their lifetimes. She sees Smart as using poetic forms in new ways and Leapor as employing new themes.

*Emma Coburn Norris*

# STEVIE SMITH

**Born:** Hull, Yorkshire, England; September 20, 1902
**Died:** Ashburton, England; March 7, 1971

PRINCIPAL POETRY

*A Good Time Was Had by All*, 1937
*Tender Only to One*, 1938
*Mother, What Is Man?*, 1942
*Harold's Leap*, 1950
*Not Waving but Drowning*, 1957
*Selected Poems*, 1962
*The Frog Prince, and Other Poems*, 1966
*The Best Beast*, 1969
*Two in One: "Selected Poems" and "The Frog
    Prince, and Other Poems,"* 1971
*Scorpion, and Other Poems*, 1972
*The Collected Poems of Stevie Smith*, 1975
*Selected Poems*, 1978
*Cats, Friends, and Lovers: For Women's Chorus*,
    1987 (music by Stephen Paulus)
*New Selected Poems of Stevie Smith*, 1988
*Stevie's Tunes: An Anthology of Nine Songs for
    Mezzo-soprano and Piano*, 1988 (music by Peter
    Dickinson)
*Two Stevie Smith Songs: For Voice and Piano*,
    1990 (music by Geoffrey Bush)

OTHER LITERARY FORMS

Stevie Smith published three autobiographical novels, the best-received of which was her first, *Novel on Yellow Paper: Or, Work It Out for Yourself* (1936). A book of her drawings (with captions) called *Some Are More Human than Others: Sketch-Book by Stevie Smith* appeared in 1958. She also wrote short stories, essays, book reviews, and a one-act radio play.

ACHIEVEMENTS

Stevie Smith's first novel received warm reviews in 1936, and she enjoyed a popularity that was sudden but relatively stable until the 1950's, when she fell out of fashion for a number of years. By the early 1960's, however, she was back in the public eye, and she remained popular, giving readings in which she some-

times sang her poems in an odd, singsong voice, until her death in 1971. She won the Cholmondeley Award for Poetry in 1966 and was awarded the Gold Medal for Poetry by Queen Elizabeth II in 1969.

BIOGRAPHY

Born Florence Margaret Smith, Stevie Smith belonged to a family made up of women from the time she was four, when her father disappeared to make a career for himself as a sailor. That year, 1906, she moved with her mother, sister, and aunt to a house on Avondale Road in the London suburb of Palmers Green. Smith lived there for the rest of her life. By 1924, her mother had died and her sister had moved to Suffolk. From then on, she shared the house with her adored Aunt Margaret, whom Smith affectionately called the Lion Aunt.

Smith was not university educated and was never married. The nickname Stevie, acquired when she was eighteen, is a reference to Steve Donaghue, a famous jockey. After her graduation from secretarial training college, she got a job as a private secretary at a publishing firm in 1923. She kept this job for thirty years, until she finally devoted herself to writing full time. She died of an inoperable brain tumor in 1971.

ANALYSIS

Stevie Smith populated the margins of her poems with idiosyncratic drawings of swimmers and potted plants, ghosts and dogs, howling children and flirting couples. She doodled this art herself, when, as she explained, she was "not thinking too much. If I suddenly get caught by the doodle, I put more effort into it and end up calling it a drawing. I've got a whole collection in boxes. Some are on tiny bits of paper and drawn on telephone and memo pads." Smith insisted that the drawings be published with her poems, even though they do not technically "illustrate" the words on the page. Instead, she chose drawings that seemed to her to illustrate "the spirit or the idea in the poem."

In some ways, reading Smith's poetry is like fishing in one of her boxes filled with drawings on loose sheets and tiny bits of paper. As one moves from one drawing to another, one poem to another, the habits of her imagination become familiar. One can identify concerns (death, spinsterhood, sexuality) that appeared early and persisted late, name maneuvers (analysis of myth, parody of family roles) that recur again and again. One learns to recognize the spatialization of her impatience with categories through images of claustrophobia ("Souvenir de Monsieur Poop"), to expect her assumption of the proximity between love and hate ("I HATE THIS GIRL"), to look for the ways in which grief feeds the heart ("So to fatness come"). She moves back and forth among forms—from rapid stanzas with fixed rhyme schemes ("Nourish Me on an Egg," "Do Take Muriel Out") to long poems constructed of rhyming couplets ("The Passing Cloud," "The Hostage"), to looser, more narrative lines ("Dear Karl," "The Abominable Lake"). Yet the procedure from one poem to another—or one collection to another—does not present itself as neat linear development.

### INHERITED STORIES

It is possible, however, to sketch out a set of preoccupations that Smith found compelling enough to return to throughout her career. One of the most conspicuous of these concerns is her investigation of inherited stories: fairy tales, narratives from the Bible, legends, and myths. Smith takes as her premise that material culture and literary culture constitute overlapping territories and is at pains in many of her poems to demonstrate the ways in which Western culture has organized itself in response to certain famous stories.

In a late poem called "How Cruel Is the Story of Eve," for example, she argues the disturbing repercussions that Genesis, with its snake and its apple and its falling woman, set in motion: "What responsibility it has/ In history/ For cruelty." She goes on to address the collective resistance of skeptical readers, who might call her estimation of the effects of Eve's story exaggerated: What is the meaning of this legend, she asks, "if not/ To give blame to women most/ And most punishment?"

Smith is interested in stories and images that have saturated the cultural imagination of her society—stories that have defined and continue to influence the position of women, to shape attitudes about animals and wildness, to teach lessons about romance and relationships. Her poems refer back in literary history to William Blake (in her "Little Boy Sick") and across

boundaries of genre when she appropriates fairy tales (in "The Frog Prince") or Arthurian legends (in "The Blue from Heaven"). As Smith points out, these stories color all human thought and are therefore important to anyone interested in disrupting some of those thoughts.

### INHERITED ROLES

If Smith's exploration of inherited stories uncovers some of the ways in which culture grids according to gender or species, her survey of the roles inherited and negotiated within families reduces the scale of the inquiry while maintaining precise attention to instances of ill fit between individuals and the roles in which they find themselves. Adults are irked at having to give up the colors and excesses of childhood ("To Carry the Child"); children with absent fathers are cynical from babyhood ("Infant"). Women with husbands and children weep over frying pans ("Wretched Woman") or lash out—"You beastly child, I wish you had miscarried,/ You beastly husband, I wish I had never married" ("Lightly Bound")—while women who refuse to compromise themselves by investing in less-than-adequate relationships doubt their own decisions and worry about isolation: "All, all is isolation/ And every lovely limb's a desolation" ("Every Lovely Limb's a Desolation"). Because Smith delights in circling round a situation, sizing it up from all angles, there also are poems that defend solitude—speakers who argue, for example, that the best personal prescription is to "shun compromise/ Forget him and forget her" ("To the Tune of the Coventry Carol"), despite the risks of isolation. The typical attitude of a wife toward her wifehood, a mother toward her motherhood, or a child toward her childhood is discomfort and cynicism. Figures in Smith's poems are perpetually chafed by the discrepancy between their needs and the roles into which they believe they have been, one way or another, stuck.

For all her self-consciousness about cultural slots, Smith feels no obligation to limit her renditions of them to tragic monotones. Her preference for reading Agatha Christie novels in translation, for example, clearly indicates that she relished the humor of a poor fit. "If you read her in French," she once remarked, "you get a most exotic flavor, because there never was anything more English than the stuff she's writing. It's great fun that the translations are rather poor." Smith administered her critical, antic judgment to anything in sight, including her own loyalties—to Anglicanism, for example. While she remained personally loyal to the church her whole life, she cheerfully poked poetic fun at the awkward positions into which God forces his underlings.

### "NATURE AND FREE ANIMALS"

Smith argues in one early poem, for example, that the human impulse to make dogs into pets has always been prompted by the unbearably cramped space of the will to which people find themselves restricted when they see, on one hand, "Nature and Free Animals" and on the other, God himself. The poem begins with God's irate pronouncement that humans have committed the one moral error he cannot abide: "they have taught [dogs] to be servile . . . To be dependent touching and entertaining." Given human pride in legal systems that articulate and protect human rights, to complain that having "rights to be wronged/ And wrongs to be righted" insults a God-given wild dogginess might strike one as ludicrous. However, Smith celebrates the possibility of uninhibited if violent life that animals represent while poking merciless fun at the ways in which human laws and orders actually trivialize death. The person God reprimands in this poem shoots back a feisty self-defense: "Nature and Free Animals/ Are all very fine," the speaker grants, but with them "on the one side/ And you on the other,/ I hardly know I'm alive." Squeezed from both directions, humans have no room to exercise either instinct or will, and it is precisely this unpleasant sensation that compels them to make dogs into pets. Having made her irreverent point, Smith undoubtedly chuckled at the anagrammatic joke of resisting God by putting a leash on his name spelled backwards.

### "THE ZOO"

Not being one to shy away from the unorthodox destinations toward which her unorthodox theories point her, Smith accepts the fact that her celebration of animals must accommodate violence. Thus, in a poem called "The Zoo," a lion "sits within his cage,/ Weeping tears of ruby rage" because he has been deprived of his natural capacity for violence. "His claws are blunt, his teeth fall out,/ No victim's flesh consoles his snout," the speaker reports sympathetically, concluding that it is no wonder that "his eyes are red/ Considering his tal-

ents are misused." Smith gives God due credit for having bestowed on the lion "lovely teeth and claws/ So that he might eat little boys."

Oddly as such a compliment rings, other of Smith's treatments of animals suggest that it is not an entirely backhanded one. The reader may wince at being made politely to admire the lion's gift for making snacks of little boys, but when one is presented with the alternative of allying oneself with pet owners as depicted in poems such as "Jumbo," the crunching of bones begins to have a certain raw dignity:

> Jumbo, Jumbo, Jumbo darling, Jumbo come to Mother.
> But Jumbo wouldn't, he was a dog who simply wouldn't
>  bother
> An ugly beast he was with drooping guts and filthy skin,
> It was quite wonderful how "mother" loved the ugly
>  thing.

What Smith ridicules here is not the ugliness of Jumbo but rather the human compulsion to assert its will even over such a mangy beast. Jumbo's unwillingness to be bothered with his yodeling "mother" is a caustic enough comment on humans' clumsy interference with naturally occurring systems in which dogs, with wonderful indifference, eat dogs. Smith takes clear delight, however, in pushing the caricature one step further. In linking humans' desire to lord it over the likes of Jumbo with the sacred job of mothering, she insinuates that perhaps people are not as far removed from the harshness of nature as they wish to believe.

### "A MOTHER'S HEARSE" AND "THE WANDERER"

Crass as one may find such an intimation, Smith doggedly pursues the possibility that "the love of a mother for her child/ Is not necessarily a beautiful thing" ("A Mother's Hearse"). "Mother, if mother-love enclosure be," one child protests, "It were enough, my dear, not quite to hate me." While another Brontë-like waif trails about tapping at windowpanes and crying that "you have weaned me too soon, you must nurse me again," the speaker corrects the misapprehension of the unhappy ghost. Would she indeed "be happier if she were within?" Smith guesses not: "She is happier far where the night winds fall,/ And there are no doors and no windows at all" ("The Wanderer").

Just as God and beasts are understood to restrict the possibility for human action by having prior claim on both divine instruction and animal instinct, claustrophobia of the will looms over the enterprise of motherhood. What Smith seems, in fact, to be suggesting is the unattractive possibility that domination is one of the primary (and primal) motivations of humankind. The desire to dominate warps even the best-intentioned of projects and even love.

### "PAPA LOVE BABY"

If mothers threaten to smother their little darlings, the conspicuous absence of paternal will allows children to rule in worlds of lopsided power. The gigantic quantity of control one presumes that parents wield over their toddlers, for example, dwindles rather rapidly in "Papa Love Baby" when the child administers judgment:

> I sat upright in my baby carriage
> And wished mama hadn't made such a foolish marriage.
> I tried to hide it, but it showed in my eyes unfortunately
> And a fortnight later papa ran away to sea.

Such radical shrinkage of adult presumption would be comic except for the child's disturbing admission that its keen and unforgiving wit carries with it the burden of responsibility: "I could not grieve/ But I think I was somewhat to blame."

Even more disturbing than this image of a preschooler having to shoulder the blame for her own abandonment, the articulate baby of "Papa Love Baby" tells her brief tale in a way that hints darkly at incest:

> What folly it is that daughters are always supposed to be
> In love with papa. It wasn't the case with me
> I couldn't take to him at all
> But he took to me
> What a sad fate to befall
> A child of three.

The shrinking line lengths of this stanza, which ends with an admission of her tender age, remind us of the inevitable physical advantage that even a stupid papa enjoys over his little girl. The sexual suggestiveness of the poem stays, by all means, at the level of nebulous suggestion: The father "took to" the child who did not "take to him." Yet the reader can hardly help wondering why such a turn of events would constitute a "sad fate" and why, despite the fact that the poem concerns itself primarily with the child's disdain for her "unrespected" father, its title should highlight the fact that in spite of that childish contempt, "Papa Love Baby."

### A GOOD TIME WAS HAD BY ALL

The place children occupy in the various structures they find themselves to have inherited from adults constitutes one of Smith's most persistent preoccupations. *A Good Time Was Had by All*, her first published volume of poetry, begins and ends with poems that treat this issue. "The Hound of Ulster" and "Louise" frame the collection, typifying her vision of how the tension between adulthood and childhood shapes most human relationships. Despite what is normally thought of as the distance separating grownups from youngsters, she was at perpetual pains to point out their complicated proximity. "We are," as she once remarked, "as much the child's old age as he is our youth."

### "THE HOUND OF ULSTER"

In "The Hound of Ulster," a "courteous stranger" urges a little boy to "take a look/ In the puppy shop," with its tantalizing array of dogs: "Could anything be merrier?" This adult script, rendered instantly suspect by the ease with which it fits the pattern parents proverbially warn their children against (never accept rides, candy, or invitations from strangers), does not, however, turn genuinely sinister until the last lines of the poem. Upon the child's polite inquiry regarding what it might be that "lurks in the gray/ Cold shadows at the back of the shop," the stranger warns that Cuchulain, the legendary Irish warrior also known as the Hound of Ulster, "lies tethered there . . . tethered by his golden hair."

As a child, the legend goes, the Irish warrior killed a fierce dog that attacked him. The dog belonged to Chulain, who grieved over the death of his pet. Upon seeing the owner's grief, the child took it upon himself to be watchdog for Chulain until a new dog could be found. Thus he earned the name of Cuchulain, which translates to "the hound of Chulain." Cuchulain is also known as the "Hound of Ulster" in reference to the Ulster cycle of Gaelic literature.

If, as "Nature and Free Animals" suggests, humans make pets of dogs as a way of securing for themselves a modicum of space within which their wills—bounded by animals from below and God from above—can operate, the childhood feat of Cuchulain represents a double seizure of power. Having been mortally threatened by the dog, the child first dispenses with the beast that dares to trespass beyond his already liberal bounds, then appropriates the bestial vigor of the dog—but only temporarily. In Smith's structure of competing territories between people and animals, then, Cuchulain's ability to negotiate his way between those territories ensures a much more spacious scope for the exercise of his strength.

In the poem, however, the hound stands as an image of paralyzed will, "tethered by his golden hair/ His eyes are closed and his lips are pale/ Hurry little boy he is not for sale." Having asked too much, the curious child is sent on his way. Only the poem's speaker, familiar with the puppy inventory and protective of the shop's tethered secret, seems to exercise any genuine control in this poem, and it is a control of exhibition. The reader's or the boy's access to dogs of the will is strictly limited to spectatorship, while the speaker extends the invitation and controls the display, blending the roles of poet and zookeeper.

### "LOUISE"

"Louise," the final poem in *A Good Time Was Had by All*, repeats the eerie childhood experience described in "Papa Love Baby": articulate intellectual power darkened by traces of sexual powerlessness. Louise sits on a suitcase in the "suburban sitting room" of Mr. and Mrs. Tease, having traveled all over Europe with her mother but having "never been long enough in any nation/ Completely to unpack." The only words she speaks in the poem are wistful ones—"Oh if only I could stay/ Just for two weeks in one place." Her thoughts are quickly followed by her mother's advice, "Cheer up girlie," because they will indeed be stopping here for at least two weeks, as it will take Louise's father that long to come up with the money they need to move on. The poem (and the collection) thus ends on a note of bewilderment colored by the reader's response to the idea of hosts called Mr and Mrs Tease: "The poor child sits in a mazy fit:/ Such a quick answer to a prayer/ Shakes one a bit." That the near-instantaneous answer to her wish should send Louise down the emotional path of something as complicated as a "mazy fit" demonstrates part of what makes Smith's abnormally astute, hyper-intuitive children such disturbing combinations of sophistication and vulnerability. While their wishes conform to a formula of Cinderella simplicity, their intuitive gifts expose the problems inherent in reductive answers. A homesick child gets to stay in one house for two weeks, but how reassuring is it when that house is presided over by hosts by the name of Mr. and Mrs. Tease? The predicament of Louise, caught between her apparent powers of shaping the adult world and her childish susceptibility to the adults who nevertheless continue to rule it, haunts the body of Smith's work right up to her death.

### "DUTY WAS HIS LODESTAR"

Sometimes children manage to elude adult authority—exhibiting, as a poem such as "Duty Was His Lodestar" gleefully demonstrates, particular skill in ducking out of verbal structures. As Smith herself has explained, the premise of this poem is a child's having "been told that duty is one's lodestar. But she is rebellious, this child, she will have none of it, so she says lobster instead of lodestar, and so makes a mock of it, and makes a monkey of the kind teacher." What readers are presented with is "A song" (the poem's subtitle) in which speaker and lobster damage their relationship but then mend it and celebrate their reunification:

Duty was my Lobster, my Lobster was she,
And when I walked with my Lobster
I was happy.
But one day my Lobster and I fell out,
And we did nothing but
Rave and shout

Rejoice, rejoice, Hallelujah, drink the flowing
 champagne,
For my darling Lobster and I
Are friends again.

The seriousness of duty as presented by adult to child is replaced by the celebration of relationship. Duty, meant to fix the child's respectful attention and serve as a sober guide, gives way to friendship, charged with gospel-choir enthusiasm.

### "OUR BOG IS DOOD"

In "Our Bog Is Dood," Smith parodies the limits of the religious imagination in a humorous anecdote about the difficulties of achieving interpretive consensus. In this poem, the children chanting "Our Bog is dood" reveal to the speaker that they know their Bog is dood "because we wish it so/ That is enough." Here, Smith lays out for the reader's amusement (or admiration; the two are neighboring concepts as far as she is concerned) the acts of sheer and reckless will by which both children and children of God collapse the distance between wish and belief, constructing verbal worlds that they inhabit with collective placidity until prodded to articulate the specifics of those worlds. "Then tell me, darling little ones," the speaker inquires, feigning innocence, "What's dood, suppose Bog is?" This flummoxes them, for though they give the irritating speaker an answer quick enough ("Just what we think it is"), they soon began arguing with one another, "for what was dood, and what their Bog/ They never could agree." The speaker proves to be exempt from this hostility not by virtue of having answers to the issues of Bog or dood but rather by a willingness to let the questions lie unanswered, to walk beside rather than into "the encroaching sea,/ The sea that soon should drown them all,/ That never yet drowned me."

### "TO CARRY THE CHILD"

It is irrepressibility that Smith celebrates in the children of "To Carry the Child," which suggests that the labor of carrying a child does not end at birth or even when the baby learns to walk but rather at the nebulous juncture separating childhood from adulthood. In this poem, she describes the moment of being allowed to stand on one's own two feet not as a moment of independence but of diminishment. Grownups are "frozen," while children are "easy in feeling, easily excessive/ And in excess powerful." Growing in this poem is an act not of growing up but of growing into, a process of entrapment: What can the poor child do, "trapped in a grown-up carapace,/ But peer outside of his prison room/ With the eye of an anarchist?" That Smith visualizes adults as a population of "handicapped" children speaks to the vigor with which she gripped onto the idea of children as a model for the independent imagination, gradually able to hold onto

their mobility of vision only from within a claustrophobic space.

### "NUMBERS"

If the encroaching rigidity of a carapace threatens to reduce the imaginative scope of a child to the rolling of eyeballs, then the architecture of domesticity constructs somewhat less restrictive but still idiosyncratic frames of reference. In "Numbers," that such frames of reference limit the bounds of the imagination becomes a matter of literal concern as well, since the information that fails to make its way into the boundaries of the poem's window frames is the small fact that the speaker's house sits on a four-hundred-foot cliff. The poem lists numbers of objects that romp about or spread outside one house:

> A thousand and fifty-one waves
> Two hundred and thirty-one seagulls
> A cliff of four hundred feet
> Three miles of ploughed fields.

Four windows provide views of the waves and the fields, while one skylight provides visual access to a square of sky. Thus the occupant of the house is able to perceive a little bit of most of what lies beyond the walls of the house: four windows' worth of the 1,051 waves, four windows' worth of the three miles of fields, and one of the 231 seagulls. Only the four-hundred-foot cliff on which the house sits is invisible, suggesting that while frames of domestic reference may indeed offer access to snippets of the world at large, they ground themselves, obliviously, on the precarious edges of things. What is disturbing about this poem is not so much the cliff as the apparent unconsciousness with which the inhabitants of the house are perched on it.

### ATTITUDE TOWARD DEATH

Harold's courage in not only confronting but also in leaping such cliffs is what stirs the admiring eulogy of acrophobic Harold in the title poem of Smith's 1950 collection, *Harold's Leap*. "Harold was always afraid to climb high,/ But something urged him on." Smith lavishes the energy of this poem not on Harold's failure to accomplish anything beyond his own death-by-leap but on the dizzying height of the rocks, the sheer will Harold mustered. That she applauds his leap in spite of its futility suggests that since death is the project looming over all other projects anyway, to take one's death into one's own legs constitutes the only possible act of frank courage.

This unblinking attitude toward death constitutes, in fact, one of the most conspicuous stripes by which Smith's work may be recognized. Her stance toward it veers from the dismissive to the devoted but always takes careful account of its reliability as a solution. In "Death Bereaves Our Common Mother, Nature Grieves for My Dead Brother," an early poem from *A Good Time Was Had by All*, death is noted as a shift in verb tense: "He was, I am." The subject is a dead lamb, a drawing of which (lying on its back with its four legs straight up like a dead bug) decorates the poem. This ditty on death is casual to the point of flippancy, despite its professed compassion—"Can I see lamb dead as mutton/ And not care a solitary button?" Lest one suspect that she reserves this easy tone for animals, Smith describes the death of one Major Spruce in another poem in the same volume in nearly identical terms. "It is a Major Spruce/ And he's grown such a bore, such a bore. . . . It was the Major Spruce./ He died. Didn't I tell you?" ("Progression").

In the title poem of *Tender Only to One*, Smith borrows a familiar convention of gooey sentimentality to demonstrate her feelings for death. Here, the petal-plucking speaker performs that hoary ritual of virginhood—loves me, loves me not—in order to discover the name of him to whom she is tender. In the end, the bald flower manages to convey the message: "Tender only to one,/ . . . His name, his name is Death." While it is difficult to tell precisely whether the speaker with such a quantity of tenderness to bestow is surprised by the outcome of her experiment, the ease with which the stanza contains the name of the beloved suggests that the news does not perturb her. The entire display, apparently, is presented for the reader's benefit.

Another poem in the same collection fancies death as stage two of a doctor's prescription. When the solicitous physician observes that "You are not looking at all well, my dear,/ In fact you are looking most awfully queer," my dear replies that yes, indeed, the pain is "more than I can bear, so give me some bromide." She will go away to the seashore, where the tides, naturally,

will take care of the situation, carrying the speaker "beyond recovery" ("The Doctor"). "Come Death (I)," meanwhile, reprimands Christianity for teaching people to be brave in facing death, for courage is not even necessary. "Foolish illusion, what has Life to give?" the speaker inquires scornfully. "Why should man more fear Death than fear to live?" "From the Coptic" shapes the relationship between life and death into a narrative, as it describes three angels trying to coax clay into manhood. The first two angels promise the clay happiness, to little effect: "the red clay lay flat in the falling rain,/ Crying, I will stay clay and take no blame." Upon identifying himself as Death, however, the third angel produces immediate results: "I am Death, said the angel, and death is the end,/ I am Man, cries clay rising, and you are my friend."

### "NOT WAVING BUT DROWNING"

Given the array of instances in which Smith warmly clasps the hand of death, that her most famous poem draws on the human dread of dying may say more about the kind of poems people wish to anthologize than it does about any alteration of her sensibility. "Not Waving but Drowning" is, however, the title poem of the 1957 collection, suggesting at the very least that she wished her readers to take a look at this fable of how gestures of despair and even catastrophe get mistaken for something else:

> Nobody heard him, the dead man,
> But still he lay moaning:
> I was much further out than you thought
> And not waving but drowning.

This poem, with its disturbing pun on panicky signal and casual acknowledgment, suggests that civilized systems of communication fail to accommodate emergencies. Schooled in polite noninterference and having no mechanism for detecting anything outside the bounds of that inarticulate propriety, one simply assumes that any waves at all are bound to be waves of greeting. This sorry state of communicative affairs is further complicated by the fact that the swimmer's ability to articulate difference is overwhelmed by the very medium through which he swims: How can he be expected to clarify for others the distinction between waves of greeting and waves of alarm when all his waves are immersed in even more and perpetual waves of water? The enterprise seems doomed from the beginning.

Smith's refusal to desert these individual victims of isolation, her cocking of the ear to the persistent voice of a dead man, offers a fragile consolation. Prodded and coached by this plucky mistress of lost voices, her readers learn at least to recognize the coarseness of their own powers of interpretation. If one fails to make out the words of the drowned swimmer, one can at least be assured that it is not for the lack of his having gurgled out a message.

OTHER MAJOR WORKS

LONG FICTION: *Novel on Yellow Paper: Or, Work It Out for Yourself*, 1936; *Over the Frontier*, 1938; *The Holiday*, 1949.

NONFICTION: *Some Are More Human than Others: Sketch-Book by Stevie Smith*, 1958, 1990.

MISCELLANEOUS: *Me Again: Uncollected Writings of Stevie Smith*, 1981; *Stevie Smith: A Selection*, 1985; *A Very Pleasant Evening with Stevie Smith: Selected Short Prose*, 1995.

BIBLIOGRAPHY

Barbera, Jack, and William McBrien. *Stevie: A Biography of Stevie Smith*. New York: Oxford University Press, 1987. Barbera and McBrien's literary biography is well researched and very readable.

Civello, Catherine A. *Patterns of Ambivalence: The Fiction and Poetry of Stevie Smith*. Columbia, S.C.: Camden House, 1997. An analysis of Smith's work using feminist theory.

Huk, Romana. *Stevie Smith: Between the Lines*. New York: Palgrave Macmillan, 2005. An assessment of the works of Smith and a study of their cultural significance.

Pumphrey, Martin. "Play, Fantasy, and Strange Laughter: Stevie Smith's Uncomfortable Poetry." *Critical Quarterly* 28 (Autumn, 1986): 85-96. Pumphrey uses some of the basic assumptions of play theory to approach Smith's poems. He discusses her use of fairy-tale elements and describes her as an "anti-confessional" poet.

Rankin, Arthur. *The Poetry of Stevie Smith, "Little Girl Lost."* Totowa, N.J.: Barnes and Noble, 1985. Clearly analyzes Smith's poetic styles, themes, and attitudes.

Severin, Laura. *Stevie Smith's Resistant Antics*. Madison: University of Wisconsin Press, 1997. Severin's extensive study challenges the notions of Smith as an apolitical and eccentric poet, instead portraying her as a well-connected literary insider who used many genres to resist domestic ideology in Britain.

Spalding, Frances. *Stevie Smith: A Biography*. Rev. ed. New York: Sutton House, 2002. A classic biography of Smith that challenges the notion that the writer was a recluse.

Sternlicht, Sanford. *Stevie Smith*. Boston: Twayne, 1990. Sternlicht's book is a good introduction to Smith's work. It includes chapters on her novels and nonfiction as well as chronological descriptions of Smith's development. The book contains a chronology of Smith's life and a selected bibliography.

_____, ed. *In Search of Stevie Smith*. Syracuse, N.Y.: Syracuse University Press, 1991. A collection of biographical and critical essays on the life and works of Smith. Includes bibliographical references and index.

Williams, Jonathan. "Much Further Out than You Thought." *Parnassus: Poetry in Review* 2 (Spring/Summer, 1974): 105-127. This article is a meditation by a personal friend of Smith, most interesting for its quotations from a 1963 interview.

*Allyson Booth*

---

# ROBERT SOUTHEY

**Born:** Bristol, England; August 12, 1774
**Died:** Greta Hall, Keswick, England; March 21, 1843

PRINCIPAL POETRY

*Poems*, 1795 (with Robert Lovell)
*Joan of Arc: An Epic Poem*, 1796, 1798, 1806, 1812
*Poems*, 1797-1799
*Thalaba the Destroyer*, 1801

*Madoc*, 1805

*Metrical Tales, and Other Poems*, 1805

*The Curse of Kehama*, 1810

*Odes to His Royal Highness the Prince Regent, His
    Imperial Majesty the Emperor of Russia, and
    His Majesty the King of Prussia*, 1814

*Roderick, the Last of the Goths*, 1814

*Minor Poems*, 1815

*The Lay of the Laureate: Carmen Nuptiale*, 1816

*The Poet's Pilgrimage to Waterloo*, 1816

*Wat Tyler: A Dramatic Poem*, 1817

*A Vision of Judgement*, 1821

*A Tale of Paraguay*, 1825

*All for Love, and the Pilgrim to Compostella*, 1829

*Poetical Works*, 1829

*The Devil's Walk*, 1830 (with Samuel Taylor
    Coleridge)

*Selections from the Poems*, 1831, 1833

*Poetical Works*, 1839

*Oliver Newman: A New-England Tale (Unfinished):
    With Other Poetical Remains*, 1845

*Robin Hood: A Fragment*, 1847 (with Caroline
    Southey)

*Robert Southey: Poetical Works, 1793-1810*, 2004
    (5 volumes)

## OTHER LITERARY FORMS

The collected prose works of Robert Southey (SOW-thee, also SUHTH-ee) comprise almost forty volumes, ranging from literary criticism to biography, from fiction to translations. *Letters from England by Don Manuel Espriella* (1807) is a satiric commentary on everyday life in contemporary England, while *Sir Thomas More* (1829) reveals Southey again examining society, this time by way of conversations between the spirit of the departed More and Montesimos (Southey himself). His so-called novel, the seven-volume *The Doctor* (1834-1847), concerns Dr. Daniel Dove of Doncaster and his horse Nobs; as a fantasy and a commentary on life, the excruciatingly lengthy piece reminds one of Laurence Sterne's *Tristram Shandy* (1759-1767)—without the artistic qualities of that remarkable work of fiction. Hidden within chapter 129 of Southey's effort lies the first-known telling of the nursery classic "The Three Bears."

*Life of Nelson* (1813) and *Life of Wesley and the Rise and Progress of Methodism* (1820) head the list of Southey's biographical studies. Others of note include *A Summary of the Life of Arthur, Duke of Wellington* (1816); the *Life of John, Duke of Marlborough* (1822); *Lives of the British Admirals* (1833-1840); and *The Life of the Rev. Andrew Bell* (1844, one volume only), the Scottish-born educationist who founded the National Society for the Education of the Poor. Southey's historical writings include the *History of Brazil* (1810-1819), *The History of Europe* (1810-1813), and the *History of the Peninsular War* (1823-1832). In 1812, Southey published *The Origin, Nature, and Object of the New System of Education*. This was followed by *The Book of the Church* (1824), *Vindiciae Ecclesiae Anglicanae* (1826), and *Essays Moral and Political* (1832).

Southey was also an editor and translator. Among his edited works are *The Annual Anthology* (1799-1800), *The Works of Chatterton* (1803, with Joseph Cottle), *Palmerin of England* (1807), Isaac Watts's *Horae Lyricae* (1834), and *The Works of William Cowper* (1835-1837). Southey's notable translations include Jacques Necker's *On the French Revolution* (1797), Vasco Lobeira's *Amadis de Gaul* (1805), the *Chronicle of the Cid* (1808), Abbe Don Ignatius Molina's *The Geographical, Natural, and Civil History of Chili* (1808), and *Memoria Sobre a Litteratura Portugueza* (1809).

## ACHIEVEMENTS

During his lifetime, Robert Southey enjoyed moments of popularity and success; there were even those among his contemporaries who believed that he ranked with the best of his nation's poets. He outlived Samuel Taylor Coleridge, Sir Walter Scott, Charles Lamb, William Hazlitt, Lord Byron, Percy Bysshe Shelley, and John Keats, yet rarely does one find mention of his name in a discussion of the significant figures and forces that shaped British Romanticism in the first part of the nineteenth century. Although Southey is deep in the shadows of William Wordsworth and Coleridge, appearing in literary histories only as their mediocre associate, his poetry deserves a careful reading, especially that written before 1801. This early work reveals an extremely high degree of versatility, not always appreciated by those who study only the first rank of nineteenth century British Romantics. The simplicity and directness of language found in Southey's early ballads and short narratives echo Wordsworth's *Lyrical Ballads* (1798), but the pieces succeed because the poet could rise above pure imitation. He could also write irregular odes and heroic epistles that demonstrated his knowledge of the Augustan Age, he knew how to create sublime imagery with the aid of biblical themes, and he could plunge downward to concoct playful exercises with pigs and gooseberry pies. He was adept in a variety of poetic forms: the elegy, the sonnet, the sapphic, the ballad, the metrical tale.

The content of Southey's poems is as varied as the form. While at Balliol College, Oxford, during the period of his enthusiasm for republicanism, he wrote a dramatic poem on Wat Tyler, the leader of the peasant revolt of 1381, while four years later, his piece on the first duke of Marlborough's victory at Blenheim (August, 1704) during the War of the Spanish Succession graphically underscored the poet's sentiments on the futility of war—"But what good came of it at last?" In what seemed a radical shift of poetical gears, Southey rode hard and fast on the waves of the Gothic horror narrative in "God's Judgment on a Wicked Bishop" (1799), in which he adapted the legendary story of a tenth century German bishop who was attacked and then devoured by a pack of rats. At the outset of the nineteenth century, he turned to a series of epic poems—*Thalaba the Destroyer* and *The Curse of Kehama* being two examples—that placed him alongside his contemporaries in the Romantic quest for glamour and the grandeur of distant places and even more distant times.

Southey's greatest weakness may have been his inability to recognize his own limitations as a poet. He remained unaware of what he could do best. He took his role as poet laureate of England far too seriously—especially in view of the fact that the honor came only because Sir Walter Scott refused to accept it. Not only did he exercise poor political and critical judgment by attacking Byron, but he also wrote, in 1821, the unnecessarily lengthy *A Vision of Judgement*, in which he attempted to transport the recently departed King George III into heaven. Byron, of course, replied in the preface to his similarly titled poem (*The Vision of Judgment*,

1822), "If Mr. Southey had not rushed in where he had no business, and where he never was before," paraphrasing Alexander Pope's *An Essay on Criticism* (1711), "the following poem would not have been written." Southey never appreciated his skill as a writer of shorter and less ambitious poems wherein, for example, he could calmly reflect on his personal love of good books in his own large library, as in "My Days Among the Dead Are Past." Perhaps, also, he never realized the extent to which he could display his talent with language, as in the onomatopoetic and highly animated "The Cataract of Ladore." Interestingly enough, when Southey could isolate himself from the perils and problems of a large, ugly world, he achieved considerable maturity as a poet. Unfortunately, the periods of imaginative seclusion were both irregular and inconsistent.

BIOGRAPHY

Although born at Bristol, the son of Robert Southey and Margaret Hill Southey, Robert Southey spent most of his first fourteen years at Bath, in the company of his mother's half-sister, Miss Elizabeth Tyler. Biographers describe Tyler as a lady endowed with strong personal attractions, ambitious ideas, an imperious temper, and a significantly large library. The last-mentioned asset allowed young Southey early introductions to dramatic literature, classical poetry, and the epics of Edmund Spenser. Thus, his entrance into Westminster School in April, 1788—after shorter terms at small schools in Corston and Bristol—found him well prepared to pursue learning. Nevertheless, he demonstrated little interest in subjects outside the narrow limits of his own idiosyncratic reading tastes: ceremony, ritual, and world mythology and religion. Four years later, the school authorities expelled him for his published essays against Westminster's system of corporal punishment, specifically the flogging of students by their masters for trivial offenses. Through the efforts of his maternal uncle, the Reverend Herbert Hill, Southey gained entrance to Balliol College, Oxford (after first having been refused admission by Christ Church because of the Westminster School incident). The significant events during his undergraduate term proved to be friendships formed with Samuel Taylor Coleridge and Robert Lovell. The three determined to emigrate to the banks of the Susquehanna River in the United States, there to embark on a scheme of an ideal life of unitarianism and pantisocracy (a Utopian community in which all members would rule equally). Interestingly enough, the relationship acquired even stronger ties (which would eventually cost Southey considerable money and labor) when the friends married the three daughters of the widow of Stephen Fricker, an unsuccessful sugar-pan merchant at Westbury. Southey's marriage to Edith Fricker occurred in November, 1795.

When Elizabeth Tyler heard of her nephew's proposal to leave England, she evicted him from her house. By that time, Southey had embarked on several literary projects, and, fortunately, a young publisher, Joseph Cottle, came to his aid and purchased the first of his epic poems, *Joan of Arc*. Moreover, his uncle, Herbert Hill, invited him to visit Lisbon, resulting in *Letters in Spain and Portugal* (1808) and *Madoc*. After returning to London, he began to study the law, but soon abandoned that exercise (as he had turned from divinity and medicine at Oxford) and once more focused his attention on poetry. Seeking seclusion, Southey moved first to Westbury, then to Burton (in Hampshire), producing additional ballads and eclogues and working hard on his *History of Brazil*. In April, 1800, serious illness forced him to seek the temperate climate of Portugal, where he remained for a year, completing *Thalaba the Destroyer* and continuing to plod along with the Brazilian history. Back in England, he settled first at Keswick, then moved to Dublin as secretary to the chancellor of the Irish exchequer, Isaac Corry. He then moved to Bristol, but the death of his mother and infant daughter drove him away from his birthplace. In 1803, partly to satisfy his wife, Southey and his family took up residence at Greta Hall, Keswick; there, practically under the same roof as his brother-in-law Coleridge, he made his home for the remainder of his life.

Work and activity at Keswick brought Southey into close association with Wordsworth and, more important, provided the motivation to produce his most ambitious poetic works. Financial pressures (particularly the support of Coleridge's family in addition to his own), however, forced him to forsake poetry temporarily for more lucrative prose projects, which he churned out in significant quantity between 1803 and 1832. At Greta Hall, he amassed a library in excess of fourteen thousand volumes, including works that he eventually edited and translated. Between 1808 and 1839, he edited and contributed to the *Quarterly Review*, the result of his association with Sir Walter Scott. That relationship proved to be most advantageous to Southey's literary career, for although Scott could not arrange to secure for his friend the post of historiographer royal, he did, in 1813, transfer the offer to be poet laureate from himself to Southey. To his credit, the latter accepted the honor only on condition that he would not be forced to write birthday odes to the sovereign or to members of the royal family. Unfortunately, however, he did manage to get into trouble with Byron and others of the liberally inclined Romantic poets when he wrote *A Vision of Judgement* and seemingly challenged liberal opinion. Despite squabbles with his contemporaries, his reputation remained high, as

*Robert Southey* (Hulton Archive/Getty Images)

witnessed by offers to edit the *Times* of London and to serve as librarian of the Advocates' Library, Edinburgh—both of which he declined.

In November, 1837, Edith Southey passed away— for years she had been failing mentally. The poet-essayist himself, according to contemporary accounts, had by this time become afflicted with softening of the brain, manifested by an obvious indifference to everyone and everything except his beloved books. Suddenly, near the end of his sixty-fourth year, Southey married (on June 4, 1839) Caroline Ann Bowles, a poet and hymnodist with whom he had maintained a close correspondence for more than twenty years. When the couple returned from their wedding tour, Southey's condition worsened; he passed gradually from insensibility to external matters into a complete trance and died on March 21, 1843. The poet laureate was buried in Crosthwaite churchyard, and friends placed memorials in Westminster Abbey and Bristol Cathedral.

## ANALYSIS

Robert Southey's poetical career proved, indeed, to have been a struggle: His desire to create from impulse and inspiration came into conflict with his duty to earn money from his pen. During his early period, he wrote a large number of ballads and metrical tales for the *Morning Post* at the then-going rate of one guinea a week. When he republished those in book form, money again became the principal motive, as it did once more in 1807 when he had to support Coleridge's family as well as his own. At that time, he announced that, if necessary, he would take on more reviews and articles for the magazines and would write additional verses for the newspapers. Thus, judgment and analysis of his poetry must balance what Southey wanted to do with what he had to do. Throughout his professional life, he tried desperately to preserve the time for literary labors worthy of his talent; as long as that division existed, he could perform his hackwork without fear of humiliation or sacrifice. Unfortunately, time and energy eventually failed him, and his poems—both serious and popular—became less salable; after 1820, he saw himself as more historian than poet.

In 1837, two years prior to the illness that would eventually incapacitate him, Southey prepared the last collected edition of his poems to be published during his lifetime. That task provided an opportunity for the poet to survey his own work, to rank as well as to analyze. Thus, concerning the narrative poems, he thought *Joan of Arc*, written when he was nineteen, to have the least merit, although the piece did constitute the first stage of his poetic development. *Thalaba the Destroyer*, published five years afterward, allowed Southey to achieve poetic maturity, to set aside the law of nature and permit his poetic fancy to wander freely. For that reason, he chose not to control the rhythmic structure of his blank verse; rather, the lines of that poem follow a spontaneous melody, dividing themselves into varying lengths. In addition, the poet tended to interrupt the ordinary iambic cadence with a sudden trochaic or dactylic movement: for example, "Lo! underneath the broadleaved sycamore/ With lids half closed he lies,/ Dreaming of days to come."

### RELIGIOUS EPICS

While a schoolboy at Westminster, Southey had formed the idea of a long poem, epic in form and content, based on each of the important religions (he considered them to be mythologies) of the world. For Islam (then called Mohammedanism), he eventually wrote *Thalaba the Destroyer*; *The Curse of Kehama*, published in 1810, focused on Hinduism. In the latter poem, he again allowed his fancy and his imagery to range freely, seemingly unconcerned with the orthodox notions and sympathies of the vast majority of his readers. For whatever the reasons, however, in *The Curse of Kehama* Southey returned to rhyme; more accurately, he attempted to compromise between the rambling blank verse of *Thalaba the Destroyer* and the symmetry of the traditional English epic form. *Madoc* had been begun before he set to work on *The Curse of Kehama*, but Southey, believing the former to have been his most significant poem, set it aside until he could devote his full attention to it. Finally published in 1805, *Madoc* evidences a pleasing melody and an easy, fluent, and graceful narrative diction. Unfortunately, it met with the least favorable reception of all his long poems.

### RODERICK, THE LAST OF THE GOTHS

The failure of *Madoc* did not deter Southey from his grand epic design. In *Roderick, the Last of the Goths*, he produced a long narrative poem that succeeded because the versification and theme managed to complement each other. Relying on the issue of subjugation and underlining it with moral grandeur and tragedy, the poet easily held the interest of his contemporary readers. He began with a single and momentary sin of the passions by an otherwise consistently virtuous monarch and proceeded to unravel the consequences: the slaughter of Christians by Moors in a battle lasting eight days; the king's escape after the battle and his deep remorse and self-inflicted penance of a long and solitary hermitage while others thought that he had been slain; the king's dream, in which his mother appears with instructions to deliver his country from the Moors; and the departure and eventual encounter with the sole survivor of a massacre, who tells the king of the tragedy and inspires him to both personal and patriotic revenge. Southey demonstrated, in *Roderick, the Last of the Goths*, his ability to sustain a narrative while at the same time developing a character, a hero, through a series of meaningful and related adventures: Roderick, in the guise of a priest, passes through the country, meets old friends, and is recognized only by his dog. Finally, the king leads his forces in triumph over the Moors, after which he disappears.

Southey achieved effective rhythm to complement the narrative of Roderick's adventures by taking full advantage of proper names derived from Spanish and from various Moorish and Gothic dialects. He sought diversity of both rhythm and language, knowing well how John Milton, for example, had underscored the substance of his theme in the opening book of *Paradise Lost* (1667, 1674) with his roll call of Satan's evil host. Thus, in a single passage of twenty-six lines from book 4, the poet relies on the effect of a dozen or so proper names to vary his rhythm, as

> Skirting the heights of *Aguiar*, he reached
> That consecrated pile amid the wild
> Which sainted *Fructuoso* in his zeal
> Reared to *St. Felix, on Visionia*'s banks.

Further, Southey reinforced his narrative with heavy descriptions of natural scenery, furnishing rhetorical respites from the action and the passion of events. He viewed such pauses as essential to the long narrative poem, particularly when they followed long episodes of emotional strain or exaltation. From a positive point of view, the descriptive respites filled the imagination with the sights and the sounds of the beauties of nature, allowing the long narrative poem to serve as a true work of creative art. Southey made such attempts in all his long poems, but he reached the highest levels of perfection in *Roderick, the Last of the Goths*.

#### "ODE, WRITTEN DURING THE NEGOTIATIONS WITH BUONAPARTE, IN JANUARY 1814"

Although Southey's occasional poetry includes his weakest efforts, there are rare moments of eloquence when the poet is able to give free rein to his emotions. Consider, for example, his "Ode, Written during the Negotiations with Buonaparte, in January 1814." Southey truly detested the diminutive emperor of the French, and he attacked his subject on moral grounds, as well as on the obvious political and patriotic levels. His passions were further aroused by the sight of those individuals who worshiped what they believed to have been the wonders of Napoleon's political and military successes. The poet saw the emperor only as a mean tyrant: "And ne'er was earth with verier tyrant curst,/ Bold man and bad,/ Remorseless, godless, full of fraud and lies"; for those personal and political crimes, demanded Southey, Napoleon must pay with his life.

#### "FUNERAL ODE ON THE DEATH OF THE PRINCESS CHARLOTTE"

Another of Southey's occasional poems, the "Funeral Ode on the Death of the Princess Charlotte," should be mentioned because its lines are as sensitive and serene as those on Napoleon are harsh and bitter. The poet gazes about the burial grounds at Windsor, where, "in thy sacred shade/ Is the Flower of Brunswick laid!" Then, further surveying the scene, he comments on others lying there—Henry, Edward, Elizabeth, Ann Seymour, and Mary Stuart. Nevertheless, the piece serves as more than a roll call of history, for Southey loses sight of neither his subject nor the tragedy of Charlotte's passing: "Never more lamented guest/ Was in Windsor laid to rest."

#### LEGACY

In the final analysis, Southey must be seen as a nineteenth century child of the Augustan Age who contributed little to the poetry of Romanticism. Confusion arises when literary historians too quickly connect him with Wordsworth and Coleridge, forgetting, perhaps, that the relationship existed on a personal rather than an artistic level. Artistically and intellectually, Southey had almost nothing in common with the major figures among the first generation of British Romantic poets. He waited until practically the end of his literary life—in the preface to the 1837-1838 edition of his *Poetical Works*—before setting forth what amounted to his poetical and intellectual declaration of independence from the new literature of pre-Victorian England. Southey chose to spend a lifetime with his books, rather than in the company of men; he would retire to a life of literary pursuit, "communing with my own heart, and taking that course which upon mature consideration seemed best to myself."

Southey further maintained that he had no need for the new schools of poetry, for he had learned poetry from the masters, confirmed it in his youth, and exemplified it in his own writing. Indeed, few would deny Professor Renwick's assertion that "No poet since Dryden wrote such pure clean English so consistently." Unfortunately, unlike his contemporaries who set and then followed new trends, Southey seemed more inclined to practice and develop the craft of poetry rather than its art. He never really learned (either in or out of school) that poetry had to come from sources other than labor and learning. Nevertheless, he possessed an ardent and genial piety, a moral strength, a poetic power of depth and variety, and an ability to develop a range of literary forms and interests. In those respects, he deserved the name and the honor of poet laureate.

OTHER MAJOR WORKS

LONG FICTION: *The Doctor*, 1834-1847 (7 volumes).

PLAY: *The Fall of Robespierre*, pb. 1794 (with Samuel Taylor Coleridge).

NONFICTION: *Letters from England by Don Manuel Espriella*, 1807; *Letters in Spain and Portugal*, 1808; *The History of Europe*, 1810-1813; *History of Brazil*, 1810-1819; *The Origin, Nature, and Object of the New System of Education*, 1812; *Life of Nelson*, 1813; *A* *Summary of the Life of Arthur, Duke of Wellington*, 1816; *Life of Wesley and the Rise and Progress of Methodism*, 1820; *History of the Expedition of Orsua and Crimes of Aguirre*, 1821; *Life of John, Duke of Marlborough*, 1822; *History of the Peninsular War*, 1823-1832; *The Book of the Church*, 1824; *Vindiciae Ecclesiae Anglicanae*, 1826; *Sir Thomas More*, 1829; *Essays Moral and Political*, 1832; *Lives of the British Admirals*, 1833-1840; *The Life of the Rev. Andrew Bell*, 1844.

TRANSLATIONS: *On the French Revolution*, 1797 (of Jacques Necker); *Amadis de Gaul*, 1805 (of Vasco Lobeira); *Chronicle of the Cid*, 1808 (of *Crónica del famoso cavallero Cid Ruy Diaz Campeador*, *La crónica de España*, and *Poema del Cid*); *The Geographical, Natural, and Civil History of Chili*, 1808 (of Abbe Don Ignatius Molina); *Memoria Sobre a Litteratura Portugueza*, 1809.

EDITED TEXTS: *The Annual Anthology*, 1700-1800; *The Works of Chatterton*, 1803 (with Joseph Cottle); *Palmerin of England*, 1807; *Horae Lyricae*, 1834 (by Isaac Watts); *The Works of William Cowper*, 1835-1837.

BIBLIOGRAPHY

Bernhardt-Kabisch, Ernest. *Robert Southey*. Boston: Twayne, 1977. A study of *Joan of Arc* follows a sketch of Southey's early life. Chapter 3 assesses his personality and lyrical poetry. The central chapters analyze his epics and the verse of his laureate years. The last chapter is a survey of Southey's prose. Contains chronology, notes, select bibliography, and index.

Bolton, Carol. *Writing the Empire: Robert Southey and Romantic Colonialism*. London: Pickering & Chatto, 2007. The author places Southey's writings, including his epic poetry, within their historical context to argue that Southey's views created a moral imperialism that shaped Victorian values.

Carnall, Geoffrey. *Robert Southey and His Age: The Development of a Conservative Mind*. Oxford, England: Clarendon Press, 1960. Part 1 focuses on Southey as Jacobin, devoted to radical reform and democracy. Part 2 analyzes Southey as Tory, advocating strong government and conservativism. Finally, the question of whether Southey should be called an apostate is examined. Supplemented by illustrations, two appendixes, and an index.

Curry, Kenneth. *Southey*. London: Routledge & Kegan Paul, 1975. Reviews Southey's life, prose, and poetry. Includes bibliography and index.

Pratt, Lynda, ed. *Robert Southey and the Contexts of English Romanticism*. Burlington, Vt.: Ashgate, 2006. A specially commissioned collection of essays on Southey that examine the links between the writer and English Romanticism. The essays focus on culture, politics, and history, although many deal with his writings, including his poetry.

Simmons, Jack. *Southey*. 1945. Reprint. Port Washington, N.Y.: Kennikat Press, 1968. A substantial biography of modest length, this book details Southey's education, his friendship with Samuel Taylor Coleridge, and his sojourn in Portugal. His fame leads to political controversies, and his declining years begin with the death of his daughter Isabel. Contains illustrations, a note on the Southey family, a list of Southey's works, notes, and an index.

Smith, Christopher J. P. *A Quest for Home: Reading Robert Southey*. Liverpool, England: Liverpool University Press, 1997. A historical and critical study of the works of Southey. Includes bibliographical references and index.

Speck, W. A. *Robert Southey: Man of Letters*. New Haven, Conn.: Yale University Press, 2006. This biography of the poet discusses his poetry but also establishes Southey as more than a poet: as essayist, reviewer, historian, biographer, and novelist. Includes bibliography and index.

Storey, Mark. *Robert Southey: A Life*. New York: Oxford University Press, 1997. Storey tells the fascinating story of a complex and contradictory man, the mirror of his age, and provides a different perspective on familiar events and figures of the Romantic period.

*Samuel J. Rogal*

# ROBERT SOUTHWELL

**Born:** Horsham St. Faith, Norfolk, England; 1561
**Died:** London, England; March 4, 1595

PRINCIPAL POETRY

*Moeoniae: Or, Certaine Excellent Poems and
    Spirituall Hymnes*, 1595
*Saint Peter's Complaint, with Other Poems*, 1595
*A Foure-Fould Meditation of the Foure Last
    Things*, 1605
*The Complete Poems of Robert Southwell*, 1872
    (Alexander B. Grosart, editor)
*The Poems of Robert Southwell*, 1967 (James H.
    McDonald and Nancy Pollard Brown, editors)
*Collected Poems*, 2007 (Peter Davidson and Anne
    Sweeney, editors)

OTHER LITERARY FORMS

Besides writing poetry Robert Southwell wrote many religious tracts, including *Mary Magdalens Funerall Teares* (1591).

ACHIEVEMENTS

Robert Southwell's reputation as a poet in his own time is difficult to determine, since he was a priest in hiding and a martyr for his Roman Catholic faith. It is natural that the five manuscript compilations of his verses do not name the author, and that the two printed volumes, both published in the year of his execution, likewise do not name the author; one of them, however, gives his initials. The publishers may have thought that readers would associate the poems with Southwell, who was of much interest at the time, although the government tried to keep his trial secret. Early references to his verse, however, with a single exception, do not indicate knowledge of authorship. Southwell's name did not appear in an edition until 1620.

The musical quality of his verse is remarkable, considering that he almost forgot his native English during his long education abroad and had to relearn it when he returned to England as a priest in hiding. He has been described by Pierre Janelle as the "leading Catholic writer of the Elizabethan age," and one who might have developed into one of the greatest English writers if it were not for his death at the age of thirty-four. His best-known poem is "The Burning Babe," and Ben Jonson is reputed to have said that if he had written that poem, he would have been content to destroy many of his.

BIOGRAPHY

Robert Southwell was born toward the end of 1561, according to evidence gathered from his admittance to the Society of Jesus and from his trial. His family was prosperous, and he spent his boyhood at Horsham St. Faith, Norfolk.

In 1576, when he was about fifteen, he entered the English College of the Jesuit school at Douai; like many young Catholics of that period, he was sent to the Continent for his later education. He studied at the Jesuit College of Clermont in Paris for a short time for his greater safety, returning to Douai in 1577, the year in which he applied to enter the Jesuit novitiate at Tournai. He was at first rejected but was accepted into the novitiate in Rome in 1578, where he was a student at the Roman College and tutor and precept of studies at the English College. Forbidden to speak English, he spoke Latin and Italian, becoming very fluent in the latter and reading a great deal of Italian literature. He wrote Latin poetry, including religious epics, elegies, and epigrams.

His poetry in English was written during his mission to England, from his return in July, 1586, to his arrest in June, 1592. He was stationed in London, working under a superior, the Reverend Henry Garnet. Southwell occupied a house in London and provided lodgings for priests, meeting those coming into the country. He corresponded with the Reverend Claudius Aquaviva, general of the Society of Jesus, giving him reports of the persecution. He received much help from the countess of Arundel, and his prose works were printed secretly. He met at intervals with his superior and other priests; one such meeting was raided, but those at the meeting managed to escape.

He was betrayed by a fellow Jesuit who had been arrested after arriving in England and who described the appearance of Southwell, and by the sister of a Catholic friend with whom he was staying in Uxenden, north of London. This Anne Bellamy, of a loyal Catholic fam-

ily, had been imprisoned and become pregnant while in prison, probably having been assaulted by the priest-hunter Topcliffe; she married Topcliffe's assistant and betrayed Southwell on the condition that her family would not be molested, a promise that was not kept. Southwell was arrested on June 25, 1592. Topcliffe wrote an exultant letter to the queen about the importance of his prisoner and his intentions. Southwell was brought to Topcliffe's house and tortured many times. One of the tortures was being hung by the hands against a wall. He refused to identify himself or admit that he was a priest; in the absence of such identification, the family that had sheltered him could not be implicated. On Queen Elizabeth's instructions, he was moved to the Gatehouse Prison, where he was tortured and questioned by the Privy Council, but he always kept his silence. After he heard that there was other evidence against the Bellamys (they had been imprisoned on Anne's evidence), he wrote to Sir Robert Cecil, a member of the Council, that he was a priest and a Jesuit. He did not want his silence to be misinterpreted as fear or shame of his profession. Imprisoned in the Tower of

*Robert Southwell* (Archive Photos/Getty Images)

London, he was arraigned under the Act of 1585 for the treason of returning to England as an ordained Catholic priest and of administering sacraments. Weak as he was, he had to conduct his own defense, but he was constantly interrupted. He was convicted, dragged through the streets, and hanged, drawn, and quartered at Tyburn Tree on March 4, 1595, after praying for his queen, his country, and himself. He was beatified by the Roman Catholic Church in 1929 and canonized as a saint in 1970.

## Analysis

Robert Southwell wrote religious poetry with a didactic purpose. In the prose preface to a manuscript, addressed to his cousin, he says that poets who write of the "follies and fayninges" of love have discredited poetry to the point that "a Poet, a Lover, and a Liar, are by many reckoned but three words of one signification." Poetry, however, was used for parts of Scripture, and may be used for hymns and spiritual sonnets. He has written his poetry to give others an example of subject matter, he says, and he hopes that other more skillful poets will follow his example. He flies from "prophane conceits and fayning fits" and applies verse to virtue, as David did. Perhaps his distaste for the stylized love poetry of his time explains the absence of sonnets in his writing. Although Southwell's purpose in writing was didactic, he was often more emotional than purely intellectual. His poems are seldom tranquil. They tend to startle through his use of the unexpected, the fantastic, and the grotesque, and may thus be described as baroque. Southwell is also linked to the baroque movement in his use of Italian models and such themes as weeping, anticipating the seventeenth century Roman Catholic poet Richard Crashaw.

As might be expected, death is a recurring theme in his poetry, yet he makes the theme universal rather than personal, for his purpose was instructive and oral rather than merely self-expressive. In "Upon the Image of Death," for example, he speaks of what is apparently a memento mori kind of picture that he often looks at, but he still does not really believe that he must die; historical personages and people he has known have all died, and yet it is difficult to think that he will die. There are personal touches, such as references to his gown, his knife, and his chair, but all are reminders to him and to all of inevitable death, "And yet my life amend not I." The poem's simplicity and universality give it a proverbial quality.

His most inspired poems were about birth rather than death, the birth of the Christ child. In part 6 of "The Sequence on the Virgin Mary and Christ," "The Nativitie of Christ," he uses the image of the bird that built the nest being hatched in it, and ends with the image of the Christ child as hay, the food for the beasts that human beings have become through sin. His image of Christ is often that of a child, as in "A Child My Choice," where he stresses the superior subject he praises in the poem, compared with the foolish praise of what "fancie" loves. While he loves the Child, he lives in him, and cannot live wrongly. In the middle two stanzas of this four-stanza poem, he uses a great deal of alliteration, parallelism, and antithesis to convey the astonishing nature of this Child, who is young, yet wise; small, yet strong; and man, yet God. At the end of the poem, he sees Christ weeping, sighing, and panting while his angels sing. Out of his tears, sighs, and throbs buds a joyful spring. At the end of the poem, he prays that this Child will help him in correcting his faults and will direct his death. The prayer was of course meant to be didactic, but it assumes a very personal meaning because of Southwell's manner of death. The themes of the Nativity and of death are thus artistically linked.

### "A vale of teares"

As Vincent Barry Leitch has stated, the Incarnation serves as a paradigm of God's love for human beings and signifies God's sanctification of human life. There is thus a strong sense of the divine in human life in most of Southwell's poems, yet some of the poems are referred to as "desolation poems" because this sense of God in human life is absent. Sin is prevalent, and the sinner feels remorse. In "A vale of teares," for example, God seems to be absent, leaving people alone to work things out for themselves. The poem is heavily descriptive, describing a valley of the Alps and painting a picture of a dreary scene that is in keeping with a sense of loneliness and desolation. It is wild, mountainous, windy, and thunderous, and although the green of the pines and moss suggests hope, hope quails when one looks at the cliffs. The poem ends with an apostrophe to

Deep Remorse to possess his breast, and bidding Delights adieu. The poem has been linked to the conventional love lyric in which the lover, in despair, isolates himself from the world, but it has also been linked to the Ignatian Exercises of the Jesuits.

### SAINT PETER'S COMPLAINT

Another poem on the theme of isolation and remorse is the long dramatic poem *Saint Peter's Complaint*, comprising 132 stanzas of six lines each, based on an Italian work by Luigi Tansillo (1510-1568), *Le Lagrime di San Pietro* (the tears of Saint Peter). Southwell wrote a translation of part of Tansillo's poem, titling it, "Peeter Playnt," and two other poems, "S. Peters complaint," a poem of eleven stanzas, and "Saint Peters Complaynte," a poem of twelve stanzas. These three apparently represent stages in the composition of the long poem. In the translation, there is an objective rather than a first-person point of view, and Peter's denying Christ was an action in the immediate past in the courtyard, while reference is made to the suffering Peter will experience in the future. In each of the three original versions, Peter is the speaker and the time and place are indefinite. Much of the material in "Saint Peters Complaynte" is incorporated in the long poem. The uneven quality of the long poem has caused Janelle to assign it to an early period of experimentation, but McDonald and Brown see it as an unpolished work left unfinished when Southwell was arrested.

In the long poem, Saint Peter indulges in an extended nautical conceit, appropriate for this speaker, of sailing with torn sails, using sighs for wind, remorse as the pilot, torment as the haven, and shipwreck as the best reward. He hopes his complaints will be heard so that others will know that there is a more sorrowful one than they, and he lists all the unfortunate things he is, one to a line for a whole stanza, including "An excrement of earth. . . ." He says that others may fill volumes in praise of "your forged Goddesse," a reference to the literary fashion of praising some supposed love, who might not be real at all. Saint Peter's griefs will be his text and his theme. Several times in his works, Southwell makes this distinction between the falseness of stylized love poetry and the reality of religious themes. Saint Peter says that he must weep, and here Southwell employs hyperbole, for a sea will hardly

rinse Peter's sin; he speaks of high tides, and says that all those who weep should give him their tears. The poem is heavily rhetorical, with many exclamations, parallelisms, repetitions, questions, and comparisons. Saint Peter had not thought that he would ever deny Christ. In lines 673-677, Southwell characteristically begins a line with a word that had already appeared toward the end of the preceding line, thus patterning Peter's "circkling griefes." Peter compares himself to a leper with sores and asks Christ's forgiveness. The taunts that Peter levels at the woman in the courtyard in the poem have been taken to suggest a parallel between the woman's actions and those of Queen Elizabeth. Alice Mary Lubin, in a study of Southwell's religious complaint lyrics, says that this poem differs from the traditional complaint poem in that the complaining figure is separated from Christ rather than from a figure such as a lover and that it differs from medieval religious complaint poems because it constitutes a statement of remorse rather than being simply a lament. A description of Peter's isolation occupies much of the pom. Lubin does not see the work as an ordered meditative poem; rather, it resembles an Italian "weeper" poem in subject, though not in treatment. She suggests analogues in *A Mirror for Magistrates* (1555) and in the Old Testament Lamentations.

### "THE BURNING BABE"

Southwell's most famous work, "The Burning Babe," combines several of his favorite themes, including the Nativity, isolation, guilt, and purification, into a vision poem that becomes a lament. He presents the material as a mystical vision. The occasion is presented dramatically, for it was a "hoary winter's night" and he was shivering in the snow when he felt the sudden heat that made him look up to see the fire. The dramatic contrasts continue, as he speaks of seeing a pretty baby; but it is in the air, not where a baby would be, and it is "burning bright," like a fire. The image is deliberately odd, ambiguous, and out of place. The next image, that the baby is "scorched" with great heat, turns the odd image into a horrible one, conveying the idea that the baby's body is no longer white but discolored from a fire that is not a mere metaphor. The fire is not from the air, but from inside the body, which means that there is no escape for the baby. The next image is ironic, for the baby cries copiously, as if the "floods" of tears could quench the flames, which they cannot do.

When the baby speaks, it is to lament that he fries in this heat although he has just been born, and yet no one seeks to warm the heart at this fire, and no one but the baby feels this fire. Here the Christ child is very much alone. It is not until the next line, however, that the baby is clearly identified as Christ, when he says that the furnace (the place where the fire is) is his breast, and the fuel is "wounding thorns." The ironic crown of thorns of the Crucifixion becomes fuel for the fire. His breast is kept burning because people wound him with thorns and hurt him through their mocking actions. The Crucifixion was a specific event, but the fire is a continuing torment, so the "wounding thorns" must be not only the crown of thorns but also the sins that people are continuing to commit.

Vision poems have often had a guide figure, someone who leads the viewer and explains the allegorical significance of the vision. Here the baby is both the vision and the guide, resulting in a kind of ironic horror. The image throughout this section of the poem is that of a furnace, a piece of technology used for creating and working things. The baby explains that the fire is love, a rather complicated idea, for it is the "wounding thorns" that keep the fire (the love) alive. Christ's love feeds on the wrongs of human beings. He loves human beings despite their sins, and indeed because of their sins. The smoke is sighs, his emotional dissatisfaction with what is happening and how people are acting. The ashes are the residue, the residual shame and scorn. The shame is Christ's embarrassment at being crucified and the equal embarrassment of the constant crucifixion He suffers because of continuing sin. The scorn is the rejection of his reality and the mission that he came into the world as a baby to accomplish, the taking of sins onto himself. Thus the residue of the fire is the shame and scorn, not entirely consumed in the fire but left over and ever present. Two personifications now enter the allegory. Justice puts the fuel on the fire, for it is not only that the sins and injustices of human beings be burnt, consumed, transformed in this way, but it is also Mercy that "blows the coals," that keeps the fire of love going strong by blowing air onto it. The imagery has changed from the "wounding thorns" causing the baby

to be on fire, to the necessity and justice of burning up and burning away the wrongs of humans in the heat of God's love, which is kept going by his mercy.

The metals that are worked in this furnace are the souls of human beings, which have been defiled, but which are to be changed in the fire, thus representing another change in the imagery. Christ is now on fire to change them into something better, and he says that he will "melt into a bath to wash them in my blood." A bath is a cleansing, a purification, and after feeling the love of God, they will be purified by a cooling liquid, ironically not water, but Christ's blood, another touch of horror but also of love and glory. Saying that he would melt, a term meaning depart or disappear, but having special imagistic significance here because of the burning, the Christ child vanishes. The reader is conscious that the baby will become the crucified Christ, and the poet realizes that it is Christmas. Southwell here makes the Christ child the isolated one, most ironically, and develops the symbolism to make the reader feel remorse for his sins. The poem's startlingly grotesque subject clearly links it to the baroque movement.

### JOY AND ALIENATION

Southwell's main themes were the opposing ones of the joyous Incarnation, with its joining of God and human beings, and the tragic desolation of feeling the alienation of self from God through sin. Striking images with strong emotion achieve a religious purpose of affecting the reader. In his short life, Southwell wrote many fine poems in a language he had once forgotten. He referred very little in his poetry to the persecution that overshadowed his life, choosing to write instead of religious experiences that transcended time and place.

### OTHER MAJOR WORKS

NONFICTION: *Epistle of a Religious Priest unto to His Father, Exhorting Him to the Perfect Forsaking of the World*, 1589; *Mary Magdalens Funerall Teares*, 1591; *Letter to Sir Robert Cecil*, 1593; *An Humble Supplication to Her Majestie*, pb. 1595 (wr. 1591); *A Short Rule of Good Life: To Direct the Devout Christian in a Regular and Orderly Course*, 1596; *The Triumphs over Death: Or, A Consolatory Epistle for Afflicted Minds, in the Affects of Dying Friends*, pb. 1596 (wr. 1591); *An Epistle of Comfort*, pb. 1605 (wr. 1591); *A Hundred*

*Meditations on the Love of God*, pb. 1873 (wr. c. 1585); *Two Letters and Short Rules of a Good Life*, 1973 (Nancy Pollard Brown, editor).

BIBLIOGRAPHY

Brownlow, F. W. *Robert Southwell*. New York: Twayne, 1996. An introductory biography and critical study of selected works by Southwell. Includes bibliographic references and an index.

Caraman, Philip. *A Study in Friendship: Saint Robert Southwell and Henry Garnet*. St. Louis, Mo.: Institute of Jesuit Sources, 1995. This slim volume from religion scholar Caraman contains a bibliography and an index.

Deane, John F. *From the Marrow-Bone: The Religion of Poetry—The Poetry of Religion*. Blackrock, Ireland: Columba Press, 2008. Part 1 contains essays by the author on a variety of aspects of religion and poetry, and part 2 contains essays on various poets, including Southwell.

Janelle, Pierre. *Robert Southwell the Writer: A Study in Religious Inspiration*. 1935. Reprint. Mamaroneck, N.Y.: Paul J. Appel, 1971. Janelle's biography—the first three chapters of the book—remains the standard account of the life of Southwell. The other chapters concerning Jesuit influence, Petrarchan origins, and Southwell's place among his contemporaries have stood the test of time. Contains an extensive bibliography.

Moseley, D. H. *Blessed Robert Southwell*. New York: Sheed & Ward, 1957. A sympathetic biography drawn from late sixteenth century writings and records, which provides an understanding of the cultural, religious, and political climate in which Southwell lived and wrote. Supplemented by a chronological select bibliography of Southwell criticism.

Pilarz, Scott R. *Robert Southwell and the Mission of Literature, 1561-1595: Writing Reconciliation*. Burlington, Vt.: Ashgate, 2003. Pilarz examines Southwell as a Catholic writer and from the standpoint of his religious mission.

Scallon, Joseph D. *The Poetry of Robert Southwell, S. J.* Salzburg: Institute for English Language and Literature, 1975. Scallon's monograph provides chapters on Southwell's biography, his short poems (particularly those concerning Christ and the Virgin Mary), and the poems on repentance. *Saint Peter's Complaint*, Southwell's best poem, receives extensive analysis. Contains a substantial bibliography.

Sweeney, Anne R. *Robert Southwell: Snow in Arcadia—Redrawing the English Lyric Landscape, 1586-1595*. New York: Manchester University Press, 2006. Sweeney, the coeditor of a collection of Southwell's poetry, examines Southwell in his role as a lyric poet.

*Rosemary Ascherl*

# STEPHEN SPENDER

**Born:** London, England; February 28, 1909
**Died:** London, England; July 16, 1995

PRINCIPAL POETRY

*Nine Experiments, by S. H. S.: Being Poems Written at the Age of Eighteen*, 1928
*Twenty Poems*, 1930
*Poems*, 1933, 1934
*Vienna*, 1935
*The Still Centre*, 1939
*Selected Poems*, 1940
*Ruins and Visions*, 1942
*Spiritual Exercises (To Cecil Day Lewis)*, 1943
*Poems of Dedication*, 1947
*Returning to Vienna 1947: Nine Sketches*, 1947
*The Edge of Being*, 1949
*Collected Poems, 1928-1953*, 1955
*Inscriptions*, 1958
*Selected Poems*, 1964
*The Generous Days*, 1971
*Recent Poems*, 1978
*Collected Poems, 1928-1985*, 1985
*Dolphins*, 1994

OTHER LITERARY FORMS

Although best known for his poetry, Stephen Spender wrote a considerable body of drama, fiction, criticism, and journalism. The first of his six plays, *Trial of a Judge* (pr. 1938), was his contribution to the Group Theatre effort, in which his friend W. H. Auden was so heavily involved, and reflected the young Spender's socialist outlook. Most of the others—notably *Danton's Death* (pr. 1939), which he wrote with Goronwy Rees; *Mary Stuart* (pr. 1957), taken from the J. C. F. Schiller play; and *Rasputin's End* (pb. 1963), a libretto to music by Nicholas Nabokov—likewise dealt with broadly political situations and problems. Spender's published fiction consists of a collection of stories, *The Burning Cactus* (1936); a novel, *The Backward Son* (1940); and two novellas, *Engaged in Writing* and *The Fool and the Princess* (published together in 1958).

Spender's nonfiction prose comprises more than a dozen books, as well as hundreds of essays contributed to periodicals. The critical works have dealt mostly with the issues and problems of modern literature, beginning with essays written for *The Criterion* in the 1930's and *The Destructive Element: A Study of Modern Writers and Beliefs* (1935), and continuing through his study of T. S. Eliot (1975) and the selection of essays from various periods of Spender's career titled *The Thirties and After: Poetry, Politics, People, 1933-1970* (1978). Especially notable among his other critical books are *The Struggle of the Modern* (1963), a study of modernism's complicated relationship to twentieth century literature in general, and *Love-Hate Relations: A Study of Anglo-American Sensibilities* (1974), which examines the connections between American and English literary sensibilities. Spender's journalistic writings include *Citizens in War and After* (1945) and *European Witness* (1946). He also published *World Within World: The Autobiography of Stephen Spender* (1951).

ACHIEVEMENTS

Several of Stephen Spender's poems stand among the most poignant of the twentieth century. Those anthology pieces with which his name is most often associated—"Not Palaces, an Era's Crown," "Beethoven's Death Mask," "I think continually of those who were truly great," "The Express," "The Landscape near an Aerodome," and "Ultima Ratio Regum"—have helped

achieve for Spender greater recognition than for any of the other British poets who came into prominence in the late 1920's and early 1930's, with the notable exception of W. H. Auden. Spender's many public and literary honors include being named a Companion in the Order of the British Empire (C.B.E.) in 1962, receiving the Queen's Gold Medal for Poetry in 1971, and being given an honorary fellowship to University College, Oxford, in 1973. He served as consultant in poetry (poet laureate) to the Library of Congress from 1965 to 1966. In 1970, he was appointed to the chair of English literature in University College, London.

Spender's stature rests also on his peculiar position among poets writing through the Great Depression and after World War II. More than the others, he emerged as an authentic voice bridging the modernist and postwar periods. Even during the 1930's—when Auden was the leader of the loose confederation of young writers to which he and Spender belonged—it was Spender who in poem after poem voiced most honestly and movingly the tensions informing the writing of poetry in that troubled time. When Auden and Christopher Isherwood departed for the United States in 1939, Spender remained as the foremost representative of the liberal values and lyric intensity that had marked the best poetry of the prewar years. Later—especially with the death of the other figures making up the so-called Auden Group—Spender's verse, as well as his prose, took on special interest, as a last link between contemporary British literature and an earlier period crucial to its development.

In many respects Spender's outlook and poetry scarcely changed after the 1930's. While many critics regarded such want of development as a mark of failure, in a sense, it represents a strength. Presumably, Spender saw little reason to change his poetic method or to go beyond those indisputably successful poems of his early adulthood because for him the fundamental problems—poetic, political, and personal—hardly changed since that time. Interestingly, an audience that grew up scarcely aware of Spender's poetic achievement became fascinated by Spender the essayist and lecturer. Because his most characteristic pronouncements to this more recently acquired audience were closely related to the viewpoint revealed in the early poems, they suggest the continuing value of those po-ems, not merely as artifacts from an increasingly dis-tant past but as permanent sources of interest and plea-sure.

BIOGRAPHY

Stephen Harold Spender was born in London on February 28, 1909. His father was Harold Spender, a noted journalist and lecturer, and his mother was Violet Hilda Schuster Spender, a painter and poet. The death of Spender's mother when he was fifteen and of his fa-ther two years later, in 1926, brought the four children, of whom he was the second-oldest, under the care of his maternal grandmother, a pair of spinster great-aunts, and an uncle.

After attending University College School in Lon-don, Spender went to University College, Oxford, in 1928, leaving in 1930 without a degree. Having begun to write poetry in childhood and having determined to be a poet, he sought out the somewhat older W. H. Auden even before beginning at Oxford. Their friend-ship, marked by a mutual awareness of their differences in temperament and outlook, apparently developed rapidly; Spender himself published Auden's first book of poems in 1928 on the same handpress he used to bring out his own first book. He spent the summer vaca-tion of 1929 in Germany, meeting many young Ger-mans and observing social and political developments that would set the stage for the next decade.

The 1930's were a time of tremendous literary ac-tivity for the young Spender, periodically punctuated by travels throughout Europe. He achieved prominence as a leading member of the group of rising young writ-ers clustered around Auden. Although Spender has claimed a singular position among the Auden group, during that time he behaved in a fashion broadly similar to that adopted by the others, briefly joining the Com-munist Party in 1936, traveling to Spain in 1937 to observe the Civil War from the Republican side, and publishing poems and essays supporting a radical viewpoint and warning of the growing Nazi menace. By late 1939, he had joined Cyril Connolly as coeditor of *Horizon*, a post he held until 1941. The war years also saw Spender in the National Fire Service and later in the Foreign Service. In 1941, he married Natasha

*Stephen Spender* (Getty Images)

Litwin, his 1936 marriage to Agnes Marie Pearn having ended in divorce.

After World War II, Spender focused on numerous writing, editing, and translating projects, on extensive travel and university lecturing—particularly in the United States—and on his family life. From 1953 to 1966, he served as coeditor of *Encounter*, resigning when he learned of the Central Intelligence Agency's financing of that magazine. He died in London on July 16, 1995.

ANALYSIS

Stephen Spender seems always to have struck his readers as halting. Even in the relatively confident writ-ing of his youth, he was the most likely of the Auden Group to avoid the extreme pronouncements to which his seemingly more self-assured contemporaries—especially Auden himself—were prone. Taken as a whole, his poetry appears to reflect a perpetual debate, an unresolved tension over what can be known, over what is worth knowing, and over how he ought to re-spond as a poet and as a citizen of a modern society.

Taken separately, his poems—particularly the best and most representative ones—exhibit an attraction or a movement sometimes toward one side of an issue, and sometimes toward the other. Almost always, however, such commitment at least implies its opposite.

This tension itself may account for the continuing appeal of so many Spender lyrics, decades after they were written and after their historical context has passed. Obviously they conform to the demand for irony and ambiguity begun in the late 1920's by I. A. Richards and William Empson and prolonged until recently by their American counterparts, the New Critics. In this respect, if not in others, Spender established a link with the seventeenth century Metaphysical wits so admired by T. S. Eliot. The qualifying tendency of Spender's poetry connects him also with the postwar movement among a younger generation of British poets—notably Philip Larkin, Donald Davie, and Kingsley Amis—who have taken issue with Eliot's modernist ambitions and with Dylan Thomas's romantic gesturing.

The tentativeness of Spender's writing connects with so many diverse and often opposing tendencies in modern literature because it has its roots in the Romanticism underlying all modern literature. Like Romanticism, Spender's verse embraces a variety of conflicting impulses. Whether to write about private subjects or to take on more public concerns, and whether to adopt a personal or an impersonal stance toward the selected subjects, become central problems for Spender. He finds himself at some times, and in some poems, drawn to life's simple, civilian joys; at other times he is moved toward the grand actions of politics. Stylistically, he can be seen vacillating between directness and obliqueness, literalness and figurativeness, and realism and imagism. The conflicting pulls of pragmatism and idealism so evident throughout his career suggest a sympathy with virtually all strains of Western philosophy, especially since René Descartes. Underlying this inability, or unwillingness, to project a set posture is the drive toward inwardness seen in nineteenth century literature, a drive at once hastened and opposed by the great Romantics. The legacy of this drive and its attendant struggle constitute much of the drama played out in Spender's poems.

His writing in the 1930's suggests the same sort of shift evident in the other Auden poets and in many prose writers, such as George Orwell. It suggests, too, a process more of accretion than of drastic change, since the seeds of Spender's discontent with the posture of his earlier political poems lay in the poems themselves. Auden's poetry probably encouraged the young Spender to move from the unfocused idealism of his teens and to write more about the real world. Spender's poetry thus became noticeably contemporary in reference, with urban scenes and crowds, to the point that he could devote entire poems to a speedy train ("The Express") or an airship ("The Landscape near an Aerodrome").

Just as Auden found Spender too romantic, Spender found Auden too cool and detached from the often grim world that Auden had induced him to consider in his poems. Even at his most topical, even when most under Auden's influence, Spender refused to indulge in Audenesque wit or satiric bite. The characteristic feeling of the *Poems* of 1933 is one of commitment and seriousness. Where Auden might concentrate on the ridiculousness of society, Spender concentrates on society's victims and their suffering.

### "MOVING THROUGH THE SILENT CROWD"

"Moving Through the Silent Crowd" illustrates well the understated poignancy of which Spender was capable at this time in his career. Nearly empty of metaphor, it gains its effect through Spender's emphasis on emblematic detail and through the development of saddening irony. He frames the poem with his own vantage point, from which he observes the idle poor. The first stanza turns on his intimation of "falling light," which represents for him the composite disillusionment and wasted potential of the men silent in the road. In the second, he notices the cynicism implicit in such gestures as shrugging shoulders and emptying pockets. Such a scene leads him, in the final two stanzas, to develop the irony of the situation and to hint at a radical political stance. He notes how the unemployed resemble the wealthy in doing no work and sleeping late. Confessing jealousy of their leisure, he nevertheless feels "haunted" by the meaninglessness of their lives.

An equally strong element of social conscience colors many other Spender poems written before 1933. Generally they exhibit more eloquence and metaphorical sweep than the rather terse "Moving Through the Silent Crowd." For example, in "Not palaces, an era's crown," he catalogs those purely intellectual or aesthetic considerations that he must dismiss in favor of social action. Such action he significantly compares to an energized battery and illustrates in a bold program of opposition to social and political tyranny. The short, forceful sentences of the poem's second section, where this program is described, contrast with the longer, more ornate syntax of the beginning. The hunger that Spender hopes to eradicate is of a more pressing order than that addressed by aesthetics or vague idealism, which he characterizes as sheer indolence. Only in the poem's final line, once his moral and political ambitions have been fully expressed, can he permit himself a Platonic image, as light is said to be brought to life.

Such insistence on social reform, shading into radical political action, probably peaked in the period of 1935 to 1938, when *Vienna* and *Trial of a Judge* were appearing. Perhaps more notable than Spender's eventual repudiation of the unsuccessful *Vienna* is the fact that in so many of the shorter poems written during these years, especially those concerned with Spain, he turned increasingly from the public subjects, the outwardly directed statements, and the didactic organization marking the earlier poems. Where his critique of life in England might be construed as supportive of Communism, the picture he draws of Spain during the Civil War largely ignores the political dimension of the struggle and focuses instead on the suffering experienced by civilians in all regions and of all political persuasions. Although a strain of political idealism continues, the enemy is no longer simply capitalism or even Adolf Hitler; rather, for Spender it has become war and those persons responsible for inflicting a state of war on the helpless and innocent.

### "ULTIMA RATIO REGUM"

One of his most effective poems from Spain, "Ultima Ratio Regum," exhibits a didactic form, even ending with a rhetorical question; but it carefully avoids condemnation or praise of either side. Read without consideration for Spender's original reasons for going to Spain, his angry and moving account of a young Spaniard's senseless death by machine-gun fire condemns the Republicans no less than the Insurgents and

ultimately centers on the impersonality of modern war, which reduces to statistical insignificance a formerly alive and sensitive young man. Similarly, "Thoughts During an Air Raid" deals with Spender's own feelings while taking cover and with the temptation to regard oneself as somehow special and therefore immune from the fate threatening all other people in time of war. If Spender here argues for a more collective consciousness, it is but a vague and largely psychological brotherhood. As in "Ultima Ratio Regum," the viewpoint here is wholly civilian and pacifist. Even "Fall of a City," which clearly and sadly alludes to a Republican defeat, suggests more the spirit of freedom that Spender sees surviving the fall than any political particulars or doctrine attending that spirit. There Spender derives his residual hope not from a party or concerted action, but from the simple handing down of memories and values from an old man to a child. If anything, this poem reflects a distrust of large-scale political ideologies and action and of the dishonesty, impersonality, and brutality that they necessarily breed.

In his autobiography, Spender writes of having been puzzled by civilian enthusiasm for both sides in the Spanish struggle. Like Orwell, he was also disturbed by Republican atrocities against civilians. Such disillusioning discoveries no doubt contributed to the reluctance with which he viewed England's struggle against the Nazis even after the war had begun. Conceding the need to counter the German threat, Spender in his war poems nevertheless stressed the pain, rather than the glory, of that necessity. Such was his perception of that pain that he found it necessary in "The War God" to ask and answer questions that, after Munich or the invasion of Poland, even the most war-wary Englishman probably would no longer have considered. One almost gets the impression that Spender is concerned with convincing, or reminding, himself more than anyone else of the reasons behind the war, so obvious is the logic of the poem. Even "Memento," his more effective response to the death camps, betrays the same lingering pacifism as its surreal images describe the victims' horror and helplessness.

### "JUNE 1940"

Perhaps Spender's most remarkable—and his most reluctant—war poem is his response to the fall of

France, "June 1940." Even as Britain is most threatened, he finds it necessary and appropriate to invoke the ghost of World War I to express his skepticism about the impending defense against Hitler. The first section of the poem combines a lyrical description of the delights of the English summer with suggestions of the war's distance from that pastoral scene. Spender has the "grey" survivors of the earlier war note the difference between the trench fighting of their youth and the newer, more mechanized European war of which they have heard only very little. He shows boys bicycling around village war memorials and the Channel "snipping" England from France. The scene and mood change drastically in the next section, with the slightly surreal account of the "caterpillar-wheeled blond" charging over birds' nests in France that very day, and with the lengthy series of voices arguing the need to counter the Nazi horde with armed resistance. Such arguments persuade the old soldiers, sitting in their deck chairs since the poem's beginning, that the struggle against Germany is just and that the alternative is an imprisoned England.

Even so, Spender characterizes the old veterans' response as "disillusioned" to prepare the reader for the poem's audacious ending. In six short lines, he overturns the style, the premises, and the conclusion of the earlier dialogue. A dead soldier from the Great War suddenly testifies to the purgatory of guilt to which participation in that earlier struggle against Germany has doomed him, to imply that the arguments justifying the current war represent only a seductive parallel to earlier warmongering, and that even defeating Hitler will not wholly justify the impending struggle or absolve the English of war guilt. While the conclusion implied by the logic of the poem may not be that England ought to surrender, it certainly cuts very thin any moral advantage the English might claim in resisting. Again Spender ultimately focuses his attention on the burden—in this case a moral one—placed on the individual by collective action.

"June 1940" represents only the most blatant evidence of Spender's departure from the spirited socialism and anti-Nazism of his earlier poems. The general drift of his writing after 1934 had been clearly in that direction. His poems had dealt increasingly with personal problems and situations. In *Forward from Liberalism* (1937), he had articulated his dissatisfaction with the socialist creed, a dissatisfaction based principally on what he saw as the necessary antipathy to the individual person that politics, and especially leftist politics, inevitably aroused. Before too long he was able, in *The Creative Element: A Study of Vision, Despair, and Orthodoxy Among Some Modern Writers* (1953), to attribute his earlier political orthodoxy to liberal guilt induced by the misery of the poor during the Great Depression.

## "An Elementary School Classroom in a Slum"

The ease with which such renunciation and self-analysis seem to have come after the late 1930's suggests the limited nature of Spender's commitment to politics even when he seemed most political. The tension between individual and collective viewpoints that becomes central to the Spanish Civil War poems and to "June 1940" is at least implicit in most of his earlier writing, as well.

It is true that in his criticism Spender repeatedly questions the wisdom of the modernists' avoidance of politics, particularly that of T. S. Eliot and William Butler Yeats, whom he so admired as a young man. In this regard, "An Elementary School Classroom in a Slum" constitutes Spender's gloss on Yeats's "Among School Children," first in the type of school the younger poet chooses to visit, and second in his refusal to turn the visit into an occasion for personal theorizing, as Yeats did. Spender's allusion to "Sailing to Byzantium"—where he asserts that he will not transform the street beggars into "birds" on his "singing-tree"—attacks Yeats even more directly.

The grammar of this assertion, however—indeed, of many ostensibly political statements by the young Spender—guarantees, perhaps intentionally, some confusion of purpose and does it so often that it seems reflective of a confusion in Spender himself.

### First-person perspective

"In railway halls, on pavement near the traffic" is the very poem in which he seems to mock Yeats for the Irishman's indifference to public affairs. The poem is governed by an "I" whose statement of poetic intent ultimately reflects more on himself than on the plight of the poor. Not only does the subject of the poem thus become poetry—something that Spender could deplore in Yeats—but also in a sense the poet becomes the hero. This is not to criticize Spender, but merely to point out, ironically, how much his focus approaches Yeats's after all. The first-person perspective of so many other early Spender poems ties the public to the private and prevents any purely political orientation from taking over.

"Moving Through the Silent Crowd" illustrates even more strikingly this same tension. While the observed poor are rendered sympathetically, the reader can never forget the observer. The marked return, in the final stanza, to his viewpoint and his troubles—where three of four lines begin with "I'm," and where each of the parallel clauses develops the poet's dilemma—clearly raises a question as to the ultimate object of sympathy here. This does not mean that the poem reflects merely self-pity or that Spender might not want to get outside himself; however, the poem finally becomes an exposure not only of poverty, but also of the poet's inability to close the perceived gap between himself and the poor. He concludes with a sense of his distance from them; all he can do is sympathize and be "haunted" by them. Because he appears as helpless as they, though in a somewhat different sense, his helplessness becomes at least as important as theirs as the subject of the poem. Without the personal perspective, the poem seems to ask, Of what validity is political or social criticism? At the same time, the poem's fixation with the observer's perspective places in serious doubt the efficacy of whatever criticism he may construct.

### "THE EXPRESS"

Another dimension of Spender's uncertainty comes in his treatment of contemporary civilization, particularly in those celebrated early poems dealing with technology. Although Auden probably influenced Spender in this direction, Spender seems never to have been so comfortable as Auden with the up-to-date world, particularly as an element of his poetry. Such discomfort largely escaped his first readers, who found his apparent acceptance of material progress a welcome departure from old-fashioned nature poetry. A. Kingsley Weatherhead rightly suggests, in *Stephen Spender and the Thirties* (1975), that many writers of that decade wrote a covert kind of nature poetry even as they purported to repudiate the values of the Georgian poets.

They did so, Weatherhead says, by taking a critical look at contemporary civilization and thereby implying retreat as the only viable alternative.

Although this no doubt is true of Spender, his retreat often takes very subtle forms. Sometimes it resides largely in the terms with which he commends an aspect of twentieth century technology. "The Express," for example, appears to celebrate the beauty and speed of a fast-moving train and, thus, to confirm the benefits of modern applied science. An examination of the poem's progression, however, reveals considerable dissatisfaction with the external world for which the train has been manufactured. Perhaps the whole idea of a lyric poem's appropriating something so utilitarian as an express train might seem an implied criticism of utility; certainly Walt Whitman's "To a Locomotive in Winter" and Emily Dickinson's "I like to see it lap the miles" can be seen as backhanded compliments. Even so, Spender's train poem seems of a different order in that it places the train much more realistically—with references to stations, to gasworks, and to Edinburgh. A good deal of the poem's language is very literal. Even Spender's initial nonliteral description ascribes utility to the train's beginning: It is cast as a queen issuing a "plain manifesto" to her subjects.

The image of such public action yields to more private behavior in the poem's second sentence, where "she" is said to "sing" with increasing abandon as she gathers speed. In the third and final sentence, she sings enraptured, exceeding the bounds of nature by flying in her music. The shape of the poem is thus the progression of its metaphors. Because that progression is vertical—away from the earth, into a state of Platonic grace suggested by music, again reminiscent of Yeats—the poem becomes a celebration of imaginative and self-absorbed retreat from the mundane and empirical reality in which the express actually resides. Even as Spender praises the train, he gives equal praise to a place where the express could not possibly exist. The two objects of praise coexist, as do the two kinds of language by which they are represented. There is no evidence that the speaker of the poem—significantly *not* represented as "I"—does not believe he is praising the express on its own terms. On the other hand, the progression of the terms he uses, particularly the metaphors, suggests that he in fact admires principles quite antipathetic to those on which the express runs, and that perhaps he can find the express tolerable only by transforming it into something it is not and cannot be.

Poems such as "The Express," "The Landscape near the Aerodrome," and "Pylons" suggest a flight from the material values on which modern popular culture is founded. In this they can have even greater pertinence now than when they were written. An examination of other early poems suggests a wish, or at least a need, to escape the human element as well. For all their apparent humanism, they propose a withdrawal from the very society that Spender would help redeem, and confirm the Marxist critique of Romanticism as an elevation of private concerns at the expense of the public good. They bring to mind, too, Hugh MacDiarmid's indictment of the Auden group's ultimate lack of political commitment.

### Platonic images

Certainly, it seems no accident that Spender wrote so much about Romanticism and especially about Percy Bysshe Shelley. His discussion of the modern poet's difficulties in reconciling the Romantic ideal of the individual imagination and sensibility with a public, collective age seems almost an abstract of poems such as "Without that one clear aim, the path of flight" or "From all these events, from the slum, from the war, from the boom." In the first of these, a sonnet, Spender complains of being choked and imprisoned by social reality, of needing desperately to escape on the "wings" of poetry. So politically suspect a motive for writing, which he reinforces by other Platonic images suggestive of Shelley, informs the second poem. There Spender expresses a faith, not in reformist action, but in the power of time to obliterate the memory not only of wrongdoing but also of those who would correct it. What might have horrified Thomas Hardy thus consoles Spender. In "Perhaps," he takes comfort in the more escapist position that troubling public events may be only fantasies. Even "I think continually of those who were truly great," so often cited as the epitome of 1930's selflessness, suggests that Spender's characteristic way of coping with social problems is to forget them: to ignore the present by dreaming of the "truly great."

Individual poems and the collective poetry of Spen-

der rarely show him consistent in this regard. His struggle with the irreconcilables of individual and group, private and public, and realism and idealism have their stylistic level, as elegances of metaphor and syntax frequently accompany and undermine his call for action in the present. To an age grown increasingly aware of the limitations, if not the futility, of collective behavior and of the traps into which both leader and follower can fall, Spender poses the dilemma of the morally and socially sensitive individual. For this reason, he commands a not inconsiderable place among the poets of the twentieth century.

### Other major works

LONG FICTION: *The Backward Son*, 1940; *The Temple*, 1988.

SHORT FICTION: *The Burning Cactus*, 1936; *"Engaged in Writing" and "The Fool and the Princess,"* 1958.

PLAYS: *Trial of a Judge*, pr. 1938; *Danton's Death*, pr. 1939 (with Goronwy Rees); *To the Island*, pr. 1951; *Mary Stuart*, pr. 1957; *Lulu*, pr. 1958; *Rasputin's End*, pb. 1963; *Oedipus Trilogy: A Play in Three Acts Based on the Oedipus Plays of Sophocles*, pr. 1983.

NONFICTION: *The Destructive Element: A Study of Modern Writers and Beliefs*, 1935; *Forward from Liberalism*, 1937; *Citizens in War and After*, 1945; *European Witness*, 1946; *Poetry Since 1939*, 1946; *World Within World: The Autobiography of Stephen Spender*, 1951; *Shelley*, 1952; *The Creative Element: A Study of Vision, Despair, and Orthodoxy Among Some Modern Writers*, 1953; *The Making of a Poem*, 1955; *The Struggle of the Modern*, 1963; *The Year of the Young Rebels*, 1969; *Love-Hate Relations: A Study of Anglo-American Sensibilities*, 1974; *Eliot*, 1975; *The Thirties and After: Poetry, Politics, People, 1933-1970*, 1978; *Letters to Christopher: Stephen Spender's Letters to Christopher Isherwood, 1929-1939, with "The Line of the Branch"—Two Thirties Journals*, 1980; *Journals, 1939-1983*, 1985.

### Bibliography

Blamires, Harry. *Twentieth Century English Literature*. Rev. ed. New York: Schocken Books, 1985. This standard account of the development of English literature devotes only four pages to Spender, but it represents the judgment of the last quarter of the century and places the poet well in his generation and cultural context. Includes an index, a list for further reading, and a chronology.

Hamilton, Ian. *Against Oblivion: Some Lives of the Twentieth-Century Poets*. London: Viking, 2002. This collection of biographies of twentieth century poets that Hamilton considers important contains a chapter on Spender.

Leeming, David Adams. *Stephen Spender: A Life in Modernism*. New York: Henry Holt, 1999. Leeming's friendship with his subject began in 1970 and lasted until Spender's death; it is a relationship that, coupled with Spender's eloquent self-disclosure in his journals, autobiography, critical writings, and poetry, makes for a fluent narrative. Leeming sees Spender as a key witness to and participant in the rise of modernism.

Sternlicht, Sanford V. *Stephen Spender*. New York: Twayne, 1992. A study of the entire Spender canon that discusses all genres of the author's work. Sternlicht begins by providing the reader with a well-researched, biographical sketch of the poet's development over several decades. He also includes a discussion of Spender's influential role as literary and political critic.

Sutherland, John. *Stephen Spender: The Authorized Biography*. New York: Viking, 2004. An engaging, readable, and substantial authorized biography. Produced with access to Spender's personal papers, and illustrated.

Thurley, Geoffrey. "A Kind of Scapegoat: A Retrospect on Stephen Spender." In *The Ironic Harvest: English Poetry in the Twentieth Century*. London: Edward Arnold, 1974. Provides a good synthesis of the changing estimate of the enduring value of Spender's poetry. This account places Spender in the context of the 1930's.

Weatherhead, A. Kingsley. *Stephen Spender and the Thirties*. Lewisburg, Pa.: Bucknell University Press, 1975. Covers most aspects of interest in Spender's work and life and is a comprehensive source. Weatherhead's bibliography is still useful.

*Bruce K. Martin*

# EDMUND SPENSER

**Born:** London, England; c. 1552
**Died:** London, England; January 13, 1599

PRINCIPAL POETRY
*The Shepheardes Calender*, 1579
*The Faerie Queene*, 1590, 1596
*Complaints*, 1591
*Daphnaïda*, 1591
*Amoretti*, 1595
*Astrophel*, 1595
*Colin Clouts Come Home Againe*, 1595
*Epithalamion*, 1595
*Fowre Hymnes*, 1596
*Prothalamion*, 1596
*The Poetical Works of Edmund Spenser*, 1912 (J. C. Smith and Ernest de Selincourt, editors)

OTHER LITERARY FORMS

Like most Renaissance writers, Edmund Spenser usually prefaced his poems with dedicatory letters that complimented the recipients and also provided helpful interpretations for other readers. Further indications of Spenser's theories about "English versifying" appear in his correspondence with Gabriel Harvey: *Three Proper, and Wittie, Familiar Letters* (1580) and *Foure Letters and Certaine Sonnets* (1586). Although *A View of the Present State of Ireland* was written in 1596, it was not published until 1633, thirty-four years after the author's death. In this treatise, Spenser presented a clear picture of Elizabethan Ireland and its political, economic, and social evils. The serious tone of this work deepens the significance of the Irish allusions and imagery throughout Spenser's poetry.

ACHIEVEMENTS

The inscription on Edmund Spenser's monument hails him as "the Prince of Poets in his time," but his reputation as "poet's poet" continued among his Romantic peers three centuries later. What was praised and imitated changed with time, but the changes themselves suggest the extent of Spenser's achievements. His popularity among his contemporaries was documented not only in commentaries written during his lifetime but also in William Camden's account of Spenser's funeral, during which mourning poets threw into his tomb their elegies and the pens with which they had written these tributes. Among his fellow Elizabethans, Spenser first gained renown as a love poet, a pastoral writer, and a restorer of the native language—all three of these roles already enacted in his early work, *The Shepheardes Calender*, in which he demonstrated the expansiveness of rural dialect and English unadulterated with continental vocabulary. Later, in a more courtly work, *The Faerie Queene*, Spenser still sought variety in language more through native archaisms than through foreign idiom. Despite its simplicity of diction, *The Shepheardes Calender* contained an elaborate academic apparatus that demanded recognition for its author as a serious poet. The fact that Spenser took his work seriously was also manifested in various levels of satire and in metrical experimentation that strengthened what Sir Philip Sidney described as his "poetical sinews."

*Edmund Spenser* (Library of Congress)

Seventeenth century imitators echoed Spenser's allegorical and pastoral elements, his sensuous description, and his archaic phrasing. These early Spenserians, however, did not fully comprehend their model. Their servile imitations of surface themes and complex metrical forms temporarily diminished Spenser's reputation and probably stimulated later eighteenth century parodies. The serious side of Spenser, however, gradually received more notice. In *Areopagitica* (1644), for example, John Milton extolled him as "a better teacher than Scotus or Aquinas," and when the neoclassicists praised him, it was primarily for allegorical didacticism. In the nineteenth century, admiration of Spenser's moral allegory yielded to delight in his metrical virtuosity and the beauties of his word-pictures. When such great Romantics as Sir Walter Scott, Lord Byron, and John Keats imitated the Spenserian or "Faerie Queene" stanza form, they demonstrated anew the strength and flexibility of Spenser's metrical inventiveness. Modern holistic criticism continues to find deeper levels of Spenserian inventiveness in structural intricacy, allegorical ingenuity, and both narrative and descriptive aptness.

BIOGRAPHY

If allusions in his own poetry can be read autobiographically, Edmund Spenser was born in London around 1552, apparently into a mercantile family of moderate income. In 1561, the Merchant Taylors' School opened with Richard Mulcaster as its first headmaster, and in that same year or shortly afterward, Spenser was enrolled, probably as a scholarship student. From Mulcaster, Spenser learned traditional Latin and Greek and also an awareness of the intricacies and beauties of the English language unusual among both schoolboys and schoolmasters of that time. Later, Spenser as "Colin Clout" paid tribute to Mulcaser as the "olde Shephearde" who had made him "by art more cunning" in the "song and musicks mirth" that fascinated him in his "looser yeares." Even before Spenser went to Cambridge, fourteen of his schoolboy verse translations had been incorporated into the English version of Jan van der Noot's *Theatre for Worldlings* (1569).

At Pembroke College, Cambridge, Spenser took his B.A. degree in 1573 and his M.A. in 1576; little else is known about his activities during that period except that he made several lifelong friends, among them Gabriel Harvey and Edward Kirke. Both Harvey and Kirke were later among Spenser's prepublication readers and critics, and Kirke today remains the most likely candidate for the role of "E. K.," the commentator whose glosses and arguments interpret enigmatic passages in *The Shepheardes Calender*. The Spenser-Harvey letters reveal young Spenser's theories on poetry and also his hopes for the patronage of Philip Sidney and Sidney's uncle, the earl of Leicester, Queen Elizabeth's favored courtier. Harvey's greetings to a woman, whom he addresses as "Mistress Immerito" and "Lady Colin Clout," also suggest that Spenser was married about 1580; nothing more is known of the first wife, but there are records of a son and a daughter at the time of Spenser's second marriage to Elizabeth Boyle in 1594.

When Spenser found himself unable to gain an appointment as a fellow at Cambridge, he accepted the post of secretary to John Young, bishop of Rochester. In 1580, he went to Ireland as secretary for Arthur Lord Grey, the newly appointed Lord Governor. When Grey was recalled from Ireland two years later because his policies did not control the Irish rebellion as the English court desired, Spenser remained behind. For several years, he moved into minor offices in different sections of the country; about 1589, he became "undertaker" of Kilcolman, an estate in Cork. As an "undertaker," Spenser received a grant of land previously confiscated from an Irish rebel, agreeing to see to the restoration of the estate and to establish tenant farmers on it. Love for Kilcolman is reflected in his poetry even though his days there were shadowed by litigation with an Irish neighbor who claimed the property and by a new outbreak of rebellion that eventually destroyed the estate and forced him to leave Ireland about a month before his death in 1599.

With the exception of *The Shepheardes Calender*, all of Spenser's major poetry was written in Ireland. The landscape and the people of his adopted country are reflected in imagery and allusions; political and economic conditions appear in various guises, perhaps nowhere so strongly and pervasively as in book 5 of *The Faerie Queene*, the Book of Justice. Although Spenser lived most of his adult life far from the court of Elizabeth, he maintained constant contact with events and friends there. His strongest bid for court recognition came in *The Faerie Queene*, with its creation of Gloriana, the Fairyland reflection of the living Queen of Britain, who rewarded him for his portrait of her by granting him an annual pension. Two of Queen Elizabeth's favorites played major roles in Spenser's later years: Sir Walter Ralegh and Robert, earl of Essex. Ralegh, who owned an estate neighboring Spenser's Kilcolman, frequently encouraged the poet's work in a general way and, if there is any validity in Spenser's famous prefatory letter, influenced specific changes in the structure of *The Faerie Queene*. Essex financed the poet's funeral and his burial in the Poet's Corner of Westminster Abbey in 1599.

ANALYSIS

By an eclectic mingling of old traditions, Edmund Spenser created new poetry—new in verse forms, in language, and in genre. From the Middle Ages, Spenser had inherited complex allegorical traditions and a habit of interlacing narrative strands; these traditions were fused with classical myth and generic conventions, some of them transformed by continental imitators before they reached Spenser. This fusion of medievalism and classicism was in turn modified by currents of thought prevalent in Tudor England, especially by the intense nationalism that manifested itself in religion, language, politics, and international affairs.

To some extent, Spenser's poetic development evolved naturally from his deliberate selection of Vergil as his model. Like Vergil, he started his published career with pastoral eclogues; like him, too, he turned, in his last major work, from shepherds to great heroes. Before Spenser evoked classical muses in his epic, however, the tradition of Vergil had picked up romantic coloring and allegorical overtones from continental epics, especially Ludovico Ariosto's highly allegorized *Orlando Furioso* (1516, 1521, 1532; English translation, 1591). Spenser himself announced the three-way pattern adopted for *The Faerie Queene*: "Fierce wars and faithful loves shall moralize my song." Long after Spenser's death, his admirers continued to compare him with Vergil, often to Spenser's advantage. Vergil provided stimulus not only for the pastoral and epic genres in which Spenser wrote his two major works but also for the mythical allusions that permeate most of his work and for the serious use of poetry, especially in political and religious satire and in the reflection of nationalistic pride. Vergil's exaltation of Augustus and the Roman Empire accorded well with the nationalism of Elizabethan England, a nationalism poetically at its zenith in *The Faerie Queene*.

Vergil's sobriquet "Tityrus" became for Spenser a means of double praise when he hailed his fourteenth century predecessor Geoffrey Chaucer as an English Tityrus, the "God of shepheards." Rustic language, interlocked narratives, and experiments in vernacular quantitative verse forms in *The Shepheardes Calender* all reflect Chaucerian influence; in a less direct way, the vogue of courtly love in medieval and Renaissance literature was also channeled partly through Chaucer. During the two centuries between Chaucer and Spenser, love poetry became permeated with a blend of Petrarchan and Neoplatonic elements. Petrarchan lovers taught Spenser's shepherds to lament over their ladies' cruelty, to extol their beauty, and to describe their own pains, anxieties, and ecstasies with conventional images. The more sensuous aspects of love remained central to many of the *Amoretti* sonnets and to several set pieces in *The Faerie Queene*, such as Acrasia's Bower of Bliss and Busiranes' Mask of Cupid, but idealistic Neoplatonic concepts also emerged here. Such Neoplatonic concepts undergird the *Fowre Hymnes*. The first two hymns praise erotic human love and the inspirational force of feminine beauty; the other two deprecate these more earthly powers, elevating in their place the heavenly love and beauty of Christ, the source of all true human love and beauty.

In *The Faerie Queene*, too, idealistic Neoplatonic elements assume more pervasive significance than do Petrarchan motifs. The Platonic identification of the good and the beautiful, for example, is often manifest, especially in Gloriana, Una, and Belphoebe; and the true and false Florimels of books 3 to 5 exemplify true

and false beauty, the former inspiring virtuous love and marriage and the second inciting sensuous lust. Although books 3 and 4 are called the Books of Chastity and Friendship, their linked story dramatically demonstrates variant forms of love. The concept of love as either debilitating or inspiring reflects one of the mythical traditions transmitted from antiquity through the Middle Ages: the double significance of Venus as good and evil love. As the goddess of good, fruitful love, Venus herself frequents the Garden of Adonis, where nature is untouched by deceptive art, where spring and harvest meet, and where love flourishes joyfully. In her own temple, Venus listens to the sound of "lovers piteously complaining" rather than rejoicing.

Renaissance pageantry and Tudor emblem books contributed to the pictorial quality with which Spenser brought myths to life—classical tales, rustic folklore, and his own mythic creations. One of the most picturesque of Spenser's new myths describes the "spousals" of the Thames and Medway rivers, a ceremony attended by such "wat'ry gods" as Neptune and his son Albion; by other rivers, remote ones such as the Nile and the Ganges, Irish neighbors such as the Liffey and the Mulla, and streams that paid tribute to one of the betrothed rivers; and by Arion, accompanied by his dolphin and carrying the harp with which he provided wedding music. Scenes like these exemplify the artistry with which Spenser created new poetry out of old traditions.

### THE SHEPHEARDES CALENDER AND COLIN CLOUTS COME HOME AGAINE

Classic and contemporary models, rural and courtly milieu, universal and occasional topics—from such a mixture Spenser formed his first major work, the "little booke," which he dedicated to Sidney and which he signed "Immerito," the Unworthy One. *The Shepheardes Calender* went through five editions between 1579 and 1597, none of them bearing Spenser's name. Such anonymity fits common Renaissance practice, but it may also have had additional motivation from Spenser's awareness of sensitive topical allusions with too thin an allegorical veil. Contemporary praise of Spenser indicates that by 1586 the anonymity was technical rather than real. In his twelve eclogues, one for each month of the year, Spenser imitated conventions that Renaissance writers attributed to Vergil and to his Greek predecessors: debates between rustic speakers in a rural setting, varied by a singing match between shepherds, a lament for the death of a beloved companion, praise of the current sovereign, alternating exultation and despair over one's mistress, and veiled references to contemporary situations. A fifteenth century French work, translated as *The Kalender and Compost of Shepherds*, probably suggested to Spenser not only his title but also the technique of emblematic illustration, the application of zodiacal signs to everyday life and to the seasons, and the arrangement of instructional commentary according to the months. Barbabe Googe's *The Zodiake of Life* (1565) strengthened the satirical and philosophical undertone of the calendar theme.

Despite the surface simplicity connoted by its nominal concern with shepherds, Spenser's book is a complex work. Not the least of its complexities are the paraphernalia added by "E. K.": the dedicatory epistle, the introductory arguments (for the whole book and for each eclogue), and the glosses. Although the initials themselves make Spenser's Cambridge friend Edward Kirke the most likely person to designate as the mysterious commentator, the Renaissance love for name-games does not exclude other possible solutions of the identity puzzle. Even Spenser himself has been suggested as a candidate for the enigmatic role. Many of E. K.'s annotations supply information essential to an understanding of the poet's cryptic allusions, to the identification of real-life counterparts for the characters, and occasionally to a modernization of archaic diction. Some annotations, however, are either accidentally erroneous or pedantically misleading: for example, several source references and the etymology for "aeglogues." E. K. derives the term "eclogues" from "Goteheardes tales" rather than from "conversations of shepherds," the more usual Renaissance understanding of the term; in actuality, "eclogues" are etymologically short selections that convention came to associate with pastoral settings.

The twelve separate selections could have produced a sense of fragmentation, but instead they create a highly unified whole. The most obvious unifying device is the calendar framework, which gives to the individual poems their titles and their moods. Another

source of unity lies in the shepherd characters who appear repeatedly, especially Colin Clout, a character borrowed from the Tudor satirist John Skelton and used by Spenser as his own persona. Colin appears in four of the eclogues and is the topic of conversation in three others; his friendship for Hobbinol (identified by E. K. as Harvey), and his love for Rosalind (unidentified) provide a thread of plot throughout the twelve poems. Moreover, the figure of Colin represents the whole life of "everyman"—or at least every poet—as he passes from the role of "shepherd boy" in "January" to that of the mature "gentle shepherd" in "December."

In his general argument, E. K. establishes three categories for the topics of the eclogues: plaintive, recreative, and moral. The four selections that E. K. classifies as plaintive are those in which Colin's is the main voice. "January" and "June" are laments about his futile love for Rosalind; "December," too, is a conventional love plaint, although it adds the dimension of Colin's approaching death. "November," one of the most highly structured eclogues, is a pastoral elegy for Dido, the daughter of one "great shephearde" and the beloved of another "great shepheard Lobbin." E. K. pleads ignorance of the identity of both shepherds, but most critics identify "Lobbin" as a typical anagram for Robin (Robert Dudley) plus Leicester, thus suggesting a covert allusion to a love interest of Elizabeth's favorite, the earl of Leicester.

The first of the three recreative selections, "March," is a sprightly, occasionally bawdy, discussion of love by two shepherd boys. "April" starts out with a description of Colin's lovesickness but then moves on to an encomium on "fayre Elissa, Queene of shepheardes all," a transparent allusion to Queen Elizabeth. The singing contest in "August" gives Spenser an opportunity to exploit shifting moods and an intricate variety of metrical patterns.

It is sometimes difficult to interpret the satire in the eclogues that E. K. classes as "moral" because of the ambivalence of the dialogue structure itself and because of the uncertain implications of the fables included in four of the five moral selections. Besides, misperception on the part of the characters or the commentator can be part of the comedy. In "May," "July," and "September," different pairs of shepherds discuss religious "shepherds," making clear allusions to contemporary churchmen. In contrast to the sometimes vehement satire in these religious eclogues, the debate on youth and age in "February" has a light, bantering tone. As a statement of Spenser's views on poetry, "October" is perhaps the most significant "moral" eclogue. When the disillusioned young poet Cuddie complains that his oaten reeds are "rent and wore" without having brought him any reward, the idealistic Piers tries to convince him that glory is better than gain. He encourages Cuddie to leave rustic life, to lift himself "out of the lowly dust," but Cuddie complains that the great worthies that "matter made for Poets on to play" are long dead. The ambivalence of the pastoral debate is particularly evident here because the two voices apparently represent a conflict within Spenser himself. The inner Piers has an almost Platonic vision of poetry and sees potential inspiration in the active life of the court; but the inner Cuddie, fearing the frustrations of the poet's role, resigns himself to the less conspicuous, less stimulating rural life.

In a sequel to the eclogues, *Colin Clouts Come Home Againe*, Colin describes to his friends a trip to London, apparently a reflection of Spenser's trip to make arrangements for the publication of *The Faerie Queene*. The question-and-answer format allows Colin to touch on varied topics: the level of poetic artistry in London, conventional satire of life at court, topographical poetry about the "marriage" of two Irish rivers, and Platonic deification of love. Although this more mature Colin is less critical of court life than the earlier one had been, Ireland rather than England is still "home" to him.

### THE FAERIE QUEENE

Any study of *The Faerie Queene* must take into account the explanatory letter to Ralegh printed in all early editions under the heading "A Letter of the Author's, Expounding his Whole Intention in the course of this Work. . . ." The fact that the letter was printed at the end rather than the beginning of the first edition (books 1-3 only) suggests that Spenser was writing with a retrospective glance at what was already in the printer's press, even though he was also looking toward the overall structure of what had not yet been assembled. Ralegh had apparently requested such an explanation, and Spenser here clarified elements that he considered essential to understanding his "continued Allegory of dark conceit." These elements can be summarized as purpose, genre, narrative structure, and allegorical significance.

In carrying out his purpose "to fashion a gentleman or noble person in vertuous and gentle discipline," Spenser imitated other Renaissance conduct books that set out to form representatives of different levels of polite society, such as those peopled by princes, schoolmasters, governors, and courtiers. By coloring his teaching with "historical fiction," Spenser obeyed Horace's precept to make poetry both useful and pleasing; he also followed the example of classic and Renaissance writers of epic by selecting for the center of that fiction a hero whose historicity was overlaid by legend: Arthur. Theoretically, an epic treats a major action of a single great man, while a romance recounts great deeds of many men. Kaleidoscopic visions of the deeds of many great knights and ladies within the separate books superimpose a coloring of romance, but the overall generic designation of *The Faerie Queene* as "epic" is possible because Arthur appears in the six books as a unifying hero. Through Arthur, the poet also paid tribute to his sovereign, whose family, according to the currently popular Tudor myth, claimed descent from Arthur's heirs.

Although the complexity of the poem stems partly from the blending of epic and romance traditions, Spenser's political concern added an even greater complication to his narrative structure. He wanted to create a major role by which he could pay tribute to a female sovereign in a genre that demanded a male hero. From this desire came two interlocked plot lines with Gloriana, the Faerie Queene, as the motivating force of both: The young Arthur "before he was king" was seeking as his bride the beautiful Queen of Fairyland whom he had seen in a vision; meanwhile, this same queen had sent out on quests twelve different knights, one for each book of the epic. At strategic points within these separate books Arthur would interrupt his quest to aid the currently central figure. Since Spenser completed only six of the proposed twelve books, the climatic wedding of Arthur and Gloriana never took place and the dramatic dispersion and reassembling of Gloriana's knights occurred only in the poet's explanation, not in his poem.

Patterns of allegory, like patterns of narrative, intertwine throughout the poem. By describing his allegory as "continued," Spenser did not imply that particular meanings were continuously retained but rather that central allegories recurred. In the letter to Ralegh, for example, Spenser explains that in his "general intention," Gloriana means glory, but in a more "particular" way, she is "the glorious person" of Elizabeth. Spenser is not satisfied to "shadow" Elizabeth only as Gloriana. In the letter and in the introduction to book 3, he invites Elizabeth to see herself as both Gloriana and Belphoebe, "In th'one her rule, in th'other her rare chastity." Less pointedly, she is also "shadowed" in Una, the image of true religion (book 1); in Britomart, the beautiful Amazonian warrior (books 3-5); and in Mercilla, the just queen (book 5). The glories of Elizabeth thus appear as a pervasive aspect of the "continued allegory," even though they are represented by different characters. Allegorical continuity also comes from Spenser's plan to have his twelve knights as "patrons" of the "twelve private moral virtues" devised by Aristotle, with Arthur standing forth as the virtue of magnificence, "the perfection of all the rest." The titles of the six completed books indicate the central virtues of their heroes: holiness, temperance, chastity, friendship, justice, and courtesy.

Historical and topical allusions appear frequently. Only when such allusions link references to Arthur and Gloriana, however, do they form a continuous thread of allegory. In the Proem to book 2, "The Legend of Sir Guyon, or of Temperance," Spenser encourages Elizabeth to see her face in the "fair mirror" of Gloriana, her kingdom in the "land of faery," and her "great ancestry" in his poem. In canto 10, he inserts a patch of "historical fiction" in which Arthur and Guyon examine the chronicles of Briton kings and elfin emperors, the first ending with the father of Arthur, Uther Pendragon, and the second with Tanaquil, called "Glorian . . . that glorious flower." Spenser prefaces his lengthy account of British history (stanzas 5-69) with a tribute to his own "sovereign queen" whose "realm and race" had been derived from Prince Arthur; he thus identifies the realm of the "renowned prince" of this story as the England of history. The second chronicle describes an idealized land where succession to the crown is peaceful, where

the elfin inhabitants can trace their race back to Prometheus, creator of Elf (Adam) and Fay (Eve), and where Elizabeth-Gloriana can find her father and grandfather figured in Oberon and Elficleos. The "continued" historical allegory looks to the wedding of Arthur and Gloriana as blending real and ideal aspects within England itself.

Topical political allegory is most sustained in book 5, "The Legend of Artegall, or of Justice." In this book Elizabeth appears as Queen Mercilla and as Britomart; Mary Stuart as Duessa (sentenced by Mercilla) and as Radigund (defeated in battle by Britomart); Arthur Lord Grey as the titular hero, Artegall; and the earl of Leicester as Prince Arthur himself in one segment of the narrative. Several European rulers whom Elizabeth had either opposed or aided also appear in varied forms. Contemporary political problems are reflected in the story of Artegall's rescue of Irena (Ireland) from the giant Grantorto (literally translated as "Great Wrong"), usually allegorically identified as the Pope. Spenser's personal defense of Lord Grey shows through the naïve allegory of canto 12, where Artegall, on the way back to Faery Court, is attacked by two hags, Envy and Detraction, and by the Blatant Beast (Calumny). Spenser thus suggests the cause of the misunderstandings that led to Elizabeth's recalling Grey from Ireland. Elizabeth's controversy with Mary Stuart, doubly reflected in book 5, also provides a significant level of meaning in book 1, "The Legende of the Knight of the Red Crosse, or of Holinesse."

A closer look at the tightly structured development of book 1 shows more clearly Spenser's approach to heroic and allegorical poetry in the epic as a whole. On the literal level of romantic epic, Gloriana assigns to an untrained knight the quest he seeks: the rescue of the parents of a beautiful woman from a dreaded dragon. The plot traces the separation of Red Cross and Una, Red Cross's travels with the deceptive Duessa (duplicity), Una's search for Red Cross, the reunion of Una and her knight, the fulfillment of the quest, and the betrothal of hero and heroine. Vivid epic battles pit Red Cross against the serpentine Error and her swarming brood of lesser monsters, against a trio of evil brothers (Sansfoy, Sansjoy, and Sansloy), against the giant Orgoglio (from whose dungeon he must be rescued by

Prince Arthur), and eventually against one of the fiercest, best-described dragons in literature. In canto 10, Red Cross learns his identity as Saint George, changeling descendant of human Saxon kings rather than rustic elfin warrior. Red Cross's dragon-fight clearly reflects pictorial representations of Saint George as dragon-slayer.

All three levels of allegory recognized by medieval exegetes are fully developed in book 1: typical, anagogical, and moral. Typically, Una is the true Church of England, and Elizabeth is the protector of this Church; Duessa is the Church of Rome and Mary Stuart, its supporter. Red Cross is both abstract holiness defending truth and a figure of Christ himself. Arthur, too, is a figure of Christ or of grace in his rescue of Red Cross—here a kind of Everyman—from Orgoglio, the forces of Antichrist.

Anagogical or apocalyptic elements appear primarily in sections treating Duessa and the dragon and in Red Cross's vision of heaven. Duessa, at her first appearance, reflects the description of the scarlet woman in the Revelation of St. John, and the mount given her later by Orgoglio is modeled on the apocalyptic seven-headed beast. The mouth of the great dragon of canto 11 belches forth flames like those often pictured erupting from the jaws of hell in medieval mystery plays. Red Cross is saved from the dragon by his contacts with the Well of Life and the Tree of Life, both borrowed from Revelation. Before Red Cross confronts the dragon, he has an apocalyptic vision of the New Jerusalem, a city rivaling in beauty even the capital of Fairyland, Cleopolis.

The moral level provides the most "continued" allegory in book 1. Red Cross-Everyman must develop within himself the virtue of holiness if he is eventually to conquer sin and attain the heavenly vision. When holiness is accompanied by truth, Error can be readily conquered. However, when holiness is deceived by hypocrisy (Archimago), it is easily separated from truth and is further deceived by duplicity (Duessa) masquerading as fidelity (Fidessa). Tempted to spiritual sloth, Red Cross removes his armor of faith and falls to pride (Orgoglio). He must then be rescued from the chains of this sin by grace (Prince Arthur), must be rescued from Despair by truth, and must be spiritually strengthened

in the House of Holiness, conducted by Dame Caelia (heaven) and her daughters Fidelia, Speranza, and Charissa (faith, hope, and charity). Only then can he repent of his own sins and become holy enough to conquer sin embodied in the dragon.

If book 1 best exemplifies self-contained, carefully structured allegorical narrative, books 3 and 4 exemplify the interweaving common in medieval and early Renaissance narrative poetry. Characters pursue one another throughout the two books; several stories are not completed until book 5. In fact, Braggadochio, the cowardly braggart associated with false Florimell in this section, steals Guyon's horse in book 2 and is judged for the crime in book 5. Belphoebe, too, introduced in a comic interlude with Braggadochio in book 2, becomes a central figure in the Book of Chastity. Belphoebe blends the beauty of Venus (Bel) with the chastity of Diana (Phoebe); her twin sister, Amoret, is a more earthly representation of Venus, destined to generate beauty and human love. Britomart, the nominal heroine of book 3, embodies the chastity of Belphoebe in her youth but the generative love of Amoret in maturity. Despite complex and not always consistent allegorical equations applicable to these central characters, Spenser moves them through their adventures with a delicate interlacing of narrative and allegorical threads typical of the romantic epic at its most entertaining level.

### AMORETTI AND EPITHALAMION

The sonnet sequence *Amoretti* (little love poems) and the *Epithalamion* (songs on the marriage bed) together provide a poetic account of courtship and marriage, an account that tradition links to actualities in Spenser's relationship with Elizabeth Boyle, whom he married in 1594. References to seasons suggest that the "plot" of the sonnet sequence extends from New Year's Day in one year (Sonnet 4) through a second New Year's Day (Sonnet 62) to the beginning of a third winter in the closing sonnet (Sonnet 89), a time frame of about two years. Several sonnets contain references that tempt readers to autobiographical interpretations. In Sonnet 60, "one year is spent" since the planet of "the winged god" began to move in the poet; even more significantly, the poet refers to the "sphere of Cupid" as containing the forty years "wasted" before this year. By simple arithmetical calculations, biographers of Spenser have deduced from his assumed age in 1593 his birth in 1552. Two sonnets refer directly to his work on *The Faerie Queene*: Sonnet 33 blames on his "troublous" love his inability to complete the "Queen of Faery" for his "sacred empress," and Sonnet 80 rejoices that having run through six books on Fairyland he can now write praises "low and mean,/ Fit for the handmaid of the Faery Queen."

Collectively and individually the *Amoretti* follow a popular Renaissance tradition established by Petrarch and imitated by numerous English sonneteers. In metrical structure, Spenser's sonnets blended Italian and English forms. The five-rhyme restriction in the Italian octave-plus-sestet pattern (*abbaabba cdecde*) was adapted to fit the English pattern of three quatrains plus couplet; instead of the seven rhymes used in most English sonnets, the interlocked rhymes of the Spenserian quatrains created a more intricate, as well as more restricted, form (*abab bcbc cdcd ee*).

Although Spenser's metrical pattern was innovative, most of his conceits and images were conventional; for example, love is related to a judicial court (Sonnet 10) and to religious worship (Sonnets 22 and 68); the beloved is a cruel causer and observer of his pain (Sonnets 20, 31, 41, 42, and 54) and the Neoplatonic ideal of beauty (Sonnets 3, 9, 45, 61, 79, and 88); love is warfare (Sonnets 11, 12, 14, and 57), a storm (Sonnet 46), sickness (Sonnet 50), and a sea journey (Sonnet 63). The poet at times promises the immortality of fame through his praise (Sonnets 27, 29, 69, 75, and 82); at other times he simply rejoices in the skill that enables him as poet to offer his gift of words (Sonnets 1 and 84). Even the kind of praise offered to his beloved is traditional. In Sonnet 40, "An hundred Graces" sit "on each eyelid" and the lover's "storm-beaten heart" is cheered "when cloudy looks are cleared." Elsewhere, eyes are weapons (Sonnets 7, 16, and 49) and a means of entanglement (Sonnet 37). The beloved is a "gentle deer" (Sonnet 67) and a "gentle bee" caught in a sweet prison woven by the spider-poet (Sonnet 71); but she is also a cruel panther (Sonnet 53) and a tiger (Sonnet 56). Physical beauties are compared to precious metals and gems (Sonnet 15), to sources of light (Sonnet 9), and to the sweet odors of flowers (Sonnet

64). Classical myths color several sonnets, identifying the beloved with Penelope, Pandora, Daphne, and the Golden Apples of Hercules (Sonnets 23, 24, 28, and 77) and the poet-lover with Narcissus, Arion, and Orpheus (Sonnets 35, 38, and 44).

In typical Petrarchan fashion, the lyrical moments in the *Amoretti* fluctuate between joy and pain, between exultation over love returned and anxiety over possible rejection. The sequence ends on a note of anxiety not in keeping with a set of poems conceived as a prelude for the glowing joy of the *Epithalamion*. Despite clear references to the 1592-1594 period of Spenser's life, it seems unlikely that all eighty-nine sonnets were written during this period or that all were originally intended for a sequence in praise of Elizabeth Boyle. The *Epithalamion*, however, is clearly Spenser's celebration of his own wedding at Kilcolman on Saint Barnabas' Day (June 11), 1594.

In its basic form and development, this marriage song is as conventional as the sonnets with which it was first published; but it is also original and personal in its variations on tradition. Classical allusions, for example, are countered by the homely invocation to nymphs of the Irish river and lake near Spenser's home (lines 56-66), by the imprecation against the "unpleasant choir of frogs still croaking" in the same lake (line 349), and by some of the attendants: "merchants' daughters," "fresh boys," and childlike angels "peeping in" the face of the bride. Although allusions to classical gods and goddesses heighten the lyric mood, other elements retain a more personal touch.

Structurally, Spenser adapted the *canzone* form. As used by Dante and Petrarch, the *canzone* consisted of a series of long stanzas followed by a short stanza (a *tornata*) responding to the preceding stanzas. Within the stanzas, one or more three-foot lines varied the basic five-foot line; the *tornata*, too, had one short line. A. Kent Hieatt has demonstrated in *Short Time's Endless Monument* (1960) the ingenuity with which Spenser varied the basic *canzone* structure to reflect units of time in general and to relate poetic divisions with night/day divisions on the longest day of the year in southern Ireland. Hieatt points out that variations in verse form correspond to days in the year (365 long lines), hours in the day (24 stanzas), spring and fall equinoxes (parallel diction, imagery, and thought in stanzas 1-12 and 13-24), degrees of the sun's daily movement (359 long lines before the *tornata*, corresponding to 359 degrees of the sun's movement as contrasted with 360 degrees of the stars' movement), and the division between waking and sleeping hours (indicated by a change in the refrain at the end of stanza 17). It is variations within stanza 17 that most personalize the time element to make the "bedding" of the bride occur at the point in the poem representing nightfall on the poet's wedding day, the day of the summer solstice in southern Ireland. At the end of the stanza, the refrain, which had for sixteen stanzas been describing the answering echo of the woods, changes to "The woods no more shall answer, nor your echo ring": All is quiet so that the poet-bridegroom can welcome night and the love of his bride.

### COMPLAINTS

The collection of moralizing, melancholy verse titled *Complaints* reflects an as yet not fully developed artistry in the author. Although published in the aftermath of fame brought by *The Faerie Queene*, most of the nine poems were probably first drafted much earlier. The most significant poem in this volume was probably the satirical beast fable, "Prosopopoia: Or, Mother Hubberd's Tale." Following the tradition of Giovanni Boccaccio and Geoffrey Chaucer, the poet creates a framework of tale-tellers, one of whom is "a good old woman" named Mother Hubberd. In Mother Hubberd's story, a Fox and an Ape gain personal prosperity through the gullibility of farmers, the ignorance and worldliness of clergymen, and the licentiousness of courtiers. About two-thirds of the way through, the satire turns more specifically to the concern of England in 1579 with a possible marriage between the twenty-four-year-old Duc d'Alencon and Queen Elizabeth, then forty-six. The marriage was being engineered by Lord Burleigh (the Fox of the narrative) and by Jean de Simier, whom Elizabeth playfully called her "Ape." This poem, even more than *The Shepheardes Calender*, demonstrates Spenser's artistic simplicity and the Chaucer-like irony of his worldview. Burleigh's later hostility to Spenser gives evidence of the pointedness of the poet's satiric barbs. "Virgil's Gnat" also exemplifies a satiric beast fable, this time with Leicester's

marriage as the target, hit so effectively that Spenser himself was wounded by Leicester's lessened patronage. In "Muiopotmos: Or, The Fate of the Butterfly," beast fable is elevated by philosophical overtones, epic machinery, and classical allusions. Some type of personal or political allegory obviously underlies the poem, but critical interpretations vary widely in attempting to identify the chief figures, the Spider and the Butterfly. Despite such uncertainty, however, one message is clear: Life and beauty are mutable.

Mutability permeates *Complaints*; it is even more central to the posthumous fragment known as the "Mutabilitie Cantos." The publisher Matthew Lownes printed these two cantos as "The Legend of Constancy," a fragmentary book 7 of *The Faerie Queene*. Lownes's identification of these two cantos with the unfinished epic was apparently based on similar poetic form, an allusion to the poet's softening his stern style in singing of hills and woods "mongst warres and knights," and a reference to the records of Fairyland as registering mutability's genealogy. There are, however, no knights, human or elf, in these cantos. Instead, Jove and Nature represent allegorically the cosmic principle of Constancy, the permanence that underlies all change. Despite the philosophical victory of Nature, one of the most effective extended passages in the cantos represents change through a processional pageant of the seasons, the months, day and night, the hours, and life and death.

The principle of underlying permanence applies to Spenser's works as well as to the world of which he wrote. In his shepherds and shepherdesses, his knights and ladies, his own personae, and even in the animal figures of his fables, images of Everyman and Everywoman still live. Time has thickened some of the allegorical veils that conceal as well as reveal, language then new has become archaic, and poetic conventions have become freer since Spenser's poetry first charmed his contemporaries. Despite such changes, however, the evocative and creative power that made Spenser "the Prince of Poets in his time" remains constant.

### OTHER MAJOR WORKS

NONFICTION: *Three Proper, and Wittie, Familiar Letters*, 1580; *Foure Letters and Certaine Sonnets*,

1586; *A View of the Present State of Ireland,* pb. 1633 (wr. 1596).

MISCELLANEOUS: *The Works of Edmund Spenser: A Variorum Edition*, 1932-1949 (Edwin Greenlaw, et al., editors).

BIBLIOGRAPHY

Burlinson, Christopher. *Allegory, Space, and the Material World in the Writings of Edmund Spenser.* Rochester, N.Y.: D. S. Brewer, 2006. An analysis of the poetry of Spenser that concentrates on the symbolism and allegory in his work.

Grogan, Jane. *Exemplary Spenser: Visual and Poetic Pedagogy in "The Faerie Queene."* Burlington, Vt.: Ashgate, 2009. Grogan examines Spenser's poetry through an analysis of *The Faerie Queene.*

Hamilton, A. C., et al., eds. *The Spenser Encyclopedia.* Toronto, Ont.: University of Toronto Press, 1990. This 858-page volume represents the cooperative efforts of Spenserian scholars to compile a series of articles on every aspect of Spenser's life and work. Also offers many articles on the history of England and on literary theory and practice. With index.

Heale, Elizabeth. *"The Faerie Queene": A Reader's Guide.* New York: Cambridge University Press, 1987. Offers an updated guide to Spenser's *The Faerie Queene*, the first great epic poem in English. Emphasizes the religious and political context for each episode. One chapter is devoted to each book of *The Faerie Queene.* Contains an index for characters and episodes.

Heninger, S. K., Jr. *Sidney and Spenser: The Poet as Maker.* University Park: Pennsylvania State University Press, 1989. In this study of mimesis, or imitation, S. K. Heninger considers the transmutation of allegory to fiction. Examines the aesthetic elements in art, music, and literature, analyzes the forms of Spenser's major works and considers the relationship between form and content. This 646-page study of Renaissance aesthetics offers an essential background for understanding Spenser's art.

Lethbridge, J. B., ed. *Edmund Spenser: New and Renewed Directions.* Madison, N.J.: Fairleigh Dickinson University Press, 2006. This collection of essays covers most of Spenser's works, including those written in later life. It also examines Spenser's friendships with Sir Walter Ralegh and Queen Elizabeth through *The Faerie Queene.*

Morrison, Jennifer Klein, and Matthew Greenfield Aldershot, eds. *Edmund Spenser: Essays on Culture and Allegory.* Burlington, Vt.: Ashgate, 2000. A collection of critical essays dealing with the works of Spenser. Includes bibliographical references and an index.

Oram, William A. *Edmund Spenser.* New York: Twayne, 1997. An introductory biography and critical study of selected works by Spencer. Includes bibliographic references and an index.

Van Es, Bart, ed. *A Critical Companion to Spenser Studies.* New York: Palgrave Macmillan, 2006. Comprising thirteen chapters, this useful resource surveys issues of gender, religion, texts, and critical analyses.

Zurcher, Andrew. *Spenser's Legal Language: Law and Poetry in Early Modern England.* Rochester, N.Y.: D. S. Brewer, 2007. Zurcher provides a look at Spenser's works in terms of what they reveal about law in early modern England.

*Marie Michelle Walsh*

---

# ROBERT LOUIS STEVENSON

**Born:** Edinburgh, Scotland; November 13, 1850
**Died:** Vailima, near Apia, Samoa; December 3, 1894

PRINCIPAL POETRY
*Moral Emblems*, 1882
*A Child's Garden of Verses*, 1885
*Underwoods*, 1887
*Ballads*, 1890
*Songs of Travel, and Other Verses*, 1896

OTHER LITERARY FORMS
Robert Louis Stevenson is primarily remembered for his prose fiction, although he was a notable essayist and enjoyed a small reputation as a poet. Stevenson also tried his hand at drama and collaborated with Wil-

liam Ernest Henley in the writing of four plays (*Deacon Brodie*, pb. 1880; *Beau Austin*, pb. 1884; *Admiral Guinea*, pb. 1884; and *Macaire*, pb. 1885), and with his wife, Fanny Van de Grift Osbourne Stevenson, on one (*The Hanging Judge*, pb. 1887). His first published works were collections of essays, which he would continue to publish throughout his career. His short stories are collected in *The New Arabian Nights* (1882), *More New Arabian Nights* (1885), *The Merry Men, and Other Tales and Fables* (1887), and *Island Nights' Entertainments* (1893). Of his novels, the four romances of adventure, *Treasure Island* (1883), *Kidnapped* (1886), *The Black Arrow: A Tale of the Two Roses* (1888), and *Catriona* (1893), along with his psychological work, *The Strange Case of Dr. Jekyll and Mr. Hyde* (1886), firmly established him as a master storyteller and ensured him a place in popular culture for the several generations of readers (and viewers of film adaptations) whose imagination he captured. His lesser romances (*Prince Otto*, 1885), and especially those written in collaboration with his stepson, Lloyd Osbourne, are of a much lower order than his major novels, *The Master of Ballantrae* (1889) and the unfinished *Weir of Hermiston* (1896).

## ACHIEVEMENTS

Robert Louis Stevenson's unquestionable literary achievements as a storyteller and as an accomplished essayist in an age of prolific essayists overshadow his prominence as a poet who excelled in occasional verse and perfectly captured the impermanent and various moods of childhood and who, in *Underwoods*, exerted a profound and lasting influence on Scots poetry of the twentieth century. Tusitala, "the teller of tales," as the Samoans called him, achieved a measure of fame as an essayist, sometimes as a controversialist, but was most at home writing the tales of adventure and romance on which his reputation justly rests.

His uncompleted masterpiece, *Weir of Hermiston*, and *The Master of Ballantrae* rank him as a serious novelist of the first order, who dealt with the complexities of human personality in its own depths and as it is subject to both inexorable fate and the buffets of history. His extraordinarily penetrating study of the divided self, "the war in the members," has made his cre-

ations Dr. Jekyll and Mr. Hyde household words. His tales of adventure, especially *Treasure Island*, *Kidnapped*, and *Catriona*, have become classics not only for youth but also for those who would recapture their youth. Enjoyment, in a word, characterizes the purpose and effect of much of Stevenson's fiction; it is also the principal object of much of his poetry.

One does not read—certainly one does not reread—Stevenson's poetry for its examination of adult life's complexities or its wrestling with the ultimate questions which each generation must ask for itself. These concerns are certainly present in some of the poetry but do not dominate it. Rather, in the bulk of Stevenson's verse, one reads to find an emotion crystallized, an occasion noted, a fleeting mood artfully captured and rendered. One reads the poetry primarily to enjoy a highly realized sense of childhood, a freshness and naïveté that is usually full of wonder, sometimes on the verge of joyous laughter, and often tinged with an almost inexpressible sadness. Stevenson is unmistakably a minor poet who has something in common with William Ernest Henley and Rudyard Kipling, other minor poets of the age, as well as with the early William Butler Yeats. A. E. Housman's poetry owes a clear debt to Stevenson's.

## BIOGRAPHY

Robert Louis Balfour Stevenson was born to Thomas and Margaret Isabella (Balfour) Stevenson in Edinburgh on November 13, 1850, the midpoint of the Victorian era. Thomas Stevenson, destined to be the last of a line of illustrious Scottish engineers, had hopes that his only child would take up that profession. His hopes proved to be unrealized when Stevenson switched from a sporadic study of engineering to a sporadic study of the law at Edinburgh University. Never a strong child, Stevenson spent much of his childhood and, indeed, much of his adulthood, either undergoing or convalescing from long and serious bouts of illness, chiefly respiratory disorders. His early life and education were overshadowed by illness, confinement, and frequent changes of climate. His youthful wanderings after health and sun led to later trips to France, Switzerland, and America, and, finally, in 1888, to the South Seas, where he ultimately built a house, "Vailima," in Samoa. There he remained until his death from a cerebral hemorrhage in 1894. His recent biographers make much of his turbulent adolescence and hint of his several early love affairs, especially the platonic affair with Fanny Sitwell, whom he met in 1873 when she was newly separated from her husband. The more important woman in his life was the American, Fanny Van de Grift Osbourne, whom he met at Grez, France, in 1876, and married in California in 1880. From the time of his marriage (which drew him away from such friends as Charles Baxter, Sidney Colvin, and William Ernest Henley) until his death, Stevenson passed his time in constant writing, constant illness, and nearly constant travel. Periodically exiled from Scotland by its harsh climate and finally leaving it forever in 1888, Stevenson often returned there imaginatively to find sources for both his prose and his poetry. He was survived by his mother, his wife, and her children, Lloyd Osbourne, and Isobel Osbourne Strong Field. The latter two wrote reminiscences of him.

*Robert Louis Stevenson* (Library of Congress)

### ANALYSIS

Robert Louis Stevenson himself, in a letter to his cousin R. A. M. Stevenson (September, 1868), wrote what is both a summary of his evaluation of Horace and Alexander Pope and a just index of his own intentions and later poetic achievement: "It is not so much the thing they say, as the way they say it. The dicta are often trivial and commonplace, or so undeniably true as to become part of orthodox boredom; but when you find an idea put in either of them, *it is put in its optimum form*." Stevenson's poetry is often about the commonplace—childhood, partings, reunions, homesickness, felicitations, greetings, friendship, the open road, the sea—but it is a crafting of common experience into heightened language and optimum form. His verse usually achieves its effects by a rigid application of meter and fixed rhyme scheme, although on occasion he breaks into a Whitmanesque style with a force far exceeding that of his more conventional poetry. Even in conventional poetic forms, however, he generally succeeds in lifting ordinary sentiment to a higher plane by the very simplicity, directness, and clarity of his language. This is one aspect, for example, of *A Child's Garden of Verses*, accounting for its appeal to adults as well as to children.

Stevenson's is a poetry of sentiment. At times, the sentiment appears to be artificial posturing that ranges from melancholy to high spirited. He does not make intellectual demands of his readers, but he does ask them to listen carefully; indeed, listening to his poems read aloud is the way most people first come to him. He also asks his readers to participate in the moment as he captures it, if only for that moment's sake. The quality of that moment is often twofold; it has the permanence that poetry can give it, and it vanishes as it is apprehended by the reader.

### A CHILD'S GARDEN OF VERSES

One can find no better starting place for examining Stevenson's poetry than his envoi "To Any Reader" in *A Child's Garden of Verses*. Here, in eight rhymed couplets, he encapsulates the sentiment of the volume. The reader is first carried back to childhood; Stevenson likens the reader's watchful care over the child in the verses to that which mothers exercise over their children as they play. Then, reminded of the commonplace event of a mother knocking at the window to get her child's attention, the reader is told that the child in the book will not respond in the familiar way. The child is there in the garden in one sense, but not there in another: "It is but a child of air." Stevenson suggests that, however much one might observe and watch over his child, he cannot successfully intervene in his child's life or break out of the historical confinement in which, as an adult, he finds himself. The moment one tries to do more than fix his attention on the child, to have the child in the verses give ear to his concerns, warnings, admonitions, or summonses, the child vanishes; he becomes "grown up," and is "gone away."

The reader must proceed warily in *A Child's Garden of Verses* and not disturb the moments of the fifty-eight poems but, rather, enjoy them for what they are, privileged to observe and fleetingly share them before they dissolve, as they will when one tries to bring adult reflection to bear on them. Stevenson creates an ideal and somewhat idealized world of childhood—a special childhood, to be sure, but also a universal one. Although it is clear that the volume has for its background his own holiday visits to his maternal grandfather's house, Colinton Manse, near the Water of Leith, and is dedicated to Alison Cunningham ("Cummy"), his childhood nurse, to read the poems for the autobiography they contain would be to miss their point as poetry. Further, the child who narrates the poems is, above all, a persona created by a man in his thirties, a persona that is sometimes the object of gentle irony (in "Looking Forward" and "Foreign Children," for example) and often (although children actually do this) speaks with a wisdom beyond his years (in "The Gardener" and "System").

Each poem, in the words of "From a Railway Carriage," "is a glimpse and gone for ever!" In those glimpses, Stevenson renders portraits that are quite new in children's literature. Neither out to produce a didactic primer nor to condescend to children, he does provide childlike insights while retaining for his narrator a sense of wonder about the world. Just as, literarily speaking, the child was the invention of nineteenth century literature, so this child is a new invention who speaks in a language that the adult has outgrown.

Where Charles Baudelaire, for example, had written of the philosophy of children's toys in "La Morale du joujou" (1853), Stevenson goes to the heart of the matter in such poems as "The Dumb Soldier," "The Land of Story Books," and "The Land of Counterpane."

### UNDERWOODS

Stevenson's *Underwoods*, best known for its Scottish dialect poems, also contains many occasional pieces in English that are of some interest, because in them is found a preeminent prose writer paying tribute, returning thanks, or commemorating a gift, a death, a visit, an illness. Much the same can be said of *Songs of Travel, and Other Verses*. The Scots poems (book 2) are, by contrast, more interesting as poems in their own right. "A Lowden Sabbath Morn" and "Embro Hie Kirk" are perfect in their resonances of Robert Burns's language, style ("the Burns stanza"), treatment of common religious themes, and, in the latter, religious controversy. Full of humor and hominess, like his earlier "pieces in Lallan" addressed to Charles Baxter, the poems in Scots lack an overall seriousness of purpose that might raise them from the status they achieve as minor poetry.

### BALLADS

Stevenson's *Ballads* amply illustrate that his forte was prose. The South Seas ballads "The Song of Rahero" and "The Feast of Famine" are, in his words, "great yarns" that suffer primarily because, as he wrote, they are "the verses of a Prosater." "Heather Ale" is a curious retelling of a Pictish legend, and "Christmas at Sea" is the story of a young man's first voyage in icy waters; it is not, except for the poignancy of the last two lines, remarkable. Stevenson is much more in his element in "Ticonderoga: A Legend of the West Highlands." Here his storytelling ability comes to the fore, as does his undoubted ability to catch the conversational tones of the Scots language. The ballad has all that one could wish for—a murder, a test of honor in the face of ghostly visitation, far-flung travel and military exploits, inevitable fate, and the eerie sense of supernatural forces at work. However, like the other ballads, "Ticonderoga" would be better suited to Stevenson's prose than to his mechanical verse.

Except for a very few poems (notably, "Requiem" and the poems in Scots), the master of prose succeeded best as a poet when he sought to recapture the evanescent moments of youth. Stevenson's poetry takes its place far below that of the greater Victorians. His poetry is not a reminder to humanity of its precarious place in the universe or of the tenuous grasp it has on civilization. His poetry does, however, express the sheer delight, the cares, the rewards, and the experience itself of childhood. Like the child of *A Child's Garden of Verses*, the reader looks to Stevenson the novelist and poet with a fondness for the magic of his "dear land of Story-books."

## OTHER MAJOR WORKS

LONG FICTION: *Treasure Island*, 1881-1882 (serial), 1883 (book); *Prince Otto*, 1885; *Kidnapped*, 1886; *The Strange Case of Dr. Jekyll and Mr. Hyde*, 1886; *The Black Arrow: A Tale of the Two Roses*, 1888; *The Master of Ballantrae*, 1889; *The Wrong Box*, 1889; *The Wrecker*, 1892 (with Lloyd Osbourne); *Catriona*, 1893; *The Ebb-Tide*, 1894 (with Osbourne); *Weir of Hermiston*, 1896 (unfinished); *St. Ives*, 1897 (completed by Arthur Quiller-Couch).

SHORT FICTION: *The New Arabian Nights*, 1882; *More New Arabian Nights*, 1885; *The Merry Men, and Other Tales and Fables*, 1887; *Island Nights' Entertainments*, 1893.

PLAYS: *Deacon Brodie*, pb. 1880 (with William Ernest Henley); *Admiral Guinea*, pb. 1884 (with Henley); *Beau Austin*, pb. 1884 (with Henley); *Macaire*, pb. 1885 (with Henley); *The Hanging Judge*, pb. 1887 (with Fanny Van de Grift Stevenson).

NONFICTION: *Edinburgh: Picturesque Notes*, 1878; *An Inland Voyage*, 1878; *Travels with a Donkey in the Cévennes*, 1879; *Virginibus Puerisque*, 1881; *Familiar Studies of Men and Books*, 1882; *The Silverado Squatters: Sketches from a Californian Mountain*, 1883; *Memories and Portraits*, 1887; *The South Seas: A Record of Three Cruises*, 1890; *Across the Plains*, 1892; *A Footnote to History*, 1892; *Amateur Emigrant*, 1895; *Vailima Letters*, 1895; *In the South Seas*, 1896; *The Letters of Robert Louis Stevenson to His Family and Friends*, 1899 (2 volumes), 1911 (4 volumes); *The Lantern-Bearers, and Other Essays*, 1988; *The Letters of Robert Louis Stevenson*, 1994-1995 (8 volumes); *R. L. Stevenson on Fiction: An Anthology of Literary and Critical Essays*, 1999 (Glenda Norquay, editor).

## BIBLIOGRAPHY

Ambrosini, Richard, and Richard Dury, eds. *Robert Louis Stevenson: Writer of Boundaries*. Madison: University of Wisconsin Press, 2006. A collection of essays reflecting a trend in Stevenson studies that can readily be appreciated by a twenty-first century reader.

Bathurst, Bella. *The Lighthouse Stevensons*. New York: HarperPerennial, 2000. A history of Stevenson's family, who built fourteen lighthouses along the Scottish coast during the nineteenth century. A fascinating insight into Stevenson's family background.

Bloom, Harold, ed. *Robert Louis Stevenson*. Philadelphia: Chelsea House, 2005. Compilation of critical essays on Stevenson's fiction, ranging in focus from the dialectic between realism and romance to Stevenson's attitude toward professionalism in authorship.

Buckton, Oliver S. *Cruising with Robert Louis Stevenson: Travel, Narrative, and the Colonial Body*. Athens: Ohio University Press, 2007. This volume looks at much of Stevenson's nonfiction and his major fictional works to examine the importance of travel in his life and his writing. Buckton shares enlightening views on the energies and desires that were released by Stevenson through travel.

Callow, Philip. *Louis: A Life of Robert Louis Stevenson*. Chicago: Ivan R. Dee, 2001. An engaging biography that draws on the work of other biographers to present for the general reader a cohesive life of the novelist.

Dunlop, Eileen. *Robert Louis Stevenson: The Travelling Mind*. Edinburgh: National Museums Scotland, 2008. A biography of the writer that looks at his travels and how they shaped his life and works.

Gray, William. *Robert Louis Stevenson: A Literary Life*. New York: Palgrave Macmillan, 2004. Focuses on how Stevenson's writing was shaped by its geographical, cultural, and political contexts.

Harman, Claire. *Myself and the Other Fellow: A Life of Robert Louis Stevenson*. New York: HarperCollins, 2005. A substantial biography, covering the writer's early family life, his writing and travels, and his curious but successful marriage. Includes bibliography and index.

McLynn, Frank. *Robert Louis Stevenson: A Biography*. New York: Random House, 1993. The author traces Stevenson's career, noting the malignant influence of his wife and stepson and concluding that Stevenson "is Scotland's greatest writer of English prose."

Reid, Julia. *Robert Louis Stevenson, Science, and the Fin de Siècle*. New York: Palgrave Macmillan, 2006. Study of the role of science, especially the theory of evolution, both in Stevenson's works and in the fin-de-siècle culture that produced them.

*John J. Conlon*

# SIR JOHN SUCKLING

**Born:** Whitton, Twickenham, Middlesex, England;
February 10, 1609 (baptized)
**Died:** Paris, France; 1642

PRINCIPAL POETRY

*Fragmenta Aurea*, 1646
*The Last Remains of Sir John Suckling*, 1659
*A Ballad Upon a Wedding*, 1927
*Love Poems*, 2008 (Anthony Astbury, editor)

OTHER LITERARY FORMS

Between 1637 and 1641, Sir John Suckling completed three plays: *Aglaura* (pr., pb. 1638), *The Goblins* (pr. 1638), and *Brennoralt* (pr. 1646). *The Sad One*, an unfinished fragment, was written sometime earlier. *Aglaura* was published in 1638 in folio format; none of the other plays was printed during the poet's lifetime. Most of Suckling's fifty-odd letters are personal in subject matter, but two of them—one to "A Gentleman in Norfolk" and one to Henry Jermyn—are essentially political tracts dealing with the Scottish Campaign of 1639 and the opening of the Long Parliament in 1640, respectively. Suckling was also the author of "An Account of Religion by Reason," a defense of Socinianism that attempts to reconcile biblical revelation with the mythologies of the ancients. Suckling's letters and "An Account of Religion by Reason" have been collected by Thomas Clayton in *The Works of Sir John Suckling: The Non-Dramatic Works* (1971).

ACHIEVEMENTS

During his lifetime, Sir John Suckling's reputation as courtier and rakehell overshadowed his literary endeavors. His attacks on the Neoplatonic amatory conventions of the 1630's led him into poetic skirmishes with Edmund Waller and a swarm of lesser poets; his much vaunted dislike of the aged and ailing Ben Jonson earned him the enmity of the Sons of Ben. In his satire "The Wits," Suckling took on the entire Caroline literary establishment, with a good word for no one but Lucius Cary, Viscount Falkland. Such combativeness, joined with the theatricality of his personal life, isolated Suckling from his fellow poets, and his work elicited few of the usual encomia from contemporaries. The raciness and adolescent flippancy that are the hallmarks of his style, moreover, constitute a reaction against the prevailing Caroline tastes that was little appreciated in his own day.

Suckling's style, however, was precisely suited to the poets of the succeeding generation, and the Restoration wits found in him a model for their own aspirations. In John Dryden's *Of Dramatic Poesie: An Essay* (1668), Eugenius argues that the ancients "can produce nothing so courtly writ, or which expresses so much the conversation of a gentleman, as Sir John Suckling"; William Congreve and John Wilmot, earl of Rochester, both praised his ease and naturalness. Restoration poets eagerly imitated "The Wits," using it as the pattern for their own literary squibs; they also appropriated the ballad stanza that Suckling introduced into formal poetry.

Although enthusiasm for Suckling waned during the eighteenth century, he continued to command a firm place in the poetic pantheon. Samuel Johnson praised him for not falling into the metaphysical excesses of poets such as Abraham Cowley. Since that time the critical estimation of Suckling has remained relatively constant: Although a minor poet, he was a good one, and several of his lyrics are frequently anthologized.

Dryden undoubtedly exaggerated Suckling's achievement, but his recognition of the part that Suckling played in transforming English poetic diction is valid.

Suckling's ability to capture the rhythms of colloquial speech in rhymed verse represents a real innovation in seventeenth century poetry. Although his attitudes toward women and love are often cynical and occasionally grating, his earthy common sense usually comes across as a necessary antidote to the stylized Neoplatonism of so much amatory verse of the 1630's. In similar fashion, Suckling's embrace of native literary forms such as the ballad and the riddle serves as a corrective to the classicizing tendencies of Renaissance poetry. Suckling's oeuvre is small, but the role he played in English poetry was a pivotal one: His experiments in diction and essays in satire furthered the shift from a Renaissance to a Restoration aesthetic.

### BIOGRAPHY

Sir John Suckling was born in February, 1609, into a prominent gentry family. His father, also Sir John, was a longtime member of Parliament who held a number of minor positions at court; in 1622, he purchased the office of Comptroller of the King's Household, which he occupied until his death in 1627. The poet's mother, Martha, was the sister of Lionel Cranfield, later first earl of Middlesex and, until his impeachment in 1624, Lord Treasurer of England. Although his mother died in 1613, Suckling maintained close ties with the Cranfield family; his uncle's disgrace, countenanced by the royal favorite the duke of Buckingham, alienated Suckling from the inner circles of the court.

Suckling matriculated at Trinity College, Cambridge, between 1623 and 1628; he was admitted to Gray's Inn in 1627. He may have served in the English expedition against the French on the Ile de Ré in 1627 and definitely fought in Lord Wimbledon's regiment in the Dutch service in 1629-1630. In October, 1631, Suckling joined the embassy to Gustavus Adolphus led by Sir Henry Vane, who was negotiating with the Swedish monarch for the return of the Palatinate to Charles I's brother-in-law, the Elector Frederick. Vane sent Suckling to England in March, 1632, with dispatches for the King. His mission complete, Suckling remained in England and plunged into a course of gambling and womanizing that lasted for the rest of the decade. During this period, according to John Aubrey, Suckling invented the game of cribbage. To recoup the

*Sir John Suckling* (Hulton Archive/Getty Images)

vast sums he lost at cards and bowling, Suckling entered into a prolonged courtship of the northern heiress Anne Willoughby. Although the king supported his suit, Suckling's prospective in laws did not; after a series of challenges, threatened lawsuits, and pitched battles between the two families and their allies, Suckling ceased his attentions. Shortly after this abortive courtship, Suckling entered into a relationship with the woman he called Aglaura, probably Mary Bulkeley of Beaumaris, Anglesey. Despite the intensity of feeling that Suckling expresses in his few surviving letters to Aglaura, the affair flickered out by 1639, when Mary married a local squire. During the remainder of his life Suckling's closest emotional ties were with his Cranfield relatives, his uncle and his cousin Martha, Lady Cary.

Suckling had begun writing poetry during adolescence, but the lyrics for which he is best known were composed during the mid-1630's. In 1637, he turned seriously to drama; his tragedy *Aglaura* was produced with great fanfare in February, 1638, by the King's Company at Blackfriars. Suckling provided *Aglaura* with a tragicomic ending for a performance before the king and queen in April, 1638; the play was printed in a lavish folio edition later that year.

The outbreak of trouble in Scotland in 1639 put an end to Suckling's literary activities. Raising a troop of one hundred horsemen, whom he clad at his own expense in white doublets and scarlet breeches, Suckling joined King Charles in the north. Because of illness, perhaps dysentery, he saw little action and was later accused of cowardice in the campaign. With the Treaty of Berwick in June, 1639, Suckling returned to London and was elected to the Short Parliament as a member of Parliament for Bramber, Sussex, in a by-election. Suckling returned to the border country in August, 1640, for the Second Bishops' War. After the defeat of the king's forces at Newburn, he participated in the general retreat, during which he reportedly lost his coach and a wardrobe worth £300 to the Scottish commander Leslie.

With the opening of the Long Parliament in November, 1640, Suckling began to assume a more active role in politics. He became involved in a conspiracy to stage a coup d'état that would have dissolved Parliament and returned effective political power to the king. The plans of the plotters were discovered; after a preliminary examination by the House of Commons, Suckling fled to France on May 5, 1641. A writ for his arrest was issued the same day. Suckling arrived in Paris on May 14, but nothing is known of his subsequent activities. Although the exact details of his death are unclear, the most plausible account is that he committed suicide by poison sometime in 1642.

## ANALYSIS

Sir John Suckling was a poet of reaction. Assuming the role of roaring boy at the Caroline court, he assaulted with an almost adolescent glee the conventions, literary and amatory, that prevailed during the 1630's. Suckling challenged the fashionable cult of Platonic Love with a pose of libertinism. He rejected the sophisticated Continental models employed by Jonson and Thomas Carew in their lyrics, introducing in their stead native, "subliterary" forms such as the ballad and the riddle. Finally, Suckling rejected the title "poet," vaunting his amateur status in a pursuit that he implied

had become increasingly dominated by ungentlemanly professionals. For the greater part of his short poetic career, Suckling was an iconoclast rather than an innovator, more certain of what he was attacking than what he proposed to offer in its place. In the final poems, however, he achieved a balance between the successive waves of idealism and cynicism that rocked his short life. This newfound confidence in his art manifests itself most clearly in the good humor and good sense of "A Ballad upon a Wedding."

Thomas Clayton divides Suckling's poetic career into four periods. The earliest poems, discovered by L. A. Beaurline in manuscript in the late 1950's, consist of a Christmas devotional sequence and two meditations on faith and salvation written before or during 1626. These pieces are derivative and not of great literary value, but they do suggest the young Suckling's receptiveness to influences and stylistic options open to him. Two of the eleven poems are important inasmuch as they forecast the themes that would run through Suckling's best-known lyrics. In "Faith and Doubt," the speaker contemplates the Christian mysteries of the incarnation and redemption; suspended between a desire to believe and an inability to move beyond the rational, he prays for the experience vouchsafed the apostle Thomas—the confirmation of faith through the senses. The speaker's troubled doubt serves as a prologue to the pose of libertine skepticism that Suckling later adopted in his amatory verse. Even more central to Suckling's poetic vision, perhaps, is the exuberant description of rustic customs and superstitions in "Upon Christmas Eve." With a sensitivity reminiscent of Robert Herrick, Suckling testified to his rural upbringing and his obvious delight in country life. Beneath the elegant courtliness of later poems this theme will persist, eventually reemerging in "A Ballad upon a Wedding."

The poems that Clayton assigns to the years 1626 to 1632 are a mixed lot, suggesting that the young Suckling was still in search of a personal style. While a number of these pieces represent essays in popular, usually humorous, forms—the riddle, the character, the ballad—others are serious attempts at the type of lyric that flourished at court. A final group fuses the popular and courtly strains in parody or, more rarely, in a delicate mixture of humor and compliment. With only a few exceptions, the poems exhibit a preoccupation with love and sexuality.

### "A CANDLE" AND OTHER BAWDY RHYMES

The short riddle "A Candle" is essentially an adolescent joke that allows the poet to talk bawdy but evade the consequences. In a series of double entendres, Suckling describes the "thing" used by "the Maiden Female crew" in the night; to the discomfiture of the reader, the answer to the riddle proves to be "a candle." The poet is obviously intensely interested in sex, but apparently too unsure of his poetic powers to deal with it directly. The same type of double entendre informs "A Barley-break" and three characters—"A Barber," "A Pedler of Small-Wares," and "A Soldier." In "A Soldier," the speaker offers his love to an audience of ladies, combining bluster with a winning naïveté. The assertion "I cannot speak, but I can doe," with its obvious pun on "doe," well describes Suckling's own position in the early 1630's—willing and eager to besiege the ladies, but unskilled in the language of amatory gallantry.

### LOVE LYRICS

Suckling's attempts to write conventional love lyrics underscore the truth of the admission in "A Soldier." While technically correct, these pieces seem flat after the exuberance and leering smuttiness of the riddles and characters. "The Miracle," for example, is an uninspired rehash of the Petrarchan fire and ice paradox. "Upon the first sight of my Lady Seimor," an exercise in Caroline Neoplatonism, is a stillborn blazon. In *Non est mortale quod opto*: Upon Mrs. A. L.," Suckling tackles the same theme that Carew treats so successfully in "A Divine Mistress," that of the woman who is so perfect that the poet can find no way to approach her. Whereas Carew wittily solves the dilemma by praying to the gods to grant his lady "some more humanitie," Suckling blunders badly with his closing couplet, "I love thee well, yet wish some bad in thee,/ For sure I am thou art too good for me." The acquisition of "some bad," unlike "humanitie," can only mar the lady's perfection. Carew effects an accommodation between poetic convention and amatory pragmatism without compromising either; Suckling, facing the same dilemma, is forced to choose between them.

What is interesting about these poems written in an unblinking Platonic vein is that they are contemporaneous with the characters and ballads. The disjunction between love and sexuality, moreover, assumes a literary form inasmuch as Suckling reserves his bawdiness for the "subliterary" genres. In Suckling's mature style, the gap is bridged: Courtly verse forms are employed to set off the very grossness of the "country matters" they discuss. In "The deformed Mistress," Suckling weds the high-flown diction and exotic imagery of the serious blazon to the most unattractive physical blemishes with striking effect:

> Her Nose I'de have a foot long, not above,
> With pimples embroder'd, for those I love;
> And at the end a comely Pearl of Snot,
> Considering whether it should fall or not.

"Upon T. C. having the P." reemploys the fire-and-water conceit of "The Miracle" in unexpected fashion: The subject of the poem is Carew's difficulties in urinating when he has the pox.

### "UPON MY LADY CARLILES WALKING IN HAMPTON-COURT GARDEN"

The best of these pieces is "Upon my Lady Carliles walking in Hampton-Court garden," a dialogue between T. C., presumably Carew, and J. S., Suckling himself. While T. C. deifies the countess and falls into raptures over her beauty, J. S. mentally strips her until she is as naked as Eve in her first state. The degradation of Lady Carlisle from goddess to mortal woman to whore becomes complete when J. S. suggests in the final lines that countless fools have enjoyed the favors of this leading court beauty; if he and T. C. are men, they will do likewise rather than contenting themselves with merely praising her charms.

The humor of the poem should not distract the reader from the serious problem it raises. J. S., claiming that he is not "born to the Bay," disavows the title of poet; instead, he assumes the role of the plain-dealer who refuses to acquiesce in the fictions purveyed by Caroline lyricists. The dialogue dramatizes the opposition between "speaking" and "doing" that first appears in "A Soldier"; it also represents the externalization of an internal conflict inasmuch as Suckling, with little success, had for several years been penning the same platonic sentiments that he here fobs off on T. C. The attack on poetic conventions seems as much designed to conceal Suckling's inability to conform to the prevailing mode as to herald a new epoch in English lyric.

### LOVE AND SEXUALITY

Between 1632 and 1637, Suckling composed the lyrics for which he is best remembered. Although most of these poems trade on the blunt, skeptical attitude toward love that he affects in "Upon my Lady Carliles walking in Hampton-Court garden," others deal with love seriously, often in terms of the amatory Platonism that he had seemingly rejected. In the mid-1630's, Suckling was still searching for a congenial lyric stance, one that would allow him to reconcile love and sexuality, innocence and experience. Both Platonism and libertinism prove in the end to be inadequate solutions to the problem, since Suckling is uneasy with the one and much too strident in the other.

In the song "Honest Lover whosoever," the speaker gently prescribes the proper Platonic behavior for the youth who aspires to amatory correctness. The effect is one of humorous indulgence; Suckling treats the absurdities of young love with the same bemused tolerance that Geoffrey Chaucer displays in book 1 of *Troilus and Criseyde* (1382). The two poems "To his Rival" display the same comic delicacy, but it is a delicacy that begins to cloy.

In "Why so pale and wan, fond Lover?," however, Suckling finds a formula that combines sympathy and humor in a winning way. After counseling a pining young lover in the arts of seduction, the long-suffering speaker finally loses patience: In the last line he dismisses the unyielding woman with the exclamation, "The Devill take her." The use of comic reversal for purposes of closure becomes a standard element in Suckling's lyrics; the formula provides the perfect means for the poet to indulge his platonic sentiments while protesting his superiority to them with a wink or a leer.

### LIBERTINE LYRICS

Darker in tone are the libertine lyrics, those that insist that love is a mere physical act without moral or spiritual implications. Suckling employs an argumentative style that superficially recalls the elegies, songs,

and sonnets of John Donne, but the argument is less metaphorical and logically innovative than that of the elder poet. The tendency of these poems is to reduce love to mere appetite. In "Sonnet II," love is described as a good meal. In "Womans Constancy," lovemaking is compared to bees extracting pollen from a flower: "One lights, one tastes, gets in, gets out." Suckling reaches his nadir in "Loves Offence," in which he arrives at the conclusion that "love is the fart/ of every heart."

### "AGAINST FRUITION"

The two "Against Fruition" poems present Suckling at his most cynical. In "Against Fruition I," the speaker argues against sexual consummation, not because of any moral or philosophical scruples, but because fruition compares unfavorably with the more exquisite delights of sexual anticipation. The speaker argues that "Women enjoy'd (what s'ere before th'ave been)/ Are like Romances read, or sights once seen." This mistress, reified rather than deified, reappears throughout Suckling's lyrics of the mid-1630's. "Against Fruition II," an address to a mistress, is disturbing in its violence. One wonders how the lady should deal with the paradox, "Shee's but an honest whore that yeelds, although/ She be as cold as ice, as pure as snow." Suckling provides no answer to the dilemma. The subversion of the platonic arguments to a libertine end renders the "Against Fruition" poems a fascinating intellectual exercise, but they prove to be a poetic dead end.

### RECONCILING CONTRARIES

In the final years of his life, Suckling at last found a framework within which he could reconcile his own hateful contraries. In the prose "Letter to a Friend" and "An Answer," both undoubtedly written by Suckling, "Jack" attempts, with the usual libertine arguments, to dissuade his friend "Tom" from marriage. Tom, however, has the last word: Turning the libertine commonplaces upside down, he argues that the "ravishing *Realities*" of marriage far surpass the "pleasing *Dreames*" of the sort that Suckling champions in "Against Fruition I." The reconciliation of idealism and skepticism is here suggested rather than achieved; yet, the recognition that love and sexuality are not necessarily incompatible prefigures the high-spirited synthesis of "A Ballad upon a Wedding."

### "A BALLAD UPON A WEDDING"

In both style and substance, "A Ballad upon a Wedding" returns to the poems of the late 1620's. Suckling revitalizes the tired tradition of the epithalamium by describing an aristocratic wedding through the eyes of a yokel. The poem, written in an eight-eight-six ballad stanza, is remarkable for its exquisite imagery; in employing the homely details of rural life—mice, Katherine pears, a young colt—to blazon the bride's beauty, Suckling rediscovers the themes and techniques of his early Christmas poems. Coupled with the freshness of the imagery is a relaxed, accepting attitude toward the problem of love and sexuality that had bedeviled Suckling throughout his career. The poem closes with a comic reversal: The naïve speaker demonstrates that he is not so naïve after all when he speculates on what takes place in the nuptial chamber once the ceremony is over:

> At length the candles out, and now
> All that they had not done, they do:
>      What that is, who can tell?
> But I beleeve it was no more
> Than thou and I have done before
>      With *Bridget*, and with *Nell*.

The speaker's sexual awareness does not vitiate his fundamental innocence, nor does the bride's sexuality vitiate the romantic idealism that she inspires in the early parts of the poem. The real and the ideal are integrated into a comprehensive vision of love.

### "THE WITS"

Aside from "A Ballad upon a Wedding" and one other epithalamium, Suckling's final poems deal primarily with literary affairs. As with love, Suckling achieves a balanced, mature outlook toward his position as a poet only with a struggle. "The Wits," probably composed during the summer of 1637, describes the scramble for the laureateship touched off by the death of Jonson in August of that year. Employing the same ballad form he had used in "A Ballad upon a Wedding," Suckling lampoons all the chief Caroline pretenders to wit. Jonson and Carew come in for some especially hard knocks; only Viscount Falkland escapes the general opprobrium, perhaps because by this time he had given over poetry for philosophy. Suckling

alone is absent from the convocation: A bystander tells Apollo,

> He loved not the muses so well as his sport;
>      And
> Prized black eyes, or a lucky hit
> At bowls, above all the Trophies of wit.

Angered at this information, the deity promptly declares Suckling an outlaw in poetry. No role, perhaps, suited Suckling better. Falling back on the role of plaindealer he had perfected in his lyrics, Suckling rejects the poetic establishment but at the same time betrays his anxiety that he does not quite measure up to its standards.

### FINAL POEMS

In the last poems, however, Suckling demonstrates a growing willingness to accept his vocation. In "An Answer to some Verses made in his praise," he sheds his customary *sprezzatura* and, with convincing modesty, accepts the tribute of another poet. Suckling at long last takes his place among the wits he had feigned to scorn less than two years earlier.

The outbreak of civil war cut short Suckling's career. Before his death in 1642, however, he had achieved a poetic and personal maturity: His last poems, which suggest a new accommodation of the conflicting motives so evident in the earlier works, are also his best. Suckling's small oeuvre of some eighty poems is erratic in quality. Those pieces that argue doctrinaire positions on love and life tend to be his worst: The poems taking the stock platonic line are insipid, the libertine exercises too often grating. Nevertheless, Suckling displays throughout his work a sure sense for the comic and a sensitivity to rural life matched in this period only by Herrick. Suckling's poems record his progress, sometimes halting but always fascinating, toward a sure sense of himself and his art.

OTHER MAJOR WORKS

PLAYS: *Aglaura*, pr., pb. 1638; *The Goblins*, pr. 1638; *Brennoralt*, pr. 1646; *The Works of Sir John Suckling: The Plays*, 1971 (L. A. Beaurline, editor).

MISCELLANEOUS: *The Works of Sir John Suckling: The Non-Dramatic Works*, 1971 (Thomas Clayton, editor).

BIBLIOGRAPHY

Beaurline, L. A. "'Why So Pale and Wan?': An Essay in Critical Method." In *Seventeenth-Century English Poetry: Modern Essays in Criticism*, edited by William R. Keast. Rev. ed. New York: Oxford University Press, 1981. Beaurline sees the poem as a dramatic lyric with a "facetious" (in the sixteenth century sense) narrator whose wit reflects unity in situation, character, argument, and language. Beaurline also discusses the poem as a response to the more complex Metaphysical poetry.

Bloom, Harold, ed. *The Best Poems of the English Language: From Chaucer Through Frost*. New York: HarperCollins, 2004. Contains some poems by Suckling, selected by Bloom and with commentary by Bloom.

Clayton, Thomas. "'At Bottom a Criticism of Life': Suckling and the Poetry of Low Seriousness." In *Classic and Cavalier: Essays on Jonson and the Sons of Ben*, edited by Claude J. Summers and Ted-Larry Pebworth. Pittsburgh, Pa.: University of Pittsburgh Press, 1982. Clayton's essay provides an overview of Suckling criticism and proceeds to analyze four poems: the early "Upon St. Thomas's Unbelief," "An Answer to some Verses made in his praise," "Why so pale and wan, fond Lover?" and "Love's Clock." Places Suckling's work in its literary context.

Squires, Charles L. *Sir John Suckling*. Boston: Twayne, 1978. Squires covers Suckling's life, plays, poems, prose, and literary reputation. He also provides careful readings of several poems, and his criticism of the four plays is detailed. Suckling emerges as the spokesperson for the Cavalier era. Includes a chronology and bibliography.

Van Strien, Kees. "Sir John Suckling in Holland." *English Studies* 76, no. 5 (September, 1995): 443. Suckling traveled in the Low Countries in the early seventeenth century yet left no record of his journeys. A letter written by Suckling and additional material are pieced together to develop a picture of the writer during a little-known period of his life.

Wilcher, Robert. *The Discontented Cavalier: The Work of Sir John Suckling in its Social, Religious, Political, and Literary Contexts*. Newark: University of Delaware Press, 2007. Endeavors to examine the works of Suckling in the context of his times—in his social circumstances and position, the religious and political views of the time, and the literary world, including the Cavalier poets.

*Michael P. Parker*

# HENRY HOWARD, EARL OF SURREY

**Born:** Hunsdon, Hertfordshire, England; 1517
**Died:** London, England; January 19, 1547

## PRINCIPAL POETRY

*An Excellent Epitaffe of Syr Thomas Wyat*, 1542
*Songes and Sonettes*, 1557 (also known as *Tottel's Miscellany*)
*The Poems of Henry Howard, Earl of Surrey*, 1920, 1928 (Frederick Morgan Padelford, editor)

## OTHER LITERARY FORMS

Henry Howard, earl of Surrey, did not contribute to English literature with any other form besides poetry. His poetic innovations, however, helped to refine and stabilize English poetry.

## ACHIEVEMENTS

As a translator and original poet, Henry Howard, earl of Surrey, prepared the way for a number of important developments in English poetry. His translations and paraphrases are not slavishly literal; they are re-creations of classical and continental works in terms meaningful to Englishmen. He naturalized several literary forms—the sonnet, elegy, epigram, and satire—and showed English poets what could be done with various stanzas, metrical patterns, and rhyme schemes, including terza rima, ottava rima, and poulter's measure. He invented the English or Shakespearean sonnet (three quatrains and a couplet) and set another precedent by using the form for subjects other than love. His poems exerted considerable influence, for they circulated in manuscript for some time before they were printed. Forty of them appear in *Songes and Sonettes* (better known as *Tottel's Miscellany*), a collection of more than 270 works which saw nine editions by 1587 and did much to establish iambic meter in English poetry. Surrey shares with Sir Thomas Wyatt the distinction of having introduced the Petrarchan mode of amatory verse in England.

His innovations in poetic diction and prosody have had more lasting significance. Surrey refined English poetry of aureate diction, the archaic and ornate language cultivated by fifteenth century writers. His elegant diction formed the basis of poetic expression until well into the eighteenth century.

His greatest achievement is his demonstration of the versatility and naturalness in English of the iambic pentameter line. Surrey invented blank verse, which later poets brought to maturity. The metrical regularity of much of his rhymed verse (a regularity perhaps enhanced by Tottel's editor) had a stabilizing effect on English prosody, which had long been in a chaotic state. In *The Arte of English Poesie* (1589), George Puttenham hailed Wyatt and Surrey as "the first reformers of our English meetre and stile," for they "pollished our rude & homely maner of vulgar poesie." Until the present century Surrey's smoothness was generally preferred to Wyatt's rougher versification.

Surrey's essential quality, a concern with style, informed his poetry, his life, and the Tudor court of which he was a brilliant representative. Consistently as a poet and frequently as a courtier, he epitomized learning and grace; for his countrymen, he was an exemplar of culture.

BIOGRAPHY

Henry Howard, earl of Surrey from 1524, was the eldest son of Thomas Howard, third duke of Norfolk. The elder Howard, one of the most powerful leaders of the old nobility, saw to it that his heir received an excellent education. At the age of twelve, Surrey was translating Latin, French, Italian, and Spanish and practicing martial skills. He was selected as the companion of Henry Fitzroy, Henry VIII's illegitimate son who had been created duke of Richmond. The youths, both proud, impetuous, and insecure, were settled at Windsor in the spring of 1530. Surrey was married in 1532 to Lady Frances de Vere; the couple began living together

a few years later, and he was evidently devoted to her for the rest of his life.

Surrey and Richmond accompanied the king to France in the autumn of 1532. The young men resided with the French court, then dominated by Italian culture, for most of the following year. Surrey acquired courtly graces and probably became acquainted with the work of Luigi Alamanni, a Florentine writer of unrhymed verse. Shortly after Surrey and Richmond returned to the English court, the king's son married Surrey's sister Mary.

In 1540, Surrey was appointed steward of the University of Cambridge in recognition of his scholarship. Having also distinguished himself in martial games, in 1541 he was made Knight of the Garter. His military education was completed when he was sent to observe the King's continental wars. The first English aristocrat to be a man of letters, statesman, and soldier, the handsome and spirited earl was esteemed as a model courtier. During his final seven years, he was occupied with courtly, military, and domestic matters, finding time to write only when he was out of favor with Henry VIII or otherwise in trouble.

Early in 1543, Surrey, Thomas Clere, Thomas Wyatt the Younger, and another young man indulged in disorderly behavior that led to the earl's brief imprisonment in the Fleet. Still in the king's good graces, he spent most of the next three years serving in France and building an elegant, costly house in the classical style. As marshal of the field and commander of Boulogne, he proved to be a competent officer who did not hesitate to risk his own life. He was wounded while leading a courageous assault on Montreuil. After a defeat in a minor skirmish, he was recalled in the spring of 1546.

By that time, he had made enemies who were intent on destroying him. He was imprisoned for threatening a courtier who had called Norfolk morally unfit to be regent during the minority of the king's son, Edward. Making much of Surrey's pride in his Plantagenet ancestry, his enemies built a case that he intended to seize power. His request to be allowed to confront his chief accuser in single combat—characteristic of his effort to live by the chivalric code of a vanishing era—was denied. His sister Mary and certain supposed friends testified against him. Maintaining his innocence, Surrey

*Henry Howard, earl of Surrey* (Hulton Archive/Getty Images)

forcefully defended himself and reviled his enemies during an eight-hour trial for treason; but, like many others whom the Tudors considered dangerous or expendable, he was condemned and beheaded on Tower Hill.

## ANALYSIS

An aristocrat with a humanistic education, Henry Howard, earl of Surrey, considered literature a pleasant diversion. As a member of the Tudor court, he was encouraged to display his learning, wit, and eloquence by writing love poems and translating continental and classical works. The poet who cultivated an elegant style was admired and imitated by his peers. Poetry was not considered a medium for self-expression. In the production of literature, as in other polite activities, there were conventions to be observed. Even the works

that seem to have grown out of Surrey's personal experience also have roots in classical, Christian, Italian, or native traditions. Surrey is classical in his concern for balance, decorum, fluency, and restraint. These attributes are evident throughout his work—the amatory lyrics, elegies, didactic verses, translations, and biblical paraphrases.

## LOVE POEMS

Surrey produced more than two dozen amatory poems. A number of these owe something to Petrarch and other continental poets. The Petrarchan qualities of his work, as well as those of his successors, should not be exaggerated, however, for Tudor and Elizabethan poets were also influenced by native tradition and by rhetorical treatises which encouraged the equating of elegance and excellence. Contemporaries admired the fluency and eloquence which made Surrey, like Petrarch, a worthy model. His sonnet beginning "From Tuscan cam my ladies worthi race," recognized in his own time as polite verse, engendered the romantic legend that he served the Fair Geraldine (Elizabeth Fitzgerald, b. 1528?), but his love poems are now recognized as literary exercises of a type common in Renaissance poetry.

Surrey's courtly lovers complain of wounds; they freeze and burn, sigh, weep, and despair—yet continue to serve Love. Representative of this mode is "Love that doth raine and live within my thought," one of his five translations or adaptations of sonnets by Petrarch. The poem develops from a military conceit: The speaker's mind and heart are held captive by Love, whose colors are often displayed in his face. When the desired lady frowns, Love retreats to the heart and hides there, leaving the unoffending servant alone, "with shamfast looke," to suffer for his lord's sake. Uninterested in the moral aspects of this situation, Surrey makes nothing of the paradox of Love as conqueror and coward. He does not suggest the lover's ambivalence or explore the lady's motives. Wyatt, whose translation of the same sonnet begins "The longe love, that in my thought doeth harbor," indicates (as Petrarch does) that the lady asks her admirer to become a better man. Surrey's speaker, taught only to "love and suffre paine," gallantly concludes, "Sweet is the death that taketh end by love."

The point is not that Surrey's sonnet should be more like Wyatt's but that in this poem and in many of his lyrics, Surrey seems less concerned with the complexity of an experience than with his manner of presenting it. Most of the lines are smooth and regularly iambic, although there are five initial trochees. The poem's matter is carefully accommodated to its form. The first quatrain deals with Love, the second with the lady, and the third with the lover's plight. His resolve is summarized in the couplet: Despite his undeserved suffering, he will be loyal. The sonnet is balanced and graceful, pleasing by virtue of its musical qualities and intellectual conceit.

Some of the longer poems do portray the emotions of courtly lovers. The speaker in "When sommer toke in hand the winter to assail" observes (as several of Surrey's lovers do) that nature is renewed in spring, while he alone continues to be weak and hopeless. Casting off his despondency, he curses and defies Love. Then, realizing the gravity of his offense, he asks forgiveness and is told by the god that he can atone only by greater suffering. Now "undone for ever more," he offers himself as a "miror" for all lovers; "Strive not with love, for if ye do, it will ye thus befall." Lacking the discipline of the sonnet form, this poem in poulter's measure seems to sprawl. Surrey's amatory verse is generally most successful when he focuses on a relatively simple situation or emotion. "When sommer toke in hand the winter to assail," not his best work, is representative in showing his familiarity with native poetry: It echoes Geoffrey Chaucer's *Troilus and Criseyde* (1382) and describes nature in a manner characteristic of English poets. In seven other love poems, Surrey describes nature in sympathy with or in contrast to the lover's condition.

### A WOMAN'S PERSPECTIVE

At a time when most amatory verse was written from the male perspective, Surrey assumed a woman's voice in three of his lyrics. The speaker in "Gyrtt in my giltlesse gowne" defends herself against a charge of craftiness pressed by a male courtier in a companion poem beginning "Wrapt in my carelesse cloke." Accused of encouraging men she does not care for, the

lady compares herself to Susanna, who was slandered by corrupt elders. Remarking that her critic himself practices a crafty strategy—trying to ignite a woman's passion by feigning indifference—she asserts that she, like her prototype, will be protected against lust and lies. This pair of poems, if disappointing because Surrey has chosen not to probe more deeply into the behavior and emotions generated by the game of courtly love, demonstrates the poet's skill in presenting a speaker in a clearly defined setting or situation. His finest lyrics may fairly be called dramatic.

Two other monologues, "O happy dames, that may embrace" and "Good ladies, ye that have your pleasure in exyle," are spoken by women lamenting the absence of their beloved lords. They may have been written for Surrey's wife while he was directing the siege of Boulogne. Long separations troubled him, but his requests to the Privy Council for permission to bring his family to France were denied. After an exordium urging her female audience to "mourne with [her] awhyle," the narrator of "Good ladies" describes tormenting dreams of her "sweete lorde" in danger and at play with "his lytle sonne" (Thomas Howard, oldest of the Surreys' five children, was born in 1536). The immediate occasion for this poem, however personal, is consciously literary: The lady, a sorrowful "wight," burns like a courtly lover when her lord is absent, comforted only by the expectation of his return and reflection that "I feele by sower, how sweete is felt the more" (the sweet-sour antithesis was a favorite with courtly poets). Despite the insistent iambic meter characteristic of poulter's measure, one can almost hear a voice delivering these lines. In the best of his love poetry, Surrey makes new wholes of traditional elements.

### ELEGIAC POEMS

Surrey's elegiac poems reflect his background in rhetoric. Paying tribute to individuals, he would persuade his readers to become more virtuous men and women. "Wyatt resteth here, that quick could never rest," the first of his works to be published, devotes more attention to praise of Wyatt than to lament and consolation. Using the figure of *partitio* (division into parts), Surrey anatomizes the physique of this complete man in order to display his virtues—prudence, integrity, eloquence, justice, courage. Having devoted eight quatrains to praise, Surrey proceeds to the lament—the dead man is "lost" to those he might have inspired—with a consolation at the thought that his spirit is now in heaven. He implies that God has removed "this jewel" in order to punish a nation blind to his worth. In so coupling praise and dispraise, Surrey follows a precedent set by classical rhetoricians. He again eulogized Wyatt in two sonnets, "Dyvers thy death do dyversely bemoan" and "In the rude age," both attacking Wyatt's enemies. The former devotes a quatrain to each of two kinds of mourners, hypocrites who only seem to grieve and malefactors who "Weape envyous teares heer [his] fame so good." In the sestet, he sets himself apart: He feels the loss of so admirable a man. Here, as in a number of his sonnets, Surrey achieves a harmony of form and content. There is no evidence that he knew Wyatt personally. His tributes to the older courtier are essentially public performances, but they convey admiration and regret and offer a stinging rebuke to courtiers who do not come up to Wyatt's standard.

Many sixteenth century poets wrote elegies for public figures; more than twenty appear in *Tottel's Miscellany*. Surrey, as indicated above, was familiar with the literary tribute. In "Norfolk sprang thee," an epitaph for his squire Thomas Clere (d. 1545), he uses some of the conventions of epideictic poetry to express esteem, as well as grief, for the dead. Developed according to the biographical method of praise (seen also in "From Tuscan cam my ladies worthi race"), the sonnet specifies Clere's origins and personal relationships; it traces his career from his birth in Norfolk to his mortal wound at Montreuil—incurred while saving Surrey's life—to his burial in the Howards' chapel at Lambeth. By "placing" Clere geographically and within the contexts of chivalric and human relationships, Surrey immortalizes a brave and noble person. He has succeeded in writing a fresh, even personal poem while observing literary and rhetorical conventions.

Personal feeling and experience certainly went into "So crewell prison," a lament for Richmond (d. 1536) and the poet's youthful fellowship with him at Windsor—ironically, the place of his confinement as a penalty for having struck Edward Seymour. Subtly alluding to the *ubi sunt* tradition, he mentions remembered places, events, and activities—green and graveled courts, dewy meadows, woods, brightly dressed ladies, dances, games, chivalric competition, shared laughter and confidences, promises made and kept—as he does so, conveying his sense of loss. He praises, and longs for, not only his friend but also the irrecoverable past. Of Richmond's soul he says nothing. His consolation, if so it may be called, is that the loss of his companion lessens the pain of his loss of freedom. "So crewell prison," perhaps Surrey's best poem, is at once conventional and personal.

### DIDACTIC POEMS

Taught to regard the courtier as a counselor, Surrey wrote a few explicitly didactic pieces. His sonnet about Sardanapalus, "Th' Assyryans king, in peas with fowle desyre," portrays a lustful, cowardly ruler. Such depravity, Surrey implies, endangers virtue itself. The poem may allude to King Henry VIII, who had executed two Howard queens. (Surrey witnessed Anne Boleyn's trial and Catherine Howard's execution.) The degenerate monarch in Surrey's sonnet, however, bears few resemblances to Henry VIII, who had often shown his regard for Norfolk's heir and Richmond's closest friend. John Gower, John Lydgate, and other poets had also told the story of Sardanapulus as a "mirror" for princes. Surrey's "Laid in my quyett bedd" draws upon Horace's *Ars poetica* (c. 17 B.C.E.; *The Art of Poetry*) and the first of his *Satires* (35 B.C.E., 30 B.C.E.; English translation, 1567). The aged narrator, after surveying the ages of man, remarks that people young and old always wish to change their estate; he concludes that boyhood is the happiest time, though youths will not realize this truth before they become decrepit. Like certain of the love poems, "Laid in my quyett bedd" illustrates Surrey's dramatic ability.

### "LONDON, HAS THOU ACCUSED ME"

The mock-heroic "London, has thou accused me" was probably written while Surrey was imprisoned for harassing and brawling with some citizens and breaking windows with a stonebow. As C. W. Jentoft points out, the satirist, presenting himself as a God-sent "scourge for synn," seems to be delivering an oration. "Thy wyndowes had don me no spight," he explains; his purpose was to awaken Londoners secretly engaged in deadly sins to their peril. Appropriating the structure of the classical oration, he becomes, in effect, not the defendant but the prosecutor of a modern Babylon. The peroration, fortified with scriptural phrasings, warns of divine judgment.

### POETRY TRANSLATIONS

Surrey's translations also reflect the young aristocrat's classical and humanistic education. He translated two poems advocating the golden mean—a Horatian ode and an epigram by Martial. In the former ("Of thy lyfe, Thomas") he imitates the terseness of the original. "Marshall, the thinges for to attayne," the first English translation of that work, is also remarkably concise. His intention to re-create in English the style of a Latin poet is evident in his translations of the second and fourth books of the *Aeneid* (c. 29-19 B.C.E.; English translation, 1553). He did not attempt to reproduce Vergil's unrhymed hexameters in English Alexandrines (as Richard Stanyhurst was to do) or to translate them into rhymed couplets (as the Scottish poet Gawin Douglas had done). Familiar with the decasyllabic line of Chaucer and other native poets and the *verso sciolto* (unrhymed verse) of sixteenth century Italy, he devised blank verse, the form that was to be refined by Christopher Marlowe, William Shakespeare, and John Milton.

Textual scholars have encountered several problems in studying Surrey's translation of the *Aeneid*. His manuscripts are not extant, and all printed versions appeared after his death. The work may have been undertaken as early as 1538 or as late as 1544; in the light of his service at court and in France, it seems likely that the translation was done intermittently. Modern scholars now favor an early period of composition, which would make this translation earlier than many of Surrey's other works and help to account for their refined, decorous style.

Another issue is the relationship of Surrey's work to the *Eneados* of Gawin Douglas (1474?-1522), whose translation had circulated widely in manuscript during Surrey's youth. Scholar Florence Ridley found evidence of Douglas's influence in more than 40 percent of Surrey's lines. In book 4, perhaps completed later than book 2, Surrey borrowed from Douglas less frequently. There is other evidence that his style was maturing and becoming more flexible: more frequent run-ons, feminine endings, pauses within the line, and metrical variations.

The distinctive qualities of Surrey's translation are largely owing to his imitation of Vergil's style. A young humanist working in an immature language and using a new form, Surrey was trying, as Italian translators had done, to re-create in the vernacular his Latin master's compactness, restraint, and stateliness. He did not always succeed. Generally avoiding both prosaic and aureate vocabulary, he uses relatively formal diction. To a modern reader accustomed to the blank verse developed by later poets, the iambic meter is so regular as to be somewhat monotonous. By means of patterned assonance, consonance, and internal rhyme, as well as the placement of caesuras, he has achieved a flowing movement that approximates Vergilian verse paragraphs. Phonetic effects often pleasing in themselves heighten emotional intensity and help to establish the phrase, not the line, as the poetic unit. It is not surprising, then, that Thomas Warton called Surrey England's first classical poet. Imitation led to innovation, the creation of a form for English heroic poetry. Even though blank verse did not come into general use until late in the sixteenth century, Surrey's achievement remains monumental.

### BIBLICAL PARAPHRASES

The paraphrases of Ecclesiastes 1-5 and Psalms 55, 73, and 88, Surrey's most nearly autobiographical works, portray the "slipper state" of life in the Tudor court. Probably written during his final imprisonment in late 1546, they speak of vanity and vexation of spirit and cry out against vicious enemies, treacherous friends, and a tyrant who drinks the blood of innocents. Like Wyatt, whose penitential psalms he admired, he used Joannes Campensis's Latin paraphrases which had been published in 1532. Surrey's translations are free, amplifying and at times departing from the Vulgate and Campensis, as in this line from his version of Ecclesiastes 2: "By princely acts [such as the pursuit of pleasure and building of fine houses] strave I still to make my fame indure." Although his background was Catholic, these poems express Protestant sentiments.

In his versions of Psalms 73 and 88, he speaks of God's "elect" and "chosen," apparently placing himself in that company. While praying for forgiveness in Psalm 73, he notes that his foes are going unscathed and asks why he is "scourged still, that no offence have doon." Psalm 55 calls for divine help as he faces death and exulting enemies; at the end of this unpolished, perhaps unfinished poem, Surrey completely departs from his printed sources to inveigh against wolfish adversaries. The time to live was almost past, but it was not yet the time to keep silence. Like the other biblical paraphrases, this work has chiefly biographical interest. Expecting imminent execution, Surrey was still experimenting with prosody: Psalm 55 is the one poem in this group to be written in unrhymed hexameters rather than poulter's measure. Even in his last works, the poet is generally detached and self-effacing. Surrey's greatest legacy to English poets is a concern for fluent, graceful expression.

OTHER MAJOR WORKS

TRANSLATIONS: *The Fourth Boke of Virgill*, 1554; *Certain Bokes of Virgiles Aenaeis*, 1557.

BIBLIOGRAPHY

Childs, Jessie. *Henry VIII's Last Victim: The Life and Times of Henry Howard, Earl of Surrey*. New York: Thomas Dunne Books/St. Martin's Press, 2007. Discusses the poet's life in detail, in particular his relationship with Henry VIII.

Heale, Elizabeth. *Wyatt, Surrey, and Early Tudor Poetry*. New York: Longman, 1998. An indispensable resource that brings together critical analysis of the early Tudor poets. Those who would study Edmund Spenser and William Shakespeare's sonnets will benefit from the reading of these wonderful authors.

Lines, Candace. "The Erotic Politics of Grief in Surrey's 'So crewell prison.'" *Studies in English Literature, 1500-1900* 46, no. 1 (2006): 1-26. Provides a close examination of Surrey's well-known poem, focusing on his expression of grief.

Sessions, William A. *Henry Howard, the Poet Earl of Surrey: A Life*. 1999. Reprint. New York: Oxford University Press, 2003. Sessions's narrative combines historical scholarship with close readings of poetic texts and Tudor paintings to reveal the unique life of the first Renaissance courtier and a poet who wrote and created radically new forms.

Spearing, A. C. *Medieval to Renaissance in English Poetry*. New York: Cambridge University Press, 1985. After discussing Renaissance classicism in Surrey's poetry, Spearing proceeds to extended analyses of three poems: two epitaphs on Sir Thomas Wyatt and "So crewell prison," the poem about Surrey's imprisonment at Windsor.

Thomson, Patricia. "Wyatt and Surrey." In *English Poetry and Prose, 1540-1674*, edited by Christopher Ricks. 1970. Reprint. London: Penguin Books, 1993. Thomson first compares Surrey and Sir Thomas Wyatt to John Skelton, whose poetry was primarily late medieval, then discusses Surrey and particularly Wyatt as inheritors of the Petrarchan tradition.

Walker, Greg. *Writing Under Tyranny: English Literature and the Henrician Reformation*. New York: Oxford University Press, 2005. Contains a chapter on Surrey and Sir Thomas Wyatt that examines their experiences writing under Henry VIII and the innovative forms that Surrey produced.

*Mary De Jong*

---

# JONATHAN SWIFT

**Born:** Dublin, Ireland; November 30, 1667
**Died:** Dublin, Ireland; October 19, 1745

PRINCIPAL POETRY

*Cadenus and Vanessa*, 1726
*On Poetry: A Rapsody*, 1733
*Verses on the Death of Dr. Swift, D.S.P.D.*, 1739
*The Poems of Jonathan Swift*, 1937, 1958 (3 volumes; Harold Williams, editor)

OTHER LITERARY FORMS

Jonathan Swift's major satires in prose are *A Tale of a Tub* (1704) and *Gulliver's Travels* (originally titled *Travels into Several Remote Nations of the World, in Four Parts, by Lemuel Gulliver, First a Surgeon, and Then a Captain of Several Ships*, 1726); both are included in the most useful general collection, *The Prose Works of Jonathan Swift* (1939-1968; 14 volumes.; Herbert Davis, editor); but *"A Tale of a Tub" to Which*

*Is Added "The Battle of the Books" and the "Mechanical Operation of the Spirit"* (1958, A. C. Guthkelch and D. Nichol Smith, editors) is also notable. Swift is also master of the short satiric treatise, as evidenced by *Argument Against Abolishing Christianity* (1708; first published as *An Argument to Prove That the Abolishing of Christianity in England May, as Things Now Stand, Be Attended with Some Inconveniences and Perhaps Not Produce Those Many Good Effects Proposed Thereby*) and *A Modest Proposal for Preventing the Children of Poor People of Ireland from Being a Burden to Their Parents or the Country, and for Making Them Beneficial to the Public* (1729; known as *A Modest Proposal*). Noteworthy as well are his comical satires in prose, best exemplified by the "Bickerstaff" pamphlets against Partridge the Almanac-Maker (such as *Predictions for the Year 1708*, 1708; *The Accomplishment of the First of Mr. Bickerstaff's Predictions*, 1708; and *A Vindication of Isaac Bickerstaff, Esq.*, 1709). Swift's major political diatribes are included in *The Drapier's Letters to the People of Ireland* (1935); other notable political writings include his contributions to *The Examiner* (1710-1711); and the treatise termed *The Conduct of the Allies and of the Late Ministry, in Beginning and Carrying on the Present War* (1711). The letters are assembled in *The Correspondence of Jonathan Swift* (5 volumes.; 1963-1965, Harold Williams, editor). Equally interesting is his chatty and informal *Journal to Stella* (1766, 1768).

ACHIEVEMENTS

By common consent, Jonathan Swift is perhaps the greatest satirist who ever lived. His prose creation *A Tale of a Tub* is clearly one of the densest and richest satires ever composed. His terse mock-treatise *A Modest Proposal* is considered the most brilliant short prose satire in the English language. The long pseudonarrative of his later years, *Gulliver's Travels*, is acknowledged to be his masterpiece.

For this very mastery, Swift was in his time considerably dreaded and feared. In his case, the pen was mightier than the sword, and politicians trembled and dunces quavered at his power. In many instances, his satire could instantly shade into invective, and Swift wrote many powerful tirades against individuals whom he openly named, reducing them to impotence by powerful mockery and public scorn. At one time, he was the most important political writer for the ruling Tory party; his essays, projects, and analyses were a potent force in the halls of government.

However, all was not terror, violence, and indecorum. In addition to his nasty side—his "serious air"—he could, as Alexander Pope acknowledged, praising him in *The Dunciad* (1728-1743), take his rightful place as a great comedian; he could "laugh and shake in Rab'lais' easy chair." Swift was terribly potent precisely because he could be so terribly funny. He was an absolute master at writing little idiotic mock-solemn invitations to dinner, in composing poetry in pig Latin, in donning masks and voices and assuming the roles of others. He will be remembered as the imitator of the voices of dunces: the perplexed but grandly complacent "Modern" hack writer of *A Tale of a Tub*; the utterly self-satisfied Isaac Bickerstaff (the Astrologer who could See Into and Predict the Future); the ceaselessly chattering poor female servant, Frances Harris; the quintessential public-defender M. B.; the "Patriot" Drapier; and the tautological and ever-to-be-befooled Lemuel Gulliver.

Finally, Swift was a poet of considerable skill. He deprecated his verse; he preferred throughout his career the jog-trot of the octosyllabic line, deliberately avoiding the heroic couplet that was in his day the reigning poetic form. He chose to treat "low" topics and paltry occasions in his verse, and he was ever fond of coarseness: Many of his poems take up nearly unmentionable topics—particularly excrement. For such reasons, Swift was for long not taken seriously as a poet; the staid Victorians, for example, found in him nothing of the Arnoldian "high seriousness" and grim cheerfulness that heralded and endorsed progress. However, there has been a renewed interest in Swift's poetry, and in this realm too, Jonathan Swift is coming to occupy his rightful—and rightfully very high—place.

BIOGRAPHY

Jonathan Swift, as Louis Bredvold has observed, was the "greatest genius" among the Augustan wits, and even more clearly "one of the most absorbing and enigmatic personalities in literature." He was a man of brute talent with the pen, a man with remarkable intensity and drive, yet one who was frequently alienated and rebuffed. Of English parentage, Swift was born in 1667 in Dublin, seven months after his father's death. In straitened circumstances, Swift was reared in Ireland. His father had settled there at the time of the Restoration of Charles II (1660); his paternal grandfather had been an Anglican minister in England. Swift and his mother were dependent on a relatively well-to-do uncle, who did see to young Jonathan's education at Kilkenny Grammar School (at that time, the best in the land). Swift's mother, Abigail, returned to England to live; Swift remained in Ireland, and subsequently, with the help of his uncle, attended Trinity College, Dublin.

Going to England in 1689, Swift obtained a secretaryship under Sir William Temple at Moor Park in Surrey, where he resided with few interruptions for some ten years. Temple had been a major diplomat, an ambassador to The Hague, and a wise conservative who had even arranged for the future King William's marriage. Twice refusing to become secretary of state, he had at last retired with dignity and honor to a rural plot. At the least, Swift could anticipate great instruction and "connections," but he never did realize any actual preferment from this affiliation. It was also at Moor Park that Swift met "Stella" (Esther Johnson), the eight-year-old daughter of Sir William's housekeeper; a compelling and intimate relationship (still not fully fathomed or explained) developed over the years between the two, which led to Stella's following Swift to Ireland and living close to him for the remainder of her life. Neither ever married. In 1694, Swift became an Anglican priest in Dublin, with a remote parish in the isolated countryside at Kilroot. Nevertheless, Swift stayed mostly at Moor Park in England until Temple's death in 1699, whereupon he accepted the chaplaincy to the earl of Berkeley, who was settling in Ireland as Lord Justice. Still, preferment and advancement eluded the young man.

After several false starts in literature, Swift found his true voice—in prose and in verse—as a satirist. He wrote many short, incisive poems in the early years of the new century, and a prose masterpiece, *A Tale of a Tub*, appeared in 1704. The next decade was perhaps the most crucial in his career, for Swift helped the Tories gain office after a lengthy absence, and he became their chief spokesperson, apologist, and potent political satirist (1710-1714). His power and success in London were inordinate; he did not lack glory. During this period, Swift held court with the brightest of the Tory wits in the so-called Scriblerus Club (the most famous of its kind in literary history), which included such distinguished authors as Alexander Pope, John Arbuthnot, Matthew Prior, and John Gay.

Ireland, however, could not be avoided for long. Swift had held (though as an absentee) a post as minister to the parish of Laracor in Ireland, and the most he could extract from his political allies (he had every reason to expect more) was the deanship of St. Patrick's in Dublin. Moreover, there were other reasons for dis-

*Jonathan Swift* (Library of Congress)

illusionment: The Tory leaders had taken to squabbling among themselves, and their authority became precarious. Unable to patch up this rift, Swift sadly withdrew from London. The Tories fell resoundingly from power in 1714, with the sudden death of Queen Anne. There were immediate political repercussions: A Whig government even went so far as to seek to imprison the Tory leadership. Swift had already retired—for safety and out of necessity—to Ireland. He would seldom be able to return.

After a period of quiet adjustment to the catastrophe that brought him to exile (1714-1720), Swift finally came to terms with his destiny and entered on a great creative period. From 1719 on, he wrote a great deal of poetry and produced his prose masterpieces, *Gulliver's Travels* in 1726 and *A Modest Proposal* in 1729. His great period culminated with *Verses on the Death of Dr. Swift, D.S.P.D.* and *On Poetry*.

In his old age, Swift was kept busy with cathedral affairs, with overseeing an extensive edition of his "Collected Works" being printed by George Faulkner in Dublin throughout the 1730's, and with polishing old works that he had not previously brought to fruition. His health—never too hardy—commenced rapidly to decline. After what is believed to have been a crippling stroke in 1742, Swift was declared incompetent, and others were assigned by a court to handle his affairs. He died in October, 1745, and was buried in St. Patrick's Cathedral. As a final touch of satiric bravado, Swift in his will left his little wealth for the establishment of a "hospital" or asylum for incurables—both fools and madmen. Jonathan Swift, if he had had the last word, would have implied that among humankind, there are fools and knaves—and little else.

## ANALYSIS

In 1689, Jonathan Swift, at the age of twenty-two, came to Moor Park to serve as secretary under Sir William Temple. It was to be Swift's brush with gentility, polite learning, and aristocracy, and it served him well. As a raw, aspiring man of letters, the youthful Swift hoped to make his name as a serious poet, and in this period, he composed a series of rather maudlin and certainly pedestrian poems that sought to soar in the panegyric strain, Pindaric odes in the manner of Abraham

Cowley (and of John Dryden in his youth): polite but plodding celebrations and praises—to King William after the Battle of the Boyne ("Ode to the King," 1690-1691), to a supposedly Learned Organization ("Ode to the Athenian Society," 1692), to William Sancroft, to the successful Irish playwright William Congreve, and two effusions to Sir William Temple himself (all in 1692 and 1693). Like many young beginners, he was rather excessively enamored of his own productions ("I am overfond of my own writings . . . and I find when I writt what pleases me I am Cowley to my self and can read it a hundred times over," he tells a relative in a letter of May 3, 1692), but by 1693 even Swift himself recognized the hopeless nature of this stiflingly formal and elevated gentlemanly verse, for he broke off rudely in the midst of his second Ode to Temple and renounced such a Muse forever.

Certainly, *politesse* and officious, gaudy, and Cavalier verse (already a mode passing out of date since the Restoration in 1660) were never to be Swift's forte, yet even in these formal pieces there are some sparks and signs of the later Swift, for he could not restrain periodic outbursts of an inborn satiric temper as in "Ode to the Athenian Society":

> *She seems a Medly of all Ages*
> With a huge Fardingal to swell her Fustian Stuff,
> A new Comode, a *Top-knot*, and a Ruff,
> Her Face patch't o'er with *Modern Pedantry*,
>     With a long sweeping Train
> Of Comments and Disputes, ridiculous and vain,
>     *All of old Cut with a new Dye. . . .*

In a rather strained posture—even for a satirist—he let himself boast of "*My hate, whose lash just heaven has long decreed/ Shall on a day make sin and folly bleed . . .*" ("To Mr. Congreve"). In his poem to Congreve, in fact, he had recommended that the writer should "*Beat not the dirty paths where vulgar feet have trod,/ But give the vigorous fancy room.*"

### ANTIPOETIC PRACTICES

Within a year Swift would take his own advice and relinquish oppressive formal structures and grand studied compliments. Indeed, throughout the remainder of his career as a poet, Swift purposely eschewed all hints of genteel elegance, polite praise, or formal density.

Thereafter, his verse was rough, chatty, and colloquial, deliberately informal, low in diction and in subject— scrupulously out of the beaten track of the faddish mode in verse, the heroic couplet. For the rest of his life, Swift's poetry took its measure instead from the witty, learned, and coyly antipoetic practices of Samuel Butler's *Hudibras* (1663, 1664, 1678), making use of the almost singsong, Mother Goose-like octosyllabic couplet, pedestrian subjects, far-fetched rhymes, and coarse mien. In addition, Swift never indulged in the longer epical modes so much in favor in his day; his poems remained prosaic and short.

### "VERSES WROTE IN A LADY'S IVORY TABLE-BOOK"

Hence, in the next extant verse of Swift to appear ("Verses wrote in a Lady's Ivory Table-Book"), the new mode is almost fully formulated and matured. He mocks the typical empty-headed young lady whose hall guest book is entirely scribbled over (by suitors and herself as well) with the muck of self-regard and of shallow tastes, flirtatious clichés, and torpid vanities; such "Brains Issue" the poet considers "Excrement"— and real gentlemen are warned to avoid such a tart:

> Whoe're expects to hold his part
> In such a Book and such a Heart,
> If he be Wealthy and a Fool
> Is in all Points the fittest Tool,
> Of whom it may be justly said,
> He's a Gold Pencil tipt with Lead.

A number of strategies in operation here are certainly worthy of note, for they remained Swift's hallmarks throughout his career. First, Swift owes many of his themes to the Restoration and its stage themes of fops, seducers, and fashionable lovers; a frequent topic of his art is the idle, frivolous, vacant, and flirtatious city maiden and her mindless, posturing fop or "gallant." Swift endows these conventional and even humdrum subjects with venomous sting: Such a woman is, in his imagery, no better than a whore, a prostitute of fashion, and her suitors are portrayed as perverse and impotent whoremasters: "tools" "tipt with Lead."

### SAVAGE SATIRE

Swift's poetry transforms the polite inanities of social intercourse into monstrosities. His poetry gains all the more telling force precisely because of its seemingly innocuous outer clothing; bobbing along in quaint, informal four-footed lines, and immersed in chatty diction, the verse promises to be no more than light and witty. However, the images soon transform such poetry into a species of savagery. Swift once mildly observed in one of his poems that "*Swift* had the Sin of Wit no venial Crime," and that "Humour, and Mirth, had Place in all he writ. . . ." It is true that Wit and Mirth are featured dramatically in virtually all Swift's creations, but let no reader be lulled into expectations of mild pleasure and repose, for the Dean's poetry often turns wit and humor deliberately sour.

### "THE DESCRIPTION OF A SALAMANDER"

A good example of this transformation may be observed in an early lampoon, "The Description of a Salamander," a deliberate cold-blooded attack on Baron Cutts the warrior, who had been nicknamed the "Salamander." In the poem, Cutts is metamorphosized into a salamander and reptile. Swift savors setting up the analogy, and does so with painstaking nicety:

> . . . should some Nymph who ne'er was cruel,
> Like *Carleton* cheap or fam'd *Duruel*,
> Receive the Filth which he ejects,
> She soon would find, the same Effects,
> Her tainted Carcase to pursue,
> As from the *Salamander*'s Spue;
> A dismal shedding of her Locks
> And, if no Leprosy, a Pox.

Although this is an early effort, there is no doubt that Swift is adept at being ruthlessly unkind: words such as *cheap, Filth, Spue,* and *Pox* are staccato-like Anglo-Saxon monosyllables, and only seemingly simplistic. What is more, they are amassed with furious delectation and vigor. Nevertheless, the poem remains tightly contained, purporting throughout to be a calm, disinterested argument, a scientific demonstration, a precise comparison. Swift's robustness arises precisely because he can interfuse the careful language of reasoning with the gross irrationality of nightmarish visions of infectious and loathsome vice and disease.

### CLASSICAL INFLUENCES

Needless to say, a number of Swift's poems are less vicious, but there is always in them a certain flickering spark that implies imminent combustion. A number of his early poems are deliberate imitations or paraphrases of Horace, and others follow Ovid in telling a far-fetched story. Swift learns much from both of these classical authors about the manipulation of animal imagery, about the handling of diverse tones, and above all about sophistication: the juggling with diction, the juxtaposition of high and low styles, and the sly use of irony and indirection. Behind these deft usages is the potential adder and spike of the Swiftian assault.

### CITY PASTORALS

Two companion pieces in this early period are almost universally admired: "A Description of the Morning" and "A Description of a City Shower." Both are studied presentations, ironic, quiet, and steady, while they also demonstrate another of Swift's strengths: parody. The two poems are species of City Pastoral, a mock-form that laughs at the fad of writing polite bucolic pieces about some never-never land of innocent shepherds and of the happy life in a pristine garden. Swift simply moves eclogues and idylls heavy-handedly indoors—and into the reeking, overcrowded, dirty London of the eighteenth century. The result (a frequent strategy in much of Swift's verse) is polite Vergilian verse that is overcome by gross content: thieving swains, whorish nymphs, and maids and apprentices too lazy to do any work.

### EXPOSING AFFECTATION

Swift likes nothing better than to puncture civilization's postures, to divulge what Henry Fielding called affectation, and to blast holes in a nation's language of hypocrisy, concealment, euphemism, and deceit. Such uncovering can take the form of exposé: polite, tedious love-verse that is merely a tissue of clichés is rigorously parodied and exposed by hilarious ineptitudes of language ("A Love Song in the Modern Taste"), or a gross physical deformity is laid bare as a "modern nymph" disrobes and reveals herself to be in the last stages of disintegration from syphilis ("A Beautiful Young Nymph Going to Bed"). Swift would argue that false and impure language is exactly as viciously deceptive as ulcerous and pox-ridden physical reality. Both are instances of human-made corruption. With satiric glee, Swift loves to paint a running sore in technicolor.

Swift is not always savage, cunning, or voracious.

Some of his most pleasant verse remains Horatian, and plays quieter games. An early piece, "Mrs. Harris' Petition," reveals his mastery of mimicry; he assumes the voice and exact intonations of a middle-aged busybody servant who has lost her purse—and considers that event the greatest cataclysm since The Flood. (For a similar tone of voice, consult "Mary the Cook-Maid's Letter to Dr. Sheridan"). One of his longest poems in the early years, *Cadenus and Vanessa* is a masterpiece of coy indirection; one Esther Vanhomrigh had indiscreetly pursued the older Swift with some heat and passion: A polite and circuitous allegorical tale is used to cool her down and warn her off.

### POEMS TO STELLA

Swift is at times at his most elegant (if such a term may be applied to his hobble-footed, four-stressed, grossly rhymed lines) in a number of poems over the years (1719-1727) to Stella. These are usually poems on slight topics, birthday celebrations, or graver reflections in the later years on her growing illness. They are always light and bantering in style, polite yet quaintly backhanded with compliments, and sometimes almost insulting. Swift was a master not only of the direct attack but also of ironic indirection, and, following Vincent Voiture, he loved what he called "raillery"—a kind of bantering jest that paid compliments by seeming complaints and mock- or near-insults. A good example would be lines from "On Stella's Birth-day 1719":

> STELLA this Day is thirty four,
> (We shan't dispute a Year or more)
> However Stella, be not troubled,
> Although thy Size and Years are doubled,
> Since first I saw Thee at Sixteen
> The brightest Virgin on the Green,
> So little is thy Form declin'd
> Made up so largely in thy Mind.

The jesting continues until that last line, and so do the whimsical inaccuracies: Stella was not thirty-four (but older), and Swift had not first met her when she was sixteen (more likely at eight); she is obviously invited to wince at the trite phrases about bright Virgins, lofty queens, village greens, and sweet sixteens, for these are the pabulum of most pedestrian Muses (even today they thrive in popular lyrics and Hallmark cards). Finally, there is the innuendo about her girth—so paradoxically multiplied but nevertheless "So little . . . declin'd." Swift could not resist in some way speaking the truth. Much of his verse is of this seriocomic, semiprivate nature (and includes epigrams, puns, some pig Latin, invitations to dinner, verse epistles, windowpane scribblings, and merest notes), but all of it has a certain effervescence—and the Stella poems are surely the most accomplished in this vein.

### POLITICAL INVECTIVE

Another body of poems, like the verse attacking Lord Cutts, consists of savage political invective, bred of the heat and animosity of factions, contentions, and parties. Some of the most acerb include a potent libel against Richard Tighe in "Mad Mullinix and Timothy," a most vicious portrayal of the duke of Marlborough, the renowned Whig general ("A Satirical Elegy on the Death of a late Famous General"), and, in his strongest poem of this type, a savage libelous attack on the Irish Parliament, in "A Character, Panegyric, and Description of the Legion Club," which indicts the group as a crowd of mad demoniacs. One of the most artful of these politically tinged poems incorporates themes about similar corruptions in the arts: *On Poetry: A Rapsody.* Like Pope's *Peri-Bathos: Or, The Art of Sinking in Poetry* (1727), this poem purports to be a manual of instruction, a how-to handbook guiding one who seeks to become a degenerate modern-day political hanger-on and hack writer. The final implication is that most men are already so degraded, abject, and profligate that there ought to be no one, really, who needs such "helpful" advice. That is exactly Swift's point: The so-called Age of Reason is in reality decimated and dissolute, the last, the Fifth or Iron Age of Vice (in Hesiod's terms): the final stage of creation's decline. Like Juvenal before him, Swift the satirist found it expedient to assume the worst about humankind's propensity for deterioration and debasement.

### SCATOLOGICAL POEMS

Perhaps Swift's most renowned poems are his most shocking; they defame women, employ scatology, and have often been considered "obscene" and even "unprintable." They use the typical Swiftian ploy of jolting the reader into paying attention by using paradoxes and coarse language, and they include in their number some of Swift's best verse. On the borderline in this category are such fine poems as "The Progress of Marriage" and "Phillis: Or, The Progress of Love," poems that speak in the crassest terms of ill-matched marriages, and which frankly wage battle against the trifling romantic slogans that presume that "true-love" and "feelings" and "good intentions" and "high hopes" will win out against all practical odds. Rather grimly, Swift shows—in gruesome detail—the fate of such marriages.

The most blatantly offensive of the scatalogical poems include "The Lady's Dressing Room," "A Beautiful Young Nymph Going to Bed," "Strephon and Chloe," and "Cassinus and Peter." Every one of these poems mocks the "double standard" that allows men to be most coarse in their everyday affairs and yet somehow naïve about the single topic of women (whom they place on pedestals in the tradition of courtly love). This self-deception leads inevitably to disillusionment, misery, and the destruction of lives, just as it has made for sheaves of tedious, lackluster love poetry. In Swift's poems, rather dirty modern urban swains are baldly confronted with nymphs who defecate and stink (as do all people) and who in extreme cases are coming apart with syphilis and gonorrhea. The bane of Venus, in short, is that she is fetid and venereal. As a consequence of such a confrontation, the knavish and foolish men in these poems usually run mad—precisely as Gulliver does when he encounters man-as-Yahoo. The lesson applies as well to these dubious Lovers as it does to Gulliver: They are so easily unhinged because their minds never were screwed very well together; they have trained themselves—and society has trained them—to ignore or distort reality, to set up screens and shields and ideals—clouds of obfuscation that cut one off from everyday physical reality. Swift implies that if such men shut out actuality, they deserve the manure and laughter he heaps rather furiously on them. These verses deserve more consideration than they usually receive.

### VERSES ON THE DEATH OF DR. SWIFT, D.S.P.D.

Swift's most fruitful years span the period from 1730 to 1733, and special notice should be given to his masterpiece, the 484-line *Verses on the Death of Dr. Swift, D.S.P.D.* In it, the Dean chooses to defend a rather nasty maxim by François La Rouchefoucauld asserting that adversities befalling our friends do not necessarily displease us. Here is a sterling opportunity to expose human perversity, and Swift rises to the occasion. He points out amicably that all people like to get ahead of their acquaintances, and especially of their friends. Then he commences to use a marvelous example to "prove" his case: the occasion of his own demise. Sure enough, as Swift would have it, all his friends in some way gloat over his passing. Even more curiously, enemies actually lament the Dean's death. Before the poem is through, it is paradoxically worked out that only men "indifferent," absolute strangers, can ever fairly assess one's merits or judge one's worth.

There is a further stickler that the reader should grasp in the thorny thicket of ironies infesting Swift's delightful poem: All men do in some way indulge in self-aggrandizement; a man naturally exalts his ego over others, and does not mind in the least treading on toes (or heads) in the implacable urge to ascend. The last touch of irony includes even Dean Swift, who was so curiously "generous" in consenting hypothetically to "sacrifice" his own life so that he might win this argument. That is the very point: Swift, like the rest of humankind, will stop at nothing to salve his ego or to engineer a victory—even the most trifling triumph in a debate. Men will sacrifice friends, relatives, and even twist and convert enemies, so that they might, in Swift's fond phrase, "lie uppermost." Men are engendered in heaps; it is each one's voracious inclination to climb to the top. Thus stands one of Swift's most pleasing (and yet vexing) conundrums.

### CRITICAL RESPONSE

For some two hundred years, Swift's poetry was seldom taken very seriously; it was, after all, not in the mainstream of the poetry of his own day, and much of it was crass and vulgar in the bargain. Swift himself had contributed to this downplaying of his talents, typically paying himself a left-handed compliment: His verse, he reports in a prose addendum to a poem ("A Left-handed Letter to Dr. Sheridan," 1718), is slight, for he composes with his "Left Hand, [when he] was in great Haste, and the other Hand was employed at the same Time in writing some Letters of Business." More and more often, however, recent criticism has been coming

to take that self-deprecation with a grain of salt. The truth is that Swift's poetry is both dexterous and sinister—full of easy grace as well as of two-fisted power. His poems are disturbing yet pleasing, and growing numbers of readers are acknowledging that vexation and that pleasure. Perhaps the oppressive reality of warfare, terrorism, and recession has suggested that Swift and La Rochefoucauld came close to putting humanity in its place.

### OTHER MAJOR WORKS

LONG FICTION: *A Tale of a Tub*, 1704; *Gulliver's Travels*, 1726 (originally entitled *Travels into Several Remote Nations of the World, in Four Parts, by Lemuel Gulliver, First a Surgeon, and Then a Captain of Several Ships*).

NONFICTION: *A Discourse of the Contests and Dissensions Between the Nobles and the Commons in Athens and Rome*, 1701; *The Battle of the Books*, 1704; *The Accomplishment of the First of Mr. Bickerstaff's Predictions*, 1708; *Argument Against Abolishing Christianity*, 1708 (first published as *An Argument to Prove That the Abolishing of Christianity in England May, as Things Now Stand, Be Attended with Some Inconveniences, and Perhaps Not Produce Those Many Good Effects Proposed Thereby*); *Predictions for the Year 1708*, 1708; *A Project for the Advancement of Religion, and the Reformation of Manners By a Person of Quality*, 1709; *A Vindication of Isaac Bickerstaff, Esq.*, 1709; *The Conduct of the Allies and of the Late Ministry, in Beginning and Carrying on the Present War*, 1711; *A Proposal for Correcting, Improving and Ascertaining the English Tongue, in a Letter to the Most Honourable Robert Earl of Oxford and Mortimer, Lord High Treasurer of Great Britain*, 1712; *The Public Spirit of the Whigs, Set Forth in Their Generous Encouragement of the Author of the Crisis*, 1714; *A Letter from a Lay-Patron to a Gentleman, Designing for Holy Orders*, 1720; *A Proposal for the Universal Use of Irish Manufacture*, 1720; *A Modest Proposal for Preventing the Children of Poor People of Ireland from Being a Burden to Their Parents or the Country, and for Making Them Beneficial to the Public*, 1729; *The Drapier's Letters to the People of Ireland*, 1735; *A Complete Collection of Genteel and Ingenious Conversation, Ac-*

*cording to the Most Polite Mode and Method Now Used at Court, and in the Best Companies of England, in Three Dialogues*, 1738; *Directions to Servants in General . . .*, 1745; *The History of the Four Last Years of the Queen, by the Late Jonathan Swift DD, DSPD*, 1758; *Journal to Stella*, 1766, 1768; *Letter to a Very Young Lady on Her Marriage*, 1797; *The Correspondence of Jonathan Swift*, 1963-1965 (5 volumes; Harold Williams, editor).

MISCELLANEOUS: *Miscellanies in Prose and Verse*, 1711; *Miscellanies*, 1727-1733 (4 volumes; with Alexander Pope and other members of the Scriblerus Club); *The Prose Works of Jonathan Swift*, 1939-1968 (14 volumes; Herbert Davis, editor).

BIBLIOGRAPHY

Barnett, Louise. *Jonathan Swift in the Company of Women*. New York: Oxford University Press, 2007. This volume takes a look at Swift's relationships with the women in his life and his attitude toward the fictional women in his texts. Barnett explores his contradictory views and illustrates how he respected and admired individual women, yet loathed the female sex in general. She offers a critical, nonjudgmental study of the misogynistic attitude Swift displays in his writing when he expresses his contempt and disgust for the female body.

Ehrenpreis, Irvin. *Swift: The Man, His Works, and the Age*. 3 vols. Cambridge, Mass.: Harvard University Press, 1962-1983. A monumental biography that rejects long-held myths, provides much new information about Swift and his works, and relates him to the intellectual and political currents of his age.

Fox, Christopher, and Brenda Tooley, eds. *Walking Naboth's Vineyard: New Studies of Swift*. Notre Dame, Ind.: University of Notre Dame Press, 1995. The introduction discusses Swift and Irish studies, and the subsequent essays all consider aspects of Swift as an Irish writer. Individual essays have notes, but there is no bibliography.

Glendinning, Victoria. *Jonathan Swift: A Portrait*. New York: Henry Holt, 1998. Glendinning illuminates this proud and intractable man. She investigates the main events and relationships of Swift's life, providing a portrait set in a tapestry of controversy and paradox.

Hunting, Robert. *Jonathan Swift*. Boston: Twayne, 1989. While primarily useful as a source for biographical information, this volume does contain much insightful, if general, analysis of Swift's art. Includes chronology, notes and references, bibliography, and index.

Nokes, David. *Jonathan Swift: A Hypocrite Reversed—A Critical Biography*. New York: Oxford University Press, 1985. Draws heavily on Swift's writings, offering a good introduction for the general reader seeking information about his life and works. Nokes views Swift as a conservative humanist.

Palmieri, Frank, ed. *Critical Essays on Jonathan Swift*. New York: G. K. Hall, 1993. Divided into sections on Swift's life and writings, *Gulliver's Travels*, *A Tale of a Tub* and eighteenth century literature, and his poetry and nonfiction prose. Includes index but no bibliography.

Rawson, Claude. *The Character of Swift's Satire: A Revised Focus*. Newark: University of Delaware Press, 1983. Presents eleven essays by Swift scholars, including John Traugatt's excellent reading of *A Tale of a Tub*, Irvin Ehrenpreis on Swift as a letter writer, and F. P. Lock on Swift's role in the political affairs of Queen Anne's reign.

Real, Hermann J., and Heinz J. Vienken, eds. *Proceedings of the First Münster Symposium on Jonathan Swift*. Munich: Wilhelm Fink, 1985. Includes twenty-four essays on all aspects of Swift's work, each preceded by an abstract. Includes index.

Swift, Jonathan. *The Correspondence of Jonathan Swift*. Edited by David Woolley. New York: Peter Lang, 1999. A collection of letters by Swift that offer insight into his life and work. Includes bibliographical references.

*John R. Clark*

# ALGERNON CHARLES SWINBURNE

**Born:** London, England; April 5, 1837
**Died:** Putney, London, England; April 10, 1909
**Also known as:** A. C. Swinburne

PRINCIPAL POETRY

*Poems and Ballads*, 1866
*A Song of Italy*, 1867
*Ode on the Proclamation of the French Republic*,
    1870
*Songs Before Sunrise*, 1871
*Songs of Two Nations*, 1875
*Poems and Ballads: Second Series*, 1878
*The Heptalogia*, 1880
*Songs of the Springtides*, 1880
*Tristram of Lyonesse, and Other Poems*, 1882
*A Century of Roundels*, 1883
*A Midsummer Holiday, and Other Poems*, 1884
*Gathered Songs*, 1887
*Poems and Ballads: Third Series*, 1889
*Astrophel, and Other Poems*, 1894
*The Tale of Balen*, 1896
*A Channel Passage, and Other Poems*, 1904
*Posthumous Poems*, 1917
*Rondeaux Parisiens*, 1917
*Ballads of the English Border*, 1925

OTHER LITERARY FORMS

The most learned and versatile of all the Victorian poets, Algernon Charles Swinburne (SWIHN-burn) tried his hand with varying degrees of success at virtually every literary form available to him. He sought to make his mark as a dramatist and novelist as well as a poet, and in the course of his career, he published twelve complete plays excluding juvenilia and fragments. They are all tragedies written predominantly in blank verse. *Atalanta in Calydon* (pb. 1865) and *Erechtheus* (pb. 1876) are based on the Greek model. *Chastelard* (pb. 1865), *Bothwell* (pb. 1874), and *Mary Stuart* (pb. 1881) constitute a trilogy that harks back in spirit and style to Swinburne's beloved Elizabethan period. *The Sisters* (pb. 1892) is his only play with a nineteenth century English setting.

He wrote two semiautobiographical novels, *Love's Cross-Currents* (1901; serialized as *A Year's Letters* in 1877) and the fragmentary *Lesbia Brandon* (1952), not published until many years after his death. The first makes use of the eighteenth century epistolary form, while the second adopts the omniscient point of view. Swinburne projected a collection of short prose tales on the model of Giovanni Boccaccio to which he gave the title *Triameron*. He left a list of nineteen titles, but only four tales have survived: "Dead Love," "The Portrait," "Queen Fredegond," and "The Marriage of Mona Lisa." In addition to numerous critical articles written for newspapers and periodicals, Swinburne left behind sixteen volumes of literary criticism, dating from 1866, when *Byron* was published, to the posthumous *Contemporaries of Shakespeare*, which appeared in 1919. *William Blake: A Critical Essay* (1868), *Essays and Studies* (1875), *A Study of Shakespeare* (1880), and *Miscellanies* (1886) are the most significant of this body of material. He was also a voluminous letter writer. Cecil Lang has collected more than two thousand of Swinburne's letters in his six-volume edition.

ACHIEVEMENTS

Algernon Charles Swinburne comes closest of all the Victorians to being a Renaissance man. John Ruskin said that he could write as well in Greek, Latin, Italian, and French as he could in English. He wrote two burlesques entirely in French, a novel titled *La Fille du Policeman* and a play, *La Soeur de la Reine*, of which only two acts are known to have survived. Swinburne was intimately familiar with five great literatures. Only John Milton among the English poets exceeded him in knowledge. Swinburne was a great parodist and translator, a prolific and fascinating letter writer, a novelist, and a voluminous dramatist and critic. His *The Heptalogia*, in addition to the well-known parody of Alfred, Lord Tennyson—"The Higher Pantheism in a Nut Shel"—contains a devastating parody of himself, the "Nephilidia," and fiendishly clever parodies of the Brownings, Coventry Patmore, "Owen Meredith," and Dante Gabriel Rossetti. Cecil Lang in his introduction to his edition of Swinburne's letters comments that Swinburne's ability to absorb the manner and reproduce the mannerisms of his targets constitutes "a miracle of 'negative capability.'" The same could be said of his border ballads, which seem more authentic than imitative or derivative. "Lord Scales," "Burd Margaret," and "The Worm of Spindlestonheugh" capture the form and essence of the early ballad as well as any modern poems.

According to Cecil Lang, Swinburne as a translator "could have ranked with the great masters." Passages from Greek and Latin poets appear in his works as well as selections from nineteenth century Italian and French writers. His only sustained translations are of François Villon, and some of them are masterpieces. His "Ballad of the Lords of Old Time" and "Ballad of the Women of Paris" capture the spirit of Villon's original poems as closely as it is possible for translations to do, and as English translations they are equaled only by Dante Gabriel Rossetti's "Ballad of Dead Ladies." Swinburne's failure to translate Villon's *The Great Testament* (1461), must be counted as a great loss to literature.

As a novelist Swinburne was the only certified aristocrat of the period to write fiction about the aristocracy. *Love's Cross-Currents* and *Lesbia Brandon*, in the words of Edmund Wilson, introduce us to "a world in which the eager enjoyment of a glorious out-of-door life of riding and swimming and boating is combined with adultery, incest, enthusiastic flagellations and quiet homosexuality" (*The Novels of A. C. Swinburne*). Wilson regards *Love's Cross-Currents* as almost a neglected masterpiece. *Lesbia Brandon* contains passages of superb description, strong characterization, and convincing dialogue. Both works suggest that Swinburne had at least the potential of being a significant novelist. Unfortunately, these novels are the most neglected of his major writings.

Although Swinburne's reputation is based primarily on his poetry, it was as the author of *Atalanta in Calydon* that he first gained fame. This little-read play is best remembered today for its choruses, which are often included in anthology collections of Swinburne, but it is a genuine tour de force: a treatment in English, on the model of Greek tragedy, of a famous myth that had not been used before as the subject of a play. It is widely regarded by critics as the finest Greek tragedy in English, although the concentration of Milton's *Samson*

*Agonistes* (1671) is closer to the Greek tragedians than the diffuse blank verse of Swinburne's work. About *Erechtheus*, Swinburne's other experiment with Greek drama, David G. Riede writes in his *Swinburne: A Study of Romantic Mythmaking* that it "is a masterpiece in all respects—it is unrivaled as a re-creation of the Greek spirit and drama, nearly untouchable as a sustained lyric effusion, astounding in its metrical variety, dazzling in its metaphoric representation, and even remarkable in its philosophical import. . . ." Unfortunately, this play today is even less read than *Atalanta in Calydon*. Swinburne's trilogy on Mary Stuart was deeply researched and created over a period of many years, but it is entirely unsuited for the theater. *Bothwell* alone has well over fifty characters, and the epic length of its five acts illustrates Swinburne's disregard for the contemporary stage. *Chastelard* is the easiest of the trilogy to read, but the extent of its preoccupation with sexual passion has prevented it from being as widely appreciated as its artistry warrants. *Mary Stuart* is given high marks by T. Earl Welby in his *A Study of Swinburne* for transforming prose matter into poetry, but Welby concludes that it "inspire[s] respect rather than enthusiasm." Of Swinburne's other plays it should perhaps be said that *Marino Faliero* (pb. 1885) compares favorably with Byron's treatment of the same subject; *The Duke of Gandia* (pb. 1908) displays the powerful concentration of style of which Swinburne was capable, and *The Sisters* provides a fascinating insight into Swinburne's strange sexual proclivities.

As a critic, Swinburne's contributions are more substantial. At his best, he is capable of judicious insights expressed in fine prose, while at his worst, his strong feelings lead to idiosyncratic pronouncements and his prose style is baroque to the point of opacity. Swinburne left behind no innovations of critical approach and no permanent principles of judgment. Critical theory did not particularly interest him. Although he is the most cosmopolitan of the Victorian critics, his attentions are directed almost exclusively to literature or in some few cases to painting. Unlike Matthew Arnold, he does not travel in the broader ranges of society and religion. Swinburne's strength as a critic rests in his abiding love of literature and his genuine respect for those who made permanent contributions. This most aristocratic of English writers created in his mind an aristocracy of genius that included not only William Shakespeare and Victor Hugo, whom he revered to the point of idolatry, but also such writers as François Villon, William Blake, Robert Burns, and Charles Baudelaire. He had a special affinity for those writers who cut across the grain of convention. His *William Blake: A Critical Essay* is immensely original, charting new paths through the wilderness of the Prophetic Books and repairing years of neglect of this poet. If the insights now appear dated, certain passages have retained the freshness of great poetry.

It was as a poet that Swinburne made his most memorable and lasting contributions to literature. The seventeen volumes of poetry he published in his lifetime, exclusive of volumes printed only for private circulation, constitute a remarkable feat of creative exuberance even in an age as prolific as the Victorian. His early poetry is sometimes characterized by such rhetorical excess that the figures of speech call attention to themselves rather than enforce wider meanings. Such uncontrolled use of rhetoric is especially pronounced in the lengthy *A Song of Italy* and in the sadomasochistic poems of the first series of *Poems and Ballads*. As he matured as a poet, Swinburne came to exercise greater imaginative control over his materials, and his finest poems display a masterful command of the resources of language to create visions of striking beauty. "A Forsaken Garden" and "Ave Atque Vale," Swinburne's magnificent elegy on Baudelaire, clearly illustrate that rhetorical richness held in check by imaginative restraint that is characteristic of Swinburne at his best. A similar progressive mellowing of subject matter is evident in Swinburne's poetry. The violent denunciations of traditional Christianity and the preoccupation with various forms of sexual perversion that mark so much of Swinburne's early work disappear from the middle and later poetry, just as the melancholy hedonism of the early poems gives place to optimistic declarations about the triumph of freedom in the political poems and to a kind of quiet stoicism in the more personal ones. That said, it should be remembered that variety of subject matter and form remains the hallmark of Swinburne's huge body of poetry, and easy generalizations about it must be regarded with suspicion.

## BIOGRAPHY

Algernon Charles Swinburne was born in London on April 5, 1837. His family on both sides was aristocratic, the Swinburnes being clearly traceable to the time of Charles I and the Ashburnhams dating back before the Norman Conquest. As the eldest of six children, Swinburne had an active childhood, spent mainly at the family seat on the Isle of Wight with regular visits to another family house in Northumberland. The contrasting beauty of these diverse parts of England left a lasting impression on Swinburne, who as a child displayed an almost Wordsworthian responsiveness to nature. He early developed a passion for the sea, which is reflected in much of his poetry.

From the beginning, Swinburne was surrounded by books and fine paintings. His mother, Lady Jane, introduced him to a wide range of literature, including the Bible, William Shakespeare, Sir Walter Scott, Charles Dickens, Dante, and Molière. She also taught her son French and Italian, laying the foundation for his cos-

*Algernon Charles Swinburne* (Library of Congress)

mopolitanism. In April of 1849, Swinburne entered Eton College. In the four years he spent there, he received a thorough grounding in Greek and Latin poetry and some acquaintance with the French and Italian classics. He independently acquired a remarkable knowledge of English literature. He was especially attracted to the Elizabethan dramatists, an interest that would remain constant for the remainder of his life. *The Unhappy Revenge*, a bloodcurdling fragment in the manner of Cyril Tourneur and John Webster, dates from about 1849. His earliest poem to survive, "The Triumph of Gloriana," was a school exercise to commemorate a visit by Queen Victoria and Prince Albert to Eton on June 4, 1851. Its stiff heroic couplets give no clue of the direction Swinburne's genius was to take.

Although his academic record at Eton was good, it was decided in August of 1853 for reasons that are not entirely clear that he would not return, much to the surprise of his classmates. Instead, he would receive private tutoring for his entrance into Oxford, where his family expected him to pursue a degree leading to a legal or ecclesiastical career. Swinburne's patriotism was fired when he learned of Balaklava in the fall of 1854, and he wished to enter the army, but his father, Admiral Charles Henry Swinburne, would not permit it, perhaps because of his son's frailty. After a summer trip to Germany in the company of an uncle, Swinburne entered Balliol College, Oxford, on January 23, 1856.

At Oxford, Swinburne fell under the influence of John Nichol, the guiding spirit of Old Mortality, a small group of student intellectuals to which Swinburne belonged. Nichol, who was to remain a lifelong friend, undermined Swinburne's religious faith and confirmed him in political republicanism. It was under Nichol's influence that Swinburne wrote the "Ode to Mazzini" and became a devotee of the Italian patriot. Later, Swinburne was to be an outspoken advocate of Italian Unity. Most of Swinburne's future political poems were either to espouse Liberty and Freedom or castigate Tyranny in equally fervent language. Percy Bysshe Shelley may have become the main spiritual presence in Swinburne's political poetry, but it was Nichol who first directed Swinburne's thought along republican lines.

Another major influence on Swinburne at Oxford was the Pre-Raphaelite Brotherhood. In 1857, he met Dante Gabriel Rossetti, William Morris, and Edward Burne-Jones and immediately fell under their spell. Morris's poems, particularly "The Defence of Guenevere," influenced Swinburne profoundly. Shortly after meeting Morris, he began *Queen Yseult*, and until 1860, his poems are, in the words of Georges Lafourcade, "a long self-imposed grind, a series of prosodic exercises" (*Swinburne: A Literary Biography*). One such exercise was *Laugh and Lie Down*, an Elizabethan pastiche written in 1858-1859, the sado masochistic elements of which anticipate Swinburne's discovery of the writings of the Marquis de Sade in 1861. In 1860, because of his preoccupation with poetry and his irregular habits, which were cause for increasing concern, Swinburne encountered serious academic difficulties at Oxford, and he left without taking a degree.

In the spring of 1861, after a visit to France and Italy, Swinburne settled in London determined to make his mark as a poet. Shortly before, he had published *The Queen-Mother. Rosamond. Two Plays*, plays that did nothing to establish his reputation. His father had reluctantly agreed to a literary career for his son and settled on him a small allowance. Swinburne quickly resumed his relations with the Pre-Raphaelites, developing a close friendship with Rossetti that was to last until 1872. He also made friends with such notable figures as Richard Burton, the explorer, and Simeon Solomon, the painter, and throughout the decade lived a bohemian life marked by increasingly severe alcoholic debauches from which he was repeatedly rescued by his father. In 1862, an affair with Jane Faulkner, the only serious love of his life, ended unhappily, causing him to write "The Triumph of Time," one of his finest poems. About this time he also wrote an autobiographical novel, *A Year's Letters*, which appeared under the pseudonym of "Mrs. Horace Manners" in 1877. Also to 1862 belongs "Laus Veneris," his first poem to crystallize many of the themes of the first series of *Poems and Ballads*: the apotheosis of female beauty, the celebration of eroticism, the wish for death, the defiance of God, and the damnation of Christianity as a religion of restraint.

Along with poetry, Swinburne wrote a number of critical reviews in the early 1860's including favorable articles on Charles Baudelaire's *Les Fleurs du mal*

(1857, 1861, 1868; *Flowers of Evil*, 1909) and George Meredith's *Modern Love* (1862). In spite of all these efforts, serious recognition continued to elude Swinburne until *Atalanta in Calydon* was published, at his father's expense, in 1865. The reviews were all but unanimously enthusiastic. Swinburne was at last established in the front ranks of Victorian poets. His triumph was marred only by the fact that Walter Savage Landor, whom he had visited in Florence the year before to dedicate the then unfinished work, had died. Also in 1865 appeared *Chastelard*, the first part of a dramatic trilogy on Mary Stuart. The next year saw the publication of *Poems and Ballads* (first series), which scandalized the reading public. The volume was widely condemned by the reviewers as immoral, heretical, and insincere. Swinburne, never one to take criticism calmly, replied in kind with *Notes on Poems and Reviews*.

After *Poems and Ballads*, Swinburne's drinking grew worse, and in 1867, he had an affair with the scandalous Adah Isaac Menkin, which was the talk of London society. Swinburne's image as the *enfant terrible* of the Victorian era was firmly established. Nevertheless, throughout this period of storm and stress, Swinburne was able to do some of his best work. After several years of writing and revising, *William Blake: A Critical Essay* made its appearance in 1868, as did "Ave Atque Vale," the serenely beautiful elegy on Baudelaire. According to Lafourcade, these two works bring an end to the Pre-Raphaelite and art-for-art's-sake phases of Swinburne's poetic growth.

In London on March 20, 1867, Swinburne met Giuseppe Mazzini, whom he had idolized since his Oxford days, and his political consciousness was intensified. He gave up writing his erotic novel, *Lesbia Brandon*, and for the next three years devoted his efforts to writing poems on political and social themes. A visit to France in the summer of 1869 confirmed his hatred of Napoleon III, which he recorded in several scathing sonnets. Swinburne's renewed interest in world affairs came to a head in 1871 with the publication of *Songs Before Sunrise*. This volume makes a dramatic shift in the direction of Swinburne's poetry. The private eroticism of *Poems and Ballads* had given way to public denunciations of political and religious repression and Shelleyan prophecies of the triumph of freedom.

After the publication of *Songs Before Sunrise*, Swinburne began to dissipate more than ever, and yet his output throughout the decade was prodigious. In the 1870's, his poetry becomes quieter in tone and more melancholy and introspective. The second series of *Poems and Ballads* is tinged with a stoical acceptance of the impermanence of youth and love that is absent from the first. *Bothwell*, the most impressive work of his dramatic trilogy, appeared in 1874, followed by *Erechtheus* in 1876. In the 1870's, Swinburne turned increasingly to criticism. His *Essays and Studies*, which contains discerning appreciations of several contemporaries, was published in 1875. From 1875 to 1880, he worked on *A Study of Shakespeare*. Always contentious, he became increasingly involved in quarrels of various kinds. His attack on Ralph Waldo Emerson in the form of a public letter was occasioned by an unfavorable remark that Emerson allegedly made about him to the press. He attacked George Eliot in his *A Note on Charlotte Brontë* (1877) and was involved in a protracted dispute with F. J. Furnival, the Shakespearean scholar, on ideological grounds. He wrote a brilliant parody of Tennyson and revised earlier ones on the Brownings, all published in *The Heptalogia* in 1880.

After his father's death in 1877, Swinburne's health broke. Through much of 1878, he was bedridden from dissipation, and the decade that began with his expulsion from the Arts Club ended with the poet prostrate in his disordered London chambers near death from alcoholism. His friend and legal adviser, Theodore Watts (later Watts-Dunton), rescued him, and for the last thirty years of his life Swinburne lived at Watts's home, The Pines, in Putney. Watts severely restricted Swinburne's social contacts, but he did accompany him to Paris in 1882 for his meeting with Victor Hugo, whom Swinburne had revered for so long. This was to be his last visit to the Continent. During his years at The Pines, Swinburne contributed well over two hundred articles to newspapers and periodicals and published more than twenty volumes. *Mary Stuart* was published in 1881, finally completing the dramatic trilogy conceived years before. Swinburne's early interest in Arthurian materials was revived and *Tristram of Lyonesse, and Other Poems* appeared in 1882 and *The Tale of Balen* in 1896. He also continued to write political poems, directed largely against Russia abroad and William Gladstone and Charles Parnell at home. His aristocratic background never allowed him to regard the liberal prime minister as anything other than a dangerous radical. He opposed Home Rule as fiercely as earlier he had advocated the liberation of Italy. He ended as a republican who was opposed to democracy.

Having outlived most of his friends and all his family except for one sister, Swinburne died at The Pines on April 10, 1909. He was buried in Bonchurch Churchyard on the Isle of Wight. Theodore Watts-Dunton, true to the poet's request, would not permit the Burial of the Dead to be read over the grave.

## ANALYSIS

The body of Algernon Charles Swinburne's poetry is so vast and varied that it is difficult to generalize about it. Swinburne wrote poetry for more than sixty years, and in that time he treated an enormous variety of subjects and employed many poetic forms and meters. He wrote English and Italian sonnets, elegies, odes, lyrics, dramatic monologues, ballads, and romances; and he experimented with the rondeau, the ballade, and the sestina. Much of this poetry is marked by a strong lyricism and a self-conscious, formal use of such rhetorical devices as alliteration, assonance, repetition, personification, and synecdoche. Swinburne's brilliant self-parody, "Nephilidia," hardly exaggerates the excessive rhetoric of some of his earlier poems. The early *A Song of Italy* would have more effectively conveyed its extreme republican sentiments had it been more restrained. As it is, content is too often lost in verbiage, leading a reviewer for *The Athenaeum* to remark that "hardly any literary bantling has been shrouded in a thicker veil of indefinite phrases." A favorite technique of Swinburne is to reiterate a poem's theme in a profusion of changing images until a clear line of development is lost. "The Triumph of Time" is an example. Here the stanzas can be rearranged without loss of effect. This poem does not so much develop as accrete. Clearly a large part of its greatness rests in its music. As much as any other poet, Swinburne needs to be read aloud. The diffuse lyricism of Swinburne is the opposite of the closely knit structures of John Donne and is akin to the poetry of Walt Whitman.

## POEMS AND BALLADS

Nowhere is this diffuseness more clearly visible than in those poems of the first series of *Poems and Ballads*, which proved so shocking to Victorian sensibilities: "Anactoria," "Laus Veneris," "Dolores," "Faustine," and "Felise." Although they all exhibit technical virtuosity, these poems are too long, and their compulsive repetition of sadomasochistic eroticism grows tiresome. Poems that celebrate the pleasures and pains of sexual love are most successful when the language is sufficiently sensuous to convey the immediacy of the experience—Ovid's *Amores* (c. 20 B.C.E.; English translation, c. 1597) comes to mind—and it is ironic that Swinburne's sensual poems in this early volume fall somewhat flat because they are not sensuous enough. Faustine and Dolores fail to come to life, just as the unnamed speakers, reveling in the pains of love, remain only voices. One feels that the dramatic form is ill-chosen. Swinburne tells us in his *Notes on Poems and Reviews* that in "Dolores" he strove "to express that transient state of spirit through which a man may be supposed to pass, foiled in love and weary of loving, but not yet in sight of rest; seeking refuge in those 'violent delights' which 'have violent ends,' in fierce and frank sensualities which at least profess to be no more than they are." This is a legitimate purpose for a poem, but it is not realized in these early works.

Still, this volume cannot be dismissed too lightly. Swinburne wrote it partly to shock and partly to accomplish what he attributed to Charles Baudelaire's *Flowers of Evil*: the transformation of ugliness into beauty, immorality into morality by the sheer power of the imagination. He certainly succeeded in shocking, and at times he was able to invest desperate and dark thoughts with a languorous beauty of sound, as in these lines from "The Garden of Proserpine":

> I am tired of tears and laughter,
> And men that laugh and weep;
> Of what may come hereafter
> For men that sow to reap:
> I am weary of days and hours,
> Blown buds of barren flowers,
> Desires and dreams and powers
> And everything but sleep.

This is quintessential early Swinburne. Nothing had been heard in English poetry quite like it. For all their defects, the longer dramatic poems in the first series of *Poems and Ballads* expanded the boundaries of the subject matter of English poetry in much the way that Whitman did for American poetry. In the shorter lyrics, such as "A Leave-taking," "Rococo," and "A Match," Swinburne created a note of elusive melancholy that had not been heard before. "Madonna Mia," one of the most exquisitely beautiful lyrics in the language, by itself compensates for the flawed longer poems and ends on a more hopeful note than the other poems of the volume.

### SONGS BEFORE SUNRISE

In Swinburne's next volume of poems, *Songs Before Sunrise*, the Femme Fatale is replaced by the goddess Freedom; the earlier obsession with flagellation is sublimated into a more acceptable form of violence—namely, the overthrow of tyranny; and the desperate hedonism of the "Hymn to Proserpine" gives way to the militant humanism of the "Hymn of Man." "A little while and we die; shall life not thrive as it may?" is changed to "Men perish, but man shall endure; lives die, but the life is not dead." The doctrine of art for art's sake evaporates in these poems of social concern as the influence of Victor Hugo and Giuseppe Mazzini replaces that of Charles Baudelaire and the Marquis de Sade. With the exception of "Before a Crucifix," a powerful attack on the Roman Catholic Church for self-aggrandizement in a suffering world, the poems of *Songs Before Sunrise* are aggressive, forward-looking accounts of the defeat of oppression and the triumph of liberty. "Hertha" affirms the immortality of humankind—"In the buds of your lives is the sap of my leaves; ye shall live and not die"—and asserts that "the morning of manhood is risen, and the shadowless soul is in sight." This philosophical poem ends, in words that echo Shelley's *Prometheus Unbound: A Lyrical Drama in Four Acts* (1820), with a revelation of the death of God and the birth of "love, the beloved Republic, that feeds upon freedom and lives." The other philosophical poems of *Songs Before Sunrise*, the "Hymn of Man," similarly asserts the immortality of the race and proclaims the demise of God, who in the figure of Christ is imaged as a tyrant: "By the spirit he ruled as his slave is he slain who was mighty to slay/ And the stone that is sealed on

his grave he shall rise not and roll not away." The poem concludes with a striking perversion of Scripture, a characteristic technique of Swinburne:

> Thou art smitten, thou God, thou art smitten; thy
>     death is upon thee, O Lord.
> And the love-song of earth as thou diest resounds
>     through the wind of her wings—
> Glory to Man in the highest! for Man is the master
>     of things.

The other poems of this volume are more closely related to the events of the day. "Super Flumina Babylonis" celebrates the release of Italy from bondage in imagery that recalls the resurrection of Christ. The open tomb, the folded graveclothes, the "deathless face" all figure in this interesting poem that sings out, "Death only dies." In "Quia Multum Amavit," France, shackled by tyranny, is personified as a harlot who has been false to liberty. She has become "A ruin where satyrs dance/ A garden wasted for beasts to crawl and brawl in." The poem ends with France prostrate before the spirit of Freedom, who speaks to her as Christ spoke to the sinful woman in the Pharisee's house, in a tone of forgiveness.

### A CHANNEL PASSAGE, AND OTHER POEMS

Although Swinburne's later political poems continued to attack tyranny abroad, especially in Russia, the emphasis in them shifted to England. In *A Channel Passage, and Other Poems*, Swinburne's last volume of poetry published in his lifetime, the poems having to do with political subjects tend to reflect Swinburne's insularity. Poems such as "The Centenary of the Battle of the Nile," "Trafalgar Day," and "Cromwell's Statue" celebrate glorious moments of England's past in language of chauvinistic hyperbole, while others such as "The Commonweal: A Song for Unionists," "The Question," and "The Transvaal" counsel the severest measures against England's enemies, who, be they Irish or Boers, are invariably depicted as the "cowardliest hounds that ever lapped/ blood" or "dogs, agape with jaws afoam." These poems lack the rhetorical richness of *Songs Before Sunrise*, suggesting that, in the twilight of his career, Swinburne's strength lay not in contention but in the peaceful lyricism that informs "The Lake of Gaube" and "In a Rosary," the finest of the poems in this volume.

### POEMS AND BALLADS: SECOND SERIES

With the publication in 1878 of *Poems and Ballads: Second Series*, Swinburne reached the height of his powers as a poet. The unhealthy eroticism and hysterical denunciations of Christianity have disappeared. The language is altogether more restrained, and there is a greater harmony of form and substance. The major themes are the impermanence of love and the inevitability of death. The predominant mood is elegiac, but the despair of "Hymn to Proserpine" has been replaced by the resignation of "At Parting," and a few of the poems hold out some hope of personal immortality, although on this subject Swinburne's private beliefs are never made clear.

In "A Forsaken Garden," one of the loveliest of Swinburne's poems, the landscape as dry as "the heart of a dead man" serves as an emblem for "lovers none ever will know/ Whose eyes went seaward a hundred sleeping/ Years ago." "Love deep as the sea as a rose must wither" and lovers now living must follow those who have gone before. The poem concludes that the forsaken garden is now beyond further change until the world itself ends, and there with the ghosts of bygone lovers "As a god self-slain on his own strange altar/ Death lies dead." This mood-piece manages to convey through the effective use of detail and tight control of rhetoric a landscape more vividly realized than is to be found in Swinburne's earlier poems. "A Vision of Spring in Winter" displays an equally rich texture of natural description brought into focus by a restrained imagination. In this lovely poem, Swinburne bids farewell to youth. The poet tells the spirit of Spring, "I would not bid thee, though I might, give back/ One good thing youth has given and borne away." The loves and hopes of youth "Lie deeper than the sea" and Spring could not restore them even if the poet wished for their return. The poem ends on a wistful note: "But flowers thou may'st and winds, and hours of ease/ And all its April to the world thou may'st/ Give back, and half my April back to me."

Virtually all the elegies in this remarkable volume merit special mention. In "Inferiae," a poem of simple and quiet beauty, Swinburne pays tribute to his father, who has just died; and in words whose marmoreal quality recalls Landor, the poet who earlier had proclaimed the death of God expresses hope of immortality. "In

Memory of Barry Cornwall" opens with a marvelous picture of a kind of Socratic paradise "where the singers whose names are deathless/ One with another make music unheard of men." "To the beautiful veiled bright world where the glad ghosts meet" has gone "Barry Cornwall." Although Time has taken him and other poets from us, the poem affirms that he shall not take away "the flower of their souls," nor will "the lips lack song for ever that now lack breath." The elegy on Baudelaire, "Ave Atque Vale," was written soon after the publication of the first series of *Poems and Ballads*, but it is closer in language and tone to this volume, where it properly appears. Swinburne's deep affection for the dead French poet is felt throughout, and the resonant poignance created by the sibilance and dark vowels of the majestic stanzas and accentuated by the speaker's apostrophe of Baudelaire as "brother" helps make this one of the great elegies of English poetry. It conveys more sincerity than either "Lycidas" or "Adonais" and it is more tender than "Thyrsis." After paying tribute to Baudelaire's genius—"Thou sawest, in thine old singing season, brother/ Secrets and sorrows unbeheld of us"—the poem affirms that even though he is "far too far for wings of words to follow," his poetry lives on. Remembering that everyone will one day meet death as the poet has, the poem concludes with a profound serenity.

There is no such serenity in "Fragment on Death," one of Swinburne's masterful translations of François Villon. Here death is depicted in all its medieval horror. This and the other translations, particularly the "Ballad of the Women of Paris," provide a contrast to the poems already discussed, but not so shocking a one as the four sonnets attacking Russia, which appear completely out of place in this volume.

### LATER WORKS

After the second series of *Poems and Ballads*, Swinburne continued to publish poems for twenty-six years in a continuing variety of subject matter and form. The Arthurian romances *Tristram of Lyonesse, and Other Poems* and *The Tale of Balen*, while containing passages of undisputed power and beauty, suggest that Swinburne's forte as a poet was not in extended narration. The many poems about babies in *A Century of Roundels* reveal a mature tenderness that one would not have expected from the author of *Songs Before*

*Sunrise*. There are beautiful passages in *Songs of the Springtides*. The second series of *Poems and Ballads*, however, remains the pinnacle of Swinburne's achievement as a poet, and if he had written no more poetry after 1878, his reputation would have been essentially unchanged.

OTHER MAJOR WORKS

LONG FICTION: *Love's Cross-Currents*, 1901 (serialized as *A Year's Letters* in 1877); *Lesbia Brandon*, 1952.

PLAYS: *The Queen-Mother*, pb. 1860; *Rosamond*, pb. 1860; *Atalanta in Calydon*, pb. 1865; *Chastelard*, pb. 1865; *Bothwell*, pb. 1874; *Erechtheus*, pb. 1876; *Mary Stuart*, pb. 1881; *Marino Faliero*, pb. 1885; *Locrine*, pb. 1887; *The Sisters*, pb. 1892; *Rosamund, Queen of the Lombards*, pb. 1899; *The Duke of Gandia*, pb. 1908.

NONFICTION: *Byron*, 1866; *Notes on Poems and Reviews*, 1866; *William Blake: A Critical Essay*, 1868; *Under the Microscope*, 1872; *Essays and Studies*, 1875; *George Chapman*, 1875; *A Note on Charlotte Brontë*, 1877; *A Study of Shakespeare*, 1880; *Miscellanies*, 1886; *A Study of Victor Hugo*, 1886; *A Study of Ben Jonson*, 1889; *Studies in Prose and Poetry*, 1894; *The Age of Shakespeare*, 1908; *Shakespeare*, 1909; *Three Plays of Shakespeare*, 1909; *Contemporaries of Shakespeare*, 1919.

MISCELLANEOUS: *The Complete Works of Algernon Charles Swinburne*, 1925-1927 (20 volumes); *New Writings by Swinburne*, 1964 (Cecil Y. Lang, editor).

BIBLIOGRAPHY

Harrison, Antony H. *Swinburne's Medievalism: A Study in Victorian Love Poetry*. Baton Rouge: Louisiana State University Press, 1988. Although most of this book deals with Swinburne's poetic dramas, the chapter on *Poems and Ballads*, "Historicity and Erotic Aestheticism," provides an illuminating discussion of the influence of "historicist, erotic, and formal concerns" on several of Swinburne's most famous medieval lyrics.

Hyder, Clyde K., ed. *Swinburne: The Critical Heritage*. New York: Barnes & Noble, 1970. This volume in the Critical Heritage series charts the reception and evolving evaluation of Swinburne's work to 1920. Authors from Henry Brooks Adams to Sir Max Beerbohm state their opinions, ranging from amusement to damnation. Notable omissions are T. S. Eliot and Ezra Pound. The controversy over *Poems and Ballads* is well represented. The introduction provides an excellent overview.

Louis, Margot Kathleen. *Swinburne and His Gods: The Roots and Growth of an Agnostic Poetry*. Montreal: McGill-Queen's University Press, 1990. An intelligent investigation of the importance of Swinburne's "religious polemics." The use of "demonic parody" and whore goddesses in the early works is compared to the biblical sources. The alternative mythologies of later works are also discussed and related, in an appendix, to the mythmaking of William Blake. Includes an extensive bibliography.

Pease, Allison. *Modernism, Mass Culture, and the Aesthetics of Obscenity*. New York: Cambridge University Press, 2000. Pease's scholarly study of erotic literature and views of obscenity looks at the works of Swinburne and others. Includes bibliography and index.

Reide, David G. *Swinburne: A Study of Romantic Mythmaking*. Charlottesville: University Press of Virginia, 1978. Reide argues that Swinburne is the link between the first English Romantics and the modern Romantics.

Rooksby, Rikky. *A. C. Swinburne: A Poet's Life*. Brookfield, Vt.: Ashgate, 1997. This biography of Swinburne looks at his life and works, focusing on his poetry and his critical writings. Includes bibliography and index.

Rooksby, Rikky, and Nicholas Shrimpton, eds. *The Whole Music of Passion: New Essays on Swinburne*. Brookfield, Vt.: Ashgate, 1993. A collection of essays providing literary criticism of Swinburne's works. Includes bibliography and index.

Thomas, Donald Serrell. *Swinburne: The Poet in His World*. New York: Oxford University Press, 1979. This volume depicts Swinburne in relation to the society in which he lived. An insightful biography of what the author deems to be one of the most eccentric and original writers of the Victorian period. Contains illustrations and a select bibliography.

*Robert G. Blake*

# T

## ALFRED, LORD TENNYSON

**Born:** Somersby, Lincolnshire, England; August 6, 1809
**Died:** Aldworth, near Haslemere, Surrey, England; October 6, 1892

PRINCIPAL POETRY

*Poems by Two Brothers*, 1827 (with Charles Tennyson and Frederick Tennyson)
*Poems, Chiefly Lyrical*, 1830
*Poems*, 1832 (imprinted 1833)
*Poems*, 1842
*The Princess*, 1847
*In Memoriam*, 1850
*Maud, and Other Poems*, 1855
*Idylls of the King*, 1859-1885
*Enoch Arden, and Other Poems*, 1864
*The Holy Grail, and Other Poems*, 1869 (imprinted 1870)
*Gareth and Lynette*, 1872
*The Lover's Tale*, 1879
*Ballads, and Other Poems*, 1880
*Tiresias, and Other Poems*, 1885
*Locksley Hall Sixty Years After, Etc.*, 1886
*Demeter, and Other Poems*, 1889
*The Death of Œnone, and Other Poems*, 1892

OTHER LITERARY FORMS

Although Alfred, Lord Tennyson (TEHN-ih-suhn), is best known today for his poetry, he wrote several dramatic works that were popular in his own day. His first play, *Queen Mary*, was published in 1875. From that time until his death he continued writing verse dramas: *Harold* (pr. 1876), *The Falcon* (pr. 1879), *The Cup* (pr. 1881), *Becket* (pb. 1884), and *The Foresters* (pr., pb. 1892). Most of these were staged very successfully. The renowned producer and actor Henry Irving starred opposite Ellen Terry in *The Cup*, which ran for more than 130 nights. Irving also produced *Becket* several times after Tennyson's death, achieving success in both England and the United States. Generally speaking, however, his contemporaries' judgment that Tennyson was a greater poet than a dramatist has been confirmed by modern critics. Tennyson's only prose composition was also a play, *The Promise of May* (pr. 1882); it was not well received by theatergoers. Although he published no criticism in his lifetime, Tennyson, like most of his contemporaries, expressed his critical opinions of his own and others' works in his conversations and in numerous letters. Hallam Tennyson's two-volume *Alfred, Lord Tennyson: A Memoir* (1897) of his father prints many of these documents, and preserves as well many of Tennyson's conversations and remarks about literature.

ACHIEVEMENTS

During his lifetime Alfred, Lord Tennyson, attracted a popular following seldom achieved by any poet in any age. Although his first four volumes received little favorable attention, the publication of *In Memoriam* in 1850 brought him overnight fame, and his subsequent works were all best sellers. His Victorian contemporaries liked all forms of his poetry: More than sixty thousand copies of *In Memoriam* were sold in the first few months after publication; ten thousand copies of the Arthurian tales titled *Idylls of the King* sold in the first week after publication in 1859, and the remainder of the first edition shortly thereafter; and the first edition, sixty thousand copies, of his volume of narrative poems and lyrics, *Enoch Arden, and Other Poems* sold out shortly after it was published. His popularity continued until his death; twenty thousand copies of *Demeter, and Other Poems* were sold before publication. Readers found in Tennyson's poetry excitement, sentiment, and moral solace; his works were a lighthouse in a stormy sea of social and moral uncertainty. Many turned to Tennyson as a teacher, seeing in his works a wisdom not available in churches, schools, or public institutions.

Perhaps because he was so popular in his own day, Tennyson became the primary target for scores of critics of the two generations that followed. Critics of the post-World War I era condemned Tennyson for pandering to public demands that poetry be "uplifting," that it contain a moral for public consumption, and that it avoid controversial subjects. During the years between the World Wars, it became fashionable to speak of "the two Tennysons"; critics condemned the public poet who preached jingoism and offered moral platitudes in works such as *Maud, and Other Poems* and *Idylls of the King*, yet found much of value in the private poet, a morbid, introverted person whose achievement lay in his lyrics, with their private symbolism developed to express personal anxieties and frustrations.

Critics writing since World War II have generally been more appreciative of the entire canon of Tennyson's poetry. Following the lead of Sir Charles Tennyson, whose sympathetic yet scholarly biography of his grandfather rekindled interest in Tennyson as a serious poet both in his public and private roles, scholars have reexamined *In Memoriam*, *Idylls of the King*, *The Princess*, and *Maud, and Other Poems* and found them to be works of considerable artistic merit. "Ulysses" is regarded as a significant short poem; *Idylls of the King* has been called one of the truly great long poems of the language; and *In Memoriam* is considered one of the world's great elegies.

BIOGRAPHY

Alfred Tennyson, first Baron Tennyson of Aldworth and Freshwater, was born at Somersby in the Lincolnshire district of England on August 6, 1809, the fourth of twelve children. His father, the Reverend George Tennyson, was a brooding, melancholic man, whose lifelong bitterness—inspired by his having been disinherited in favor of a younger brother—manifested itself in his behavior toward his family. Alfred was spared much of his father's wrath, however, because George Tennyson apparently recognized his fourth son's special brilliance and took pains to tutor him in history, science, and literature. Tennyson spent five years at Louth Grammar School (1815-1820), then returned home to continue his studies under his father's personal guidance.

Tennyson began writing poetry at an early age; at eight, he was imitating James Thomson, and at twelve, he was writing romances in the manner of Sir Walter Scott. In 1827, the year he entered Trinity College,

Cambridge, he and his brothers Charles and Frederick published *Poems by Two Brothers*.

At Cambridge, Tennyson was an undisciplined student. He was well received by his fellow students, however, and in 1829, he was elected a member of the Apostles, a club devoted to intellectual inquiry. Through this association, he met Arthur Henry Hallam, who was to figure prominently in his life. In 1829, Tennyson won the Chancellor's Medal for his poem "Timbuctoo," and in 1830, he published *Poems, Chiefly Lyrical*. In March, 1831, George Tennyson died, and shortly afterward Tennyson left Cambridge without a degree.

Tennyson's 1832 volume, *Poems*, like his earlier one, was treated rather roughly by reviewers. Their comments, coupled with the death of Hallam in 1833, caused him to avoid publication for ten years. Hallam's death was an especially severe blow to Tennyson. Hallam had been engaged to Tennyson's sister, and the two men had become very close friends. The poet suffered prolonged fits of depression after receiving the news of

*Alfred, Lord Tennyson* (Library of Congress)

Hallam's death. Eventually, however, he was able to transform his grief into a series of lyrics that he published in 1850, titling the elegy *In Memoriam A. H. H.*

During the years between Hallam's death and the publication of *In Memoriam*, Tennyson was far from inactive. He lived with his mother and other members of his family, assisting in their moves from Somersby to Tunbridge Wells, then to Boxley. During these years, he spent time in London, Cornwall, Ireland, and Switzerland, gathering material for his poems. In 1834, he fell in love with Rosa Baring, and when that relationship cooled, he lighted on Emily Sellwood, whose sister had married his brother Charles. Tennyson had no real means of supporting a family at that time, so he was forced to wait fourteen years to marry. He returned to publishing in 1842, issuing a two-volume set titled simply *Poems*; it contained both new materials and revisions of previously published poems. In 1847, he published *The Princess*, a long narrative exploring the roles of men and women in modern society.

Months after *In Memoriam* appeared in May, 1850, Tennyson's fortunes rose meteorically. In June of that year, he married Emily Sellwood. In November, he was named poet laureate, succeeding the recently deceased Wordsworth. During his forty-two years as laureate, he wrote numerous poems commemorating various public events, among them some of his more famous works, including "Ode on the Death of the Duke of Wellington" (1852) and "The Charge of the Light Brigade" (1854). He came to be lionized by the British public, and even the Royal Family made numerous personal requests for him to commemorate events of importance.

The 1850's was a productive and important decade for Tennyson. In 1855, he published *Maud, and Other Poems*; in 1859, he brought out a volume containing the first four Arthurian stories that would be joined by eight others during the next twenty-five years to form *Idylls of the King*.

The Tennysons' first child was stillborn, but in 1852, Hallam Tennyson was born. The family moved to Farringford on the Isle of Wight in 1853. The following year a second son, Lionel, was born.

The remainder of Tennyson's life can be characterized as personally stable but artistically tumultuous.

During the 1860's, 1870's, and 1880's, several collections of his poems were issued. The poet added eight new volumes to his growing list of works. Beginning in the mid-1870's, Tennyson turned to drama, writing several successful plays and taking great interest in the details of their production. In 1886, his son Lionel died while returning from India. His elder son, Hallam, remained with the poet, serving as a kind of secretary and executor. In the early months of 1892, Tennyson's health began to fail, and he died in bed in October of that year, his hand resting on a volume of Shakespeare.

## ANALYSIS

Always praised for his ability to create musical lyrics, Alfred, Lord Tennyson, is now recognized as a master of a number of verse forms and a thinker who brooded deeply over the problems of his age, attempting to capture these problems and deal with them in his poetry. He is also credited with being one of the few poets whose works demonstrate a real assimilation of the poetic tradition that preceded him. His poems reflect an insight into the crises of his own age, as well as an appreciation of problems that have faced all people, especially the problems of death, loss, and nostalgic yearning for a more stable world.

Early works such as "The Palace of Art" and "The Two Voices" are clear examples of the kind of poem for which Tennyson traditionally has been acclaimed. In each, the poet presents a sensitive person who faces a crisis and is forced to choose between radical alternatives. In "The Palace of Art," the speaker must choose between self-indulgence in a world of artistic beauty and commitment to a life of service; in "The Two Voices," the speaker's choice is either to escape the harsh realities of an oppressive world through suicide, or to continue living with only the faintest glimmer of hope.

### "THE LOTOS-EATERS"

Tennyson's highly regarded classical poem "The Lotos-Eaters" explores similar themes to "The Palace of Art" and "The Two Voices." For his subject, the poet drew on the incident in the *Odyssey* (c. 725 B.C.E.; English translation, 1614) in which Odysseus's men disembark in the paradisiacal land of the lotus-eaters and fall under the enchantment of the lotus fruit. The poem is also influenced by Edmund Spenser's *The Faerie Queene* (1590, 1596), where the figure of Despair argues for the same kind of languid repose that the mariners sing of in "The Lotos-Eaters." Tennyson uses all his powers of description and his special command of the language to select words and phrases whose tonal qualities and connotative meanings strongly suggest the sense of repose and stasis. The musical quality of the poem is enhanced by the meter, the effectiveness of caesura and enjambment, and the varying line lengths used throughout, especially the extensive use of long lines broken by numerous caesuras near the end of the lyric. "The Lotos-Eaters," a combination of narrative and choric song, describes the arrival of the mariners in a land that appears to be perpetually "afternoon," where "all things always seemed the same." Here the "wild-eyed melancholy Lotos-eaters" bring to the travelers the food that will dull their desire to continue on to Ithaca. Having partaken of the fruit of the lotus, the mariners begin to think of their homeland as merely a dream, too distant a goal, no longer worth striving for. As they lie on the beach, one suggests that they "return no more," and the others quickly take up the chant; their choric song, in eight sections, makes up the remainder of the poem. In the song, the mariners review the many hardships they have faced and the many more that await them if they continue their journey. About them they see that "all things have rest"; they ask "Why should we toil alone?" Rather than continue, they beg to be given "long rest or death, dark death, or dremful ease." The poem's final statement is an exhortation to "rest, ye brother mariners, we will not wander more." It is unwise, however, to assume that the mariners' decision to opt for "dreamful ease" over a life of "toil" is Tennyson's own position. Rather, "The Lotos-Eaters" explores, from only one perspective, the dilemma of commitment versus retreat. The poet treats the same theme in many other poems in which the speaker takes a decidedly different view.

### "ULYSSES"

Tennyson's complex treatment of this theme of commitment to ideals can be seen in one of his most famous shorter works, "Ulysses." This poem also exemplifies numerous other characteristics common to much of Tennyson's poetry, particularly his use of

irony. Indeed, in "Ulysses" the reader can see the glimmerings of the essentially ironic poetic form that emerged during the nineteenth century, made popular by Robert Browning—the dramatic monologue. "Ulysses" is a poem inspired by Tennyson's personal experiences; yet in the poem Tennyson transforms his experiences into a work of art that speaks of an issue that concerns all people. In "Ulysses," Tennyson is both typically Victorian and still a poet for all times. The call to action at the end of the poem and the emphasis on each man's "work" was no doubt appealing to the poet's contemporaries. In the twentieth century, under the scrutiny of critics more aware of the subtleties of Tennyson's ironic vision, the poem provides pleasure for its refusal to yield to a simplistic reading.

In "Ulysses," the reader discovers how Tennyson uses the poetic tradition, especially the legacy of classical and Renaissance poets. Like "The Lotos-Eaters," "Ulysses" is based in part on Homer's *Odyssey*. The classical epic is not the only source, however, for by the poet's own admission, the poem owes much to the portrait of Ulysses in Dante's *Inferno* (in *La divina commedia*, c. 1320; *The Divine Comedy*, 1802). In Dante's poem, Ulysses is found in hell, condemned as a deceiver for having led his men away from Ithaca in search of vain glories. That Tennyson chose to draw his own hero from sources that present such radically different views of Ulysses suggests that he wanted to create an ironic tension in his own work. In the *Inferno*, Ulysses tells Dante that, unable to remain at home, he was compelled by wanderlust to set forth in search of new adventures. The spirit of Homer's unconquerable quester is captured in Tennyson's poem, but Dante's condemned spirit is always there to remind the reader that there may be dangers in pursuing the ideal at the expense of other considerations.

When one first reads "Ulysses" one can easily be swept along by the apparent vigor of the hero's argument. His description of life in his native Ithaca, where he is "matched with an aged wife," forced to "meet and dole/ Unequal laws" in a land whose people he regards as "savage," makes it easy for the reader to understand Ulysses' wish to return to a life of seafaring adventure. Among these people, Ulysses is not appreciated for the adventures that have caused him to "become a name" throughout the Mediterranean world. His experiences have become absorbed into the very fiber of his being; he reflects that "I am a part of all that I have met." Small wonder that the confines of his island home seem to imprison him! He realizes that his many exploits are only doorways to future experiences, an "arch" beyond which "gleams/ That untravelled world" he has yet to see. At home he finds himself becoming "dull," like a weapon left to "rust unburnished."

Realizing that he can no longer be happy as ruler in such a land, Ulysses declares that he will leave his "sceptre and the isle" to his son Telemachus, a man more capable and more patient than his father when operating in the "sphere/ Of common duties." Ulysses recognizes that he and his son are different—"He works his work, I mine"—and it is best for all if each man follow his own destiny. This difference is easy for the modern reader to accept, as it suggests a truism about human nature that those imbued with the Romantic desire for self-fulfillment find immediately palatable.

Having passed on his kingship to his son, Ulysses turns to the companions who have "toiled, and wrought, and thought" with him, and calls them to one last voyage. As night draws near, he urges them to embark once more in the ship that will carry them to lands where "some work of noble note, may yet be done." "'Tis not too late," he exhorts them, "to seek a newer world." His purpose is to "sail beyond the sunset" until he dies. The unextinguishable spirit of adventure, burning still in the heart of this old warrior, is summed up best in the closing lines, where he proclaims to those who accompany him that, although they are no longer young, they can still be men of "heroic hearts," "strong in will,/ To strive, to seek, to find, and not to yield."

Because the poem was composed shortly after the death of Tennyson's friend Arthur Henry Hallam, some critics have seen "Ulysses" as a statement of the poet's personal commitment to continue living and writing even after suffering a great personal tragedy that seemed to have robbed life of its meaning. Looking at himself as an old man who had been deprived of the spark of adventure and facing a fast-approaching death of his creative self, Tennyson chose to continue living and working. Only through an active commitment to life itself could he hope one day to see "the great Achil-

les," here meant to represent Hallam. Such a biographical interpretation is supported by Tennyson's comment, preserved in Hallam Tennyson's *Alfred, Lord Tennyson: A Memoir*, that "Ulysses" expressed his "feeling about the need of going forward, and braving the struggle of life" after Hallam's death.

The biographical interpretation can be supported in part by a close reading of the text. The resounding note of optimism, at least on the surface of the poem, is apparent. All the images associated with life on the isle of Ithaca suggest dullness, a kind of death-in-life. Tennyson displays his mastery of the single line in his withering description of the people of Ithaca; ten monosyllables capture the essence of those whom Ulysses has come to despise: They "hoard, and sleep, and feed, and know not me." Here is avarice, indolence, a suggestion of animal satisfaction with physical ease, and, most important, a lack of appreciation for the man who has raised himself from the multitude and won fame through bravery, cleverness, and other distinctly human qualities. Similarly, Tennyson has Ulysses describe the life of wandering and the yearning for further adventures in most appealing terms, both sensual and intellectual. Ulysses is a "hungry heart"; he wishes to "drink/ Life to the less," having previously "drunk delight of battle with my peers." In a single phrase borrowed from Homer, Tennyson's Ulysses recalls the great struggle in which he first won fame, far away from home on the "ringing plains of windy Troy." The excitement of battle serves as a counterpoint to the dullness of life in Ithaca. The hero's excitement is captured in his final exhortation, in which the poet once again resorts to a line of monosyllables that bombard the reader in staccato fashion: "To strive, to seek, to find, and not to yield." Active verbs call the mariners to action and the reader to acceptance of the hero's decision.

Despite the stirring note of optimism in this final line, however, the poem cannot be accepted simply as another example of strident Victorian rhetoric aimed at encouraging one to have faith in oneself and one's God and press on in the face of uncertainties. In fact, when the uncertainties in the poem are considered carefully, the reader begins to see another side of the aged hero. Ulysses is certain of his boredom with having to govern the "savage race" and of the resentment he harbors toward them because they fail to honor him for his past exploits. What Ulysses will substitute for his present life, and what good he will accomplish in leaving Ithaca, is not at all clear. Some notable work "may yet be done," but he cannot be certain that his new wanderings will lead to anything but death: "It may be that the gulfs will wash us down," he cautions. Of course, he and his mariners may "touch the Happy Isles" where they will be reunited with "the great Achilles," but the chance of such a reunion is at best tenuous. In fact, such a desire implies a kind of death wish, since Achilles has departed this life for Elysium.

One may sympathize with Ulysses, seeing that his present life is unfulfilling, and agree that pursuing tenuous goals is better than stagnating. At this point, though, one must recall that the dreary condition on Ithaca is not related by the poet as factual, but rather is described by Ulysses himself. Because the poem is dramatic in nature, only the hero's own word provides a touchstone for judging things as they really are, and it is possible that Ulysses' view is jaundiced. One must consider, too, that Tennyson draws not only from Homer but also from Dante for his portrait of Ulysses; the Dantean quality of the hero cannot be overlooked, and in the *Inferno*, Ulysses is found in hell, having led his mariners to their doom. In the version of the *Inferno* that Tennyson probably read, that by H. F. Cary (1805), Ulysses tells Dante that no familial feelings could overcome the "zeal" he had to explore the world, a feeling that he calls "man's evil and his virtue." Tennyson's Ulysses may also be a victim of this curse and blessing. Despite his pronounced enthusiasm for a life of heroic adventure, Ulysses may in fact merely be running away from his responsibilities. If the reader recalls from the *Odyssey* the hero's struggles to return to his wife and son, Ulysses' behavior in Tennyson's poem must appear a little suspect. The beloved and faithful Penelope is now scorned as an "aged wife." Telemachus, although praised for his sagacity and patience, is still not of the heroic mold.

A word of caution is in order here. In the past, critics have been quick to call Ulysses' description of his son a thinly disguised piece of sarcasm, but this reading smuggles twentieth century notions into a nineteenth century context. Words such as "blameless" and "de-

cent" were not terms of disapprobation in the nineteenth century, nor would Tennyson have been denigrating Telemachus by pointing out that he worked best in the sphere of "common duties." In fact, in his other poetry and in the writings preserved in Hallam Tennyson's *Alfred, Lord Tennyson: A Memoir*, Tennyson clearly had great respect for men and women who served society at the expense of personal gratification. Precisely because the duties that Ulysses turns over to Telemachus are ones that Tennyson and his contemporaries considered important for the continuation of ordered society, Ulysses' decision to abdicate them makes his motives questionable. It is at least possible to see that behind the hero's rhetoric lies a clever scheme to convince his listeners, and the reader, that his actions are motivated by the highest intentions, when in fact he is abandoning a job he finds distasteful and difficult to pursue a lifestyle he finds more gratifying. Such a possibility makes it difficult to see Ulysses as a hero; rather, he appears to be an irresponsible villain for whom Tennyson and the critical reader can have little sympathy. That Tennyson would have held such a man in low regard is evident from his own remarks; as recorded in Hallam Tennyson's *Alfred, Lord Tennyson: A Memoir*, he once told a young aspirant to university life that a man "should embark on his career in the spirit of selfless and adventurous heroism and should develop his true self by not shirking responsibility."

In the light of this ambiguity, it is easy to construe Ulysses' real decision as an affirmation not of life but of death, and to see his desire to journey forth again as a kind of death wish. Whether one adopts such a reading depends largely on the way one views the tone of the final segments of the poem, in which Ulysses states publicly his reasons for undertaking such a voyage. If this public harangue is merely a rhetorical pose intended to win over skeptical followers so that they will man the hero's ship on this futile journey, then "Ulysses" is a poem of deceit and despair, a warning to the reader of the hypnotic power of such rhetoric to sway listeners into a mood of naïve optimism. On the other hand, if one is convinced of the hero's sincerity in his call to strive, seek, find, and not yield, one cannot help considering "Ulysses" another of the many poems in which Tennyson offers hope and support to his fellow Victorians, tempering such optimism with the notion that one can never be absolutely certain whether the journey through life will lead to paradise or merely to death, adrift on an angry sea.

The dilemma may never be solved satisfactorily, for in "Ulysses," Tennyson is experimenting with a relatively new poetic form, the dramatic monologue, in which ambiguity and ironic distance are characteristic. Although "Ulysses" does not possess all the formal qualities of the dramatic monologue, it does contain the essentials. Situation and action are inferred only from the speech of the main character, and the reader's assessment of motives rests on his estimation of the character of the speaker. The hero's exhortation is intended not only to be heard by his fellow mariners but also to be overheard by the reader; one feels compelled to judge the merits of the hero's philosophy. What one brings to the poem—knowledge of the *Odyssey* or *The Divine Comedy*, or of Tennyson's life—may help to determine whether one should accept or reject Ulysses' call. In any case, the act of choosing demanded by the poem forces one to make a moral commitment of some kind. The need for making such judgments, and the complexities involved in making them, are matters that concern Tennyson in all his poetry. The ambiguity of the poem is intentional, reflecting the dilemmas faced in the real world by Tennyson and his readers.

### THE PRINCESS

The same concerns that one finds in Tennyson's shorter compositions, such as "Ulysses," are also reflected in the poet's longer works. Tennyson wrote four long poems: *The Princess, In Memoriam, Maud,* and *Idylls of the King*. None of these is typical of traditional narrative poetry, and in several ways, they anticipate the long poems of the twentieth century. All four are fragmented in some way; none tells a single story from a consistent perspective. *The Princess* is the most tightly constructed of Tennyson's long poems. In this medley, a group of seven young men and women each create part of a tale about a princess who has removed herself from the world of men to establish a college for women. Princess Ida and the prince who comes to "rescue" her and win her love are the products not of a single creator but of seven, as each young person participating in the game adds to both story line and character

development. As a result, the poem is actually two stories—that of the princess whose tale is created by the young people, and that of the young people who are themselves very like the characters they create. Throughout the poem songs are interspersed to serve as counterpoint to the narrative and to highlight major themes.

### IDYLLS OF THE KING AND MAUD

*Maud* is also a medley. Here, however, the variation is in the verse form, and the fragmentary structure mirrors the nature of the hero, a man poised on the edge of disaster and dementia.

*Idylls of the King*, Tennyson's Arthurian poem, consists of twelve separate pieces tied together by the overarching structure provided by the legend itself—the rise and fall of Arthur and his Round Table. Within this framework, individual idylls remain relatively self-contained units. The poet's examination of the downfall of a society that abandons its ideals is carried forward through an intricate patterning of repeated images and parallel scenes.

### IN MEMORIAM

Tennyson's most fragmented long poem is the one for which he is best remembered and most praised. *In Memoriam* is a collection of more than 130 lyrics, composed by the poet over seventeen years and finally pieced together to record his reaction to the death of his dearest friend. Rather than being a continuous narrative, *In Memoriam* is a loosely assembled collage that, when read as a whole, reflects the varied emotions that one man experiences when prompted by the death of a loved one to face the reality of death and change in the world and the possibilities for life after death. Like "Ulysses," the poem is inspired by Tennyson's personal grief, yet it uses this personal experience as a touchstone for examining an issue that plagued all people of his era: humanity's ability to cling to faith in God and an afterlife in the face of the challenges of the new science.

The "I" of *In Memoriam* is not always to be identified with the poet himself; rather, as Tennyson himself said, the speaker is sometimes "the voice of the human race speaking thro' him [that is, the poet]." Nine years before Charles Darwin published *On the Origin of Species by Means of Natural Selection* (1859), Tennyson was questioning the value of the individual human life in the light of scientific discoveries proving that whole species of animals that once roamed the earth had long ago become extinct. In the much-anthologized middle section of *In Memoriam*, Tennyson's narrator observes of nature, "So careful of the type she seems,/ So careless of the single life," only to cry despairingly in the next lyric,

> "So careful of the type?" but no.
> From scarpéd cliff and quarried stone
> She cries, "A thousand types are gone:
> I care for nothing, all shall go."

Here is the "Nature, red in tooth and claw" that people of Tennyson's age, nurtured on faith in a benevolent God, found impossible to comprehend.

Tennyson sees his personal dilemma over the loss of Hallam and the larger problem involving the conflict between the biblical account of creation and scientific discoveries as essentially similar. The speaker of *In Memoriam* passes through several emotional stages: from grief and despair over his loss; to doubt, which presumes that all is not lost in death; to hope, based not solely on blind trust but also on "intuition," people's sense that a higher person exists to guide their lives and the life of nature itself; to, finally, faith, an acceptance of the notion of immortality and permanence even in the face of changes in nature that the speaker cannot deny. In the poem, Tennyson's friend Hallam becomes a symbol of a "higher Race," a harbinger of a better life, one sent to earth ahead of his time to offer hope to all people that the changes and impermanences of life exhibit not chaos but rather a divine pattern of progress, a movement toward God himself. In terms that anticipate the twentieth century theologian and mystic, Pierre Teilhard de Chardin, Tennyson concludes his elegy with a tribute to his friend who appeared on earth "ere the times were ripe," and who now lives with the beneficent God who guides this process of evolution, "who ever lives and loves,/ One God, one law, one element,/ And one far-off divine event,/ To which the whole creation moves."

The note of optimism at the end of *In Memoriam* is achieved only after a great deal of agonizing doubt. In fact, T. S. Eliot believed that the strength of Tennyson's elegy lay not in its final affirmation of faith, but rather in the quality of its doubt. The fragmentary nature of the poem allows Tennyson to explore that doubt with much greater range and intensity than would a more typical narrative structure. For example, Section LX begins with two lines that refer directly to the speaker's grief over his lost friend: "He past; a soul of nobler tone:/ My spirit loved and loves him yet." The remaining fourteen lines, however, are an extended simile, in which the speaker compares his grief to the feelings of a young girl for a boy who is above her in social status. The girl's "heart is set/ On one whose rank exceeds her own." Seeing the young man "mixing with his proper sphere," and recognizing "the baseness of her lot," the girl experiences jealousy, without knowing what she should be jealous of, and envy of those who are fortunate enough to be near her beloved. She goes about her life in the "little village" that "looks forlorn" to her, feeling that her days are "narrow" as she performs her common household chores in "that dark house where she was born." From her friends, she receives no pity (they "tease her" daily), and she is left alone at night to realize the impossibility of ever achieving the union she desires: "How vain am I," she weeps, "How should he love a thing so low?"

The link to the larger themes of the poem, the speaker's grief over the loss of his friend, is found most obviously in the lyric's opening lines. Once that link is established, the parallels between the feelings of the speaker and the young girl he describes in the remaining lines become apparent at numerous points. The different "spheres" in which the girl and her beloved live represent the difference the speaker sees between himself and his friend, whom he calls elsewhere the "herald of a higher race." The "little village" is the speaker's world, into which the dead friend will no longer come. The most important image used to link this lyric with the other sections of *In Memoriam* is the "dark house" in which the girl must pass her days. That image, first appearing in section 7 when the speaker stands before his friend's house in London shortly after learning that his friend has died, recurs in several other sections and always suggests the loss the speaker feels at his friend's death.

Section 60, then, is typical of many lyrics that Tennyson pieced together to form *In Memoriam*. In it, the speaker's grief, inexpressible in its magnitude, is made realizable by comparison with feelings that immediately touch the reader. One develops a sense of the speaker's loss, and his friend's greatness, through the process of empathetic association with more familiar feelings of loss and pain experienced in the sphere of everyday life. Similarly, when the speaker begins to understand that the loss of his friend should not be cause for despair, but rather for joy, that joy is transmitted to the reader by associating the speaker's feelings with traditional symbols of happiness—the three Christmas seasons that form important structural links within *In Memoriam* and the wedding celebration that closes the poem. The celebration of the wedding is a most appropriate close for this poem: the union of two lives to form a single unit from which new life will spring mirrors man's ultimate union with God, "To which the whole creation moves."

## OTHER MAJOR WORKS

PLAYS: *Queen Mary*, pb. 1875; *Harold*, pb. 1876; *The Falcon*, pr. 1879 (one act); *The Cup*, pr. 1881; *The Promise of May*, pr. 1882; *Becket*, pb. 1884 (wr. 1879); *The Foresters*, pr., pb. 1892 (wr. 1881); *The Devil and the Lady*, pb. 1930 (unfinished).

NONFICTION: *The Letters of Alfred Lord Tennyson: Volume 1, 1821-1850*, 1981 (Cecil Y. Lang and Edgar F. Shannon, editors); *The Letters of Alfred Lord Tennyson: Volume 2, 1851-1870*, 1987 (Lang and Shannon, editors); *The Letters of Alfred Lord Tennyson: Volume 3, 1871-1892*, 1990 (Lang and Shannon, editors).

MISCELLANEOUS: *The Works of Tennyson*, 1907-1908 (9 volumes; Hallam, Lord Tennyson, editor).

## BIBLIOGRAPHY

Barton, Anna. *Tennyson's Name: Identity and Responsibility in the Poetry of Alfred Lord Tennyson*. Burlington, Vt.: Ashgate, 2008. An examination of the poetry by Tennyson in terms of the topics of identity and responsibility.

Hood, James W. *Divining Desire: Tennyson and the Poetics of Transcendence*. Burlington, Vt.: Ashgate, 2000. Hood examines religious transcendence in the works of Tennyson. Includes bibliography and index.

Jordan, Elaine. *Alfred Tennyson*. New York: Cambridge University Press, 1988. Jordan devotes individual chapters to the English idylls, the dramatic monologues, and the major poems (*The Princess*, *In Memoriam*, *Maud*, and *Idylls of the King*) to illustrate her thesis that Tennyson was intensely interested in gender issues and was ambivalent regarding the validity of patriarchal methods of governing society.

Joseph, Gerhard. *Tennyson and the Text: The Weaver's Shuttle*. New York: Cambridge University Press, 2005. Joseph starts with the weaving figure of the Lady of Shalott to focus on poetic texture and a sense of textuality in Tennyson's poetry.

Ledbetter, Kathryn. *Tennyson and Victorian Periodicals: Commodities in Context*. Burlington, Vt.: Ashgate, 2007. This study of Tennyson looks at the popularity of his writings and his relationship with the publishers of journals and other periodicals.

Lovelace, J. Timothy. *The Artistry and Tradition of Tennyson's Battle Poetry*. New York: Routledge, 2003. Examines Tennyson's lesser studied battle poems and argues that they present elements of the Homeric epics.

Mazzeno, Laurence W. *Alfred Tennyson: The Critical Legacy*. Rochester, N.Y.: Camden House, 2004. Mazzeno focuses on the critical evaluation of the works of Tennyson during his life and after, as well as the poet's influence on other writers.

Perry, Seamus. *Alfred Tennyson*. Tavistock, England: Northcote House/British Council, 2005. A biography of the famous poet that also presents analyses of his works.

Shaw, W. David. *Alfred Lord Tennyson: The Poet in an Age of Theory*. New York: Twayne, 1996. An introductory biography and critical study of selected works by Tennyson. Includes bibliographical references and index.

Thorn, Michael. *Tennyson*. New York: St. Martin's Press, 1993. A biography of Tennyson that covers his life and works. Includes bibliography and index.

*Laurence W. Mazzeno*

# DYLAN THOMAS

**Born:** Swansea, Wales; October 27, 1914
**Died:** New York, New York; November 9, 1953

PRINCIPAL POETRY

*Eighteen Poems*, 1934
*Twenty-five Poems*, 1936
*The Map of Love*, 1939
*New Poems*, 1943
*Deaths and Entrances*, 1946
*Twenty-six Poems*, 1950
*Collected Poems, 1934-1952*, 1952
*In Country Sleep*, 1952
*The Poems of Dylan Thomas*, 1971, rev. ed. 2003
    (Daniel Jones, editor)

OTHER LITERARY FORMS

Dylan Thomas wrote one novel, *The Death of the King's Canary* (1976), in collaboration with John Davenport. His stories and collections of stories include the very popular, essentially autobiographical, *Portrait of the Artist as a Young Dog* (1940) and many posthumous publications. Scripts include the extremely popular *Under Milk Wood* (pr. 1953); *The Doctor and the Devils* (1953), which has been translated into German, Czech, and Spanish and was republished with four additional scripts in 1966; and *Quite Early One Morning* (1944), which has variant English and American versions. Thomas's letters are rich with biographical materials and critical insights. There are three important collections: *Letters to Vernon Watkins* (1957), written to, and edited by, Vernon Watkins, his friend and fellow poet; *Selected Letters of Dylan Thomas* (1966), edited by Constantine FitzGibbon, his "official" biographer; and *Twelve More Letters by Dylan Thomas* (1969), a limited edition supplemental to the FitzGibbon collection. Many other articles, poems, letters, scripts, and stories are widely scattered in manuscripts, anthologies, newspapers, and magazines.

ACHIEVEMENTS

Whatever else may be said about the poetry of Dylan Thomas, it had the qualities needed to bring its author to the attention of the English-speaking world by the time he was twenty-two years old. Whether it was simply his tone, his subject matter, or a bit of both, Thomas's poems elicited a marked response in readers caught in a fierce economic depression. In any immediate sense, the poems were not optimistic; they sang of no golden age in the offing. Instead, mildly outrageous in subject matter and language, defiant of the ugly processes of life and death, and apparently even more defiant of conventional poetic forms, they seemed to project a knowledge of the inner workings of the universe denied to other mortals but toughly shared.

Small wonder, then, that Thomas gained a hearing as poet and seer in the literary world and among general readers. Although the initial impact of *Eighteen Poems* was slight, *Twenty-five Poems* established Thomas as a writer to be reckoned with. The book generated several critical questions. Did the world have a new John Keats on its hands, a poet who came almost at once to literary maturity and whose works would be permanent? Was Thomas simply a minor poet who had struck a rich topical vein that would soon be exhausted? Was Thomas, worst of all, as seemed to some most likely, a mere wordmonger whose obscure rantings would soon become mere curiosities, interesting, if at all, only to literary historians? He received the Levinson Prize from *Poetry* magazine in 1945. By the twenty-first century, Thomas had been firmly established as a true poet, but discussion of the ultimate value of his poetry continues. What is clear is that he had a strong hold on the public imagination for roughly two decades and, during that time, helped to shape the idea of what poetry is or can aspire to be.

BIOGRAPHY

Dylan Marlais Thomas is firmly identified in many minds as the Welsh poet par excellence, as the voice of modern Wales speaking in the bardic tradition of *The Mabinogion* (c. twelfth and thirteenth centuries) and in the Renaissance tradition of William Shakespeare's mystic, Owen Glendower. In fact, Thomas's poetry is scarcely Welsh at all, although the poet loved Wales. Biographers have noted that Thomas's life and times have only a limited relevance to his poetry, and what influence there is, is transformed into a personal inner

*Dylan Thomas* (Library of Congress)

world. "Fern Hill," "Over Sir John's Hill," and a few other poems are set in the countryside and seashore that Thomas knew, and "Hold Hand, These Ancient Minutes in the Cuckoo's Month" speaks accurately of the brutality of the Welsh winter and spring, but rarely does Thomas's poetry treat in any serious way either the real or mythical history and countryside of Wales, the realities of the depressed industrial Wales he knew as an adolescent, or the postwar Wales he returned to after the horrors of the London bombing or the triumph of the American tours. The rough and intimate life of the family and village he treats so graphically in other genres seems to lie outside his idea of poetic fitness.

Thomas was born and reared in Swansea, in southern Wales, east by a few miles from Carmarthen and its environs, Fern Hill and Laugharne, which were to play such an important part in his personal life. Swansea, urban and industrial, contrasts strongly with the idyllic Carmarthenshire. Thomas's immediate family consisted of his father, David John Thomas; his mother, Florence Thomas (née Williams); and an older sister, Nancy. He was liberally supplied with aunts, uncles, and cousins of all sorts, and shared the usual

family closeness of the Welsh, though his wife, Caitlin, recorded in *Leftover Life to Kill* (1957) that he tried hard but unsuccessfully to free himself from its puritanical background.

Thomas's paternal grandfather was, among a number of other vocations, a poet, not especially distinguished, who took for himself the bardic name "Gwilym Marles." "Gwilym" is William and "Marles" was taken from the Welsh stream Marlais, which, in its proper spelling, later became Thomas's middle name. Thomas's father had poetic ambitions of his own and was determined that his son should have his chance to become a poet. Disappointed in his hope for a distinguished career in education, he had settled with some lasting bitterness for a schoolmastership in the south of Wales. Thomas's poem "Do Not Go Gentle into That Good Night" furnishes some measure of his bitterness at his father's lingering death from cancer and of the son's reciprocation of the father's love.

Thomas's school days were unusual only in that he began to write poetry early. His close friend in grammar school was Daniel Jones, who was later to edit *The Poems of Dylan Thomas*. They wrote more than two hundred poems together, each contributing alternate lines—Jones odd, Thomas even.

Thomas left school in 1931 and worked until 1932 for the *South Wales Daily Post*. The period of his most intense activity as a poet had already begun in 1930 and was to extend to 1934. Daniel Jones calculated that during this period Thomas's output was four times greater than that of the last nineteen years of his life. Ralph Maud edited the four so-called Buffalo Notebooks, which contain working drafts of Thomas's poems from 1930 to August, 1933—except for the period of July, 1932, to January, 1933—publishing them, with other manuscript material, in *Poet in the Making: The Notebooks of Dylan Thomas* (1968). Maud observed that Thomas came to think of these poems as a sort of mine of early drafts and drew on them, generally with some revision, for a number of poems in *Twenty-five Poems*; he continued to do so until the notebooks were purchased in 1941 by the State University of New York at Buffalo.

Thomas's last two years in Swansea, 1932 to 1934, foreshadowed the importance of the theater in his life.

Thomas was actively interested in acting and playwriting while he was still in school, then joined a community theater group, the Mumbles Stage Society. By all accounts, Thomas rapidly became a competent actor, but the bohemianism that was to mar his personal life had already become established and caused his expulsion from the group.

In 1933, Thomas began to place poems in British papers and magazines that had more than local circulation. In September, 1933, he began a correspondence with the future novelist Pamela Hanford Johnson, who eventually married another novelist, C. P. Snow. The correspondence ripened into a friendship, which in turn became a love affair after visits in 1934. In November, Thomas moved to London, the center of his activities until 1937.

*Eighteen Poems* appeared in December, 1934. Although the book caused hardly a ripple, when it was followed in 1936 by *Twenty-five Poems*, Thomas's reputation was established, helped not a little when the book was received by the prestigious poet Edith Sitwell.

*Twenty-five Poems* contains a rich trove of some of Thomas's best work. The sonnet sequence "Altarwise by Owl-Light," for example, has still not been exhausted by critical study. The sequence is generally viewed as containing the elements that make Thomas's poetry at once difficult and rewarding: religious, overtly Christian, motifs; packed metaphor and imagery, some of it traditional, some of it esoteric in various ways; high style mixed with colloquial phrasing; and the always-present theme of life and death as a process centered around, informed by, and powered through, sexuality.

Perhaps the central event of Thomas's personal life was his meeting with Caitlin Macnamara at a London pub party in April, 1936. The daughter of the eccentric Yvonne Majolier and Francis Macnamara, Caitlin was immediately drawn to Thomas, and the affair quickly became serious. By all accounts, Caitlin's temperament was as mercurial as Thomas's own. After a trip together to Cornwall, they married on July 11, 1937, in Penzance, without any visible means of support or any moral support from Thomas's family. They lived at first in Hampshire, southwest of London, with Caitlin's

mother. It was a relatively happy and carefree time.

In the fall of 1938, Thomas and his wife moved to Wales, living at first with Thomas's parents, then alone in Laugharne, where their first son, Llewelyn, was born in January, 1939. In August, *The Map of Love* was published, complete with Augustus John's portrait of Thomas. This book contains a number of more or less surrealistic stories plus sixteen poems. In spite of the celebrated episode of Thomas's participation in the Surrealist Exhibition of June 26, 1936, where he read poetry and passed around a cup of strong tea, the notion that Thomas was at any time a surrealist writer has been thoroughly exploded. G. S. Fraser argued that *The Map of Love* generated the New Apocalypse movement, later the New Romanticism, which was, in turn, superficially influenced by Surrealism and Dadaism. H. H. Kleinman, in *The Religious Sonnets of Dylan Thomas* (1963), argued that Thomas could not have been a Surrealist because he was essentially nonliterary as a reader. Earlier than either, Marshall Stearns, in "Unsex the Skeleton: Notes on the Poetry of Thomas" (1944), placed a high value on Thomas's poetry because of its originality and because of the influence it had on the Apocalypse group, specifically Henry Treese, Fraser, and J. F. Hendry. When Richard Church, a Dent publishing company official, objected to some of Thomas's poems as surrealistic, Thomas rejected the charge and described Surrealism as a "pernicious experiment" which was beneath him, adding that "every line of his poetry was to be understood by the reader thinking and feeling." In any case, the book was well received and contained at least two outstanding poems, the brittle elegy "After the Funeral (In Memory of Ann Jones)" and the splendid compact birthday piece, "Twenty-four Years."

On September 3, 1939, Great Britain declared war against Nazi Germany, beginning a struggle from which the world as Thomas had known it would never reemerge. During the relatively quiet early stages, before the German drives in the spring of 1940 that led first to the evacuation of Dunkirk and then to the surrender of France, Thomas registered shock about the war and determined not to be involved in it. Called up for military service in April, just after *Portrait of the Artist as a Young Dog* was published, he was found unfit for service. In June, he moved to an artists' colony in the Cotswolds and thence to London in the fall. There began a long period of poverty and writing scenarios for war documentaries, an occupation that may have been emotionally damaging, but that also stood him in good stead as preparation for later participation in filmmaking. His personal life continued to be on the windy side of bohemianism, especially during the periods when Caitlin was in Wales. On March 3, 1943, his daughter Aeron was born while Caitlin was still in London. The Thomases were to have no more children until their second son, Colm, was born in Carmarthen on July 24, 1949, less than five years before his father's death.

The war years saw only a single slim volume of poetry produced, *New Poems*. Included in this book were several poems of first importance: "And Death Shall Have No Dominion," "The Marriage of a Virgin," "The Hunchback in the Park," the long and controversial "Ballad of the Long-Legged Bait," "Once Below a Time," "Deaths and Entrances," and one of his few war poems, "Among Those Killed in the Dawn Raid Was a Man Aged One Hundred." In spite of the title, the poems were not "new"; they were drawn from earlier publication in scattered periodicals.

In the spring of 1945, the European phase of the war was finished, and the Thomases returned once more to Wales, settling this time in New Quay on the western coast and moving from there to Oxford in 1946, and finally, in the spring of 1949, to the Boat House in Laugharne, with which Thomas is, perhaps, most often associated. He produced one book of poetry during this period, *Deaths and Entrances*. Meanwhile, he was busy writing and acting for the British Broadcasting Corporation, writing filmscripts, and traveling abroad to Italy, Czechoslovakia, and, finally, the United States, on the first of four tours.

In August, 1950, after his return from the United Staes, *Twenty-six Poems* was published. This limited edition, printed by hand in Italy, signed by Thomas, and in all ways a pretentious production, signaled a new sort of arrival. Rather a large number of people were now willing to pay handsomely for the status conferred by owning a copy of a limited edition of his work.

The American tours were triumphs for Thomas. He appears to have basked in the adoration of American society and academic groups. From the detailed accounts of his mentor, John Malcolm Brinnin, recorded in his biographical *Dylan Thomas in America: An Intimate Journal* (1955), Thomas worked very hard while at the same time continuing to behave in off-hours in the feckless manner for which he was now notorious.

Even so, in February, 1952, a second handsome edition appeared, the six poems of *In Country Sleep*. This book was almost immediately eclipsed by the publication in November of Thomas's most important book, *Collected Poems, 1934-1952*. Again, the format was impressive and the edition included a number of specially bound copies. This volume includes nearly all of Thomas's poetry and forms the point of departure for any serious study of his work.

While the fourth American tour was under way, Thomas was taken ill in New York, lapsed into a coma, and died on November 9, 1953. He was buried on November 24 in St. Martin's Churchyard, Laugharne, Wales.

ANALYSIS

In placing Dylan Thomas as a poet, critics have generally recognized that he wrote some poems of lasting value, although they do not highly rate his poetic output as a whole. However, even if Thomas's poetry comes down to no more than that, a few lasting poems, still, to have caught the imagination and the spirit, if not fully the understanding, of the people who endured the Depression and World War II, to have embodied in his poetry a fearless, if bitter, search for reality and a limited hope in a world bereft of its traditional theological certainties, is no mean feat. This much, at least, Thomas achieved.

Three poems will serve to illustrate, provisionally, the range in theme and technique of Dylan Thomas's poetry: "And Death Shall Have No Dominion," "Altarwise by Owl-Light," and "Over Sir John's Hill." All three deal with the life-in-death theme that permeates Thomas's work. The first is a very early poem, rather clear and personal in its statement; the second, consisting of ten sonnets treated as a single entity, involves a great deal of Christian material, though it is not incontrovertibly a Christian poem and presents many problems of analysis and interpretation; the third is a "Welsh" poem inasmuch as it is set in Wales and may well spring from Welsh folk material. While the middle poem is considered to be difficult, the last is sequentially clear in its narrative progression, panorama of images, and vivid descriptions.

### "AND DEATH SHALL HAVE NO DOMINION"

"And Death Shall Have No Dominion" appears in the "Buffalo Notebooks" dated April, 1933, and was published in *The New English Weekly* on May 18, 1933, and in *Collected Poems, 1934-1952*. It consists of three stanzas, each beginning and ending with the phrase "And death shall have no dominion." The rhythm is based on a four-stress count with enough variations to intrigue the serious prosodist. These may involve eccentric massing of stresses, as in the title line, or stressing or not stressing the same word in a single line, as in "When their bones are picked cleán and the cleán bones goñe." Aside from the title-refrain, the poem does not lend itself to simple syllable count, though lines two and six consistently have eight syllables and line five has nine. The other four lines are more or less irregular. For the most part, the lines tend to fall irregularly into the iambic and anapestic patterns common to English versification. Alliteration runs throughout the poem. End-rhyme, assonance, and consonance also play a part in the sound pattern. Lines two and three of the second stanza, for example, substitute alliteration for end rhyme with "windily" and "way," while "way" is assonant with "break" in line five. Moreover, "windily" is assonant with the first word of the following line, "twisting," which, in turn, is assonant with both words of the phrase "sinews give." More alliteration is found in line three in "lying long," and "lying" echoes "windings" in line two. Such intricacy of sound patterning is the rule in Thomas's poetry.

This rhythmical music contributes much to the readability and understanding of the poem. Prosed, the first stanza says little more than that human beings will die in many ways and places and their bodies will return to the elements and be scattered. The elements, however, will live again because love will continue its purpose of regeneration, and death will not rule life. Of course, prosing cannot indicate the cosmic triumph of "They shall have stars at elbow and foot." The second paragraph works with images of sea death and of torture, and plays on the paradox that the broken will remain whole. The third stanza picks up a minor theme of madness and couples it with a wasteland setting. In spite of madness, in spite of burial and dissolution, the poem insists that something will continue to hammer the elements into life until the sun itself breaks down. Again, the prosing gives little notion of the desolation evoked by "Where blew a flower may a flower no more/ Lift its head to the blows of the rain."

In an essay in the *Explicator* (1956), Thomas E. Connolly professed to see both Christian and Platonic elements in the poem and suggested the influence of Percy Bysshe Shelley's *Adonais* (1821) and John Milton's "Lycidas" (1645) as well. The Christian note is at best vague, while the breaking down of the sun and the persistence with which the elements return to the flesh instead of to the godhead seems clearly enough to refute Platonism. Whatever the merits of the *Adonais* identification may be, Thomas's resources would be poor indeed if he had to depend on "Lycidas" for sea-drowning imagery. On the other hand, other critics have agreed with Connolly's identification of Saint Paul's Epistle to the Romans as the source of the title-refrain and the language indicating that the dead in the sea will rise again. They reject the idea that the lines Christianize the poem and sees them, instead, as part of a "more generalized mysticism."

### "ALTARWISE BY OWL-LIGHT"

"Altarwise by Owl-Light" is a much more difficult and controversial poem. The first seven of its ten sonnets were published in *Life and Letters Today* (1935) and the last three were published at various times during 1936 in *Contemporary Poetry and Prose*. They were printed later as a sequence in *Twenty-five Poems*.

The poems composing "Altarwise by Owl-Light" are traditional sonnets mainly inasmuch as they have fourteen lines each; they do not follow the rhyme scheme of either the English or the Italian form. In fact, their rhyme is of the incidental and varied pattern characteristic of so much of Thomas's poetry. Terminal sounds are patterned, but hardly enough so to be considered formalized. The rhythm is equally irregular. Most lines contain five stressed syllables, many of them iambic, but that the overall pattern is dominated by iambs is doubtful. Even so, the poems are recognizable as variants of the twentieth century sonnet.

Elder Olson, in *The Poetry of Dylan Thomas* (1954), developed what must be by far the most intricate analysis of the poems' symbolism. He assembled charts to demonstrate that the poems are based on astrology, basically Herculean in identity. Olson's interpretation has been rejected for the most part by other critics. On a different tack, Bernard Knieger, in an essay in the *Explicator* (1956), offered an interpretation to counter a rather muddled one by R. N. Maud earlier in the same periodical. Knieger defined the themes of "Altarwise by Owl-Light" as being simultaneously Christian and sexual. E. H. Essig, again in the *Explicator* (1958), built on Olson's and Knieger's interpretations to demonstrate a fully Christian poetry. In 1965, G. S. Fraser rejected Olson's position out of hand and joined David Daiches in the opinion, expressed in *College English* (1954), that, although splendid in parts, the sonnets are, as wholes, "oppressive and congested." At the same time, he declared that the sonnets "are important because they announce the current orthodox Christian feeling . . . which was henceforth increasingly to dominate Thomas's work in poetry." The opinion is interesting in the face of Thomas's remark, reported by J. M. Brinnin in an article in *The Atlantic Monthly* (1955), that he now intended to write "poems in praise of God's world by a man who doesn't believe in God." Daniel Jones, perhaps, deserves the last word. He argued that "Altarwise by Owl-Light" could be termed "absolute poetry," held together, not by ordinary logic, but by a pattern of words and images joined by a common relationship with such things as "sex, birth, death, Christian and pagan religion and ritual." He saw the poem as "sustained by a single metaphor" and as beyond translation into other words or thoughts. Like Fraser, he saw the poem marking a change in Thomas's poetry, but unlike Fraser, he saw it as moving away from the extravagant expression of the earlier work and toward economy.

It is clear that "Altarwise by Owl-Light" demonstrates Thomas's concern for the life-death paradox taken on the grandest scale and illuminated, at least in part, by the Christian mythos. Also helpful is the understanding that the persona of the poem is a universalized character who is at once himself and the Christ who dies, and who is also all the human beings who have ever died and who will ever die. With their insistence on the mysteries of life in death, mercy in destruction, God in man, the sonnets are quintessentially Thomas.

### "OVER SIR JOHN'S HILL"

"Over Sir John's Hill" first appeared in *Botteghe Oscure* in 1949 and was later included in the *Collected Poems, 1934-1952*. Daniel Jones pointed out that the poem was written during Thomas's residence at Laugharne. The area of "Sir John's Hill" borders an estuary east of the outlet of the River Towy, a semi-wilderness area supporting many wildfowl and birds of prey. The poem, then, reflects a setting that was intimately familiar to Thomas; even so, except for the place-names, the setting could be nearly any waste area in the world where land and a large body of water meet.

Jones's detailed study of the prosody of "Over Sir John's Hill" is interesting. He has noted the varied but exact patterning of the long and short lines based on a syllabic count, the longest line containing fifteen syllables, the shortest containing only one; lines of either thirteen and fourteen syllables, or four to six syllables are the most common line lengths. Jones also observed that the poem's four stanzas have a rhyme pattern of *aabbccbxdadxx*, *a*, *b*, *c*, and *d* being either full-rhymes or half-rhymes, and *x* indicating alliteration with first-syllable assonance. Jones considered the verse form to be representative of Thomas's work at its best and most mature. Although he conceded that such intricacy is open to the charge of artificiality and that syllabic verse tends to be "easily overcome by the natural patterns of the English language, based upon combinations of weak and strong stresses," he argued that all artists must work within "self-imposed discipline."

While "Over Sir John's Hill" exists on many levels, it can be approached quite usefully from the point of view of allegory. Allegory works by having each actor's part function on several levels simultaneously in a linear story. The trick is to see that each actor functions differently, though interrelatedly, in several stories at once. Thus, an actor may be a bird, functioning as a bird, and a bird functioning as a mortal man, and a man functioning as an immortal soul, all at the same time.

Put another way, one actor plays three parts in three stories, all fully coherent, in the telling of one tale. In "Over Sir John's Hill," there is a persona who narrates the action, observes it, and participates in it. The "young Aesop fabling" watches the drama of birdlife and bird death on the estuary shortly before sunset. On the literal level, the persona watches while a hawk, during last light, is destroying sparrows. A fishing heron watches and grieves, and the grief is echoed by the "tear" of the river. The birdlife then settles down, an owl hoots, and the persona hears the sound of the river in the willows just before the plunge of night.

On the ethical level, "Over Sir John's Hill" is a grim sort of parody of the legal system and of institutionalized religion. The birds and the countryside echo human behavior. The hill itself represents a judge who has, on evidence which is never presented in the poem, reached a verdict of condemnation; thus, he is sitting with the symbol of the death sentence on his head, the "black cap of jackdaws." That the cap is formed of jackdaws is instructive. The jackdaw's habit of playing jokes on people is reflected in the term "gulled birds," which Thomas may have picked up from his interest in Jacobean tragedy. "Gulled," in that context, means "fooled" and here functions to undercut the quality of human justice. As jackdaws are also minor carrion birds, their use as a "black cap" heightens the grim note. The hawk represents the executioner, as is indicated by the adjective "tyburn," an allusion to the Tyburn Tree or Tyburn Elms, a thirteenth century place of execution on the River Tybourne and later the slang name for the gallows built near the site of London's Marble Arch. The identification is intensified by an immediate reference to "wrestle of elms" and the "noosed" hawk. The law, it would seem, chooses its victims at random, and the victims themselves are by nature young and silly, foredoomed and courting death. They sing "dilly dilly, come let us die," and are described by the persona and the heron as "led-astray birds." The saintly heron, at the ethical level, stands for the church, which observes the workings of human justice without protest, though it grieves for the victims. The heron, like the church, continues to carry on its own business in spite of the mundane horrors about it. On the ethical level, then, society is formal, filled with sorrow but not with mercy, and its conceptions of justice, death, and divinity are at once structured and casual.

The divine level is still more disquieting. The persona regards nature in an old-fashioned way, his words couched in fresh metaphor, as he describes nature as the Book in which divinity can be read. He opens "the leaves of water" and reads psalms there, and in a shell, he reads "death." He and the heron-church ask for God's mercy, the God who, in silence, observes the sparrow's "hail," a term implying not only the sparrows' song of praise but also the numbers in which their dead bodies pelt the earth. If the God of the poem is more merciful than the indifferent hill-judge, the poem does not say so. Of salvation and an afterlife there is no affirmation; the "lunge of night" seems dreadfully final, not Thomas's more usual affirmation of a circular process in which death is the entrance to life, in which life is repeated rather than translated to a divine realm. It may be that, after the war, Thomas was no longer able to see the cycle of nature as an endlessly repeating pattern. If "Over Sir John's Hill" is in fact a celebration, it is an unusually dark one, even for Thomas.

OTHER MAJOR WORKS

LONG FICTION: *The Death of the King's Canary*, 1976 (with John Davenport).

SHORT FICTION: *Portrait of the Artist as a Young Dog*, 1940; *Selected Writings of Dylan Thomas*, 1946; *A Child's Christmas in Wales*, 1954; *Adventures in the Skin Trade, and Other Stories*, 1955; *A Prospect of the Sea, and Other Stories*, 1955; *Early Prose Writings*, 1971; *The Followers*, 1976; *The Collected Stories*, 1984.

PLAY: *Under Milk Wood: A Play for Voices*, pr. 1953 (public reading), pr. 1954 (radio play), pb. 1954, pr. 1956 (staged; musical settings by Daniel Jones).

SCREENPLAYS: *No Room at the Inn*, 1948 (with Ivan Foxwell); *Three Weird Sisters*, 1948 (with Louise Birt and David Evans); *The Doctor and the Devils*, 1953; *The Beach at Falesá*, 1963; *Twenty Years A'Growing*, 1964; *Me and My Bike*, 1965; *Rebecca's Daughters*, 1965.

RADIO PLAYS: *Quite Early One Morning*, 1944; *The Londoner*, 1946; *Return Journey*, 1947; *Quite Early One Morning*, 1954 (twenty-two radio plays).

NONFICTION: *Letters to Vernon Watkins*, 1957 (Vernon Watkins, editor); *Selected Letters of Dylan Thomas*, 1966 (Constantine FitzGibbon, editor); *Poet in the Making: The Notebooks of Dylan Thomas*, 1968 (Ralph Maud, editor); *Twelve More Letters by Dylan Thomas*, 1969 (FitzGibbon, editor); *The Collected Letters*, 1985 (Paul Ferris, editor).

MISCELLANEOUS: *"The Doctor and the Devils," and Other Scripts*, 1966 (2 screenplays and one radio play).

## BIBLIOGRAPHY

Ackerman, John. *Dylan Thomas: His Life and Work*. New York: St. Martin's Press, 1996. A biography describing the life and writings of Thomas.

_____. *Welsh Dylan: Dylan Thomas's Life, Writing, and His Wales*. 2d ed. Bridgend, Wales: Seren, 1998. This biography of Dylan looks at his homeland, Wales, and shows how the area influenced his writings.

Davies, Walford. *A Reference Companion to Dylan Thomas*. Westport, Conn.: Greenwood Press, 1998. A valuable aid to understanding Thomas's troubled life and enduring body of work. Begins with an insightful biography that provides a useful context for studying his writings. The second section provides a systematic overview of his works, while the third section summarizes the critical and scholarly response to his writings. The volume concludes with a bibliography of the most helpful general studies.

Ferris, Paul. *Dylan Thomas: The Biography*. Washington, D.C.: Counterpoint, 2000. This excellent biography contains material found in American archives and also those of the British Broadcasting Corporation. Ferris interviewed more than two hundred people who either knew Thomas or worked with him. He attempts to separate the facts from the legendary reputation of Thomas. This book elaborates on, and enhances, the "approved" biography by Constantine FitzGibbon (*The Life of Dylan Thomas*, 1965), the personal memoirs by Caitlin Thomas (*Leftover Life to Kill*, 1957), and John Malcolm Brinnin (*Dylan Thomas in America*, 1955).

Hardy, Barbara Nathan. *Dylan Thomas: An Original Language*. Athens: University of Georgia Press, 2000. Hardy looks at Thomas's use of language in his writings, including his use of Welsh-derived terms. Includes bibliography and index.

Korg, Jacob. *Dylan Thomas*. Rev. ed. New York: Twayne, 1992. A basic biography of Thomas that covers his life and works. Includes bibliography and index.

Lycett, Andrew. *Dylan Thomas: A New Life*. Woodstock, N.Y.: Overlook Press, 2005. A major Thomas biography, well-researched and acclaimed.

Sinclair, Andrew. *Dylan the Bard: A Life of Dylan Thomas*. New York: Thomas Dunne Books, 2000. Sinclair provides the story of Thomas's life as a poet and writer. Includes bibliography and index.

Thomas, Caitlin. *My Life with Dylan Thomas: Double Drink Story*. London: Virago, 2008. This memoir by Thomas's wife discusses their life together.

Wigginton, Christopher. *Modernism from the Margins: The 1930's Poetry of Louis MacNeice and Dylan Thomas*. Cardiff: University of Wales Press, 2007. Places the poetry of Louis MacNeice and Thomas in historical time and argues that W. H. Auden's domination of the period was not as extensive as many critics believe.

*B. G. Knepper*

---

# EDWARD THOMAS

**Born:** London, England; March 3, 1878
**Died:** Arras, France; April 9, 1917

PRINCIPAL POETRY

*Six Poems*, 1916
*Poems*, 1917
*Last Poems*, 1918
*Collected Poems*, 1920, 1928
*The Poetry of Edward Thomas*, 1978

OTHER LITERARY FORMS

Although Edward Thomas is remembered today as a poet, throughout his working life, he supported himself and his family by writing various sorts of prose. He always considered himself to be a writer, and the lasting tragedy of his life was that he never seemed able, until the outbreak of World War I, to buy enough time to devote himself to the art of writing as he obviously wished to do. Ironically, the war in which he died also provided him with the structured, organized environment and the freedom from financial anxiety that enabled him to produce the work which has secured his reputation.

His entire prose opus runs to nearly forty volumes, most of which were published during his lifetime. The titles cover a variety of subjects. It is also possible to see what a remarkable volume of work he produced in the years 1911 to 1912, a productivity that culminated, after nine published works, in a breakdown in 1912. Although the prose work of Thomas is often dismissed as being unimportant, it is obvious from merely reading the titles where his main interests lay. Themes of nature and of the British countryside predominate, together with literary criticism.

In fact, Thomas was a remarkably perceptive literary critic. He was among the first reviewers to appreciate the work of Robert Frost, and he also recognized Ezra Pound's achievement in *Personae* (1909), which he reviewed in its first year of publication. When he began to write, he was heavily influenced by Walter Pater's code of aesthetics, his love of rhetoric, and his formality. He was later to have to work hard to rid his prose of those features, which he recognized as being alien to his own poetic voice.

## ACHIEVEMENTS

In his poetry, Edward Thomas succeeded in realizing two ambitions, which another poet of nature set out as his aims more than a century earlier. In the preface to the *Lyrical Ballads* (1798), William Wordsworth stated that his intent in writing poetry was "to exalt and transfigure the natural and the common" and also to redefine the status of the poet so that he would become "a man speaking to men." Wordsworth's poetry received both acclaim and abuse when it first appeared and formed an expectation of poetry that continued until the end of the nineteenth century. By that time, the aesthetic movement had come to the fore, and poetry was well on its way, at the outbreak of World War I, toward suffocating itself with overblown rhetoric.

Thomas is not generally regarded as a war poet, being discussed more often in conjunction with Thomas Hardy and Walter de la Mare than with Wilfred Owen, Siegfried Sassoon, and Isaac Rosenberg. By combining his acute perceptions of both nature and political events, however, Thomas produced poetry in which evocations of place and detailed descriptions of nature become a metaphor for humanity's spiritual state. F. R. Leavis, writing in *New Bearings in English Poetry* (1932) made this observation: "He was exquisitely sincere and sensitive, and he succeeded in expressing in poetry a representative modern sensibility. It was an achievement of a very rare order, and he has not yet had the recognition he deserves." Thomas's poetry has become widely known, and he has become almost an establishment figure in the literature of the early twentieth century. It is a measure of his achievement that in returning to his slender *Collected Poems*, it is always possible to be stimulated and surprised by his work.

## BIOGRAPHY

Edward Philip Thomas was born in London, the eldest of six boys. Both of his parents were Welsh, and Thomas always had an affinity with the principality, spending much time there during his childhood, although the landscapes of his poetry are predominantly those of the south of England. Thomas's father was a stern, unyielding man who had risen by his own efforts to a social position far above that which might be expected from his poor background. Having succeeded in elevating himself, he was naturally very ambitious for his eldest son, and Thomas received an excellent education, attending St. Paul's School, Hammersmith (as a contemporary of G. K. Chesterton and E. C. Bentley, among others), and going on from there to Jesus College, Oxford.

Shortly before going to Oxford, Thomas met Helen Noble; it was one of the momentous events in his life. Both he and Noble had very advanced ideas for their time; they were already lovers while Thomas was still an undergraduate. They discussed their future lives together and how they would bring up their children in accordance with Richard Jeffries's theories of freedom and the open-air life. Noble herself said, "We hated the thought of a legal contract. We felt our love was all the bond there ought to be, and that if that failed it was immoral to be bound together. We wanted our union to be free and spontaneous." In the spring of 1899, Noble discovered that she was pregnant and was rather appalled to discover that Edward himself, as well as her friends in the bohemian community in which she lived, thought that they should be married. Noble's family were shocked to learn of her pregnancy, insisting on a hurried marriage and refusing to help the young couple in any way. Thomas's family was more sympathetic, allowing Noble to live with them and helping Thomas while he worked toward his degree.

Once he graduated, the need to earn money to support his family became pressing, and determined not to become submerged in the drudgery of an office job, Thomas solicited work from publishers. Until the time that he joined the Artists' Rifles, Thomas supported himself and his family by writing. They were always poor, and he often reproached himself bitterly because he had no regular source of income.

Writing became a chore to him, something to be done merely for the sake of the money. In 1912, he suffered a breakdown brought on by overwork. At about that time, also, he met Frost and formed a close friendship with the American poet. Thomas was among the first to appreciate Frost's poetry, and Frost encouraged Thomas to try his hand at writing poetry himself; Thomas gradually gained confidence in his ability to say what he wanted in poetry. When he was killed by a bombshell in the spring of 1917, what might have become a considerable voice in English poetry was tragically silenced.

ANALYSIS

Perhaps the most notable feature of Edward Thomas's poetry, which strikes the reader immediately, is its characteristic quietness of tone and its unassertive, gentle quality. He is primarily a poet of the country, but through his descriptions of the English landscape, impressionistic and minutely observed, he also attempts to delineate some of the features of his own inner landscape.

As may be seen from the titles of the many books of prose that he wrote before beginning to write poetry at the behest of Frost, he was always deeply interested in nature and the land. Many of the fleeting observations in his poetry are drawn from his notebooks, in which he recorded such things as the first appearance of a spring blossom and the first sightings of various species of birds. In his prose, as opposed to the notebooks, his style was highly rhetorical, so that the keen observations that make his poetry so effective are lost in a plethora of adjectival excess. In one of his reviews, he wrote that "The important thing is not that a thing should be small, but that it should be intense and capable of unconsciously symbolic significance." In his poetry, by the acuity of his observation and the spareness and tautness of his language, he certainly achieves remarkable—if low-key—intensity. He also achieves, in his best work, an unforced symbolic resonance.

### "AS THE TEAM'S HEAD-BRASS"

"As the Team's Head-Brass" is one of Thomas's most impressive achievements; at first reading, it may appear to be only an account of a rural dialogue between the poet and a man plowing a field. It begins with a reference to the plowman, and to some lovers who are seen disappearing into the wood behind the field being plowed. The lovers are not directly relevant to the substance of the poem, but they are an important detail. The poem begins and ends with a reference to them, and although they are in no sense representative of a Lawrentian "life-force," their presence in the poem does suggest the triumph of life and love over death and destruction. The very mention of the lovers reinforces the image of the plow horses "narrowing a yellow square of charlock"—that is, destroying the (living) weeds, that better life may grow.

"If we could see all all might seem good" says the plowman, and this seems to be Thomas's contention in this poem. The writing throughout is highly controlled, the structure of the poem reinforced with alliteration and internal rhyme—seeming to owe something to Gerard Manley Hopkins and ultimately even to the Welsh *cynghanedd* form, with the use of "fallen/fallow/plough/narrowing/yellow/charlock" all in four lines, and then later in the same opening section, "word/weather/war/scraping/share/screwed/furrow." Leavis observes that "we become aware of the inner life which the sensory impressions are notation for." This is particularly true of "As the Team's Head-Brass." The closing lines bring the whole poem together most succinctly—the lovers, forgotten since the opening lines, emerge from the wood; the horses begin to plow a new furrow; "for the last time I watched" says Thomas, and the reader must pause here to ask whether he means "for the last time on this particular occasion" or "for the last time ever." All the conversation in the poem has been about war, and in the last two lines come the words "crumble/topple/stumble," which, although used ostensibly with reference to the horses and the soil, may equally be taken to refer back to the fallen tree on which the poet is sitting, the plowman's workmate who has been killed in the war, the changing state of society, and the relentless passage of time.

### "ADLESTROP"

"As the Team's Head-Brass" is not typical of Thomas's work, however, for it is longer and much more detailed and elaborate than most of his poems. More typical of his work are poems such as "Tall Nettles" and "Adlestrop," which evoke the moment without attempting to do more than capture the unique quality of one particular place or one particular moment in time. "Adlestrop" is a poem much anthologized and much appreciated by those who love the English countryside. It has been described as the most famous of modern "place" poems, and yet it also seems to conjure up an almost sexual tension (perhaps by the use of the words "lonely fair"?) of a kind that is often implicit in such hot summer days. This is a sense of the poem that the contemporary poet Dannie Abse has obviously found, for he has written a poem titled "Not Adlestrop," in which the unspecified lady actually makes an appearance in a train going in the opposite direction. Abse's poem is something of a literary joke, but it does pinpoint an element of unresolved sexual tension in several of Thomas's poems. "Some Eyes Condemn," "Celandine," and "The Unknown" all seem to be worlds away in mood from "And You, Helen," a poem written for his wife.

### "NO ONE SO MUCH AS YOU"

The poignant "No One So Much as You," a kind of apologia for an imperfectly reciprocated love, was written for Mary Elizabeth Thomas, the poet's mother, although it has often been mistaken for a love poem to his wife. In either case it would seem that familiarity did not necessarily increase Thomas's love for his family—in fact, it was obvious, both from his despairing reaction to the news of his wife's second pregnancy and from his well-documented impatience with domestic life—that distance and mystery were important elements of attraction for him. Perhaps fortunately for all concerned, Thomas's dissatisfactions and unfulfilled longings seem to have made up only a very small part of his nature. Having come to poetry late, he wastes little time in cataloging regrets for what he might have been and concentrates mainly on what he was able to do best—that is, to capture his own impressions of English rural life and country landscapes and combine them in poetry with various insights into his own personality.

### AFFINITY FOR COUNTRY LIFE

It would not be possible to offer a succinct analysis of Thomas's poetry without referring to his deeply felt patriotism. In *Edward Thomas: A Poet for His Country* (1978), Jan Marsh describes an incident that occurred soon after Thomas enlisted in the British army, although he was in fact over the usual age limit for enlistment. A friend asked the poet what he thought he was fighting for; Thomas bent down and picked up a pinch of earth and, letting it crumble through his fingers, answered, "Literally, for this."

This is the predominant impression that the reader carries away from an encounter with Thomas's poetry, for here is a sensitive, educated man who, despite his cultivation, is deeply attuned to the land. This affinity is particularly clear in the country people who inhabit Thomas's poetry, for they are always portrayed as being part of a long and noble tradition of rural life. Thomas does not romanticize his vision: He portrays the cruelties of nature as well as its beauties. A recurring image in his poetry is that of the gamekeeper's board, hung with trophies in an attempt to discourage other predators. Perhaps because he makes an honest attempt to describe the reality of country life without attempting to gloss over or soften its less attractive aspects, he succeeds superbly. Since his life, when his poetry was scarcely known, Thomas's work has become steadily more popular, so that he has become known as one of England's finest nature poets.

OTHER MAJOR WORKS

NONFICTION: *The Woodland Life*, 1897; *Horae Solitariae*, 1902; *Oxford*, 1903; *Rose Acre Papers*, 1904; *Beautiful Wales*, 1905; *The Heart of England*, 1906; *Richard Jeffries*, 1909; *The South Country*, 1909; *Feminine Influence on the Poets*, 1910; *Rest and Unrest*, 1910; *Rose Acre Papers*, 1910; *Windsor Castle*, 1910; *Celtic Stories*, 1911; *The Isle of Wight*, 1911; *Light and Twilight*, 1911; *Maurice Maeterlinck*, 1911; *The Tenth Muse*, 1911; *Algernon Charles Swinburne*, 1912; *George Borrow: The Man and His Books*, 1912; *Lafcadio Hearn*, 1912; *Norse Tales*, 1912; *The Country*, 1913; *The Happy-Go-Lucky Morgans*, 1913; *The Icknield Way*, 1913; *Walter Pater*, 1913; *In Pursuit of Spring*, 1914; *The Life of the Duke of Marlborough*, 1915; *A Literary Pilgrim in England*, 1917; *Cloud Castle, and Other Papers*, 1922; *Chosen Essays*, 1926; *Essays of Today and Yesterday*, 1926; *The Last Sheaf*, 1928; *The Childhood of Edward Thomas*, 1938; *The Prose of Edward Thomas*, 1948 (Roland Gant, editor); *Letters from Edward Thomas to Gordon Bottomley*, 1968; *Letters to America, 1914-1917*, 1978.

CHILDREN'S LITERATURE: *Four-and-Twenty-Blackbirds*, 1915.

BIBLIOGRAPHY

Cuthbertson, Guy, and Lucy Newlyn, eds. *Branch-Lines: Edward Thomas and Contemporary Poetry*. Chester Springs, Pa.: Dufour Editions, 2007. Contains essays on Thomas and poems by him and the poets he influenced.

Emeny, Richard, comp. *Edward Thomas, 1878-1917: Towards a Complete Checklist of His Publications*. Edited by Jeff Cooper. Blackburn, Lancashire, England: White Sheep Press, 2004. A bibliography of Thomas's numerous publications, from the poetry to the many prose writings.

Farjeon, Eleanor. *Edward Thomas: The Last Four Years*. Rev. ed. Foreword by P. J. Kavanagh. Edited by Anne Harvey. Stroud, Gloucestershire, England: Sutton, 2007. A double memoir that uses Thomas's letters and Farjeon's diaries to provide a candid account of their developing friendship. Offers a unique account of Thomas's development as a poet, including his meeting Robert Frost, whose encouragement led to Thomas's first poems. Thomas's letters describe his family, his friendships with other writers, and provides a detailed account of his experiences in World War I.

Frost, Robert, and Edward Thomas. *Elected Friends: Robert Frost and Edward Thomas to One Another*. Edited by Matthew Spencer. New York: Handsel Books, 2003. Contains the letters and poems that Frost and Thomas wrote to each other. Frost's influence helped Thomas develop as a poet.

Kirkham, Michael. *The Imagination of Edward Thomas*. New York: Cambridge University Press, 1986. Kirkham ignores chronology as he explores Thomas's imagination by identifying the characteristic style that is evidenced in his poetry. Augmented with a solid bibliography and an index, this book is extremely helpful for an in-depth study of Thomas.

Motion, Andrew. *The Poetry of Edward Thomas*. 1980. Reprint. London: Hogarth, 1991. Motion approaches Thomas's poetry as drawing from the Georgian tradition while anticipating the arrival of the modernists in content and in form. Motion examines the subtle style of Thomas and introduces him as an evolutionary poet.

Smith, Stan. *Edward Thomas*. London: Faber & Faber, 1986. Thomas is considered in this book as the "quintessential English poet," whose devotion to the rural countryside is reflected in his poetry. Presents several critical approaches. Helpful selected bibliography.

Thomas, R. George. *Edward Thomas: A Portrait*. 1985. Reprint. Oxford, England: Clarendon Press, 1987. This book provides rare insight into the life and work of Thomas by making use of letters, memoirs, and personal papers. Biographical in nature, and supported by an excellent bibliography, the book gives a solid foundation for the study of his prose and poetry.

Wiśniewski, Jacek. *Edward Thomas: A Mirror of England*. Newcastle upon Tyne, England: Cambridge Scholars, 2009. Critical analysis of the works of Thomas, whom the author finds to be representative of England.

*Vivien Stableford*

# R. S. THOMAS

**Born:** Cardiff, Wales; March 29, 1913
**Died:** Pentrefelin, Wales; September 25, 2000

PRINCIPAL POETRY

*The Stones of the Field*, 1946
*An Acre of Land*, 1952
*The Minister*, 1953
*Song at the Year's Turning: Poems, 1942-1954*, 1955
*Poetry for Supper*, 1958
*Tares*, 1961
*The Bread of Truth*, 1963
*Pietà*, 1966
*Not that He Brought Flowers*, 1968
*H'm*, 1972
*Young and Old*, 1972
*Selected Poems, 1946-1968*, 1973
*What is a Welshman?*, 1974
*Laboratories of the Spirit*, 1975
*The Way of It*, 1977
*Frequencies*, 1978
*Between Here and Now*, 1981
*Later Poems, 1972-1982*, 1983
*Destinations*, 1985
*Ingrowing Thoughts*, 1985
*Experimenting with an Amen*, 1986
*Welsh Airs*, 1987
*The Echoes Return Slow*, 1988
*Counterpoint*, 1990
*Mass for Hard Times*, 1992
*Collected Poems, 1945-1990*, 1993
*No Truce with the Furies*, 1995
*Residues*, 2002
*Selected Poems*, 2003
*Collected Later Poems, 1988-2000*, 2004

OTHER LITERARY FORMS

Apart from minor prose pieces, R. S. Thomas's other creative works have been autobiography, talks, and a number of radio and television broadcasts. His main autobiographical apologia, *Neb* (1985), meaning "nobody," was written in Welsh, and in the third person. He also edited a number of volumes of verse, including the *Batsford Book of Country Verse* (1961) and *The Penguin Book of Religious Verse* (1963). He also edited selected volumes of Edward Thomas, a fellow Anglo-Welsh poet, George Herbert, and William Wordsworth. His best-known talk was that given at the National Eisteddford in 1976, entitled "Abercuawg," about the search for the ideal Welsh village. None of his sermons has been recorded.

ACHIEVEMENTS

Over R. S. Thomas's long poetic career, he won acclaim as the leading Anglo-Welsh poet and, for a period of that time, as one of the leading British poets. His first public recognition was in 1962, when his works were included in the first volume of *Penguin Modern Poets*. By then, his *Song at the Year's Turning* had won the Heinemann Award of the Royal Society of Literature. In 1964, he was offered the Queen's Medal for Poetry by poet laureate John Masefield. He received the Cholmondeley Award for 1978, and subsequently, three Welsh Arts Council Literary Awards. In 1996, he was nominated for the Nobel Prize in Literature and was given the Lannan Lifetime Achievement Award.

After his death in 2000, a memorial service was held in Westminster Abbey. Leading Anglo-Irish poet Seamus Heaney read some of his poetry, as did poet laureate Andrew Motion. The R. S. Thomas Research Centre has been set up at the University of Wales, Bangor, where many of his private papers are kept.

BIOGRAPHY

Ronald Stuart Thomas was born in South Wales. His father, Thomas Hubert Thomas, was a seaman and frequently absent. Thomas, an only child, found himself in a close but uneasy relationship with his mother, Peggy. When he was five years old, the family moved to Holyhead, North Wales, the major port to Ireland. Although the county was largely Welsh speaking, Holyhead itself was English speaking, as were his parents, and the high school he attended from 1925 to 1931.

It was decided he should enter the church in Wales. To pursue this career, he first attended University College, Bangor, where he majored in Latin, and then spent a year at theological college in South Wales. His first post was in 1936 at Chirk, on the English-Welsh border north of Shrewsbury. While there, he met Mildred Elsie "Elsi" Eldridge, an artist and art teacher. They were married July 5, 1940. As an ordained minister, he was excused from wartime service. Later, Thomas became an ardent pacifist and antinuclear campaigner.

After another curacy in the area, Thomas and his wife wanted to discover a "truer" Wales, with mountains and speakers of Welsh. He thought he had found such an area in 1942, when he was appointed to Manafon, a small parish in mid-Wales in a secluded valley with hills all round. The couple's only son, Gwydion, was born there in 1945.

Thomas began making rounds to visit the many hill farmers of the area and to learn Welsh. His poetry changed to focus on these very different farmers and villagers, and they formed the core of his earlier and better-known work.

However, Thomas began to feel the drawbacks of such a remote parish. He moved to Eglwys Fach, a small village north of Aberystwyth, the other side of mid-Wales. The scenery of estuary, sea, and mountains was stunning. An added attraction was the bird sanctuary, as by now Thomas had become an avid bird-watcher. His congregation was mainly older, retired English or Anglo-Welsh people, very different from the members of the farming community of Manafon. Opinions about him were divided. By all accounts, he could be a silent and difficult man, though an expert visitor of the sick.

Thomas stayed for thirteen years, from 1954 to 1967, before moving on to his final parish of Aberdaron, at the end of the Lleyn Peninusla in North Wales. The Lleyn is a twenty-five-mile-long neck of land sticking out into the Irish Sea. It is remote, has some of the world's oldest rocks, and is predominantly Welsh speaking except for three summer months, when English tourists invade the area. He became increasingly pro-Welsh and anti-English, though he preached and wrote in English.

He retired in 1978 but continued to live in the parish in a small cottage, his output of poetry unabated. His wife, Elsi, died in 1991. After a short while, he started a relationship with a former parishioner from Eglwys Fach, Betty Vernon, also widowed. They married in 1996. By that time, he was suffering from a heart condition and had to curtail the traveling he had been doing as a recognized man of letters. In 2000, after a short illness, he died at the age of eighty-seven.

ANALYSIS

R. S. Thomas's output—more than twenty-five volumes of poetry—was substantial. However, Thomas was careless of his own compositions, reluctant to explain difficult passages, and revised very little. Most of his poems were less than thirty lines. He wrote no long poems, although he did create several sequences.

In many ways, it is best to see each small poem as part of one grand, lifelong work. There is never any great philosophical statement, but many detailed observations of life, the cycle of the seasons, the ordinary people he met in his parishes, their joys and griefs, and moments of religious or philosophical insight. Although he was a priest, his faith was more one of uneasy questionings, with black humor substituting for a theology. In real life, he preached the doctrines of his church; but as a poet, he looked enigmatically at each attempt to portray God. As a nature mystic, he is nearer to Ted Hughes, a contemporary from northern England, than to any tradition of religious poetry. Although he was a provincial poet, unashamedly Welsh, his perceptions and questions are universal, with a probing of modernism. Paradox was his hallmark, both in real life and in his poetry, with an ironic perception of his own persona and speaking voice. His poetry is imagistic and Romantic.

Recognition came comparatively late for Thomas. His first two volumes were printed at his own expense. Through the influence of friends, his first acclaimed volume, *Song at the Year's Turning*, was published by a small but reputable London publisher, Hart-Davis. That volume proved to be typical of the poetry he published over the next fifteen years, giving him national standing as a poet of Wales, its people, culture, and landscapes.

After his removal to Aberdaron, where he found a truly Welsh milieu, he no longer felt the need to write on obviously Welsh matters. He turned to theological issues, as in *H'm*. On his retirement, he continued to develop poems on his own spiritual journey, intermixed with autobiographical memories, starting with *Laboratories of the Spirit* and *Frequencies*. Longer sequences began to develop, for example a series of meditations on famous paintings in *Between Here and Now*, and especially in *The Echoes Return Slow* and *Counterpoint*. The latter probably represents his most coherent attempt to state a philosophical/religious viewpoint. He continued producing poetry until his death.

### SONG AT THE YEAR'S TURNING

*Song at the Year's Turning*, published in 1955 when Thomas was already forty-two years old, is the volume that brought him to the attention of the general public. It consists of poems written while he was at Manafon, in the Welsh hill country. The title poem, addressed to himself, suggests the end of idealistic dreams of a Welsh pastoral; in their place is a grittiness, a disillusionment expressed in Romantic imagery of seasonal change. He asks, "Is there blessing?" It could be said that the rest of Thomas's poetry is an attempt to find the answer to that question. The Wordsworthian optimism in nature has been put aside in Thomas's ironic perceptions of the rural countryside, just as it was in the writings of Thomas Hardy.

This is most clearly seen in the character Thomas invented in "A Peasant" (from *The Stones of the Field*), Iago Prytherch, an independent small farmer of the infertile hills. Once he may have been prosperous; now time works against him and his way of life, which has become a physical, ugly fight for survival. "The Last of the Peasantry" in *Song at the Year's Turning* echoes this. As a priest, he, the poet, feels unable to find any point of contact, but the reader senses Thomas's deep compassion.

### H'M

This sense of searching for the lost Wales and portraying a very unromantic present is the main theme of the poems written up until *H'm*. This volume introduced quite a new voice, a move that parallels that of Thomas's contemporary, Hughes. Like Thomas, after a number of volumes of nature poetry, Hughes also discovered a new voice—blatant, anarchistic, and God defying. Hughes's *Crow* (1970, revised 1972) and Thomas's *H'm* were published within two years of each other.

The word "H'm"—a noncommital utterance—is apparently the expression Thomas used to signify he had heard the speaker but did not want to agree or disagree. In the context of his poetry, however, it could also suggest the word "Him," in the sense of God, but as an abbreviated perception. The title poem depicts the priest-poet trying to utter a truth about God's love, but the "big bellies" of the starving children take away the utterance. The poems become, then, a theodicy, that is, a speaking well of God in a world of evil. First, however, the evil has to be spoken about. For Hughes, the evil suggest anarchy and nonexistence; Thomas still hung on grimly to a truth of God, even if it can never be expressed in Romantic terms of presence and beauty.

Thomas's other concern was with the "machine," the new religion of technology: "The machine . . . cannot absolve us," though it tries to dismantle religious faith. The shiny machine is opposed to the dark suffering cross and the wounded side of Christ. The poems are thus far more obviously religious than the earlier ones.

### LABORATORIES OF THE SPIRIT

Three years later, Thomas continues his theodicy, but at a more personal level in *Laboratories of the Spirit*. The mood is set by the first poem in the collection, "Emerging." There is more address to God; the poetry is not just about him: "Not as in the old days I pray,/ God." This wrestling with God, as found in Herbert and Gerard Manley Hopkins, is part of a long tradition that Thomas joins. The poem ends with the phrase "the laboratory of the spirit," which suggests the need to use modern scientific metaphors to come to terms with God anew in a machine age.

The Hughes-like "Hand" wrestles with the independence of the poet to make sense of the world and to find truth. Somehow God is still in the creative process and cannot be written out of it. In the end, there is an uneasy truce: God gives the poet his freedom but on the condition that he "tell them I am," just as in the burning bush episode, another poet-priest, Moses, was given the name "I am" by which to call God. It would seem that Thomas, no longer needing to preach about God, felt the need to write about him more and more explicitly in Christian terms.

## OTHER MAJOR WORKS

NONFICTION: *Selected Prose*, 1983, 1995 (Sandra Anstey, editor); *Neb*, 1985; *Autobiographies*, 1997 (Jason Walford Davies, translator); *R. S. Thomas: Letters to Raymond Garlick, 1951-1999*, 2009 (Davies, editor).

EDITED TEXTS: *Batsford Book of Country Verse*, 1961; *The Penguin Book of Religious Verse*, 1963.

## BIBLIOGRAPHY

Anstey, Sandra, ed. *Critical Writings on R. S. Thomas.* Rev. ed. Chester Springs, Pa.: Dufour Editions, 1992. A collection of essays on Thomas's poetry dating from 1952 to 1991, including two by A. M. Allchin, and one by Peter Abbs, a fellow Anglo-Welsh poet. The essays are taken from Anglo-Welsh literary journals.

Brown, Tony. *R. S. Thomas.* Cardiff: University of Wales Press, 2003. This introductory work, part of the Writers of Wales series, deals with biography and critical assessments and analyses.

Davis, William V. *R. S. Thomas: Poetry and Theology.* Baylor, Texas: Baylor University Press, 2007. This is an introductory work on Thomas's poetry, especially his more obviously religious poetry.

McGill, William J. *Poets' Meeting: George Herbert, R. S. Thomas, and the Argument with God.* Jefferson, N.C.: McFarland, 2003. This compares the two Anglican priest-poets and the way they address God, either from faith or doubt.

Morgan, Christopher. *R. S. Thomas: Identity, Environment, Deity.* New York: Manchester University Press, 2003. Deals with common themes in Thomas's volumes of verse, especially those that focus on the philosophical and practical aspects of science and technology ("machine").

Rogers, Byron. *The Man Who Went into the West: The Life of R. S. Thomas.* London: Aurum Press, 2006. This is the authorized biography of Thomas, supported with a major research grant from the Welsh Books Council. It includes extensive interviews with Thomas's son and many others, and the finding of extensive correspondence and documentation not hitherto available.

*David Barratt*

# JAMES THOMSON

**Born:** Ednam, Roxburgh, Scotland; September 7, 1700
**Died:** Richmond, Surrey, England; August 27, 1748

## PRINCIPAL POETRY

*Winter*, 1726
*Summer*, 1727
*Spring*, 1728
*Autumn*, 1730
*A Hymn*, 1730
*The Seasons*, 1730, 1744, 1746 (includes *Winter*, *Summer*, *Spring*, and *Autumn*)
*Liberty*, 1735-1736
*The Castle of Indolence: An Allegorical Poem*, 1748

## OTHER LITERARY FORMS

Although James Thomson's reputation is as a poet, he also wrote plays that were generally successful in their day. He wrote five plays and coauthored a sixth. *The Tragedy of Sophonisba*, a tragedy about the Carthaginian queen Sophonisba, was performed and published in 1730. Thomson's second tragedy, *Agamemnon*, appeared in 1738. His next two plays followed rapidly: *Edward and Eleonora* (pb. 1739) was prohibited by censorship, and *Alfred* (pr., pb. 1740) was coauthored with David Mallet. The play about King Alfred contains Thomson's famous ode "Rule, Britannia," still well known in England, especially the refrain: "Rule, Britannia, rule the waves;/ Britons never will be slaves." Thomson's most successful play, the tragedy *Tancred and Sigismunda* (pr., pb. 1745), continued to be performed in the second half of the eighteenth century and was translated into French and German. His final play, the tragedy *Coriolanus* (pr., pb. 1749), was not performed until after Thomson's death.

## ACHIEVEMENTS

For more than a century, James Thomson's most famous work, *The Seasons*, was among the most widely read poems in English. It went through more than two hundred editions in the eighteenth century. Even though

William Wordsworth replaced Thomson as the poet of nature for English readers beginning in the nineteenth century, *The Seasons* remained popular; there have been more than four hundred editions of the poem since the eighteenth century.

BIOGRAPHY

James Thomson was born in the village of Ednam, Roxburgh, in Scotland, close to the border with England. His father, Thomas Thomson, was a minister. The poet's mother, Beatrix Trotter Thomson, communicated enthusiasm for religious devotion to her children. James was the fourth of nine children. When he was an infant, Thomson's family moved to the nearby hamlet of Southdean. Here the future poet of nature roamed a varied landscape that included snow on the Cheviot Hills, the Jed Water, and a pastoral setting in which light and shade, cloud and horizon, wind and weather, and greens and browns produce an environment of remarkable variety and dramatic vividness.

Thomson was a student for almost ten years at Edinburgh University, beginning in 1715. He studied for the Presbyterian ministry, but poetry, which he began writing before college, became increasingly important to him. By early 1725, Thomson had decided to go to London to attempt a literary career. His successes were quick by any standards. The first version of what would become his immensely popular *The Seasons* was the 406-line poem *Winter*, published in April, 1726. This was followed by a second edition just two months later. *Summer* appeared in 1727, *Spring* in 1728, and *Autumn* in 1730 as part of the first edition of *The Seasons*. During these first five years in England, Thomson also wrote "Poem to the Memory of Sir Isaac Newton" (1727), "Britannia" (1729), and his first play, *The Tragedy of Sophonisba.*

From 1730 to 1733, Thomson took a Grand Tour as the traveling companion and tutor to Charles Richard Talbot, eldest son of the Solicitor-General Charles Talbot. Between his return from the Grand Tour and his death fifteen years later, Thomson wrote five plays and produced *The Castle of Indolence: An Allegorical Poem*, his imitation of the Spenserian stanza from *The Faerie Queene* (1590, 1596) of the Renaissance poet Edmund Spenser.

*James Thomson* (Hulton Archive/Getty Images)

The poet moved to the village of Richmond, Surrey, in 1736, and spent the last twelve years of his life there. Richmond was about ten miles from London, with rural beauty and reasonable proximity to the capital. There Thomson enjoyed friendships with the writers Alexander Pope, John Dyer, Aaron Hill, Mallet, Richard Savage, William Shenstone, and Tobias Smollett. Thomson courted Elizabeth Young, the sister-in-law of Thomson's old Scottish friend William Robertson. He wrote her tortured love letters, which became more desperate as her indifference continued. Thomson did not give up until she married someone else. Thomson never married. He died just two weeks before his forty-eighth birthday of a fever on August 27, 1748.

ANALYSIS

The plays of James Thomson are largely forgotten, as is the poem Thomson regarded as his finest work, *Liberty*. His reputation rests on *The Seasons* and, to a lesser extent, *The Castle of Indolence*. Thomson critics and scholars generally agree, as Richard Terry puts it, that there is no doubt that "Thomson is a major poet of his time . . . but there is still scope for the nature of his individual achievement to be redefined." Whatever redefinition future scholarship on Thomson attempts, *The Seasons* will remain his distinctive contribution to English poetry.

### THE SEASONS

The main debate in Thomson scholarship about *The Seasons* concerns whether or how thoroughly this long poem is unified. Scholar David Anderson claims that the poem demonstrates a structural principle that gives an effective direction to the reader about how to comprehend the many topics that appear in Thomson's poem. Anderson describes the structure of the poem as leading readers from "landscape description, through emotional response to landscape, to enthusiastic praise of the landscape's Creator." He names this structure an "emotive theodicy." Since any theodicy attempts to justify the ways of God to human beings, Anderson is being logical when he argues that the central fact of *The Seasons* is contained in the following lines: ". . . tho' conceal'd, to every purer Eye/ Th' informing Author in his Works appears:/ Chief, lovely Spring, in thee, and thy soft Scenes,/ The SMILING GOD is seen. . . ."

The first collected edition of *The Seasons* was published in 1730. Its total length was 4,569 lines. Thomson produced a major revision of his most famous poem, which appeared in 1744; this edition is a quarter longer, adding about 1,000 lines. These are certainly not two different poems, but much changed in the intervening fourteen years. The 1744 edition makes *Spring* and *Autumn* only about 100 lines longer. About 300 lines are added to *Winter*, and approximately 600 to *Summer*. Scholar James Sambrook notes that the later edition extends the historical and geographical material. He also notes that in *Winter* Thomson doubles the number of ancient heroes and makes the passage five times longer than in the 1730 text. Sambrook emphasizes that in *Summer*, the 1744 edition more evenly balances pleasures and pains as well as horrors and delights in nature. This attempt at a balancing act in the revisions of *The Seasons* serves both a religious and a political purpose.

If religion and praise of God are important to *The Seasons*, so is politics. Scholar Tim Fulford emphasizes that Thomson's landscapes in *The Seasons*, especially in the 1744 edition, are imagined by the poet as political spaces. Thomson sees wild landscapes as bastions of natural British freedom, and he presents cultivated landscapes as indexes of the virtues of the patrons whose political commitments Thomson shared. The poet perceives this wild native freedom and cultivated virtues of British landscapes as threatened by the spreading corruption of Prime Minister Robert Walpole's government of arbitrary and abusive power. This corruption is literally covering the landscape, attacking both natural freedom and the civil freedoms of a just society. In *Winter*, Thomson describes the arrogance and barbarism of corrupt power: "AH little think the gay licentious Proud,/ Whom Pleasure, Power, and Affluence surround," while others "feel, this very Moment, Death/ And all the sad Variety of Pain." Thomson, in trying to marry religious and political commitments in his presentation of natural and cultivated landscapes, risks both the unity of his poem and the integrity of his poetic vision.

### LIBERTY

Thomson's time in France and Italy inspired him to write what he regarded as his most important poem, *Liberty*. Thomson originally intended *Liberty* to be a "poetical landscape of countries, mixed with moral observations on their governments and people." This approach would have identified the poem as by the author of the highly successful *The Seasons*, but Thomson did not follow this plan. The poet who reestablished natural description in English poetry in *The Seasons* barely mentions nature in *Liberty*, which was an utter failure with the public. It was published in separate parts: Three thousand copies of part 1 were printed, two thousand copies of parts 2 and 3, and only one thousand copies of parts 4 and 5, indicating the failure of the poem. However, Thomson considered it his most important and finest poem. Scholar Samuel Kliger feels that it is understandable that Thomson considered it his greatest poem; he said, *Liberty* "could be considered great because its theme—the increment of history turned back to enrich the lives of England's humblest citizens—was great."

*Liberty* argues against luxury and corruption as the causes of tyranny. This 3,378-line poem describes the cyclical rise and fall of freedom in various states, principally Greece and Rome. Thomson feared that Great Britain was beginning to decline because of indulgence in luxury and party faction by eminent Britons. The poem is a dissuasion against self-interest, attempting to show that freedom is a delicate condition that must be nurtured and maintained with great care. The poem deals with the necessity of harmonizing all aspects of the personality so that one will not be susceptible to corruption in any of its forms. *Liberty* is a fable about political virtue that embodies Thomson's conception of spiritual evolution and that holds up the ideal of "*boundless Good without the power of Ill*."

### THE CASTLE OF INDOLENCE

In April, 1748, Thomson wrote a letter to his friend William Paterson about what would be Thomson's last major poem: "after fourteen or fifteen Years, the Castle of Indolence comes abroad in a Fortnight." Thomson's friend Patrick Murdoch described the genesis of the poem as a mockery of himself and some friends whom he thought indolent. This playful origin of the poem and a more serious application of the moral of the poem— to live an active life of public service—are both present in the tone of *The Castle of Indolence*. In the same letter about the poem, Murdoch added: "But he saw very soon, that the subject deserved to be treated more seriously, and in a form fitted to convey one of the most important moral lessons."

*The Castle of Indolence* consists of two cantos. It is a poem of 1,422 lines. The first canto is composed of seventy-seven Spenserian stanzas, or 693 lines. The Spenserian stanza uses 8 iambic lines of ten syllables and a ninth line of twelve syllables, and its rhyme scheme is *ababbcbcc*. Canto 1 describes a castle where imagination and romantic images create earthly paradises suggested by the Bower of Bliss in Spenser's *Faerie Queene*. This castle is ruled by the Wizard of Indolence, who uses Nepenthe, the drink from the *Faerie Queene*, to enchant people and draw them into the luxurious ease of the castle. The influence of the drink is to provide "sweet Oblivion of vile earthly Care;/ Fair gladsome waking Thoughts, and joyous Dreams more fair." The inhabitants of the cas-

tle, however, become ill and are left in a dungeon to languish.

The second canto is composed of eighty-one stanzas, or 729 lines. It presents the Knight of Arts and Industry destroying the romantic imagination and replacing it with moral responsibility and hard work. This commitment to hard work, public service, and progress leads to eternal activity: "Heirs of Eternity! yborn to rise/ Through endless States of Being, still more near/ To Bliss approaching, and Perfection clear . . ."

*The Castle of Indolence* was praised by Wordsworth. Another nineteenth century English poet, Percy Bysshe Shelley, said that "the Enchanter in the first canto was a true philanthropist, and the Knight in the second an oligarchical imposter, overthrowing truth by power." Sambrook argues that the achievement of Thomson's poem "is to make us feel the power of romanticism and respond with delight to its appeal, while at the same time we judge it, and know the dangers of its rejection of responsibility and reality."

### OTHER MAJOR WORKS

PLAYS: *The Tragedy of Sophonisba*, pb. 1730; *Agamemnon*, pr., pb. 1738; *Edward and Eleonora*, pb. 1739; *Alfred*, pr., pb. 1740 (with David Mallet); *Tancred and Sigismunda*, pr., pb. 1745; *Coriolanus*, pr., pb. 1749.

### BIBLIOGRAPHY

Goodman, Kevis. *Georgic Modernity and British Romanticism: Poetry and the Mediation of History*. New York: Cambridge University Press, 2008. Examines the poetry and writings of Thomson (*The Seasons*), William Wordsworth, William Cowper, and Joseph Addison.

Irlam, Shaun. *Elations: The Poetics of Enthusiasm in Eighteenth-Century Britain*. Stanford, Calif.: Stanford University Press, 1999. Takes the concept of enthusiasm and examines the aesthetic theory and poetry of Thomson and Edward Young.

Lethbridge, Stefanie. *James Thomson's Defence of Poetry: Intertextual Allusion in "The Seasons."* Tübingen, Germany: Max Niemeyer, 2003. Examines aesthetics in Thomson's *The Seasons*.

Sambrook, James. *James Thomson, 1700-1748: A Life.*

New York: Clarendon Press, 1991. This extensive biography places Thomson in his social and cultural context, explores his relationships with fellow writers such as Alexander Pope, and thoroughly examines Thomson's Whig politics and relationship with Frederick, Prince of Wales, leader of the opposition to Prime Minister Robert Walpole. Sambrook supplies biography, history, and literary criticism by producing a detailed analysis of the whole body of Thomson's writings.

Scott, Mary Jane W. *James Thomson, Anglo-Scot.* Athens: University of Georgia Press, 1988. This book argues for the importance of the Scottish dimensions of Thomson's writings. For example, although Anthony Ashley-Cooper, third earl of Shaftesbury, has always been considered a major influence on Thomson's ideas about benevolence and the poetry of sensibility, this book shows that the Scottish writer Francis Hutcheson, a follower of Shaftesbury, was the more important influence. Hutcheson had a Calvinist interpretation of benevolence, which moved Thomson to his frequent promotion in his poetry of sympathy as a universal social duty.

Terry, Richard, ed. *James Thomson: Essays for the Tercentenary.* Liverpool, England: Liverpool University Press, 2000. This is the first book of essays devoted to Thomson's works. Part 1 focuses on Thomson's poetry and drama, and part 2 examines Thomson's influences on later writers and his reputation. There is a useful introduction that gives a good overview of Thomson scholarship. This book offers a reappraisal of Thomson from the perspective of the early twenty-first century, to show how he transcends his own time, as well as being a barometer of the trends of his day.

*Robert Eddy*

# JAMES THOMSON

**Born:** Port Glasgow, Scotland; November 23, 1834
**Died:** London, England; June 3, 1882

PRINCIPAL POETRY

*The City of Dreadful Night, and Other Poems*, 1880
*Vane's Story, Weddah and Om-el Bonain, and Other Poems*, 1881
*A Voice from the Nile, and Other Poems*, 1884
*Shelley, a Poem: With Other Writings Relating to Shelley*, 1884
*The Poetical Works of James Thomson*, 1895
(2 volumes; Bertram Dobell, editor)

OTHER LITERARY FORMS

James Thomson wrote criticism, journalism, essays, and imaginative prose works from the early 1860's through his last years, primarily for magazines dedicated to the Free Thought movement, including the *London Investigator* and *National Reformer*. His subjects were often literary, as in his essays on Walt Whitman and fellow atheist poet George Meredith. One selection of Thomson's essays, *Essays and Phantasies* (1881), appeared in book form in the poet's lifetime. Several posthumous volumes followed, including one volume of his translations.

ACHIEVEMENTS

James Thomson's long narrative poem "The City of Dreadful Night" established the poet's reputation, although many critics were slow to recognize its qualities. In its monumental depiction of a lone soul's journey through a city bathed in darkness, it communicated a melancholy yet beautiful vision of the human condition, a vision distinctively different from those offered by Thomson's contemporaries. The poem earned him the appellation "laureate of pessimism," given him by Bertram Dobell.

The poem's impact was acknowledged by such contemporaries as George Eliot and George Meredith, and by such later figures as Rudyard Kipling and T. S. Eliot, the latter whose *The Waste Land* (1922) is considered by some critics a direct literary descendent. In this and others of his works, in both subject and literary tone, Thomson expressed a sensibility more akin to that found in the poetry of the twentieth century than in that of the nineteenth.

BIOGRAPHY

James Thomson was born to Scottish parents whose chief characteristics became some of his own. His father, an officer of the merchant marine, was known for his geniality and love of drink, while his mother was known for her melancholy.

Thomson's father was a chief officer in a ship out of Greenock, Scotland, when he was disabled by a paralytic stroke in 1840. He moved the family to London, where within two years the young Thomson was admitted to the Royal Caledonian Asylum, an institution for the children of indigent Scottish servicemen. His ailing mother died soon thereafter, in 1842.

Thomson's relatives determined his future as an army schoolmaster and in 1850 enrolled him in the military normal school of the Royal Military College at Chelsea. Successful in his studies, Thomson was posted in 1851 as assistant teacher in a regimental school in Ballincollig, near Cork, Ireland. His nearly year-and-a-half stay there proved pivotal. He made friends with a trooper in the dragoons, Charles Bradlaugh, who later would become an editor and leading proponent of the Free Thought movement in England. He also fell in love with the young Matilda Weller. To Thomson's great despair, she died soon after his duties took him back to Chelsea. To his dying day, he kept a curl of her hair in a locket.

Made an army schoolmaster in 1854, for the next eight years he served in Devonshire, Dublin, Aldershot, Jersey, and Portsmouth. He also began his career as a poet. His works appeared in periodicals including the *Edinburgh Magazine* above the signature "B. V." The first initial represented "Bysshe," to invoke Percy Bysshe Shelley, while the second represented "Vanolis," an anagram on Novalis, pseudonym of German Romantic poet Friedrich von Hardenberg. Thomson's identification with the latter was strengthened by the fact that Hardenberg's one love had also died in childhood.

In 1862, Thomson was court-martialed and dis-missed from the army along with several companions, ostensibly for a minor rules infraction. Thomson's dismissal also may have been due to his increasing suffering from melancholy and bouts of drunkenness.

Bradlaugh came to his aid, taking him in and helping him locate work, initially as a clerk and later as a journalist. Thomson wrote for the freethinker journal *London Investigator* and subsequently for *National Reformer*, which eventually came under Bradlaugh's sole editorship. In these journals Thomson, as "B. V.," enjoyed a growing, if still small, reputation as both poet and dedicated proponent of rationalism. Conversant in several languages, he also translated the works of Giacomo Leopardi, Heinrich Heine, and Novalis, among others.

Earning only a meager living through these writings, Thomson was forced to live in single-room apartments in the London slums. He briefly held two promising positions in the early 1870's. In 1872-1873, he served as secretary for London's Champion Gold and Silver Mines Company, which sent him to Central City, Colorado, for nine months to inspect its holdings. These being worthless, the company went into bankruptcy soon after Thomson's return.

Later in 1873, Bradlaugh helped Thomson obtain a post with the *New York World* to report on the Spanish civil conflict between Royalists and Republicans, a conflict that proved of such low intensity it provided inadequate material for coverage, leading to his recall after six weeks.

The following year brought Thomson new recognition, however. His masterwork, *The City of Dreadful Night, and Other Poems*, appeared in serial form in the weekly *National Reformer*, in issues from March 22 through May 17, 1874. Among those taking notice was Dobell, who met the poet and arranged for the publication of Thomson's first book in 1880. By then, however, Thomson and Bradlaugh had broken off their friendship, in part due to the influence of Bradlaugh's new associate and future theosophist, Annie Besant. Thereafter Thomson's writings appeared in another Free Thought magazine, the *Secularist*, and a combination trade and literary journal, *Cope's Tobacco Plant*. Dobell helped secure publication of two more volumes of collected works.

Thomson, who had long struggled with insomnia, melancholy, and alcoholism, enjoyed some spells of happiness in 1881 and 1882 but suffered a hemorrhage after a drunken bout and died June 3, 1882, in University College Hospital, London. He was buried in Highgate Cemetery.

ANALYSIS

While Dobell dubbed James Thomson the "laureate of pessimism," a title that accurately captures the initial impression given by some of his works, the appellation has the unfortunate effect of leading readers to ignore one of Thomson's major concerns. The poet spoke of despair, undoubtedly, but he did so to seek a way past the pessimism that pure rationalism had a tendency to produce.

While "The City of Dreadful Night" seems outwardly about despair, it pointedly concerns itself with questions about the meaning and purpose of life in an indifferent universe. The narrator of the poem and many of its other shadowy characters persist with their lives despite the prevailing despair, a fact in keeping with the conclusion stated in the poem's final lines: while the weak despair, the strong endure. Facing the mystery central to existence, "The strong . . . drink new strength of iron endurance,/ The weak new terrors."

Perceiving the oppositions at work within the human mind as well as within the larger universe, Thomson embraced rationalism without dismissing the simple joys possible in life. In both shorter and longer works, he concerned himself with topics born of rationalism, in terms that are deeply emotional. His attitude is most clearly summed up in "Philosophy" (1866).

Thomson's poetry is marked by a measured clarity of image and language, guided by a strong narrative instinct. The poems are largely stanzaic, often structured with repeating motifs or phrases to help emphasize their dramatic movement.

### "THE DOOM OF A CITY"

Subtitled "A Fantasia," the early long poem "The Doom of a City" (1857) anticipated "The City of Dreadful Night" in its imagery and thematic elements. Divided into the three sections, "The Voyage," "The City," and "The Judgments," the poem offers a journey across a strange, storm-tossed sea to a darkness-shrouded city whose inhabitants have been frozen into stonelike stillness. The tragedy the traveler discovers, which the reader takes to be the source of the city's doom, is the motionless funeral procession for a beautiful young girl.

The traumatic experience of having a loved one die too young and too soon, Thomson would later address directly in his short poem "Indeed You Set Me in a Happy Place" (1862), which ends with the lines, "Ah, ever since her eyes withdrew their light,/ I wander lost in blackest stormy night." In the earlier "The Doom of a City," the vision of the dead girl evokes the transitory nature of beauty and youth, and the fleeting pleasures of life. The early date of this poem's composition reveals the lifelong nature of Thomson's struggle to deal with the opposition between a relentlessly changing universe and the ephemeral possibility of personal joy.

### "PHILOSOPHY"

The four-canto poem "Philosophy" presents in capsule form Thomson's concern with the implications of rational or scientific thought and embodies many of his major thematic concerns. The unidentified central character of the poem "Looked through and through the specious earth and skies," making him akin to the "City of Dreadful Night" inhabitants who see that "all is vanity and nothingness." The question he faces, "How could he vindicate himself?," parallels the struggle to find solace and meaning in the longer poem of 1874.

"Philosophy" presents an optimistic vision, even in its rationality, and makes an argument for the importance of human love, echoing his earlier poem "The Deliverer" (1859). It ends with one of the most charming moments in Thomson's works, a quatrain on an insect:

> If Midge will pine and curse its hours away
> Because Midge is not Everything For-aye,
> Poor Midge thus loses its one summer day;
> Loses its all—and winneth what, I pray?

### "IN THE ROOM"

A subdued yet powerful poem, "In the Room" (1867-1868) is a tour de force in which the objects of a room speak to one another, as though animate beings equipped with speech and memory. The object of their conversation is their sense of a change having occurred in the room, which is revealed to be the death of the room's lone inhabitant, whose life had been quiet and unhappy. Remarkable not only for its conceit but also for its execution, "In the Room" is a focused and unsentimental exploration of the theme of isolation, found in many other Thomson poems.

### "THE CITY OF DREADFUL NIGHT"

A long poem of unusual emotional strength, thematic consistency, and intellectual rigor, "The City of Dreadful Night" offers the tale of a man consigned to existence in a "City of the Night," whose only dwellers are "melancholy Brothers." Divided into twenty-one cantos, the poem alternates between sections of a descriptive and reflective nature, and of a narrative nature.

The unfortunate main character travels through a series of telling situations and incidents, first overhearing conversations alongside a darkened river, unveiling the nature of the city. He discovers a palace lighted as for a festival and finds inside a bier with a dead young girl, over whom a young man kneels in sorrow. He then approaches a cathedral, whose doorkeeper demands each entrant's story. Each of these brief stories ends with what amounts to an invocation: "I wake from daydreams to this real night."

Inside the cathedral, he listens to a "great sad voice" from the pulpit who raises the question of the search for meaning that propels the poem and speaks of the beckoning solace of oblivion, an idea introduced in the poem's first canto as the "One anodyne for torture and despair." The speaker at the pulpit leaves a message ringing in the ears of his listeners: "End it when you will," he says, perhaps referring to the river in canto 19.

The poem ends with a series of striking tableaux. Canto 19 speaks of the "River of Suicides" and describes the ways different suffering souls enter its waters. Canto 20 describes a silent confrontation between an armed angel and an impassive sphinx, in which the latter, whose "vision seemed of infinite void space," emerges the motionless victor. The final canto, 21, describes a great "bronze colossus of a winged Woman," named Melancolia. It is to her the strong turn their eyes, "to drink new strength of iron endurance," while the weak look to her for "new terrors."

Like the much shorter "Philosophy," "The City of Dreadful Night" both reaffirms and issues a challenge to the Deist rationalism and free thinking Thomson embraced in his own life. In the poem, God is a "dark delusion of a dream," yet the poem warns both specifically and in its imagery against a way of thinking "most rational and yet insane" and embodies the search for meaning and solace in an indifferent universe found also in "Philosophy."

### "A VOICE FROM THE NILE"

Written in 1881, "A Voice from the Nile" (from *A Voice from the Nile, and Other Poems*) strikes a different chord from many of Thomson's other works, the central conceit being that the river Nile itself is the poem's speaker. The great river observes the various animal inhabitants on its shores and notes how they exist contentedly within their various spheres of existence. The river then observes the "children of an alien race," the people who built great structures along its shores. ". . . Man, this alien in my family,/ Is alien most in this, to cherish dreams/ And brood on visions of eternity . . ." More than any other characteristic in humankind, the river Nile focuses on the "religions in his brooding brain" as the characteristic that estranges humankind from the rest of nature. "O admirable, pitiable Man," the river says. The poem has unusual rhetorical impact, establishing a nearly pastoral tone before developing its rationalist theme with increasing incisiveness.

### OTHER MAJOR WORKS

NONFICTION: *Essays and Phantasies*, 1881; *Satires and Profanities*, 1884 (G. W. Foote, editor); *Biographical and Critical Studies*, 1896 (Bertram Dobell, editor); *Walt Whitman, the Man and the Poet*, 1910 (Dobell, editor).

TRANSLATION: *Essays, Dialogues, and Thoughts*, 1905 (of Giacomo Leopardi; Dobell, editor).

### BIBLIOGRAPHY

Dobell, Bertram. *The Laureate of Pessimism: A Sketch of the Life and Character of James Thomson ("B. V."), Author of "The City of Dreadful Night."* 1910. Reprint. Charleston, S.C.: BiblioLife, 2009. Dobell was the editor of some of Thomson's work and helped him in his career. His biography provides an interesting perspective on Thomson.

Gerould, Gordon Hall. *Poems of James Thomson "B. V."* New York: Henry Holt, 1927. Gerould's early evaluation of Thomson's poetry remains valuable for its balanced defense and consideration of poems beyond the most frequently considered works. He observes that Thomson pursued his art for twenty-five years. Thomson's finest work, he also argues, was not the product of bursts of inspiration. "It was the work of a man whose capacity for steady effort was as marked as his imaginative power," a fact made more striking in that it "continued without the stimulus of an audience." Gerould notes the "austere but melodic dignity" found in Thomson's works.

Leonard, Tom. *Places of the Mind: The Life and Work of James Thomson ("B. V.")*. London: Cape, 1993. Leonard's carefully researched, documentary account gives factual depth to the story of Thomson and his times, shedding light on the poet's surroundings, friends, and writings. The book includes extensive writings and letters by both Thomson and his friends.

Moore, Dafydd. "'The Truth of Midnight' and 'The Truth of Noonday': Sensation and Madness in James Thomson's *The City of Dreadful Night*." In *Victorian Crime, Madness, and Sensation*, edited by Andrew Maunder and Grace Moore. Burlington, Vt.: Ashgate, 2004. Provides an in-depth look at madness and sensation in the most famous poem by Thomson. Moore says Thomson creates an "abyss of despair" that is understandable and even appealing to those who have never experienced anything like it.

Morgan, Edwin. Introduction to *The City of Dreadful Night, and Other Poems*, by James Thomson. Reprint. Edinburgh: Canongate Classics, 1998. In a wide-ranging and insightful essay, Morgan explores the nature of Thomson's poetry, challenging the notion of Thomson as the "laureate of pessimism" and examining some of Thomson's legacy.

Paolucci, Henry. *James Thomson's "The City of Dreadful Night": A Study of the Cultural Resources of Its Author and a Reappraisal of the Poem*. 2000.

Reprint. Wilmington, Del.: Griffin House, 2005. Provides a reassessment of the quality of Thomson's poetry, finding his poem to be a modern rendering of what Saint Augustine described as the City of Man.

Salt, H. S. *The Life of James Thomson ("B. V.")*. 1889. Reprint. Whitefish, Mont.: Kessinger, 2006. One of the earliest accounts of Thomson's life, and the primary source of many subsequent biographies.

*Mark Rich*

---

# CHARLES TOMLINSON

**Born:** Stoke-on-Trent, Staffordshire, England; January 8, 1927

PRINCIPAL POETRY

*Relations and Contraries*, 1951
*The Necklace*, 1955, 1966
*Seeing Is Believing*, 1958, 1960
*A Peopled Landscape*, 1963
*American Scenes, and Other Poems*, 1966
*The Way of a World*, 1969
*Renga: A Chain of Poems*, 1971 (with Octavio Paz, Jacques Roubaud, and Edoardo Sanguineti)
*Written on Water*, 1972
*The Way In, and Other Poems*, 1974
*Selected Poems, 1951-1974*, 1978
*The Shaft*, 1978
*Airborn = Hijos del Aire*, 1981 (with Octavio Paz)
*The Flood*, 1981
*Notes from New York, and Other Poems*, 1984
*Collected Poems*, 1985, expanded 1987
*The Return*, 1987
*Annunciations*, 1989
*The Door in the Wall*, 1992
*Jubilation*, 1995
*Selected Poems, 1955-1997*, 1997
*The Vineyard Above the Sea*, 1999
*Skywriting, and Other Poems*, 2003
*Cracks in the Universe*, 2006

OTHER LITERARY FORMS

Charles Tomlinson has published much work of translation, including *Versions from Fyodor Tyutchev, 1803-1873* (1960, with Henry Gifford), *Translations* (1983), and *Selected Poems* (1993; of Attilio Bertolucci's poetry). Among Tomlinson's many essays of commentary and criticism, the most significant are found in *The Poem as Initiation* (1967), *Some Americans: A Personal Record* (1981), *Poetry and Metamorphosis* (1983), and *American Essays: Making It New* (2001). As an editor, Tomlinson has introduced British readers to the work of poets previously little known in England. His editions include *Marianne Moore: A Collection of Critical Essays* (1969), *William Carlos Williams: A Critical Anthology* (1972), *Selected Poems* (1976, 1985; of William Carlos Williams's poetry), *Selected Poems* (1979; of Octavio Paz's poetry), and *Poems of George Oppen, 1908-1984* (1990). Tomlinson has also edited volumes of translations, *The Oxford Book of Verse in English Translation* (1980) and *Eros English'd: Classical Erotic Poetry in Translation from Golding to Hardy* (1992). Finally, Tomlinson has collaborated with other poets in writing experimental poetic sequences: the multilingual *Renga* (1971; with Octavio Paz, Jacques Roubaud, and Edoardo Sanguineti) and the bilingual *Airborn – Hijos del Aire* (1981; with Paz).

ACHIEVEMENTS

Charles Tomlinson is generally recognized as a major English poet of the postmodern era. His work in traditional forms with conservative themes has set him apart from apocalyptic poets such as Dylan Thomas, as well as from the poets of the Movement, such as Philip Larkin. Tomlinson, a successful painter, has achieved recognition for his style of precise vision in poetry, and he has been often noticed as a seminal force in bringing the work of William Carlos Williams and other American writers to the serious attention of British poets and critics.

His achievements in poetry (as well as in painting) have won Tomlinson many awards and honors, including the Bess Hokin Prize for Poetry in 1956, a traveling fellowship from the Institute of International Education in 1959-1960, the Levinson Prize for Poetry in 1960, the Union League Civic and Arts Poetry Prize in 1961, the Frank O'Hara Prize in 1968, election as fellow of the Royal Society of Literature in 1974, an honorary doctorate in literature from Colgate University in 1981, the Wilbur Award for Poetry in 1982, election as an honorary fellow of Royal Holloway and Bedford New College (London University) in 1981, and the Bennett Award for achievement in literature in 1993.

BIOGRAPHY

Born in the English Midlands into a lower-class family, Alfred Charles Tomlinson was restless to escape the confinements of a mining community. The political conservatism of his father, Alfred Tomlinson, an estate agent's clerk, had a strong influence on the development of young Tomlinson's sensibility. Tomlinson attended Queen's College, University of Cambridge, from 1945 to 1948; while there he studied under Donald Davie, who became a lifelong friend and colleague. After receiving his degree, Tomlinson was married to Brenda Raybould. They moved to London, where Tomlinson taught in an elementary school and worked at his painting. In 1951, he published his first collection of poems, *Relations and Contraries*.

In 1951-1952, he traveled in Italy, where he worked briefly as private secretary to Percy Lubbock. While in Italy, he gradually abandoned his painting in favor of composing poems. After returning to London, he earned a master's degree from London University in 1954. In 1956, he took a position as lecturer in English poetry at the University of Bristol, where he later became a reader and then professor.

Tomlinson's next volume of poetry, *Seeing Is Believing*, attracted the attention of several American critics. In 1959, he fulfilled a long-held wish to meet William Carlos Williams, whom he visited in Rutherford, New Jersey. On the same trip to the United States, made possible by a fellowship, he also visited Yvor Winters in California. Before returning home, he visited Marianne Moore in Brooklyn, New York, and returned for a second visit with Williams in New Jersey.

With Henry Gifford, he published the first of several joint projects of translation, *Versions from Fyodor Tyutchev, 1803-1873*, in 1960. Tomlinson was invited to serve as visiting professor at the University of New

Mexico in 1962-1963. During this year, he met two persons who would prove to be very important for his career, the Objectivist poets Louis Zukofsky and George Oppen. He was introduced to other young American writers, Robert Duncan and Robert Creeley, and he visited the painter Georgia O'Keeffe at her home in New Mexico.

His poems collected for *A Peopled Landscape* in 1963 showed how important William Carlos Williams had become for Tomlinson's style. After a reading tour of New York State for the Academy of American Poets, in 1967, Tomlinson went back to Italy, where he met Ezra Pound and Octavio Paz, who would become a valued friend.

Returning to the United States as Olive B. O'Connor Professor of Literature at Colgate University, Tomlinson delivered the Phi Beta Kappa lecture, which was published as *The Poem as Initiation*. He continued to travel in the United States and Europe, lecturing and working on his translations, from 1969 to 1971. Tomlinson's painting and poetry were brought together in *Words and Images* in 1972, and some of his poems

*Charles Tomlinson*

were set to music by Stephen Strawley and recorded by Jane Manning in 1974. After another reading tour in the United States, his poetry and graphics were collected by the Arts Council of Great Britain as an exhibition at Hayward Gallery in 1978 in London and then toured Great Britain until 1981. Although Tomlinson did not cease his international traveling, his graphic work continued to bring him more recognition to match his reputation as a poet.

In 1982, he received the prestigious Wilbur Award for Poetry and delivered the Clark Lectures at Cambridge, titled "Poetry and Metamorphosis." Some of his poems were again set to music, in a song cycle that was performed in Belgium in 1985. The next year, Keele University held an exhibit, "Charles Tomlinson: A Celebration," of his books, manuscripts, photographs, and graphics, and then established an archive of his poetry recorded for commercial issue on audio cassettes. Also in the 1980's, Tomlinson published a selection of his poems in French and Italian, served as visiting professor at McMaster University, Canada, and delivered the Edmund Blunden Lecture in Hong Kong.

In 1992, he retired as professor of English from the University of Bristol. After his retirement, Tomlinson has continued to travel, lecture, paint, and write poems. Bilingual selections of his poetry appeared in Spain, Germany, Italy, Portugal, and Mexico, and in 1997 his *Selected Poems, 1955-1997* was published in England and in the United States. This work was followed by several other poetry collections, including *Cracks in the Universe*.

ANALYSIS

Throughout his career, Charles Tomlinson has used his arts of poetry and painting to challenge nature's objectivity with the shaping powers of human (subjective) imagination. He has spoken of the invitation to make meaning out of apparent meaninglessness, by discovering that "chance" rhymes with "dance," and that "chance" interrupts and enlivens the deadening effects of certitude. Therefore, in volume after volume, Tomlinson tests the proposition expressed by the title of his third collection, *Seeing Is Believing*. At first, this seems to limit one's imaginative capacity (to believe) to the outlines of things in sight, to the exteriors of being. Gradually, however, it becomes clear that Tomlinson's aesthetic detachment is an illusion of objectivity, that his art warms with the energies of combating objects in natural settings, negotiating space for culture and ritual, and rescuing values from history to compensate for anger at what humankind threatens to waste through ignorance and brutality.

The only poem that Tomlinson chose to rescue from his first collection, *Relations and Contraries*, to include in his *Collected Poems* is one simply titled "Poem." Short though it is, "Poem" suggests a major interest of the early poetry: It describes a sequence of sounds heard by an "unstopped ear" from a winter scene of activity, including horses' hooves making "an arabesque on space/ A dotted line in sound." This containment of space with sound, to make "space vibrate," is an effort that Tomlinson's next volume, *The Necklace*, continues to make, as in "Aesthetic," where "reality is to be sought . . . in space made articulate." Imagination uses language to establish an order of things, set firmly in their own world, though subject to human play, as in "Nine Variations in a Chinese Winter Setting."

### SEEING IS BELIEVING

This last poem takes its title from one by Wallace Stevens, the American poet whose work was an early important influence on Tomlinson. That influence continued to show in the third collection, *Seeing Is Believing*, which uses the painter's experience to capture an essential artistic attitude toward objects or acts in space. Thus "Object in a Setting" achieves the sense of being in a piece of glass that resists all efforts "to wish it a more human image," and "Paring the Apple" illustrates the beauty of art that forces "a recognition" of its charm even from those who look for a more "human" art in portraits. Still, the paring is an act of "human gesture," which compels its own recognition that art requires the human to be, and so all art is essentially a human endeavor. The poem, "A Meditation on John Constable," is art re-creating art: a poem about a painter making a painting. The title reinforces the very human essence of the artistic process: meditating about a human being who is an artist.

This is even more clear in those poems of *Seeing Is Believing* that occur as the consequence of visits to places. Although "At Holwell Farm" seeks to capture the "brightness" of air that is gathered "within the stone" of the farm's wall and buildings, it moves to a gentle observation that it is a "dwelling/ Rooted in more than earth," guarding an "Eden image." "On the Hall at Stowey" records a visit to a deserted house, allowed to fall into ruin while the fields about it continue to be fruitful and well attended. The poet is angry that five centuries of culture have fallen into decay here, where once pride of tradition was boldly beautiful. What humanity bestowed upon the objective space of nature, humanity has taken away through the objective distancing of time.

### A PEOPLED LANDSCAPE

*A Peopled Landscape* takes the concerns of place and time more warmly into more poems, as in "Harvest Festival: At Ozleworth." The poet notices the ironic juxtaposition of remnants from both Roman and Christian history in the market scene of this country village: A harvest festival of pagan origins is conducted beneath the stone arch of a Christian church, to deepen the scene of space with the complexities of history. Working with juxtapositions of this kind, Tomlinson uses his return from a trip to the United States to observe differences between modern and traditional values in "Return to Hinton," where he lovingly catalogs the details of his home, whose "qualities/ are like the land/ —inherited." These are contrasted with life in a "rich and nervous land" where "locality's mere grist/ to build." This poem uses the three-layered verse form of Tomlinson's American model William Carlos Williams; the preference for the American style of poetry is a complication of the poem's theme, which admits its complicity in the process of modern detachment from traditional "farmbred certainties." This same sense of separateness from tradition, along with a yearning to enjoy the pleasures of the past, is a strong element of "The Farmer's Wife" in the same volume.

### AMERICAN SCENES, AND OTHER POEMS

The impact and importance of American experience are dramatized by the title of Tomlinson's next volume, *American Scenes, and Other Poems*, which nevertheless includes poems not immediately referring to American scenes or settings, such as "A Given Grace." This is one of Tomlinson's most discussed poems, partly because it continues to show the influence of Stevens as well as that of Williams and Moore. It does not use the three-layered form, but it establishes an Imagist posture associated with the Americans. The title, deliberately tautological, derives from the beauty of "two cups" set on a mahogany table; the "grace" given is a power of evocation from form to imagination, aptly recorded as the poem itself.

In "The Hill," a woman gives grace to the poet's perception. She climbs a hill, making it yield to her human pressure and take its shape of meaning from her presence. A more explicitly American scene is exploited in "The Cavern," which recounts a descent that begins as a tourist's jaunt but ends as a press toward "a deeper dark" where the self discovers its "unnameable and shaping home." The poem works with gentle irony as it works out the myth of Theseus exploring the labyrinth: It acquires additional force if the final discovery of the self in its "shaping home" also suggests that the self is the minotaur as well as, or instead of, the heroic Theseus. However, there is further irony here, since the poem derives from Tomlinson's travels through the American Southwest, where he records a discovery about his deepest self (repeating the experience of his predecessor D. H. Lawrence). This self-discovery is repeated in other poems, such as "Idyll," which describes how the poet is drawn by the creative contrasts of quiet Washington Square in the heart of loud, bustling San Francisco. Here is not a desert cavern, but there is nevertheless a similar sense of self renewed by its identity in distance: A boy reading (beneath the lintel of a church upon which is carved a verse from Dante) draws the poet into a sympathetic identification as universal reader, for whom the message of the square is a "poised quiescence, pause and possibility."

### THE WAY OF A WORLD

One of Tomlinson's most acclaimed volumes is *The Way of a World*, which includes the lovely "Swimming Chenango Lake," a poem about establishing an artful relationship between human subjectivity and nature's objectivity. It sympathetically observes the poise of a swimmer, who has paused in a quiescent moment to study possibilities before leaping into an autumn lake. The swimmer is like an artist, measuring the "geometry of water" before attempting to master it with his skill,

but the swimmer is also all humanity participating in the challenging processes of all nature. In this poem, Tomlinson has brought together many of his career's themes: aesthetic observation through detachment, cold reflectiveness, and human calculation. Like the swimmer, human beings "draw back" from the cold mercilessness of nature, even as they force a kind of "mercy" from it, making nature sustain the human experience.

In this volume, Tomlinson demonstrates more decisively his strong distaste for extremism of all kinds, whether political or artistic, even though he has himself explored the use of American experimental aesthetic practices. His poem "Prometheus" is a strong work of imagination in which the poet listens to a radio broadcast of music by the Russian composer Aleksandr Scriabin; since there is a storm outside his house at the time, the poet can juxtapose the two events, artistic and natural, to each other. Because Scriabin's *Prometheus* is a work intended to help further the apocalypse of revolution, his music is examined as an exercise in political irony. This is made possible by the mockery of "static" in the radio's transmission during an electrical storm; the static is a figurative vehicle for the poet's mockery of art in the service of political propaganda. Music is the source of inspiration for another poem of the volume, "Night Transfigured," which derives from a work by Arnold Schoenberg. This poem is a kind of conclusion to a three-poem sequence beginning with "Eden" and followed by "Adam," as the poet becomes a new Adam-artist transfiguring the night of modernism with his light of imagination.

Tomlinson includes in *The Way of a World* two interesting experiments of his art, "Skullshapes" and "To be Engraved on the Skull of a Cormorant." The former is one of the poet's several exercises in "prose poem," which escape rigid classification because they are not measured in verse but neither are they merely prose. "Skullshapes" is a meditation on the shapes of different kinds of skulls; these are shapes of nature that summon imagination to fill "recess and volume" and to trace the "lines of containment, lines of extension." This is what Tomlinson does with his short poem "To Be Engraved on the Skull of a Cormorant," in which he accepts nature's challenge to turn a space of death into a rhythm of living affirmation.

### WRITTEN ON WATER

Tomlinson has said in interviews that he learned to be a poet by watching the water in canals running through his home village; the title of his collection *Written on Water* captures some of the feeling he has for that time of his childhood. The title also carries other levels of meaning, including the interest a painter has in working with water (the source of life itself) and the chance an artist takes in any medium that his or her work will not last. From among the poems that focus on the element of water, "Mackinnon's Boat" is an idyllic review of a day's work of fishing, sometimes presented from the view of a dog that lies in the bow of the boat, seemingly eager for return to land. This poem echoes the theme of "Swimming Chenango Lake," with its passage through and over a medium of nature as a mastery of its force. This same move of transcendence by human art, via imagination, occurs in "Hawks," which negotiates the element of air in its metaphors of achieving a right relationship between contraries.

### THE WAY IN, AND OTHER POEMS

Several of his poems in *The Way In, and Other Poems* have brought Tomlinson much appreciative critical attention, particularly the sequence that begins with "Under the Moon's Reign." Other poems, however, continue the nostalgic review of the past that has often been a manner of his writing. There is a sharper edge to some of these poems, as the poet's sorrow turns more often into anger at what modern life has done to traditional values and ancient landscapes. "The Way In" ironically notices two old people, like an ancient Adam and Eve, puttering about in the waste regions of the city where the poet drives to work. He may regret what humans have done to the landscape and he may deplore the empty lives the old couple seem to live, but he feels himself contributing to the devastation as he depresses the accelerator of his automobile. "Gladstone Street" and "At Stoke" take him back to scenes of his youth, where there is no improvement of an industrial wasteland and where the changes are few; still, it brings evidence that whatever the poet has accomplished, he owes much to his origin in that place of "grey-black." These poems of return and observation often follow the shape of experience drawn from driving. In "Night Ride," the poet sees well by artificial lighting but de-

plores the loss of vision to see the stars. Progress may make "our lights seem more beautiful than our lives," but it can also blacken the optimistic planners of the past, such as Josiah Wedgwood's utopian schemes in "Etruria Vale." Tomlinson dates the beginning of a new era for Great Britain from the end of World War II, which is marked in "Dates: Penkhull New Road." He sees it as a place that expresses a time: "Something had bitten a gap/ Out of the stretch we lived in." This is a commentary on postwar Great Britain as much as it is an observation about the physical disruption of a street in an English village.

Space for imagination to work across landscapes of special places can be found in revisiting scenes of youth and childhood, but it can also be discovered without leaving a present scene. This is the tactic of the four-poem sequence beginning with "Under the Moon's Reign." Moonlight transfigures the landscape to create a new world, after the *Götterdämmerung* of twilight's apocalypse; this is the closest Tomlinson can come to acceptance of extremism, and he does so in a tone of quiet irony. It is in such a moonlit terrain that "Foxes' Moon" is set, to allow an interruption of England's "pastoral" existence by an alien, intruding presence: the foxes who "go/ In their ravenous quiet"—utterly different modes of being for humanity to contemplate. The third poem, "The Dream," takes the speaker into a wider world of contemplation, where new spaces are made of cities within cities; dreams are the proportioning of sleep that "replenishes/ To stand reading with opened eyes/ The intricacies of the imagined spaces." No amount of dreaming, however, nor any amount of artful creation, can relieve the anguish and pain of one who stands over the "little ash" of a loved one, in "After a Death." Articulating the space of words does not assuage the burden of vision that feels "the imageless unnaming upper blue" of "this burial place" straddling a green hill.

Perhaps ends of things, ends of lives, establish important terms of definition, as Tomlinson writes often on this theme. As he puts it in his prose-poem of this volume, "The Insistence of Things," there is an "insistence of things" that "face us with our own death, for they are so completely what we are not." Thus moonlight shows, as does the grim determination of the foxes' barking between dreams, that death is a function of "the insistence of things."

### THE SHAFT

The hard outline of this insistence can be observed in history as well as across the spaces of the present. *The Shaft* collects poems that drive a shaft through time as well as into the dark depths of the earth. Extremist leaders of the French Revolution are presented in "Charlotte Corday," "Marat Dead," and "For Danton," to show the insufficiency of lives devoted to desperate deeds. At the real center of being is a fecund darkness, as in the title poem, "The Shaft," which is a womblike cavity (reached through a "cervix of stone"); as one bends to enter, one feels "a vertigo that dropped through centuries." One cannot remain there for long; it is "a place of sacrifice," but it allows escape and rebirth, as there is a return to "the sun of an unfinished summer." One may draw upon the dark energies of being in one's quest for a way back into the realm of light, where work is to be done.

### THE FLOOD AND THE RETURN

In both *The Flood* and *The Return*, Tomlinson's poetry acquires more religious qualities, as he describes the renovating experience of fighting destruction from the very water that inspired his work as a poet and painter, and as he ritualizes his life to receive the gifts of loving human companions as well as coldly indifferent natural forces. "The Flood" describes how taken by surprise he was when the stream near his house broke its banks in a flood that swept through his stone wall and across the lower floor of his home; it shook his "trust in stone" and "awakened" his eyes to fresh perceptions of nature's force. That there is compensation from nature is celebrated in a poem that echoes William Wordsworth's "The Recompense," which follows the route of expectation of viewing a comet, being disappointed, and then discovering new energies from a moonrise to reward the efforts of unnourished hope. The same appreciation for compensations drives the imagination in "The Return," which prepares the poet for the return of his wife on a winter's journey after a time of separation from each other.

These volumes, *The Flood* and *The Return*, embody contrasting themes constant throughout Tomlinson's career as poet: the concern for values of historical culture that are threatened with annihilation and the opportunity for renewal that nature constantly offers to the human imagination. The poet refuses to be intimidated by apocalypses of nature or of history. Instead, he keeps his artist's eye alert for new objects to replenish his hunger for fresh experience to nourish his poetry and his painting.

### ANNUNCIATIONS

The religious qualities that emerged in Tomlinson poetry during the 1980's become more explicit in *Annunciations*, a volume whose title suggests one of its chief themes: the "blessedness" of the physical world, a secular blessedness analogous to, yet profoundly different from, the divine blessedness announced by the Archangel Michael to the Virgin Mary. In "Annunciation," the volume's opening poem, a "flashing wing of sunlight" appears in an ordinary kitchen to announce an "unchaptered gospel." The sunlight comes not as a divine revelation but as a "domestic miracle" that will not "wait for the last day" to return. "[E]very day," the sunlight tells us, "is fortunate even when you catch/ my ray only as a gliding ghost." For Tomlinson, the momentary, accidental, yet recurrent visitation of sunlight, its play upon the surfaces of the world, is sufficient consolation, is miracle enough.

Many of the subsequent poems in *Annunciations* disclose similar "miracles," revealing a presence in the world that, in the words of critic Michael Edwards, "has preceded and will outlast us." This presence, says Edwards, is "ceaselessly entering local chance and circumstance" and "comes not from beyond but from within the world." Like the "flashing wing of sunlight" in "Annunciation," the presence revealed in other poems is naturalistic, not transcendent. Nevertheless, Tomlinson draws from it a sense of "religious" awe and comfort. The given world is revelation enough.

In several of the poems from *Annunciations*, the luminosity of the natural world takes the form of sunlight or moonlight. In "Variation," for example, a rising moon is "an unpausing visitant" that gradually illuminates the trees, one by one, "Setting each trunk alight, then hurrying on/ To shine back down over the entire wood." Near the end of this poem, Tomlinson shifts from the moon's illumination of a physical landscape to its illumination of human consciousness as it "pours/

Into the shadows and the watcher's mind." Similarly, in "Moonrise," the "watcher" of the moon is illuminated by "Its phosphor burning back our knowledge to/ The sense that we are here, that it is now." For Tomlinson, the mysterious presence of moonlight is an "annunciation" that, rather than take one out of the world, grounds one in it. Tomlinson suggests that the here and now is—or ought to be—sufficient.

### THE DOOR IN THE WALL

Many poems in *The Door in the Wall*, like those in *Annunciations*, contemplate the world with a sense of religious awe, recording the passing of the seasons (geese "planing in" on "autumn gusts") or the strangeness of the natural world closely observed (mushrooms, gathered by moonlight, looking like "tiny moons," like "lunar fruits"). These two books also take readers to places less luminous and strange. Tomlinson not only writes powerfully about the natural landscapes of the New Mexican desert and the Canadian wilderness but also takes his readers to crowded, often troubled, urban centers like New York, San Francisco, and Tübingen. He is not in any conventional sense a political poet, but two pieces from *The Door in the Wall* explore leftist politics of the late 1960's: "Paris in Sixty-nine" and "Siena in Sixty-eight," the latter closing with a powerful image of the 1968 Soviet invasion of Czechoslovakia.

### JUBILATION AND THE VINEYARD ABOVE THE SEA

*Jubilation* and *The Vineyard Above the Sea* include work written during the 1990's, the years following Tomlinson's retirement from academic life. The poems in these books remind readers that one of Tomlinson's great strengths as a poet is his capacity for precise, detailed description of the physical world. His "descriptions," however, are never mere renderings of the world's surfaces. Poems such as "The Cypresses," from *Jubilation*, and "On the Downs," from *The Vineyard Above the Sea*, are complex meditations on the world's "otherness." Such poems reveal in their "descriptions" a carefully established relation between observer and observed, a relation in which the world's otherness is given its due. In muting the claims of the perceiving self, Tomlinson enacts what he calls his "basic theme—that one does not need to go beyond sense experience to some mythic union, that the 'I' can be responsible only in relationship and not by dissolving itself away into ecstasy or the Over-soul."

These volumes also reconfirm Tomlinson as quintessentially a poet of landscape, of place. Like his earlier collections, *Jubilation* and *The Vineyard Above the Sea* contain a large number of poems, often sequences of poems, about the many places he has visited: Italy (a setting that appears repeatedly throughout his work), Greece, Portugal, and Japan, as well as his native England. All these locations—their physical contours, their languages, their cultures—enrich Tomlinson's poetry, making his work perhaps the least insular, least provincial, of any English poet writing since World War II.

While he remains an avid traveler, Tomlinson also acknowledges in these poems a competing urge: a homing instinct. "Against Travel," from *Jubilation*, celebrates the virtues of domesticity: "Those days are best when one goes nowhere,/ The house a reservoir of quiet change." At several points in *Jubilation*, the world out there gives way to a personal, domestic, closed-in world that Tomlinson has never before admitted so fully to his poetry. In "For a Granddaughter," a series of six "domestic poems," Tomlinson speaks in a self-revealing voice and from a private perspective rarely found in his earlier work. These poems and others suggest a sense of acceptance, a feeling of fulfillment, an easing into a new phase of life. Indeed, the book's title, *Jubilation*, puns on the word *jubilación*, Spanish for retirement, and in a poem called "Jubilación," Tomlinson celebrates his retirement in gently rhymed, easygoing, often humorous couplets addressed to a friend.

Tomlinson writes that his life has become an essentially domestic existence shared with his wife: "Books, music, and our garden occupy me./ All these pursuits I share (with whom you know)/ For Eden always was a place for two." In the new millennium, he has continued to write poetry, publishing the collections *Skywriting, and Other Poems*, and *Cracks in the Universe*.

### OTHER MAJOR WORKS

NONFICTION: *The Poem as Initiation*, 1967; *Some Americans: A Personal Record*, 1981; *Isaac Rosenberg of Bristol*, 1982; *Poetry and Metamorphosis*, 1983; *The Sense of the Past: Three Twentieth Century British Poets*, 1983; *The Letters of William Carlos Williams and Charles Tomlinson*, 1992; *William Carlos Williams and Charles Tomlinson: A Transatlantic Connection*, 1998; *American Essays: Making It New*, 2001; *Metamorphoses: Poetry and Translation*, 2003.

TRANSLATIONS: *Versions from Fyodor Tyutchev, 1803-1873*, 1960 (with Henry Gifford); *Castilian Ilexes: Versions from Antonio Machado, 1875-1939*, 1963 (with Gifford); *Ten Versions from "Trilce" by César Vallejo*, 1970 (with Gifford); *Translations*, 1983; *Selected Poems*, 1993 (of Attilio Bertolucci).

EDITED TEXTS: *Marianne Moore: A Collection of Critical Essays*, 1969; *William Carlos Williams: A Critical Anthology*, 1972; *Selected Poems*, 1976, 1985 (by William Carlos Williams); *Selected Poems*, 1979 (poems by Octavio Paz); *The Oxford Book of Verse in English Translation*, 1980; *Poems of George Oppen, 1908-1984*, 1990; *Eros English'd: Classical Erotic Poetry in Translation from Golding to Hardy*, 1992.

MISCELLANEOUS: *Words and Images*, 1972; *In Black and White: The Graphics of Charles Tomlinson*, 1976; *Eden: Graphics and Poetry*, 1985.

BIBLIOGRAPHY

Clark, Timothy. *Charles Tomlinson*. Plymouth, England: Northcote House, 1999. Clark gives a brief but wide-ranging introduction to Tomlinson's career, covering not only his poetry but also his work as a translator, as a graphic artist, and as a collaborator in writing experimental, multilingual poetic sequences. Features a detailed biographical outline, examples of Tomlinson's graphics, a bibliography, notes, and index.

John, Brian. *The World as Event: The Poetry of Charles Tomlinson*. Montreal: McGill-Queen's University Press, 1989. John says that Tomlinson's poetry creates a language of the senses, enlarges definitions, and pursues understanding of experience. Includes a photograph, notes, a bibliography, and an index.

Kirkham, Michael. *Passionate Intellect: The Poetry of Charles Tomlinson*. Liverpool, England: Liverpool University Press, 1999. This book provides a detailed critical reading of Tomlinson's poetry from the 1950's through the 1980's. Kirkham presents Tomlinson's work in an "unfolding sequence," focusing on the poet's "unified vision of the natural-human world." Includes a bibliography, notes, and an index.

O'Gorman, Kathleen, ed. *Charles Tomlinson: Man and Artist*. Columbia: University of Missouri Press, 1988. Eleven essays, two interviews, a poem, a chronology, and a foreword by Donald Davie cover Tomlinson's career. Six essays present different perspectives on his poetry, and two provide overviews of his development. Three essays study interrelationships of his painting and poetry. Illustrations, bibliography, and index.

Saunders, Judith P. *The Poetry of Charles Tomlinson: Border Lines*. Madison, N.J.: Fairleigh Dickinson University Press, 2003. Focuses narrowly on the theme of "boundaries" that Saunders sees as a key element in the poetry of Tomlinson.

Spiegelman, Willard. *How Poets See the World: The Art of Description in Contemporary Poetry*. New York: Oxford University Press, 2005. Spiegelman examines the works of poets such as Tomlinson who start with descriptions of the ordinary world to produce very different poetry.

Swigg, Richard. *Charles Tomlinson and the Objective Tradition*. Lewisburg, Pa.: Bucknell University Press, 1994. Swigg explores Tomlinson's place in an Anglo-American poetic tradition of objectivity that values the world's otherness, its existence apart from the ego of the poet. Focuses on the ways in which various writers within this tradition have influenced Tomlinson. A bibliography, notes, and index are included.

_____. *Look with the Ears: Charles Tomlinson's Poetry of Sound*. New York: Peter Lang, 2002. This analysis of Tomlinson's poetry focuses less on its well-known visual aspects and more on how it sounds.

Weatherhead, A. Kingsley. "Charles Tomlinson." In *The British Dissonance: Essays on Ten Contemporary Poets*. Columbia: University of Missouri Press, 1983. Explores the question raised by Tomlinson about whether form is in objective reality or imposed by subjective perception. Presents Tomlinson as a poet who bridges many of the divisions separating contemporary poets and their themes. Includes notes, a bibliography, and an index.

*Richard D. McGhee*
*Updated by Michael Hennessy*

---

# THOMAS TRAHERNE

**Born:** Herefordshire, England; c. 1637
**Died:** Teddington, England; October, 1674

PRINCIPAL POETRY

*A Serious and Patheticall Contemplation of the Mercies of God*, 1699 (better known as *Thanksgivings*)
*The Poetical Works of Thomas Traherne*, 1903
*Traherne's Poems of Felicity*, pb. 1910 (wr. c. 1655-1674)

OTHER LITERARY FORMS

The reputation of Thomas Traherne (truh-HURN) is based primarily on his religious works, both in poetry and prose. His treatises include *Roman Forgeries* (1673); *Christian Ethicks* (1675); and the meditation *Centuries of Meditations* (1908). His works have been collected as *The Works of Thomas Traherne* (2005-2009).

ACHIEVEMENTS

Thomas Traherne is usually categorized with the seventeenth century Metaphysical poets, although his poetry lacks the quality of wit that characterizes John Donne's and George Herbert's work. His poetry is religious and philosophical and bears closest comparison with that of Henry Vaughan, to whom it was attributed when first discovered in a London bookstall in 1896. Plato is the ultimate source of Traherne's thinking, both in verse and prose, and his works demonstrate his reading of many other writers in the Platonic tradition, including Saint Augustine, Saint Bonaventure, Marsilio Ficino, Giovanni Pico della Mirandola, and the Cambridge Platonists. Scholars have generally judged

Traherne to be more interested in philosophy than poetry. Perhaps as a consequence, his prose works have received more critical attention than his poetry, especially *Centuries of Meditations*, a devotional work in the Anglican tradition of Lancelot Andrewes and Donne. *Christian Ethicks*, published the year after Traherne's death, was the only systematic treatise intended for the educated English layman to appear in the thirty years following the Restoration. Because of the attention he paid to infant and childhood experiences and the importance he ascribed to them in the development of an understanding of divinity, Traherne has been suspected of the Pelagian heresy (which denies the doctrine of Original Sin). His name is frequently linked with such Romantic poets as William Blake and William Wordsworth, who also praised childhood innocence as the state in which humans are most closely in touch with the eternal.

BIOGRAPHY

The few bits of information known about Thomas Traherne's life come principally from John Aubrey's *Miscellanies* (1696), which reveals that Traherne was twice visited by apparitions, and from Anthony à Wood's *Athenae Oxoniensus* (1691-1692), where he is identified as a son of John Traherne, a shoemaker who was related to Philip Traherne, twice mayor of Hereford. Traherne also had a brother Philip, who revised and edited some of his poems. Traherne was educated at Brasenose College, Oxford, where he took his B.A. degree on October 13, 1656. He was ordained and, on December 30, 1657, was appointed to the Rectory at Credenhill, County Hereford. While at Credenhill, Traherne became spiritual adviser to Susanna Hopton. She had become a Roman Catholic after the execution of Charles I but rejoined the Church of England after the Restoration and became the center of a religious society for which Traherne wrote *Centuries of Meditations*. Hopton's niece married Traherne's brother Philip. Traherne returned to Oxford to take his M.A. on November 6, 1661, and his B.D. (Bachelor of Divinity) on December 11, 1669. In 1667, he became chaplain to Sir Orlando Bridgman, Keeper of the Seals in the Restoration. Traherne's death occurred three months after his patron's, and he was buried beneath the reading desk in the church at Teddington on October 10, 1674. *Roman Forgeries*, the equivalent of a modern B.D. thesis, was his only work published in his lifetime, although he was preparing *Christian Ethicks* for publication at the time of his death. There may yet be more works of Traherne to be discovered; manuscripts of his works have come to light in 1964, 1981, and 1996-1997.

## ANALYSIS

Modern readers first encountered Thomas Traherne as a poet, and the publication of his poems fortuitously coincided with the renewed interest in the seventeenth century poets signaled by H. J. C. Grierson's 1912 edition of Donne. Although Traherne was not included in Grierson's famous 1921 anthology of Metaphysical poetry, he has always been categorized with those poets, although in the second rank. Traherne might be surprised to find himself among the ranks of the poets at all, for his verse, at least as much of it as has been discovered, comprises only a portion of his known writings, and there is reason to believe that he placed more importance on two of his prose works, *Christian Ethicks* and *Centuries of Meditations*. Thematically, and even stylistically, his poetry is of a piece with his prose, which deserves some consideration here, both for the light it throws on his poetry and for its own sake.

Widely and deeply read, intellectually eclectic, and religiously heterodox, Traherne reminds one of John Milton, whom he preceded in death by less than a month. Both were modernists, sharing in the new Humanist emphasis of their era. Traherne, however, found a place in the established Church, something that the great Puritan poet would have found impossible. Traherne lacked the genius that made Milton an original, and readers of the younger poet are always conscious of his debts to thinkers and writers greater than he. He copied into his Commonplace Book from those whom he especially admired, many of whom are in the Platonic tradition, such as Hermes Trismegistus, whose *Divine Pymander* Traherne copied in its 1657 English translation, and Henry More, the Cambridge Platonist, from whose *Divine Dialogues* (1668) Traherne copied extracts. Another unpublished manuscript (British Museum Manuscript Burney 126) is known informally as

the Ficino Notebook because it consists of extracts from Ficino's Latin epitomes and translations of Plato. It also contains a long Latin life of Socrates and an otherwise unidentified work titled "Stoicismus Christianus."

Traherne's writings are almost exclusively religious, and the influence of Plato, without whom Christianity would be a very different religion, is therefore unsurprising. What is surprising is Traherne's apparent acceptance of Platonic doctrines usually rejected by the Christian Fathers, such as the doctrine of the soul's preexistence, and his modification of other doctrines, such as the traditional Platonic opposition of the material and spiritual worlds, from their usual adaptation to Christian dogma. Hints of the soul's memory of an existence previous to the earthly one is one of the motifs in Traherne's poetry that reminds readers of the Romantic poets, especially Wordsworth of the "Ode: Intimations of Immortality from Recollections of Early Childhood." Were it not for the fact that Traherne's work was not discovered until nearly fifty years after Wordsworth's death, scholars would doubtless have searched for the Trahernian influence on him. In *Centuries of Meditations*, 3.2, Traherne marvels, "Is it not strange that an infant should be heir of the whole world, and see those mysteries which the books of the learned never unfold?" His exaltation of infancy and childhood in particular makes him seem a precursor of the Romantic movement. Like Wordsworth, Traherne values childhood innocence because the "Infant-Ey," as he says in a poem of that title, "Things doth see/ Ev'n like unto the Deity." Attributing such power to the child requires, as he paradoxically says, "a learned and a Happy Ignorance" and is one of the indications that Traherne believed in the preexistence of the soul. Although he never expressly states such a belief, it can be inferred from his writings, particularly *Centuries of Meditations* and *Christian Ethicks*, where he discusses other aspects of Neoplatonic mysticism.

On the other hand, Traherne rejects the traditional Platonic preference for the ideal world over the real. In fact, Traherne holds that the spiritual world is enhanced by its physical actualization. Another way in which Traherne departs from strict Platonism is in his conception of time and eternity. For Platonic philosophers, time is the earthly, mortal image of eternity, but for Traherne, this is part of eternity, just as the physical world is part of God's unified creation. Here again, Traherne is reacting against the medieval emphasis on the opposition between this world and the next, finding instead a reconciliation.

His reaction to the Aristotelian dichotomies of the Scholastic philosophers is one of the affinities between Traherne and the Cambridge Platonists. He also shared their distaste for the Calvinist preoccupation with Original Sin and, like them, focused on humanity's potential, through the exercise of reason, to achieve happiness. In fact, as more than one scholar has suggested, Traherne's theology may have been Pelagian; his heavy stress on the power of childhood innocence almost requires a denial of the doctrine of Original Sin. Scholar Patrick Grant asserts that Traherne's theology is indebted to Saint Irenaeus, one of the pre-Nicene Fathers to whom the Cambridge Platonists also looked for a method whereby pagan philosophy could be incorporated into Christianity. Scholar Stanley Stewart finds Traherne aligned with the Arminians at Oxford who struck a balance between Pelagian "secularism" and Calvinistic determinism. Traherne's emphasis on humanity's potential for creation, which humanity shares with God, and his slight attention to sin, certainly distinguish him from Donne and Herbert. Traherne's accommodation of less traditional religious views probably was one of the factors that earned for him the position as chaplain to Bridgman, who allied himself overtly with the Latitudinarian cause and, before Traherne, had employed a Latitudinarian divine.

### SEARCH FOR RELIGIOUS TRUTH

Traherne's approach to theology was essentially exploratory, searching for truth rather than dogma. "Let it be your Care to dive to the Bottom of true Religion, and not suffer your Eyes to be Dazzled with its Superficial Appearance," he wrote in *Christian Ethicks*. That attitude is evident in *Roman Forgeries*, a polemic with the ostensible purpose of indicting the Roman church for its flagrant forgeries of documents and falsification of historical facts. Stewart's book sets the work in the rhetorical context of the antipapist tracts of the late Tudor and Stuart dynasties, but goes on to argue the preeminent influence of a 1611 work by Thomas James

lengthily titled *A Treatise of the Corruption of Scripture, Councels, and Fathers, by the Prelats, Pastors, and Pillars of the Church of Rome for Maintenance of Popery and Irreligion*. Like James, Traherne's purpose is less to vent anti-Catholic vitriol, although *Roman Forgeries* observes convention in that regard, than to reexamine, scientifically, texts condemned as false, with an eye toward religious certainty.

Renaissance Platonists, such as those at Cambridge and such as Traherne, asserted that humankind was the bond of the universe, the link between the spiritual and the material, between the Creation and the Creator; that belief probably accounts for the self-centered quality of much of Traherne's work, especially *Centuries of Meditations*. The notion of humankind as microcosm is found in many places, but a probable source for Traherne is Pico della Mirandola's *Oratio de hominis dignitate* (pb. 1496; *Oration on the Dignity of Man*, 1940), which he especially praised. For Pico della Mirandola and others, when humanity was created in the image of God, humans were also made the quintessence of the universe. Thus, although Traherne's philosophy of life seems rather self-centered, as more than one critic has pointed out, it is possible that he was using himself as microcosmic man. Stewart finds that the *Centuries of Meditations* is a self-centered work and yet not egotistic; rather, Traherne indulges in "a process of perfect narcissism," for in self-love one finds the beginning of love of the universe, created by God.

### CENTURIES OF MEDITATIONS

Despite Traherne's identification as a poet, scholarly attention has concentrated on *Centuries of Meditations*, particularly in the years since the publication of Louis L. Martz's two studies, *The Poetry of Meditation: A Study in English Religious Literature of the Seventeenth Century* (1954) and, especially, *The Paradise Within* (1964), in which Martz places *Centuries of Meditations* in the tradition of the Augustinian meditative exercise. Much of Traherne's writing, including his poetry, derives from that tradition, including *Meditations on the Six Days of the Creation* (1717) and an unpublished work, *The Church's Year-Book*. The century was an established subgenre of the Anglican manual of meditation. Earlier examples include Thomas Wilson's *Theological Rules* (1615), organized in four centuries, and Alexander Ross's *A Centurie of Divine Meditations* (1646). Traherne's work is divided into five centuries, all except the fifth containing one hundred short meditations. Since the fifth century ends with the tenth meditation followed by the numeral "11," scholars have felt obliged to ponder whether the work is unfinished or whether perhaps Traherne purposely ended abruptly so that the reader (or perhaps his patron, Hopton), having become adept at meditation through studying the first four centuries, could complete the fifth meditation for himself on the forty-eight blank pages remaining in the manuscript. Such a fanciful explanation, the ultimate in self-effacement in an otherwise self-centered work, seems unlikely. Some scholars have felt that the blank pages produced an eloquent silence. Indeed, Traherne was not unaware of the importance of silence for the mystic, as demonstrated in his poem "Silence": "A quiet Silent Person may possess/ All that is Great or High in Blessedness." This poem, however, is followed in the Dobell Folio by other poems, not blank pages.

The most influential discussion of the source of the *Centuries of Meditations* is by Martz, who sees it as an Anglican adaptation of the Augustinian meditative mode, particularly as exemplified by Saint Bonaventure's *Itinerarium Mentis in Deum* (1259, *Journey of the Mind to God*). Martz finds a basis for Traherne's optimism in Augustine's discussion of the power of the human mind in *De Trinitate* (c. 419; *On the Trinity*, 1873), and he identifies the *Centuries of Meditations* as a "confessional" work, moving through the three stages of confession of sin, confession of praise, and confession of faith that Augustine's *Confessiones* (397-401; *Confessions*, 1620) moves through. Traherne's five-part division mirrors Saint Bonaventure's *Journey of the Mind to God*. Bonaventure's journey opens with a Preparation, corresponding to Traherne's first century. Traherne prepares for the meditative exercise by meditating on the cross and by introducing one of his most important images, Adam in Paradise. The central sections of Bonaventure's work set forth the Threefold Way to God, which is accomplished by Traherne's three central centuries. Traherne begins his contemplative journey autobiographically, drawing in centuries two and three on personal experience in this world,

taken as a mirror of the divine world. In the fourth century, he leaves personal experience behind and attempts to discuss the divine principles themselves. Bonaventure's *Journey of the Mind to God* closes with a Repose, which corresponds to Traherne's fifth century.

Most subsequent commentators on the *Centuries of Meditations* pay homage to Martz, even when they disagree with him. Scholar Isabel MacCaffrey suggests that Traherne's plan was not simply Augustinian but Ignatian, an idea that gains support from the knowledge that Traherne used an English translation of a meditative work by a Spanish Jesuit in the composition of the *Thanksgivings* and especially in the *Meditations on the Six Days of the Creation* and in *The Church's Year-Book*. Gerard Cox, who calls the application of Bonaventure and Augustine to Traherne "highly questionable," argues instead that the *Centuries of Meditations* is organized according to Platonic principles derived from the Cambridge Platonists Theophilus Gale and Benjamin Whichcote. Cox, however, undercuts his own discussion by conceding that there are significant deviations from the Platonic organizing principle in the *Centuries of Meditations*. Scholar Richard Jordan argues for a three-part structure for the work, each part devoted, respectively, to the world, the individual soul, and God, and points out that in his promised discussion of the attributes of God, Traherne never mentions love, which he had discussed in relation to the other two topics. Century five, then, Jordan suggests, must have been intended as a meditation on God's love. Although his three-part division of a work divided by its author into five parts seems strained, his explanation for the incomplete state of the fifth century is reasonable. Stewart dismisses all attempts to find or impose an order on the work as symptomatic of modern expectations of literature and claims that the *Centuries of Meditations* proceeds by accretion.

### CHRISTIAN ETHICKS

Stewart claims that basically the same principle underlies the organization of *Christian Ethicks*, a collection of Baconian essays on various virtues, theological and moral. Although each chapter does proceed in the exploratory fashion of Francis Bacon's essays, each one is self-contained so that there is no particular necessity to the organization of most of the book—indeed the discussion of the cardinal virtues justice and prudence is interrupted by the discussion of the theological virtues, faith, hope, charity, and (Traherne's addition) repentance—Traherne nevertheless sees the whole as governed by a general purpose, as his preface "To the Reader" makes clear. One tradition from which *Christian Ethicks* derives is the gentleman's handbook, which instructed Renaissance men in the attainment of the various virtues required of a gentleman. Traherne's handbook, however, will be different. He will not treat the virtues "in the ordinary way," he says, as that has already been done; rather, he seeks "to satisfie the Curious and Unbelieving Soul, concerning the reality, force, and efficacy of *Vertue*" as a means to felicity. As Carol Marks says in the general introduction to the 1968 edition of *Christian Ethicks*, the work is distinguished by "persuasive emotion, rather than intellectual originality." Rhetorically speaking, "persuasive emotion" is an aim ascribed by seventeenth century rhetoricians to poetry, and indeed the work may be compared with Edmund Spenser's *The Faerie Queene* (1590, 1596), whose end was also "to fashion a gentleman." Traherne echoes, as well, Milton's purpose in *Paradise Lost* (1667, 1674) when he says, "You may easily discern that my Design is to reconcile Men to GOD."

Spenser claimed that the virtues celebrated by his poem were such "as Aristotle hath devised," and Marks asserts that ethical textbooks in seventeenth century England all derived from Aristotle's *Ethica Nicomachea* (n.d.; *Nicomachean Ethics*, 1797). Traherne's organizational plan, however, as outlined in the preface, is not really Aristotelian. He divides human history into four parts, according to the "estates" of Innocence, Misery, Grace, and Glory, and assigns to each its appropriate virtues. He emphasizes in his preface his reluctance to speak of vice, claiming to be completely occupied with the discussion of virtues. The arduous *via negativa* through the circles of hell was not for him. Rather, as Anne Ridler says in the introduction to her edition of the poems, Traherne is a "master of the Affirmative Way."

### TRAHERNE'S POEMS OF FELICITY

Traherne's Platonism and Neoplatonic mysticism

and his interests in meditation and ethical instruction recur throughout his poetry, and, indeed, there are occasional poems scattered among the prose works already discussed. The only poems published before the twentieth century are those known as the *Thanksgivings*, nine psalmlike poems praising God's creation. Traherne's other lyrics are in two different manuscripts known as the Dobell Folio, named for the bookseller who first identified the author, and *Traherne's Poems of Felicity*, a group of poems selected and transcribed by Traherne's brother Philip, who also edited them very heavily, as duplicate poems from the Dobell Folio demonstrate. He smoothed out rhythms, mended defective rhymes, regularized stanza forms, and made the expression "plainer" by substituting the literal for the metaphorical. Two versions of a line from one of Traherne's best-known poems, "Wonder," demonstrate Philip's method. In the Dobell Folio version, the line is "The Streets were pav'd with golden Stones." In *Traherne's Poems of Felicity*, only one word is changed, but it is a significant one: "The Streets seem'd paved with Golden Stones." Philip has changed the metaphor into a simile, making the line safer, less bold. The Dobell Folio comprises thirty-seven poems. All but six are also in *Traherne's Poems of Felicity*. The latter manuscript is, however, the only source for thirty-eight of its sixty-one poems. Because of the extensiveness of Philip's emendations to the poems also contained in the Dobell Folio, the textual accuracy of the poems for which Philip's version is the only source is clearly unreliable.

The Dobell Folio is a holograph, so it is likely that the poems in it were arranged in their present order by the author. The general plan seems to be a person's spiritual biography from infancy to maturity. The opening poem is appropriately titled "The Salutation," although it is not a greeting to the reader, but the child's greeting to life. Childhood innocence, especially as it resembles the state of Adam in Paradise, is the subject of the first four poems. The next six, from "The Preparative" to "The Approach," concern ways of coming to know God, chiefly through appreciation of his works, a theme that recurs throughout the poems and is frequently expressed by catalogs of God's works. Traherne's reading of philosophers and theologians is everywhere apparent, most obtrusively in a poem called "The Anticipation" employing technical terminology from the Aristotelian tradition to exploit the paradox that God is at once the end, the means, and the cause of natural law. The titles of the last eight poems in the sequence reveal Traherne's Christianized Platonism. There are four, titled, respectively, "Love," "Blisse," "Desire," and "Goodnesse," among which are interposed four poems, each titled "Thoughts." Love and desire, according to Platonic doctrine, are the forces that motivate people to seek bliss and goodness, and thoughts are the means, the "Engines of Felicitie," to use one of his rare Metaphysical conceits. Thoughts are the means to a mystical apprehension of God, as quotations from "Thoughts: III" and "Thoughts: IV" exemplify: "Thoughts are the Angels which we send abroad,/ To visit all the Parts of Gods Abode." They are "the Wings on which the Soul doth flie."

Traherne's emphasis on "thoughts" in these poems is another reminder of Traherne's familiarity with the meditative tradition; scholar John Malcolm Wallace has argued that the poems of the Dobell Folio constitute a five-part meditation in the Augustinian-Jesuit tradition, as described by Martz. Whether such a process was the poet's intention cannot be proved. Scholar A. L. Clements has interpreted the Dobell Folio using a somewhat simpler three-part framework. He sees the poems moving from childlike innocence, through fallen adult experience, to blessed felicity, the traditional Christian life-pilgrimage. Scholars seem to agree, in any case, that the manuscript is a patterned work of art and not simply a random collection of poems.

The same cannot be said about *Traherne's Poems of Felicity*. There can be little doubt of Traherne's authorship of all the poems of the manuscript, for they express the same themes and exhibit the same stylistic features as those in the holograph manuscript. Nevertheless, it cannot be said with certainty that choice lines are not Philip's revisions.

### CRITICAL RECEPTION

Stylistically, Traherne's poetry has never received much critical approbation, although some recent critics have argued that New Critical tenets have made it impossible for modern readers to appreciate Traherne.

Two primary characteristics of his poetics—his heavy reliance on abstractions and his frequent catalogs of, for example, God's creations do not make for vivid verse. His relative avoidance of imagery is deliberate, as the well-known poem on his poetics, "The Author to the Critical Peruser," attests. Traherne specifically rejects "curling Metaphors" in favor of "naked Truth." It may be, as some sympathetic scholars have thought, that his style represents his attempt to transcend imagistic language in an effort to apprehend Platonic ideas, but he is a difficult poet to enjoy for readers who have learned to admire concrete diction and sensual imagery. Such imagery as he does use is often biblical and Christian—images of light, fire, water, mirrors, and, from the Neoplatonic tradition, the eye and the circle. Like other contemporary Christian poets, he makes frequent use of paradoxes, a figure fundamental to Christian theology. One particularly striking hyperbolic, oxymoronic example is "Heavenly Avarice," which he uses to describe "Desire" in the poem of that title. Paradoxes, like abstractions, are part of his effort to raise the mind to the level where apparent opposites are seen to be one.

In English literary history, Traherne is himself something of a paradox. He has achieved a reputation as a poet, and yet his best work was done in prose. As a thinker, he did not achieve anything new, and yet his work demonstrates more consistently than any of the other Metaphysical poets that he was a serious student of philosophy and religion. He was a sort of quiet rebel, remaining in the established church and yet fearlessly examining, and sometimes abandoning, its doctrines. Traherne was not unique; he was very much a man of the Renaissance and Reformation; yet, to study him is to achieve a new insight into the intellectual life of seventeenth century England.

### OTHER MAJOR WORKS

NONFICTION: *Roman Forgeries*, 1673; *Christian Ethicks*, 1675; *Meditations on the Six Days of the Creation*, 1717; *Centuries of Meditations*, 1908 (revised as *Waking up in Heaven: A Contemporary Edition of Centuries of Meditation*, 2002).

MISCELLANEOUS: *The Works of Thomas Traherne*, 2005-2009 (4 volumes).

BIBLIOGRAPHY

Blevins, Jacob. *An Annotated Bibliography of Thomas Traherne Criticism: 1900-2003*. Lewiston, N.Y.: Edwin Mellen Press, 2006. This bibliography focuses on critical works analyzing Traherne.

_____, ed. *Re-reading Thomas Traherne: A Collection of New Critical Essays*. Tempe: Arizona Center for Medieval and Renaissance Studies, 2007. This volume contains nine well researched essays that take a modern approach to the reading of Traherne's poetry and prose, making it more relevant in the twenty-first century.

Cefalu, Paul. "Infinite Love and the Limits of Neo-Scholasticism in the Poetry and Prose of Thomas Traherne." In *English Renaissance Literature and Contemporary Theory: Sublime Objects of Theology*. New York: Palgrave Macmillan, 2007. Cefalu finds elements of neo-Scholasticism and Aristotelianism in Traherne's writings, especially his poetry, rather than mysticism and Neoplatonism.

Day, Malcolm M. *Thomas Traherne*. Boston: Twayne, 1982. Day's study of Traherne's meditations and poems focuses on his use of abstraction, paradox, and repetition to evoke in his readers a sight of eternity unlike the childlike vision earlier critics described in his work. Day provides a biographical chapter, thoughtful analyses of Traherne's work, a chronology, and an annotated select bibliography.

De Neef, A. Leigh. *Traherne in Dialogue: Heidegger, Lacan, and Derrida*. Durham, N.C.: Duke University Press, 1988. De Neef's study investigates the applicability to Traherne's work of three popular theories, with their themes of being, psychic identity, desire, and "the discursive economy of supplementarity."

Inge, Denise. *Re-examining the "Poet of Felicity": Desire and Redemption in the Theology of Thomas Traherne*. London: University of London Press, 2002. Examines the religious views of Traherne as revealed in his poetry and prose.

_____. *Wanting Like a God: Desire and Freedom in Thomas Traherne*. London: SCM Press, 2009. Inge examines two important concepts in the poems of Christian poet Traherne, who argues that want is the very essence of God's being.

Johnston, Carol Ann. "Thomas Traherne's Yearning Subject." In *John Donne and the Metaphysical Poets*, edited by Harold Bloom. Rev. ed. New York: Bloom's Literary Criticism, 2010. Examines the religious poetry and writing of Traherne, focusing on want and yearning.

Sluberski, Thomas Richard. *A Mind in Frame: The Theological Thought of Thomas Traherne (1637-1674)*. Cleveland, Ohio: Lincoln Library Press, 2008. A biography that examines Traherne's religious beliefs through his writings.

*John Thomson*

# V

## HENRY VAUGHAN

**Born:** Newton-on-Usk, Wales; April 17, 1622
**Died:** Llansantffraed, Wales; April 23, 1695

### PRINCIPAL POETRY

*Poems*, 1646
*Silex Scintillans*, parts 1 and 2, 1650, 1655
*Olor Iscanus*, 1651
*Thalia Rediviva*, 1678
*The Secular Poems of Henry Vaughan*, 1958 (E. L.
   Marilla, editor)
*The Complete Poetry of Henry Vaughan*, 1964
   (French Fogle, editor)

### OTHER LITERARY FORMS

Henry Vaughan (vawn, also von), whose religious poetry reflects the influence of John Donne and George Herbert, published translations of several religious and medical treatises.

### ACHIEVEMENTS

Henry Vaughan is usually grouped with the Metaphysical poets, anthologized particularly with Donne, Herbert, Richard Crashaw, and Andrew Marvell. While there is some justification for this association, in Vaughan's instance it has resulted in a somewhat too narrow estimation of his work and its historical context. In the Metaphysical collections, to be sure, Vaughan has been represented by some of his best poems, such as "Regeneration," "The World," or "Affliction," drawn from *Silex Scintillans*. These works, however, have often been grouped in contrast with the lyrics from Herbert's *The Temple* (1633). Invariably Vaughan has been admired only as a lesser foil to his great predecessor; while admittedly Vaughan had his great moments, he lacked the sustained intensity of Herbert. Moreover, Vaughan's gracious preface to the 1655 edition of *Silex Scintillans* shows much regard for the creator of *The Temple*. Given such authority, it is not surprising that Vaughan's modern reputation, emerging in the Metaphysical revival of the twentieth century, has been overshadowed by the accomplishments of Herbert.

Fortunately, recent scholarship has begun to redress the imbalances concerning Vaughan with thorough study of his work and his milieu. By his own admission, Vaughan lived "when religious controversy had split the English people into factions: I lived among the furious conflicts of Church and State" ("Ad Posteros" in *Olor Iscanus*). His was the time that saw a people indict, condemn, and execute its monarch in the name of religious fervor and political expedience. His was the time that saw the final vestiges of ancient families' power supplanted by parliamentary prerogatives of a potent middle class. Vaughan defined his place outside the struggle in order to take part in it as conservator of the Anglican-Royalist cause, a defender of the British Church in poetry and prose tied closely to the attitudes and values of pagan and Christian pastoral literature. Moreover, in his own Welsh countryside and lineage, Vaughan found the touchstone for his conservatorship, an analogue of the self-imposed exiles of early church fathers who took refuge from the conflicts and hazards of the world.

### BIOGRAPHY

Henry Vaughan was one of twins born to Thomas Vaughan and Denise Vaughan in 1622, ten years after a union that brought the elder Vaughan into possession of house and lands at Trenewydd (Newton-on-Usk). The father of the poet apparently had no calling except that of a gentleman, and in later life, he seems to have been fond of suing and being sued by his relatives. The Vaughan family had resided in the Brecknock region of Wales for generations and traced their line back to David ap Llwellen, known as Davey Gam, who was knighted and slain at the Battle of Agincourt in 1415. The poet's twin, also named Thomas, obtained a greater measure of fame in his own lifetime than Henry did. He was a philosopher of the occult sciences who at one point engaged in a pamphlet war with Henry More, the noted Cambridge Platonist writer. He settled near Oxford and died in 1666. Contemporary scholars have suggested that the elaborate pastoral eclogue, *Daphnis*, appearing in *Thalia Rediviva*, was the poet's farewell to his twin.

As befit the heirs of a minor country gentleman, the twins began their formal studies about 1632 with the rector of Llangatock, Matthew Herbert, continuing until 1638. The poet recalls that Herbert, "Though one man . . . gave me double treasure: learning and love." Following this tutelage, the twins were sent off to Jesus College, Oxford. They were seventeen; they had grown up steeped in Welsh language and culture. While the record of Thomas Vaughan's matriculation at Jesus College survives, no similar record exists for the poet. He apparently remained in Oxford until 1640, when he set forth to London with the intention of studying law. Shortly after his arrival, the king's favorite, the earl of Stafford, and Archbishop Laud were indicted. Stafford was executed by a reluctant monarch in the following May. Perhaps at this time Vaughan began translating Juvenal's tenth satire on the vanity of human wishes. While at London, Vaughan began his poetic "apprenticeship," steeping himself in the writings of Ben Jonson and his Cavalier followers such as Thomas Randolph. These efforts were published in the *Poems* of 1646. One imagines the young Vaughan's brief tenure in London as preparation for a respectable civic life, perhaps dividing his time between the city and the Welsh countryside. It was not to be.

In the summer of 1642, the first civil war erupted; Vaughan hastened to Wales. There he accepted the post of secretary to the chief justice of the Great Sessions, Sir Marmaduke Lloyd, probably retaining it until 1645. At the same time, Vaughan courted Catherine Wise, the daughter of a Warwickshire family. The "Amoret" poems in the 1646 volume were probably written and arranged in honor of his courtship and subsequent marriage to her. With the outbreak of the second civil war, Vaughan left the service of the law to join the Royalist army.

The appearance of the first part of *Silex Scintillans* in 1650, arguably the finest volume of poetry published by anyone in the years of the Interregnum, was unspectacular. Not until 1655, when he added several poems and a revealing preface, did Vaughan provide posterity with the ill-conceived notion of his religious "conversion." Of all the facts concerning Vaughan's life, no

nonevent is as important as the "conversion." It was invented in the nineteenth century by the Reverend H. F. Lyte, who edited the first publication of Vaughan's work since the poet's lifetime. Lyte took remarks in the 1655 preface concerning Vaughan's illness as a metaphor for a spiritual malaise cured by a heavy dose of Protestant piety. As a result of Lyte's homily, Vaughan's secular poetry suffered absolute neglect until the mid-twentieth century. *Silex Scintillans* was considered artistic proof of a conversion because it is Vaughan's best, most sustained work. A more accurate reading of what happened to Vaughan was that he matured, as a man and as an artist. He found his unique voice in the urgency of the moment, in the defeat of his religious and political party, in the example of Herbert's poetry, in the pastoralism of passages in the Bible, in the whole tradition of finding the virtuous life in rural surroundings.

One senses, throughout his mature work, Vaughan's urgent defense of the values of simplicity and rural piety tempered from within by resolve. Vaughan included translations of Boethius and Maciej Kazimierz Sarbiewski (Mathias Casimirus Sarbievius) in *Olor Iscanus*. They offer a pattern of stoic acceptance of this world's reversals by seeking virtue in retirement. Retirement, as Vaughan sees it, is not passive, however. It is a conscious choice. Thus, his allusions to illness in his preface to *Silex Scintillans* must be regarded within the larger context of his discovery of Herbert's poems and his condemnation of trifling, uncommitted poetry. Vaughan was always an Anglican and a Royalist. He did not convert: He simply found his way to fight back. From the remove of the country, Vaughan discovered a role for himself in a strife-torn society more potent than that of soldier or solicitor: as a poetic defender of God and king.

No doubt other events contributed to Vaughan's recognition of his poetic mission, including the death of a younger brother, William, in 1648, and of his first wife, Catherine, five years later. He married her sister Elizabeth in 1655, the same year that his translation of Heinrich Nolle's *Hermetical Physick* appeared. By then Vaughan had elected medicine as a new career. That he continued to write verse is evidenced by the dates of poems in Vaughan's final collection, *Thalia Rediviva*. Thalia is the Muse of pastoral poetry. Vaughan continued to see himself in terms of the rural tradition of poetry because he found there a synthesis of images, metaphors, and implied or explicit values that harmonized with his religious and political beliefs. He continued to practice medicine, according to one contemporary account, as late as autumn, 1694. When he died the following spring, he was buried overlooking the countryside he so long celebrated, in the churchyard of the faith he so vehemently defended, his stone reciting his link to the Silures, the ancient Welsh tribe from which he took his epithet, "The Silurist," by which he was often known.

## ANALYSIS

Henry Vaughan's first collection, *Poems*, is very derivative; in it can be found borrowings from Donne, Jonson, William Hobington, William Cartwright, and others. It contains only thirteen poems in addition to the translation of Juvenal. Seven poems are written to Amoret, believed to idealize the poet's courtship of Catherine Wise, ranging from standard situations of thwarted and indifferent love to this sanguine couplet in "To Amoret Weeping": "Yet whilst Content, and Love we joyntly vye,/ We have a blessing which no gold can buye." Perhaps in "Upon the Priorie Grove, His Usuall Retirement," Vaughan best captures the promise of love accepted and courtship rewarded even by eternal love:

> So there again, thou 'It see us move
> In our first Innocence, and Love:
> And in thy shades, as now, so then
> Wee'le kisse, and smile, and walke again.

The lines move with the easy assurance of one who has studied the verses of the urbane Tribe of Ben. That other favorite sport of the Tribe—after wooing—was drink, and in "*A Rhapsodie*, Occasionally written upon a meeting with some friends at the Globe Taverne, . . ." one sees the poet best known for his devout poems celebrating with youthful fervor all the pleasures of the grape and rendering a graphic slice of London street life. Though imitative, this little volume possesses its own charm. Perhaps it points to the urbane legal career that Vaughan might have pursued had not the conflicts of church and state driven him elsewhere.

## OLOR ISCANUS

The poet of *Olor Iscanus* is a different man, one who has returned from the city to the country, one who has seen the face of war and defeat. Nowhere in his writing does Vaughan reject the materials of his poetic apprenticeship in London: He favors, even in his religious lyrics, smooth and graceful couplets where they are appropriate. This volume contains various occasional poems and elegies expressing Vaughan's disgust with the defeat of the Royalists by Oliver Cromwell's armies and the new order of Puritan piety. The leading poem, "To the River *Isca*," ends with a plea for freedom and safety, the river's banks "redeem'd from all disorders!" The real current pulling this river—underscoring the quality of *Olor Iscanus* which prompted its author to delay publication—is a growing resolve to sustain one's friends and one's sanity by choosing rural simplicity. The idea of this country fortitude is expressed in many ways. For example, the Cavalier invitation poem, "To my worthy friend, *Master T. Lewes*," opens with an evocation of nature "Opprest with snow," its rivers "All bound up in an *Icie Coat*." The speaker in the poem asks his friend to pass the harsh time away and, like nature itself, preserve the old pattern for reorder:

> Let us meet then! and while this world
> In wild *Excentricks* now is hurld,
> Keep wee, like nature, the same *Key*,
> And walk in our forefathers way.

In the elegy for Lady Elizabeth, daughter of the late Charles I, Vaughan offers this metaphor: "Thou seem'st a Rose-bud born in *Snow*,/ A flowre of purpose sprung to bow/ To headless tempests, and the rage/ Of an Incensed, stormie Age." Then, too, in *Olor Iscanus*, Vaughan includes his own translations from Boethius's *De consolatione philosophiae* (523; *The Consolation of Philosophy*, late ninth century) and the Horatian odes of the seventeenth century Polish writer Sarbiewski. In these, the "country shades" are the seat of refuge in an uncertain world, the residence of virtue, and the best route to blessedness. Moreover, affixed to the volume are three prose adaptations and translations by Vaughan: *Of the Benefit Wee may get by our Enemies*, after Plutarch; *Of the Diseases of the Mind and the Body*, after Maximum Tirius; and *The Praise and Happiness of the Countrie-Life*, after Antonio de Guevera. In this last, Vaughan renders one passage: "*Pietie and Religion* may be better Cherish'd and preserved in the Country than any where else."

The themes of humility, patience, and Christian stoicism abound in *Olor Iscanus* in many ways, frequently enveloped in singular works praising life in the country. The literary landscape of pastoral melds with Vaughan's Welsh countryside. For Vaughan, the enforced move back to the country ultimately became a boon; his retirement from a "world gone mad" (his words) was no capitulation, but a pattern for endurance. It would especially preserve and sustain the Anglican faith that two civil wars had challenged. In Vaughan's greatest work, *Silex Scintillans*, the choices that Vaughan made for himself are expressed, defended, and celebrated in varied, often brilliant ways.

### SILEX SCINTILLANS

New readers of *Silex Scintillans* owe it to themselves and to Vaughan to consider it a whole book containing engaging individual lyrics; in this way its thematic, emotional, and Imagistic patterns and cross references will become apparent. The first part contains seventy-seven lyrics; it was entered in the Stationers' Register on March 28, 1650, and includes the anonymous engraving dramatizing the title. Fifty-seven lyrics were added for the 1655 edition, including a preface. The first part appears to be the more intense, many of the poems finding Vaughan reconstructing the moment of spiritual illumination. The second part finds Vaughan extending the implications of the first. Above all, though, the whole of *Silex Scintillans* promotes the active life of the spirit, the contemplative life of natural, rural solitude.

Some of the primary characteristics of Vaughan's poetry are prominently displayed in *Silex Scintillans*. First, there is the influence of the Welsh language and Welsh verse. Welsh is highly assonant; consider these lines from the opening poem, "Regeneration": "Yet *it* was frost w*it*h*in*/ And surly w*in*ds/ Blasted my *in*fant buds, and s*in*ne/ L*i*ke clouds eccl*i*ps'd my m*in*d." The *dyfalu*, or layering of comparison upon comparison, is a technique of Welsh verse that Vaughan brings to his English verse. A second characteristic is Vaughan's

use of Scripture. For example, the idea of spiritual espousal that informs the Song of Solomon is brought forward to the poet's own time and place. "Hark! how his *winds* have chang'd their *note*,/ And with warm *whispers call* thee out" ("The Revival") recalls the Song of Solomon 2:11-12. In "The Dawning," Vaughan imagines the last day of humankind and incorporates the language of the biblical Last Judgment into the cycle of a natural day. Will man's judge come at night, asks the poet, or "shal these early, fragrant hours/ Unlock thy bowres? . . ./ That with thy glory doth best chime,/ All now are stirring, ev'ry field/ Ful hymns doth yield."

Vaughan adapts and extends scriptural symbols and situations to his own particular spiritual crisis and resolution less doctrinally than poetically. In this practice, Vaughan follows Herbert, surely another important influence, especially in *Silex Scintillans*. Nearly sixty poems use a word or phrase important to *The Temple*; some borrowings are direct responses, as in the concluding lines of "The Proffer," recalling Herbert's "The Size." Sometimes the response is direct; Vaughan's "The Match" responds to Herbert's "The Proffer." Herbert provided Vaughan with an example of what the best poetry does, both instructing the reader and communicating one's own particular vision. This is Vaughan's greatest debt to Herbert, and it prompts his praise for the author of *The Temple* in the preface to *Silex Scintillans*. Further, Vaughan emulates Herbert's book of unified lyrics, but the overall structure of *The Temple*—governed by church architecture and by the church calendar—is transformed in Vaughan to the Temple of Nature, with its own rhythms and purposes.

The Temple of Nature, God's "second" book, is alive with divinity. The Welsh have traditionally imagined themselves to be in communication with the elements, with flora and fauna; in Vaughan, the tradition is enhanced by Hermetic philosophy, which maintained that the sensible world was made by God to see God in it. The poet no doubt knew the work of his brother Thomas, one of the leading Hermetic voices of the time. Henry Vaughan adapts concepts from Hermeticism (as in the lyric based on Romans 8:19), and also borrows from its vocabulary: Beam, balsam, commerce, essence, exhalations, keys, ties, sympathies occur throughout *Silex Scintillans*, lending force to a poetic vision already imbued with natural energy. "Observe God in his works," Vaughan writes in "Rules and Lessons," noting that one cannot miss "his Praise; Each *tree, herb, flowre*/ Are shadows of his wisedome, and his *Pow'r*."

Vaughan is no pre-Romantic nature lover, however, as some early commentators have suggested. Rather, *Silex Scintillans* often relies on metaphors of active husbandry and rural contemplation drawn from the twin streams of pagan and biblical pastoral. Many of the lyrics mourn the loss of simplicity and primitive holiness; others confirm the validity of retirement; still others extend the notion of husbandry to cultivating a paradise within as a means of recovering the lost past. Drawing on the Cavalier poets' technique of suggesting pastoral values and perspective by including certain details or references to pastoral poems, such as sheep, cots, or cells, Vaughan intensifies and varies these themes. Moreover, he crosses from secular traditions of rural poetry to sacred ones. "The Shepheards"—a nativity poem—is one fine example of Vaughan's ability to conflate biblical pastoralism asserting the birth of Christ with "literary" conventions regarding shepherds.

Several poems illuminating these important themes in *Silex Scintillans*, are "Religion," "The Brittish Church," "Isaac's Marriage," and "The Retreate" (loss of simplicity associated with the primitive church); "Corruption," "Vanity of Spirit," "Misery," "Content," and "Jesus Weeping" (the validity of retirement); "The Resolve," "Love, and Discipline," "The Seed Growing Secretly," "Righteousness," and "Retirement" (cultivating one's own paradise within). These are, of course, not the only lyrics articulating these themes, nor are these themes "keys" to all the poems of *Silex Scintillans*, but Vaughan's treatment of them suggests a reaffirmation of the self-sufficiency celebrated in his secular work and devotional prose. In his finest volume of poems, however, this strategy for prevailing against unfortunate turns of religion and politics rests on a heartfelt knowledge that even the best human efforts must be tempered by divine love.

## THALIA REDIVIVA

Vaughan's last collection of poems, *Thalia Rediviva*, was subtitled *The Pass-times and Diversions of a Countery-Muse*, as if to reiterate his regional link with the Welsh countryside. The John Williams who wrote the dedicatory epistle for the collection was probably Prebendary of Saint David's, who within two years became archdeacon of Cardigan. He was probably responsible for soliciting the commendatory poems printed at the front of the volume. That Vaughan gave his endorsement to this Restoration issue of new lyrics is borne out by the fact that he takes pains to mention it to his cousin John Aubrey, author of *Brief Lives* (1898) in an autobiographical letter written June 15, 1673. Moreover, when it finally appeared, the poet probably was already planning to republish *Olor Iscanus*. Thus, though his great volume of verse was public reading for more than two decades, Vaughan had not repudiated his other work.

Nor would he have much to apologize for, since many of the finest lyrics in this miscellany are religious, extending pastoral and retirement motifs from *Silex Scintillans*: "Retirement," "The Nativity," "The True Christmas," "The Bee," and "To the pious memorie of C. W. . . ." Moreover, *Thalia Rediviva* contains numerous topical poems and translations, many presumably written after *Silex Scintillans*. The most elaborate of these pieces is a formal pastoral eclogue, an elegy presumably written to honor the poet's twin, Thomas. It is Vaughan's most overt treatment of literary pastoral; it closes on a note that ties its matter to the diurnal rhythms of the world, but one can recognize in it the spirit of *Silex Scintillans*: "While feral birds send forth unpleasant notes,/ And night (the Nurse of thoughts,) sad thoughts promotes./ But Joy will yet come with the morning-light,/ Though sadly now we bid good night!" Though not moving in the dramatic fashion of *Silex Scintillans* through a reconstruction of the moment and impact of divine illumination, the poems of *Thalia Rediviva* nevertheless offer further confirmation of Vaughan's self-appointed place in the literature of his age.

OTHER MAJOR WORKS

NONFICTION: *The Mount of Olives: Or, Solitary Devotions*, 1652.

TRANSLATIONS: *Hermetical Physick*, 1655 (of Heinrich Nolle); *The Chymists Key to Open and to Shut*, 1657 (of Nolle).

MISCELLANEOUS: *The Works of Henry Vaughan*, 1914, 1957 (L. C. Martin, editor).

BIBLIOGRAPHY

Davies, Stevie. *Henry Vaughan*. Chester Springs, Pa.: Dufour Editions, 1995. A concise historical narrative of the life and works of Vaughan. Includes an index and a bibliography.

Dickson, Donald R., and Holly Faith Nelson, eds. *Of Paradise and Light: Essays on Henry Vaughan and John Milton in Honor of Alan Rudrum*. Newark: University of Delaware Press, 2004. A collection of essays on Vaughan and Milton; topics include *Silex Scintillans*, nature, and religion.

Manning, John. *The Swan of Usk: The Poetry of Henry Vaughan*. Lampeter: Trivium, University of Wales, Lampeter, 2008. Part of the Tucker Lecture series, this work examines the poetry of Vaughan in detail.

Nelson, Holly Faith. "Historical Consciousness and the Politics of Translation in the Psalms of Henry Vaughan." In *John Donne and the Metaphysical Poets*, edited by Harold Bloom. New York: Bloom's Literary Criticism, 2010. Examines Vaughan's psalms and treats Vaughan as a Metaphysical poet.

Post, Jonathan F. S. *Henry Vaughan: The Unfolding Vision*. Princeton, N.J.: Princeton University Press, 1982. Post, who divides his emphasis between Vaughan's secular and religious poems, declares the heart of his study is *Silex Scintillans*. Although he covers many of Vaughan's poems, some—among them "The Night" and "Regeneration"—receive lengthy analysis. Contains a general index, as well as an index to Vaughan's poems.

Shawcross, John T. "Kidnapping the Poets: The Romantics and Henry Vaughan." In *Milton, the Metaphysicals, and Romanticism*, edited by Lisa Low and Anthony John Harding. New York: Cambridge University Press, 2009. Looks at the influence of Vaughan and other Metaphysicals on Romanticism.

Sullivan, Ceri. *The Rhetoric of the Conscience in Donne, Herbert, and Vaughan*. New York: Oxford University Press, 2009. Notes that these poets—Vaughan, John Donne, and George Herbert—see the conscience as only partly under their own control. Finds similarities in the ways these poets seek their authentic nature in relation to the divine.

Young, R. V. *Doctrine and Devotion in Seventeenth-Century Poetry: Studies in Donne, Herbert, Crashaw, and Vaughan*. Rochester, N.Y.: D. S. Brewer, 2000. Young provides a critical interpretation of English early modern and Christian poetry. Includes bibliographical references and index.

*Kenneth Friedenreich*

# W

## EDMUND WALLER

**Born:** Coleshill, Hertfordshire, England; March 3, 1606

**Died:** Hall Barn, Beaconsfield, Buckinghamshire, England; October 21, 1687

PRINCIPAL POETRY

*Poems*, 1645, 1664, 1686, 1690, 1693

"A Panegyrick to My Lord Protector," 1655

"A Poem on St. James' Park as Lately Improved by His Majesty," 1661

"Instructions to a Painter," 1666

*Divine Poems*, 1685

*The Second Part of Mr. Waller's Poems*, 1690

OTHER LITERARY FORMS

In 1664, Edmund Waller collaborated with Charles Sackville, the earl of Dorset, Sir Charles Sedley, and several other young wits in translating Pierre Corneille's play as *Pompey the Great* (c. 1642). He also had a hand in a Restoration adaptation of Francis Beaumont and John Fletcher's play *The Maid's Tragedy* (pr. 1610-1611); his revisions were printed in the second 1690 edition of the *Poems*. Three of Waller's speeches before the Short and Long Parliaments are reprinted by Elijah Fenton in *The Works of Edmund Waller, Esq., in Verse and Prose* (1729); extracts from speeches made in the Restoration parliaments can be found in Anchitell Grey's ten-volume *Debates of the House of Commons, from the Year 1667 to the Year 1694* (1763). Waller's extensive correspondence, both personal and political, has not been collected in any one edition.

ACHIEVEMENTS

Although his poems were circulating in manuscript form from the late 1620's, Edmund Waller garnered little critical attention until nearly twenty years later. The discovery of his plot against Parliament in 1643 pushed

him into the political limelight; the publication of his poems in 1645 in four separate editions is in part attributable to the desire of the booksellers to capitalize on his public notoriety. The innovations of Waller's poetry—his peculiar style of classical allusion and his perfection of the heroic couplet—were fully appreciated only with the Restoration. As Francis Atterbury remarked in his "Preface to the Second Part of Mr. Waller's *Poems*" (1690), Waller stands "first in the list of refiners" of verse and ushers in the Augustan Age of English poetry. John Dryden's comment in the "Preface to Walsh's Dialogue concerning Women"—"Unless he had written, none of us could write"—pays full tribute to Waller's role in charting the public mode so essential to Restoration and eighteenth century poetry. The Augustans continued to laud Waller; as late as 1766, the *Biographica Britannica* described him as "the most celebrated Lyric Poet that ever England produced."

With the Romantic reaction against neoclassical taste, Waller's reputation plummeted. Critics condemned his poetry as vacuous and artificial; doubts about the probity of his actions during the civil war reinforced the aesthetic judgments. Elizabeth Barrett Browning's dismissal of Waller in *The Greek Christian Poets and the English Poets* (1863)—"He is feeble poetically, quite as surely as morally and politically"—exemplifies how biographical considerations distorted the critical picture. Edmund Gosse, the most important nineteenth century critic of Waller, savaged his subject in *From Shakespeare to Pope* (1885). Although Gosse argued that Waller's role in the rise of neoclassicism was lamentable, he did at least recognize that Waller had played a crucial role in that movement.

Despite the resurgence of interest in seventeenth century poetry led by Sir Herbert Grierson and T. S. Eliot early in the twentieth century, Waller's reputation continued to languish until the 1960's. Since then, several book-length studies and articles have examined the precise character and extent of Waller's influence on Augustan verse. His position in the history of English poetry now appears fairly secure.

Waller was certainly not the inventor of the heroic couplet, but he played a critical part in gaining its acceptance as the preferred verse form for neoclassical poetry. His style of classical allusion, singular in the 1620's and 1630's, provided the model for English poets of the succeeding century. Waller's innovations, however, were more valuable for public, political poetry than for meditative or amatory verse; Gosse's complaint that his technique proved deadly to eighteenth century lyric is more than a little justified. Waller's glory and his bane lie in his position as one of the truly transitional figures in English literature. Because he straddles the Renaissance and the Restoration, critics have been hard put to decide where to place him. As recent studies suggest, however, this transitional position renders Waller's works all the more important. The current interest in periodization will continue to make Waller the focus of critical scrutiny.

BIOGRAPHY

Edmund Waller was born on March 3, 1606, into a wealthy landowning family. John Hampden, the future parliamentary leader, was a maternal first cousin; Oliver Cromwell was a more distant kinsman. The death of Robert Waller in 1616 left his ten-year-old son the heir to an estate worth £3,500 per annum. Anne Waller, the poet's mother, sent him to Eton, and from there he proceeded to Cambridge. In 1620, he was admitted a Fellow-Commoner of King's College, but appears to have left without taking a degree. Waller may have represented Agmondesham, Buckinghamshire, in the Parliament of 1621; it is certain that he sat for Ilchester in the Parliament of 1624 at the age of eighteen.

In July, 1631, Waller married Anne Bankes, the wealthy heiress of a London mercer, against the wishes of her guardians. The Court of Aldermen, which had jurisdiction over the wardship of Mistress Bankes, instituted proceedings against Waller in Star Chamber; only the personal intervention of King Charles I appeased the aldermen and they dropped their suit upon payment of a fine by the young bridegroom. Anne Waller died in October, 1634, after bearing a son and a daughter.

Waller had begun writing verses at a young age. What is generally supposed to be his earliest poem, "On the Danger of His Majesty (Being Prince) Escaped in the Road at St. Andrews," was composed sometime during the late 1620's. A series of occasional poems on Charles I and Henrietta Maria constituted the bulk of

Waller's literary production during the late 1620's and early 1630's. With his good friend George Morley, later bishop of Winchester, the poet joined the philosophic and literary circle that Lucius Carey, Viscount Falkland, gathered about him at Great Tew. During this period Waller also became an intimate of Algernon Percy, who succeeded to the earldom of Northumberland in 1632, and his sisters Lucy Hay, countess of Carlisle, and Dorothy Sidney, countess of Leicester. Sometime after the death of his wife, Waller commenced a prolonged poetic courtship of Lady Leicester's daughter Dorothy, whom he celebrated under the name of Sacharissa (from the Latin *sacharum*, "sugar"). Many, though by no means all, of Waller's best-known lyrics are addressed to Lady Dorothy. It is questionable whether the Sidneys ever took Waller seriously as a suitor; in any event, with the marriage in July, 1639, of Lady Dorothy to Lord Spencer of Wormleighton, later created earl of Sunderland, the poet was disappointed in his hopes. Waller and Lady Sunderland were frequent correspondents for the remainder of their lives. An anecdote relates that the pair

*Edmund Waller* (©Michael Nicholson/CORBIS)

met at the house of Lady Woburn after both had attained old age. The widowed Lady Sunderland asked, presumably in jest, "When, Mr. Waller, I wonder, will you write such beautiful verses to me again?" "When, Madam," replied the poet, "your ladyship is as young and handsome again."

With the political upheavals of the early 1640's, Waller entered on the most active phase of his public career. He sat in the Short Parliament of 1640 as the member for Agmondesham; he was returned to the Long Parliament, which convened in November, 1640, for St. Ives. Waller at first aligned himself with the constitutional moderates who resisted the abuses of the royal prerogative, but as the temper of Parliament grew more radical, he increasingly took the side of the king. Waller played a prominent role in the attack on ship-money, of which his cousin Hampden was the most prominent opponent; his speech condemning what he considered an unlawful tax was immensely popular and reportedly sold twenty thousand copies in one day. On the other hand, Waller attacked the proposals to abolish the episcopacy, arguing that such tinkering with fundamental institutions would lead to the abolition of private property and undermine the basis of English society. With the outbreak of the civil war in August, 1642, Waller remained in the parliamentary stronghold of London, but soon became embroiled in a scheme to end the conflict by delivering the city to the king. Waller's Plot was discovered in May, 1643, and its leaders arrested. Waller confessed all, an action that alienated him from many royalists; his brother-in-law, an accomplice in the plot, was hanged on the basis of Waller's testimony. Waller himself escaped execution by paying a fine of ten thousand pounds and reportedly spending three times that amount in bribes. After a year and a half in prison, the poet was released and banished to the Continent.

Waller spent the next six years in France and Italy. During that period, he married his second wife, Mary Bracey, and his poems were published, purportedly without his permission, in England. In 1651, Waller received a pardon from Parliament and returned to England in January, 1652. He soon reached an accommodation with the Cromwell regime, and in 1665, published his famous "A Panegyrick to My Lord Protector." In the same year, he was appointed a Commissioner of Trade.

When the monarchy was later restored, Waller made the transition easily, he being among the first to greet the newly arrived Charles II with a poem titled "Upon His Majesty's Happy Return." When Charles complained that this panegyric was inferior to that composed for Cromwell five years earlier, Waller made the celebrated reply, "Poets, Sir, succeed better in fiction than in truth." Waller's wit ensured his retention of a firm position at court during the reign of Charles and during that of his brother James II. The poet also continued to serve in Parliament, steering a moderate course between the court and country parties and periodically reminding his colleagues of the importance of trade to England's greatness. He was a primary supporter of measures to extend religious toleration to Catholics and to Protestant dissenters.

Waller's second wife died in 1677, and soon afterward, he retired to his home at Hall Barn, renowned for the woods and gardens that the poet had laid out himself. In his last years, Waller apparently underwent a religious conversion; rejecting his earlier works, he turned to composing hymns and meditations on spiritual themes. He died at Hall Barn on October 21, 1687, surrounded by his children and grandchildren, at the age of eighty-one.

ANALYSIS

Edmund Waller's poetic corpus is singular in its homogeneity. Although his career spanned more than half a century, it is difficult to trace any stylistic development; as Samuel Johnson remarks in his "Life of Waller," "His versification was, in his first essay, such as it appears in his last performance." What changes do appear in Waller's poetry are primarily thematic rather than technical and can be attributed to the demands of genre rather than to any maturation in style. An examination of several poems composed at different periods of Waller's life and for very different occasions demonstrates this uniformity and, at the same time, demonstrates the innovations that Waller brought to seventeenth century verse.

## "OF HIS MAJESTY'S RECEIVING THE NEWS OF THE DUKE OF BUCKINGHAM'S DEATH"

Waller's earliest poems are mainly panegyrics composed on Charles I and Henrietta Maria. In "Of His Majesty's Receiving the News of the Duke of Buckingham's Death," one of the best of these pieces, Waller charts the program that English poets would follow for the next century in celebrating the virtues of the Stuart monarchs. The assassination of George Villiers, duke of Buckingham, in 1628 constituted a major blow, both political and emotional, to the young king. According to the earl of Clarendon, Charles publicly received the news with exemplary calm. When a messenger interrupted the monarch at prayers to blurt out the report of Buckingham's death, Charles continued to pray without the least change of expression; only when the service was completed and his attendants dismissed did he give way to "much passion" and "abundance of tears." In his panegyric, Waller celebrates the king's public response to the assassination and suppresses the unedifying private sequel. Charles's refusal to suspend his household's devotions is viewed as an act of heroic piety:

> So earnest with thy God! can no new care,
> No sense of danger, interrupt thy prayer?
> The sacred wrestler, till a blessing given,
> Quits not his hold, but halting conquers Heaven.

The conceit of the "sacred wrestler," which implicitly identifies Charles with the biblical patriarch Jacob, emphasizes that it is only through exertion that the king masters his natural impulses of grief and fear. His outward composure proceeds from a tenacious courage rather than from any lack of feeling. The direct address of the first line and the succession of present tense active verbs inject the description with dramatic urgency. Although threatened by personal harm and lamed ("halting") by the loss of his chief minister, Charles struggles and triumphs. By subordinating his personal grief to a faith in divine providence, the king "conquers" no mere earthly kingdom, but heaven itself.

Waller provides a context for Charles's heroism by comparing his response to Buckingham's death with the behavior of Achilles and of David in similar circumstances. While Achilles reacts to the death of Patroclus with "frantic gesture," Charles maintains a princely serenity; while David "cursed the mountains" for the death of Jonathan, Charles prays. The English king represents the ideal Christian hero, of which David and Achilles were but imperfect types: His absolute self-control and religious faith crown those virtues that he shares with the heroes of biblical and classical antiquity.

Charles's composure in the face of adversity constitutes both the justification and the outward manifestation of his kingship. Waller's contemplation of Charles Stuart's simultaneous humanity and divinity explodes in a final burst of compliment:

> Such huge extremes inhabit thy great mind,
> Godlike, unmoved, and yet, like woman, kind!
> Which of the ancient poets had not brought
> Our Charles's pedigree from Heaven, and taught
> How some bright dame, compressed by mighty Jove,
> Produced this mixed Divinity and Love?

The poet's initial sympathy with the king in his effort to master his grief and fear gradually shades into an awed recognition of his godhead: Dramatic struggle concludes in masquelike apotheosis.

Several aspects of Waller's technique in "Of His Majesty's Receiving the News of the Duke of Buckingham's Death" constitute innovations in Caroline verse. Although nearly every seventeenth century poet employed classical and biblical mythology in his work, Waller exploits this legacy in a new way; the detailed comparisons between Charles and Achilles and David anticipate the elaborate typological schemes used so effectively by poets such as John Dryden in *Absalom and Achitophel* (1681, 1682) or Alexander Pope in his ethical epistles. Accompanying this predilection for allusion is Waller's use of the extended simile and the Homeric epithet. All these devices derive from classical epic: By his own admission, Waller's early reading consisted mainly of Vergil, George Chapman's translation of Homer, and Edward Fairfax's translation of Torquato Tasso's *Gerusalemme liberata* (1581, *Jerusalem Delivered*, 1600).

More striking than the presence of sustained classical allusion, perhaps, is the regularity of Waller's verse. Of the nineteen couplets in the poem, all but one is closed; the individual lines are by and large end-stopped and the few instances of enjambment are not particularly dramatic. In short, Waller is using the heroic couplet with sophisticated ease in this poem of 1628-1629. Waller's sense of balance within individual lines is no less precise: Rhetorical devices such as zeugma and chiasmus lend the poem an unmistakable Augustan ring.

### "OF THE LADY WHO CAN SLEEP WHEN SHE PLEASES"

The presence of these devices in panegyrics on the monarchs seems appropriate, but their translation to lyric is a surprising development. "Of the Lady Who Can Sleep When She Pleases," for example, addresses the conventional amatory situation of the indifferent mistress and the love-harried suitor, but the classical frame of reference imparts an unwonted air of formality to the lover's plaint:

> No wonder sleep from careful lovers flies,
> To bathe himself in Sacharissa's eyes.
> As fair Astraea once from earth to heaven,
> By strife and loud impiety was driven;
> So with our plaints offended, and our tears,
> Wise Somnus to that paradise repairs.

In the remaining fourteen lines of the poem, Waller introduces yet another four deities and several more extended similes. Johnson notes with approval that Waller avoids Petrarchan and Metaphysical conceits and that his amorous verses "are less hyperbolical than those of some other poets. Waller is not always at the last gasp; he does not die of a frown, nor live upon a simile." Allusion, in fact, appears to fill the void left by Waller's abandonment of more traditional amatory conceits. The epic style brings with it an almost epic detachment; even when treating the most emotionally charged situations or intimate passions, Waller maintains a tone of cool suavity. The seduction poem "To Phyllis," for example, opens dramatically—"Phyllis! why should we delay/ Pleasures shorter than the day?"—but the ensuing arguments are abstract, general, and lifeless. It is hard to imagine that a real woman or a real love is in question. After pointing out the insignificance of the past and the uncertainty of the future, Waller's speaker makes his climactic appeal: "For the joys we now may prove,/ Take advice of present love." It is instructive to compare the parallel plea made by the lover in Thomas Carew's nearly contemporary poem, "To A. L. Perswasions to love":

> Oh love me then, and now begin it,
> Let us not loose this present minute:
> For time and age will worke that wrack
> Which time or age shall ne're call backe.

Waller's poem is smooth and precise, but Carew's *suasoria* is more impassioned and psychologically sensitive. Carew here imparts an urgency to his request that Waller, for all his rhetorical skill, never quite musters.

### "THE STORY OF PHOEBUS AND DAPHNE, APPLIED"

Waller himself suggests the rationale behind his detachment in one of his best-known poems, "The Story of Phoebus and Daphne, Applied." The opening lines establish the parallel between the classical myth and the speaker's own love affair:

> Thyrsis, a youth of the inspired train,
> Fair Sacharissa loved, but loved in vain.
> Like Phoebus sung the no less amorous boy;
> Like Daphne she, as lovely, and as coy!

Her suitor's poetic gifts notwithstanding, Sacharissa refuses to yield. After a long chase, Thyrsis achieves a wholly unexpected prize:

> All but the nymph that should redress his wrong,
> Attend his passion, and approve his song.
> Like Phoebus thus, acquiring unsought praise,
> He catched at love, and filled his arm with bays.

The theory that poetry springs from a sublimated passion is hardly new, but the equanimity with which the speaker accepts his fate surprises the reader. Apparently no regret accompanies the loss of Sacharissa. Despite its frigid conclusion, "The Story of Phoebus and Daphne, Applied" contains a valid psychological insight. Amatory poetry is grounded in aspiration rather than in fulfillment; the pursuit of Sacharissa brings its own reward, though not the one for which the speaker had hoped. In "When He Was at Sea," however, Waller denies even this relation between poetry and love:

Whilst I was free I wrote with high conceit,
And love and beauty raised above their height;
Love that bereaves us both of brain and heart,
Sorrow and silence doth at once impart.

"Passion" is denied even a catalytic role in the composition of poetry; Waller's antithesis not only distinguishes between, but also absolutely opposes, the two realms of experience. In insisting on this separation, Waller denies amatory verse any effective role in courtship. The love poem becomes a mere literary exercise. Viewed in the light of "When He Was at Sea," Waller's response when Charles II questioned the inferiority of his panegyric on the Restoration to that on Cromwell—"Poets, Sir, succeed better in fiction than in truth"—seems less a politic evasion than an accurate statement of his artistic principles.

### "Go, Lovely Rose"

Waller's avowed detachment from "passion," however, at times renders him an astute observer of amatory psychology. "Go, Lovely Rose," perhaps the most frequently anthologized of Waller's lyrics, revitalizes a traditional topos:

> Go, lovely Rose!
> Tell her that wastes her time and me
> That now she knows,
> When I resemble her to thee,
> How sweet and fair she seems to be.

The surprising yet apt zeugma of line 2 and the graceful intimation of mortality in the word "seems," which foreshadows the *carpe florem* admonition in the final stanza, exemplify the witty economy that the poet displays in his best work. In "To a Fair Lady, Playing with a Snake," Waller contemplates with bemused detachment the "innocence, and youth, which makes/ In Chloris' fancy such mistakes,/ To start at love, and play with snakes." A comic delicacy suffuses the treatment of the adolescent's simultaneous repulsion from and attraction to sexuality. "The fall" similarly integrates first love into the larger natural patterns of creation and decay. Waller's gentle eroticism and deft wit, sharpened by absolute rhetorical control, render his lyrics eminently memorable and eminently quotable.

### "A Panegyrick to My Lord Protector"

With his return to England in 1655, Waller again resumed the public and political poetry that had been the object of his earliest work. In technique, "A Panegyrick to My Lord Protector" resembles the pieces written on Charles I in the 1620's and 1630's: the mixture of biblical and classical allusion, the typological mode, and the epic similes combine to heroize Cromwell and legitimate his government. Waller's central conceit is an extended comparison between England and ancient Rome. As the death of Julius Caesar initiated a period of civil strife that ceased only with the emergence of Augustus, so Cromwell triumphs over the factious Parliament that assumed control after the execution of Charles. Waller retains a certain sympathy for Charles, as the parallel with the great Caesar makes clear, but his major concern is with the new, imperialistic England that Cromwell strives to forge. "A Panegyrick to My Lord Protector" is a strong poem, but more a public performance than an investigation of the crisis in loyalties that Cromwell's rule provoked. It lacks the rich ambiguities in perspective that distinguish Andrew Marvell's poem on the same theme, "An Horatian Ode upon Cromwell's Return from Ireland."

Waller's willingness to pen panegyrics for both Cromwell and the Stuarts disgruntled royalists in his own day and gave him a reputation as a venal time-server that has persisted into the twentieth century. It can be plausibly argued, however, that the poet's devotion is to England rather than to its rulers, and Waller was not alone in recognizing how Cromwell's capable rule quashed faction at home and raised the nation's prestige abroad. With the political chaos that succeeded Cromwell's death in 1658 and the emergence of Charles II as the one leader who could reunite Englishmen, Waller was quick to reassert his loyalties to the house of Stuart.

### "A Poem on St. James' Park as Lately Improved by His Majesty"

The panegyrics that form the greatest part of Waller's Restoration poetry are, with a few exceptions, competent but undistinguished. "A Poem on St. James' Park as Lately Improved by His Majesty" is a panegyric *cum* topographical poem in the tradition of Sir John Denham's "Cooper's Hill." Drawing on the classical tradition of *concordia discors*, Waller presents the order of the park as a harmonious microcosm of the universal order. Structures in the landscape such as the Palace of Whitehall and Westminster Abbey assume a symbolic function, becoming reminders of the eternal values on which England's greatness is based, whoever the ruler.

### "INSTRUCTIONS TO A PAINTER"

The willingness to experiment with a new genre that Waller demonstrates in "A Poem on St. James' Park as Lately Improved by His Majesty" is also evinced by "Instructions to a Painter," a poem in which he "advises" an artist how to depict the British naval victory at Lowestoft in June, 1665. Waller's panegyric, which omits the less edifying details of the sea fight, elicited a series of satiric rejoinders that served to establish the "advice to a painter" trope as a standard motif in Restoration poetry.

### "OF THE LAST VERSES IN THE BOOK"

The religious pieces of Waller's last years betray no flagging in poetic energy; as Atterbury remarks in his "Preface" to the 1690 *Poems*, "Were we to judge barely by the wording, we could not know what was wrote at twenty and what at fourscore." Perhaps the most moving passage of the religious poems is the final conceit in "Of the last verses in the book":

> The soul's dark cottage, battered and decayed,
> Lets in new light through chinks that time has made;
> Stronger by weakness, wiser men become,
> As they draw near to their eternal home.
> Leaving the old, both worlds at once they view,
> That stand upon the threshold of the new.

The fine image of the battered cottage in many ways sums up Waller's poetic career. Without forfeiting his basic values, Waller nevertheless learned to adjust to the shifting circumstances of seventeenth century England. Like "The Trimmer" popularized by George Savile, marquess of Halifax, Waller retained an allegiance to moderation and balance in an age in which strong loyalties and excessive partisanship were the political and literary norm. Although his individual poems rarely achieve greatness, they are consistently witty, perceptive, and stylistically distinguished. The

homogeneity of Waller's achievement, in fact, may be said to be his greatest triumph inasmuch as it provided one of the few fixed standards of excellence in a period of radical change. Waller's emphasis on balance and harmony, coupled with a willingness to incorporate new genres into his repertory, rendered him a fitting figure to usher in the new Augustan Age.

### OTHER MAJOR WORKS

PLAYS: *Pompey the Great*, pb. 1664 (translation of Pierre Corneille); *The Maid's Tragedy*, pb. 1690 (adaptation of Francis Beaumont and John Fletcher's play).

NONFICTION: *The Workes of Edmund Waller in This Parliament*, 1645; *Debates of the House of Commons from the Year 1667 to the Year 1694*, 1763 (10 volumes; with others).

MISCELLANEOUS: *The Works of Edmund Waller, Esq., in Verse and Prose*, 1729 (Elijah Fenton, editor).

### BIBLIOGRAPHY

Chernaik, Warren L. *The Poetry of Limitation: A Study of Edmund Waller*. New Haven, Conn.: Yale University Press, 1968. Vividly depicts the political, cultural, and literary context in which Waller wrote his Cavalier lyric poetry, formal occasional poems, and heroic satire, but there are few extended analyses of his works. Contains a chapter accounting for the rise and fall of Waller's literary reputation.

Cummings, R. M., ed. *Seventeenth-Century Poetry: An Annotated Anthology*. Malden, Mass.: Blackwell, 2000. Contains a short biography of Waller and a selection of his poems, with annotations that inform and analyze.

Davison, Sarah. "Ezra Pound's Esteem for Edmund Waller: A New Source for *Hugh Selwyn Mauberley*." *Review of English Literature* 60, no. 247 (November, 2009): 785. Davison argues that Pound may have had a more favorable impression of Waller than is generally thought and that Edmund Gosse's work on Waller may have influenced Pound.

Gilbert, Jack G. *Edmund Waller*. Boston: Twayne, 1979. Gilbert explores the complex relationship between Waller's political career and poetry, devotes separate chapters (with extended analyses of some poems) to the lyric and the political poems, and concludes by defining Waller's view of art and fixing his position in English literature. Includes a chronology and an annotated select bibliography.

Hager, Alan. *The Age of Milton: An Encyclopedia of Major Seventeenth-Century British and American Authors*. Westport, Conn.: Greenwood Press, 2004. Contains a brief biography of Waller, as well as critical analysis.

Hillyer, Richard. "Edmund Waller's Sacred Poems." *Studies in English Literature, 1500-1900* 39, no. 1 (Winter, 1999): 155-169. At age seventy-nine, Waller published *Divine Poems*, the fruits of his late rebirth that crowned the final collected edition of his works printed during his lifetime. Waller's sacred poems are discussed.

Jason, Philip K., ed. *Masterplots II: Poetry Series*. Rev. ed. Pasadena, Calif.: Salem Press, 2002. This set contains a summary and analysis of "Go, Lovely Rose."

Kaminski, Thomas. "Edmund Waller, English Precieux." *Philological Quarterly* 79, no. 1 (Winter, 2000): 19-43. Kaminski places Waller in a seventeenth century context that should enable the reader to grasp both what was new in his poetry and why it should have been praised so highly during his life and for nearly a century after his death.

Richmond, H. M. "The Fate of Edmund Waller." In *Seventeenth-Century English Poetry: Modern Essays in Criticism*, edited by William R. Keast. Rev. ed. New York: Oxford University Press, 1971. Richmond attributes Waller's decline in popularity and in literary merit to his faults as a person (his feigned madness, bribery, and informing to save his life), rather than to his poetic talents and the lack of the thought/feeling tension associated with the Metaphysical poets.

*Michael P. Parker*

# ISAAC WATTS

**Born:** Southampton, England; July 17, 1674
**Died:** London, England; November 25, 1748

PRINCIPAL POETRY

*Horae Lyricae*, 1706, 1709
*Hymns and Spiritual Songs*, 1707, 1709
*Divine and Moral Songs for Children*, 1715
*The Psalms of David*, 1719
*Reliquiae Juveniles: Miscellaneous Thoughts in Prose and Verse*, 1734

OTHER LITERARY FORMS

Isaac Watts's verse and prose is almost exclusively religious, although—as a practicing divine interested in the instruction of youth—he authored tracts that could be classified as pedagogical and theological. Foremost among these is a collection of prayers for little children titled *The First Catechism* (1692). This collection was followed by *The Art of Reading and Writing English* (1721), *The Christian Doctrine of the Trinity* (1722), *Logick: Or, The Right Use of Reason* (1725), *An Essay Towards the Encouragement of Charity Schools* (1728), *A Caveat Against Infidelity* (1729), and his last work, *Useful and Important Questions Concerning Jesus, the Son of God* (1746). Watt's *Sermons on Various Subjects*, in three volumes, appeared between 1721 and 1727.

ACHIEVEMENTS

Isaac Watts, the founder of English hymnody, ranks as the highest among the Nonconformist writers of divine poetry during the eighteenth century. For more than a century he held the respect of those British and American Nonconformists who sought spiritual uplift from the worship services of their particular denominations. Although Watts established his literary reputation as a hymnodist, as a writer of divine odes for congregational worship, he saw himself as a poet, although one who later renounced poetry for the sake of edification. Among lower-class Christians, Watts sought to promote what he termed "pious entertainment," which, unfortunately, prevented him from achieving his potential as a pure literary artist. Indeed, on more than one occasion he felt the need to apologize for being so easily understood, for having written poetry that could be read without difficulty.

In addressing the simpler souls of the English-speaking world, Watts managed to fuse image with thought and emotion, attaining a level of intensity not often reached by his more learned Augustan colleagues. In so doing, he relieved the English hymn of considerable poetic excess—complex theology and imagery that, during the late seventeenth and early eighteenth centuries, were regarded as essential ingredients of divine poetry. Watts, however, recognized immediately the difference between the high aesthetic level of divine poetry and the practical regions in which congregational song had, out of necessity, to function. Thus, he set out to compose a body of verse representative of the vigorous human spirit. He aimed at poetry and song that applied the Gospels to the various experiences of life. He strived for clarity of language, simplicity of diction, and sympathy of understanding so that thousands of English worshipers, both within and without the religiosocial establishment, could lean on his hymns as the natural expression of their own religious feelings.

Watts combined, in his hymnody, the soul of a poet and the conviction of a preacher. As a recognized cleric, he cast aside the theological mantle and reached down to the humblest of Christians, beckoning them to walk with God on the high ground of Christian piety. Thus, he set a fashion and provided a model; for the last half of the eighteenth century, a whole school of hymnodists would continue his vitality and his directness. The key to Watts's legacy was the relationship of hymnody to literature. He stood as one of the few poets of the Augustan Age who managed to preserve the spiritual enthusiasm of Protestant dissent and at the same time demonstrate that such enthusiasm could achieve some semblance of poetic expression. As both Independent divine and classical poet, he formed an obvious link between the zeal of the seventeenth century and the evangelical revival of George Whitefield and John and Charles Wesley. Most important, that link—that transition—was built on Watts's conviction that poetic and religious inspiration could be harnessed and combined by a person such as himself: a learned man, competently able to draw from tradition ideas congenial to his own times and his own temperament.

BIOGRAPHY

Isaac Watts was born at Southampton on July 17, 1674, the eldest of his father's nine children. Isaac Watts, senior, stood as a respected Nonconformist, one so serious about his essentially Puritan religious convictions that he served two prison terms rather than conform to the establishment. After his release, he maintained a successful boarding school at Southampton. Young Watts began his education under the direction of the Reverend John Pinhorne, rector of All Saints Church and headmaster of the Southampton Grammar School, who taught him Greek, Latin, and Hebrew. The boy's talent for learning and his taste for verse prompted citizens of the city to offer him a university education for eventual ordination into the Church of England. Of course he refused, which meant that he drifted, in 1690, toward the Nonconformist academy at Stoke Newington, London, under the care of Thomas Rowe, pastor of the Independent congregation at Girdler's Hall. Watts joined that congregation three years later.

In 1694, at the age of twenty, Watts left Rowe's academy and returned to Southampton. During this period, he wrote the majority of the hymns that would appear in *Hymns and Spiritual Songs*: "Behold the glories of the Lamb" was supposedly the first, composed in an attempt to elevate the standards of praise and prayer. Others followed, principally the results of requests from friends: "There is a land of pure delight" came from an uplifting experience on viewing the scene across Southampton Water. Watts, however, returned to the district of Stoke Newington as tutor to the son of a prominent London Puritan, Sir John Hartropp. The tutor pursued his own investigations into theology and philosophy with the same intensity as his pupil, which may have been the principal reason for the eventual decline in his health.

In the meantime, Watts turned his attention from pedagogy to divinity. He preached his first sermon in 1698 and continued that activity for the next three years. Then, in 1702, he was ordained minister of the Independent congregation at Mark Lane, a pulpit that had been filled by such eminent Nonconformist orators as Joseph Caryl and his successor, John Owen. Watts's congregation reflected the prominence and affluence of London Nonconformity, and the diminutive divine presided over it for the next ten years. In 1712, he became seriously ill with a fever, and his assistant, Samuel Price, assumed the role of copastor at the time when the congregation moved to another chapel just built in Bury Street. At that point, Sir Thomas Abney took the ailing Watts into his home, and Watts remained with the family until his death (Sir Thomas died in 1722). Indeed, the *Divine and Moral Songs for Children* was written for and dedicated to Sir Thomas's daughters.

Because of his illness and general state of incapacity, there is really nothing to note concerning the last thirty-five years of Watts's life. He spent his days largely in study and in preparing his poetry and prose for publication. In 1728, Edinburgh University bestowed, unsolicited, the degree of doctor of divinity on the poet, who died at Stoke Newington on November 25, 1748. He was buried at Bunhill Fields, the London resting place of Nonconformists, and a monument was erected to him in Westminster Abbey.

*Isaac Watts* (Hulton Archive/Getty Images)

ANALYSIS

Criticism of Isaac Watts's poetry has ranged from what could be termed "kind" to that which is obviously and totally negative. In his *Life of Watts* (1781), Samuel Johnson set the critical tone by complaining of the irregularity of his measures, his blank verse, and his insufficiently correspondent rhymes. As was his method, however, Johnson did find merit in Watts's smooth and easy lines and religiously pure thoughts, combined with ample piety and innocence. Still, the London sage wished for greater vigor in the hymnodist's verse. In the nineteenth century, critical commentators made sport of the sing-song patterns of Watts's children's hymns, while Lewis Carroll delighted in parodies of such pieces as "Let dogs delight to bark and bite," "'Tis the voice of the sluggard," and the "Busy bee." Such

strokes secured for Watts the lasting reputation of an Independent minister who accomplished little, poetically, beyond penning stiff moral verses for little children in his spare moments.

Careful reading of the poet's prefaces to those collections intended for mature minds, however, reveals him to have been his own rather stern critic. As late as 1734, with his major poetry already published, Watts proclaimed (in *Reliquiae Juveniles*) that he had made no pretense to the name of poet, especially since the age and the nation had produced so many superior writers of verse. More than the mere conventional expression of humility, the statement leads directly to an examination of those "superior" souls steeped in classicism who helped Watts develop his poetic theories and practices. One, Maciej Kazimierz Sarbiewski (Mathias Casimirus Sarbievius; 1595-1640)—although outside both Watts's age and his nation—demonstrated the advantages of a form, the ode, that he could easily adapt to congregational and private worship. The other, John Milton—like Watts a Nonconformist and a classicist—

proved that blank verse could convey both meaning and elegance.

### HORAE LYRICAE

Sarbiewski—the Polish Jesuit, classical reviser of the breviary hymns under Pope Urban VIII, and known generally as the Christian Horace—wrote Latin odes and biblical paraphrases that became popular shortly after their publication in England in 1625 and 1628. Watts translated certain of those odes in his *Horae Lyricae* (both 1706 and 1709 editions); many other poets, both earlier and later, also translated some of Sarbiewski's works: Among them were Henry Vaughan (in 1651), Sir Edward Sherburne (1651), the compilers of *Miscellany Poems and Translations by Oxford Hands* (1685), Thomas Browne (1707-1708), and John Hughes (1720). Even Samuel Taylor Coleridge translated Sarbiewski's "Ad Lyram," but after the early nineteenth century little interest was expressed in the works of the Polish Jesuit. Watts probably discovered Sarbiewski sometime between 1680 and 1690, when studying Latin at the Free School at Southampton under the tutelage of the Reverend Pinhorne. The earliest printed evidence of Sarbiewski's influence appeared in book 2 of *Horae Lyricae* in the form of an ode to Pinhorne, in which the young Watts thanked his schoolmaster for introducing him to the Latin poets, particularly Sarbiewski. The extravagant praise of Sarbiewski and the translation of his poetry make it clear that Watts never really lost his schoolboy regard for that poet. In fact, in the preface to the 1709 edition of *Horae Lyricae*, Watts admitted that he often added or deleted as many as ten or twenty lines in order to fit the original sense to his own design. Further, he apologized for not having been able to capture Sarbiewski's force, exactness, and passion of expression.

Thirteen acknowledged translations and imitations of modern Latin appear throughout Watts's poems and hymns; ten of these come from Sarbiewski. The Sarbiewski translations may be found in both the 1706 and 1709 editions of *Horae Lyricae*: "The fairest and only beloved," "Mutual love stronger than death," "Converse with Christ," "Forsaken yet helping," "Meditation in a Grove," "Come, Lord Jesus," "Love to Christ present or absent," and the long narrative that received considerable praise from Robert Southey, "The

Dacian Battle." In *Reliquiae Juveniles*, a collection of earlier poetry and prose, Watts included translations of "To Dorio" and "The Hebrew Poet." In the first piece, Watts reacted to what he termed the softness and the beauty of two four-line stanzas describing a lyric poet's first attempts on the "harp" and his introduction to the lyric form. He complained, however, of the difficulties of translation. "The Hebrew Poet" is very long—thirty four-line stanzas. Again, Watts notes the difficulty of accurate translation from the Old Testament Psalms: How does the translator Christianize the piece, yet at the same time retain the "Hebrew glory" and the quality of the original Latin ode? Early in the poem, he mentions "The Bard that climb'd to Cooper's-Hill," referring to Sir John Denham, who succeeded as a poet concerned with meditative and speculative subjects but who failed as a translator of the psalms of David.

Despite his misgivings, Watts managed to do justice to Sarbiewski's Latin poetry. His study of Sarbiewski and the practical exercise of translating his odes taught the Nonconformist poet to think in terms of higher nature while praising God. Thus, his hymns challenged the Augustans to regard natural objects closely and with a certain degree of enjoyment, a characteristic found lacking in the vast majority of Watts's less pious contemporaries—principally John Sheffield, William Wycherley, Bishop Thomas Sprat, William Walsh, Bernard Mandeville, and, foremost among them, Jonathan Swift.

In upbringing and training and in conception of the poet's purpose, certain tantalizing parallels exist between the early careers of Watts and Milton. Milton died the same year that Watts was born. Both emerged from Puritan homes, having been exposed to the dominant literary and cultural traditions of their times. After classical educations (although Milton's was longer and perhaps more formal), both returned to their homes for further study, meditation, and work. As students, they both wrote Latin verse dedicated to their tutors: Milton's "Ad Thomas Iunium, Praeceptorem Suum" (1627) when he was nineteen, Watts's corresponding "Ad Reverendum Virum Dom. Johannem Pinhorne" (1694) at the age of twenty. Finally and more significantly, the two poets proclaimed the merits of biblical poetry and paraphrase; both determined that the poet's work was a divine mission, inspired by the love of God.

In an essay "Of the Different Stops and Cadences in Blank Verse" (1734), Watts acknowledged his debt to Milton, a debt that may appear to counter the criticism of Johnson. He labeled Milton the esteemed parent and author of blank verse, of which *Paradise Lost* (1667, 1674) must stand as the noblest example. Milton, according to the Nonconformist hymnodist, assured his readers that true musical delight need not consist of rhyme, or even in the jingling sounds of like endings. Instead, that pleasure could easily be found in appropriate numbers, fit quantity of syllables, and the principal theme of the piece as it proceeds from one segment of a poem to another. Watts, however, must not be identified as an imitator of Milton or even as a follower; rather, his reliance on Miltonic blank verse provided a sharp point of departure from the predominant form of the Augustan Age. He wrote blank verse when almost every other poet sped forward on the quick airs of the couplet. His particular blank verse, however, was indeed distinct from anything previously written in the form. It was neither epic, as was Milton's, nor dramatic, as was the verse of William Shakespeare and his successors. Instead, Watts's lines were lyrical and meditative blank verse, in the manner that William Cowper and then William Wordsworth would develop so brilliantly.

Watts acknowledged the superiority of Milton's verse to his own; nevertheless, he formulated five specific rules whereby the legacy of the great Puritan epic poet could be maintained but improved. Watts's criticism of Milton's blank verse began in *Horae Lyricae*, in which he declared that Milton's lengthy periods and parentheses ran him out of breath, while certain of his numbers seemed too harsh and uneasy. Watts refused to believe that roughness and obscurity added anything to the grandeur of a poem—even to an epic. Furthermore, he could not understand how archaisms, exoticisms, and "quaint uncouthness of speech" could be affected by poets merely for the sake of being labeled "Miltonian." Thus, instead of imitating Milton, Watts chose to experiment with his meter, producing in *Horae Lyricae* a combination of religious and poetic earnestness with great vividness and intensity.

## RELIQUIAE JUVENILES

Watts advanced his own theories of prosody, generally opposing the neoclassical traditions of the early eighteenth century—which may well be a major reason for his neglect today. In his *Reliquiae Juveniles*, Watts argued that a writer of verse should be attentive to the ear as well as to the eye. Challenging the dominance of the couplet, he complained that the form tended to end too abruptly and often without necessity. Such practice (he believed) produced poems that proceeded with excessive regularity; this uniformity, according to Watts, becomes tiresome and offensive to every sensitive ear. His criticism of the closed couplet, then, was tied to rhyme, punctuation, and general sentence sense, and he argued that poets often ended their couplets without being attentive to meaning.

In "Of the Different Stops and Cadences in Blank Verse," published in *Reliquiae Juveniles*, Watts set down five extremely exact rules (which he had followed in composing the majority of his congregational hymns) whereby the tiresome and offensive uniformity of the couplet could be avoided. First, he suggested that the poetic sentence be extended to between six and ten lines. Second, although he could identify at least ten places within a line where the sentence could end with the inclusion of a fixed stop, Watts cautioned against that stop occurring too early or too late. Third, he argued that two lines in which the poet places a strong stop at the first or the ninth syllable ought not to appear in succession. Most important to his argument was the fourth rule, which held that the final line in a poetic sentence or poetic paragraph should contain the sense of that passage and that the next line should introduce a new scene, episode, or idea. Finally, Watts believed that every line should end with a short pause, which would provide respite, but not an end to the sense. In that fifth rule, the reader immediately sees Watts's concern for a poem in blank verse—a divine ode—that is to be written for or adapted to congregational worship.

Perhaps the most outstanding example of Watts's ability to apply his rules to his own poetry is his most anthologized piece, "The Day of Judgment," from the 1706 edition of *Horae Lyricae*. In both content and form, those thirty-six lines have received more critical attention than any other Watts poem or hymn. Amy

Reed, in relating "The Day of Judgment" to the various influences on Thomas Gray's "Elegy Written in a Country Churchyard" (1751), emphasizes Watts's skill in consistently offsetting the negative aspects of life: human vanity and the horrors of death and judgment. In their place, he introduced the thought of the saving power of Christ and the bliss of the righteous in heaven. Unfortunately, the lowest among the humble Christians who came into contact with Watts's poems relied only on their uncontrolled imaginations and saw only the gruesome elements of his Judgment Day: the fierce north wind, red lightning, bloody trumpets, and gaping waters quick to devour sinners. Another scholar, Enid Hammer, views the poem as a leap into the nineteenth century, believing it to be the link between the sapphics of Sir Philip Sidney and those of Robert Southey and Charles Lamb. Watts himself was so dedicated to the idea of the poem that he produced a prose version for the introduction to an essay, "Distant Thunder" (1734), another commentary on the theme of judgment.

Watts must be given credit for poetic and critical skills beyond a single poem on judgment or a single essay on the stops and cadences in blank verse. As a writer of religiously inspired odes and hymns for congregational worship, he stood almost alone, promoting the spiritual ardor of Protestant dissent. No doubt the eighteenth century reader and worshiper must have stood in awe at the wide range of that expression. Watts could, for example, strike fear into the hearts of children with his description of hell (as in "Heaven and Hell"); he could ascend to heights of extreme tenderness (as in the well-known cradle hymn, "Hush, my dear, lie still and slumber"); he could visualize eternity in the hand of the very God that made all people (as in his most noted hymn, "O God, our help in ages past").

Although Watts set out to Christianize the Old Testament Psalms and to make David speak as a Christian, Watts also needed to consider those eighteenth century Britons who would be his readers and his singers. Thus, in his hymns, he saw clear parallels between Judea and Great Britain; historical events such as the gunpowder plot, the coming of William III and Mary to England, the end of the Stuarts and the accession of the Hanoverians, and the Jacobite uprisings were occasions to set forth, poetically, clear lessons, sound political doctrine, and general thanksgiving. Watts had no real interest in limited or local occurrences; his primary focus was on the larger issues that concerned, politically and intellectually, the citizens of a legitimate Christian nation. He limited his hymnody to the same three or four general areas: the weakness of humans, the imperfections of society, the transience of human existence, and the hopes and fears of common creatures. Watts was nondenominational as long as he remained within those perimeters; he could rightfully claim that his hymns and psalm paraphrases held fast to the common denominators of universal Christianity.

In his three major hymn collections (*Horae Lyricae*, *Hymns and Spiritual Songs*, and *Divine and Moral Songs for Children*), Watts developed a complete system of praise, a process by which persons at all stages of their lives could come together to express their feelings, experiences, and beliefs. Watts sought to make the divine ode representative of the individual worshiper's response to the word of God. *The Psalms of David* and the *Hymns and Spiritual Songs* became the poetical guidebooks by which the diverse denominations of British and American Nonconformity achieved fullness and directness of religious and ethical thought, especially during the eighteenth and early nineteenth centuries when authority and direction were lacking.

Despite the reception of Watts's hymns and psalms in England and America during the eighteenth and nineteenth centuries, modern age seems unwilling or unable to determine the poet's rightful place in British literary history. Although evangelical churchmen continue to hold him in esteem, his literary position is less secure. Nevertheless, few will challenge Watts's capabilities as a poet or his skills in prosody; all will accept him as an experimenter, willing to challenge the popular poetic forms of his era. Watts was a wise and discriminating theorist who developed rules of prosody patterned after the brightest lights of the seventeenth century. Despite his credentials, however, literary historians have not willingly allowed him to represent both English hymnody and English poetry. Watts wrote verse that consciously explicated the doctrines of religious nonconformity and applied them to almost every facet of human experience. For that reason, the poems have not always been easily separated from the hymns, thus detracting from a full understanding of his verse. Watts intended a fusion between the poem and the congregational hymn, and a careful reading of his prose and poetry reveals his total concept of literature: He held it to be a repository wherein poetry and hymnody could eventually meet. Unfortunately, such a concept never has found a large audience, and Watts remains an Augustan poet of the second rank.

OTHER MAJOR WORKS

NONFICTION: *The First Catechism*, 1692; *A Guide to Prayer*, 1715; *The Art of Reading and Writing English*, 1721; *Sermons on Various Subjects*, 1721-1727 (3 volumes); *The Christian Doctrine of the Trinity*, 1722; *Logick: Or, The Right Use of Reason*, 1725; *An Essay Towards the Encouragement of Charity Schools*, 1728; *A Caveat Against Infidelity*, 1729; *Philosophical Essays on Various Subjects*, 1733; *The World to Come*, 1739, 1745 (2 volumes); *Useful and Important Questions Concerning Jesus, the Son of God*, 1746.

BIBLIOGRAPHY

Adey, Lionel. *Class and Idol in the English Hymn*. Vancouver: University of British Columbia Press, 1987. This history of English hymnody places Watts's remarkable career in theological and historical perspectives while explaining the role hymns occupied in the church life of eighteenth century England. Adey's particular contribution is his argument that Watts's stern Calvinist upbringing determined his portrait of a Father God in his psalms and hymns. Adey's bibliography is a gold mine of primary sources related to Watts and the hymnody of his era.

Argent, Alan. *Isaac Watts: Poet, Thinker, Pastor*. London: Congregational Memorial Hall Trust, 1999. A brief biographical study of Watts and his work.

Bailey, Albert Edward. *The Gospel in Hymns*. New York: Charles Scribner's Sons, 1950. A standard history of gospel hymnody places Watts at the center of the revolution in church music through his "rhymed theology." Bailey's extensive catalog of Watts's hymns, psalms, and poems is especially useful to researchers.

Fountain, David. *Isaac Watts Remembered*. 1978. 2d ed. Reprint. Southhampton, Hants, England: Mayflower Christian Bookshop, 1998. This biography of Watts examines his life from beginning to end, with an emphasis on his Christian beliefs and how they shaped his life and works.

Hood, John Paxton. *Isaac Watts: His Life and Hymns*. Greenville, S.C.: Ambassador, 2001. A biography of Watts that examines his life philosophy and religious views and how they informed his hymns.

Maclear, J. F. "Isaac Watts and the Idea of Public Religion." *Journal of the History of Ideas* 53, no. 1 (January, 1992): 25. Watts's ideas about public religion are discussed. Watts developed a comprehensive and detailed formulation of national religion.

Stackhouse, Rachelle A. *The Language of the Psalms in Worship: American Revisions of Watts' Psalter*. Lanham, Md.: Scarecrow Press, 1997. Part of the Drew Studies in Liturgy series, this work examines the psalms by Watts and the language used.

Woychuk, N. A. *Isaac Watts: The Father of English Hymnology*. St. Louis, Mo.: SMF Press, 2002. This biography of Watts looks at him as a writer of hymns.

*Samuel J. Rogal*

---

# OSCAR WILDE

**Born:** Dublin, Ireland; October 16, 1854
**Died:** Paris, France; November 30, 1900

PRINCIPAL POETRY

*Ravenna*, 1878
*Poems*, 1881
*Poems in Prose*, 1894
*The Sphinx*, 1894
*The Ballad of Reading Gaol*, 1898

OTHER LITERARY FORMS

Oscar Wilde wrote a number of plays produced successfully in his lifetime: *Lady Windermere's Fan* (pr. 1892), *A Woman of No Importance* (pr. 1893), *An Ideal Husband* (pr. 1895), and *The Importance of Being Earnest: A Trivial Comedy for Serious People* (pr. 1895).

Banned in London, his play *Salomé* was produced in 1893 in Paris with Sarah Bernhardt. Two plays, *Vera: Or, The Nihilists* (pb. 1880) and *The Duchess of Padua* (pb. 1883), were produced in New York after publication in England. Finally, two plays, *A Florentine Tragedy* (pr. 1906) and *La Sainte Courtisane*, were published together in the collected edition of Wilde's works in 1908. Wilde published one novel, *The Picture of Dorian Gray* (1891), serially in *Lippincott's Magazine*. Commercially and artistically successful with a number of his plays and his one novel, Wilde reached his peak in the early 1890's when he wrote little poetry. Wilde also wrote short stories and a number of fairy tales. His last prose work is a long letter, *De Profundis*, an apologia for his life. Parts of it were published as early as 1905, but the full work was suppressed until 1950.

ACHIEVEMENTS

G. F. Maine states that the tragedy of Oscar Wilde is that he is remembered more as a criminal and a gay man than as an artist. Readers still feel overwhelmed by Wilde's life just as his personality overwhelmed his contemporaries. His greatest achievement is in drama, and his only novel–*The Picture of Dorian Gray*—is still widely read. In comparison, his poetry is essentially derivative.

Wilde modeled himself on the poets of a tradition that was soon to end in English literature, and most of his poetry appears in the earlier part of his career. Within this Romantic tradition, Wilde had a wider range than might be expected; he could move from the limited impressions of the shorter poems to the philosophic ruminations of the longer poems. Yet behind each poem, the presence of an earlier giant lurks: John Keats, William Wordsworth, Algernon Charles Swinburne. Wilde's most original poem, *The Ballad of Reading Gaol*, is not derivative, and its starkness shows a side of Wilde not generally found in his other poems. Wilde's poetry is a coda, then, to the end of a tradition.

BIOGRAPHY

Oscar Fingal O'Flahertie Wills Wilde was born in Dublin, Ireland, on October 16, 1854. Flamboyance, so characteristic of the adult Wilde, was an obvious quality of both of his parents. His father was noted for physical dirtiness and love affairs, one of which led to a lawsuit and public scandal. Something of a social revolutionary, his mother published poetry and maintained a salon for intellectual discussion in her later years. Wilde grew up in this environment, showing both insolence and genius. He was an excellent student at all his schools. He attended Portora Royal School, Trinity College in Dublin, and then won a scholarship to Magdalen College, Oxford. At this time, John Ruskin was lecturing, and Wilde was influenced by Ruskin's ideas and style. More important, he heard and met Walter Pater, who had recently published his *Studies in the History of the Renaissance* (1873). It is Pater's influence that is most obvious in Wilde's development as a poet. While at Oxford, Wilde visited Italy and Greece, and this trip strengthened the love of classical culture so obvious in his poetry.

In the 1880's, as he developed as a writer, he also became a public personality. He toured the United States for about a year, and in both the United States and England, he preached an aesthetic doctrine that had its origins in the Pre-Raphaelites and Pater. He married in 1883 and had two sons. Wilde serially published his only novel, *The Picture of Dorian Gray*, which immediately created a sensation with the public. Thereafter, he wrote a number of plays, most notably *Lady Windermere's Fan* and *The Importance of Being Earnest*.

Wilde's last decade involved the scandal over his sexuality. His chief male lover was Lord Alfred Douglas, whose father, the marquess of Queensberry, tried to end Wilde's liaison with his son and ruin Wilde socially. Consequently, Wilde sued the marquess of Queensberry for libel but lost the case and also had his sexuality revealed. Tried twice for homosexuality, a crime in England at the time, he was found guilty and sentenced to two years at hard labor. From his prison experiences, Wilde wrote his most famous poem, *The Ballad of Reading Gaol*. Released from prison, he wandered over the Continent for three years, broken physically and ruined financially. He died in Paris at the age of forty-six.

ANALYSIS

Oscar Wilde's poetry derives from the rich tradition of nineteenth century poetry, for, as Richard Aldington shows, Wilde imitated what he loved so intensely in the great poets of his century. Drawing from John Keats, Dante Gabriel Rossetti, William Morris, and Algernon Charles Swinburne, Wilde demonstrated an aestheticism like theirs in his lush imagery and in his pursuit of the fleeting impression of the moment. His poetry tries to capture the beautiful, as the Victorian critic John Ruskin had urged a generation earlier, but generally lacks the moral tone that Ruskin advocated. Wilde's poetry best fulfills the aesthetic of Walter Pater, who, in his *Studies in the History of the Renaissance*, advocated impressionism and art for art's sake. Indeed, Wilde paraphrased Pater's famous line of burning with a "hard, gemlike flame" in several of his poems.

Wilde published many poems individually before 1881, but his *Poems* of 1881 included almost all these poems and many new ones. With this collection, he published more than half of the poetry that he was to produce. The collection of 1881 is a good representation of his aestheticism and his tendency to derivativeness. Wilde avoided the overtly autobiographical and confessional mode in these poems, yet they mirror his attitudes and travels as impressions of his life. The forms he tried most often in the collection were the Italian sonnet and, for longer poems, a six-line stanza in pentameter with an *ababcc* rhyme scheme. The smaller poetic output that followed the 1881 collection consists of a number of shorter poems, two longer poems, and *Poems in Prose*. The short poems break no new ground, *The Sphinx* heralds a decadence and a celebration of pain unequaled in the nineteenth century except by Swinburne a generation earlier. *The Ballad of Reading Gaol*, however, builds on Wilde's earlier efforts. Again, he avoids the confessional mode that one would expect, considering the horrors of incarceration out of which the poem grew. The persona of the poem is no longer an urbane mind observing nature and society, but a common prisoner at hard labor generalizing about the cruelties of humans and their treatment of those they love. In this poem, despite its shrillness and melodrama, Wilde struck a balance between his own suffering and art, a balance that the impressionism of his poetic talents made easier. He dealt, as an observer, with the modern and the sordid as he had dealt earlier with art and nature. *Poems in Prose* is Wilde's effort at the short parable,

*Oscar Wilde* (Library of Congress)

offering neither the impressionism nor the formal qualities of his other poems, but ironic parables that refute the pieties of his era. Here Wilde is at his wittiest.

### RAVENNA

*Ravenna* was Wilde's first long poem to be published, and it won the Newdigate prize for poetry while he was still at Oxford. Written in couplets, the poem deals with many of the themes that he developed for the 1881 collection; thus, *Ravenna* is the starting point in a study of Wilde's poetry. Like the later long poems, *Ravenna* develops through contrasts: northern and southern European cultures, innocence and experience, past and present, classical and Christian. As a city, Ravenna evokes all these contrasts to the youthful Wilde.

The opening imagery is of spring, with a tendency to lushness typical of Keats. The boyish awe that Wilde felt in Ravenna is tempered, however, by recollection, for in the poem he is recalling his visit a year later. It is through recollection that he understands the greatness of the city, for in his northern world he has no such symbol of the rich complexity of time. What he learns from the English landscape is the passage of seasons that will mark his aging. He is sure, though, that with his love for Ravenna he will have a youthful inspiration despite his aging and loss of poetic powers.

Most of the poem is a poetic recounting of Ravenna's history. Wilde discusses the classical past of the city with reference to Caesar, and when he refers to Lord Byron's stay in the city, by association with Byron's last days in Greece, he imagines the region peopled with mythological figures; but the evening convent bell returns him to a somber Christian world. Recounting the Renaissance history of the city, Wilde is most moved by Dante's shrine. He closes the poem with references to Dante and Byron.

Wilde published twenty-eight sonnets in the 1881 collection, *Poems*, all of them Italian in form. Like his mentor Keats, Wilde used the sonnet to develop themes that he expanded in his longer poems.

### SONNETS

"Hélas," an early sonnet not published in the 1881 collection, is his artistic manifesto that sets the tone for all the poems that followed. "Hélas" finds Wilde rhetorically questioning whether he has bartered wisdom for the passion or impression of the moment. In the sonnets that follow, he clearly seems to have chosen such moments of vivid impression.

In several sonnets, Wilde alludes to the poets who molded his style and themes, including two sonnets about visiting the graves of Keats and Percy Bysshe Shelley in the Protestant cemetery in Rome. He identifies himself with Keats as he never identifies with Shelley, and rightly so, for Keats's style and themes echo throughout the 1881 collection. Wilde also refers directly to Keats in another sonnet, "Amor Intellectualis," and to other poets important to him: Robert Browning, Christopher Marlowe, and particularly Dante and John Milton. The sonnet "A Vision" is a tribute to Aeschylus, Sophocles, and Euripides. On a larger scale than the sonnets, the longer poem "The Garden of Eros" presents Wilde's pantheon of poets with his feelings about them.

Some of the sonnets have political themes; in a number of these, Wilde advocates freedom, occasion-ally sounding like a Victorian Shelley. He is concerned with the political chaos of nineteenth century Italy, a land important to him for its classical past; "Italia" is a sonnet about the political venality in Italy, but it stresses that God might punish the corrupt. In his own country, Wilde idealizes the era of the Puritans and Oliver Cromwell; the sonnet "To Milton" laments the loss of democracy in England and advocates a return to the ideals of the Puritan revolution. In "Quantum Mutata," he admires Cromwell for his threat to Rome, but the title shows how events have changed, for Victorian England stands only for imperialism. This attack on British imperialism informs the long poem "Ave Imperatrix," which is far more emotional in tone than the political sonnets.

A number of Wilde's sonnets express his preference for the classical or primitive world and his antipathy for the modern Christian world. These poems have a persona visiting Italy, as Wilde did in 1877, and commenting on the Christian elements of the culture; "Sonnet on Approaching Italy" shows the speaker longing to visit Italy, yet, in contemplating far-off Rome, he laments the tyranny of a second Peter. Three other sonnets set in Italy, "Ave Maria, Gratia Plena," "Sonnet Written in Holy Week in Genoa," and "Urbs Sacra Aeterna," have Wilde contrasting the grandeur and color of the classical world with the emptiness and greyness of the Christian world. It is in these poems that Wilde is most like Swinburne. In other sonnets, he deals with religious values, often comparing the Christian ideal with the corruption of the modern Church he sees in Italy, or Christ's message with the conduct of his sinful followers. In "Easter Day," Wilde depicts the glory of the Pope as he is borne above the shoulders of the bearers, comparing that scene with the picture of Christ's loneliness centuries before. In "E Tenebris," the speaker appeals for help to a Christ who is to appear in weary human form. In "Sonnet, On Hearing the Dies Irae Sung in the Sistine Chapel," Wilde criticizes the harsh picture of a fiery day of judgment and replaces it with a picture of a warm autumn harvest, in which humankind awaits reaping by and fulfillment in God.

Wilde's best religious sonnet, "Madonna Mia," avoids the polemicism of some of his other religious sonnets, showing instead an affinity with the Pre-Raphaelite painting and poetry of a generation earlier. This sonnet is Pateresque in its hard impression, and it fulfills the credo suggested by the sonnet "Hélas." The picture Wilde paints in words is detailed: braided hair, blue eyes, pale cheeks, red lips, and white throat with purple veins; Wilde's persona is a worshiper of Mary, as Dante was of Beatrice.

### "THE BURDEN OF ITYS"

"The Burden of Itys" is one of several long philosophic poems about nature and God to be found in the 1881 collection. Each of these poems has the same stanza form, a six-line stanza with an *ababcc* rhyme scheme; the first five lines are iambic pentameter, and the sixth is iambic heptameter. The stanza form gives a lightness which does not perfectly fit the depth of the ideas the poems present; it seems a form better suited to witticism than to philosophy.

Set in England close to Oxford, "The Burden of Itys" is similar in imagery and setting to Matthew Arnold's poems "The Scholar Gypsy" and "Thrysis." Wilde piles image on image of the flora of the region to establish the beauty of the setting, suggesting that the beauty of the countryside (and thus of nature in general) is holier than the grandeur of Rome. Fish replace bishops and the wind becomes the organ for the persona's religious reverie. By stanza 13, Wilde shifts from his comparison between Rome and nature to a contrast between the English landscape and the Greek. Because England is more beautiful than Greece, he suggests that the Greek pantheon could fittingly be reborn in Victorian England. A bird singing to Wilde, much like the nightingale singing to Keats, is the link between the persona imagining a revival of classical gods and actually experiencing one in which he will wear the leopard skin of a follower of Bacchus. This spell breaks, though, with another contrast, for a pale Christ and the speaker's religion destroy the classical reverie.

Brought back then to the Victorian world, as Keats was brought back to his world at the end of "Ode to a Nightingale," Wilde philosophizes and fixes the meaning of his experience in a way Keats never would have done. He stresses that nature does not represent the lovely agony of Christ but warm fellowship both in and between the worlds of humankind and animal. Even Oxford and nature are linked to each other, Wilde implies, as the curfew bell from his college church calls him back.

### PHILOSOPHICAL POEMS

"Panthea" also works through dissimilarity, this time between southern and northern Europe, passion and reason, and classical and Christian thought. Wilde's rejection of the Church in "The Burden of Itys" is gentle, but in "Panthea" it is blatant. The gods have simply grown sick of priests and prayer. Instead, people should live for the passion and pleasure of an hour, those moments being the only gift the gods have to give. The poem emphasizes that the Greek gods themselves dwell in nature, participating fully in all the pleasures there. Their natural landscape, though, is not the bleak landscape of northern Europe, but the warm rich landscape of southern Europe.

Wilde proceeds to the philosophical theme of the poem, that one great power or being composes nature, and Nature, thus, subsumes all lives and elements and recycles them into various forms. For people to be reborn as flower or thrush is to live again without the pain of mortal existence; yet, paradoxically, without human pain, nature could not create beauty. Pain is the basis of beauty, for nature exists as a setting for human passion. Nature, in Wilde's words, has one "Kosmic Soul" linking all lives and elements. Wilde echoes lines of Keats and Pater, and, uncharacteristically, William Wordsworth; Wilde's affirmation proceeds with lines and images from Wordsworth's "Ode: Intimations of Immortality from Recollections of Early Childhood."

"Humanitad" is the longest of the philosophical poems in the 1881 collection, and it has much less in common with the other two philosophical poems than they have with each other. While spring is imminent, the speaker responds only to the winter elements still persisting. He emphasizes (paraphrasing Pater) that he has no fire to burn with a clear flame. The difference here is with the renewal of spring and spiritual exhaustion, and the speaker must look outside himself for some source of renewal. At one point, the poem turns topical by referring to ideals of simplicity and freedom: Switzerland, Wordsworth, and Giuseppe Mazzini. Wilde invokes the name of Milton as epitomizing the fight for freedom in the past; and, at the same time, he laments that there are no modern Miltons. Having no modern exemplar, Wilde also dismisses death and love as possible solutions for his moribund life. Turning to science, Wilde also rejects it. Wilde then has no recourse, and he faces a meaningless universe until he touches on mere causality after having rejected science.

Causality leads to God and creed, for causality is a chain connecting all elements. Nature, as in "Panthea," cannot help the speaker, for he has grown weary of mere sensation. Accordingly, he turns to the force behind nature (in this instance, God as Christ), although he rejects orthodoxy. He sees modern humanity's creed as being in process, for humanity is in the stage of crucifixion as it tries to discover the human in Christ and not the divine. The persona then sees his emptiness as the suffering leading to renewal. It is the full discovery of Christ's humanity that will make modern human beings masters of nature rather than tormented, alienated outcasts.

### The Sphinx

Just as Wilde drew from classical mythology for many of his poems and then contrasted the gray Christian world with the bright pagan world, he used Egyptian mythology in *The Sphinx* to picture a decadent sadistic sensuality as distinguished from a tortured Christian suffering. The situation in the poem is that a cat has crept into the speaker's room; to the speaker, the cat represents the Sphinx. Now, giving his imagination play, the speaker reveals his own sadistic eroticism, a subject that Wilde had not developed in other poems. The style also represents a departure for him; the stanzas consist of two lines of iambic octameter with no rhyme, resulting in a languorous slow rhythm in keeping with the speaker's ruminations about sensuality and sadism.

The cat as Sphinx represents the lush, decadent, yet appealing sensuality found in Egyptian mythology. In half of the poem, Wilde rhetorically questions the Sphinx about mythological figures of ancient Egypt, asking who her lovers were and at the same time cataloging the most famous myths of Egypt. Wilde settles on Ammon as the Sphinx's lover, but then he discusses how Ammon's statue has fallen to pieces, thus suggesting that the lover might be dead. Yet the Sphinx has the power to revive her lover; Ammon is not really dead. Having earlier referred to the holy family's exile in Egypt, Wilde now mentions that Christ is the only god who died, having let his side be pierced by a sword. Christ then is weaker than Ammon, and, in this way, Wilde suggests that pagan mythology is more vital than Christian mythology. The speaker's reflections on love become orthodox at the end; he feels he should contemplate the crucifix and not the Sphinx. He returns to a world of penitence where Christ watches and cries for every soul, but the speaker sees the tears as futile. The poem then raises the question of whether human beings can be redeemed from their fallen condition.

### The Ballad of Reading Gaol

Wilde's most famous poem, *The Ballad of Reading Gaol*, is a departure from any of the poems he had published previously. Sometimes overdone emotionally, the poem uses the prison as a metaphor for life and its cruelties. Wilde is the observer rather than the subject; in this way, he distances himself from his own experiences. The poem raises the thematic question of why humans are cruel to other human beings, so cruel that they always destroy what they love. It is through cruelty that people kill or destroy the ones they love, just as the prisoner whom Wilde observes, and who is soon to hang, murdered his lover. The mystery of human cruelty was the mystery of the Sphinx in Wilde's previous poem, but here the issue is the agony of the mystery rather than the decadent glory of cruelty, as in *The Sphinx*.

Wilde exploits the Gothic elements of the situation, dwelling on the macabre details of the grave of quicklime that dissolves the murderer's body. He uses the dread and gloom of the prisoners' lives to heighten the tone, but he often becomes shrill and melodramatic by emphasizing details such as the bag that covers the head of the condemned, tears falling like molten lead from the other prisoners as they observe the condemned, terror personified as a ghost, and the greasy rope used for the hanging. Ironically, the surviving prisoners are bedeviled by terror and horror, while the condemned dies calmly and serenely. Wilde uses a simple six-line stanza for a forcefully direct effect. The short lines alternate three and four feet of iambic pentameter with masculine rhyming of the second, fourth, and sixth lines. The stanza form is not one that suggests a reflective tone but rather a direct, emotional one.

The concluding motif of the poem is religious. The prison is a place of shame, where brother mistreats brother. Christ could feel only shame at what he sees his children do to each other there; but he rescues sinful humankind when he is broken by suffering and death. Even though the body of the hanged had no prayers said over it before interment in the quicklime, Christ rescued his soul. The surviving prisoners, their hearts broken and contrite, also gain salvation from the effects of their suffering.

### POEMS IN PROSE

Wilde's *Poems in Prose* was the last collection published of all his poems except *The Ballad of Reading Gaol*, and the reader hears a different voice from that of the other poems, satirical and paradoxical like William Blake's in *The Marriage of Heaven and Hell* (1790). In Wilde's hands, the prose poem is a debonair and provocative parable on religious subjects. More often than not in his six prose poems, Wilde is trying to shock the bourgeoisie out of complacency and religious orthodoxy.

"The Artist" sets the tone of the prose poems; in this piece, the artist forsakes the oppressive sorrow of Christianity for the pursuit of hedonism. It is this kind of ironic reversal that the other prose poems also develop. In "The Doer of Good," Christ returns to find sinners and lepers he has saved or cured delighting in the sin, no longer wrong, from which he saved them. The one person whom Christ saved from death wishes that Christ had left him dead. "The House of Judgment" ironically shows the sinner complaining that his earthly life was hellish, and confronted now with Heaven, he has no conception of it after his life of suffering. The most moving of the six is "The Teacher of Wisdom," in which Wilde shows that the finest act of humankind is to teach the wisdom of God. A hermit, having attained the knowledge of God, refuses to part with it by giving it to the young sinner who is imploring him. Frustrated, the sinner returns to sin, but, in so doing, extracts the knowledge from the hermit, who hopes to turn the sinner away from more sin. Fearing that he has parted with his knowledge, the hermit is consoled by God, who now, for his sacrifice, grants him a true love of God. In this parable, Wilde has transcended the satiric wit of the other parables to teach through irony.

### OTHER MAJOR WORKS

LONG FICTION: *The Picture of Dorian Gray*, 1890 (serial), 1891 (expanded).

SHORT FICTION: "The Canterville Ghost," 1887; *The Happy Prince, and Other Tales*, 1888; *A House of Pomegranates*, 1891; *Lord Arthur Savile's Crime, and Other Stories*, 1891.

PLAYS: *Vera: Or, The Nihilists*, pb. 1880; *The Duchess of Padua*, pb. 1883; *Lady Windermere's Fan*, pr. 1892; *Salomé*, pb. 1893 (in French), pb. 1894 (in English); *A Woman of No Importance*, pr. 1893; *An Ideal Husband*, pr. 1895; *The Importance of Being Earnest: A Trivial Comedy for Serious People*, pr. 1895; *A Florentine Tragedy*, pr. 1906 (one act; completed by T. Sturge More); *La Sainte Courtisane*, pb. 1908.

NONFICTION: *Intentions*, 1891; *De Profundis*, 1905; *The Letters of Oscar Wilde*, 1962 (Rupert Hart-Davis, editor); *The Complete Letters of Oscar Wilde*, 2000 (Merlin Holland and Hart-Davis, editors).

MISCELLANEOUS: *Works*, 1908; *Complete Works of Oscar Wilde*, 1948 (Vyvyan Holland, editor); *Plays, Prose Writings, and Poems*, 1960.

### BIBLIOGRAPHY

Belford, Barbara. *Oscar Wilde: A Certain Genius*. New York: Random House, 2000. An examination of Wilde's life with a somewhat revisionist view of Wilde's post-prison years.

Bloom, Harold, ed. *Oscar Wilde*. New York: Bloom's Literary Criticism, 2008. A collection of literary criticism on Wilde's body of work.

Canning, Richard. *Brief Lives: Oscar Wilde*. London: Hesperus, 2008. A biography of Wilde that covers his short life and his works.

Guy, Josephine, and Ian Small. *Studying Oscar Wilde: History, Criticism, and Myth*. Greensboro, N.C.: ELT Press, 2006. This volume attempts to provide a guide to studying the poet that distinguishes between the myth and history as well as provides literary criticism.

Harris, Frank. *Oscar Wilde: Including My Memories of Oscar Wilde by George Bernard Shaw*. 2d ed. New York: Carroll & Graf, 1997. Harris was one of the few friends who remained loyal to Wilde after his downfall. His biography, although highly readable and full of interesting anecdotes, is not always reliable. Shaw's afterward is a shrewd assessment of Wilde.

McKenna, Neil. *The Secret Life of Oscar Wilde*. New York: Basic Books, 2005. This controversial and groundbreaking biography focuses on how Wilde's homosexuality influenced the writer's life and work. Illustrated.

Nunokawa, Jeff, and Amy Sickels. *Oscar Wilde*. Philadelphia: Chelsea House, 2005. A portrait of Wilde that examines his rise to fame, his sexuality, and the difficulties he experienced, especially after his fall.

Pearce, Joseph. *The Unmasking of Oscar Wilde*. San Francisco: Ignatius Press, 2004. Pearce avoids lingering on the actions that brought Wilde notoriety and instead explores Wilde's emotional and spiritual search. Along with a discussion of *The Ballad of Reading Gaol* and the posthumously published *De Profundis*, Pearce also traces Wilde's fascination with Catholicism.

Stokes, Anthony. *Pit of Shame: The Real Ballad of Reading Gaol*. Winchester, England: Waterside Press, 2007. Looks at Wilde's poem and also the actual jail that held the poet.

Wilde, Oscar. Interviews. *Oscar Wilde in America: The Interviews*. Edited by Matthew Hofer and Gary Scharnhorst. Urbana: University of Illinois Press, 2009. A collection of interviews from the time Wilde spent in the United States.

*Dennis Goldsberry*

---

# WILLIAM WORDSWORTH

**Born:** Cockermouth, Cumberland, England; April 7, 1770

**Died:** Rydal Mount, Westmorland, England; April 23, 1850

## PRINCIPAL POETRY

*Descriptive Sketches*, 1793

*An Evening Walk*, 1793

*Lyrical Ballads*, 1798 (with Samuel Taylor Coleridge)

*Lyrical Ballads, with Other Poems*, 1800 (with Coleridge, includes Preface)

*Poems in Two Volumes*, 1807

*The Excursion*, 1814

*Poems*, 1815

*The White Doe of Rylstone*, 1815

*Peter Bell*, 1819

*The Waggoner*, 1819

*The River Duddon*, 1820

*Ecclesiastical Sketches*, 1822

*Poems Chiefly of Early and Late Years*, 1842

*The Prelude: Or, The Growth of a Poet's Mind*, 1850

*The Recluse*, 1888

*Poetical Works*, 1940-1949 (5 volumes; Ernest de Selincourt and Helen Darbishire, editors)

## OTHER LITERARY FORMS

In addition to his poetry, William Wordsworth's preface to the second edition of his *Lyrical Ballads* is the single most important manifesto of the Romantic position in English, defining his ideas of the primary laws of nature, the working of the imagination, the process of association of ideas, and the balance of passion and restraint in human conduct.

## ACHIEVEMENTS

William Wordsworth was one of the leading English Romantic poets. Along with William Blake, Samuel Taylor Coleridge, Lord Byron, Percy Bysshe Shelley, and John Keats, Wordsworth created a major revolution in ideology and poetic style around 1800. The Romantic writers rebelled against the neoclassical position exemplified in the works of Alexander Pope (1688-1744) and Samuel Johnson (1709-1784). Although all such broad generalizations should be viewed with suspicion, it is generally said that the neoclassical writers valued restraint and discipline, whereas the Romantic poets favored individual genius and hoped to follow nature freely. Wordsworth's poetry praises the value of the simple individual, the child, the helpless, the working class, and the natural man. Such sentiments were explosive in the age of the French Revolution, when Wordsworth was young. He helped to define the attitudes that fostered the spread of democracy, of more humane treatment of the downtrodden, and of respect for nature.

BIOGRAPHY

The northwestern corner of England, which contains the counties of Northumberland and Westmorland, is both mountainous and inaccessible. The cliffs are not as high as those in Switzerland, but they are rugged, and the land is settled mainly by shepherds and by isolated farmers. The valleys have long, narrow, picturesque lakes, and so the region is called the English Lake District. William Wordsworth was born and lived much of his life among these lakes. Many of the English Romantic writers are sometimes called lake poets because of their association with this area. Wordsworth was born in 1770 in the small town of Cockermouth in Cumberland. Although he later wrote about the lower classes, his own family was middle class, and the poet never actually worked with his hands to make his living. His father was a lawyer who managed the affairs of the earl of Lonsdale. The poet had three brothers (Richard, John, and Christopher) and a sister (Dorothy). For the first nine years of his life, the family inhabited a comfortable house near the Derwent River. William attended Anne Birkett's school in the little town of Penrith, where Mary Hutchinson, whom he married in 1802, was also a student. His mother died when he was seven. The two brothers, William and Richard, then boarded at the house of Ann Tyson while attending grammar school in the village of Hawkshead.

Apparently this arrangement was a kindly one, and the boy spent much time happily roaming the nearby fields and hills. He also profited from the teaching of his schoolmaster William Taylor, who encouraged him to write poetry. In 1783, his father died and the family inheritance was tied up in litigation for some twenty years. Only after the death of the earl of Lonsdale in 1802 was Wordsworth able to profit from his father's estate. With the help of relatives, he matriculated at St. John's College, Cambridge University. Although he did not earn distinction as a student, those years were fertile times for learning.

*William Wordsworth* (Library of Congress)

While he was a student at St. John's, between 1787 and 1791, the French Revolution broke out across the English Channel. During his summer vacation of 1790, Wordsworth and his college friend, Robert Jones, went on a walking tour across France and Switzerland to Italy. The young students were much impressed by the popular revolution and the spirit of democracy in France at that time. Wordsworth took his degree at St. John's in January, 1791, but had no definite plans for his future. The following November, he went again to revolution-torn France with the idea of learning the French language well enough to earn his living as a tutor. Passing through Paris, he settled at Blois in the Loire Valley. There he made friends with Captain Michael Beaupuy and became deeply involved in French Republican thought. There, too, he fell in love with Annette Vallon, who was some four years older than the young poet. Vallon and Wordsworth had an illegitimate daughter, Caroline, but Wordsworth returned to England alone in December, 1792, probably to try to arrange his financial affairs. In February, 1793, war broke out between France and England so that Wordsworth was not able to see his baby and her mother again until the Treaty of Amiens in 1802 made it possible for him to visit them. His daughter was then ten years old.

In 1793, Wordsworth must have been a very unhappy young man: His deepest sympathies were on the side of France and democracy, but his own country was at war against his French friends such as Captain Michael Beaupuy; he was separated from Annette and his baby, and his English family associates looked on his conduct as scandalous; the earl of Lonsdale refused to settle his father's financial claims, so the young man was without funds and had no way to earn a living, even though he held a bachelor's degree from a prestigious university. Under these conditions, he moved in politically radical circles, becoming friendly with William Godwin, Mary Wollstonecraft, and Thomas Paine. In 1793, he published his first books of poetry, *An Evening Walk* and *Descriptive Sketches*.

Wordsworth and his younger sister, Dorothy, were close friends. In 1795, the poet benefited from a small legacy to settle with her at Racedown Cottage in Dorset, where they were visited by Mary Hutchinson and Samuel Taylor Coleridge. In 1797, they moved to Alfoxden, near Nether Stowey in Somerset, to be near Coleridge's home. Here a period of intense creativity occurred: Dorothy began her journal in 1798 while Wordsworth and Coleridge collaborated on *Lyrical Ballads*. A walking trip with Dorothy along the Wye River resulted in 1798 in "Lines Composed a Few Miles Above Tintern Abbey." That fall, Coleridge, Dorothy, and Wordsworth went to study in Germany. Dorothy and the poet spent most of their time in Goslar, where apparently he began to write *The Prelude*, his major autobiographical work which he left unfinished at his death. Returning from Germany, he and Dorothy settled in Dove Cottage in the Lake District. In 1800, he completed "Michael" and saw the second edition of *Lyrical Ballads* published. With the end of hostilities in 1802, Wordsworth visited Vallon and their daughter in France, arranging to make an annual child-support payment. Upon his return to England, he married Mary Hutchinson. During that year, he composed "Ode: Intimations of Immortality from Recollections of Early Childhood."

In 1805, his brother John was drowned at sea. Words-worth often looked on nature as a kindly force, but the death of his brother in a shipwreck may have been a powerful contribution to his darkening vision of nature as he grew older. In 1805, he had a completed draft of *The Prelude* ready for Coleridge to read, although he was never satisfied with the work as a whole and rewrote it extensively later. It is sometimes said that when Wordsworth was a "bad" man, fathering an illegitimate child, consorting with revolutionaries and drug addicts, and roaming the countryside with no useful occupation, he wrote "good" poetry. When he became a "good" man, respectably married and gainfully employed, he began to write "bad" poetry. It is true that, although he wrote prolifically until his death, not much of his work after about 1807 is considered remarkable. In 1813, he accepted the position of distributor of stamps for Westmorland County, the kind of governmental support he probably would have scorned when he was younger. His fame as a writer, however, grew steadily. In 1842 when his last volume, *Poems Chiefly of Early and Late Years*, was published, he accepted a government pension of three hundred pounds sterling per annum, a considerable sum. The next year, he succeeded Robert Southey as poet laureate of England. He died April 23, 1850, at Rydal Mount in his beloved Lake District.

ANALYSIS

When the volume of poetry called the *Lyrical Ballads* of 1798 was published in a second edition (1800), William Wordsworth wrote a prose preface for the book that is the single most important statement of Romantic ideology. It provides a useful introduction to his poetry.

LYRICAL BALLADS

Wordsworth's preface to *Lyrical Ballads* displays the idea of primitivism as the basis of the Romantic position. Primitivism is the belief that there is some primary, intrinsically good "state of nature" from which adult, educated, civilized humankind has fallen into a false or wicked state of existence. When Jean-Jacques Rousseau began *The Social Contract* (1762) with the assertion that "Man was born free, and yet we see him everywhere in chains," he concisely expressed the primitivist point of view. The American and French revolutions were both predicated on Romantic primitivism, the idea that humanity was once naturally free, but that corrupt kings, churches, and social customs held it enslaved. The Romantic typically sees rebellion and breaking free from false restraint to regain a state of nature as highly desirable; Wordsworth's preface shows him deeply committed to this revolutionary ideology. He says that he is going to take the subjects of his poems from "humble and rustic life" because in that condition humankind is "less under restraint" and the "elementary feelings" of life exist in a state of simplicity.

Many writers feel that serious literature can be written only about great and powerful men, such as kings and generals. Some writers apparently believe that wounding a king is tragic, while beating a slave is merely funny. Wordsworth's preface firmly rejects such ideas. He turns to simple, common, poor people as the topic of his poetry because they are nearer a "state of nature" than the powerful, educated, and sophisticated men who have been corrupted by false customs of society. Many writers feel that they must live in the centers of civilization, London or Paris, for example, to be conversant with new ideas and the latest fashions. Wordsworth turns away from the cities to the rural scene. He himself lived in the remote Lake District most of his life, and he wrote about simple shepherds, farmers, and villagers. He explains that he chooses for his topics

> humble and rustic life . . . because, in that condition, the essential passions of the heart find a better soil in which they can attain their maturity, are less under restraint, and speak a plainer and more emphatic language; because in that condition of life our elementary feelings coexist in a state of greater simplicity, and consequently may be more accurately contemplated.

He sees a correspondence between the unspoiled nature of humankind and the naturalness of the environment. Romantic ideology of this sort underlies much of the contemporary environmentalist movement: the feeling that humans ought to be in harmony with their environment, that nature is beneficent, that people ought to live simply so that the essential part of their human nature may conform to the grand pattern of nature balanced in the whole universe.

The use of the words "passion" and "restraint" in Wordsworth's quotation above is significant. English neoclassical writers such as Alexander Pope tended to be suspicious of human passions, arguing that anger and lust lead people into error unless such passions are restrained by right reason. For Pope, it is necessary to exercise the restraint of reason over passion for people to be morally good. "Restraint" is good; "passion" bad. Wordsworth reverses this set of values. Humans' natural primitive feelings are the source of goodness and morality; the false restraints of custom and education are what lead people astray from their natural goodness. In his preface, Wordsworth seems to be following the line of thought developed by Anthony Ashley-Cooper, the third earl of Shaftesbury (1671-1713) in his *An Inquiry Concerning Virtue or Merit* (1709). Shaftesbury asks his readers to imagine a "creature who, wanting reason and being unable to reflect, has notwithstanding many good qualities and affections,—as love to his kind, courage, gratitude or pity." Shaftesbury probably is thinking of creatures such as a faithful dog or a child too young to reason well. In such cases, one would have to say that the creature shows good qualities, even though he or she lacks reasoning power. For Shaftesbury, then, to reason means merely to recognize the already existing good impulses or feelings naturally arising in such a creature. Morality arises from natural feeling, evidently present in creatures with little reasoning power.

Wordsworth's preface is heavily influenced by Shaftesbury's argument. He turns to simple characters for his poems because they exhibit the natural, primary, unspoiled states of feeling that are the ultimate basis of morality. Wordsworth's characters are sentimental heroes, chosen because their feelings are unspoiled by restraints of education and reason: children, simple shepherds and villagers, the old Cumberland Beggar, Alice Fell, and so on. While William Shakespeare often puts a nobleman at the center of his plays and relegates the poor people to the role of rustic clowns, Wordsworth takes the feelings of the poor as the most precious subject of serious literature.

The preface displays two kinds of primitivism. Social primitivism is the belief that humankind's state of nature is good and that it is possible to imagine a social setting in which humans' naturally good impulses will flourish. Social primitivism leads to the celebration of the "noble savage," perhaps an American Indian or a Black African tribesman, who is supposed to be morally superior to the sophisticated European who has been corrupted by the false restraints of his own society. Social primitivism was, of course, one of the driving forces behind the French Revolution. The lower classes rose up against the repression of politically powerful kings and destroyed laws and restraints so that their natural goodness could flourish. Unfortunately, the French Revolution did not produce a morally perfect new human being once the corrupt restraints had been destroyed. Instead, the French Revolution produced the Reign of Terror, the rise of Napoleon to military dictatorship, and the French wars of aggression against relatively democratic states such as the Swiss Republic. With unspeakable shock, Wordsworth and the other Romantics saw the theory of social primitivism fail in France. The decline of Wordsworth's poetic power as he grew older is often explained in part as the result of his disillusionment with revolutionary France.

A second kind of primitivism in the preface is psychological. Psychological primitivism is the belief that there is some level in the mind that is primary, more certain than everyday consciousness. In the preface, Wordsworth says that humble life displays "the primary laws of our nature; chiefly, as far as the manner in which we associate ideas." Here Wordsworth refers to a very important Romantic idea, associational psychology, which developed from the tradition of British empirical philosophy—from John Locke's *Essay Concerning Human Understanding* (1690), David Hume's *Enquiry Concerning Human Understanding* (1748), and especially David Hartley's *Observations on Man* (1749).

When Wordsworth speaks in the preface to the *Lyrical Ballads* about tracing in his poems the "manner in which we associate ideas," he is endorsing the line of thought of the associational psychologists. Poems trace the process by which the mind works. They help people to understand the origins of their own feelings about what is good and bad by demonstrating the way impressions from nature strike the mind and by showing how the mind associates these simple experiences, forming complex attitudes about what proper conduct is, what fidelity and love are, what the good and the true are. In *The Prelude*, one of Wordsworth's main motives is to trace the history of the development of his own mind from its most elementary feelings through the process of association of ideas until his imagination constructs his complex, adult consciousness.

Wordsworth's preface to the second edition of *Lyrical Ballads* set out a series of ideas that are central to the revolutionary Romantic movement, including both social and psychological primitivism, the state of nature, the "noble savage," the sentimental hero, the power of the imagination, and the association of ideas. These concepts are basic to understanding his poetry.

### "LINES COMPOSED A FEW MILES ABOVE TINTERN ABBEY"

Wordsworth's "Lines Composed a Few Miles Above Tintern Abbey" (hereafter called simply "Tintern Abbey") was composed on July 13, 1798, and published that same year. It is one of the best-known works of the English Romantic movement. Its poetic form is blank verse, unrhymed iambic pentameter, in the tradition of John Milton's *Paradise Lost* (1667, 1674). In reading any poem, it is important to define its dramatic situation and to consider the text as if it were a scene from a play or drama and determine who is speaking, to whom, and under what circumstances. Wordsworth is very precise in telling the reader when and where these lines are spoken. Tintern Abbey exists, and the poet Wordsworth really visited it during a tour on July 13, 1798. Because the poem is set at a real point in history rather than once upon a time, and in a real place rather than in a kingdom far away, it is said to exhibit "topographic realism." The speaker of the poem reveals that this is his second visit to this spot; he had been there five years earlier. At line 23, he reveals that he has been away from this pleasant place for a long time and, at lines 50-56, that while he was away in the "fretful stir" of the world he was unhappy. When he was depressed, his thoughts turned to his memory of this natural scene, and he felt comforted. Now, as the poem begins, he has come again to this beautiful site with his beloved younger sister, whom he names directly at line 121. The dramatic situation involves a speaker, or persona, who tells the reader his thoughts and feelings as if he were addressing his younger sister, who is "on stage" as his dramatic audience. Although the poem is autobiographical, so that the speaker resembles Wordsworth himself and the sister resembles Dorothy Wordsworth, it is better to think of the speaker and his listener as two invented characters in a little play. When William Shakespeare's Hamlet speaks to Ophelia in his play, the audience knows that Hamlet is not the same as Shakespeare although he surely must express some of Shakespeare's feelings and ideas. So, too, the reader imagines that the speaker in "Tintern Abbey" speaks for Wordsworth, but is not exactly the same as the poet himself.

The poem displays many of the ideas stated in the preface to the *Lyrical Ballads*. It begins with a description of a remote rural scene, rather than speaking about the latest news from London. In this rustic setting, the speaker discovers some essential truths about himself. The first twenty-two lines describe the natural scene: the cliffs, orchards, and farms. This is a romantic return to nature, the search for the beautiful and permanent forms that incorporate primitive human goodness. The speaker not only describes the scene, but also tells the reader how it generates feelings and sensations in him. In lines 23-56, the speaker says that his memory of this pure, natural place had been of comfort to him when he was far away. Lines 66-90 trace the speaker's memory of his process of growing up: When he first came among these hills as a boy, he was like a wild animal. He was filled with feelings of joy or fear by wild nature. As a boy, nature was to him "a feeling and a love" that required no thought on his part. That childish harmony with nature is now lost. His childish "aching joys" and "dizzy raptures" are "gone by." As he fell away from his unthinking harmony with nature, his power of thought developed. This power is "abundant recompense" for the childish joys of "thoughtless youth." Now he understands nature in a new way. He hears in nature "The still sad music of humanity." At line 95, he explains that his intellect grasps the purpose and direction of nature, whereas his childish experience was more intense and joyous but incomplete. Now, as an adult, he returns to this natural scene and understands what he had only felt as a child, that nature is the source

of moral goodness, "the nurse, the guide, the guardian of my heart, and soul of all my moral being."

At line 110, he turns to his younger sister and sees in her wild eyes his own natural state of mind in childhood. He foresees that she will go through the same loss that he experienced. She too will grow up and lose her unthinking harmony with the natural and the wild. He takes comfort in the hope that nature will protect her, as it has helped him, and in the knowledge that the memory of this visit will be with her when she is far away in future years. Their experience of this pastoral landscape is therefore dear to the speaker for its own sake, and also because he has shared it with his sister. He has come back from the adult world and glimpsed primitive natural goodness both in the scene and in his sister.

The poem employs social and psychological primitivism. The rural scene is an imagined state of primitive nature where human goodness can exist in the child, like Adam in the garden of Eden before the Fall of Man. The poem shows how the primitive feelings of the boy are generated by the forms of nature and then form more and more complex ideas until his whole adult sense of good and bad, right and wrong, can be traced back to his elementary childish experiences of nature. Reason is not what makes beauty or goodness possible; natural feelings are the origin of the good and the beautiful. Reason merely recognizes what the child knows directly from his feelings.

Critics of Wordsworth point out that the "natural" scene described in the opening lines is, in fact, not at all "natural." Nature in this scene has been tamed by man into orchards, hedged fields, and cottage farms. What, critics ask, would Wordsworth have written if he had imagined nature as the struggling jungle in the Congo where individual plants and animals fight for survival in their environmental niche and whole species are brought to extinction by the force of nature "red in tooth and claw"? If Wordsworth's idea of nature is not true, then his idea of human nature will likewise be false. While he expects the French Revolution to lead to a state of nature in joy and harmony, in fact it led to the Reign of Terror and the bloodshed of the Napoleonic wars. Critics of Romantic ideology argue that when the Romantics imagine nature as a "kindly nurse," they unthinkingly accept a false anthropomorphism. Nature is not like a kindly human being; it is an indifferent or neutral force. They charge that Wordsworth projects his own feelings into the natural scene, and thus his view of the human condition becomes dangerously confused.

### "MICHAEL"

"Michael: A Pastoral Poem" was composed between October 11 and December 9, 1800, and published that same year. It is typical of Wordsworth's poetry about humble and rustic characters in which the sentiments or feelings of human beings in a state of nature are of central importance. The poem is written in blank verse, unrhymed iambic pentameter, again the meter employed in Milton's *Paradise Lost*. Milton's poem explores the biblical story of the fall of Adam from the Garden of Eden. Michael's destruction in Wordsworth's poem shows a general similarity to the tragedy of Adam in *Paradise Lost*. Both Michael and Adam begin in a natural paradise where they are happy and good. Evil creeps into each garden, and through the weakness of a beloved family member, both Adam and Michael fall from happiness to misery.

The poem "Michael" has two parts: the narrative frame and the tale of Michael. The frame occupies lines 1-39 and lines 475 to the end, the beginning and ending of the text. It relates the circumstances under which the story of Michael is told. The tale occupies lines 40-475, the central part of the text, and it tells the history of the shepherd Michael; his wife, Isabel; and their son Luke. The frame of the poem occurs in the fictive present time, about 1800, whereas the tale occurs a generation earlier. The disintegration of Michael's family and the destruction of their cottage has already happened years before the poem begins. The frame establishes that the poem is set in the English Lake District and introduces the reader to the "I-persona" or speaker of the poem. He tells the story of Michael and knows the geography and history of the district. A "You-character" who does not know the region is the dramatic audience addressed by the "I-persona." In the frame, "I" tells "You" that there is a hidden valley up in the mountains. In that valley, there is a pile of rocks, which would hardly be noticed by a stranger; but there is a story behind that heap of stones. "I" then tells "You" the story of the shepherd Michael.

Michael is one of the humble and rustic characters whose feelings are exemplary of the natural or primitive state of human beings. He has lived all his life in the mountains, in communion with nature, and his own nature has been shaped by his natural environment. He is a good and kindly man. He has a wife, Isabel, and a child of his old age named Luke. The family works from morning until far into the night, tending their sheep and spinning wool. They live in a cottage far up on the mountainside, and they have a lamp that burns late every evening as they sit at their work. They have become proverbial in the valley for their industry, so that their cottage has become known as the cottage of the evening star because its window glimmers steadily every night. These simple, hardworking people are "neither gay perhaps, nor cheerful, yet with objects and with hopes, living a life of eager industry." The boy is Michael's delight. From his birth, the old man had helped to tend the child and, as Luke grew, his father worked with him always at his side. He made him a perfect shepherd's staff and gave it to his son as a gift. Now the boy has reached his eighteenth year and the "old man's heart seemed born again" with hope and happiness in his son.

Unfortunately, Michael suffers a reversal of his good fortune, for news comes that a distant relative has suffered an unforeseen business failure, and Michael has to pay a grievous penalty "in surety for his brother's son." The old man is sorely troubled. He cannot bear to sell his land. He suggests that Luke should go from the family for a time to work in the city and earn enough to pay the forfeiture. Before his beloved son leaves, Michael takes him to a place on the farm where he has collected a heap of stones. He tells Luke that he plans to build a new sheepfold there and asks Luke to lay the cornerstone. This will be a covenant or solemn agreement between the father and son: The boy will work in the city, and meanwhile the father will build a new barn so that it will be there for the boy's return. Weeping, the boy puts the first stone in place and leaves the next day for his work far away. At first, the old couple get a good report about his work, but after a time Luke "in the dissolute city gave himself to evil courses; ignominy and shame fell on him, so that he was driven at last to seek a hiding-place beyond the sea." After the loss of his son,

Michael still goes to the dell where the pile of building stones lies, but he often simply sits the whole day merely staring at them, until he dies. Some three years later, Isabel also dies, and the land is sold to a stranger. The cottage of the evening star is torn down and nothing remains of the poor family's hopes except the straggling pile of stones that are the remains of the still unfinished sheepfold. This is the story that the "I-persona," who knows the district, tells to the "You-audience," who is unacquainted with the local history and geography.

The poem "Michael" embodies the ideas proposed in Wordsworth's preface to the *Lyrical Ballads*. He takes a family of simple, rural people as the main characters in a tragedy. Michael is a sentimental hero whose unspoiled contact with nature has refined his human nature and made him a good man. Nature has imprinted experiences on his mind that his imagination has built into more and more complex feelings about what is right and wrong. The dissolute city, on the other hand, is confusing, and there Luke goes astray. From the city and the world of banking and finance, the grievous forfeiture intrudes into the rural valley where Michael was living in a state of nature, like a noble savage or like Adam before his fall.

The poem argues that nature is not a neutral commodity to be bought and sold. It is man's home. It embodies values. The poem demands that the reader consider nature as a living force and demonstrates that once one knows the story of Luke, one never again can look on a pile of rocks in the mountains as worthless. That pile of rocks was a solemn promise of father and son. It signified a whole way of life, now lost. It was gathered for a human purpose, and one must regret that the covenant was broken and the sheepfold never completed. Likewise, all nature is a covenant, an environment, filled with human promise and capable of guiding human feelings in a pure, simple, dignified, and moral way. The function of poetry (like the "I-persona's" story of Michael) is to make the reader see that nature is not neutral. The "I-persona" attaches the history of Michael to what otherwise might be merely a pile of rocks and so makes the "You-audience" feel differently about that place. Likewise, the poem as a whole makes the reader feel differently about nature.

"Tintern Abbey" and "Michael" both explore the important question of how human moral nature develops. What makes humans good, virtuous, or proper? If, as the preface argues, people are morally best when most natural, uncorrupted by false custom and education, then the normal process of growing up in the modern world must be a kind of falling away from natural grace.

### "ODE: INTIMATIONS OF IMMORTALITY FROM RECOLLECTIONS OF EARLY CHILDHOOD"

Wordsworth's "Ode: Intimations of Immortality from Recollections of Early Childhood" (hereafter called "Ode: Intimations of Immortality") is also concerned with the process of growing up and its ethical and emotional consequences. The poem is written in eleven stanzas of irregular length, composed of lines of varying length with line-end rhyme. The core of the poem is stanza 5, beginning "Our birth is but a sleep and a forgetting." Here the poet discusses three stages of growth: the infant, the boy, and the man. The infant at birth comes from God, and at the moment when life begins the infant is still close to its divine origin. For this reason, the newborn infant is not utterly naked or forgetful, "but trailing clouds of glory do we come from God." The infant is near to divinity; "Heaven lies about us in our infancy," but each day leads it farther and farther from its initial, completely natural state. As consciousness awakens, "Shades of the prison house begin to close upon the growing boy." In other words, the natural feelings of the infant begin to become constrained as man falls into consciousness. A boy is still near to nature, but each day he travels farther from the initial source of his natural joy and goodness. The youth is like a priest who travels away from his Eastern holy land, each day farther from the origin of his faith, but still carrying with him the memory of the holy places. When a man is fully grown, he senses that the natural joy of childish union with nature dies away, leaving him only the drab ordinary "light of common day" unilluminated by inspiration. This process of movement from the unthinking infant in communion with nature, through the stage of youth filled with joy and natural inspiration, to the drab adult is summarized in stanza 7, from the "child among his new-born blisses" as he or she grows up playing a series of roles "down to palsied Age."

The poem as a whole rehearses this progression from natural infant to adulthood. Stanzas 1 and 2 tell how the speaker as a child saw nature as glorious and exciting. "There was a time when meadow, grove, and stream . . . to me did seem apparelled in celestial light." Now the speaker is grown up and the heavenly light of the natural world has lost its glory. Even so, in stanza 3, his sadness at his lost childhood joys is changed to joy when he sees springtime and thinks of shepherd boys. Springtime demonstrates the eternal rebirth of the world, when everything is refreshed and begins to grow naturally again. The shepherd boys shouting in the springtime are doubly blessed, for they are rural characters, and moreover, they are young, near the fountainhead of birth. In stanza 4, the adult speaker can look on the springtime or on rural children and feel happy again because they signify the experience he has had of natural joy. Even though, as he says in stanza 10, "nothing can bring back the hour of splendour in the grass, of glory in the flower," the adult can understand with his "philosophic mind" the overall design of the natural world and grasp that it is good.

### THE PRELUDE

*The Prelude* is Wordsworth's longest and probably his most important work. It is an autobiographical portrait of the artist as a young man. He was never satisfied with the work and repeatedly rewrote and revised it, leaving it uncompleted at his death. He had a fairly refined draft in 1805-1806 for his friend Coleridge to read, and the version he left at his death in 1850 is, of course, the chronologically final version. In between the 1805 and 1850 versions, there are numerous drafts and sketches, some of them of the whole poem, while others are short passages or merely a few lines. When a reader speaks of Wordsworth's *The Prelude*, therefore, he is referring not so much to a single text as to a shifting, dynamic set of sometimes contradictory texts and fragments. The best edition of *The Prelude* is by Ernest de Selincourt, second edition revised by Helen Darbishire (Oxford University Press, 1959), which provides on facing pages the 1805-1806 text and the 1850 text. The reader can open the de Selincourt/Darbishire edition and see side by side the earliest and the latest version of every passage, while the editors' annotations indicate all significant intermediate steps.

The 1805 version is divided into thirteen books, while the 1850 version has fourteen. Book 1, "Introduction, Childhood and Schooltime," rehearses how the poet undertook to write this work. He reviews the topics treated in famous epic poems, in Milton's *Paradise Lost*, Edmund Spenser's *The Faerie Queene* (1590, 1596), and other works. He concludes that the proper subject for his poem should be the process of his own development. He therefore begins at line 305 of the 1805 version to relate his earliest experiences, following the ideas explored above in "Tintern Abbey" and his "Ode: Intimations of Immortality." He traces the earliest impressions on his mind, which is like the tabula rasa of the associational psychologists. "Fair seed-time had my soul, and I grew up/ Foster'd alike by beauty and by fear." He tells of his childhood in the lakes and mountains, of stealing birds from other hunters' traps, of scaling cliffs, and especially a famous episode concerning a stolen boat. At line 372, he tells how he once stole a boat and rowed at night out onto a lake. As he rowed away from the shore facing the stern of the boat, it appeared that a dark mountain rose up in his line of vision as if in pursuit. He was struck with fear and returned with feelings of guilt to the shore. Experiences like this "trace/ How Nature by extrinsic passion first peopled my mind." In other words, impressions of nature, associated with pleasure and pain, provide the basic ideas that the imagination of the poet uses to create more and more complex attitudes until he arrives at his adult view of the world. The process described in the stolen boat episode is sometimes called the "discipline of fear."

Book 2 concerns "School-Time." It corresponds to the three stages of life outlined in "Ode: Intimations of Immortality": infant, youth, and adult. As in "Tintern Abbey," in *The Prelude*, book 2, Wordsworth explains that his early experiences of nature sustained him when he grew older and felt a falling off of the infant's joyful harmony with the created universe. Book 3 deals with his "Residence at Cambridge University," which is like a dream world to the youth from the rural lakes: "I was a Dreamer, they the dream; I roamed/ Delighted through the motley spectacle." He talks of his reading and his activities as a student at St. John's College, concluding that his story so far has been indeed a heroic argument, as important as the stories of the ancient epics, tracing the development of his mind up to an eminence, a high point of his experience.

Book 4 recounts his summer vacation after his first year of college, as he returns to the mountains and lakes of his youth, a situation comparable to the return of the persona in "Tintern Abbey" to the rural scene he had previously known. He notes the "inner falling-off" or loss of joy and innocence that seems to accompany growing up. Yet at line 344, he tells of a vision of the sun rising as he walked homeward after a night of gaiety and mirth at a country dance, which caused him to consider himself a "dedicated spirit," someone who has a sacred duty to write poetry. Later in this book, he recounts his meeting with a tattered soldier returned from military service in the tropics and how he helped him find shelter in a cottage nearby. Book 5 is simply titled "Books" and examines the role of literature in the poet's development. This book contains the famous passage, beginning at line 389, "There was a boy, ye knew him well, ye Cliffs/ And Islands of Winander." There was a youth among the cliffs of the Lake District who could whistle so that the owls would answer him. Once when he was calling to them the cliffs echoed so that he was struck with surprise and wonder. This boy died while he was yet a child and the poet has stood "Mute—looking at the grave in which he lies." Another recollection concerns the appearance of a drowned man's body from the lake.

Book 6, "Cambridge and the Alps," treats his second year at college and the following summer's walking tour of France and Switzerland. When the poet first arrived at Calais, it was the anniversary of the French Revolution's federal day. The young man finds the revolutionary spirit with "benevolence and blessedness/ spread like a fragrance everywhere, like Spring/ that leaves no corner of the land untouched." Frenchmen welcome the young Englishman as brothers in the struggle for freedom and liberty and they join in a common celebration. The Alps were a formidable barrier in the nineteenth century, seeming to separate the Germanic culture of northern Europe from the Mediterranean. Crossing the Alps meant passing from one culture to a totally different one. Ironically, the poet records his errant climb, lost in the fog and mist, as he approached Italy, so that the English travelers cross the Alps without even knowing what they had done. Perhaps the crossing of the Alps unaware is like his observation of the French Revolution. The poet *sees* more than he *understands*. Book 7 treats of the poet's residence in London. As one would expect, the city is unnatural and filled with all kinds of deformed and perverted customs, epitomized at the Bartholomew Fair, "a hell/ For eyes and ears! what anarchy and din/ Barbarian and infernal! 'tis a dream/ Monstrous in colour, motion, shape, sight, sound."

Book 8, "Retrospect—Love of Nature Leading to a Love of Mankind," is in contrast to book 7. Opposed to the blank confusion of the city, book 8 returns to the peaceful, decent rural scenes of the Lake District. It contrasts a wholesome country fair with the freak shows of London. Nature's primitive gift to the shepherds is beauty and harmony, which the poet first experienced there. Such "noble savages," primitive men educated by nature alone, are celebrated as truly heroic.

Book 9 tells of the poet's second visit to France and residence in the Loire Valley. It suppresses, however, all the real biographical details concerning Wordsworth's affair with Annette Vallon and his illegitimate daughter. As he passes through Paris, the poet sees "the revolutionary power/ Toss like a ship at anchor, rock'd by storms." He arrives at his more permanent home in the Loire Valley and makes friends with a group of French military officers there. One day as he wanders with his new friends in the countryside, he comes across a hunger-bitten peasant girl, so downtrodden that she resembles the cattle she is tending. His French companion comments, "'Tis against *that* which we are fighting," against the brutalization of humankind by the monarchical system. In later versions, at the conclusion of this book, Wordsworth inserts the story of "Vaudracour and Julia." This love story seems to stand in place of Wordsworth's real-life encounter with Vallon. Book 10 continues his discussion of his visit to France, including a second visit to Paris while the Reign of Terror is in full cry and the denunciation of Maximilien Robespierre takes place. This book also traces his return to England and the declaration of war by England against France, which caused the young Wordsworth deep grief. The French Revolution was probably the most important political event in the poet's life. His initial hopes for the French cause were overshadowed by the outrages of the Reign of Terror. His beloved England, on the other hand, joined in armed opposition to the cause of liberty. In the numerous reworkings of this part of his autobiography, Wordsworth steadily became more conservative in his opinions as he grew older. Book 10 in the 1805 text is split into books 10 and 11 in the 1850 version. In this section, he explains that at the beginning of the French Revolution, "Bliss was it in that dawn to be alive,/ But to be young was very heaven." Yet the course of the revolution, running first to despotic terror and ending with the rise of Napoleon, brought Wordsworth to a state of discouragement and desolation.

Book 11 in the 1805 text (book 12 in the 1850 version) considers how one may rise from spiritual desolation: Having lost the innocent joy of primitive youth and having lost faith in the political aims of the French Revolution, where can the soul be restored? At line 74, the poet tells how "strangely he did war against himself," but nature has a powerful restorative force. At line 258, he enters the famous "Spots of time" argument, in which he maintains that there are remembered experiences that "with distinct preeminence retain/ A vivifying Virtue" so that they can nourish one's depleted spirits. Much as in "Tintern Abbey," a remembered experience of nature can excite the imagination to produce a fresh vitality. Book 12 in the 1805 version (book 13 in the 1850) begins with a summary of nature's power to shape man's imagination and taste:

> From nature doth emotion come, and moods
> of calmness equally are nature's gift,
> This is her glory; these two attributes
> Are sister horns that constitute her strength.

The concluding book tells of the poet's vision on Mount Snowdon in Wales. On the lonely mountain, under the full moon, a sea of mist shrouds all the countryside except the highest peaks. The wanderer looks over the scene and has a sense of the presence of divinity. Nature has such a sublime aspect "That men, least sensitive, see, hear, perceive,/ And cannot choose but feel" the intimation of divine power. In this way, Nature feeds the imagination, and a love of nature leads to a

sense of humankind's place in the created universe and a love for all humankind. The poem ends with an address to the poet's friend Coleridge about their mutual struggle to keep faith as true prophets of nature.

It is often said that Wordsworth's *The Prelude*, written in Miltonic blank verse, is the Romantic epic comparable to *Paradise Lost* of Milton. Other critics point to a similarity between *The Prelude* and the bildungsroman, or novel of development. *The Prelude* is subtitled "The Growth of a Poet's Mind" and bears considerable resemblance to such classic stories as Stendhal's *The Red and the Black* (1830), in which the author traces the development of the hero, Julien Sorel, as he grows up. Finally, most readers find an important pastoral element in *The Prelude*. The "pastoral" occurs whenever an author and an audience belonging to a privileged and sophisticated society imagine a more simple life and admire it. For example, sophisticated courtiers might imagine the life of simple shepherds and shepherdesses to be very attractive compared to their own round of courtly duties. They would then imagine a pastoral world in which shepherdesses with frilly bows on their shepherds' crooks and dainty fruits to eat would dally in the shade by fountains on some peaceful mountainside. Such a vision is termed pastoral because it contrasts unfavorably the life of the real author and audience with the imagined life of a shepherd. *The Prelude* makes such pastoral contrasts frequently: for example, in the depiction of rural shepherds in the Lake District compared with urban workers; in the comparison of the life of a simple child with that of the adult; and in the comparison of the working classes of France and England with their masters. The pastoral elements in *The Prelude* are a natural consequence of the primitivism in the poem's ideology.

Wordsworth is one of the recognized giants of English literature, and his importance is nearly equal to Milton's or Shakespeare's. Even so, his work has been the subject of sharp controversy from its first publication until the present. William Hazlitt in his *Lectures on the English Poets* (1818) argues that Wordsworth is afflicted with a false optimism and that his idea of nature is merely a reflection of the human observer's feelings. Aldous Huxley in "Wordsworth in the Tropics" in *Holy*

*Face and Other Essays* (1929) attacks the unnaturalness of Wordsworth's view of nature. John Stuart Mill's *Autobiography* (1873), on the other hand, discusses the restorative power of Romantic poetry and the capacity of Wordsworth to relieve the sterility of a too "scientific" orientation. Later critics have continued the controversy.

The apparent decline of Wordsworth's poetic powers in his later years has occasioned much debate. Was he disillusioned with the course of the French Revolution so that he could no longer bear to praise humankind's primitive nature? Was he so filled with remorse over his affair with Annette Vallon that his inspiration failed? Was he a living demonstration of his own theory of the development of man from infant, to boyhood, to adult: that as man grows older he becomes more and more remote from the primitive feelings of the infant who comes into this world trailing clouds of glory, so that old men can never be effective poets? In any case, the young Wordsworth writing in the 1790's and the first decade of the nineteenth century was a voice calling out that life can be joyful and meaningful, that humankind's nature is good, and that people are not alone in an alien world, but in their proper home.

OTHER MAJOR WORKS

NONFICTION: *The Prose Works of William Wordsworth*, 1876; *Letters of William and Dorothy Wordsworth*, 1935-1939 (6 volumes; Ernest de Selincourt, editor).

BIBLIOGRAPHY

Barker, Juliet. *Wordsworth: A Life*. New York: Viking, 2002. This biography traces Wordsworth's life over eight decades, shedding light on his relationship with his family, his early poetic career, and his politics.

Bloom, Harold, ed. *William Wordsworth*. New York: Chelsea House, 2009. A collection of critical essays on Wordsworth, with an introduction by Bloom.

Bromwich, David. *Disowned by Memory: Wordsworth's Poetry of the 1790's*. Chicago: University of Chicago Press, 1998. Bromwich connects the accidents of Wordsworth's life with the originality of his works, tracking the impulses that turned him to poetry after the death of his parents and during his years as an enthusiastic disciple of the French Revolution.

Gill, Stephen. *William Wordsworth: A Life*. New York: Oxford University Press, 1989. This first biography of Wordsworth since 1965 makes full use of information that came to light after that time, including the 1977 discovery of Wordsworth's family letters as well as more recent research on his boyhood in Hawkshead and his radical period in London.

_____, ed. *The Cambridge Companion to Wordsworth*. New York: Cambridge University Press, 2003. The fifteen essays in this compilation provide excellent introductions to Wordsworth's works.

Johnston, Kenneth R. *The Hidden Wordsworth: Poet, Lover, Rebel, Spy*. New York: W. W. Norton, 1998. A thoroughgoing reexamination of the poet's life that places him far more firmly in the tradition of liberal Romanticism than previous twentieth century critics or even his own contemporaries might have thought.

Liu, Yü. *Poetics and Politics: The Revolutions of Wordsworth*. New York: Peter Lang, 1999. Liu focuses on the poetry of Wordsworth in the late 1790's and the early 1800's. In the context of Wordsworth's crisis of belief, this study shows how his poetic innovations constituted his daring revaluation of his political commitment.

Simpson, David. *Wordsworth, Commodification, and Social Concern: The Poetics of Modernity*. New York: Cambridge University Press, 2009. A discussion of Wordsworth and his works that looks at how his political and philosophical views affected his writings.

Sisman, Adam. *The Friendship: Wordsworth and Coleridge*. New York: Viking, 2007. An intimate examination of Wordsworth and Samuel Taylor Coleridge's friendship and its deterioration.

Worthen, John. *The Gang: Coleridge, the Hutchinsons, and the Wordsworths in 1802*. New Haven, Conn.: Yale University Press, 2001. Worthen describes the relationships among Samuel Taylor Coleridge and his wife, Sarah; William Wordsworth and his sister, Dorothy; and the Hutchinson sisters, Mary and Sara.

*Todd K. Bender*

# SIR THOMAS WYATT

**Born:** Allington, near Maidstone, Kent, England; 1503
**Died:** Sherborne, Dorset, England; October, 1542

PRINCIPAL POETRY

*The Courte of Venus*, c. 1539 (includes three to ten Wyatt poems)
*Certayne Psalmes Chosen out of the Psalter of David*, 1549
*Songes and Sonettes*, 1557 (also known as *Tottel's Miscellany*, Richard Tottel, editor; includes ninety to ninety-seven Wyatt poems)
*Collected Poems of Sir Thomas Wyatt*, 1949 (Kenneth Muir, editor)
*Sir Thomas Wyatt and His Circle: Unpublished Poems*, 1961 (Muir, editor)
*Collected Poems*, 1975 (Joost Daalder, editor)

OTHER LITERARY FORMS

Sir Thomas Wyatt's *Plutarckes Boke of the Quyete of Mynde*, a prose translation of Plutarch's essay on the quiet of mind, which he read in Guillaume Budé's Latin version, was made at the request of Queen Katherine of Aragon and published in 1528—his only notable work published in his lifetime. His original prose works are interesting in their own right. The state papers contain several fine examples of his correspondence. His most polished prose works are the defense he prepared for his trial in 1541 and his two letters of moral advice to his son. These letters make explicit the moral stance that underlies his poems, especially extolling honesty, which comprises "wisdome, gentlenes, sobrenes, disire to do good, frendlines to get the love of many, and trough above all the rest." Wyatt's prose is distinguished by its clarity and directness, its easy, colloquial use of language, its lively intelligence, and its wit. Often in the diplomatic letters he makes his style more immediate by using direct discourse to report conversations.

ACHIEVEMENTS

The best of the court poets who wrote under Henry VIII, Sir Thomas Wyatt stands at a crossroads in English poetry, looking both backward and forward. His fluent native lyrics, perhaps written for musical accompaniment, show direct continuity with medieval popular song and with Chaucerian love imagery. At the same time, he opened the door to the Renaissance in English poetry, importing Italian and French forms and naturalizing them. His most influential innovation was the sonnet. Experimenting with translations from Petrarch's sonnets, he invented both the Italian and the English or "Shakespearean" sonnet forms. His successors—among them Henry Howard, earl of Surrey, Sir Philip Sidney, Samuel Daniel, Michael Drayton, and William Shakespeare—adopted and refined the sonnet form for their own famous sequences of love poems.

Wyatt introduced virtually every new stanza form that appeared in the sixteenth century. As the first English satirist, he experimented with terza rima, and in his epigrams with ottava rima. He also wrote several rondeaux after French models. His verse translations from the Psalms are the finest in the language, written at a time when English versions of biblical literature were few.

Comments by his contemporaries and the high degree of preservation of his works—he is, for example, by far the largest contributor to *Tottel's Miscellany*—testify to his high reputation in his own day. When Wyatt wrote, there were no formal standards of prosody in English. Soon after his death, metrical regularity, which he had helped to establish, prevailed. Unfortunately, Tottel's editors blurred some of his most powerful effects by regularizing his meter, and his younger and smoother contemporary, Surrey, came to be regarded as a better poet. To critics of the eighteenth and nineteenth centuries, Wyatt's poems, read in the light of their successors, appeared rough and jarring. The last century, with its interest in "organic" rhythm as opposed to fixed rules of meter, and in dramatic compression and conversational immediacy as opposed to formal diction, has reevaluated Wyatt and granted him precedence as the greatest poet of his age, not only as an innovator in form but also as an original explorer of the effect on the individual mind of the insecurities and tensions inherent in love and politics.

BIOGRAPHY

Sir Thomas Wyatt was born into a family already in favor with the court. His father had served and prospered under Henry VII and Henry VIII, holding a series of important offices, and purchasing as his principal residence Allington Castle in Kent, where the poet was born. Young Wyatt made his first court appearance in 1516 and probably entered St. John's College, Cambridge, the same year. He was suitably married in 1520 to Elizabeth Brooke, the daughter of Lord Cobham, with whom he had a son; but in 1526, they separated because of her infidelity. He was sent on important diplomatic missions, in 1526 to France and in 1527 to Italy, where he traveled extensively.

It is plausibly conjectured that Wyatt was a lover of Anne Boleyn before her marriage to Henry VIII. Some of his poems were probably written to or about her, and his imprisonment in 1536 seems to have been connected with her downfall. He was quickly released to his father's custody, however, and continued to enjoy the king's favor. Knighted, he was sent as ambassador to Spain to improve relations between Henry VIII and Emperor Charles V and to prevent an alliance of the latter with France. On later embassies to France and Flanders, he continued this mission. In 1540, because of a shift in policy, his patron, Thomas Cromwell, was arrested and executed. Slanderous accusations found among Cromwell's papers led to Wyatt's imprisonment in 1541 and his subsequent preparations to reply to the charges. He was soon released, however, on condition that he leave his mistress, Elizabeth Darrell, who had borne him a son, and return to his wife. He continued to occupy important offices, serving as member of Parliament for Kent and vice admiral of the fleet. At about age thirty-nine, he died in Sherborne, Dorset, of a sudden fever contracted on a diplomatic mission to meet the Spanish envoy at Falmouth.

## ANALYSIS

Sir Thomas Wyatt was esteemed in his time for all the best qualities associated with the Renaissance courtier: military prowess, grace in art, skill in language, intelligence in council, and loyalty to his sovereign. The court of Henry VIII, himself a poet and musician, was receptive to the literary talents of such a man and capable of nourishing his worldly gifts, but the ways of politics and love were fraught with risks, as Wyatt's own career shows. It is against the back-

ground of this court, with its political and amorous intrigues, the insecurities of favor both in love and in worldly ambitions, that Wyatt's poetry can best be considered.

Wyatt is known primarily as a poet of love. The conventions of courtly love, deriving from twelfth century Provençal poetry, are the usual basis of his imagery. This tradition concerns the relationship between the great lady and her courtier "servant." Love is treated variously as sickness, servitude, worship, and war. The lover is in agony, the lady disdainful, her beauties idealized by comparisons with nature. The tradition reached Wyatt through two main sources, Geoffrey Chaucer and Francesco Petrarch, the Italian strain developing more fully the spiritual aspect of courtly love.

Wyatt's treatment of the tradition he inherited adapts to it the conditions of his own insecure times. He uses the love convention to speak not only of his lack of satisfaction in love but also about his unhappiness at other aspects of ill fortune. Since a direct judgment on contemporary events could have been dangerous to his

*Sir Thomas Wyatt* (Hulton Archive/Getty Images)

political career, even to his life, it is likely that Wyatt used the guise of a disappointed lover to interpret the sense of betrayal, the melancholy, and the insecurity inherent in his career. Life and death lay at the king's whim. Friendship was risky and tenuous, since the adherents of those who fell in favor were in danger themselves. Although Wyatt's own career was generally successful, he suffered two severe setbacks. From his prison cell, he may have watched Boleyn and her former lovers, his friends and acquaintances—persons once high in fortune and favor—go to the block. Later, his life was endangered by friendship with Cromwell. Such experiences fostered a deep sense of insecurity, which he expresses in several ways: by use of love conventions, in which he explores and comes to terms with the feeling of betrayal; by satire, in which he can compare the dangers and deceptions of court life with the peace of the country; and by seeking God's support, in his translations of the Psalms. In all his works, even in translations, it is clear that he is doing far more than merely following established forms. He is bringing stanzaic and rhythmic patterns, compression and directness of language, as well as the motif of disappointed love, to bear on the problems of expressing the strong and deep emotions of a sensitive individual, the complexities of a divided mind.

Looking at Wyatt's translations, one can see what kinds of changes he made to naturalize and individualize what he derived from his Italian models. It is impossible to determine an exact chronology for his poems, but it seems likely that those sonnet translations that are closest to their originals are earlier than those he adapts more fully to his own form and expression.

There was no equivalent in English of the sonnet form; Wyatt had to discover and invent it. For Petrarch's hendecasyllabic line, Wyatt devised a normally decasyllabic substitute, probably developed from Chaucerian models. Iambic pentameter was not, as it later was, a prescribed form, and Wyatt's lines must not be read as incompetent iambics. There are manuscript examples of his revisions away from metrical regularity, showing that the irregularity often criticized as "roughness" was intentional. Wyatt's line is open to variable stress, which allows for dominance of speech rhythms and expression of nuances of feeling. While Petrarch's

rhyme scheme divided the sonnet between octave in braced rhyme and sestet in alternative rhyme, Wyatt's three quatrains in braced rhyme allow for his rational progression of thoughts and images. The series of braced rhymes gives him several couplets with which to work as the poem progresses, to reinforce his contrasts and hammer home his feelings. He introduces a concluding couplet, which he employs with great flexibility and variety of effect—unlike Shakespeare, who too often used it lamely as a detached tag.

In several of the courtly love sonnets that Wyatt translates, he sharpens Petrarch's images and makes their expression more vivid while carefully pursuing an elaborate conceit. "The long love that in my thought doth harbor" explores love as war; Wyatt, who had participated in chivalric tournaments, conveys a vigorous, dramatic atmosphere of action in the field by use of energetic words and rhythmic pressure. "My galley charged with forgetfulness" pursues the conventional conceit of love as a ship in dangerous seas. Again, Wyatt achieves a feeling of energy, of rushing forward, opening with two run-on lines and blurring the Italian's sharp distinction between octave and sestet. This poem does not actually mention love, allowing wider application to the dangers of political life.

Another probably early translation shows how Wyatt uses courtly love conventions to focus attention more on the sufferer's state of mind than on the love situation. The original Petrarchan version of the sonnet "I find no peace, and all my war is done" appealed to Wyatt for its antithetical construction, portraying a divided mind; Wyatt's version shows how intricately he uses form to convey the sense of internal division. An essential aspect of much of his poetry is the "broken-backed" line, deriving from Anglo-Saxon through medieval lyric and still prevalent before metrical regularity became the norm. This line is divided sharply into two segments by a pronounced caesura. Each of the two resulting half-lines, containing two or three stresses, has an integrity related more to speech rhythm than to syllable counts. The divided lines point and balance the antitheses of the lover's internal division, but his balance is conveyed more intricately than in the original by the weaving together of phrases throughout the octave. The first three half-lines are parallel in structure:

"I find," "I fear," "I fly." The first and last lines of the first quatrain are united by parallel sounds and structure: "and all my war is done," "and all the world I season"; a similar effect parallels the third line of the first quatrain and the second line of the second quatrain: "yet can I not arise," "yet can I scape no-wise." The imagery is traditional in the courtly love convention, but the structure dramatizes the tension in a mind whose suffering, itself, rather than the cause of his suffering, is the poem's focus.

Wyatt uses the conventions of the suffering lover but turns them around in "Was I never yet of your love grieved." Petrarch's lover, worn out with sighing, longs for death as a release and plans a beautiful sepulchre with his lady's name engraved on it; yet if she will be satisfied with his faithful love, he may survive. Wyatt says that he is not prepared to die and have a tomb with an inscription naming the lady as the cause of his demise. Such a tomb, in any case, far from being a monument to her, would be an indictment of her cruelty. Wyatt discards Petrarch's physical description of the tomb to focus on the lover's mood. That mood is one of independent cynicism: The lady may choose to accept his love and faith, but if she chooses instead to continue acting out her disdain, she will not succeed, and that will be her own fault. There is no Petrarchan veneration of the lady here. The lover, having exhausted himself trying, has reached the conclusion that the prize is really not worth the chase. Using the couplets formed by the braced rhyme of the quatrains, he produces a powerful stress on "past" in the third line, and increases the tension between the courtly love expectation and his own rebellion against it through the rhyme of "wearied" and "buried"—an association belied by the unexpected "not."

### "WHOSO LIST TO HUNT"

A sonnet of similar subject and tone, whose subtlety and smoothness show Wyatt's confidence in having made the form his own, is "Whoso list to hunt." The Petrarchan sonnet on which this is based has a visionary, dreamlike quality, picturing the lady as a white hind in a beautiful spring landscape disappearing from the poet's ken because Caesar (presumably God) has set her free (presumably by death). The tone of Wyatt's version is quite different. The mention of the hind is de-

veloped into an extended hunting metaphor. Instead of the solitary lover, he becomes a member of a crowd of hunters (suitors). He has thus introduced a dramatic situation, plunging into it abruptly and colloquially with direct address. The natural description of the original is replaced by the immediate, realistic atmosphere of the hunt, into which Petrarch's mention of the mind has led him: the pressing rivals, the net, the hot pursuit. His use of rhythm conveys this physical experience, as heavy stresses on the alliterated "Fainting I follow" suggest limping or labored breath, with the poet's abrupt about-face, the "turn" in the poem, coming in the middle of the sharply divided line. Wyatt attacks the artificiality of the courtly love tradition, remarking that to pursue this lady is "in vain," as in the preceding sonnet—a waste of effort. Unlike Petrarch's modest Laura, this lady is wild and spirited. She is inaccessible not because she is called by God but because she has already been claimed by his social superior (it is usually assumed that "Caesar" is Henry VIII, the hind Boleyn). He further strains the convention by seeking reciprocity of affection, as opposed to one-sided worship of an ideal; to the Petrarchan lover, the pursuit, the service, is its own reward.

The structural pattern portrays the stages of the poet's argument: the first quatrain defining his plight; the second focusing more sharply on his feelings, from which he abruptly breaks; the third explaining why the case is hopeless; and the couplet giving the explanation an epigrammatic and ironic punch. With the awareness that pursuit of a highborn lady was often an essential stepping-stone to court favor, it is not straining interpretation to see in this particular love pursuit—in which idealized description of the lady has yielded to focus on the lover's feelings—a more general pursuit of fortune and success with the frustrations encountered in that struggle.

Some of Wyatt's lyrics seem to bear particular relation to his work on foreign models, such as the *strambotti* of the Italian poet Serafino de Ciminelli. Light in tone, the *strambotto* is an eight-line poem with six alternate rhymes and a concluding couplet. Examples in Wyatt's work are "Who hath heard of such cruelty before" and "Alas, madame! for stealing of a kiss?" Two of his finest lyrics which relate closely in mood to his sonnets and in form to his *strambotti* are "They flee from me, that sometime did me seek" and "It may be good, like it who list." Both use three seven-line stanzas to portray intellectual or emotional development: A problem stated in the first stanza is reexamined in the third in the light of the second. Both have the rhyme scheme *ababbcc*.

### "THEY FLEE FROM ME, THAT SOMETIME DID ME SEEK"

In Wyatt's most famous poem, "They flee from me, that sometime did me seek," the description of a specific experience may in part function as a figure to express general feelings about good fortune and its loss. This is especially likely if—as is often assumed—the poem refers to Boleyn. Although the situation is a conventional one of courtly love, the setting and experience are real and immediate, the diction that of everyday speech. The dominant image, like that of "Whoso list to hunt," is of animals, but it is uncertain what animal the poet has in mind: deer, birds, or simply women. The wild and bestial is contrasted with the tame, courtly, and civilized quality suggested by the words "gentle" and "gentleness." The main rhetorical device is a simple contrast of past with present tense, past joys with present loss. The use of "they" in the first line may point to a sense of desertion by all the speaker's friends, similar to that expressed in the epigram, "Lux, my fair falcon," in which an animal image is used in more complex fashion, as an ironic contrast between loyal animals and disloyal men. The men are ultimately seen as even lower on the animal scale than the falcons, as the men are compared to lice leaving a dead body.

The first stanza of "They flee from me, that sometime did me seek" establishes the focal point of the speaker's mood, his sense of desertion. The remarkable second stanza recalls in minute detail and tingling immediacy a specific experience, in the light of which a new mood, irony, emerges in the third stanza. This final stanza begins with the rhythmic subtlety of abrupt conversational rhythm, the jolting caesura, and the insistence of many stressed monosyllables. In this line, the dream-vision of Petrarchan convention and the erotic dream of Chaucerian romance are banished. Once again the poet's insistence on reciprocity in affection has been violated, yet he reacts not with vengefulness or

even rebellion, but with ironic detachment. He, with his humanity, his gentleness, has kept his part of the bargain. She, however, who once appeared "gentle, tame and meek," has now reverted to her wild animal nature. "Kindly" may be taken both in the sense of "according to nature" and ironically in its modern sense. The suggestion that he should be served better recalls ironically the courtly love tradition of the man's service to his lady on her pedestal, and thus Wyatt drives home again his insistence on reciprocity: Should service be given if not deserved? His conclusion is not, as in the courtly love tradition, and as the poem's opening suggests, one of sentimental agony, but musing, perhaps even amused understatement. One is left with a question: What does one deserve who repays loyalty with disloyalty? However, there remains some sense of the reality and intensity of loss from the vividness of the scene described in the second stanza. Wyatt's ideal of a reciprocal and permanent love is more of this world than Petrarch's one-sided idealization, and its existence belies a charge against him of cynicism.

### "IT MAY BE GOOD, LIKE IT WHO LIST"

"It may be good, like it who list" opens with a striking colloquial tone in mid-conversation. The debate symbolized by this dramatic situation is an internal one: The poet is uncertain whether to believe signs of friendship or affection in words and looks. He would like to, but having seen so many changes in human favor, fears to commit himself. The form perfectly conveys the thought-movement, with its seesawing rhythm, produced by the broken-backed line, used with effect similar to that in "I find no peace, and all my war is done." Stanza 1 begins with half-lines strongly set off against each other by caesuras, on either side of which are stressed syllables, so that the movement seems to be first a pressing toward a decision, then a receding from it, a depiction in sound of the mind swinging back and forth between the desire to believe and the impulse to doubt—opposites that the poet cannot reconcile—with a question to reinforce his uncertainty. The second stanza states the doctrine of contrarieties more objectively, yet four lines of it maintain structurally and rhythmically the sensation of vacillation. The final stanza resolves the argument into another question, directed to the imaginary interlocutor, and the poet seems firmly to resolve the argument in the spondaic "Nay sir." The next line opening, "And yet," sets off the whole argument again, however, to leave it seesawing still in the concluding broken-backed line—"For dread to fall I stand not fast"—which has served as a refrain in the two preceding stanzas. The paradox is stressed in union by alliteration of opposite-meaning words, "fall" and "fast," which occupy corresponding positions in their respective half-lines.

The use of a refrain connects this poem with the other main lyrical form for which Wyatt is famous, sometimes called the "ballette." This form had its origin in popular song, toward which the musical impetus of Henry VIII's court drew the courtly minds of the time. Wyatt's ballettes probably had a social function: They may have been composed for musical accompaniment to be sung in company and were certainly circulated privately. They have short stanzas and simple meters, with short lines and often a refrain. Wyatt's tendency to compression is here at its finest, as he expresses strong and deep emotion in a simple manner and brief compass.

### "SUCH HAP AS I AM HAPPED IN"

Wyatt's use of the refrain is exquisitely subtle and varied. He may, as in "Such hap as I am happed in," retain for the final line of each stanza the same rhythm and line length but alter the words of the refrain, then echo it at the beginning of the next stanza. By this means the intensity of feeling and the details of the mind's torture are progressively built up, until the poem comes to rest in its opening words, with the tortured mind drawn taut and caught in a circular trap, with no hope of escape. The poem's circularity depicts the speaker's plight.

Wyatt may repeat the same or similar words at the end of each stanza, letting them accumulate meaning and force in each recurrence from the stanza they follow, and progressively from all the preceding stanzas. "My lute awake" explores, with the subtle variations of its refrain, the relationship between the sufferer and his instrument. The first and final stanzas, almost identical, frame the poem, their minor variations exhibiting the effect of the mental progression through the intervening six. The second, third, and fourth stanzas explore the lover's plight, hinting at the possibility of retribu-

tion. The fifth, sixth, and seventh turn the tables and imagine the once-disdainful lady old and deserted, longing but daring not to express her desires (as he, ironically, is able to express his in the present poem). In the second two revenge stanzas, the poet discards the lute altogether and speaks for himself: "I have done" (finished) caring for you; you will suffer "as I have done." The sense of the opening refrain, "My lute be still, for I have done," is that the lover is finished with life. When he returns to echo it at the end, the accumulation of meanings makes it plain that he is finished with the lady. Though the last stanza echoes the first verbally, its sounds are brisker. The word "waste" now carries the full sense of time wasted in the love pursuit (similar to "As well as I may spend his time in vain" in "Whoso list to hunt"). The poet has moved from a pathetic opening through an emotional progression to a detached conclusion, a progress like that exhibited in "They flee from me, that sometime did me seek." The poem has served to delineate the lover's hurt feelings and, in a way, to cure them.

Wyatt's satires and psalms explore in their own way his basic problem of insecurity in public and private life. The satires were probably written in a period directly following one of his imprisonments, when he was relegated or had temporarily retired to his home in Kent. There he examines at length, in epistolary form addressed to his closest friends, the contrasts between courtly and country virtues, comparing the simple honesty of the country to the practiced dissimulation of the court.

### SATIRES

Wyatt's own imprisonment and the death of Boleyn and her lovers had introduced a somber gloom, which he explored in shorter poems such as "Who list his wealth and ease retain," in which he urges sequestration and anonymity as a means of holding onto life and safety. In the satires, he moves forward from this position, working through his disillusion to a contentment derived from interior strengths and virtues. This process is similar to that of the love poems, in which he works from a mood of despair or grief to one of detachment.

The satires are based on the models of Luigi Alamanni, a contemporary Italian poet, whose terza rima

Wyatt imitates, and on the satiric moods and techniques of Horace and Juvenal. The first satire especially ("Mine own John Poyntz") and the other two less overtly employ Wyatt's favorite antithetical manner, using it not to portray a divided mind but to contrast two lifestyles, public and private. Despite the difficulty of the verse form (there are far fewer available rhymes in English than in Italian), the opening of this poem based on Alamanni's tenth satire is smooth, colloquial, and ruminative. As Wyatt catalogs the courtly vices, what stings him most, as in the love poetry, is the deceit that leads to a betrayal of friendship, of "gentleness": "The friendly foe with his double face/ [I cannot] Say he is gentle, and courteous there-withal." Two series of catalogs, the first of courtly "arts" that he cannot affect—five tercets beginning "I cannot"—and the second of foreign countries where he might be ("I am not . . . Nor am I") are joyously resolved both rhetorically and metrically in the regular iambic line, "But here I am in Kent and Christendom," where he invites Poyntz to visit him and share his attractive life of independence, hunting in good weather, reading in bad.

### "MY MOTHER'S MAIDS, WHEN THEY DID SEW AND SPIN"

The second, and perhaps most attractive of the three satires, "My mother's maids, when they did sew and spin," again addressed to Poyntz, is the most effective, for instead of the catalog of vices paraded in the other two at some risk of monotony, it uses the Horatian fable of the town mouse and the country mouse to expound a moral. The language is appealingly homely, the approach intimate, and the poem's directness is assisted—like that of some of the love poems—by direct discourse: "'Peep,' quod the other, 'sister I am here.'/ 'Peace,' quod the towny mouse, 'why speakest thou so loud?'" The moral is that people should content themselves with and use well the lot assigned them and, instead of outward reward, seek inward peace. A religious note is introduced here as Wyatt asks of God a punishment for seekers after worldly gain—a punishment that resembles what he imagines for the lady in "My lute awake": that they shall behold virtue and regret their loss.

Wyatt's versions of seven psalms were probably written, like his satires, during or after one of his imprisonments. The narrative prologues that introduce them and the conception of them as expressions of penitence are derived from Pietro Aretino's prose translations into Italian. This framework probably appealed to Wyatt because it places the psalms in the context of David's love for Bathsheba and the resultant sickness of heart and soul which he strives to cure with the aid of his harp. The verse is powerful and fluid; the rhyme scheme, as in the satires, is terza rima. An examination of Psalm 38 ("O Lord, as I thee have both prayed and pray") shows how the psalms develop and continue the preoccupations expressed in the love poems and satires. As in the love poems, the focus of attention, the diction, rhetorical devices, and movement of the verse, is on depicting internal conflict, the movement of the suffering and divided mind: "O Lord, thou knowst the inward contemplation/ Of my desire, thou knowst my sighs and plaints,/ Thou knowst the tears of my lamentation." This might be part of a love lament. So might the following description of agony, where meter and imagery unite to depict a profound emotional crisis: "My heart panteth, my force I feel it quail,/ My sight, mine eyes, my look decays and faints." Broken-backed lines divided in two reinforce the poet's desperation as the second half-lines rhythmically duplicate each other. There follows a detailed description of the evils and dangers of courtly life: Friendship is betrayed, "kin unkind" desert him, slander assails him, he is in danger of his life. Like the lover, he fears rejection and seeks—this time with God—the succor of a reciprocal relationship.

The poet of individual consciousness has tested his strength against the courtly love tradition, which, in its lack of reciprocity, fails him and against court manners, which, in their lack of honesty and loyalty, appall him. He thus seeks reciprocity, trust, and affection by turning his "inward contemplation" to God.

### OTHER MAJOR WORK

TRANSLATION: *Plutarckes Boke of the Quyete of Mynde*, 1528 (of Plutarch).

### BIBLIOGRAPHY

Blevins, Jacob. "Catullus, the Early Tudors, and Wyatt's Deviation from Petrarch." In *Catullan Conscious-*

*ness and the Early Modern Lyric in England: From Wyatt to Donne*. Burlington, Vt.: Ashgate, 2004. Blevins examines how Wyatt adapted the Petrarchan sonnet form, among other topics. Other poets discussed in the book are Catullus and John Donne.

Estrin, Barbara L. *Laura: Uncovering Gender and Genre in Wyatt, Donne, and Marvell*. Durham, N.C.: Duke University Press, 1994. A study acknowledging the tyranny to women that most Petrarchan poems impose. Includes bibliographical references and index.

Foley, Stephen Merriam. *Sir Thomas Wyatt*. Boston: Twayne, 1990. Examines the meaning of Wyatt's poetry and, more important, how he came to write in such pioneering forms in Tudor England.

Heale, Elizabeth. *Wyatt, Surrey, and Early Tudor Poetry*. New York: Longman, 1998. An indispensable resource containing critical interpretation of the works of two early English sonneteers. Includes bibliographical references and index.

Jentoft, Clyde W. *Sir Thomas Wyatt and Henry Howard, Earl of Surrey: A Reference Guide*. Boston: G. K. Hall, 1980. An invaluable book for the student of Wyatt. Contains annotated information from books, magazines, studies, and monographs as well as introductions and commentaries from important editions of Wyatt's work and sections about him that appeared in other scholarly works.

Ross, Diane M. *Self-Revelation and Self-Protection in Wyatt's Lyric Poetry*. New York: Garland, 1988. This book examines how Wyatt's attempts to express his themes relate to the lyric genre. Ross accomplishes this primarily by contrasting Wyatt's work to other Renaissance lyric poetry.

Szalay, Krisztina. *The Obstinate Muse of Freedom: On the Poetry of Sir Thomas Wyatt*. Budapest: Akadémiai Kiadó, 2000. Part of the Studies in Modern Philology series, this work looks at the concept of freedom in Wyatt's poetry.

Thomson, Patricia, ed. *Wyatt: The Critical Heritage*. 1975. Reprint. New York: Routledge, 1995. The critical tradition of Wyatt's poetry is presented in sixteen commentaries on his work ranging from an unsigned 1527 preface to *Plutarckes Boke of the Quyete of Mynde*, to C. S. Lewis's comments written in 1954. Includes an informative introduction to this material.

*Arthur Kincaid*

# Y

## WILLIAM BUTLER YEATS

**Born:** Sandymount, near Dublin, Ireland; June 13, 1865

**Died:** Roquebrune-Cap-Martin, France; January 28, 1939

PRINCIPAL POETRY

*Mosada: A Dramatic Poem*, 1886

*Crossways*, 1889

*The Wanderings of Oisin, and Other Poems*, 1889

*The Countess Kathleen and Various Legends and Lyrics*, 1892

*The Rose*, 1893

*The Wind Among the Reeds*, 1899

*In the Seven Woods*, 1903

*The Poetical Works of William B. Yeats*, 1906, 1907 (2 volumes)

*The Green Helmet, and Other Poems*, 1910

*Responsibilities*, 1914

*Responsibilities, and Other Poems*, 1916

*The Wild Swans at Coole*, 1917, 1919

*Michael Robartes and the Dancer*, 1920

*The Tower*, 1928

*Words for Music Perhaps, and Other Poems*, 1932

*The Winding Stair, and Other Poems*, 1933

*The Collected Poems of W. B. Yeats*, 1933, 1950

*The King of the Great Clock Tower*, 1934

*A Full Moon in March*, 1935

*Last Poems and Plays*, 1940

*The Poems of W. B. Yeats*, 1949 (2 volumes)

*The Collected Poems of W. B. Yeats*, 1956

*The Variorum Edition of the Poems of W. B. Yeats*, 1957 (P. Allt and R. K. Alspach, editors)

*The Poems*, 1983

*The Poems: A New Edition*, 1984

OTHER LITERARY FORMS

William Butler Yeats (yayts) was a playwright as well as a poet. During certain periods in his career, he devoted more time and energy to the composition, publication, and production of plays in verse or prose than to the writing of nondramatic poetry. These plays, excluding several early closet dramas, were republished singly or in various collections from 1892 through the year of his death. *The Collected Plays of W. B. Yeats* was published in 1934, and a "new edition with five additional plays" appeared in 1952 (London) and 1953 (New York), the former being the "basic text." The genuinely definitive publication, however, is the admirably edited *Variorum Edition of the Plays of W. B. Yeats* (1966).

In addition to poems and plays, Yeats published prolifically during the course of his life in almost every imaginable genre except the novel. Numerous prose tales, book reviews, nationalistic articles, letters to editors, and so on far exceeded poems and plays in volume in the early stages of Yeats's career. In 1908, *The Collected Works in Verse and Prose of William Butler Yeats*—including lyrics, narrative poems, stories, plays, essays, prefaces, and notes—filled eight volumes, of which only the first contained predominantly nondramatic poetry. Previously, stories and sketches, many of them based wholly or in part on Irish folk tales, had been collected in *The Celtic Twilight* (1893) and *The Secret Rose* (1897). Rewritten versions of those tales from *The Secret Rose* that featured a roving folk poet invented by Yeats were later published as *Stories of Red Hanrahan* (1904). Similarly, relatively formal critical and philosophical essays were collected and published as *Ideas of Good and Evil* (1903), *The Cutting of an Agate* (1912), and *Essays, 1931-1936* (1937).

A slender doctrinal book, *Per Amica Silentia Lunae* (1918), is generally regarded as something of a precursor to *A Vision* (1925). The first edition of *A Vision* itself, an exposition of Yeats's mystical philosophy, appeared in 1925. A considerably revised edition first published in 1937 has revealed to scholars that while the book unquestionably owes much to his wife's "automatic writing," as avowed, more than a little of its content is generally based on Yeats's or his and his wife's earlier occult interests and contacts. In 1926, Yeats published a volume titled *Autobiographies*. In 1938, an American edition titled *The Autobiography of*

*William Butler Yeats* was released, with the addition of several sections or units that had been published separately or in groups in the interim. Then, in 1955 a final British issue appeared with the original title and one sub-unit not included in the American edition. A posthumous supplement to *Autobiographies* is *Memoirs* (1972), combining the draft of an earlier unpublished autobiography with a complete transcription of the private journal from which Yeats had used only selected portions in the post-1926 versions of his original book. A large and carefully edited collection of Yeats's correspondence, *The Letters of W. B. Yeats*, was published in 1954, and various smaller collections of correspondence with certain people have been published from time to time since the poet's death.

Most of Yeats's major prose, other than *A Vision*, *Autobiographies*, and his editor's introduction to *The Oxford Book of Modern Verse* (1936), has been collected and republished in three volumes printed simultaneously in London and New York. *Mythologies* (1959) includes *The Celtic Twilight*, *The Secret Rose*, *Stories of Red Hanrahan*, the three so-called Rosa Alchemica stories from 1897 (which involve Yeats's fictional personae Michael Robartes and Owen Aherne), and *Per Amica Silentia Lunae*. *Essays and Introductions* (1961) incorporates *Ideas of Good and Evil*, most of *The Cutting of an Agate, Essays, 1931-1936*, and three introductions written in 1937 for portions of a projected edition of Yeats's works that never materialized. *Explorations* (1962) brings together a number of miscellaneous items, most of them previously not readily accessible. There are three introductions to books of legend and folklore by Lady Augusta Gregory, introductions to some of Yeats's own plays, a sizable body of his early dramatic criticism, the essay "If I Were Four and Twenty," *Pages from a Diary Written in Nineteen Hundred and Thirty* (1944), and most of the author's last prose piece *On the Boiler* (1939), a potpourri including late political philosophy.

As to fiction not already mentioned, two stories from 1891—a long tale and a short novel—have been republished in a critical edition, *John Sherman and Dhoya* (1969), and a fine scholarly edition of Yeats's early unfinished novel, *The Speckled Bird* (published in a limited edition in Dublin in 1974), was printed in

1976 as an item in the short-lived *Yeats Studies* series. In another highly competent piece of scholarship, almost all the previously mentioned early book reviews, nationalist articles, and so on, as well as some later essays, have been edited and republished in *Uncollected Prose by W. B. Yeats*, Volume 1 in 1970 and Volume II in 1976. Finally, the bewildering mass of Yeats's unpublished materials—thousands of pages of working drafts, notebooks, proof sheets, personal and family letters and papers, occult documents, automatic scripts, and the like—were made available on microfilm by the poet's son, Senator Michael Yeats, in 1975. Two sets of these films are housed, one each, at the National Library of Ireland and the State University of New York at Stony Brook. With the generous permission of Yeats's daughter and son, Anna and Michael, scholars are currently studying, transcribing, and editing many of these materials. Several books that employ or reproduce portions of them have been published. Several volumes of Yeats's letters, *The Collected Letters of W. B. Yeats*, trace his life and poetic influences between the years 1865 and 1904. Most of the letters included are from Yeats's twenties, when he was passionately involved with furthering two causes: his own career and Irish literature as a whole.

ACHIEVEMENTS

William Butler Yeats is generally regarded as one of the major English-speaking poets of the "modern" era (approximately 1890 to 1950). Some authorities go even further, designating him the most important twentieth century poet in any language. Although in his late career and for some time thereafter, he was overshadowed by the poetic and critical stature of T. S. Eliot, in the years since Eliot's death, Yeats's reputation has continued to grow whereas Eliot's has declined. Like most modern poets, writing in a period labeled the age of the novel, Yeats has been relatively obscure and inaccessible to the general reader, but among academicians his eminence has flourished, and, even more significant, his influence on other poets has been both broad and deep.

Even though he was never very robust, suffering from chronic respiratory problems and extremely poor eyesight throughout much of his adult life, Yeats lived a long, productive, and remarkably multifaceted life. How one person could have been as completely immersed in as many different kinds of activity as he was is difficult to conceive. Throughout his life, he was involved in occult pursuits and interests of one kind or another, a preoccupation that has long been considered by many authorities (especially early ones) as more an impediment than a contribution to his literary career. Of more "legitimate" significance, he was, with a handful of associates, a leading figure in the initiation of the related movements that have come to be known as the Irish Renaissance and the Celtic Revival. Especially as a cofounder and codirector of the Irish National Theatre—later the famous Abbey Theatre—he was at the center of the literary movement, even aside from his prolific publication of poems, plays, essays, and reviews and the editorship of his sisters' artistically oriented Cuala Press. Moreover, between 1903 and 1932, Yeats conducted or participated in a series of five theater or lecture tours in America, thereby enhancing his renown in English-speaking countries on both sides of the Atlantic.

Major expressions of national and international recognition for such endeavors and achievements were forthcoming in the last decades of Yeats's life in such forms as honorary degrees from Queen's University (Belfast) and Trinity College (Dublin) in 1922, Oxford University in 1931, and Cambridge University in 1933; appointment as senator for the newly established Irish Free State in 1922; and, most gratifying of all, the Nobel Prize in Literature in 1923. Furthermore, in 1935 Yeats was designated editor of the *Oxford Book of Modern Verse*, having declined previously an offer of knighthood in 1915 and an invitation to lecture in Japan in 1919. From young manhood, Yeats had lived and played out the role of the poet in society, gesturing, posing, and dressing for the part. In middle years and old age, he experienced genuine fulfillment of his dream and enjoyed self-realization as "the great man" of Anglo-Irish literature within his own lifetime.

Yeats's greatest accomplishment, however, was the achievement, in both his life and his work, of an astonishing singleness or oneness in the midst of myriad activities. Driven by an obsessive precept that he labeled "Unity of Being," he strove unceasingly to "hammer" his thoughts into "unity." Though never a masterful thinker in terms of logic or ratiocination, Yeats possessed unequivocal genius of the kind recognized by today's psychologists as imaginative or creative, if not visionary. In addition to an almost infallible gift for the precisely right word or phrase, he had a mind awesomely capacious in its ability to conceive and sustain complexly interwoven structures of symbolic suggestion, mythic significance, and allusive associations. He used these abilities to link poems to plays, and oeuvre to a self-consciously dramatic life, which was itself hardly other than a supremely sculpted *objet d'art*. By the time of his death at the age of seventy-three, Yeats had so completely interfused national interests, philosophical convictions, theories of symbolic art, and mythopoeic techniques of literary composition that he had indeed fulfilled his lifelong quest to master experience by wresting unity from multiplicity, achieving an intricately wrought identity of life and work in the midst of almost unimaginably manifold diversity.

Biography

The eldest son of an eldest son of an eldest son, William Butler Yeats was born on June 13, 1865, in Sandymount, Ireland, a small community on the outskirts of Dublin that has since been absorbed by that sprawling metropolis. His father, paternal grandfather, and great-grandfather Yeats were all graduates of Trinity College, Dublin, but only his father, John Butler Yeats, had begun his postcollegiate career in the city where he had studied. Both the great-grandfather and the grandfather had been clergymen of the Protestant Church of Ireland, the latter in county Down, near Northern Ireland, and the former at Drumcliff, near the west-Irish port town of Sligo, with which the poet is so thoroughly identified.

The reason for the identification with Sligo is that John Butler Yeats married the sister of his closest collegiate schoolmate, George Pollexfen, whose family lived in Sligo. Dissatisfied with the courts as a fledgling barrister, J. B. Yeats abandoned law and Dublin to follow in London his inclinations as a graphic artist in sketches and oils. The combination of limited finances and his wife's dislike of urban life resulted in numerous extended visits by her and the growing family of children back to Sligo at the home of the poet's maternal grandfather, a sea captain and partner in a shipping firm. Thus, Yeats's ancestral line doubled back on itself in a sense. In the Sligo area, he became acquainted with Yeats descendants of the Drumcliff rector, and in memory and imagination the west-Irish valley between the mountains Ben Bulben and Knocknarea was always his spiritual home.

Yeats's formal education was irregular, at best. His earliest training was in London at the hand of his father, who read to him from English authors such as Sir Walter Scott and William Shakespeare. He did not distinguish himself at his first school in London or at Erasmus High School when the family returned to Dublin in 1880. Declining to matriculate at Trinity in the tradition of his forebears, he took up studies instead at the Metropolitan School of Art, where he met George Russell (later Æ), who was to become a lifelong close acquaintance. Yeats soon found that his interests inclined more toward the verbal arts than toward the visual, however, and by 1885, he had discontinued his studies in painting and had published some poems. At this same relatively early time, he had also become involved in occult interests, being among the founders of the Dublin Hermetic Society.

In 1887, the family returned to London, where Yeats was briefly involved with the famous Madame Blavatsky's Theosophical Society. The years 1889 to 1892 were some of the most important in this crucially formative period of his life. He was active in the many diverse areas of interest that were to shape and color the remainder of his career. In rapid succession, he became a founding member of the Rhymers Club (a young group of Pateresque fin de siècle aesthetes) and of the Irish Literary Society of London and the Irish Literary Society of Dublin (both devoted to reviving interest in native Irish writers and writing). He also joined the newly established Hermetic Order of the Golden Dawn, a Rosicrucian secret society in which he became an active leader for a number of years and of which he remained a member for more than two decades. In 1889, Yeats published *The Wanderings of Oisin, and Other Poems* and became coeditor of an edition of William Blake's work, an experience that was to influence greatly much of his subsequent thought and writing. No

*William Butler Yeats* (©The Nobel Foundation)

event in this period, however, had a more dramatic and permanent effect on the rest of his life than his introduction in the same year to Maud Gonne, that "great beauty" of Ireland with whom Yeats fell immediately and hopelessly in love. The love was largely unrequited, although Maud allowed the one-sided relationship to continue for a painfully long time throughout much of the poet's early adult life—in fact, even after her marriage and widowhood.

From this point on, Yeats's life was a whirlwind of literary, nationalistic, and occult activity. In 1896, he met Lady Augusta Gregory and John Millington Synge, with both of whom he was later to be associated in the leadership of the Abbey Theatre, as well as in investigation of the folklore and ethos of west-Irish peasants. The purpose of the Abbey Theatre, as far as these three were concerned, was to produce plays that combined Irish interests with artistic literary merit. The acquaintance with Lady Gregory also initiated a long series of summer visits at her estate in Coole Park, Galway, where his aristocratic inclinations, as well as his frequently frail physical being, were nurtured. During parts of 1895 and 1896, Yeats shared lodgings in London briefly with Arthur Symons, of the Rhymers

Club, who, as author of *The Symbolist Movement in Literature* (1899), helped to acquaint him further with the French Symbolist mode. Actually, however, through his intimate relationships with Hermetic lore and the English Romantics—especially Blake and Percy Bysshe Shelley—Yeats was already writing poetry in a manner much like that of his continental contemporaries. Later in 1896, Yeats moved in to 18 Woburn Buildings, Dublin, which came to be his permanent residence, except for rather frequent travels abroad, for an extended period.

At about the turn of the century and just after, Yeats abandoned his Pre-Raphaelite aestheticism and adopted a more "manful" style. Not wholly unrelated to this was his more outgoing involvement in the daily affairs of the nationalist theater movement. The fact should be remembered—for it is easy to forget—that at this time Yeats was in his late thirties, already moving into a somewhat premature middle age. In 1909 he met Ezra Pound, the only other major figure in the modernist movement with whom he was ever to develop an acquaintance to the point of literary interaction and influence. The relationship reached its apex in the years from 1912 to 1915, during which Pound criticized Yeats's romantic tendencies and, perhaps more important, encouraged the older poet's interest in the highly stylized and ritualistic Nō drama of Japan.

In the same years, another important aspect of Yeats's life and interests had been developing in new directions as well. Beginning about 1908-1909, his esoteric pursuits shifted from active involvement in the Order of the Golden Dawn to investigations in spiritism, séances, and "psychical research." This preoccupation continued until 1915 or 1916, at which point some biographers seem to indicate that it ended. Yet, in one sense, spiritism as an obsessive concern simply redoubled itself about this time on the occasion of Yeats's late-life marriage, for his wife turned out to be the "mystic" *par excellence*, through whose mediumship came the ultimate flowering of his lifelong prepossession with occult aspects of human—and superhuman—experience.

After Maud Gonne MacBride's husband was executed for his participation in Dublin's 1916 Easter uprising, Yeats visited Maud in Paris and proposed to her, only to be rejected as on previous occasions years before. He then became attracted to her daughter Iseult and proposed to her in turn. Once again rejected, he decided to marry an English woman whom he had known in occult circles for some years and who was a close friend of mutual acquaintances—Georgie Hyde-Less. On their honeymoon in 1917, Georgie began to experience the first of what came to be a voluminous and almost literally fantastic collection of "automatic writings," the basis of Yeats's famous mystic system, as elaborated in his book *A Vision*.

The various honors that Yeats received in the 1920's and 1930's have been outlined already under "Achievements." Ironically, from these same years, not earlier ones, came most of the poems and collections by which his importance as a major modern literary figure is to be measured. Two interrelated experiences were very likely the chief contributors to the newfound vigor, imagery, and stylistic devices characteristic of these late works—his marriage and the completion of his mystic system in *A Vision*. The nature and degree of indebtedness to the latter of these influences, however, has often been both misunderstood and overestimated. The connection can probably never be assessed with complete accuracy, whereas various other possible factors, such as his renewed interest in the writings of John Donne and Jonathan Swift, should not be ignored or minimized.

In 1926 and 1927, Yeats's health became a genuinely serious problem, and at times in the last dozen years of his life, to live seemed to him to be almost more difficult than to die. There can be little question that such prolonged confrontation with that ultimate of all human experiences is responsible for some of the combined profundity, choler, and—paradoxically—wit of his last poems and plays. During this period, winters were usually spent in various Mediterranean locales for climatic reasons. Death eventually came in the south of France in January, 1939. With characteristic doggedness, Yeats continued working to the very end; he wrote his last poem only a week before his death and dictated to his wife some revisions of a late poem and his last play after the onset of his final illness, only two days before he died. Because of transportation difficulties at the beginning of World War II, Yeats was initially buried at Roquebrune, France. His body was exhumed in 1948, however, and transported aboard an Irish corvette for reburial at Drumcliff Churchyard, as he had specified at the end of his valedictory poem, "Under Ben Bulben." As his friend and fellow author Frank O'Connor said on the occasion, that event brought to its appropriate and symbolic conclusion a life that was itself a work of art long planned.

ANALYSIS

The complexity and fullness of William Butler Yeats's life was more than matched by the complexity and fullness of his imaginative thought. There are few poets writing in English whose works are more difficult to understand or explain. The basic problems lie in the multiplicity and intricacies of Yeats's own preoccupations and poetic techniques, and all too often the reader has been hindered more than helped by the vagaries of criticism and exegesis.

A coincidence of literary history is partly responsible for the latter problem. The culmination and conclusion of Yeats's career coincided with the advent of the New Criticism. Thus, in the decades following his death, some of his most important poems became exercise pieces for "explication" by commentators whose theories insisted on a minimum of attention to the author's cultural background, philosophical views, personal interests, or even thematic intentions (hence their odd-sounding term "intentional fallacy"). The consequence has been critical chaos. There simply are no generally accepted readings for some of Yeats's major poems. Instead, there have been ingenious exegeses, charges of misapprehension, countercharges, alternative analyses, then the whole cycle starting over again—in short, interpretational warfare.

Fortunately, in more recent years, simultaneously with decline of the New Critical movement, there has been increasing access to Yeats's unpublished materials—letters, diaries, and especially the manuscript drafts of poems and plays—and more scholarly attention has been paid to the relationships between such materials and the probable themes or meanings in the completed works. Even so, critical difficulties of no small magnitude remain because of continuing widespread disagreement among even the most highly re-

garded authorities about the basic metaphysical vision from which Yeats's poetic utterances spring, variously interpreted as atheism, pagan theism, quasi-Christian theism, Theosophy, sheer aestheticism, Platonic dualism, modern humanist monism, and existentialism.

SHIFTING PHILOSOPHIES

Added to the problems created by such a critical reception are those deriving from Yeats's qualities as an imaginative writer. Probably the most obvious source of difficulty is the highly allusive and subtly symbolic mode in which Yeats so often expressed himself. Clearly another is his lifelong practice of infusing many of his poems and plays with elements of doctrine, belief, or supposed belief from the various occult sources with which he was so thoroughly imbued. Furthermore, as to doctrine or belief, Yeats was constantly either apparently or actually shifting his ground (more apparently than actually). Two of his better-known poems, for example, are appropriately titled "Vacillation" and "A Dialogue of Self and Soul." In these and numerous others, he develops and sustains a running debate between two sides of an issue or between two sides of his own truth-seeking psyche, often with no clear-cut solution or final stance made unequivocally apparent.

Related to this—but not simply the same—is the fact that Yeats tended to change philosophical or metaphysical views throughout a long career, again either actually or apparently, and, also again, sometimes more apparently than actually. One disquieting and obfuscating consequence of such mental habits is that one poem will sometimes seem flatly to contradict another, or, in some cases even aside from the dialogue poems, one part of a given poem may appear to contradict a different part of the same poem. Adjacent passages in the major piece "The Tower," involving apparent rejection of Plato and Plotinus alongside apparent acceptance of Platonic or Neoplatonic reincarnation and "translunar paradise," constitute a case in point.

To quibble at much length about Yeats's prevailing metaphysical vision is to indulge in delusive sophistry, however, if his more than moderate pronouncements on such matters in prose are taken at anything approaching face value. What emerges from the prose is the virtually unequivocal proposition that—having rejected orthodox Christianity—the poet developed his own theistic "religion." His ontology and cosmology are made from many pieces and parts of that almost unimaginably multiplex body of lore—exoteric and esoteric—sometimes referred to as the *philosophia perennis*: Platonism, Neoplatonism, Hermetic symbolism, spiritual alchemy, Rosicrucianism, and certain elements of cabalism. Moreover, as Yeats stated in several essays, he found still further parallel and supporting materials at almost every turn—in Jakob Boehme, Emanuel Swedenborg, and William Blake; in the folklore of the Irish peasantry; in classical mythology, Irish legends, and the seasonal rituals examined by Sir James George Frazer; and in Asian religions, among other places. In two different senses Yeats found in all these materials convincing bases for the perpetuation of his obsession with extracting unity from multiplicity. For one thing, all the similarities and parallels in theme and motif from the many diverse sources constituted in themselves a kind of unity within multiplicity. Furthermore, the "philosophies" involved were largely oriented toward oneness—Plato's idea of the good, alchemy's distillation of the immutable *lapis* from the world of flux, Hermetism's theory of symbolic correspondences (as above, so below), Hinduism's Brahma, and so on.

In both thought and work, however, the unresolved opposites sometimes seem to loom as large as—or even larger than—the union itself. From this context came the so-called doctrine of the mask or anti-self (though not actually wholly original with Yeats). From that in turn, or alongside it, came the concept of the daimon, "guardian genius," or minor deity for each human being, a concept fundamental to a number of the traditional sources already cited. The greatest of all possible unions, of course, was the ultimate one of human beings with God, natural with supernatural, or temporal with eternal. Because of the *scintilla* principle, however, also inherent in parts of the tradition (the universe's permeation with tiny fragments of the godhead), the union of human being and daimon became virtually equivalent to the ultimate divine union. This concept helps to explain a handful of otherwise misleading passages where Yeats occasionally seemed to be rejecting his usually dominant dualism for a mo-

mentary monism: For example, in "The Tower," man creates everything in the universe from his own soul, and in "Two Songs from a Play" whatever illuminates the darkness is from man's own heart. Such human wholeness and power, however, are not possible, Yeats would probably say, without communion with daimon.

In spirit, doctrine, or belief, then, Yeats remained preponderantly a romantic and a nineteenth century spiritualist as he lived on into the increasingly positivistic and empirically oriented twentieth century. It was in form, not content, that he gradually allowed himself to develop in keeping with his times, although he abjured *vers libre* and never wholly relinquished his attachment to various traditional poetic modes. In the direction of modernism, he adopted or employed at various times irregular rhythms (writing by ear, declaring his ignorance of the technicalities of conventional metrics), approximate rhymes, colloquial diction, some Donnean or "metaphysical" qualities, and, most important of all, symbolic techniques much like those of the French movement, though not from its influence alone. The inimitable Yeatsian hallmark, however, remained a certain romantic rhetorical quality (despite his own fulminations against rhetoric), what he called passionate syntax, that remarkable gift for just the right turn of phrase to express ecstatic emotional intensity or to describe impassioned heroic action.

To suggest that Yeats consistently achieved great poetry through various combinations of these thematic elements and stylistic devices, however, would be less than forthright. Sometimes doctrinal materials are indeed impediments. Sometimes other aspects of content are unduly personal or sentimental. At times the technical components seem to be ill-chosen or fail to function as might have been expected, individually or conjointly. Thoroughly capable of writing bad poetry, Yeats has by no means been without his detractors. The poems for which he is famous, however—even those which present difficulties of understanding—are masterpieces, alchemical transformations of the raw material of his art.

### "THE LAKE ISLE OF INNISFREE"
Probably the most famous of all Yeats's poems, especially from his early period and with popular audiences, is "The Lake Isle of Innisfree." A modern,

middle-income Dublin homemaker, chosen at random, has said on mention of Yeats's name: "Oh, yes; I like his 'Lake Isle of Innisfree'; yes, I always did like 'The Lake Isle of Innisfree.'" Such popularity, as well as its representative quality among Yeats's early poems, makes the piece a natural choice for initial consideration here.

On the surface, there seems to be little that is symbolic or difficult about this brief lyric, first published in 1890. The wavering rhythms, syntactical inversions, and colorful but sometimes hazy images are characteristic of much of Yeats's youthful verse. So too are the Romantic tone and setting, and the underlying "escape motif," a thematic element or pattern that pervades much of Yeats's early work, as he himself realized and acknowledged in a letter to a friend.

The island of the title—real, not imaginary—is located in Lough Gill near the Sligo of Yeats's youth. More than once he mentioned in prose a boyish dream of living on the wooded isle much as Henry David Thoreau lived at Walden Pond, seeking wisdom in solitude. In other passages, he indicates that while homesick in London he heard the sound of a small fountain in the window of a shop. The experience recalled Lough Gill's lapping waters, he says, and inspired him to write the poem. The most important factor for Yeats's emerging poetic vision, however, was his long-standing fascination with a legend about a supernatural tree that once grew on the island with berries that were food for the Irish fairy folk. Thus in the poet's imaginative thought, if not explicitly in the poem itself, esoteric or occult forces were at play, and in a figurative sense, at least, the escape involved was, in the words of the letter to his friend, "to fairyland," or a place much like it.

One of the most notable sources of praise for "The Lake Isle of Innisfree" was a letter from Robert Louis Stevenson in distant Samoa. Stevenson wrote that only two other passages of literature had ever captivated him as Yeats's poem did. Yeats himself said later that it was the earliest of his nonnarrative poems whose rhythms significantly manifested his own music. He ultimately developed negative feelings, however, about his autobiographical sentimentality and about instances of what he came to consider unduly artificial syntax. Yet in late life when he was invited to recite some of his own poems for radio programs, he more than once chose to include "The Lake Isle of Innisfree." Evidently he wished to offer to that audience what he felt it probably wanted to hear. Evidently he realized that the average Irish homemaker or ordinary working man, then as later, would say in response to the name Yeats: "Oh, yes, I like his 'Lake Isle of Innisfree.'"

## "LEDA AND THE SWAN"

Technically, "Leda and the Swan" (1923) is a sonnet, one of only a few that Yeats ever composed. The spaces between quatrains in the octave and between the octave and the sestet—not to mention the break in line eleven—are evidently Yeats's innovations, characteristic of his inclination toward experimentation within traditional frameworks in the period of the poem's composition. The story from Greek mythology on which the poem is based is well known and much treated in the Western tradition. In the tale from antiquity, a Spartan queen, Leda, was so beautiful that Zeus, ruler of the gods, decided that he must have her. Since the immortals usually did not present themselves to humankind in their divine forms, Zeus changed himself into a great swan and in that shape ravished the helpless girl. The story has often been portrayed pictorially as well as verbally; Yeats himself possessed a copy of a copy of Michelangelo's lost painting on the subject. There has been considerable critical discussion of the degree of interrelationship between the picture or other graphic depictions and Yeats's poem, but to no very certain conclusion, except that Leda seems much less terrified in Michelangelo's visual version—where perhaps she might even seem to be somewhat receptive—than in Yeats's verbal one.

The poem has been one of Yeats's most widely praised pieces from the time of early critical commentaries in the first decade after his death. Virtually all commentators dwell on the power, economy, and impact of the poem's language and imagery, especially in the opening sections, which seem to be concerned predominantly, if not exclusively, with mere depiction of the scene and events themselves. The poem's apparent simplicity, especially by Yeatsian standards, however, is decidedly deceptive. The greatest problem in interpretation is with the sestet's images of Troy in flames and with Agamemnon's death.

To understand the importance of these allusions to Greek history—and the deeper meanings of the poem—the reader must realize that Yeats intended the poem to represent the annunciation of a new era of civilization in his cyclic vision of history, the two-thousand-year-period of pagan polytheism that preceded the present age of Christian monotheism. As emphasized in Giorgio Melchiori's book *The Whole Mystery of Art* (1961), the poet later imaginatively balanced a second poem against "Leda and the Swan": "The Mother of God," in which another woman, Mary, is visited by another deity, the Holy Ghost, in the form of another bird, the divine dove, to initiate another period of history, the Christian era. The conscious intention of such a parallel between the two poems is attested by Yeats's having printed "Leda and the Swan" at the head of the chapter in *A Vision* titled "Dove or Swan," with a sentence on the next page stating explicitly that he thought of the annunciation that began Grecian culture as having been made to Leda. Equally unequivocal evidences are Melchiori's citation of a letter in which Yeats called the poem a classic annunciation, Yeats's note for the poem that speaks of a violent annunciation, and the fact that the poem's first submission to a publisher was under the title "Annunciation."

This last-mentioned fact relates to another point of critical disagreement. In a note, Yeats says that the poem was written in response to a request from the editor of a political review. As he worked, though, the girl and the swan took over the scene, he says, and all politics fell away. Some commentators have accepted or reaffirmed this assertion, failing to realize that Yeats—intentionally or unintentionally—overstated the case. Bird and woman did indeed so dominate the poet's imagination in the first eight lines that one critical consequence has been undue attention to the language and imagery of the surface there. When one recalls, however, that the pre-Christian era in Yeats's system was governmentally monarchical or totalitarian while the present era was imagined (however erroneously) as predominantly democratic, the perception dawns that the affairs of Leda's progeny, especially Helen as a causal factor in the Trojan war and Clytemnestra as a figure involved in its aftermath, constitute, in truth, "politics" enough. Otherwise, the allusions to the burn-

ing city and deceased king would be gratuitous deadwood in the poem, unaccountable anomalies, which is just exactly what they remain in those analyses that disregard them or minimize their importance.

Even recognition and acceptance of the themes of annunciation and history do not reveal the poem's full complexity, however, as the average reader may well sense on perusal of the final interrogative sentence. This concluding question seems to constitute a third unit in the piece, as well as the basis of some third level of significance. The traditional octave-sestet relationship of the Italian sonnet created for Yeats a division into two parts with two different but related emphases. It is his unconventional break in line 11, however, which achieves a tripartite structure at the same time that it introduces the thematic bases for an amalgamating—if not resolving—unity for all three parts of the poem and for all their interrelated levels of symbolic implication.

If the octave can be said to focus predominantly on the "surface" level of "Leda and the Swan," with the allusions to antiquity adumbrating a historical level, then the final question—a real one rather than the rhetorical sort with which Yeats sometimes concluded poems—can be seen as the introduction of a philosophical or metaphysical level. Given the possibility of such consort or interaction between the human and the divine, what supernatural effects—if any—are consequent for the mortal party? This issue, so relevant to the rest of this poem, is raised not only here or a few times in related pieces like "The Mother of God," but rather over and over again throughout the entirety of Yeats's canon. More than that, it is frequently voiced in those other places in surprisingly similar terms.

### SEEKING A TRANSCENDENT UNION

The possibility of union between humankind and God, between natural and supernatural, is probably the most persistent and pervasive theme in all of Yeats's oeuvre. It is the strongest of those threads woven throughout the fabric of his work that create the unity within multiplicity previously considered. It was also unquestionably the motivating factor in his relentlessly moving from one occult preoccupation to the other. Moreover, the conviction that artistic inspiration was one of the more readily observable manifestations of such divine visitation on the human sensibility was what made Yeats philosophically a confessed Romantic for life, regardless of what modernist elements of style or technique he may have allowed to emerge in the poetry of his later years.

A major emblem for such miraculous converse, elsewhere in Yeats just as in "Leda and the Swan," is sexual union. In several prose passages, for example, he draws explicit parallels between human interaction with the daimon or semidivine guardian spirit and a man's relationship with his sweetheart or lover. In another place, he conjectures that the "mystic way" and physical love are comparable, which is not surprising in the light of the fact that most of his occult sources employed the same analogy and frequently spoke of the moment of union—mortal with immortal—as the "mystic marriage." Yeats's utilization of this particular sexual symbology is apparent in pieces such as "Solomon and the Witch," "A Last Confession," "Chosen," and *The Player Queen*, among others. Equally relevant is the fact that Yeats repeatedly used birds as symbols of discarnate spirits or deities. Finally, the two motifs—sexual union as an analogue for supernatural union and avian symbolism for the divine—occur together in at least two works by Yeats other than "Leda and the Swan": the plays *At the Hawk's Well* (pr. 1916) and *The Herne's Egg* (pb. 1938), in the latter of which, copulation between a woman and a great white bird is similarly fundamental to the piece's philosophical implications.

In Yeats's imaginative thought, such moments of transcendent union leave behind in the physical world some vestige of the divine condescension—the art object's "immortality" in the case of inspiration, for example. In more portentous instances, however, such as those imaged in "Leda and the Swan" and "The Mother of God"—with clear metaphorical interplay between the phenomena of creation and procreation, even if not voiced in so many words—the remnant is the conception of some demigod or incarnate divinity such as Helen or Christ, whose beauty, perfection, or power is so great that its presence on earth inaugurates a whole new cultural dispensation.

What one ultimately finds in "Leda and the Swan," then, is Yeats hammering out, in the midst of manifold antinomy, two kinds of unity at a single stroke. The three somewhat separate parts of the poem are joined in unity with one another, and, simultaneously, the poem as a unified whole is united to some of the most important themes that recur throughout his canon. This unity within multiplicity is achieved through Yeats's ingeniously imaginative manipulation of a single famous myth chosen from many that involve—either or both—godhead manifested in avian form and divine visitation on humankind cast in the image of sexual conjugation.

### "THE SECOND COMING"

Almost as synonymous with Yeats's name as "The Lake Isle of Innisfree" is the unusual and foreboding poem "The Second Coming," which was composed in January, 1919, and first published in 1920. It is one of Yeats's few unrhymed poems, written in very irregular blank verse whose rhythms perhaps contribute to the ominous effect created by the diction and imagery. The piece has had a strange critical reception, deriving in part from the paradox that it is one of Yeats's works most directly related to the system of history in *A Vision*, but at the same time appears to offer reasonably accessible meanings of a significant kind to the average reader of poetry in English.

The more obvious "meanings," generally agreed on, are implications of disorder, especially in the first section, in which the falcon has lost touch with the falconer, and impressions of horror, especially in the second section, with its vision of the pitiless rough beast slouching through the desert. In the light of the date of composition, the validity of such thematic elements for both Yeats and his audience is immediately evident. World War I had just ended, leaving the Western world in that continuing mood of despondency voiced also in T. S. Eliot's *The Waste Land* (1922) (which shares with Yeats's poem the desert image) and in Gertrude Stein's—and Ernest Hemingway's—epithet of "a lost generation." In other words, despite the author's considerable further concerns, the piece on this level "caught a wave," as it were, so that it quickly came to be regarded by commentators and the author alike as prophetic—an attitude enhanced, of course, by the richly allusive title.

### HISTORY AS SPIRAL

On a deeper level, "The Second Coming" is directly related to the cyclical conception of history that Yeats delineated in *A Vision*. As seen in the discussion of "Leda and the Swan," Yeats envisioned history in terms of two-thousand-year eras, each of which was ushered in by a portentous annunciation of some sort. If Zeus's descent on Leda initiated the period from about 2000 B.C.E. to the year zero, and if the Holy Ghost's descent to Mary initiated the subsequent period from the year zero to approximately 2000 C.E., then in 1919, the poet could speculate that the next such annunciation might occur either just barely within his lifetime or else not very long thereafter. These two-thousand-year periods of culture were characterized, like so many other things in Yeats's imaginative thought, by opposition to each other, with the main oppositions in *A Vision* designated as antithetical (or "subjective") and primary (or "objective"). These labels, or tinctures as Yeats called them, are not always easy to define, but from reading *A Vision* one begins to sense their nature. In general, theantithetical is individualistic (self-centered), heroic, aristocratic, emotional, and aesthetic. It is concerned predominantly with inner being and is symbolized by a full moon. The primary, by contrast, is anti-individualistic (mass-oriented), saintly or sagelike, democratic, rational, and moral. It is associated mainly with external existence and is symbolized by either the sun or the dark of the moon. Yeats identified himself with the antithetical and associated many things that he disliked (such as democracy and "fact-finding" science) with the primary. Thus he favored the polytheistic era of Homeric and classical Greece (antithetical), whereas he rejected or spurned the moral and anti-individualistic monotheism (primary) which began with the birth of Christ.

Borrowing from Swedenborg and other esoteric sources, Yeats conceptualized the growth of these historical movements in terms of gyres or spirals, a feature of the system rather difficult to discuss without reference to diagrams. (One may see *A Vision* for diagrams in great sufficiency.) For the sake of convenience in depiction, the spirals (widening from vertex in larger and larger circles) are imaged as the outer "shells" surrounding them—that is, as cones. Furthermore, for purposes of two-dimensional representation on a book's page, each cone is usually regarded simply in terms of its profile—that is, as a triangle. However, since the entire system of *A Vision* is based on the proposition that the universe consists of numberless pairs of antinomies or contraries, no cone or triangle exists in isolation; instead, everyone is in locked interpenetration with an opposing cone or triangle, each with its vertex or narrowest point at the center of the other's widest expansion or base. Thus, Yeats conceived of the present two-thousand-year era not simply as one set of interlocked cones, but rather as two sets of one thousand years each, as is made quite explicit in the chapter that reviews history under the title "Dove or Swan." Thus, instead of the Christian gyre or cone sweeping outward toward its widest expansion at the year 2000 C.E., as most commentators seem to have assumed, the widest expansion of the triangle representing that primary religious dispensation occurred at about the year 1000 C.E., completely in keeping with the medieval Church's domination of virtually all aspects of life at that time. For the period following 1000 C.E., that religion's declining movement is represented by a contracting gyre, its base set against the base of its predecessor, forming, in two-dimensional terms, a figure that Yeats speaks of as shaped like an ace of diamonds. The Christian dispensation, then, is at dwindling to its cone's or triangle's narrowest point, at the center of the opposing gyre's widest expansion, completely in keeping with the post-Darwinian upheaval in Victorian England about science's undermining the foundations of the Church, subsequent notions of the "death of God," and so on.

What, then, is spiraling outward to its widest expansion in the twentieth century, the falcon's gyring flight having swept so far from the falconer that "the centre cannot hold"? The answer to this question lies in recognition of a point that appears rather clearly at various places in *A Vision*. In Yeats's system of history, every cone representing a religious dispensation has as its interlocking counterpart a cone that represents the secular culture of the same period. Thus, the two movements, religious and secular, live each other's death and die each other's life, to use an expression from Heraclitus that Yeats repeated time and again, in creative pieces as well as in his discursive prose. The birth of Christ came, then, as Yeats indicates with unequivocal clarity, at the time of an antithetical secular or political phenomenon at the very height of its development, at the widest expansion of its cone—the Roman Empire. As the gyre representing the primary Christian religious movement revolved outward toward its widest expansion in the Middle Ages, the power of the Roman Empire gradually declined until it vanished at about 1000 C.E. (Yeats uses the year 1050 in "Dove or Swan"). Then both movements reversed directions, with primary Christianity beginning to dwindle at the same time that a new secular life of antithetical nature started and gyred outward up to the present day. This—the widest expansion of an antithetical secular or political gyre in the twentieth century—is almost certainly what Yeats identified with fascism, not the new annunciation to come. Such a collapsing and reexpansion of the antithetical spirals in the two-thousand-year period since the birth of Christ—two one-thousand-year cones tip to tip—created what Yeats called an hourglass figure superimposed on (or, more accurately, interlocked with) the diamond shape of Christianity's primary religious dispensation.

### TINCTURES

The crucial point in interpreting "The Second Coming" is that the annunciation of every new religious dispensation involves what Yeats calls an interchange of the tinctures. In other words, at 2000 B.C.E., at the year zero, and at 2000 C.E., religion changes from primary to antithetical in quality, or vice versa, while secular life and politics change tinctures just oppositely. (Yeats was explicit about identification of the secular with politics.) No such interchange occurs, however, at the initiation of new secular gyres, as at 1000 B.C.E. or 1000 C.E. At those points the expanding or collapsing gyres of both aspects of life—religious and secular—simply reverse directions without their tinctures changing from primary to antithetical or the other way around. The importance of this feature of the system for meanings in "The Second Coming" can hardly be overstated. The interchange is sudden and cataclysmic, causing such strife in human history as the Trojan War soon after the annunciation to Leda from Zeus or the widespread battles of the Roman Empire soon after the annunciation from the Holy Ghost to the Virgin Mary. The abrupt change near the end of the twentieth century, of the antithetical tincture from secular life's widely expanded cone to religion's extremely narrowed one (and, vice versa, of the primary tincture almost instantaneously from the nearly extinguished religious gyre to the widest expansion of the counterpoised secular or political gyre), could in and of itself be catastrophic enough to warrant most of the portentous imagery and diction in Yeats's poem. Fearful concerns even more specifically related to the system than that, however, were involved in the piece's genesis and evolution. The annunciation of a new religious dispensation, antithetical in nature, would not have been anticipated by Yeats with foreboding, for he simultaneously favored the antithetical tincture and held in low regard the existing primary religious movement which was to be displaced. The only disappointing thing for Yeats about the forthcoming antithetical religion was that it would have no more than its merest beginnings within his lifetime or shortly thereafter, reaching its fullest expansion as a historical gyre not until the year 3000 C.E. The sudden imposition on the world of a primary political system, on the other hand, at its widest expansion from the very outset, was quite another matter.

What might constitute such an ultra-primary or super-"democratic" political phenomenon for the aristocratic-minded Yeats as he looked about the European world in 1919? Other than the last stages of World War I, one particular violent upheaval had just occurred: the Bolshevik Revolution. Communism was for Yeats the horrifying rough beast slouching through the postwar wasteland to be born, its politically primary hour come round exactly as predicted by the gyres and cycles of history available to him from the "automatic scripts" that his wife had begun to write out more than a year before the poem's composition.

Although this interpretational conclusion can be reached through a careful reading of *A Vision*'s sections on history, its validity has been made virtually unequivocal by Jon Stallworthy's publication of the poem's manuscript drafts (originally in his book *Between the Lines: Yeats's Poetry in the Making*, 1963, and again with fuller transcription of some partially illegible passages in the journal *Agenda*, 1971/1972). Along with several other convincing clues in these drafts occurs one line that leaves little to the imagination: "The Germany of Marx has led to Russian Com."

Working with these same unpublished drafts as well as other materials, Donald Torchiana has made a persuasive case for the proposition that what upset Yeats most of all was the possibility that Ireland's civil strife in this same period made his country a highly vulnerable tinderbox for the spread of Marxist factions or Communistic forces (*W. B. Yeats and Georgian Ireland*, 1966). A letter by Yeats written later in 1919 makes this thesis virtually incontrovertible. In it the poet states that his main concern was for Ireland to be saved from Marxist values, because he felt that their fundamental materialism could only lead to murder. Then he quotes a catchphrase that seems to echo lines from "The Second Coming": "Can the bourgeois be innocent?"

The manuscripts reveal much else as well. They show, for example, that from its earliest inception—a brief prose draft of the opening portion—"The Second Coming" was a decidedly political poem, not one concerned with some antithetical religious annunciation. Even the highly effective—though intentionally ironical—religious allusions to Bethlehem and Christ's return emerged relatively late in the poem's development. Moreover, the politics of concern are plainly of the primary tincture; the word "mob" appears repeatedly. When the expression "surely" occurred for the first time, it was followed by "the great falcon must come." Yeats, however, having said in a much-quoted passage elsewhere that he often used large noble birds to represent the subjective or antithetical and beasts that run on the ground to symbolize the objective or primary, realized his momentary drift toward depiction of the birth of an antithetical religious entity and struck the line. Then later came the famous beast, with its blank solar (primary) gaze.

Although it might shock some readers to think that Yeats would identify Christ with a beast, and with a political ideology such as Marxism, the point that should not be overlooked is that while Christ may be alternately sacred or secular in Yeats's imaginative thought, he is always unalterably primary. *A Vision* is quite explicit in several places about Christ's being primary. The poem is therefore, about his second coming, although in a frighteningly unfamiliar secular guise: a mass-oriented and anti-individualistic political materialism that paradoxically corresponds to but simulta-

neously contravenes his previous mass-oriented and anti-individualistic spiritual teachings. After twenty centuries of religious equality urged by Christ the Lamb, a cataclysmic and leveling social anarchy is about to be loosed on the world by Christ the Lion.

### "AMONG SCHOOL CHILDREN"

Composed in 1926 and published in 1927, "Among School Children" is another of Yeats's most widely acclaimed and extensively studied poems. The two most famous interpretative readings are by Cleanth Brooks in *The Well Wrought Urn: Studies in the Structure of Poetry* (1947) and John Wain in *Interpretations: Essays on Twelve English Poems* (1955). Although both essays are almost belligerently New Critical, each sees as the overall theme the relationships between natural and supernatural, or between matter and spirit, and the ravages wrought on humankind by the passage of time. Most other analyses tend to accept this same general meaning for the poem as a whole, although almost inevitably there have been some who see the subject as the triumph of art, or something of that sort. With this poem, the problems and difficulties of interpretation have been not so much with larger suggestions of significance as with individual lines or passages in their relationships—or supposed relationships—to the poem's broadest meanings. Such tendencies toward agreement about the piece's general thematic implications are fortunate since they are in keeping with Yeats's own comments in notes and letters: that physical or temporal existence will waste the youthful students and that the poem is one of his not infrequent condemnations of old age.

The inspirational matrix for the poem was literal enough—a visit by Yeats in his role as senator in the newly established Irish Free State to a quite progressive school administered by a Catholic convent. Given this information, the reader will have no problems with stanza 1. (Any analysis, incidentally, which suggests that Yeats felt that the children depicted were being taught the wrong kinds of things is open to question, for Yeats subsequently spoke to the Senate about the convent school in highly laudatory terms.) The next three stanzas, however, although they are generally thought to be less problematical than the last part of the poem, are somewhat more opaque than the casual-toned and low-keyed opening. In stanza 2, the sight of the schoolchildren suddenly brings to the poet-senator's memory (with little transition for the reader) a scene in which a beautiful woman had told him of some childhood chastisement, probably by a schoolteacher. That memory, in turn, evokes for him a vision of what she must have looked like at such an age, perhaps not too much unlike the girls standing before him in the convent's hall.

There can be little doubt that the beautiful woman in question is the one by whom Yeats's aching "heart" was "driven wild" for a large part of his adult life—Maud Gonne. Time and time again throughout his canon, Yeats compares that special woman's almost divine or superhuman beauty to the beauty of Helen of Troy, who, in Greek mythology, was born to Leda after her visitation by Zeus. This information, then, helps to clarify such characteristically allusive terms in stanzas 2 through 4 as "Ledaean body," "daughters of the swan," "every paddler's heritage," "Ledaean kind," and "pretty plumage." The alteration of Plato's parable (in the *Symposium*, probably one of the middle dialogues, where the basis of love is explained as the desire in divinely separated humankind for reunion in a sphere) to union in the white and yellow of a single egg, rather than the myth's division, also fits into this pattern of Ledaean imagery, at the same time that it looks forward to images and suggestions of generation or birth in subsequent stanzas.

Then, in stanza 4, with still another shift, the beautiful woman's present visage drifts before the poet's eyes. Surprisingly, despite the rather heavily connotative language of lines 3 and 4, along with Yeats's comparison in the second quatrain of his own youth with his present old age (not to mention similar thematic implications in the entire poem), there has been some controversy about line one. The issue is whether Yeats meant to convey a vision of the woman still young and beautiful or, instead, ravaged by time and decrepitude. The word "Quattrocento," denoting fifteenth century Italian art and artists, might be taken to substantiate either side of such a debate, depending on how it itself is construed; but along with virtually everything else in the stanza, the concluding—and later recurring—scarecrow image would seem to lend support to the suggestion of deterioration and decay.

If lines 2 through 4 of stanza 5 were removed, the stanza not only would be completely intelligible, but it would also be a rather concise statement of one of the poem's two main themes—the effects on humankind of time's passage. Since lines 2 through 4 were included, however, along with other characteristically Yeatsian elements akin to them in subsequent stanzas, the poem's real difficulties begin to manifest themselves in its second half. In a note to the poem, Yeats indicates that the honey of generation is an image that he borrowed from Porphyry's essay "The Cave of the Nymphs," almost certainly with an intended symbolic suggestion, on one level, of the pleasures of sexual union. The same note, however, also indicates explicitly that the recollection mentioned is the soul's memory—à la William Wordsworth's "Ode: Intimations of Immortality from Recollections of Early Childhood"—of a prenatal condition higher and freer than earthly incarnation. At this point, Yeats's occult and esoteric beliefs that so many critics have found difficult to accept enter the poem. Brooks's reaction, for example, is virtual incredulity. To make interpretational matters even worse, Yeats evidently employed the honey image ambiguously to relate also to "the drug," presumably physically procreated or temporal existence, which allows or causes the prenatal memory to fade. Both the note and the draft versions of the poem (reproduced in Thomas Parkinson's *W. B. Yeats: The Later Poetry*, 1964) suggest the likelihood of such intentional or semi-intentional ambiguity. All this, along with what is probably the poem's least felicitous line—"sleep, shriek, struggle . . ."—has led to considerable exegetical dispute about who or what was betrayed—mother or shape? The ambiguity seems less intentional in this particular case, however, and the drafts, along with a certain amount of common sense, tend to indicate the child, a soul entrapped in flesh by the mother's generatively honeyed act.

Stanza 6 is perhaps not too difficult once the reader realizes that the final line is, in effect, appositionally related to the main nouns in the other seven lines. In other words, the generally accepted thrust of meaning is that even the greatest and presumably wisest of men come to be, in time, like elderly poet-senators and everyone else, dilapidated old scarecrows. There is, however, a bit more wit and symbolism at work—or at play—in the stanza. For one thing, Yeats has chosen men who were teachers or students or—in two cases—both in turn: Plato, Aristotle, Alexander the Great, and Pythagoras. Furthermore, three of these four men spent their lives contemplating and theorizing about the same crucial and fundamental aspects of human experience which are the subjects of the poem—the relationships between spirit and matter and between being and becoming.

The second half of stanza 7 is the most problematical unit in the poem. The first quatrain, however, gives little trouble. With a pun on the word "images," Yeats refers both to pictures in the maternal mind's eye and to religious icons or statuary. The "Presences" of line 5 are what create interpretational difficulties, again because here Yeats's occult views become involved, views that too few exegetes have been willing to address even as accepted by the poet himself. Yeats's use of a capital *P* and the expression "self-born" (compare "self-sown," "self-begotten," and "miracle-bred" on the very next page of *The Collected Poems of W. B. Yeats*) should be clues that some kind of divinity is being apostrophized in this stanza about worship. That, in turn, can lead to recognition of a third level of meaning for the punword "images." The mask, the antiself, and especially the daimon (not synonymous terms, but kindred ones in Yeats's esoteric thought and vocabulary) were sometimes referred to as the image, for they are, like a mirror image, simultaneously like and yet exactly opposite to the human individual. Furthermore, with the daimon, that special semidivine guiding or misguiding spirit, each man or woman is involved in an exasperating attraction-repulsion relationship which explains the poet's emphasis upon heartbreak and mockery. Fleetingly known—in actuality or by analogy—through such heightened experiences as the earlier stanzas' sexual love (passion), religious love (piety), or maternal love (affection), these hatefully loving guardian geniuses draw man onward from the flesh toward spiritual glory at the same time that they do all they can to frustrate every inch of his progress or enterprise along the way.

The first half of the closing stanza would be much more readily comprehensible if Yeats had retained his draft's version of the opening line, which began with the word "all" instead of "labor." That would have agreed with a draft line relating to the dancer, "all so smoothly runs," and would justify the status *usually* attributed to the concluding quatrain: perhaps the most successful of Yeats's famous passages whose antinomy-resolving symbols or images lift poet, poem, and reader above the strife of physical existence to a condition of triumphant affirmation or realm of artistically perfected unity. Dance and dancer are indivisibly—almost divinely—one. The tree—and the poem—are supremely organic wholes, greater than the sums of their parts. This seems to be Romantic lyricism at its transcendent best.

Such a conclusion, however, is too hasty. When its initial word was "all," the first quatrain of the final stanza rather plainly meant something like "Life in this world is best when and where humankind achieves a balance between body and soul, between spirit and flesh." Yeats's eventual substitution of the word "labor," however, could well have been intended to add, among other things, the idea that such a balance is never easily come by nor readily sustained in this life. That would echo in one sense the feminine persona in "Adam's Curse," who says that women have to labor to become beautiful, as well as her interlocutor's rejoinder that subsequent to Adam's fall nothing very fine can be achieved or created without a great deal of labor. How, then, did the poet move so suddenly from the broken hearts and mockery of stanza 7 to some rhapsodically evoked unity or triumph in the last four lines of stanza 8? Perhaps the poem was never meant to suggest such a leap. There is, after all, no journey in this poem from one realm to another, as there is in "Sailing to Byzantium." The tree and the dancer are still very much in the sensuous physical realm. Perhaps the supposed transition has been only through some strange magic as unsavory to common sense as Yeats's occult inclinations were to the critics who have perpetrated this illusory transmutation. Perhaps, ironically, the unRomantic critics have made Yeats much more Romantic in this particular poem than he ever intended to be. In all fairness, the point must be acknowledged, however, that Brooks and Wain themselves read the final stanza in much more neutral or negative terms than many of the commentators who have written subsequently. Almost unquestionably the chief influence on numerous analyses of the final stanza in terms of transcendence and artistic unity has been Frank Kermode's book *Romantic Image* (1957), which takes the passage as a virtual epitome of the opposition-resolving powers of the symbolic mode, as the image of the Image.

"Among School Children" has a rather high incidence of puns and intentional ambiguities in addition to the ones already noted. The two most obvious further instances involve the words "labor" and "play," which have been commented on both separately and together. Perhaps insufficient attention has been given, however, to possibilities of multiple meanings in that salient feature, the title. Yeats, an inveterate reviser, was well capable of changing a title if it no longer best suited the interests of his poem. Why would he have retained the title here if it did not fit the finished piece—the whole work as well as the opening portions? Some continuing concern with the symbolic implications of students and teachers has already been observed in stanza 6. Why would not or could not the same kind of thing be appropriate for that very important portion of the poem, its conclusion? Suppose, in contrast to prevalent interpretations of the last quatrain, that the questions asked there are real questions, such as schoolchildren ask, rather than rhetorical ones implying some transcendence or triumph over the rest of the poem's concerns. Like a staring schoolchild, man might well ask—in fact, for centuries he has asked—where the material world ends and the spiritual world begins, and how, in this temporal realm, he can separate the one from the other. The great rooted blossomer, then, may be more an emblem of the puzzles and problems studied in life's schoolroom than of some artistically achieved solution to them. Is man the newborn infant, the adolescent pupil, the youthful procreator, or the white-haired elder statesman—or none of these or all of these or more than all of these? In the face of such conundrums, all men are "among school children," seeking and inquiring, frequently without finding or being given reassuring answers.

### "SAILING TO BYZANTIUM" AND "BYZANTIUM"

No work in Yeats's canon has won more renown or elicited more controversy than the so-called Byzantium poems, "Sailing to Byzantium" (1927) and "Byzan-

tium" (1930). Critical opinion as to which is poetically superior has been almost, if not quite, equally divided. There is almost universal agreement, however, that the earlier and more frequently reprinted piece, "Sailing to Byzantium," is the easier to understand.

Several authorities, in fact, have gone so far as to say that "Sailing to Byzantium" explains itself or needs no extensive clarification; but if such were actually the case, the amount of commentary that it has generated would clearly constitute an anomaly. If nothing else, the general reader ought to have some answer to the almost inevitable question, "Why Byzantium?" Though it does not provide every possible relevant response to such a query, a much-quoted passage from *A Vision* indicates some of the more important reasons why and how Yeats came to let that great Near Eastern city of medieval times represent in his imagination a cultural, artistic, and spiritual ideal. He believes, he says, that one might have found there "some philosophical worker in mosaic" with "the supernatural descending nearer to him than to Plotinus even," that in "early Byzantium" perhaps more than at any other time in history "religious, aesthetic and practical life were one." Artists of all kinds expressed "the vision of a whole people," "the work of many that seemed the work of one" and was the "proclamation of their invisible master."

Although there is no question whatever that "Sailing to Byzantium" is a richly symbolic poem, its genesis apparently involved a more or less literal level that, even though it has not been ignored, may not have been stressed in all its particulars as much as might be warranted. Yeats was first exposed to Byzantine art during a Mediterranean tour in 1907 that included Ravenna, where he saw mosaics and a frieze in the Church of San Apollinare Nuovo that is generally regarded as the chief basis of imagery in stanza 3 of "Sailing to Byzantium." Years later, however, two factors coincided to renew his interest, one of them involving a voyage in certain respects interestingly akin to that in the poem. In the first half of the 1920's, Yeats had read rather widely about Byzantium in connection with his work on the historical "Dove or Swan" section of *A Vision*. Then in 1924, nearing sixty years of age, he became somewhat ill and suffered high blood pressure and difficulty in breathing. He was advised to stop work and was taken by his wife on another Mediterranean tour, this time seeking out other Byzantine mosaics, and similar craftsmanship that sharply contrasted art with nature, at places such as Monreale and Palermo, Sicily. As at least one commentator has pointed out, Yeats had no great regrets about leaving home at this time because of dissatisfaction with the political situation and depression about his health. The first legible words in the drafts of "Sailing to Byzantium" are "Farewell friends," and subsequent early portions make unequivocal the fact that "That country" in the finished poem is (or at least originally was) Ireland. Thus, the imaginative and poetic voyage of a sick old man leaving one locale for a more desirable one very probably had at least some of its antecedents in a rather similar actual journey a few years earlier.

Two symbolic interpretations of "Sailing to Byzantium" have been predominant by a considerable margin: Either the poem is about the state of the poet's spirit or soul shortly before and after death, or it is about the creative process and artistic achievement. A choice between the two might be said to pivot on response to the question, "How ideal is the ideal?" In other words, does Byzantium represent this-worldly perfection on the aesthetic level or perfection of an even greater kind in a transcendent realm of existence? A not insignificant amount of the massive critical commentary on the poem (as well as on its sequel "Byzantium") has been in the way of a war of words about the "proper" reply to such a question, with surprisingly inflexible positions being taken by some of the combatants. Fortunately, however, a number of authorities have realized that there is no reason at all why both levels of meaning cannot obtain simultaneously and that, as a matter of fact, the poem becomes much more characteristically Yeatsian in its symbolic complexity and wealth of import if such a reading is accepted.

### RETURN TO PHYSICALITY, SEXUALITY

About 1926 or 1927 and thereafter, an apparent major change—with emphasis on apparent—seems to have taken place in Yeats's attitude toward life. On the surface, "Sailing to Byzantium" may look and sound like the culmination of a long line of "escape" poems, while many poems or passages written after it (for ex-

ample, "A Dialogue of Self and Soul") seem to stress instead a plunge into the physicality of this world, even a celebration of earthly existence. Even though Yeats continued to write poems very much concerned with transcendence, supernaturalism, and otherworldliness, he developed in his late career a "new" kind of poem. These poems were often short, were frequently presented in series or sequences, and were frequently—but not always—concerned with a particularly physical aspect of worldly existence, sex.

These poems also share other attributes, a number of them related to Yeats's revived interest at the time in the ballad form. One group is titled, for example, *Words for Music Perhaps, and Other Poems*, indicating their songlike qualities. In addition to the poems themselves being brief, the lines and stanza patterns are also short, the lines sometimes having as few as two stresses. Diction, syntax, and idiom are—again as in the ballad or folk song—colloquial and uncomplicated. Imagery, too, is earthy, sometimes stark or blunt. At times sound patterns other than rhyme contribute to the songlike effects, and some pieces, although not all, make effective use of the refrain as a device. In these verses, Yeats has come a long way from the amorphous Pre-Raphaelitism of his early lyrics. In them, in fact, he achieves some of the most identifiably "modern" effects in his entire canon.

Related to that modernity is the fact that these late-life songs are anything but simple in content and meaning. Their deceptiveness in this regard has led some early critics to label them—especially the scatological ones—as tasteless and crude. More recent and perceptive analysts, however, have found them to be, in the words of one commentator, more nearly eschatological. What Yeats is doing thematically in such pieces, in fact, is by no means new to him. As in "Solomon and the Witch," "Leda and the Swan," and some other earlier pieces, he is using the sexual metaphor to explore some of the metaphysical mysteries of human existence. One significant difference, however, is that now the sexual experience itself sometimes seems to be regarded as something of a mystery in its own right.

### CRAZY JANE POEMS

Almost as well known as Yeats himself is his fictive persona Crazy Jane, evidently based compositely on two old Irish women from the poet's experience, one early, one late. Like Shakespeare's—and Yeats's—fools, however, Jane is usually "crazy like a fox." In her series of poems, in the "Three Bushes" sequence, and in poems such as "Chosen," "A Last Confession," "Her Anxiety," "Consolation," and "The Wild Old Wicked Man," Yeats considers or deals with sexuality and sexual imagery in some six or seven different, though frequently interrelated, ways. At times, the poet seems to vacillate or contradict himself from one poem to another, a habit that at first makes understanding these pieces rather difficult. After a while, however, the phenomenon can be recognized for what it is: Yeats's characteristic technique of shifting ground or altering angle of vision in order to explore his subject the more completely.

One basic use of the sexual image has already been seen: The union of man and woman is parallel to or representative of the union of natural with supernatural, human with divine, or man with daimon. In some of these poems, however, the union seems to be so overwhelming that it almost ceases to be mere symbol and becomes the thing in itself, as in the last stanza of "Chosen" or in an unpublished poem where even the gyres are laid to rest in the bed of love. On the other hand (and at the other extreme) are poems that suggest that sex just does not accomplish very much at all, as in "The Chambermaid's Second Song" (last in the "Three Bushes" sequence), where after mere physical pleasure, man's spirit remains "blind as a worm." A poem of this kind echoes a reported statement by Yeats that the most unfortunate thing about coitus is the continuing "virginity of the soul." In between the two extremes are poems that see sex as little better than a *pis aller*—"Consolation," for example, or "The Wild Old Wicked Man," whose protagonist chooses "the second-best" on "a woman's breast." Then there are poems that contemplate the pleasures or problems of sexuality in this life in the light of a Swedenborgian intercourse of the angels ("A Last Confession" and "Crazy Jane on the Day of Judgment") or the Hermetic paradigm—as above, so below ("Ribh Denounces Patrick," though this piece is not in the ballad tradition). Still other poems in the collection, instead of comparing bodies in this world with spirits in the other world, use sexual symbolism to ponder the conundrums of the body-soul relationship here on earth, a theme reminiscent of "Among School Children." The Lady's three songs in the "Three Bushes" series fall into this category. Finally, Yeats sometimes uses the transience of sexual experience to parallel the ephemeral nature of all human experience, especially such heightened moments as mystic vision or artistic inspiration. Such an ironic self-consuming quality inherent in the sex act is touched on in the first stanza of "Crazy Jane and Jack the Journeyman" and in "Her Anxiety," among other places.

### "UNDER BEN BULBEN"

As indicated earlier in the biographical section, Yeats continued to work on poems and plays right down to the last day but one before his death. Although "Under Ben Bulben" was not his last poem, it was written quite consciously as a valedictory or testamentary piece in the summer and fall of 1938, when Yeats knew that death was not far away. Although such a status for the poem has been widely recognized by authorities from a very early date, surprisingly little has been written about it until relatively recently.

Ben Bulben is the impressive west-Irish headland "under" whose shadow Yeats specified that his body be buried in the churchyard at Drumcliff where his great-grandfather had been rector a century earlier. In draft versions, "Under Ben Bulben" had two previous titles: "His Convictions" and "Creed." Furthermore, the opening lines that read "Swear by" in the finished poem originally read "I believe." Here, then, presumably, if anywhere, one should be able to find Yeats's final views on life and the human condition. Because the poem goes on, however, to indicate quite candid belief in the existence of supernatural spirits and, further still, in reincarnation or transmigration of the soul, modern critics who do not accept such quasireligious views have evidently declined to take the piece very seriously. One apparent consequence has been that they have had little adequate basis for understanding or glossing the epitaph with which the poem concludes.

Ironically, the epitaph has been very often quoted: "Cast a cold eye/ On life, on death./ Horseman, pass by!" Exegetical commentary on these three lines, however, has been almost as rare as that on the larger poem.

Explication has been so minimal and inconclusive, in fact, that as late as 1974 one spokesperson, Edward Malins, asserted that determination of the epitaph's meaning and its intended audience "is anybody's guess." In terms of the framing poem's thesis of transmigration, however, along with evidence from other sources, the horseman can be identified as Yeats himself, a cosmic journeyer engaged in a vast round of cyclical deaths and rebirths, as outlined in *A Vision*. A cold eye is cast on both life and death because the point of possible release from the wheel of reincarnation to some ultimate beatific state such as that imaged in "Sailing to Byzantium" is at such great distance that the grave is little more than a way station on the cosmic odyssey. Thus, there is time or place for little more than a passing nod or glance toward either life or death. In the words of a passage from *A Vision* that is virtually a prose counterpart of the epitaph's verse, man's spirit can know nothing more than transitory happiness either between birth and death or between death and rebirth; its goal is to "pass rapidly round its circle" and to "find freedom from that circle."

The means of passing rapidly around *A Vision*'s great wheel is to live each incarnation properly "in phase." Failure in this endeavor can cause rebirth again into the same phase, thus slowing progress toward "freedom" or release. From his youthful days as a disciple of Walter Pater, Yeats had long regarded the living of life itself as an art. With the coming of *A Vision*, teleological impetus was added to this aesthetic conviction. In a note on "Sailing to Byzantium" from a radio script and in several poems, Yeats exclaims that he must "make his soul." In the terms of *A Vision*, then, once he knew the prescribed qualities of his current incarnation or phase on the wheel, he must shape and sculpt his very life until it becomes a concrete manifestation of that phase, a mythopoeic *objet d'art*.

In *Autobiographies*, on the other hand, Yeats states that when great artists were at their most creative, the rest was not simply a work of art, but rather the "re-creation of the man through that art." Similarly, in a scrap of verse, he said that whenever he remade a poem, the real importance of the act was that, in the event, he actually remade himself. Thus emerged the ultimate unity. Yeats's life and his work became two sides of the

one coin. The phenomena were mutually interdependent, the processes mutually interactive. As he forged his poems, Yeats also created his self. That created self, a living myth, was in turn the image reflected in his poetry, the center of vision embodied in the verbal constructs of his art.

## Other major works

SHORT FICTION: *John Sherman and Dhoya*, 1891, 1969; *The Celtic Twilight*, 1893; *The Secret Rose*, 1897; *The Tables of Law; The Adoration of the Magi*, 1897; *Stories of Red Hanrahan*, 1904; *Mythologies*, 1959.

PLAYS: *The Countess Cathleen*, pb. 1892; *The Land of Heart's Desire*, pr., pb. 1894; *Cathleen ni Houlihan*, pr., pb. 1902; *The Pot of Broth*, pr. 1902 (with Lady Augusta Gregory); *The Hour-Glass*, pr. 1903, 1912; *The King's Threshold*, pr., pb. 1903 (with Lady Gregory); *On Baile's Strand*, pr. 1904; *Deirdre*, pr. 1906 (with Lady Gregory); *The Shadowy Waters*, pr. 1906; *The Unicorn from the Stars*, pr. 1907 (with Lady Gregory); *The Golden Helmet*, pr., pb. 1908; *The Green Helmet*, pr., pb. 1910; *At the Hawk's Well*, pr. 1916; *The Dreaming of the Bones*, pb. 1919; *The Only Jealousy of Emer*, pb. 1919; *The Player Queen*, pr. 1919; *Calvary*, pb. 1921; *Four Plays for Dancers*, 1921 (includes *Calvary*, *At the Hawk's Well*, *The Dreaming of the Bones*, and *The Only Jealousy of Emer*); *The Cat and the Moon*, pb. 1924; *The Resurrection*, pb. 1927; *The Words upon the Window-Pane*, pr. 1930; *The Collected Plays of W. B. Yeats*, 1934, 1952; *A Full Moon in March*, pr. 1934; *The King of the Great Clock Tower*, pr., pb. 1934; *The Herne's Egg*, pb. 1938; *Purgatory*, pr. 1938; *The Death of Cuchulain*, pb. 1939; *Variorum Edition of the Plays of W. B. Yeats*, 1966 (Russell K. Alspach, editor).

NONFICTION: *Ideas of Good and Evil*, 1903; *The Cutting of an Agate*, 1912; *Per Amica Silentia Lunae*, 1918; *Essays*, 1924; *A Vision*, 1925, 1937; *Autobiographies*, 1926, 1955; *A Packet for Ezra Pound*, 1929; *Essays, 1931-1936*, 1937; *The Autobiography of William Butler Yeats*, 1938; *On the Boiler*, 1939; *If I Were Four and Twenty*, 1940; *The Letters of W. B. Yeats*, 1954; *The Senate Speeches of W. B. Yeats*, 1960 (Donald R. Pearce, editor); *Essays and Introductions*, 1961; *Ex-*

*plorations*, 1962; *Ah, Sweet Dancer: W. B. Yeats, Margot Ruddock—A Correspondence*, 1970 (Roger McHugh, editor); *Uncollected Prose by W. B. Yeats*, 1970, 1976 (2 volumes); *Memoirs*, 1972; *The Collected Letters of W. B. Yeats*, 1986-2005 (4 volumes); *Early Articles and Reviews: Uncollected Articles and Reviews Written Between 1886 and 1900*, 2004 (John P. Frayne and Madeleine Marchaterre, editors).

MISCELLANEOUS: *The Collected Works in Verse and Prose of William Butler Yeats*, 1908; *The Collected Works of W. B. Yeats*, 1989-2008 (13 volumes).

BIBLIOGRAPHY

Chaudhry, Yug Mohit. *Yeats, the Irish Literary Revival, and the Politics of Print*. Cork, Ireland: Cork University Press, 2001. A study of Yeats's political and social views as well as a critique of his writings. Bibliography and index.

Foster, R. F. *W. B. Yeats: A Life*. 2 vols. New York: Oxford University Press, 1997-2003. An excellent, extensive guide to Yeats and his work.

Greaves, Richard. *Transition, Reception, and Modernism in W. B. Yeats*. New York: Palgrave, 2002. In examining Yeats's poetry of 1902 to 1916, Greaves rejects the label of "modernist" and instead analyzes Yeats's poetry from the context of the poet's life.

Grene, Nicholas. *Yeats's Poetic Codes*. New York: Oxford University Press, 2008. Grene examines the key words and habits of speech that shape Yeats's poetry, focusing on poetic technique to understand the work.

Holdeman, David. *The Cambridge Introduction to W. B. Yeats*. New York: Cambridge University Press, 2006. Examines Yeats's poems, drama, and stories in their cultural, historical, and literary contexts.

Howes, Marjorie, and John Kelly, eds. *The Cambridge Companion to W. B. Yeats*. New York: Cambridge University Press, 2006. Yeats scholars from the United States, England, and Ireland contributed eleven essays to this work, illuminating the personal and political events in Yeats's life. Howes and Kelly chronicle his early interests in theater, politics, and the occult, along with the portrayal of these topics in his writing. Includes a detailed time line, bibliography, and index.

Jeffares, A. Norman. *W. B. Yeats: A New Biography*. New York: Continuum, 2001. A biography of Yeats by a leading scholar of the writer.

Ross, David. *Critical Companion to William Butler Yeats: A Literary Reference to His Life and Work*. New York: Facts On File, 2008. A reference work that provides information on his life and critical analysis of his writings.

Vendler, Helen. *Our Secret Discipline: Yeats and Lyric Form*. Cambridge, Mass.: Harvard University Press, 2007. A guide to Yeats' poetry that focuses exclusively on his use of form and the ways in which meaning is derived from it. Useful to scholars and students of poetry.

*James Lovic Allen*

---

# EDWARD YOUNG

**Born:** Upham, England; July 3, 1683 (baptized)
**Died:** Welwyn, England; April 5, 1765

PRINCIPAL POETRY

*An Epistle to the Right Honourable the Lord Landsdowne*, 1713

*A Poem on the Last Day*, 1713

*The Force of Religion: Or, Vanquished Love, a Poem, in Two Books*, 1714

*On the Late Queen's Death, and His Majesty's Accession to the Throne*, 1714

*A Letter to Mr. Tickell Occasioned by the Death of Joseph Addison*, 1719

*A Paraphrase on Part of the Book of Job*, 1719

*The Instalment to the Right Honourable Sir Robert Walpole, Knight of the Most Noble Order of the Garter*, 1726

*Cynthio*, 1727

*Love of Fame, the Universal Passion: In Seven Characteristical Satires*, 1728 (verse satires)

*Ocean: An Ode Occasion'd by His Majesty's Late Royal Encouragement of the Sea-Service*, 1728

*Imperium Pelagi: A Naval Lyrick, Written in Imitation of Pindar's Spirit*, 1730

*Two Epistles to Mr. Pope, Concerning the Authors of the Age*, 1730

*The Foreign Address: Or, The Best Argument for Peace*, 1735

*The Poetical Works of the Reverend Edward Young*, 1741

*The Complaint: Or, Night-Thoughts on Life, Death, and Immortality*, 1742-1744 (commonly known as *Night-Thoughts*)

*Resignation: In Two Parts, and a Postscript*, 1762

## Other literary forms

Although Edward Young is known primarily for his poetry, he was also a successful playwright, theologian, and literary theorist. In 1719, Young's first play, *Busiris, King of Egypt* (pr., pb. 1719) had a successful run at the Theatre Royal in Drury Lane. His second play, *The Revenge* (pr., pb. 1721) was less successful in its initial production but more enduring. Declared by the great actor David Garrick to be "the best modern play," *The Revenge* was frequently revived throughout the eighteenth and nineteenth centuries. In 1753, Garrick produced Young's final tragedy, *The Brothers* (pr., pb. 1753).

In several prose works, Young addressed the religious controversies of his age. Anticipating the themes of his later poetry, *A Vindication of Providence: Or, A True Estimate of Human Life* (1728) examines the effect of passion on human happiness. *The Centaur Not Fabulous: In Six Letters to a Friend on the Life in Vogue* (1755) uses satire to defend Christianity from the assaults of deism and licentiousness.

In 1728, Young completed his first work of literary theory, "A Discourse on Ode," which was published with *Ocean*. In 1759, at the age of seventy-six, Young published *Conjectures on Original Composition in a Letter to the Author of Sir Charles Grandison* (1759; better known as *Conjectures on Original Composition*), a work that anticipates many ideas associated with Romanticism.

## Achievements

During his lifetime, Edward Young established connections with some of the leading authors of his time, including Joseph Addison, Alexander Pope, Jonathan Swift, Joseph Warton, and Samuel Richardson. Because of his achievements both as a member of the clergy and as a poet, Young was well respected by his contemporaries, and his poems were successful.

Unlike other poets of his age, Young rejected many of the principles of neoclassicism. Whereas poets like Pope sought to imitate classical authors and replicate the order they found in nature, Young believed poetry should explore the experiences of the individual, especially those experiences that remain inexplicably mysterious. As he wrote in *Night-Thoughts*, "Nothing can satisfy, but what confounds;/ Nothing, but what astonishes, is true." Recognizing the unique quality of his work, Warton described Young as a "sublime and original genius." Samuel Johnson remained more guarded, concluding, "with all his defects, he was a man of genius and a poet."

Young's work had considerable influence on later poets, especially those associated with British Romanticism (notably William Blake and Samuel Taylor Coleridge) and with the Storm and Stress movement in Germany (Friedrich Gottlieb Klopstock and Johann Wolfgang von Goethe).

## Biography

Edward Young was born in July, 1683, the son of a prominent clergyman and godson of Princess Anne. At age eleven, he enrolled in Winchester College. In 1702, Young was admitted to New College, Oxford, but he left without a degree after his father's death in 1705. He eventually completed both the bachelor of laws degree in 1714 and the doctor of laws degree in 1719 at All Souls College, Oxford. While working on his degrees, Young established himself as a poet and sought to secure financial support from a patron. In 1713, he published his first poem, *An Epistle to the Right Honourable the Lord Landsdowne*. During that same year, Young completed *A Poem on the Last Day*, which was dedicated to Queen Anne, whose illness and subsequent death provided the occasions for Young's next poems in 1714: *The Force of Religion* and *On the Late Queen's Death, and His Majesty's Accession to the Throne*.

Young continued his search for patronage, eventually receiving an annuity from the duke of Wharton. In

1719, Young published *A Paraphrase on Part of the Book of Job*, which shows his continued interest in the religious sublime, and *A Letter to Mr. Tickell Occasioned by the Death of Joseph Addison*, a loving tribute to Young's friend Addison, who died in 1719. Over the next several years, Young completed three plays and took deacon's orders in the Anglican Church. Turning his attention toward satire, Young completed several works that were collectively published in 1728 under the title *Love of Fame, the Universal Passion*. These satires helped Young secure a royal pension of two hundred pounds per year. He became a royal chaplain to the king in 1728 and published a patriotic poem, *Ocean*. In 1730, Young became rector at Welwyn, Hertfordshire. He continued writing both satire (*Two Epistles to Mr. Pope*) and occasional verse (*Imperium Pelagi*), hoping to receive more substantial preferment.

In 1731, Young married Lady Elizabeth Lee, a widow with three children and the granddaughter of Charles II. Young's son Frederick was born in 1732. After suffering the loss of his stepdaughter, his friend Henry Temple, and his wife, Young began writing his most famous poetry, *Night-Thoughts*, which was published between 1742 and 1744 and collected in a single edition in 1750. During this time, Young established friendships with the duchess of Portland, who campaigned in vain for his advancement, and the novelist Richardson, who contributed to *The Centaur Not Fabulous* and *Conjectures on Original Composition*. In 1762, at the age of seventy-nine, Young published his last poem, *Resignation*. Following a long illness, Young died on April 5, 1765.

## ANALYSIS

Focusing attention exclusively on his most distinctive work, *Night-Thoughts*, modern readers frequently overlook much of Edward Young's achievement. By the time he began writing *Night-Thoughts* in the 1740's, Young had been a successful poet for almost thirty years. Although there are common thematic concerns present in many of Young's works, his poetry is most notable for its diversity.

### A POEM ON THE LAST DAY

One of Young's first published works, *A Poem on the Last Day* celebrates the Peace of Utrecht (1713),

*Edward Young* (©Michael Nicholson/CORBIS)

which ended the War of the Spanish Succession. Rather than offering a simple patriotic poem, Young uses the occasion of peace to explore the impermanence of all worldly things. The three-book poem, written with epic tone and in heroic couplets, begins with a survey of the natural world. Although nature seems to assert God's continual presence—"How great, how firm, how sacred, all appears!"—the world remains mutable and full of sin. Individuals, Young argues, should never forget the judgment of the last day. Recognizing that true greatness cannot be achieved during life, Young instructs his reader to tread on "virtues path" and to inherit divine knowledge and eternal salvation after death: "Thou, minor, canst not guess thy vast estate,/ What stores, on foreign coasts, thy landing wait."

### THE FORCE OF RELIGION

A narrative poem written in heroic couplets, *The Force of Religion* recalls Lady Jane Grey's final hours before being executed by Mary Tudor. Celebrating the spiritual triumph of Protestantism over Catholicism, the poem addresses England's fear of Jacobism during the final days of Queen Anne's reign. Young's purpose, however, exceeds the immediate political crises of his time. *The Force of Religion*, like *A Poem on the Last Day* and much of Young's later poetry, ultimately explores the conflict between the earthly and the eternal.

### LOVE OF FAME, THE UNIVERSAL PASSION

Satire, the most characteristic form of eighteenth century literature, can be divided into two forms: Horatian and Juvenalian. In the preface to *Love of Fame, the Universal Passion*, Young places his work within the good-natured Horatian tradition:

> laughing satire bids the fairest for success. . . . This kind of satire only has any delicacy in it. . . . Horace is the best master: he appears in good humour while he censures.

In contrast to harsh, vituperative Juvenalian satirists like Swift, Young assumes that human folly can be corrected through humor. Like Addison and Richard Steele, who also wrote Horatian satire, Young structures his work around fictional characters who exemplify the specific follies. Although Young's use of character is unique in verse satire, he follows the traditions of his age by writing in heroic couplets and including elements of the mock epic.

For modern readers, the most interesting—and perhaps infuriating—satires are those that address women. Like other eighteenth century writers, Young calls for women to accept a subordinate role and warns them against worldly and intellectual ambition. For Young, "Women were made to give our [male] eyes delight," and they should "Beware the fever of the mind!" At times Young's satire loses its Horatian tone and becomes distinctly Juvenalian as he oscillates between celebrating feminine virtue and ridiculing feminine vice.

Young's satire ends with an acknowledgment that the love of fame is, if rightly applied, a divine gift that can lead individuals, such as George II, Queen Caroline, and Robert Walpole, to great and benevolent accomplishments.

### NIGHT-THOUGHTS

Critics have argued that *Night-Thoughts* originated as a response to Pope's *An Essay on Man* (1733-1734), which urges the reader to focus attention on the earthly and knowable. Hoping to show his reader the significance of the mysterious and sublime, Young reverses Pope's earthbound approach and sings of "immortal man." Through a series of nine meditative poems, an older speaker, sometimes assumed to be Young himself, councils Lorenzo, a younger man of pleasure who is inclined toward both atheism and deism.

Like other eighteenth century writers, Young initially argues for God's presence and human immortality from empirical evidence. Proclaiming that devotion is the "daughter of astronomy," Young suggests that the divine can be discovered through science. This argument, however, cannot persuade Lorenzo, who, as David B. Morris states, "will not be *argued* into faith." The speaker then explores the mysterious world of the night. In so doing, he does not reject reason but asserts that it must be aided by passion and feeling: "to feel, is to be fir'd;/ And to believe, Lorenzo! is to feel."

Although Young's poetry explores mortality and grief, his night is not a gloomy, melancholy place. Unlike the graveyard poets, such as Robert Blair and Thomas Parnell, who were fascinated by the physical and psychological horror of death, Young finds reconciliation and spiritual resurrection in the night. Near the end of the poem, the speaker proclaims, "Of darkness, now, no more:/ Joy breaks; shines; triumphs; 'tis eternal day." Having experienced the night in an emotional and deeply personal way, the speaker ends the poem with a hopefulness that sees beyond mortality.

OTHER MAJOR WORKS

PLAYS: *Busiris, King of Egypt*, pr., pb. 1719; *The Revenge*, pr., pb. 1721; *The Brothers*, pr., pb. 1753 (wr. 1724).

NONFICTION: *A Vindication of Providence: Or, A True Estimate of Human Life*, 1728; *An Apology for Princes: Or, The Reverence Due to Government*, 1729; *The Centaur Not Fabulous: In Six Letters to a Friend on the Life in Vogue*, 1755; *An Argument Drawn from the Circumstances of Christ's Death for the Truth of His Religion*, 1758; *Conjectures on Original Composition in a Letter to the Author of Sir Charles Grandison*, 1759 (better known as *Conjectures on Original Composition*).

MISCELLANEOUS: *The Complete Works, Poetry and Prose, of the Rev. Edward Young*, 1854.

BIBLIOGRAPHY

Edgecombe, Rodney Stenning. "Edward Young, William J. Cory, Virgil, and Callimachus." *Notes and Queries* 55, no. 4 (December, 2008): 408-410. Takes a phrase on the passage of time that Young, Cory, Vergil, and Callimachus used, with the more modern poets borrowing from Callimachus.

_____. "Some Youngian Echoes in Wordsworth." *Notes and Queries* 56, no. 3 (September, 2009): 364. Argues that influences from the poetry of Young can be found in the work of William Wordsworth.

Forester, Harold. *Edward Young: The Poet of "The Night Thoughts," 1683-1765*. New York: Erskin, 1986. Containing a wealth of information, this biography provides a thorough investigation of Young's career and his position within eighteenth century British culture.

Irlam, Shaun. *Elations: The Poetics of Enthusiasm in Eighteenth-Century Britain*. Stanford, Calif.: Stanford University Press, 1999. Takes the concept of enthusiasm and examines the aesthetic theory and poetry of Young and James Thomson.

Morris, David B. *The Religious Sublime: Christian Poetry and Critical Tradition in Eighteenth Century England*. Lexington: University Press of Kentucky, 1972. Morris's study provides a particularly useful reading of *Night-Thoughts* and positions Young's work within the context of eighteenth century religious controversies.

Nussbaum, Felicity. *The Brink of All We Hate: English Satires on Women, 1660-1750*. Lexington: University Press of Kentucky, 1984. Nussbaum provides a cogent discussion of Young's frequently overlooked satire, *Love of Fame, the Universal Passion*.

Patey, Douglas Lane. "Art and Integrity: Concepts of Self in Alexander Pope and Edward Young." *Modern Philology* 83, no. 4 (1986): 364-378. Patey's essay examines the relationship between Alexander Pope's *An Essay on Man* and Young's *Night-Thoughts*.

St. John Bliss, Isabel. *Edward Young*. New York: Twayne, 1969. This older study still provides an excellent starting point for readers of Young's poetry.

Wanko, Cheryl L. "The Making of a Minor Poet: Edward Young and Literary Taxonomy." *English Studies* 72, no. 4 (1991): 355-367. Wanko argues convincingly that Young's reputation suffered throughout the twentieth century because of "our system of literary taxonomy." She demonstrates how eighteenth and nineteenth century appraisals of Young's work made him appear to be a literary anomaly.

*Christopher D. Johnson*

# RESOURCES

# EXPLICATING POETRY

Explicating poetry begins with a process of distinguishing the poem's factual and technical elements from the readers' emotional ones. Readers respond to poems in a variety of ways that may initially have little to do with the poetry itself but that result from the events in their own lives, their expectations of art, and their philosophical/theological/psychological complexion.

All serious readers hope to find poems that can blend with the elements of their personal backgrounds in such a way that for a moment or a lifetime their relationship to life and the cosmos becomes more meaningful. This is the ultimate goal of poetry, and when it happens—when meaning, rhythm, and sound fuse with the readers' emotions to create a unified experience—it can only be called the magic of poetry, for something has happened between reader and poet that is inexplicable in rational terms.

When a poem creates such an emotional response in readers, then it is at least a partial success. To be considered excellent, however, a poem must also be able to pass a critical analysis to determine whether it is mechanically superior. Although twenty-first century criticism has tended to judge poetic works solely on their individual content and has treated them as independent of historical influences, such a technique often makes a full explication difficult. The best modern readers realize that good poetry analysis observes all aspects of a poem: its technical success, its historical importance and intellectual force, and its effect on readers' emotions.

Students of poetry will find it useful to begin an explication by analyzing the elements that poets have at their disposal as they create their art: dramatic situation, point of view, imagery, metaphor, symbol, meter, form, and allusion. The outline headed "Checklist for Explicating a Poem" (see page 1358) will help guide the reader through the necessary steps to a detailed explication.

Although explication is not a science, and a variety of observations may be equally valid, these step-by-step procedures can be applied systematically to make the reading of most poems a richer experience for the reader. To illustrate, these steps are applied below to a difficult poem by Edwin Arlington Robinson.

### Luke Havergal

Go to the western gate, Luke Havergal,
There where the vines cling crimson on the wall,
And in the twilight wait for what will come.
The leaves will whisper there of her, and some,   4
Like flying words, will strike you as they fall;
But go, and if you listen, she will call.
Go to the western gate, Luke Havergal—
Luke Havergal.         8

No, there is not a dawn in eastern skies
To rift the fiery night that's in your eyes;
But there, where western glooms are gathering,
The dark will end the dark, if anything:   12
God slays Himself with every leaf that flies,
And hell is more than half of paradise.
No, there is not a dawn in eastern skies—
In eastern skies.       16

Out of a grave I come to tell you this,
Out of a grave I come to quench the kiss
That flames upon your forehead with a glow
That blinds you to the way that you must go.   20
Yes, there is yet one way to where she is,
Bitter, but one that faith may never miss.
Out of a grave I come to tell you this—
To tell you this.       24

There is the western gate, Luke Havergal
There are the crimson leaves upon the wall.
Go, for the winds are tearing them away,—
Nor think to riddle the dead words they say,   28
Nor any more to feel them as they fall;
But go, and if you trust her she will call.
There is the western gate, Luke Havergal—
Luke Havergal.

E. A. Robinson, 1897

## STEP I-A: *Before reading*

1. "Luke Havergal" is a strophic poem composed of four equally lengthened stanzas. Each stanza is long enough to contain a narrative, an involved description or situation, or a problem and resolution.

2. The title raises several possibilities: Luke Havergal

# CHECKLIST FOR EXPLICATING A POEM

I. THE INITIAL READINGS

A. Before reading the poem, the reader should:
1. Notice its form and length.
2. Consider the title, determining, if possible, whether it might function as an allusion, symbol, or poetic image.
3. Notice the date of composition or publication, and identify the general era of the poet.

B. The poem should be read intuitively and emotionally and be allowed to "happen" as much as possible.

C. In order to establish the rhythmic flow, the poem should be reread. A note should be made as to where the irregular spots (if any) are located.

II. EXPLICATING THE POEM

A. *Dramatic situation*. Studying the poem line by line helps the reader discover the dramatic situation. All elements of the dramatic situation are interrelated and should be viewed as reflecting and affecting one another. The dramatic situation serves a particular function in the poem, adding realism, surrealism, or absurdity; drawing attention to certain parts of the poem; and changing to reinforce other aspects of the poem. All points should be considered. The following questions are particularly helpful to ask in determining dramatic situation:
1. What, if any, is the narrative action in the poem?
2. How many personae appear in the poem? What part do they take in the action?
3. What is the relationship between characters?
4. What is the setting (time and location) of the poem?

B. *Point of view*. An understanding of the poem's point of view is a major step toward comprehending the poet's intended meaning. The reader should ask:
1. Who is the speaker? Is he or she addressing someone else or the reader?
2. Is the narrator able to understand or see everything happening to him or her, or does the reader know things that the narrator does not?
3. Is the narrator reliable?
4. Do point of view and dramatic situation seem consistent? If not, the inconsistencies may provide clues to the poem's meaning.

C. *Images and metaphors*. Images and metaphors are often the most intricately crafted vehicles of the poem for relaying the poet's message. Realizing that the images and metaphors work in harmony with the dramatic situation and point of view will help the reader to see the poem as a whole, rather than as disassociated elements.
1. The reader should identify the concrete images (that is, those that are formed from objects that can be touched, smelled, seen, felt, or tasted). Is the image projected by the poet consistent with the physical object?
2. If the image is abstract, or so different from natural imagery that it cannot be associated with a real object, then what are the properties of the image?
3. To what extent is the reader asked to form his or her own images?

4. Is any image repeated in the poem? If so, how has it been changed? Is there a controlling image?
5. Are any images compared to each other? Do they reinforce one another?
6. Is there any difference between the way the reader perceives the image and the way the narrator sees it?
7. What seems to be the narrator's or persona's attitude toward the image?

D. *Words*. Every substantial word in a poem may have more than one intended meaning, as used by the author. Because of this, the reader should look up many of these words in the dictionary and:
1. Note all definitions that have the slightest connection with the poem.
2. Note any changes in syntactical patterns in the poem.
3. In particular, note those words that could possibly function as symbols or allusions, and refer to any appropriate sources for further information.

E. *Meter, rhyme, structure, and tone*. In scanning the poem, all elements of prosody should be noted by the reader. These elements are often used by a poet to manipulate the reader's emotions, and therefore they should be examined closely to arrive at the poet's specific intention.
1. Does the basic meter follow a traditional pattern such as those found in nursery rhymes or folk songs?
2. Are there any variations in the base meter? Such changes or substitutions are important thematically and should be identified.
3. Are the rhyme schemes traditional or innovative, and what might their form mean to the poem?
4. What devices has the poet used to create sound patterns (such as assonance and alliteration)?
5. Is the stanza form a traditional or innovative one?
6. If the poem is composed of verse paragraphs rather than stanzas, how do they affect the progression of the poem?
7. After examining the above elements, is the resultant tone of the poem casual or formal, pleasant, harsh, emotional, authoritative?

F. *Historical context*. The reader should attempt to place the poem into historical context, checking on events at the time of composition. Archaic language, expressions, images, or symbols should also be looked up.

G. *Themes and motifs*. By seeing the poem as a composite of emotion, intellect, craftsmanship, and tradition, the reader should be able to determine the themes and motifs (smaller recurring ideas) presented in the work. He or she should ask the following questions to help pinpoint these main ideas:
1. Is the poet trying to advocate social, moral, or religious change?
2. Does the poet seem sure of his or her position?
3. Does the poem appeal primarily to the emotions, to the intellect, or to both?
4. Is the poem relying on any particular devices for effect (such as imagery, allusion, paradox, hyperbole, or irony)?

could be a specific person; Luke Havergal could represent a type of person; the name might have symbolic or allusive qualities. Thus, "Luke" may refer to Luke of the Bible or "Luke-warm," meaning indifferent or showing little or no zeal. "Havergal" could be a play on words. "Haver" is a Scotch and Northern English word meaning to talk foolishly. It is clear from the rhyme words that the "gal" of Havergal is pronounced as if it had two "l's," but it is spelled with one "l" for no apparent reason unless it is to play on the word "gal," meaning girl. Because it is pronounced "gall," meaning something bitter or severe, a sore or state of irritation, or an impudent self-assurance, this must also be considered as a possibility. Finally, the "haver" of "Havergal" might be a perversion of "have a."

3. Published in 1897, the poem probably does not contain archaic language unless it is deliberately used. The period of writing is known as the Victorian Age. Historical events that may have influenced the poem may be checked for later.

## STEP I-B: *The poem should be read*

## STEP I-C: *Rereading the poem*

The frequent use of internal caesuras in stanzas 1 and 2 contrast with the lack of caesuras in stanzas 3 and 4. There are end-stopped lines and much repetition. The poem reads smoothly except for line 28 and the feminine ending on lines 11 and 12.

## STEP II-A: *Dramatic situation*

In line 1 of "Luke Havergal," an unidentified speaker is addressing Luke. Because the speaker calls him by his full name, there is a sense that the speaker has assumed a superior (or at least a formal) attitude toward Luke and that the talk that they are having is not a casual conversation.

In addition to knowing something about the relationship in line 1, the reader is led to think, because of the words "go to the western gate," that the personae must be near some sort of enclosed house or city. Perhaps Luke and the speaker are at some "other" gate, since the western gate is specifically pointed out.

Line 2 suggests that the situation at the western gate is different from that elsewhere—there "vines cling crimson on the wall," hinting at some possibilities

about the dramatic situation. (Because flowers and colors are always promising symbols, they must be carefully considered later.)

The vines in line 2 could provide valuable information about the dramatic situation, except that in line 2 the clues are ambiguous. Are the vines perennial? If so, their crimson color suggests that the season is late summer or autumn. Crimson might also be their natural color when in full bloom. Further, are they grape vines (grapes carry numerous connotations and symbolic values), and are the vines desirable? All of this in line 2 is ambiguous. The only certainty is that there is a wall—a barrier that closes something in and something out.

In lines 1-3, the speaker again commands Luke to go and wait. Since Luke is to wait in the twilight, it is probably now daylight. All Luke must do is be passive because whatever is to come will happen without any action on his part.

In line 4, the speaker begins to tell Luke what will happen at the western gate, and the reader now knows that Luke is waiting for something with feminine characteristics, possibly a woman. This line also mentions that the vines have leaves, implying that crimson denotes their waning stage.

In line 5, the speaker continues to describe what will happen at the western gate: The leaves will whisper about "her," and as they fall, some of them will strike Luke "like flying words." The reader, however, must question whether Luke will actually be "struck" by the leaves, or whether the leaves are being personified or being used as an image or symbol. In line 6, the speaker stops his prophecy and tells Luke to leave. If Luke listens, "she" will call, but if he does not, it is unclear what will happen. The reader might ask the questions, to whom is "she" calling, and from where?

In summarizing the dramatic situation in stanza 1, one can say that the speaker is addressing Luke, but it is not yet possible to determine whether he or she is present or whether Luke is thinking to himself (interior monologue). The time is before twilight; the place is near a wall with a gate. Luke is directed to go to the gate and listen for a female voice to call.

From reading the first line in the second stanza, it is apparent that Luke has posed some kind of question, probably concerned with what will be found at the western gate. The answer given is clearly not a direct answer to whatever question was asked, especially as the directions "east" and "west" are probably symbolic. The reader can expect, however, that the silent persona's response will affect the poem's progress.

Stanza 3 discloses who the speaker is and what his relationship is to Luke. After the mysterious discourse in stanza 2, Luke has probably asked "Who are you?" The equally mysterious reply in stanza 3 raises the issue of whether the voice speaking is a person or a spirit or whether it is Luke's imagination or conscience.

Because the voice says that it comes out of the grave, the reader cannot know who or what it is. It may be a person, a ghost, or only Luke's imagination or conscience. Obviously the answer will affect the dramatic situation.

In line 18, the reader learns that the speaker is on a particular mission: "to quench the kiss," and the reader can assume that when the mission is complete he or she will return to the grave. This information is sudden and shocking, and because of this sharp jolt, the reader tends to believe the speaker and credit him or her with supernatural knowledge.

In stanza 4, it becomes apparent that Luke and the speaker have not been stationary during the course of the poem because the western gate is now visible; the speaker can see the leaves upon the wall (line 26).

The wind is blowing (line 27), creating a sense of urgency, because if all the leaves are blown away they cannot whisper about "her." The speaker gives Luke final instructions, and the poem ends with the speaker again pointing toward the place where Luke will find the female persona.

In summary, one can say that the dramatic situation establishes a set of mysterious circumstances that are not explained or resolved on the dramatic level. Luke has been told to go to the western gate by someone who identifies himself or herself as having come from the grave in order to quench Luke's desire, which seems to be connected with the estranged woman, who is, perhaps, dead. The dramatic situation does not tell whether the commanding voice is an emissary from the woman or from the devil, or is merely Luke's conscience; nor does it suggest that something evil will happen to Luke at the western gate, although other elements in the poem make the reader afraid for him.

The poet, then, is using the dramatic situation to draw the reader into questions which will be answered by other means; at this point, the poem is mysterious, obscure, ambiguous, and deliberately misleading.

## STEP II-B: *Point of view*

There are a number of questions that immediately come to mind about the point of view. Is the speaker an evil seducer, or is he or she a friend telling Luke about death? Why is the poem told from his or her point of view?

From a generalized study, readers know that the first-person singular point of view takes the reader deep into the mind of the narrator in order to show what he or she knows or to show a personal reaction to an event.

In "Luke Havergal," the narrator gives the following details about himself and the situation: a sense of direction (lines 1 and 9); the general type and color of the vegetation, but not enough to make a detailed analysis of it (line 2); a pantheistic view of nature (line 4); a feeling of communication with the leaves and "her" (lines 5 and 6); a philosophic view of the universe (stanza 2); the power to "quench the kiss," a sense of mission, and a home—the grave (line 18); special vision (line 20); a sense of destiny (lines 21 and 22); and a sense of time and eternity (lines 27 through 29).

Apparently, the narrator can speak with confidence about the western gate, and can look objectively at Luke to see the kiss on his forehead. Such a vantage point suggests that the speaker might represent some aspect of death. He also knows the "one way to where she is," leaving it reasonable to infer that "she" is dead.

There is another possibility in regard to the role of the speaker. He might be part of Luke himself—the voice of his thoughts, of his unconscious mind—or of part of his past. This role might possibly be combined with that of some sort of spirit of death.

The poem, then, is an internal dialogue in which Luke is attempting to cope with "she," who is probably dead and who might well have been his lover, though neither is certain. He speaks to another persona, which is probably Luke's own spirit which has been deadened by the loss of his lover.

Once it is suggested that Luke is a man who is at the depth of despair, the dramatic situation becomes very important because of the possibility that Luke may be driving himself toward self-destruction.

The dramatic situation, therefore, may not be as it originally seemed; perhaps there is only one person, not two. Luke's psychological condition permits him to look at himself as another person, and this other self is pushing Luke toward the western gate, a place that the reader senses is evil.

If the voice is Luke's, then much of the mystery is clarified. Luke would have known what the western gate looked like, whereas a stranger would have needed supernatural powers to know it; furthermore, Luke had probably heard the leaves whispering before, and in his derangement he could believe that someone would call to him if he would only listen.

Establishing point of view has cleared up most of the inconsistencies in this poem's dramatic situation, but there is still confusion about the grave and the kiss. It is easy to make the grave symbolically consistent with point of view, but the reader should look for other possibilities before settling on this explanation.

In stanzas 1 and 2, there is no problem; the dramatic situation is simple and point of view can be reconciled since there is no evidence to prove that another person is present. If, however, the voice is that of Luke's other self, then why has it come from the grave, and where did the kiss come from? At this point, it is not possible to account for these inconsistencies, but by noting them now, the reader can be on the alert for the answers later. Quite possibly accounting for the inconsistencies will provide the key for the explication.

**STEP II-C: *Images and metaphors***

Finding images in poems is usually not a difficult task, although seeing their relation to the theme often is. "Luke Havergal" is imagistically difficult because the images are introduced, then reused as the theme develops.

In stanza 1, the reader is allowed to form his or her own image of the setting and mood at the western gate; most readers will probably imagine some sort of mysterious or supernatural situation related to death or the dead. The colors, the sound of the words, and the particular images (vines, wall, whispering leaves) establish the relationship between the living and the dead as the controlling image of the entire poem.

Within the controlling death-in-life image, the metaphors and conceits are more difficult to handle. Vines clinging crimson on the wall (line 2) and waiting in the twilight for something to come (line 3) are images requiring no particular treatment at this point, but in lines 4 and 5 the reader is forced to contend directly with whispering leaves that are like flying words, and there are several metaphorical possibilities for this image.

First, there is the common image of leaves rustling in a breeze, and in a mysterious or enchanted atmosphere it would be very easy to imagine that they are whispering. Such a whisper, however, would ordinarily require a moderate breeze, as a fierce wind would overpower the rustling sound of leaves; but there is more ambiguity in the image: "The leaves will whisper there for her, and some,/ Like flying words, will strike you as they fall."

Because of the syntactical ambiguity of "some,/ Like flying words, will strike," the reader cannot be sure how close or literal is the similarity or identity of "leaves" and "words." The reader cannot be completely sure whether it is leaves or words or both that will strike Luke, or whether the sight of falling leaves might be forcing him to recall words he has heard in the past. There is a distinct metaphoric connection between leaves and words, however, and these in some way strike Luke, perhaps suggesting that the words are those of an argument (an argument in the past between Luke and "her" before her death) or perhaps meant to suggest random words which somehow recall "her" but do not actually say anything specific.

In stanza 2, the poet forces the reader to acknowledge the light and dark images, but they are as obscure as the falling leaves in stanza 1. The dawn that the reader is asked to visualize (line 9) is clear, but it is immediately contrasted with "the fiery night that's in your eyes"; Luke's smoldering, almost diabolic eyes are imagistically opposed to the dawn.

Line 11 returns to the western gate, or at least to the "west," where twilight is falling. The "western glooms" become imagistic as the twilight falls and depicts Luke's despair. Twilight is not "falling," but dark is "gathering" around him, and glooms not only denotes darkness but also connotes Luke's emotional state.

The paradox in line 12, "The dark will end the dark," beckons the reader to explore it imagistically, but it is not easy to understand how darkness relieves darkness, unless one of the two "darknesses" is symbolic of death or of Luke's gloom. With this beckoning image, the poet has created emphasis on the line and teases with images which may really be symbols or paradoxes. The same thing is true for lines 13 and 14, which tempt the reader to imagine how "God slays Himself" with leaves, and how "hell is more than half of paradise."

The beginning of stanza 3 does not demand an image so much as it serves to tell where the narrator comes from, and to present the narrator's method for quenching the kiss. Line 19, however, presents an image that is as forceful as it is ambiguous. The kiss, which may be the kiss of the estranged woman, or "the kiss of death," or both, flames with a glow, which is also paradoxical. The paradox, however, forms an image which conveys the intensity of Luke's passion.

Stanza 4 returns to the imagery of stanza 1, but now the whispering leaves take on a metaphorical extension. If the leaves are whispering words from the dead, and if the leaves are "her" words, then once the wind tears all the leaves away, there will no longer be any medium for communication between the living and the dead. This adds a sense of urgency for Luke to go to the western gate and do there what must be done.

In summary, the images in "Luke Havergal" do more than set the mood; they also serve an important thematic function because of their ambiguities and paradoxical qualities.

## STEP II-D: *Words*

Because the poem is not too old, the reader will find that most of the words have not changed much. It is still important, however, for the reader to look up words as they may have several diverse meanings. Even more important to consider in individual words or phrases, however, is the possibility that they might be symbolic or allusive.

"Luke Havergal" is probably not as symbolic as it at first appears, although poems that use paradox and allusion are often very symbolic. Clearly the western gate is symbolic, but to what degree is questionable. No doubt it represents the last light in Luke's life, and once he passes beyond it he moves into another type of existence. The west and the twilight are points of embarka-

tion; the sun is setting in the west, but even though the sun sets, there will not be a dawn in the east to dispel Luke's dark gloom. Traditionally the dark, which is gathering in the west, is symbolic of death (the west is also traditionally associated with death), and only the dark will end Luke's gloom in life, if anything at all can do it.

There is one important allusion in the poem, which comes in stanza 3; the kiss which the speaker is going to quench may be the "kiss of death," the force that can destroy Luke.

In both concept and language, stanza 3 is reminiscent of the dagger scene and killing of Duncan (act 2, scene 1) in William Shakespeare's *Macbeth* (pr. 1606). Just before the murder, Macbeth has visions of the dagger:

> Art thou not, fatal vision, sensible
> To feeling as to sight? or art thou but
> A dagger of the mind, a false creation,
> Proceeding from the heat-oppressed brain?
> I see thee yet, in form as palpable
> As this which now I draw.
> Thou marshall'st me the way that I was going

And a few lines later (act 2, scene 2) Lady Macbeth says:

> That which hath made them drunk hath made me bold;
> What hath quench'd them hath given me fire.

The reversal in point of view in "Luke Havergal" gives the poem added depth, which is especially enhanced by the comparison with Macbeth. The line, "That blinds you to the way that you must go" is almost a word-for-word equivalent of "Thou marshall'st me the way that I was going," except that in "Luke Havergal" whoever is with Luke is talking, while Macbeth himself is talking to the dagger.

The result of the allusion is that it is almost possible to imagine that it is the dagger that is talking to Luke, and the whole story of Macbeth becomes relevant to the poem because the reader suspects that Luke's end will be similar to Macbeth's.

The words of Lady Macbeth strengthen the allusion's power and suggest a male-female relationship that is leading Luke to his death, especially since, in the resolution of *Macbeth*, Lady Macbeth goes crazy and whispers to the spirits.

If the reader accepts the allusion as a part of the poem, the imagery is enhanced by the vivid descriptions in *Macbeth*. Most critics and writers agree that if a careful reader finds something that fits consistently into a poem, then it is "there" for all readers who see the same thing, whether the poet consciously put it there or not. Robinson undoubtedly read and knew Shakespeare, but it does not matter whether he deliberately alluded to *Macbeth* if the reader can show that it is important to the poem.

There is a basic problem with allusion and symbol that every explicator must resolve for himself: Did the poet intend a symbol or an allusion to be taken in the way that a particular reader has interpreted it? The New Critics answered this question by coining the term "intentional fallacy," meaning that the poet's *intention* is ultimately unimportant when considering the finished poem. It is possible that stanza 3 was not intended to allude to *Macbeth*, and it was simply by accident that Robinson used language similar to Shakespeare's. Perhaps Robinson never read *Macbeth*, or perhaps he read it once and those lines remained in his subconscious. In either case, the reader must decide whether the allusion is important to the meaning of the poem.

**STEP II-E:** *Meter, rhyme, structure, and tone*

Because "Luke Havergal" is a poem that depends so heavily on all the elements of prosody, it should be scanned carefully. Here is an example of scansion using the second stanza of the poem:

No, there/ is not/ a dawn/ in eas/tern skies
To rift/ the fie/ry night/ that's in/ your eyes;
But there,/ where wes/tern glooms/ are gath/ering,
The dark/ will end/ the dark,/ if an/ything:
God slays/ Himself/ with eve/ry leaf/ that flies,
And hell/ is more/ than half/ of par/adise.
No, there/ is not/ a dawn/ in east/ern skies—
In eas/tern skies.

The basic meter of the poem is iambic pentameter, with frequent substitutions, but every line except the last in each stanza contains ten syllables.

The stanza form in "Luke Havergal" is very intri-cate and delicate. It is only because of the structure that the heavy *a* rhyme (*aabbaaaa*) does not become monotonous; yet it is because of the *a* rhyme that the structure works so well.

The pattern for the first stanza works as follows:

| Line | Rhyme | Function |
|------|-------|----------|
| 1 | a | Sets up ideas and images for the stanza. |
| 2 | a | Describes or complements line 1. |
| 3 | b | Lines 3, 4, and 5 constitute the central part of the mood and the fears. The return to the a rhyme unifies lines 1-5. |
| 4 | b | |
| 5 | a | |
| 6 | a | Reflects on what has been said in lines 1-5; it serves to make the reader stop, and it adds a mysterious suggestion. |
| 7 | a | Continues the deceleration and reflection. |
| 8 | a | The repetition and dimeter line stop the stanza completely, and the effect is to prepare for a shift in thought, just as Luke's mind jumps from thought to thought. |

Stanza 2 works in a similar manner, except for lines 13 and 14, which tie the stanza together as a couplet. Thus, lines 13 and 14 both unify and reflect, while lines 15 and 16 in the final couplet continue to reflect while slowing down.

| Lines | Rhyme | Function |
|-------|-------|----------|
| 9 and 10 | a | Opening couplet. |
| 11 and 12 | b | Couplet in lines 11-12 contains the central idea and image. |
| 13 and 14 | a | Couplet in 13-14 reflects on that in 11-12, but the autonomy of this third couplet is especially strong. Whereas in stanza 1, only line 5 reflects on the beginning of the stanza to create unity, this entire couplet is now strongly associated with the first, with the effect of nearly equating Luke with God. |
| 15 and 16 | a | Final couplet reflects on the first and completes the stanza. |

Stanza 3 works in the same manner as stanza 2, while stanza 4 follows the pattern of stanza 1.

Each stanza is autonomous and does not need the others for continuation or progression in plot; each stanza appears to represent a different thought as Luke's mind jumps about.

The overall structure focuses on stanza 3, which is crucial to the theme. Stanzas 1 and 2 clearly present the problem: Luke knows that if he goes he will find "her," and the worst that can happen is that the darkness will remain. With stanza 3, however, there is a break in point of view as the narrator calls attention to himself.

With stanza 4 there is a return to the beginning, reinforced by the repetition of rhyme words; the difference between stanzas 4 and 1 is that the reader has felt the impact of stanza 3; structurally, whatever resolution there is will evolve out of the third stanza, or because of it.

The stanza form of "Luke Havergal" achieves tremendous unity and emphasis; the central image or idea presented in the *b* lines is reinforced in the remainder of the stanza by a tight-knit rhyme structure. There are several types of rhymes being used in the poem, all of which follow the traditional functions of their type. Stanza 1 contains full masculine end rhyme, with a full masculine internal rhyme in line 2 (*There where*). Lines 2 and 3 contain alliteration (*c* in line 2, *t* in line 3) also binding the lines more tightly.

With "go" occurring near the end of stanza 1 and "No" appearing as the first word in stanza 2, this rhyme becomes important in forming associations between lines. Lines 9, 10, 15, 16, and 18 form full masculine end rhyme, with line 14 "paradise" assonating with a full rhyme. Lines 11 and 12 are half falling rhymes; these lines also contain a full internal rhyme ("there," "where") and alliteration (*g* and *w* in line 11). "Dark" in line 12 is an exact internal rhyme. The *l* and *s* in "slays" and "flies" (line 14) create an effect similar to assonance; there is also an *h* alliteration in line 15.

In stanza 3, the plosive consonants *c* and *q* make an alliterative sound in line 18, binding "come" and "quench" together; there is also an *f* alliteration in line 19. All the end rhymes are full masculine in stanza 3 except line 21, which assonates. Stanza 4 contains full masculine end rhyme, with one internal rhyme ("they

say") in line 28, one alliteration in line 29, and consonance ("will call") in line 30.

In addition to its function in developing the stanza, rhyme in "Luke Havergal" has important influence on sound, and in associating particular words and lines.

In lines 1 and 2 of "Luke Havergal," there are a number of plosive consonants and long vowels, in addition to the internal rhyme and *c* alliteration. The cadence of these lines is slow, and they reverberate with "cling" and "crimson." The tone of these lines is haunting (which is consistent with the situation), and the rhythm and sound of the poem as a whole suggest an incantation; the speaker's voice is seductive and evil, which is important to the theme, because if Luke goes to the gate he may be persuaded to die, which is what the voice demands.

Through its seductive sound, the poem seems to be having the same effect on the reader that it does on Luke; that is, the reader feels, as Luke does, that there is an urgency in going to the gate before all the leaves are blown away, and that by hearing "her" call, his discomfort will be relieved. The reader, unable to see the evil forces at work in the last stanza, sympathizes with Luke, and thinks that the voice is benevolent.

Whereas sound can be heard and analyzed, tone is a composite of a number of things that the reader can feel only after coming to know the poem. The poet's attitude or tone may be noncommittal or it may be dogmatic (as in allegory); sometimes the tone will affect the theme, while at other times it comes as an aside to the theme.

Poems that attempt to initiate reform frequently have a more readily discernible tone than poems that make observations without judging too harshly, although this is not always true. "Luke Havergal" is, among other things, about how the presence of evil leads toward death, but the poet has not directly included his feelings about that theme. If there is an attitude, it is the poet's acceptance of the inevitability of death and the pain that accompanies it for the living.

Perhaps the poet is angry at how effectively death can seduce life; it is obvious that Robinson wants the poem to haunt and torment the reader, and in doing so make him or her conscious of the hold death has on humanity.

Luke must meet death part way; he must first go to

the gate before he can hear the dead words, which makes him partly responsible for death's hold over him. The tone of "Luke Havergal" is haunting and provocative.

## STEP II-F: *Historical context*

Finished in December, 1895, "Luke Havergal" was in Robinson's estimation a Symbolist poem. It is essential, then, that the explicator learn something about the Symbolist movement. If his or her explication is not in accord with the philosophy of the period, the reader must account for the discrepancy.

In a study of other Robinson poems, there are themes parallel to that of "Luke Havergal." One, for example, is that of the alienated self. If Robinson believes in the alienated self, then it is possible that the voice speaking in "Luke Havergal" is Luke's own, but in an alienated state. This view may add credence to an argument that the speaker is Luke's past or subconscious, though it by no means proves it. Although parallelisms may be good support for the explication, the reader must be careful not to misconstrue them.

## STEP II-G: *Themes and motifs, or correlating the parts*

Once the poem has been placed in context, the prosodic devices analyzed, and the function of the poetical techniques understood, they should be correlated, and any discrepancies should be studied for possible errors in explication. By this time, every line should be understood, so that stating what the poem is about is merely a matter of explaining the common points of all the area, supporting it with specific items from the poem, secondary sources, other poems, other critics, and history. The reader may use the specific questions given in the outline to help detail the major themes.

BIBLIOGRAPHY

Coleman, Kathleen. *Guide to French Poetry Explication.* New York: G. K. Hall, 1993.

Gioia, Dana, David Mason, and Meg Schoerke, eds. *Twentieth-Century American Poetics: Poets on the Art of Poetry.* Boston: McGraw-Hill, 2003.

Hirsch, Edward. *How to Read a Poem and Fall in Love with Poetry.* New York: Harcourt Brace, 1999.

Kohl, Herbert R. *A Grain of Poetry: How to Read Contemporary Poems and Make Them a Part of Your Life.* New York: HarperFlamingo, 1999.

Lennard, John. *The Poetry Handbook: A Guide to Reading Poetry for Pleasure and Practical Criticism.* 2d ed. New York: Oxford University Press, 2006.

Martínez, Nancy C., and Joseph G. R. Martínez. *Guide to British Poetry Explication.* 4 vols. Boston: G. K. Hall, 1991-1995.

Oliver, Mary. *A Poetry Handbook.* San Diego, Calif.: Harcourt Brace, 1994.

Preminger, Alex, et al., eds. *The New Princeton Encyclopedia of Poetry and Poetics.* 3d rev. ed. Princeton, N.J.: Princeton University Press, 1993.

Ryan, Michael. *A Difficult Grace: On Poets, Poetry, and Writing.* Athens: University of Georgia Press, 2000.

Statman, Mark. *Listener in the Snow: The Practice and Teaching of Poetry.* New York: Teachers & Writers Collaborative, 2000.

Steinman, Lisa M. *Invitation to Poetry: The Pleasures of Studying Poetry and Poetics.* Walden, Mass.: Wiley-Blackwell, 2008.

Strand, Mark, and Eavan Boland, eds. *The Making of a Poem: A Norton Anthology of Poetic Forms.* New York: W. W. Norton, 2000.

Wolosky, Shira. *The Art of Poetry: How to Read a Poem.* New York: Oxford University Press, 2001.

*Walton Beacham*

# LANGUAGE AND LINGUISTICS

Most humans past the infant stage have a spoken language and use it regularly for understanding and speaking, although much of the world's population is still illiterate and cannot read or write. Language is such a natural part of life that people tend to overlook it until they are presented with some special problem: They lose their sight or hearing, have a stroke, or are required to learn a foreign language. Of course, people may also study their own language, but seldom do they stand aside and view language for what it is—a complex human phenomenon with a history reaching back to humankind's beginnings. A study of the development of one language will often reveal intertwinings with other languages. Sometimes such knowledge enables linguists to construct family groups; just as often, the divergences among languages or language families are so great that separate typological variations are established.

True language is characterized by its systematic nature, its arbitrariness of vocabulary and structure, its vocality, and its basis in symbolism. Most linguists believe that language and thought are separate entities. Although language may be necessary to give foundation to thought, it is not, in itself, thinking. Many psychologists, however, contend that language is thought. An examination of language on the basis of these assertions reveals that each language is a purely arbitrary code or set of rules. There is no intrinsic necessity for any word to sound like or mean what it does. Language is essentially speech, and symbolism is somehow the philosophical undergirding of the whole linguistic process. The French author Madame de Staël (1766-1817) once wrote, in describing her native language, that language is even more: "It is not only a means of communicating thoughts, feeling and acts, but an instrument that one loves to play upon, and that stimulates the mental faculties much as music does for some people and strong drink for others."

## ORIGIN OF LANGUAGE

How did language originate? First, the evidence for the origin of language is so deeply buried in the past that it is unlikely that people shall ever be able to do more than speculate about the matter. If people had direct knowledge of humankind's immediate ancestors, they should be able to develop some evolutionary theory and be able to say, among other things, how speech production and changes in the brain are related. Some linguists maintain that language ability is innate, but this assertion, true though it may be, rests on the assumption of a monogenetic theory of humanity's origin. Few scholars today are content with the notion that the human race began with Adam and Eve.

According to the Bible, Adam is responsible for human speech. Genesis reports:

> And out of the ground the Lord God formed every beast of the field, and every fowl of the air, and brought them unto Adam to see what he would call them; and whatsoever Adam called every creature, that was the name thereof. And Adam gave names to all cattle, and to the fowl of the air, and to every beast of the field.

If the story of Adam and Eve is taken literally, one might conclude that their language was the original one. Unfortunately, not even the Bible identifies what this language was. Some people have claimed that Hebrew was the first language and that all the other languages of the world are derived from it; Hebrew, however, bears no discernible relationship to any language outside the Hamito-Semitic group. Besides, any so-called original language would have changed so drastically in the intervening millennia before the onset of writing that it would not bear any resemblance to ancient Hebrew. Whatever the "original" language was—and there is every reason to believe that many languages sprang up independently over a very long span of time—it could not sound at all like any language that has been documented.

Many theories of the origin of language have been advanced, but three have been mentioned in textbooks more frequently than others. One, the "bow-wow" or echoic theory, insists that the earliest forms of language were exclusively onomatopoeic—that is, imitative of the sounds of animals and nature, despite the fact that the so-called primitive languages are not largely composed of onomatopoeic words. Furthermore, some measure of conventionalization must take place before echoisms become real "words"; individual young children do not call a dog a "bow-wow" until they hear an older child or adult use the term. Another theory, called the "pooh-pooh" or interjectional theory, maintains that language must have begun with primitive grunts and groans—that is, very loose and disjointed utterances. Many have held that such a theory fits animals better than humans; indeed, this kind of exclamatory speech probably separates humans quite clearly from the animals. Still another theory, dubbed the "ding-dong" theory, claims that language arose as a response to natural stimuli. None of these theories has any strong substantiation. Some linguists have suggested that speech and song may have once been the same. The presence of tones and pitch accent in many older languages lends some plausibility to the idea; it is likely that language, gestures, and song, as forms of communication, were all intertwined at the earliest stages.

Is it a hopeless task to try to discover the origin of language? Linguists have continued to look into the question again, but there is little chance that more than a priori notions can be established. It has been suggested, for example, that prehumans may have gradually developed a kind of grammar by occasionally fitting together unstructured vocal signals in patterns that were repeated and then eventually understood, accepted, and passed on. This process is called compounding, and some forms of it are found in present-day gibbon calls.

## THE HISTORY OF LANGUAGE STUDY

In the history of language study, a number of signposts can be erected to mark the path. The simplest outline consists of two major parts: a prescientific and a scientific period. The first can be dispensed with in short order.

The earliest formal grammar of any language is a detailed analysis of classical Sanskrit, written by the Indian scholar Pānini in the fourth century B.C.E. He called it the Sutras (instructions), and in it, he codified the rules for the use of proper Sanskrit. It is still an authoritative work. Independently of Pānini, the ancient

Greeks established many grammatical concepts that strongly influenced linguistic thinking for hundreds of years. Platonic realism, although by today's standards severely misguided in many respects, offered a number of useful insights into language, among them the basic division of the sentence into subject and predicate, the recognition of word stress, and the twofold classification of sounds into consonants and vowels. In the third century B.C.E., Aristotle defined the various parts of speech. In the next century, Dionysius Thrax produced a grammar that not only improved understanding of the sound system of Greek but also classified even more clearly the basic parts of speech and commented at length on such properties of language as gender, number, case, mood, voice, tense, and person. At no time, though, did the Hindu and Greek scholars break away from a focus on their own language to make a comparison with other languages. This fault was also largely one of the Romans, who merely adapted Greek scholarship to their own needs. If they did any comparing of languages, it was not of the languages in the Roman world, but only of Latin as a "corrupt" descendant of Greek. In sum, the Romans introduced no new concepts; they were, instead, content to synthesize or reorganize their legacy from ancient Greece. Only two grammarians come to mind from the fourth and fifth centuries of the Roman Empire—Priscian and Donatus, whose works served for centuries as basic texts for the teaching of Latin.

The scientific period of language study began with a British Sanskrit scholar, Sir William Jones, who headed a society organized in Calcutta for the exploration of Asia. In 1786, he delivered a paper in which he stated that

> the Sanskrit language . . . [was] more perfect than the Greek, more copious than the Latin, and more exquisitely refined than either; yet [bore] to both of them a stronger affinity . . . than could possibly have been produced by accident; so strong, indeed, that no philologer could examine them all three without believing them to have sprung from some common source, which, perhaps, no longer exists.

He went on to say that Germanic and Celtic probably had the same origin. His revolutionary assertion that Sanskrit and most of the languages of Europe had descended from a single language no longer spoken and never recorded first produced considerable scholarly opposition, but shortly thereafter set the stage for comparative analysis. He insisted that a close examination of the "inner structures" of this family of languages would reveal heretofore unsuspected relationships.

Franz Bopp, a German born in 1791 and a student of Oriental languages, including Sanskrit, was the founder of comparative grammar. In his epochmaking book *Über das Conjugationssystem der Sanskritsprache in Vergleichung mit jenem der griechischen, lateinischen, persischen und germanischen Sprache* (1816), he demonstrated for all time what Jones and Friedrich von Schlegel and other researchers had only surmised. A young Danish contemporary named Rasmus Rask corroborated his results and established that Armenian and Lithuanian belong to the same language group, the Indo-European. The tool to establish these relationships was the "comparative method," one of the greatest achievements of nineteenth century linguistics. In applying this method, linguists searched in the various languages under investigation for cognates—words with similar spelling, similar sound, and similar meaning. They then set up sound correspondences among the cognates, much like looking for the lowest common denominator in a mathematical construction, from which the original linguistic forms could be constructed.

The German linguist Jakob Grimm (one of the Brothers Grimm known for books of fairy tales) took Rask's work one step further and, in a four-volume work published between 1819 and 1822, showed conclusively the systematic correspondences and differences between Sanskrit, Greek, and Latin, on one hand, and the Germanic languages, on the other hand. The formulation of this system of sound changes came to be known as Grimm's law, or the First Sound Shift, and the changes involved can be diagrammed as follows:

Proto-Indo-European: *bh dh gh b d g p t k*
Proto-Germanic:    *b  d  g  p t k f Θ h*

Where the Indo-European, as transmitted through Latin or Greek, had a *p* sound (as in *piscis* and *pēd*), the German-based English word has an *f* ("fish" and "foot");

the Latinate *trēs* becomes the English "three." In addition to the changes described above, another important change took place in the Germanic languages. If the *f Θ h* resulting from the change of *p t k* stood after an unaccented vowel but before another vowel, they became voiced fricatives, later voiced stops, as in the pair *seethe : sodden*. This change also affected *s*, yielding *z*, which later became *r* (Rhotacism) and explains, for example, the alternations in *was : were*. It was described by Karl Verner, a Danish linguist, and is known appropriately as Verner's law. There are one or two other "laws" that explain apparent exceptions to Grimm's law, illustrating the basic regularity of Grimm's formulations. At the very end of the nineteenth century, the neo-Grammarians, led by Karl Brugmann, insisted that all exceptions could be explained—that, in fact, "phonetic laws are natural laws and have no exceptions." Even those studying the natural sciences do not make such a strong assertion, but the war cry of the neo-Grammarians did inspire scholars to search for regularity in language.

The German language itself underwent a profound change beginning probably in the far south of the German-speaking lands sometime during the fifth century, causing a restructuring of the sounds of all of the southern and many of the midland dialects. These became known, for geographical reasons, as High German, while those dialects in the north came to be known as Low German. Six consonants in various positions were affected, but the most consistently shifted sounds were the Indo-European *b*, which in English became *p* and in German *pf*, and the *d* to *t* and *ts*. For example, the Latin *decim* became the English "ten" and the German *zehn*.

In the course of the nineteenth century, all such changes were recognized, and scholars were enabled to identify and diagram the reflex languages of Indo-European into five subgroups known as *satem* languages and four known as *centum* languages. This division is significant both geographically—the *satem* languages are located clearly to the east of where the original home of the Indo-Europeans probably was—and linguistically—the *satem* languages have, among other characteristics, *s* sounds where the *centum* languages have *k* sounds (the word *centum* is pronounced

---

## THE *SATEM* LANGUAGES

| | |
|---|---|
| Indo-Iranian | Earliest attested form, Sanskrit; modern languages include Hindi, Bengali, and Persian. |
| Albanian | Spoken by a small number of Balkan people. |
| Armenian | Spoken by a small number of people in that country. |
| Slavic | Divided into East Slavic (Great Russian, the standard language; Little Russian or Ukrainian; White Russian, spoken in the region adjacent to and partly in modern-day Poland); West Slavic (Czech, Slovak, Polish); South Slavic (Slovenian and Serbo-Croatian; Bulgarian). |
| Baltic | Lithuanian and Lettic, spoken in the Baltic states. |

---

with an initial hard *c*). The very words *satem* and *centum*, meaning "hundred" in Avestan (an Indo-Iranian language) and Latin, respectively, illustrate the sound divergence.

### INDO-EUROPEAN LANGUAGES

The original home of the Indo-Europeans is not known for certain, but it is safe to say that it was in Europe, and probably close to present-day Lithuania. For one thing, the Lithuanians have resided in a single area since the Neolithic Age (2500-2000 B.C.E.) and speak a language of great complexity. Furthermore, Lithuania is situated on the dividing line between *centum* and *satem* languages. One would also assume that the original home was somewhere close to the area where the reflex languages are to be found today and not, for example, in Africa, Australia, or North or South America. For historical and archaeological reasons, scholars have ruled out the British Isles and the peninsulas of southern Europe. Last, there are indications that the Indo-Europeans entered India from the northwest, for there is no evidence of their early acquaintanceship with the Ganges River, but only with the Indus (hence "Indo-"). Certain common words for weather conditions, geography, and flora and fauna militate in favor of a European homeland.

Scholars have classified the Indo-European languages as a family apart from certain other languages on the basis of two principal features: their common word stock and their inflectional structure. This type of classification, called genetic, is one of three. Another, called geographical, is usually employed initially. For example, if nothing whatsoever was known about American Indian languages, one might divide them into North American and South American, Eastern North American and Western North American, and perhaps some other geographical categories. A third variety of classification, called typological, is possible only when a good deal is

---

## THE *CENTUM* LANGUAGES

| | |
|---|---|
| Greek (Hellenic) | Attic, Ionic, and Doric, formerly spoken throughout the eastern areas around the Mediterranean; modern Greek. |
| Italic | Latin; modern Italian, French, Spanish, Portuguese, Catalan, Sardinian, Romanian, and Rhaeto-Romanic. |
| Celtic | Modern Welsh, Cornish, Breton, Irish, and Scots Gaelic. |
| Germanic (Teutonic) | East Germanic (Gothic, now extinct); North Germanic (Danish, Norwegian, Swedish, Icelandic); West Germanic (Low German: English, Dutch, Frisian, Plattdeutsch; High German: standard German). |
| In addition | Several extinct Indo-European languages, such as Tocharian and the Anatolian languages, especially Hittite. |

---

known about the structure of a language. The four main types of languages arrived at through such classification are inflectional, meaning that such syntactic distinctions as gender, number, case, tense, and so forth are usually communicated by altering the form of a word, as in English when -*s* added to a noun indicates plurality but, when added to a verb, singularity; agglutinative, meaning that suffixes are piled onto word bases in a definite order and without change in phonetic shape (for example, Turkish *evlerimden*, "house-s-my-from"); isolating, meaning that invariable word forms, mostly monosyllabic, are employed in variable word order (for example, Chinese *wŏ*, meaning, according to its position in the utterance, "I," "me," "to me," or "my"); and incorporating or polysynthetic, meaning that a sentence, with its various syntactic features, may be "incorporated" as a single word (for example, Eskimo /a: wlisa-utiss?ar-siniarpu-na/, "I am looking for something suitable for a fish-line").

## OTHER LANGUAGES

Although the Indo-European languages have been studied in more detail than other language families, it is possible to classify and describe many of the remaining language families of the world, the total comprising more than twenty-seven hundred separate languages. In Europe and Asia, relatively few languages are spoken by very large numbers of people; elsewhere many distinct languages are spoken by small communities. In Europe, all languages are Indo-European except for Finnish, Estonian, Hungarian, and Basque. The last-named is something of a mystery; it appears to predate Indo-European by such a long period that it could conceivably be descended from a prehistoric language. The first three belong to the same family, the Finno-Urgic. Sometimes Turkish is added to the group, and the four are called the Ural-Altaic family. All are agglutinative.

The most extensive language family in eastern Asia is the Sino-Tibetan. It consists of two branches, the Tibeto-Burman and Chinese. Mandarin is the language of the northern half of China, although there are three different varieties—northern, southwestern, and southern. In the south, there is a range of mutually unintelligible dialects. All are isolating in structure.

In other parts of Asia are found the Kadai family, consisting of Thai, Laotian, and the Shan languages of Burma, and in southern Asia, the Munda languages and Vietnamese. The latter has a considerable number of speakers.

Japanese and Korean are separate families, even though cultural relationships between the two countries have produced some borrowing over the years. Japanese is essentially agglutinative.

On the continent of Africa, the linguistic family of prime importance is the Hamito-Semitic family. Hebrew, Arabic, and some of the languages of Ethiopia make up the Semitic side. There are four Hamitic languages: Egyptian, Berber, Cushitic, and Chad. All exhibit some inflectional characteristics. In addition to these languages, Hausa, an important trade language, is used throughout the northern part of the continent.

In central and southern Africa, the Niger-Congo language family is dominant. The largest subgroup of this family is Bantu, which includes Swahili in central and eastern Africa, Kikuyu in Kenya, and Zulu in the south. Most appear to be either agglutinative or polysynthetic.

The Malayo-Polynesian languages are spoken as original tongues all the way from Madagascar to the Malay Peninsula, the East Indies, and, across the Pacific, to Hawaii. Many seem to be isolating with traces of earlier inflections.

The Indian languages of the Americas are all polysynthetic. Until recently, these Indian languages were classified geographically. Many of the North American languages have been investigated, and linguists group them into distinct families, such as Algonquian, Athabaskan, Natchez-Muskogean, Uto-Aztecan, Penutian, and Hokan.

## MODERN LANGUAGES

In addition to the distinction between prescientific and scientific periods of language study, there are other divisions that can help clarify the various approaches to this vast topic. For example, the entire period from earliest times until the late nineteenth century was largely historical, comparative at best, but scarcely truly scientific in terms of rigor. Beginning with the neo-Grammarians Brugmann and Delbrück, the stage was set for what may be called a period of general or descriptive linguistics. Languages were examined not only diachronically—that is, historically—but also synchronically, where a segment or feature of language was scrutinized without regard to an earlier stage. The most important names associated with this descriptive school are those of N. S. Trubetzkoy and Roman Jakobson. Strongly influenced by the theories of the Swiss linguist Ferdinand de Saussure, they examined each detail of language as a part of a system. In other words, they were ultimately more interested in the system and the way it hung together than in each individual detail. These scholars were members of the European school of linguistic thought that had its origin in Jakobson's Prague circle. Across the Atlantic, their most important counterpart was Leonard Bloomfield, who, in 1933, published his classic linguistics text, *Language*. Like his contemporary, Edward Sapir, Bloomfield began as a comparativist in Germanic linguistics, then studied American Indian languages, and finally became an expert in the general principles of language. Bloomfield's theory of structuralism has been criticized for its resemblance to the psychological theory of behaviorism, which restricts itself to the observable and rejects the concept of mind.

Since the 1930's, there has been a steady procession of American linguists studying and reporting on the sounds and grammatical features of many different languages, in some sense all derivative from the foundation laid by the phonemicists beginning with Saussure and Bloomfield. Kenneth Pike's tagmemics, in part an attempt to present language behavior empirically through a description at each level of grammatical form, evolved directly out of descriptive linguistics. In 1957, Noam Chomsky launched transformational-generative grammar, concerned at first only with syntax, but later also with phonology. Considerable tension has developed between structuralists and transformational-generative grammarians, concerning not only syntactic analysis but also the representation of sounds. For some, stratificational grammar provides a connection, through strata or levels of description, among descriptive, tagmemic, and computational analyses.

## THE TECHNICAL SIDE OF LANGUAGE

A language is made up of its sound system, grammar, and vocabulary. The former two may differ considerably from language family to language family, but there is a workable range in the extent and type of sounds and grammatical functions. The inventory of significant sounds in a given language, called phonemes, extends from about twenty to about sixty. English has forty-six, including phonemes of pitch, stress, and juncture. If the grammatical facts of a complicated language can be written out on one or two sheets of paper, the grammar of English can be laid out on the back of an envelope. In short, some languages are simpler phonologically or grammatically than others, but none is so complicated in either respect that every child cannot learn his or her language in about the same time.

The study of the sounds of which speech is made up became scientific in method by the end of the nineteenth century, when Paul Passy founded the International Phonetic Association. Down to the present day, articulatory phonetics has borne a close relationship to physiology in the description of the sounds of speech according to the organs producing them and the position of these organs in relation to surrounding structures.

By the mid-1920's, phoneticians realized that the unit of description of the phonology of a language had to be a concept rather than some physical entity. The term phoneme was chosen; it designates a minimally significant sound unit, an abstraction around which cluster all the phonetic realizations of that generalized sound. Thus, the English phoneme /p/ represents all recognizably similar pronunciations of [p], with more or less or no aspiration depending on position within a word or the speech habits of a given speaker. In other words, it designates a class of sounds distinct from others in the language. It carries no meaning as such, but it serves to distinguish one sound from another and, together with other phonemes, produces morphemic, or meaning, differences. Thus /p/, /i/, and /n/ are separate phonemes, but, taken together, make up a morpheme— the word *pin*—which is distinct, by virtue of a single phoneme, from, say, /bin/, "bin," or /tin/ "tin." Sometimes, morphemes show relations between words, as when -*s* is added to a noun to indicate plurality or possession or to a verb to indicate singularity.

The sound system and grammar of a language are thus closely related. Grammar, at least for Indo-European languages and many others, can be defined as consisting of a morphology and syntax, where, expressed simply, the former refers to the words and their endings and the latter to the order of words. Accompanying the words are, however, other features of language that can alter meaning. It matters, for example, whether the stress occurs on the first or second syllable of the word *pervert* or *permit*. If the stress falls on the first syllable, the word is a noun; if on the second, it is a verb. It matters whether the last few sounds of an utterance convey an upturn or a downturn and trail-off, for a question or a statement may result. It matters also what the pitch level is and whether juncture is present. These features, too, are phonemic.

To function in a language, one must have control of close to 100 percent of the phonology and 75 percent or more of the grammar, but a mere 1 percent of the vocabulary will enable the speaker to function in many situations. For a speaker of a language the size of English, a vocabulary of six thousand words will suffice. Possessing a vocabulary implies an unconscious knowledge of the semantic relationship to the phonology and grammar of the language. One theory of the word regards the word as a compound formed of two components: a physical element, the sequence of sounds of speech; and a semantic element, the amount of meaning expressed by the segment of speech. The first is called the formant, the second the morpheme. The word "cook" /kuk/ is one morpheme expressed by one formant—the formant consisting of one syllable, a sequence of three phonemes. In the plural of "cook," -*s* is a formant that is not even a syllable. In fact, a formant is not even necessarily a phoneme, but can be the use of one form instead of another, as in "her" instead of "she." There is no reason that the same formant, such as -*s*, cannot express more than one morpheme: "cooks" (noun) versus "cook's" versus "cooks" (verb). The same morpheme can also be expressed by more than one formant; there are, for example, many different formants for the plural, such as basis/bases, curriculum/curricula, datum/data, ox/oxen, child/children, man/men, woman/women, cherub/cherubim, monsignore/monsignori.

The distinction in morphology made above between words and their endings needs further amplification. An examination of a stanza from Lewis Carroll's "Jabberwocky" (from *Alice's Adventures in Wonderland*, 1865) illustrates the manner in which the poet uses formants with no evident meaning to the average speaker:

> 'Twas brilling, and the slithy toves
> Did gyre and gimble in the wabe;
> All mimsy were the borogoves,
> And the mome raths outgrabe.

Alice herself remarks that the words fill her head with ideas, but she does not know what they are. There is a rightness about the way the poem sounds because the endings, the structural morphemes, are correctly placed. When the message is of primary importance and the speaker knows the language only imperfectly, the structural morphemes may be incorrect or missing and a string of pure message morphemes may be the result: Her give man bag money.

Message morphemes have their own peculiar properties, limiting their use to certain contexts, regardless of the accuracy of the combined structural morphemes. To illustrate this principle, Chomsky composed the sentence "Colorless green ideas sleep furiously." The subject is "colorless green ideas"; the predicate, "sleep furiously." This sentence has the same structure as any sentence of the shape: adjective/adjective/noun/intransitive verb/adverb. However, there is something semantically troubling. How can one describe something green as colorless? Can ideas be green? How can an intransitive verb that describes such a passive activity be furiously involved in an action?

Chomsky's example was designed to combine structural familiarity with semantic impossibility. It is possible to devise similar sentences that, though semantically improbable, could conceivably be used by an actual speaker. The sentence "Virtue swims home every night" attributes to an abstract noun an action performed by animate beings, and poses other difficulties as well (in what setting can one swim home?), yet such strange semantic violations, given a meaningful context, are the stuff of poetry.

Indeed, semantic change actually occurs with a

measure of frequency in the history of a language. It is usually of two types. Words that are rather specific in meaning sometimes become generalized; for example, Latin *molīna* (gristmill) originally meant "mill" but expanded to cover "sawmill," "steel mill," even "diploma mill." Many words in English of very broad meanings, such as "do," "make," "go," and "things," derive from words of more specific notions. At the same time, the opposite often happens. Words that once were very general in meaning have become specific. Examples include *deer*, which formerly meant merely "animal" (compare German *Tier*), and *hound*, "dog," now a particular kind of dog. Sometimes, words undergo melioration, as in the change in *knight*, meaning originally a "servant," to "king's servant," or pejoration, as in the change in *knave*, meaning "boy" (compare German *Knabe*), to "rascal."

Perhaps the most significant force for change in language is analogy. It is occasioned by mental associations arising because of similarity or contrast of meaning and may affect the meaning or the form of words or even create new words. Most verbs in English are regular and form their preterit and past participles by the addition of *-ed* (or *-t*), as "dream, dreamed, dreamt," and not by vowel change, as in "drink, drank, drunk." New words taken into the language, as well as some of the irregular ones already in use, will usually become regular. It is by no means unusual to hear a child use analogy in forming the past of, say, "teach" or "see" as "teached" and "see'd" instead of "taught" and "saw." Since most English nouns form their plural by the addition of *-s*, it is to be expected that unfamiliar words or words with little-used, learned plural forms will be pluralized in the same way: for example, "memorandums" (or "memos") for *memoranda*, "stadiums" for *stadia*, "gymnasiums" for *gymnasia*, "prima donnas" for *prime donne*, and "formulas" for *formulae*. Sometimes a resemblance in the form of a word may suggest a relationship that causes a further assimilation in form. This process is known as folk etymology and often occurs when an unfamiliar or foreign word or phrase is altered to give it a more meaningful form. There are many examples: "crayfish" comes from Old French *crevisse* (crab), but *-visse* meant nothing and thus was changed to the phonetically similar *-fish*; a hangnail is not a (fin-

ger)nail that hangs, but one that hurts (from Old English *ang*); the second element of "titmouse" has nothing to do with a mouse, but comes from Middle English *mose*, the name for several species of birds.

There are many other processes in language by which changes are brought about. Among them are several of great importance: assimilation, dissimilation, conversion, back formation, blending, and the creation of euphemisms and slang.

Assimilation causes a sound to change in conformance with a neighboring sound, as in the plural of "kit" with [-s] (/kits/), as opposed to the plural of "limb" with [-z] (/limz/), or in the preterit and participial forms of regular verbs: "grazed" [greyzd], but "choked" [čowkt].

Dissimilation is the opposite process, whereby neighboring sounds are made unlike, as in "pilgrim" from Latin *peregrīnus*, where the first *r* dissimilates.

Conversion is the change of one part of speech or form class into another, as the change from noun to verb: The nouns "bridge," "color," and "shoulder" are converted to verbs in "to bridge a gap," "to color a book," and "to shoulder a load."

A back formation occurs when a word is mistakenly assumed to be the base form from which a new word is formed, as in "edit" from "editor," "beg" from "beggar," "peddle" from "pedlar."

Some words are blends: "flash" + "blush" = "flush"; "slight" (slim) + "tender" = "slender"; "twist" + "whirl" = "twirl"; "breakfast" + "lunch" = "brunch."

Euphemisms are words and expressions with new, better-sounding connotations—for example, to "pass away" or "breathe one's last" or "cross the river" for "to die"; "lingerie" or "intimate wear" for "underwear"; "acute indigestion" for "bellyache."

Slang consists of informal, often ephemeral expressions and coinages, such as "turkey" for "stupid person," "blow away" for "to kill," and "kook," meaning "odd or eccentric person," from "cuckoo."

All three constituents of language change over a long period of time—sounds, structure, and vocabulary—but each language or dialect retains its distinctiveness. The most durable and unchanging aspect of language is writing, of which there are two major varieties: picture writing, also called ideographic writing, and alphabetic writing. The former kind of writing began as actual pictures and developed gradually into ideograms linked directly to the objects or concepts and having no connection with the sounds of the language. The latter variety began as symbols for syllables, until each symbol was taken to represent a single spoken sound. Although alphabetic writing is much more widespread and easier to learn and use, ideographic writing has the advantage of maintaining cultural unity among speakers of dialects and languages not mutually intelligible. An alphabetic writing system can, over time, act as a conservative influence on the spoken language as well as provide valuable etymological clues. Ideographic writing can be, and often is, seen as art capable of conveying messages separate from speech. Both systems are vehicles for the transmission of history and literature without which civilization would falter and perish.

## THE SOCIAL SIDE OF LANGUAGE

The social side of language is inextricably linked to behavior. It is concerned with the use of language to create attitudes and responses toward language, objects, and people. For example, certain overt behaviors toward language and its users can create unusual political pressures. The insistence by the Québecois on French as the primary, if not sole, language of their province of Canada has led to near secession and to bitter interprovincial feelings. The creation of modern Hebrew has helped to create and sustain the state of Israel. The Irish are striving to make Irish the first language of that part of the British Isles. The Flemish urge full status for their variety of Dutch in the Brussels area. African Americans sometimes advocate clearer recognition of black English. Frisians, Bretons, Basques, Catalans, and Provençals are all insisting on greater acceptance of their mother tongues.

Within a language or dialect, there can be specialized vocabulary and pronunciation not generally understood. The term "dialect" is commonly taken to mean a regional variety of language or one spoken by the undereducated, but, strictly speaking, it is differentiated from language as such, being largely what people actually speak. Some dialects differ so substantially from standard, national tongues that, to all intents and

purposes, they are languages in their own right. The term "vernacular" is similar in that it designates everyday speech as opposed to learned discourse. "Lingo" designates, somewhat contemptuously, any dialect or language not readily comprehended. "Jargon" is specialized or professional language, often of a technical nature; in this context, the term "cant," as in "thieves' cant," is virtually synonymous with "jargon." Closely related to these two terms is the term "argot," referring to the idiom of a closely knit group, as in "criminal argot." Finally, "slang," discussed above, refers to the colorful, innovative, often short-lived popular vocabulary drawn from many levels of language use, both specialized and nonspecialized.

Words, like music, can produce moods. They can raise one's spirits or lower them. They can stir up discontent or soothe human anger. They can inspire and console, ingratiate and manipulate, mislead and ridicule. They can create enough hatred to destroy but also enough trust to overcome obstacles. While a mood may originate in physical well-being or physical discomfort and pain, language can express that mood, intensify it, or deny it. Language can be informative (emotionally neutral), biased (emotionally charged), or propagandistic (informatively neutral).

Language is informative when it states indisputable facts or asks questions dealing with such facts, even though those facts are very broad and general. One can also inform with misstatements, half-truths, or outright lies. It does not matter whether the statement is actually true or false, only that the question can be posed.

Language often reflects bias by distorting facts. Frequently, the substitution of a single derogatory term is sufficient to load the atmosphere. Admittedly, some words are favorably charged for some people, unfavorably for others. Much depends on the context, word and sentence stress, gestures, and former relationship.

Language can be propagandistic when the speaker desires to promote some activity or cause. The load that propaganda carries is directly proportional to the receiver's enthusiasm, bias, or readiness to be deceived. Almost invariably, propaganda terms arise out of the specialized language of religion, art, commerce, education, finance, government, and so forth. Propaganda is a kind of name calling, using words from a stock of esoteric and exclusive terms. Not many people are thoroughly familiar with the exact meanings of words such as "totalitarian," "fascist," "proletarian," and "bourgeois," but they think they know whether these words are good or bad, words of approval or disapproval. The effect is to call forth emotions as strong as those prompted by invectives.

The language of advertising achieves its effectiveness by conveniently combining information, bias, and propaganda. A good advertisement must gain immediate attention, make the reader or listener receptive to the message, ensure its retention, create a desire, and cause the person to buy the product without setting up resistance. Advertising must, moreover, link the product to "pleasant" or "healthy" things. In advertising circles, there is no widespread agreement as to which is more important: the avoidance of all associations that can create resistance or the creation of desire for a particular object. Even if the latter is regarded as the prime objective, it is still important to avoid resistance. The most powerful tools of the advertiser are exaggeration and cliché. The words generally used in ads deal with the basic component and qualities of a product, while the qualifiers are hackneyed and overblown: lather (rich, creamy, full-bodied); toothpaste (fights cavities three ways, ten ways, tastes zesty); cleanser (all-purpose, powerful, one-step); coffee (full of flavor buds, brewed to perfection, marvelous bouquet). The danger of advertising is evident when its pathology carries over into other areas of life. Every culture must be on guard against the effect of advertising on the health of its citizenry and the shaping of its national image. Even foreign policy can be the victim of advertising that stresses youth over maturity, beauty of body over soundness of mind, physical health over mental serenity, or the power of sex appeal over everything else.

In the latter part of the twentieth century, language began to be closely examined by certain groups aiming to rid it of inherent prejudice. Of all of these groups, perhaps feminists have had the greatest effect on the vocabulary, and even the structure, of languages that differentiate along sex lines. A vociferous contingent of women contend that the symbols of perception—words—give both meaning and value to the objects they define and that many of these words are loaded

with a male-chauvinist aspect. For example, words with the affix *-man* are being avoided or paired with *-woman* or *-person:* "congressman"/"congresswoman," "chairman"/"chairwoman"/"chairperson." In some instances, gender is eliminated altogether: "humankind" for "mankind," "chair" for "chairman" or "chairwoman." There are many more techniques employed to desexualize English; some even involve tampering with personal pronouns, a much less likely area for success. Nevertheless, any language can cope with any pressing linguistic problem. The impetus for a solution begins with the individual or a small group, but the community as a whole often applies brakes to change that is too rapid or drastic, dramatizing the fact that language exists not for the individual alone but for the community as a whole.

## APPLICATIONS

Almost everybody is intimately acquainted with at least one language. Everybody can produce the sounds and sound combinations of his or her language and understand the meanings of the sounds produced by other speakers. Everybody knows which sounds and sound combinations are allowable and which do not fit the language. Sentences that are grammatically or semantically unacceptable or strange are easily recognized. Despite this intuitive or unconscious knowledge of one's language, the average native speaker cannot comment authoritatively on the sound system or the structure of his or her language. Furthermore, there are no books containing the complete language of English or Arabic or Mandarin Chinese in which all possible sentences and sound combinations are listed. Instead, people must rely largely on dictionaries for a list of words and on grammars and linguistic texts for a statement of rules dealing with sounds, morphology, and syntax. To study one's language as an object or phenomenon is to raise one's consciousness of how language functions.

Some people have a professional need to know a lot about a language as opposed to simply being able to use it. Some of the more obvious examples include language teachers, speech therapists, advertising writers, communications engineers, and computer programmers. Others, such as the anthropologist or the historian, who often work with documents, employ their knowledge as an ancillary tool. The missionary may have to learn about some very esoteric language for which there is no grammar book and perhaps even no writing. The psychologist studies language as a part of human behavior. The philosopher is often primarily interested in the "logical" side of language. Students of foreign languages can benefit greatly from linguistic knowledge; they can often learn more efficiently and make helpful comparisons of sounds and structures between their own and the target language.

Translation and interpretation are two activities requiring considerable knowledge about language. Strictly speaking, the terms are not interchangeable; translation refers to the activity of rendering, in writing, one language text into another, whereas interpretation is oral translation. Translation is of two kinds, scientific and literary, and can be accomplished by people or machines. In general, machine translation has been a disappointment because of the grave difficulties involved in programming the many complexities of natural language. Interpretation is also of two kinds: legal and diplomatic. Whereas the legal interpreter requires a precise knowledge of the terminology of the court and must tread a thin line between literal and free interpretation, the diplomatic interpreter has the even more difficult task of adding, or subtracting, as circumstances dictate, allusions, innuendos, insinuations, and implications. Interpretation is accomplished in two ways: simultaneously with the speaker, or consecutively after a given segment of speech.

One of the important questions before linguistics is: Does linguistics aid in the study and appreciation of literature? Many would automatically assume that the answer is an unqualified yes, since the material of which literature is made is language. There are others, however, who find linguistic techniques of analysis too mechanical and lacking in the very feeling that literature tries to communicate. Probably most thoughtful people would agree that linguistics can make a contribution in tandem with more traditional analytical approaches, but that alone it cannot yet, if ever, disclose the intrinsic qualities of great literary works.

By one definition at least, literature consists of texts constructed according to certain phonological, morpho-

logical, and syntactic restrictions, where the result is the creation of excellence of form and expression. For poetry in the Western tradition, for example, the restriction most frequently imposed is that of rhythm based on stress or vowel quantity. In other cultures, syntactic and semantic prescriptions can produce the same effect.

For both poetic and prose texts, the discovery and description of the author's style are essential to analysis. In contrast to the methods of traditional literary criticism, linguistics offers the possibility of quantitative stylistic analysis. Computer-aided analysis yields textual statistics based on an examination of various features of phonology and grammar. The results will often place an author within a literary period, confirm his region or dialect, explain the foreign-vocabulary influences, describe syllabication in terms of vowel and consonant count, list euphemisms and metaphors, and delineate sentence structure with regard to subordinating elements, to mention some of the possibilities. All of these applications are based on the taxemes of selection employed by an individual author.

Of all literary endeavors, literary translation seems to stand in the closest possible relationship to linguistics. The translator must perform his task within the framework of an awareness, be it conscious or intuitive, of the phonology, syntax, and morphology of both the source language and the target language. Like the linguist, he should also be acquainted in at least a rudimentary fashion with the society that has produced the text he is attempting to translate. His work involves much more than the mechanical or one-to-one exchange of word for word, phrase for phrase, or even concept for concept. The practice of translation makes possible the scope and breadth of knowledge encompassed in the ideal of liberal arts, and without translation relatively few scholars could claim knowledge and understanding of many of the world's great thinkers and literary artists.

BIBLIOGRAPHY

Akmajian, Adrian, et al. *Linguistics: An Introduction to Language and Communication*. Cambridge, Mass.: MIT Press, 2001. The first part of this work deals with the structural and interpretive parts of language, and the second part is cognitively oriented and includes chapters on pragmatics, psychology of language, language acquisition, and language and the brain.

Beekes, Robert S. P. *Comparative Indo-European Linguistics: An Introduction*. Philadelphia: John Benjamins, 1996. Examines the history of Indo-European languages and explores comparative grammar and linguistics.

Cavalli-Sforza, L. L. *Genes, Peoples, and Languages*. Berkeley: University of California Press, 2001. Cavalli-Sforza was among the first to ask whether the genes of modern populations contain a historical record of the human species. This collection comprises five lectures that serve as a summation of the author's work over several decades, the goal of which has been nothing less than tracking the past hundred thousand years of human evolution.

Chomsky, Noam. *Language and Thought*. Wakefield, R.I.: Moyer Bell, 1998. Presents an analysis of human language and its influence on other disciplines.

Lycan, William G. *Philosophy of Language: A Contemporary Introduction*. 2d ed. New York: Routledge, 2008. Introduces nonspecialists to the main issues and theories in the philosophy of language, focusing specifically on linguistic phenomena.

Pinker, Stephen. *The Language Instinct: How the Mind Creates Language*. New York: HarperPerennial Modern Classics, 2009. Explores how humans learn to talk, how the study of language can provide insight into the way genes interact with experience to create behavior and thought, and how the arbitrary

sounds people call language evoke emotion and meaning.

Ruhlen, Merritt. *The Origin of Language: Tracing the Evolution of the Mother Tongue*. New York: John Wiley & Sons, 1996. Provides an accessible examination of nearly 100,000 years of human history and prehistory to uncover the roots of the language from which all modern tongues derive.

Trudgill, Peter. *Sociolinguistics: An Introduction to Language and Society*. 4th ed. New York: Penguin Books, 2007. Examines how speech is deeply influenced by class, gender, and ethnic background and explores the implications of language for social and educational policy.

Vygotsky, Lev S. *Thought and Language*. Edited by Alex Kozulin. Rev. ed. Cambridge, Mass.: MIT Press, 1986. A classic foundational work of cognitive science. Vygotsky analyzes the relationship between words and consciousness, arguing that speech is social in its origins and that only as a child develops does it become internalized verbal thought. Revised edition offers an introductory essay by editor Kozulin that offers new insight into the author's life, intellectual milieu, and research methods.

Yule, George. *The Study of Language*. 4th ed. New York: Cambridge University Press, 2010. Revised edition includes a new chapter on pragmatics and an expanded chapter on semantics; incorporates many changes that reflect developments in language study in the twenty-first century.

*Donald D. Hook*

# GLOSSARY OF POETICAL TERMS

*Accentual meter:* A base meter in which the occurrence of a syllable marked by a stress determines the basic unit, regardless of the number of unstressed syllables. It is one of four base meters used in English (accentual, accentual-syllabic, syllabic, and quantitative). An example from modern poetry is "Blue Moles" by Sylvia Plath, the first line of which scans: "They're out of the dark's ragbag, these two." Because there are five stressed syllables in this accentually based poem, the reader can expect that many of the other lines will also contain five stresses. See also *Scansion.*

*Accentual-syllabic meter:* A base meter that measures the pattern of stressed syllables relative to the unstressed ones. It is the most common base meter for English poetry. In the first line of William Shakespeare's sonnet 130, "My mistress' eyes are nothing like the sun," there is a pattern of alternating unstressed with stressed syllables, although there is a substitution of an unstressed syllable for a stressed syllable at the word "like." In the accentual-syllabic system, stressed and unstressed syllables are grouped together into feet.

*Allegory:* A literary mode in which a second level of meaning—wherein characters, events, and settings represent abstractions—is encoded within the surface narrative. The allegorical mode may dominate the entire work, in which case the encoded message is the work's primary excuse for being, or it may be an element in a work otherwise interesting and meaningful for its surface story alone.

*Alliteration:* The repetition of consonants at the beginning of syllables; for example, "Large *m*annered *m*otions of his *m*ythy *m*ind." Alliteration is used when the poet wishes to focus on the details of a sequence of words and to show relationships between words within a line. Because a reader cannot easily skim over an alliterative line, it is conspicuous and demands emphasis.

*Allusion:* A reference to a historical or literary event whose story or outcome adds dimension to the poem. "Fire and Ice" by Robert Frost, for example, alludes to the biblical account of the flood and the prophecy that the next destruction will come by fire, not water. Without recognizing the allusion and understanding the bib-

lical reference to Noah and the surrounding associations of hate and desire, the reader cannot fully appreciate the poem.

*Anacrusis:* The addition of an extra unstressed syllable to the beginning or end of a line; the opposite of truncation. For example, anacrusis occurs in the line: "their shoul/ders held the sky/suspended." This line is described as iambic tetrameter with terminal anacrusis. Anacrusis is used to change a rising meter to falling and vice versa to alter the reader's emotional response to the subject.

*Anapest:* A foot in which two unstressed syllables are associated with one stressed syllable, as in the line, "With the sift/ed, harmon/ious pause." The anapestic foot is one of the three most common in English poetry and is used to create a highly rhythmical, usually emotional, line.

*Anaphora:* The use of the same word or words to begin successive phrases or lines. Timothy Steele's "Sapphics Against Anger" uses anaphora in the repetition of the phrase "May I."

*Approximate rhyme:* Assonance and half rhyme (or slant rhyme). Assonance occurs when words with identical vowel sounds but different consonants are associated. "Stars," "arms," and "park" all contain identical *a* (and *ar*) sounds, but because the consonants are different the words are not full rhymes. Half rhyme or slant rhymes contain identical consonants but different vowels, as in "fall" and "well." "Table" and "bauble" constitute half rhymes; "law," "cough," and "fawn" assonate.

*Archetype:* 1) Primordial image from the collective unconscious of humankind, according to psychologist Carl Jung, who believed that works of art, including poetry, derive much of their power from the unconscious appeal of these images to ancestral memories. 2) A symbol, usually an image, that recurs so frequently in literature that it becomes an element of the literary experience, according to Northrop Frye in his extremely influential *Anatomy of Criticism* (1957).

*Assonance:* See *Approximate rhyme*

*Aubade:* A type of poem welcoming or decrying the arrival of the dawn. Often the dawn symbolizes the separation of two lovers. An example is William Empson's "Aubade" (1937).

*Ballad:* A poem composed of four-line stanzas that alternate rhyme schemes of *abab* or *abcb*. If all four lines contain four feet each (tetrameter), the stanza is called a long ballad; if one or more of the lines contain only three feet (trimeter), it is called a short ballad. Ballad stanzas, which are highly mnemonic, originated with verse adapted to singing. For this reason, the poetic ballad is well suited for presenting stories. Popular ballads are songs or verse that tell tales, usually impersonal, and they usually impart folk wisdom. Supernatural events, courage, and love are frequent themes, but any experience that appeals to people is acceptable material. A famous use of the ballad form is *The Rime of the Ancient Mariner* (1798), by Samuel Taylor Coleridge.

*Ballade:* A popular and sophisticated French form, commonly (but not necessarily) composed of an eight-line stanza rhyming *ababbcbc*. Early ballades usually contained three stanzas and an envoy, commonly addressed to a nobleman, priest, or the poet's patron, but no consistent syllable count. Another common characteristic of the ballade is a refrain that occurs at the end of each stanza.

*Base meter:* Also called metrical base. The primary meter employed in poems in English and in most European languages that are not free verse. Based on the number, pattern, or duration of the syllables within a line or stanza, base meters fall into four types: accentual, accentual-syllabic, syllabic, or quantitative. Rhythm in verse occurs because of meter, and the use of meter depends on the type of base into which it is placed.

*Blank verse:* A type of poem having a base meter of iambic pentameter and with unrhymed lines usually arranged in stichic form (that is, not in stanzas). Most of William Shakespeare's plays are written in blank verse; in poetry it is often used for subject matter that requires much narration or reflection. In both poetry and drama, blank verse elevates emotion and gives a dramatic sense of importance. Although the base meter of blank verse is iambic pentameter, the form is very flexible, and substitution, enjambment, feminine rhyme, and extra syllables can relax the rigidity of the base. The flexi-

bility of blank verse gives the poet an opportunity to use a formal structure without seeming unnecessarily decorous. T. S. Eliot's "Burnt Norton," written in the 1930's, is a modern blank-verse poem.

*Cadence:* The rhythmic speed or tempo with which a line is read. All language has cadence, but when the cadence of words is forced into some pattern, it becomes meter, thus distinguishing poetry from prose. A prose poem may possess strong cadence, combined with poetic uses of imagery, symbolism, and other poetic devices.

*Caesura:* A pause or break in a poem, created with or without punctuation marks. The comma, question mark, colon, and dash are the most common signals for pausing, and these are properly termed caesuras; pauses may also be achieved through syntax, lines, meter, rhyme, and the sound of words. The type of punctuation determines the length of the pause. Periods and question marks demand full stops, colons take almost a full stop, semicolons take a long pause, and commas take a short pause. The end of a line usually demands some pause even if there is no punctuation.

*Cinquain:* Any five-line stanza, including the madsong and the limerick. Cinquains are most often composed of a ballad stanza with an extra line added to the middle.

*Classicism:* A literary stance or value system consciously based on the example of classical Greek and Roman literature. Although the term is applied to an enormous diversity of artists in many different periods and in many different national literatures, classicism generally denotes a cluster of values including formal discipline, restrained expression, reverence for tradition, and an objective rather than a subjective orientation. As a literary tendency, classicism is often opposed to Romanticism, although many writers combine classical and romantic elements.

*Conceit:* A type of metaphor that uses a highly intellectualized comparison; an extended, elaborate, or complex metaphor. The term is frequently applied to the work of the Metaphysical poets, notably John Donne.

*Connotation:* An additional meaning for a word other than its denotative, formal definition. The word "mercenary," for example, simply means a soldier who is paid to fight in an army not of his own region, but connotatively a mercenary is an unprincipled scoundrel who kills for money and pleasure, not for honor and patriotism. Connotation is one of the most important devices for achieving irony, and readers may be fooled into believing a poem has one meaning because they have missed connotations that reverse the poem's apparent theme.

*Consonance:* Repetition or recurrence of the final consonants of stressed syllables without the correspondence of the preceding vowels. "Chair/star" is an example of consonance, since both words end with *r* preceded by different vowels. Terminal consonance creates half or slant rhyme (see *Approximate rhyme*). Consonance differs from alliteration in that the final consonants are repeated rather than the initial consonants. In the twentieth century, consonance became one of the principal rhyming devices, used to achieve formality without seeming stilted or old-fashioned.

*Consonants:* All letters except the vowels, *a, e, i, o, u*, and sometimes *y*; one of the most important sound-producing devices in poetry. There are five basic effects that certain consonants will produce: resonance, harshness, plosiveness, exhaustiveness, and liquidity. Resonance, exhaustiveness, and liquidity tend to give words—and consequently the whole line if several of these consonants are used—a soft effect. Plosiveness and harshness, on the other hand, tend to create tension. Resonance is the property of long duration produced by nasals, such as *n* and *m*, and by voiced fricating consonants such as *z, v*, and the voiced *th*, as in "them." Exhaustiveness is created by the voiceless fricating consonants and consonant combinations, such as *h, f*, and the voiceless *th* and *s*. Liquidity results from using the liquids and semivowels *l, r, w*, and *y*, as in the word "silken." Plosiveness occurs when certain consonants create a stoppage of breath before releasing it, especially *b, p, t, d, g, k, ch*, and *j*.

*Controlling image/controlling metaphor:* Just as a poem may include as structural devices form, theme, action, or dramatic situation, it may also use imagery for structure. When an image runs throughout a poem, giving unity to lesser images or ideas, it is called a controlling image. Usually the poet establishes a single idea and then expands and complicates it; in Edward Taylor's "Huswifery," for example, the image of the spinning wheel is expanded into images of weaving until the reader begins to see life as a tapestry. Robert Frost's "The Silken Tent" is a fine example of a controlling image and extended metaphor.

*Couplet:* Any two succeeding lines that rhyme. Because the couplet has been used in so many different ways and because of its long tradition in English poetry, various names and functions have been given to types of couplets. One of the most common is the decasyllabic (ten-syllable) couplet. When there is an end-stop on the second line of a couplet, it is said to be closed; an enjambed couplet is open. An end-stopped decasyllabic couplet is called a heroic couplet, because the form has often been used to sing the praise of heroes. The heroic couplet was widely used by the neoclassical poets of the eighteenth century. Because it is so stately and sometimes pompous, the heroic couplet invites satire, and many poems have been written in "mock-heroic verse," such as Alexander Pope's *The Rape of the Lock* (1712, 1714). Another commonly used couplet is the octasyllabic (eight-syllable) couplet, formed from two lines of iambic tetrameter, as in "L'Allegro" by John Milton: "Come, and trip as we go/ On the light fantastic toe." The light, singsong tone of the octasyllabic couplet also invited satire, and Samuel Butler wrote one of the most famous of all satires, *Hudibras* (1663, 1664, 1678), in this couplet. When a couplet is used to break another rhyme scheme, it generally produces a summing-up effect and has an air of profundity. William Shakespeare found this characteristic particularly useful when he needed to give his newly invented Shakespearean sonnet a final note of authority and purpose.

*Dactyl:* A foot formed of a stress followed by two unstressed syllables (′ ◡ ◡). It is fairly common in isolated words, but when this pattern is included in a line of poetry, it tends to break down and rearrange itself into components of other types of feet. Isolated, the word "meaningless" is a dactyl, but in the line "Políte/ meaning/less words," the last syllable becomes attached to the stressed "words" and creates a split foot, forming a trochee and an iamb. Nevertheless, a few dactylic poems do exist. "After the/pangs of a / desperate/lover" is a dactyllic line.

*Deconstruction:* An extremely influential contemporary school of criticism based on the works of the French philosopher Jacques Derrida. Deconstruction treats literary works as unconscious reflections of the reigning myths of Western culture. The primary myth is that there is a meaningful world that language signifies or represents. The deconstructionist critic is most often concerned with showing how a literary text tacitly subverts the very assumptions or myths on which it ostensibly rests.

*Denotation:* The explicit formal definition of a word, exclusive of its implications and emotional associations (see *Connotation*).

*Depressed foot:* A foot in which two syllables occur in a pattern in such a way as to be taken as one syllable without actually being an elision. In the line: "To each/ he boul/ders (that have)/fallen/to each," the base meter consists of five iambic feet, but in the third foot, there is an extra syllable that disrupts the meter but does not break it, so that "that have" functions as the second half of the iambic foot.

*Diction:* The poet's "choice of words," according to John Dryden. In Dryden's time, and for most of the history of English verse, the diction of poetry was elevated, sharply distinct from everyday speech. Since the early twentieth century, however, the diction of poetry has ranged from the banal and the conversational to the highly formal, and from obscenity and slang to technical vocabulary, sometimes in the same poem. The diction of a poem often reveals its persona's values and attitudes.

*Dieresis:* Caesuras that come after the foot (see *Split foot* for a discussion of caesuras that break feet). They can be used to create long pauses in the line and are often used to prepare the line for enjambment.

*Dramatic dialogue:* An exchange between two or more personas in a poem or a play. Unlike a dramatic monologue, both characters speak, and in the best dramatic dialogues, their conversation leads to a final resolution in which both characters and the reader come to the same realization at the same time.

*Dramatic irony:* See *Irony*

*Dramatic monologue:* An address to a silent person by a narrator; the words of the narrator are greatly influenced by the persona's presence. The principal reason for writing in dramatic monologue form is to control the speech of the major persona through the implied reaction of the silent one. The effect is one of continuing change and often surprise. In Robert Browning's "My Last Duchess," for example, the duke believes that he is in control of the situation, when in fact he has provided the emissary with terrible insights about the way he treated his former duchess. The emissary, who is the silent persona, has asked questions that the duke has answered; in doing so he has given away secrets. Dramatic monologue is somewhat like hearing one side of a telephone conversation in which the reader learns much about both participants.

*Duration:* The length of the syllables, which is the measure of quantitative meter. Duration can alter the tone and the relative stress of a line and influence meaning as much as the foot can.

*Elegy:* Usually a long, rhymed, strophic poem whose subject is meditation on death or a lamentable theme. The pastoral elegy uses the natural setting of a pastoral scene to sing of death or love. Within the pastoral setting the simplicity of the characters and the scene lends a peaceful air despite the grief the narrator feels.

*Elision:* The joining of two vowels into a single vowel (synaeresis) or omitting of a vowel altogether (syncope), usually to maintain a regular base meter. Synaeresis can be seen in the line "Of man's first disobedience, and the fruit," in which the "ie" in "disobedience" is pronounced as a "y" ("ye") so that the word reads dis/o/bed/yence, thereby making a five-syllable word into a four-syllable word. An example of syncope is when "natural" becomes "nat'ral" and "hastening" becomes "hast'ning." Less frequent uses of elision are to change the sound of a word, to spell words as they are pronounced, and to indicate dialect.

*Emphasis:* The highlighting of or calling attention to a phrase or line or a poem by altering its meter. A number of techniques, such as caesura, relative stress, counterpointing, and substitution can be used.

*End rhyme:* See *Rhyme*

*End-stop:* A punctuated pause at the end of a line in a poem. The function of end-stops is to show the relationship between lines and to emphasize particular words or lines. End-stopping in rhymed poems creates more emphasis on the rhyme words, which already carry a great deal of emphasis by virtue of their rhymes. Enjambment is the opposite of end-stopping.

*Enjambment:* When a line is not end-stopped—that is, when it carries over to the following line—the line is said to be "enjambed," as in John Milton's: "Avenge, O Lord, thy slaughtered saints, whose bones/ Lie scattered on the Alpine mountains cold." Enjambment is used to change the natural emphasis of the line, to strengthen or weaken the effect of rhyme, or to alter meter.

*Envoy:* Any short poem or stanza addressed to the reader as a beginning or end to a longer work. Specifically, the envoy is the final stanza of a sestina or a ballade in which all the rhyme words are repeated or echoed.

*Epic:* A long narrative poem that presents the exploits of a central figure of high position.

*Extended metaphor:* Metaphors added to one another so that they run in a series. Robert Frost's poem "The Silken Tent" uses an extended metaphor; it compares the "she" of the poem to the freedom and bondage of a silken tent. See also *Controlling image/controlling metaphor*.

*Eye rhyme:* Words that appear to be identical because of their spelling but that sound different. "Bough/ enough/cough" and "ballet/pallet" are examples. Because of changes in pronunciation, many older poems appear to use eye rhymes but do not. For example, "wind" (meaning moving air) once rhymed with "find." Eye rhymes that are intentional and do not result from a change in pronunciation may be used to create a disconcerting effect.

*Fabliau:* A bawdy medieval verse, such as many found in Geoffrey Chaucer's *The Canterbury Tales* (1387-1400).

*Falling rhyme:* Rhyme in which the correspondence of sound comes only in the final unstressed syllable, which is preceded by another unstressed syllable. T. S. Eliot rhymes "me-tic-u-lous" with "ri-dic-u-lous" and creates a falling rhyme. See also *Feminine rhyme*; *Masculine rhyme*.

*Falling rhythm:* A line in which feet move from stressed to unstressed syllables (trochaic or dactyllic). An example can be seen in this line from "The Naming

of Parts," by Henry Reed: "Glistens/like cor/al in/all of the/neighboring/gardens." Because English and other Germanic-based languages naturally rise, imposing a falling rhythm on a rising base meter creates counterpointing.

*Feminine rhyme:* A rhyme pattern in which a line's final accented syllable is followed by a single unaccented syllable and the accented syllables rhyme, while the unaccented syllables are phonetically identical, as with "flick-er/snick-er" and "fin-gers/ma-lin-gers." Feminine rhymes are often used for lightness in tone and delicacy in movement.

*Feminist criticism:* A criticism advocating equal rights for women in a political, economic, social, psychological, personal, and aesthetic sense. On the thematic level, the feminist reader should identify with female characters and their concerns. The object is to provide a critique of phallocentric assumptions and an analysis of patriarchal ideologies inscribed in male-centered and male-dominated literature. On the ideological level, feminist critics see gender, as well as the stereotypes that go along with it, as a cultural construct. They strive to define a particularly feminine content and to extend the canon so that it might include works by lesbians, feminists, women of color, and women writers in general.

*First person:* The use of linguistic forms that present a poem from the point of view of the speaker. It is particularly useful in short lyrical poems, which tend to be highly subjective, taking the reader deep into the narrator's thoughts. First-person poems normally, though not necessarily, signal the use of the first person through the pronoun "I," allowing the reader direct access to the narrator's thoughts or providing a character who can convey a personal reaction to an event. See also *Third person*.

*Foot/feet:* Rhythmic unit in which syllables are grouped together; this is the natural speech pattern in English and other Germanic-based languages. In English, the most common of these rhythmic units is composed of one unstressed syllable attached to one stressed syllable (an iamb). When these family groups are forced into a line of poetry, they are called feet in the accentual-syllabic metrical system. In the line "My mis/tress' eyes/are noth/ing like/the sun" there are four iambic feet (◡´) and one pyrrhic foot (◡◡), but in the line "Thére where/the vínes/cling crím/son ón/the wáll," there are three substitutions for the iamb—in the first, third, and fourth feet. The six basic feet in English poetry are the iamb (◡´), trochee (´◡), anapest (◡◡´), dactyl (´◡◡), spondee (´´), and pyrrhus (◡◡).

*Form:* The arrangement of the lines of a poem on the page, its base meter, its rhyme scheme, and occasionally its subject matter. Poems that are arranged into stanzas are called strophic, and because the strophic tradition is so old, a large number of commonly used stanzas have evolved particular uses and characteristics. Poems that run from beginning to end without a break are called stichic. The form of pattern poetry is determined by its visual appearance rather than by lines and stanzas, while the definition of free verse is that it has no discernible form. Some poem types, such as the sestina, sonnet, and ode, are written in particular forms and frequently are restricted to particular subject matter.

*Formalism, Russian:* A twentieth century Russian school of criticism that employed the conventional devices used in literature to defamiliarize that which habit has made familiar. The most extreme formalists treated literary works as artifacts or constructs divorced from their biographical and social contexts.

*Found poetry:* Poems created from language that is "found" in print in nonliterary settings. They can use any language that is already constructed, but usually use language that appears on cultural artifacts, such as cereal boxes. The rules for writing a found poem vary, but generally the found language is used intact or altered only slightly.

*Free verse:* A poem that does not conform to any traditional convention, such as meter, rhyme, or form, and that does not establish any pattern within itself. There is, however, great dispute over whether "free" verse actually exists. T. S. Eliot said that by definition poetry must establish some kind of pattern, and Robert Frost said that "writing free verse is like playing tennis with the net down." However, some would agree with Carl Sandburg, who insisted that "you can play a better game with the net down." Free verse depends more on cadence than on meter.

*Ghazal:* A poetic form based on a type of Persian poetry. It is composed of couplets, often unrhymed,

that function as individual images or observations but that also interrelate in sometimes subtle ways.

*Gnomic verse:* Poetry that typically includes many proverbs or maxims.

*Haiku:* A Japanese form that appeared in the sixteenth century and is still practiced in Japan. A haiku consists of three lines of five, seven, and five syllables each; in Japanese there are other conventions regarding content that are not observed in Western haiku. The traditional haiku took virtually all of its images from nature, using the natural world as a metaphor for the spiritual.

*Half rhyme:* See *Approximate rhyme*

*Heroic couplet:* See *Couplet*

*Historical criticism:* A school of criticism that emphasizes the historical context of literature. Ernst Robert Curtius's *European Literature and the Latin Middle Ages* (1940) is a prominent example of historical criticism.

*Hymn stanza:* See *Ballad*

*Hyperbole:* A deliberate overstatement made in order to heighten the reader's awareness. As with irony, hyperbole works because the reader can perceive the difference between the importance of the dramatic situation and the manner in which it is described.

*Iamb:* A foot consisting of one unstressed and one stressed syllable (◡´) The line "So long/as men/can breathe/or eyes/can see" is composed of five iambs. In the line "Acold/coming/we had/of it," a trochaic foot (a trochee) has been substituted for the expected iamb in the second foot, thus emphasizing that this is a "coming" rather than a "going," an important distinction in T. S. Eliot's "The Journey of the Magi."

*Iambic pentameter:* A very common poetic line consisting of five iambic feet. The following two lines by Thomas Wyatt are in iambic pentameter: "I find no peace and all my war is done,/ I fear and hope, I burn and freeze like ice." See also *Foot/feet*; *iamb*.

*Identical rhyme:* A rhyme in which the entire final stressed syllables contain exactly the same sounds, such as "break/brake," or "bear" (noun), "bear" (verb), "bare" (adjective), "bare" (verb).

*Imagery:* The verbal simulation of sensory perception. Like so many critical terms, imagery betrays a visual bias: It suggests that a poetic image is necessarily visual, a picture in words. In fact, however, imagery calls on all five senses, although the visual is predominant in many poets. In its simplest form, an image re-creates a physical sensation in a clear, literal manner, as in Robert Lowell's lines, "A sweetish smell of shavings, wax and oil/ blows through the redone bedroom newly aged" ("Marriage"). Imagery becomes more complex when the poet employs metaphor and other figures of speech to re-create experience, as in Seamus Heaney's lines, "Right along the lough shore/ A smoke of flies/ Drifts thick in the sunset" ("At Ardboe Point"), substituting a fresh metaphor ("A smoke of flies") for a trite one (a cloud of flies) to help the reader visualize the scene more clearly.

*Interior monologue:* A first-person representation of a persona's or character's thoughts or feelings. It differs from a dramatic monologue in that it deals with thoughts rather than spoken words or conversation.

*Internal rhyme:* See *Rhyme*

*Irony:* A figure of speech in which the speaker's real meaning is different from (and often exactly opposite to) the apparent meaning. Irony is among the three or four most important concepts in modern literary criticism. Although the term originated in classical Greece and has been in the vocabulary of criticism since that time, only in the nineteenth and twentieth centuries did it assume central importance. In Andrew Marvell's lines, "The Grave's a fine and private place,/ But none I think do there embrace" ("To His Coy Mistress"), the speaker's literal meaning—in praise of the grave—is quite different from his real meaning. This kind of irony is often called verbal irony. Another kind of irony is found in narrative and dramatic poetry. In the *Iliad* (c. 750 B.C.E.; English translation, 1611), for example, the reader is made privy to the counsels of the gods, which greatly affect the course of action in the epic, while the human characters are kept in ignorance. This discrepancy between the knowledge of the reader and that of the character (or characters) is called dramatic irony. Beyond these narrow, well-defined varieties of irony are many wider applications.

*Limerick:* A comic five-line poem rhyming *aabba* in which the third and fourth lines are shorter (usually five syllables each) than the first, second, and last lines, which are usually eight syllables each. The limerick's anapestic base makes the verse sound silly; modern limericks are almost invariably associated with bizarre indecency or with ethnic or anticlerical jokes.

*Line:* A poetical unit characterized by the presence of meter; lines are categorized according to the number of feet (see *Foot/feet*) they contain. A pentameter line, for example, contains five feet. This definition does not apply to a great deal of modern poetry, however, which is written in free verse. Ultimately, then, a line must be defined as a typographical unit on the page that performs various functions in different kinds of poetry.

*Lyric poetry:* Short poems, adaptable to metrical variation, and usually personal rather than having a cultural function. Lyric poetry developed when music was accompanied by words, and although the lyrics were later separated from the music, the characteristics of lyric poetry have been shaped by the constraints of music. Lyric poetry sings of the self, exploring deeply personal feelings about life.

*Mad-song:* Verse uttered by someone presumed to have a severe mental illness that manifests in a happy, harmless, inventive way. The typical rhyme scheme of the mad-song is *abccb*, and the unrhymed first line helps to set a tone of oddity and unpredictability, since it controverts the expectation that there will be a rhyme for it. The standard mad-song has short lines.

*Marxist criticism:* A school of criticism based on the nineteenth century writings of Karl Marx and Friedrich Engels that views literature as a product of ideological forces determined by the dominant class However, many Marxists believe that literature operates according to its own autonomous standards of production and reception: It is both a product of ideology and able to determine ideology. As such, literature may overcome the dominant paradigms of its age and play a revolutionary role in society.

*Masculine rhyme:* A rhyme pattern in which rhyme exists in the stressed syllables. "Men/then" constitute masculine rhyme, but so do "af-ter-noons/spoons." Masculine rhyme is generally considered more forceful than feminine rhyme, and while it has a variety of uses, it generally gives authority and assurance to the line, especially when the final syllables are of short duration.

*Metaphor:* A figure of speech in which two strikingly different things are identified with each other, as in "the waves were soldiers moving" (Wallace Stevens). Metaphor is one of a handful of key concepts in modern literary criticism. A metaphor contains a "tenor" and a "vehicle." The tenor is the subject of the metaphor, and the vehicle is the imagery by which the subject is presented. In D. H. Lawrence's lines, "Reach me a gentian, give me a torch/ let me guide myself with the blue, forked torch of this flower" ("Bavarian Gentians"), the tenor is the gentian and the vehicle is the torch. This relatively restricted definition of metaphor by no means covers the usage of the word in modern criticism. Some critics argue that metaphorical perception underlies all figures of speech. Others dispute the distinction between literal and metaphorical description, saying that language is essentially metaphorical. Metaphor has become widely used to identify analogies of all kinds in literature, painting, film, and even music. See also *Simile.*

*Meter:* The pattern that language takes when it is forced into a line of poetry. All language has rhythm; when that rhythm is organized and regulated in the line so as to affect the meaning and emotional response to the words, then the rhythm has been refined into meter. Because the lines of most poems maintain a similar meter throughout, poems are said to have a base meter. The meter is determined by the number of syllables in a line and by the relationship between them.

*Metrical base.* See *Base meter*

*Metonymy:* Using an object that is closely related to an idea stand for the idea itself, such as saying "the crown" to mean the king. Used to emphasize a particular part of the whole or one particular aspect of it. See also *Synecdoche.*

*Mnemonic verse:* Poetry in which rhythmic patterns aid memorization but are not crucial to meaning. Ancient bards were able to remember long poems partly through the use of stock phrases and other mnemonic devices.

*Mock-heroic:* See *Couplet*

*Modernism:* An international movement in the arts that began in the early years of the twentieth century. Although the term is used to describe artists of widely varying persuasions, modernism in general was characterized by its international idiom, by its interest in cultures distant in space or time, by its emphasis on for-mal experimentation, and by its sense of dislocation and radical change.

*Multiculturalism:* The tendency to recognize the perspectives of works by authors (particularly women and non-European writers) who, until the latter part of the twentieth century, were excluded from the canon of Western art and literature. To promote multiculturalism, publishers and educators have revised textbooks and school curricula to incorporate material by and about women, ethnic and racial minorities, non-Western cultures, gays, and lesbians.

*Myth:* Anonymous traditional stories dealing with basic human concepts and antinomies. Claude Lévi-Strauss says that myth is that part of language where the "formula *tradutore, tradittore* reaches its lowest truth value. . . . Its substance does not lie in its style, its original music, or its syntax, but in the story which it tells."

*Myth criticism:* A school of criticism concerned with the basic structural principles of literature. Myth criticism is not to be confused with mythological criticism, which is primarily concerned with finding mythological parallels in the surface action of a narrative.

*Narrator:* The person who is doing the talking—or observing or thinking—in a poem. Roughly synonymous with persona and speaker. Lyric poetry most often consists of the poet expressing his or her own personal feelings directly. Other poems, however, may involve the poet adopting the point of view of another person entirely. In some poems—notably in a dramatic monologue—it is relatively easy to determine that the narrative is being related by a fictional (or perhaps historical) character, but in others it may be more difficult to identify the "I."

*New Criticism:* A formalist movement whose members held that literary criticism is a description and evaluation of its object and that the primary concern of the critic is with the work's unity. At their most extreme, these critics treated literary works as artifacts or constructs divorced from their biographical and social contexts.

*Occasional verse:* Any poem written for a specific occasion, such as a wedding, a birthday, a death, or a public event. Edmund Spenser's *Epithalamion* (1595), which was written for his marriage, and John Milton's "Lycidas," which commemorated the death of his schoolmate Edward King, are examples of occasional verse, as are W. H. Auden's "September 1, 1939" and Frank O'Hara's "The Day Lady Died."

*Octave:* A poem in eight lines. Octaves may have many different variations of meter, such as ottava rima.

*Ode:* A lyric poem that treats a unified subject with elevated emotion, usually ending with a satisfactory resolution. There is no set form for the ode, but it must be long enough to build intense emotional response. Often the ode will address itself to some omnipotent source and will take on a spiritual hue. When explicating an ode, readers should look for the relationship between the narrator and some transcendental power to which the narrator must submit to find contentment. Modern poets have used the ode to treat subjects that are not religious in the theological sense but that have become innate beliefs of society.

*Ottava rima:* An eight-line stanza of iambic pentameter, rhyming *abababcc*. Probably the most famous English poem written in ottava rima is Lord Byron's *Don Juan* (1819-1824), and because the poem was so successful as a spoof, the form has come to be associated with poetic high jinks. However, the stanza has also been used brilliantly for just the opposite effect, to reflect seriousness and meditation.

*Oxymoron:* The juxtaposition of two paradoxical words, such as "wise fool" or "devilish angel."

*Pantoum:* A French form of poetry consisting of four quatrains in which entire lines are repeated in a strict pattern of 1234, 2546, 5768, 7183. Peter Meinke's "Atomic Pantoum" is an example.

*Paradox:* A statement that contains an inherent contradiction. It may be a statement that at first seems true but is in reality contradictory. It may also be a statement that appears contradictory but is actually true or that contains an element of truth that reconciles the contradiction.

*Pentameter:* A type of rhythmic pattern in which each line consists of five poetic feet. See also *Accentual-syllabic meter*; *Foot/feet*; *Iamb*; *Iambic pentameter*; *Line*.

*Periphrasis:* The use of a wordy phrase to describe something that could be described simply in one word.

*Persona:* See *Narrator*

*Phenomenological criticism:* A school of criticism that examines literature as an act and focuses less on individual works and genres. The work is not seen as an object, but rather as part of a strand of latent impulses in the work of a single author or an epoch. Proponents include Georges Poulet in Europe and J. Hillis Miller in the United States.

*Point of view:* The mental position through which readers experience the situation of a poem. As with fiction, poems may be related in the first person, second person (unusual), or third person. (The presence of the words "I" or "we" indicates singular or plural first-person narration.) Point of view may be limited or omniscient. A limited point of view means that the narrator can see only what the poet wants him or her to see, while from an omniscient point of view the narrator can know everything, including the thoughts and motives of others.

*Postcolonialism:* The literature that emerged in the mid-twentieth century when colonies in Asia, Africa, and the Caribbean began gaining their independence from the European nations that had long controlled them. Postcolonial authors, such as Salman Rushdie, V. S. Naipaul, and Derek Walcott, tend to focus on both the freedom and the conflict inherent in living in a postcolonial state.

*Postmodernism:* A ubiquitous but elusive term in contemporary criticism that is loosely applied to the various artistic movements that followed the era of so-called high modernism, represented by such giants as writer James Joyce and painter and sculptor Pablo Picasso. In critical discussions of contemporary fiction, postmodernism is frequently applied to the works of writers such as Thomas Pynchon, John Barth, and Donald Barthelme, who exhibit a self-conscious awareness of their modernist predecessors as well as a reflexive treatment of fictional form. Such reflexive treatments can extend to poetry as well.

*Prose poem:* A poem that looks like prose on the page, with no line breaks. There are no formal characteristics by which a prose poem can be distinguished from a piece of prose. Many prose poems employ rhythmic repetition and other poetic devices not normally found in prose, but others use such devices sparingly if at all. Prose poems range in length from a few lines to three or four pages; most prose poems occupy a page or less.

*Psychological criticism:* A school of criticism that places a strong emphasis on a causal relation between the writer's psychological state, variously interpreted, and his or her works. A notable example of psychological criticism is Norman Fruman's *Coleridge, the Damaged Archangel* (1971).

*Pun:* The use of words that have similar pronunciations but entirely different meanings to establish a connection between two meanings or contexts that the reader would not ordinarily make. The result may be a surprise recognition of an unusual or striking connection, or, more often, a humorously accidental connection.

*Pyrrhus:* A poetic foot consisting of two unstressed syllables, as in the line "Appear/and dis/appear/in the/ blue depth/of the sky," in which foot four is a pyrrhus.

*Quatrain:* Any four-line stanza. Aside from the couplet, it is the most common stanza type. The quatrain's popularity among both sophisticated and unsophisticated readers suggests that there is something inherently pleasing about the form. For many readers, poetry and quatrains are almost synonymous. Balance and antithesis, contrast and comparison not possible in other stanza types are indigenous to the quatrain.

*Realism:* A literary technique in which the primary convention is to render an illusion of fidelity to external reality. Realism is often identified as the primary method of the novel form: It focuses on surface details, maintains a fidelity to the everyday experiences of middle-class society, and strives for a one-to-one relationship between the fiction and the action imitated. The realist movement in the late nineteenth century coincides with the full development of the novel form.

*Regular meter:* A line of poetry that contains only one type of foot. Only the dullest of poems maintain a regular meter throughout, however; skillful poets create interest and emphasis through substitution.

*Relative stress:* The degree to which a syllable in pattern receives more or less emphasis than other syllables in the pattern. Once the dominant stress in the line has been determined, every other syllable can be assigned a stress factor relative to the dominant syllable. The stress factor is created by several aspects of prosody: the position of the syllable in the line, the position of the syllable in its word, the surrounding syllables,

the type of vowels and consonants that constitute the syllable, and the syllable's relation to the foot, base meter, and caesura. Because every syllable will have a different stress factor, there could be as many values as there are syllables, although most prosodists scan poems using primary, secondary, and unstressed notations. In the line "I am there like the dead, or the beast," the anapestic base meter will not permit "I" to take a full stress, but it is a more forceful syllable than the unstressed ones, so it is assigned a secondary stress. Relative to "dead" and "beast," it takes less pressure; relative to the articles in the line, it takes much more.

*Resolution*: Any natural conclusion to a poem, especially to a short lyric poem that establishes some sort of dilemma or conflict that the narrator must solve. Specifically, the resolution is the octave stanza of a Petrarchan sonnet or the couplet of a Shakespearean sonnet in which the first part of the poem preents a situation that must find balance in the resolution.

*Rhyme:* A correspondence of sound between syllables within a line or between lines whose proximity to each other allows the sounds to be sustained. Rhyme may be classified in a number of ways: according to the sound relationship between rhyming words, the position of the rhyming words in the line, and the number and position of the syllables in the rhyming words. Sound classifications include full rhyme and approximate rhyme. Full rhyme is defined as words that have the same vowel sound, followed by the same consonants in their last stressed syllables, and in which all succeeding syllables are phonetically identical. "Hat/ cat" and "laughter/after" are full rhymes. Categories of approximate rhyme are assonance, slant rhyme, alliteration, eye rhyme, and identical rhyme.

Rhyme classified by its position in the line includes end, internal, and initial rhyme. End rhyme occurs when the last words of lines rhyme. Internal rhyme occurs when two words within the same line or within various lines recall the same sound, as in "Wet, below the snow line, smelling of vegetation" in which "below" and "snow" rhyme. Initial rhyme occurs when the first syllables of two or more lines rhyme. See also *Masculine rhyme*; *Feminine rhyme*.

*Rhyme scheme:* A pattern of rhyme in a poem, designated by lowercase (and often italicized) letters. The letters stand for the pattern of rhyming sounds of the last word in each line. For example, the following A. E. Housman quatrain has an *abab* rhyme scheme.

> Into my heart an air that kills
> From yon far country blows:
> What are those blue remembered hills,
> What spires, what farms are those?

As another example, the rhyme scheme of the poetic form known as ottava rima is *ababab cc*. Traditional stanza forms are categorized by their rhyme scheme and base meter.

*Rime royal:* A seven-line stanza in English prosody consisting of iambic pentameter lines rhyming *ababbcc*. William Shakespeare's *The Rape of Lucrece* (1594) is written in this form. The only variation permitted is to make the last line hexameter.

*Romanticism:* A widespread cultural movement in the late eighteenth and early nineteenth centuries, the influence of which is still felt. As a general literary tendency, Romanticism is frequently contrasted with classicism or neoclassicism. Although there were many varieties of Romanticism indigenous to various national literatures, the term generally suggests an assertion of the preeminence of the imagination. Other values associated with various schools of Romanticism include primitivism, an interest in folklore, a reverence for nature, and a fascination with the demoniac and the macabre.

*Rondeau:* One of three standard French forms assimilated by English prosody; generally contains thirteen lines divided into three groups. A common stanzaic grouping rhymes *aabba, aabR, aabbaR*, where the *a* and *b* lines are tetrameter and the *R* (refrain) lines are dimeter. The rondel, another French form, contains fourteen lines of trimeter with alternating rhyme (*ababab bababab*) and is divided into two stanzas. The rondeau and rondel forms are always light and playful.

*Rondel:* See *Rondeau*

*Rubaiyat stanza:* An iambic pentameter quatrain that has a rhyme scheme of *aaba*.

*Scansion:* The assigning of relative stresses and meter to a line of poetry, usually for the purpose of determining where variations, and thus emphasis, in the base meter occur. Scansion can help explain how a poem generates tension and offer clues as to the key words. E. E. Cummings's "singing each morning out of each night" could be scanned in two ways: (1) sing̍ing/each mor̍n/ing̍ out/of each night or (2) sing/ing each/ morning/out of/each night. Scansion will not only affect the way the line is read aloud but also influences the meaning of the line.

*Secondary stress:* See *Relative stress*

*Seguidilla:* An imagistic or mood poem in Spanish, which, like a haiku, creates emotional recognition or spiritual insight in the reader. Although there is no agreement as to what form the English seguidilla should take, most of the successful ones are either four or seven lines with an alternating rhyme scheme of *ababcbc*. Lines 1, 3, and 6 are trimeter; lines 2, 4, 5, and 7 dimeter.

*Semiotics:* The science of signs and sign systems in communication. Literary critic Roman Jakobson says that semiotics deals with the principles that underlie the structure of signs, their use in language of all kinds, and the specific nature of various sign systems.

*Sestet:* A six-line stanza. A Petrarchan or Italian sonnet is composed of an octave followed by a sestet.

*Sestina:* Six six-line stanzas followed by a three-line envoy. The words ending the lines in the first stanza are repeated in different order at the ends of lines in the following stanzas as well as in the middle and end of each line of the envoy. Elizabeth Bishop's "Sestina" is a good example.

*Shakespearean sonnet:* See *Sonnet*

*Simile:* A type of metaphor that signals a comparison by the use of the words "like" or "as." William Shakespeare's line "My mistress' eyes are nothing like the sun" is a simile that establishes a comparison between the woman's eyes and the sun. See also *Metaphor*.

*Slant rhyme:* See *Approximate rhyme*

*Sonnet:* A poem consisting of fourteen lines of iambic pentameter with some form of alternating rhyme and a turning point that divides the poem into two parts. The sonnet is the most important and widely used of traditional poem types. The two major sonnet types are the Petrarchan (or Italian) sonnet and the Shakespearean sonnet. The original sonnet form, the Petrarchan (adopted from the poetry of Petrarch), presents a problem or situation in the first eight lines, the octave, then resolves it in the last six, the sestet. The octave is composed of two quatrains (*abbaabba*), the second of which complicates the first and gradually defines and heightens the problem. The sestet then diminishes the problem slowly until a satisfying resolution is achieved.

During the fifteenth century, the Italian sonnet became an integral part of the courtship ritual, and most sonnets during that time consisted of a young man's description of his perfect lover. Because so many unpoetic young men had generated a nation full of bad sonnets by the end of the century, the form became an object of ridicule, and the English sonnet developed as a reaction against all the bad verse being turned out in the Italian tradition. When Shakespeare wrote "My mistress' eyes are nothing like the sun," he was deliberately negating the Petrarchan conceit, rejoicing in the fact that his loved one was much more interesting and unpredictable than nature. Shakespeare also altered the sonnet's formal balance. Instead of an octave, the Shakespearean sonnet has three quatrains of alternating rhyme and is resolved in a final couplet. During the sixteenth century, long stories were told in sonnet form, one sonnet after the next, to produce sonnet sequences. Although most sonnets contain fourteen lines, some contain as few as ten (the curtal sonnet) or as many as seventeen.

*Speaker:* See *Narrator*

*Split foot:* The alteration of the natural division of a word as a result of being forced into a metrical base. For example, the words "point/ed," "lad/der," and "stick/ing" have a natural falling rhythm, but in the line "My long/two-point/ed lad/der's stick/ing through/a tree" the syllables are rearranged so as to turn the falling rhythm into a rising meter. The result of splitting feet is to create an uncertainty and delicate imbalance in the line.

*Spondee:* When two relatively stressed syllables occur together in a foot, the unit is called a spondee or spondaic foot, as in the line "Appear/and dis/appear/in the/blue depth/of the sky."

*Sprung rhythm:* An unpredictable pattern of stresses in a line, first described near the end of the nineteenth century by Gerard Manley Hopkins, that results from taking accentual meter is to its extreme. According to Hopkins, in sprung rhythm "any two stresses may either follow one another running, or be divided by one, two, or three slack syllables."

*Stanza:* A certain number of lines meant to be taken

as a unit, or that unit. Although a stanza is traditionally considered a unit that contains rhyme and recurs predictably throughout a poem, the term is also sometimes applied to nonrhyming and even irregular units. Poems that are divided into fairly regular and patterned stanzas are called strophic; poems that appear as a single unit, whether rhymed or unrhymed, or that have no predictable stanzas, are called stichic. Both strophic and stichic units represent logical divisions within the poem, and the difference between them lies in the formality and strength of the interwoven unit. Stanza breaks are commonly indicated by a line of space.

*Stichic verse:* See *Stanza*

*Stress:* See *Relative stress*

*Strophic verse:* See *Stanza*

*Structuralism:* A movement based on the idea of intrinsic, self-sufficient structures that do not require reference to external elements. A structure is a system of transformations that involves the interplay of laws inherent in the system itself. The study of language is the primary model for contemporary structuralism. The structuralist literary critic attempts to define structural principles that operate intertextually throughout the whole of literature as well as principles that operate in genres and in individual works. The most accessible survey of structuralism and literature is Jonathan Culler's *Structuralist Poetics* (1975).

*Substitution:* The replacement of one type of foot by another within a base meter. One of the most common and effective methods by which the poet can emphasize a foot. For example, in the line "Thy life/a long/dead calm/of fixed/repose," a spondaic foot ( ′ ′ ) has been substituted for an iambic foot ( ⌣ ′ ). Before substitution is possible, the reader's expectations must have been established by a base meter so that a change in those expectations will have an effect. See also *Foot/feet; iamb; spondee.*

*Syllabic meter:* The system of meter that measures only the number of syllables per line, without regard to stressed and unstressed syllables.

*Symbol:* Any sign that a number of people agree stands for something else. Poetic symbols cannot be rigidly defined; a symbol often evokes a cluster of meanings rather than a single specific meaning. For example, the rose, which suggests fragile beauty, gentleness, softness, and sweet aroma, has come to symbolize love, eternal beauty, or virginity. The tide traditionally symbolizes, among other things, time and eternity. Modern poets may use personal symbols; these take on significance in the context of the poem or of a poet's body of work, particularly if they are reinforced throughout. For example, through constant reinforcement, swans in William Butler Yeats's poetry come to mean as much to the reader as they do to the narrator.

*Synaeresis:* See *Elision*

*Synecdoche:* The use of a part of an object to stand for the entire object, such as using "heart" to mean a person. Used to emphasize a particular part of the whole or one particular aspect of it. See also *Metonymy*.

*Tenor:* See *Metaphor*

*Tercet:* Any form of a rhyming triplet. Examples are *aaa bbb*, as used in Thomas Hardy's "Convergence of the Twain"; *aba cdc*, in which *b* and *d* do not rhyme; *aba bcb*, also known as terza rima.

*Terza rima:* A three-line stanzaic form in which the middle line of one stanza rhymes with the first line of the following stanza, and whose rhyme scheme is *aba bcb cdc*, and so on. Since the rhyme scheme of one stanza can be completed only by adding the next stanza, terza rima tends to propel itself forward, and as a result of this strong forward motion it is well suited to long narration.

*Theme:* Recurring elements in a poem that give it meaning; sometimes used interchangeably with motif. A motif is any recurring pattern of images, symbols, ideas, or language, and is usually restricted to the internal workings of the poem. Thus, one might say that there is an animal motif in William Butler Yeats's poem "Sailing to Byzantium." Theme, however, is usually more general and philosophical, so that the theme of "Sailing to Byzantium" might be interpreted as the failure of human attempts to isolate oneself within the world of art.

*Third person:* The use of linguistic forms that present a poem from the point of view of a narrator, or speaker, who has not been part of the events described and is not probing his or her own relationship to them; rather, the speaker is describing what happened without the use of the word "I" (which would indicate first-person narration). A poet may use a third-person point of view, either limited or omniscient, to establish a distance between the reader and the subject, to give credi-

bility to a large expanse of narration, or to allow the poem to include a number of characters who can be commented on by the narrator.

*Tone:* The expression of a poet's attitude toward the subject and persona of the poem as well as about himself or herself, society, and the poem's readers. If the ultimate aim of art is to express and control emotions and attitudes, then tone is one of the most important elements of poetry. Tone is created through the denotative and connotative meanings of words and through the sound of language (principally rhyme, consonants, and diction). Adjectives such as "satirical," "compassionate," "empathetic," "ironic," and "sarcastic" are used to describe tone.

*Trochee:* A foot with one stressed syllable and one unstressed syllable (/‿), as in the line: "Double/double toil and/trouble." Trochaic lines are frequently substituted in an iambic base meter in order to create counterpointing. See also *Foot/feet*; *iamb*.

*Truncation:* The omission of the last, unstressed syllable of a falling line, as in the line: "Tyger,/tyger/ burning/bright," where the "ly" has been dropped from bright.

*Vehicle:* See *Metaphor*

*Verse:* A generic term for poetry, as in *The Oxford Book of English Verse* (1939); poetry that is humorous or superficial, as in light verse or greeting-card verse; and a stanza or line.

*Verse drama:* Drama that is written in poetic rather than ordinary language and characterized and delivered by the line. Verse drama flourished during the eighteenth century, when the couplet became a standard literary form.

*Verse paragraph:* A division created within a stichic poem (see *Stanza*) by logic or syntax, rather than by form. Such divisions are important for determining the movement of a poem and the logical association between ideas.

*Villanelle:* A French verse form that has been assimilated by English prosody, usually composed of nineteen lines divided into five tercets and a quatrain, rhyming *aba*, *bba*, *aba*, *aba*, *abaa*. The third line is repeated in the ninth and fifteenth lines. Dylan Thomas's "Do Not Go Gentle into That Good Night" is a modern English example of a villanelle.

# BIBLIOGRAPHY

## CONTENTS

## ABOUT THIS BIBLIOGRAPHY

This bibliography contains three main sections. The first, "General Reference Sources," lists books that treat poetry of all time periods and countries, including British, Irish, and Commonwealth poets. The section "History of British, Irish, and Commonwealth Poetry" includes sources primarily relevant to poetry from these countries written in five different eras. The final section, "Poets by Country," is divided geographically, with added subdivisions for most countries.

## GENERAL REFERENCE SOURCES

BIOGRAPHICAL SOURCES

Bold, Alan. *Longman Dictionary of Poets: The Lives and Works of 1001 Poets in the English Language.* Harlow, Essex: Longman, 1985.

Colby, Vineta, ed. *World Authors, 1975-1980.* Wilson Authors Series. New York: H. W. Wilson, 1985.

_____. *World Authors, 1980-1985.* Wilson Authors Series. New York: H. W. Wilson, 1991.

_____. *World Authors, 1985-1990.* Wilson Authors Series. New York: H. W. Wilson, 1995.

*Cyclopedia of World Authors.* 4th rev. ed. 5 vols. Pasadena, Calif.: Salem Press, 2003.

*Dictionary of Literary Biography.* 254 vols. Detroit: Gale Research, 1978-    .

*International Who's Who in Poetry and Poets' Encyclopaedia.* Cambridge, England: International Biographical Centre, 1993.

Riggs, Thomas, ed. *Contemporary Poets.* Contemporary Writers Series. 7th ed. Detroit: St. James Press, 2001.

Seymour-Smith, Martin, and Andrew C. Kimmens, eds. *World Authors, 1900-1950.* Wilson Authors Series. 4 vols. New York: H. W. Wilson, 1996.

Thompson, Clifford, ed. *World Authors, 1990-1995.*

Wilson Authors Series. New York: H. W. Wilson, 1999.

Wakeman, John, ed. *World Authors, 1950-1970.* New York: H. W. Wilson, 1975.

_____. *World Authors, 1970-1975.* Wilson Authors Series. New York: H. W. Wilson, 1991.

Willhardt, Mark, and Alan Michael Parker, eds. *Who's Who in Twentieth Century World Poetry.* New York: Routledge, 2000.

CRITICISM

Alexander, Harriet Semmes, comp. *American and British Poetry: A Guide to the Criticism, 1925-1978.* Manchester, England: Manchester University Press, 1984.

_____. *American and British Poetry: A Guide to the Criticism, 1979-1990.* 2 vols. Athens, Ohio: Swallow Press, 1995.

*Annual Bibliography of English Language and Literature.* 1921-   .

Brooks, Cleanth, and Robert Penn Warren. *Understanding Poetry.* 4th ed. Reprint. Fort Worth, Tex.: Heinle & Heinle, 2003.

Childs, Peter. *The Twentieth Century in Poetry: A Critical Survey.* New York: Routledge, 1999.

*Classical and Medieval Literature Criticism.* Detroit: Gale Research, 1988-   .

Cline, Gloria Stark, and Jeffrey A. Baker. *An Index to Criticism of British and American Poetry.* Metuchen, N.J.: Scarecrow Press, 1973.

Coleman, Arthur. *Epic and Romance Criticism: A Checklist of Interpretations, 1940-1972.* New York: Watermill Publishers, 1973.

*Contemporary Literary Criticism.* Detroit: Gale Research, 1973-   .

Day, Gary. *Literary Criticism: A New History.* Edinburgh, Scotland: Edinburgh University Press, 2008.

Donow, Herbert S., comp. *The Sonnet in England and America: A Bibliography of Criticism.* Westport, Conn.: Greenwood Press, 1982.

Draper, James P., ed. *World Literature Criticism 1500 to the Present: A Selection of Major Authors from Gale's Literary Criticism Series.* 6 vols. Detroit: Gale Research, 1992.

Habib, M. A. R. *A History of Literary Criticism: From Plato to the Present.* Malden, Mass.: Wiley-Blackwell, 2005.

Jason, Philip K., ed. *Masterplots II: Poetry Series, Revised Edition.* 8 vols. Pasadena, Calif.: Salem Press, 2002.

Kuntz, Joseph M., and Nancy C. Martinez. *Poetry Explication: A Checklist of Interpretation Since 1925 of British and American Poems Past and Present.* 3d ed. Boston: Hall, 1980.

*Literature Criticism from 1400 to 1800.* Detroit: Gale Research, 1984-   .

Lodge, David, and Nigel Wood. *Modern Criticism and Theory.* 3d ed. New York: Longman, 2008.

Magill, Frank N., ed. *Magill's Bibliography of Literary Criticism.* 4 vols. Englewood Cliffs, N.J.: Salem Press, 1979.

*MLA International Bibliography.* New York: Modern Language Association of America, 1922-   .

*Nineteenth-Century Literature Criticism.* Detroit: Gale Research, 1981-   .

Roberts, Neil, ed. *A Companion to Twentieth-Century Poetry.* Malden, Mass.: Blackwell Publishers, 2001.

*Twentieth-Century Literary Criticism.* Detroit: Gale Research, 1978-   .

Vedder, Polly, ed. *World Literature Criticism Supplement: A Selection of Major Authors from Gale's Literary Criticism Series.* 2 vols. Detroit: Gale Research, 1997.

Walcutt, Charles Child, and J. Edwin Whitesell, eds. *Modern Poetry.* Vol. 1 in *The Explicator Cyclopedia.* Chicago: Quadrangle Books, 1968.

_____. *Traditional Poetry: Medieval to Late Victorian.* Vol. 2 in *The Explicator Cyclopedia.* Chicago: Quadrangle Books, 1968.

*The Year's Work in English Studies.* 1921-   .

Young, Robyn V., ed. *Poetry Criticism: Excerpts from Criticism of the Works of the Most Significant and Widely Studied Poets of World Literature.* 29 vols. Detroit: Gale Research, 1991.

DICTIONARIES, HISTORIES, AND HANDBOOKS

Carey, Gary, and Mary Ellen Snodgrass. *A Multicultural Dictionary of Literary Terms.* Jefferson, N.C.: McFarland, 1999.

Deutsch, Babette. *Poetry Handbook: A Dictionary of Terms*. 4th ed. New York: Funk & Wagnalls, 1974.

Draper, Ronald P. *An Introduction to Twentieth-Century Poetry in English*. New York: St. Martin's Press, 1999.

Drury, John. *The Poetry Dictionary*. Cincinnati, Ohio: Story Press, 1995.

Gingerich, Martin E. *Contemporary Poetry in America and England, 1950-1975: A Guide to Information Sources*. American Literature, English Literature, and World Literatures in English: An Information Guide Series 41. Detroit: Gale Research, 1983.

Hamilton, Ian, ed. *The Oxford Companion to Twentieth-Century Poetry in English*. New York: Oxford University Press, 1994.

Kinzie, Mary. *A Poet's Guide to Poetry*. Chicago: University of Chicago Press, 1999.

Lennard, John. *The Poetry Handbook: A Guide to Reading Poetry for Pleasure and Practical Criticism*. New York: Oxford University Press, 1996.

Matterson, Stephen, and Darryl Jones. *Studying Poetry*. New York: Oxford University Press, 2000.

Packard, William. *The Poet's Dictionary: A Handbook of Prosody and Poetic Devices*. New York: Harper & Row, 1989.

Perkins, David. *A History of Modern Poetry: From the 1890's to the High Modernist Mode*. Vol. 1 in *A History of Modern Poetry*. Cambridge, Mass.: Belknap-Harvard University Press, 1976.

_____. *A History of Modern Poetry: Modernism and After*. Vol. 2 in *A History of Modern Poetry*. 2 vols. Cambridge, Mass.: Belknap-Harvard University Press, 1987.

Preminger, Alex, et al., eds. *The New Princeton Encyclopedia of Poetry and Poetics*. 3d rev. ed. Princeton, N.J.: Princeton University Press, 1993.

Shipley, Joseph Twadell, ed. *Dictionary of World Literary Terms, Forms, Technique, Criticism*. Rev. ed. Boston: Writer, 1970.

INDEXES OF PRIMARY WORKS

Frankovich, Nicholas, ed. *The Columbia Granger's Index to Poetry in Anthologies*. 11th ed. New York: Columbia University Press, 1997.

_____. *The Columbia Granger's Index to Poetry in Collected and Selected Works*. New York: Columbia University Press, 1997.

Guy, Patricia. *A Women's Poetry Index*. Phoenix, Ariz.: Oryx Press, 1985.

Hazen, Edith P., ed. *Columbia Granger's Index to Poetry*. 10th ed. New York: Columbia University Press, 1994.

Hoffman, Herbert H., and Rita Ludwig Hoffman, comps. *International Index to Recorded Poetry*. New York: H. W. Wilson, 1983.

Kline, Victoria. *Last Lines: An Index to the Last Lines of Poetry*. 2 vols. Vol. 1, *Last Line Index, Title Index*; Vol. 2, *Author Index, Keyword Index*. New York: Facts On File, 1991.

Marcan, Peter. *Poetry Themes: A Bibliographical Index to Subject Anthologies and Related Criticisms in the English Language, 1875-1975*. Hamden, Conn.: Linnet Books, 1977.

*Poem Finder*. Great Neck, N.Y.: Roth, 2000.

*Poetry Index Annual: A Title, Author, First Line, Keyword, and Subject Index to Poetry in Anthologies*. Great Neck, N.Y.: Poetry Index, 1982-    .

POETICS, POETIC FORMS, AND GENRES

Attridge, Derek. *Poetic Rhythm: An Introduction*. New York: Cambridge University Press, 1995.

Brogan, T. V. F. *English Versification, 1570-1980: A Reference Guide with a Global Appendix*. Baltimore: Johns Hopkins University Press, 1981.

_____. *Verseform: A Comparative Bibliography*. Baltimore: Johns Hopkins University Press, 1989.

Fussell, Paul. *Poetic Meter and Poetic Form*. Rev. ed. New York: McGraw-Hill, 1979.

Hollander, John. *Rhyme's Reason*. 3d ed. New Haven, Conn.: Yale University Press, 2001.

Malof, Joseph. *A Manual of English Meters*. Bloomington: Indiana University Press, 1970.

Padgett, Ron, ed. *The Teachers and Writers Handbook of Poetic Forms*. 2d ed. New York: Teachers & Writers Collaborative, 2000.

Pinsky, Robert. *The Sounds of Poetry: A Brief Guide*. New York: Farrar, Straus and Giroux, 1998.

Preminger, Alex, and T. V. F. Brogan, eds. *New Princeton Encyclopedia of Poetry and Poetics*. 3d ed. Princeton, N.J.: Princeton University Press, 1993.

Shapiro, Karl, and Robert Beum. *A Prosody Handbook*. New York: Harper, 1965.

Spiller, Michael R. G. *The Sonnet Sequence: A Study of Its Strategies*. Studies in Literary Themes and Genres 13. New York: Twayne, 1997.

Turco, Lewis. *The New Book of Forms: A Handbook of Poetics*. Hanover: University Press of New England, 1986.

Williams, Miller. *Patterns of Poetry: An Encyclopedia of Forms*. Baton Rouge: Louisiana State University Press, 1986.

### POSTCOLONIAL ANGLOPHONE POETRY

Benson, Eugene, and L. W. Connolly. *Encyclopedia of Post-Colonial Literatures in English*. 2 vols. London: Routledge, 1994.

Bery, Ashok. *Cultural Translation and Postcolonial Poetry*. New York: Palgrave Macmillan, 2007.

Keown, Michelle. *Pacific Islands Writing: The Postcolonial Literatures of Aotearoa/New Zealand and Oceania*. New York: Oxford University Press, 2007.

Lawson, Alan, et al. *Post-Colonial Literatures in English: General, Theoretical, and Comparative, 1970-1993*. A Reference Publication in Literature. New York: G. K. Hall, 1997.

Mohanram, Radhika, and Gita Rajan, eds. *English Postcoloniality: Literatures from Around the World*. Contributions to the Study of World Literature 66. Westport, Conn.: Greenwood Press, 1996.

Patke, Rajeev S. *Postcolonial Poetry in English*. New York: Oxford University Press, 2006.

Ramazani, Jahan. *The Hybrid Muse: Postcolonial Poetry in English*. Chicago: University of Chicago Press, 2001.

Williams, Mark. *Post-Colonial Literatures in English: Southeast Asia, New Zealand, and the Pacific, 1970-1992*. Reference Publications in Literature. New York: G. K. Hall, 1996.

### WOMEN WRITERS

Davis, Gwenn, and Beverly A. Joyce, comps. *Poetry by Women to 1900: A Bibliography of American and British Writers*. Toronto: University of Toronto Press, 1991.

Mark, Alison, and Deryn Rees-Jones. *Contemporary Women's Poetry: Reading, Writing, Practice*. New York: St. Martin's Press, 2000.

# HISTORY OF BRITISH, IRISH, AND COMMONWEALTH POETRY

### OLD AND MIDDLE ENGLISH

Aertsen, Hank, and Rolf H. Bremmer, eds. *Companion to Old English Poetry*. Amsterdam: VU University Press, 1994.

Beale, Walter H. *Old and Middle English Poetry to 1500: A Guide to Information Sources*. American Literature, English Literature, and World Literatures in English: An Information Guide Series 7. Detroit: Gale Research, 1976.

Brown, Carleton, and Rossell Hope Robbins. *The Index of Middle English Verse*. New York: Columbia University Press for the Index Society, 1943.

Cooney, Helen, ed. *Nation, Court, and Culture: New Essays on Fifteenth Century Poetry*. Dublin: Four Courts Press, 2001.

Hirsh, John C., ed. *Medieval Lyric: Middle English Lyrics, Ballads, and Carols*. Annotated edition. Malden, Mass.: Blackwell, 2005.

Jost, Jean E. *Ten Middle English Arthurian Romances: A Reference Guide*. Boston: G. K. Hall, 1986.

Mapstone, Sally, ed. *Older Scots Literature*. Edinburgh: John Donald, 2005.

Martin, Joanna. *Kingship and Love in Scottish Poetry, 1424-1540*. Farnham, Surrey, England: Ashgate, 2008.

Martinez, Nancy C., and Joseph G. R. Martinez. *Old English-Medieval*. Vol. 1 in *Guide to British Poetry Explication*. Boston: G. K. Hall, 1991.

O'Keeffe, Katherine O'Brien, ed. *Old English Shorter Poems: Basic Readings*. Garland Reference Library of the Humanities 1432. New York: Garland, 1994.

Palmer, R. Barton, ed. and trans. *Medieval Epic and*

*Romance: An Anthology of English and French Narrative*. Glen Allen, Va.: College Publishing, 2007.

Pearsall, Derek. *Old English and Middle English Poetry*. Vol. 1 in *The Routledge History of English Poetry*. London: Routledge, 1977.

Scanlon, Larry, ed. *The Cambridge Companion to Medieval Literature, 1100-1500*. New York: Cambridge University Press, 2009.

## RENAISSANCE TO 1660

Cheney, Patrick, Andrew Hadfield, and Garrett A. Sullivan, Jr., eds. *Early Modern English Poetry: A Critical Companion*. New York: Oxford University Press, 2006.

Frank, Joseph. *Hobbled Pegasus: A Descriptive Bibliography of Minor English Poetry, 1641-1660*. Albuquerque: University of New Mexico Press, 1968.

Gutierrez, Nancy A. *English Historical Poetry, 1476-1603: A Bibliography*. Garland Reference Library of the Humanities 410. New York: Garland, 1983.

Martinez, Nancy C., and Joseph G. R. Martinez. *Renaissance*. Vol. 2 in *Guide to British Poetry Explication*. Boston: G. K. Hall, 1991.

Post, Jonathan F. S., ed. *Green Thoughts, Green Shades: Essays by Contemporary Poets on the Early Modern Lyric*. Berkeley: University of California Press, 2002.

Ringler, William A., Jr. *Bibliography and Index of English Verse Printed 1476-1558*. New York: Mansell, 1988.

Ringler, William A., Michael Rudick, and Susan J. Ringler. *Bibliography and Index of English Verse in Manuscript, 1501-1558*. New York: Mansell, 1992.

Rivers, Isabel. *Classical and Christian Ideas in English Renaissance Poetry: A Student's Guide*. 2d ed. New York: Routledge, 1994.

## RESTORATION (1660) THROUGH EIGHTEENTH CENTURY

Fairer, David. *English Poetry of the Eighteenth Century, 1700-1789*. Annotated edition. Harlow, Essex, England: Longman, 2003.

Foxon, D. F. *English Verse 1701-1750: A Catalogue of Separately Printed Poems with Notes on Contem-*

*porary Collected Editions*. 2 vols. Cambridge, England: Cambridge University Press, 1975.

Healy, John Joseph. *Literature and the Aborigine in Australia, 1770-1975*. New York: St. Martin's Press, 1978.

Jackson, J. R. de J. *Annals of English Verse, 1770-1835: A Preliminary Survey of the Volumes Published*. Garland Reference Library of the Humanities 535. New York: Garland, 1985.

Martinez, Nancy C., Joseph G. R. Martinez, and Erland Anderson. *Restoration-Romantic*. Vol. 3 in *Guide to British Poetry Explication*. Boston: G. K. Hall, 1991.

Nokes, David, and Janet Barron. *An Annotated Critical Bibliography of Augustan Poetry*. Annotated Critical Bibliographies. New York: St. Martin's Press, 1989.

Rothstein, Eric. *Restoration and Eighteenth-Century Poetry, 1660-1780*. Vol. 3 in *The Routledge History of English Poetry*. Boston: Routledge & Kegan Paul, 1981.

Samuels, Selina, ed. *Australian Literature, 1788-1914*. Dictionary of Literary Biography 230. Detroit: Gale Group, 2001.

Sitter, John, ed. *The Cambridge Companion to Eighteenth-Century Poetry*. New York: Cambridge University Press, 2001.

Starr, G. Gabrielle. *Lyric Generations: Poetry and the Novel in the Long Eighteenth Century*. Baltimore: Johns Hopkins University Press, 2004.

## NINETEENTH CENTURY

Blyth, Caroline, ed. *Decadent Verse: An Anthology of Late-Victorian Poetry, 1872-1900*. London: Anthem Press, 2009.

Bristow, Joseph, ed. *The Cambridge Companion to Victorian Poetry*. New York: Cambridge University Press, 2000.

Chapman, Alison, ed. *Victorian Women Poets*. Cambridge, England: D. S. Brewer, 2003.

Faverty, Frederic E., ed. *The Victorian Poets: A Guide to Research*. 2d ed. Cambridge, Mass.: Harvard University Press, 1968.

Healy, John Joseph. *Literature and the Aborigine in Australia, 1770-1975*. New York: St. Martin's Press, 1978.

Jackson, J. R. de J. *Poetry of the Romantic Period*. Vol.

4 in *The Routledge History of English Poetry*. Boston: Routledge & Kegan Paul, 1980.

Jordan, Frank, ed. *The English Romantic Poets: A Review of Research and Criticism*. 4th ed. New York: MLA, 1985.

McLane, Maureen N., and James Chandler, eds. *The Cambridge Companion to British Romantic Poetry*. New York: Cambridge University Press, 2008.

Martinez, Nancy C., Joseph G. R. Martinez, and Erland Anderson. *Victorian-Contemporary*. Vol. 4 in *Guide to British Poetry Explication*. Boston: G. K. Hall, 1991.

O'Gorman, Francis, ed. *Victorian Poetry: An Annotated Anthology*. Malden, Mass.: Wiley-Blackwell, 2004.

O'Neill, Michael, and Charles Mahoney, eds. *Romantic Poetry: An Annotated Anthology*. Malden, Mass.: Wiley-Blackwell, 2008.

Reilly, Catherine W. *Late Victorian Poetry, 1880-1899: An Annotated Biobibliography*. New York: Mansell, 1994.

_____. *Mid-Victorian Poetry, 1860-1879: An Annotated Biobibliography*. New York: Mansell, 2000.

Reiman, Donald H. *English Romantic Poetry, 1800-1835: A Guide to Information Sources*. American Literature, English Literature, and World Literature in English: An Information Guide Series 27. Detroit: Gale Research, 1979.

Richards, Bernard Arthur. *English Poetry of the Victorian Period, 1830-1890*. 2d ed. New York: Longman, 2001.

Roberts, Adam. *Romantic and Victorian Long Poems: A Guide*. Brookfield, Vt.: Ashgate, 1999.

Samuels, Selina, ed. *Australian Literature, 1788-1914*. Dictionary of Literary Biography 230. Detroit: Gale Group, 2001.

TWENTIETH CENTURY AND CONTEMPORARY

Anderson, Emily Ann. *English Poetry, 1900-1950: A Guide to Information Sources*. American Literature, English Literature, and World Literatures in English: An Information Guide Series 33. Detroit: Gale Research, 1982.

Blouin, Louise, Bernard Pozier, and D. G. Jones, eds. *Esprit de Corps: Québec Poetry of the Late Twentieth Century in Translation*. Winnipeg, Man.: Muses, 1997.

Bradley, Jerry. *The Movement: British Poets of the 1950's*. New York: Twayne, 1993.

Brins, Nicholas, and Rebecca McNeer, eds. *A Companion to Australian Literature Since 1900*. Rochester, N.Y.: Camden House, 2007.

Broom, Sarah. *Contemporary British and Irish Poetry: An Introduction*. Illustrated edition. New York: Palgrave Macmillan, 2006.

Corcoran, Neil, ed. *The Cambridge Companion to Twentieth-Century English Poetry*. New York: Cambridge University Press, 2007.

Davie, Donald. *Under Briggflatts: A History of Poetry in Great Britain, 1960-1988*. Chicago: University of Chicago Press, 1989.

Dowson, Jane, and Alice Entwistle. *A History of Twentieth-Century British Women's Poetry*. New York: Cambridge University Press, 2005.

Gray, Robert, and Geoffrey Lehmann, eds. *Australian Poetry in the Twentieth Century*. Port Melbourne: William Heinemann Australia, 1991.

Healy, John Joseph. *Literature and the Aborigine in Australia, 1770-1975*. New York: St. Martin's Press, 1978.

Lehmann, John. *The English Poets of the First World War*. New York: Thames and Hudson, 1982.

Lever, Richard, James Wieland, and Scott Findlay. *Post-colonial Literatures in English: Australia, 1970-1992*. A Reference Publication in Literature. New York: G. K. Hall, 1996.

Martinez, Nancy C., Joseph G. R. Martinez, and Erland Anderson. *Victorian-Contemporary*. Vol. 4 in *Guide to British Poetry Explication*. Boston: G. K. Hall, 1991.

Persoon, James. *Modern British Poetry, 1900-1939*. Twayne's Critical History of Poetry Studies. New York: Twayne, 1999.

Reilly, Catherine W. *English Poetry of the Second World War: A Biobibliography*. Boston: G. K. Hall, 1986.

Samuels, Selina, ed. *Australian Literature, 1788-1914*. Dictionary of Literary Biography 230. Detroit: Gale Group, 2001.

Schmidt, Michael. *A Reader's Guide to Fifty Modern British Poets*. New York: Barnes & Noble, 1979.

Shields, Ellen F. *Contemporary English Poetry: An Annotated Bibliography of Criticism to 1980.* Garland Reference Library of the Humanities 460. New York: Garland, 1984.

Thwaite, Anthony. *Poetry Today: A Critical Guide to British Poetry, 1960-1992.* New York: Longman with the British Council, 1996.

Tuma, Keith, ed. *Anthology of Twentieth-Century British and Irish Poetry.* Annotated edition. New York: Oxford University Press, 2001.

# POETS BY COUNTRY

## AUSTRALIA

### Bibliographies

Hergenhan, Laurie, and Martin Duwell, eds. *The ALS Guide to Australian Writers: A Bibliography.* UQP Studies in Australian Literature. Queensland: University of Queensland Press, 1992.

Webby, Elizabeth. *Early Australian Poetry: An Annotated Bibliography of Original Poems Published in Australian Newspapers, Magazines, and Almanacks Before 1850.* Sydney: Hale, 1982.

### Biographical sources

*Who's Who of Australian Writers.* 2d ed. Clayton: National Centre for Australian Studies, 1995.

### Dictionaries, histories, and handbooks

Andrews, B. G., and William H. Wilde. *Australian Literature to 1900: A Guide to Information Sources.* American Literature, English Literature, and World Literatures in English: An Information Guide Series 22. Detroit: Gale Research, 1980.

Brins, Nicholas, and Rebecca McNeer, eds. *A Companion to Australian Literature Since 1900.* Rochester, N.Y.: Camden House, 2007.

Elliott, Brian Robinson. *The Landscape of Australian Poetry.* Melbourne: Cheshire, 1967.

Gray, Robert, and Geoffrey Lehmann, eds. *Australian Poetry in the Twentieth Century.* Port Melbourne: William Heinemann Australia, 1991.

Green, H. M. *A History of Australian Literature: Pure and Applied—A Critical Review of All Forms of Literature Produced in Australia from the First Books Published After the Arrival of the First Fleet Until 1950.* Revised by Dorothy Green. 2 vols. London: Angus & Robertson, 1984.

Hergenhan, Laurie. *The Penguin New Literary History of Australia.* Victoria: Penguin, 1988.

Hooton, Joy, and Harry Heseltine. *Annals of Australian Literature.* 2d ed. Melbourne: Oxford University Press, 1992.

Jaffa, Herbert C. *Modern Australian Poetry, 1920-1970: A Guide to Information Sources.* American Literature, English Literature, and World Literatures in English: An Information Guide Series 24. Detroit: Gale Research, 1979.

Lever, Richard, James Wieland, and Scott Findlay. *Post-colonial Literatures in English: Australia, 1970-1992.* A Reference Publication in Literature. New York: G. K. Hall, 1996.

Lock, Fred, and Alan Lawson. *Australian Literature: A Reference Guide.* 2d ed. Australian Bibliographies. New York: Oxford University Press, 1980.

Pierce, Peter, ed. *The Cambridge History of Australian Literature.* New York: Cambridge University Press, 2009.

Samuels, Selina, ed. *Australian Literature, 1788-1914.* Dictionary of Literary Biography 230. Detroit: Gale Group, 2001.

Wilde, W. H., Joy Hooton, and Barry Andrews. *The Oxford Companion to Australian Literature.* 2d ed. New York: Oxford University Press, 1994.

### Women writers

Adelaide, Debra. *Bibliography of Australian Women's Literature, 1795-1990: A Listing of Fiction, Poetry, Drama, and Non-Fiction Published in Monograph Form Arranged Alphabetically by Author.* Port Melbourne: Thorpe with National Centre for Australian Studies, 1991.

Hampton, Susan, and Kate Llewellyn, eds. *The Penguin Book of Australian Women Poets.* Victoria: Penguin Ringwood, 1986.

### Aboriginal poets

Healy, John Joseph. *Literature and the Aborigine in Australia, 1770-1975*. New York: St. Martin's Press, 1978.

Schurmann-Zeggel, Heinz. *Black Australian Literature: A Bibliography of Fiction, Poetry, Drama, Oral Traditions and Non-Fiction, Including Critical Commentary, 1900-1991*. New York: Peter Lang, 1997.

Shoemaker, Adam. *Black Words, White Page*. UQP Studies in Australian Literature. St. Lucia: University of Queensland Press, 1989.

## CANADA

### Biographical sources

Lecker, Robert, Jack David, and Ellen Quiqley, eds. *Canadian Writers and Their Works: Poetry Series*. Downsview, Ont.: ECW Press, 1983.

McLeod, Donald, ed. *Canadian Writers and Their Works Cumulated Index Volume: Poetry Series*. Toronto, Ont.: ECW Press, 1993.

New, W. H., ed. *Canadian Writers Before 1890*. Dictionary of Literary Biography 99. Detroit: Gale Research, 1990.

_____. *Canadian Writers, 1890-1920*. Dictionary of Literary Biography 92. Detroit: Gale Research, 1990.

_____. *Canadian Writers, 1920-1959: First Series*. Dictionary of Literary Biography 68. Detroit: Gale Research, 1988.

_____. *Canadian Writers, 1920-1959: Second Series*. Dictionary of Literary Biography 88. Detroit: Gale Research, 1989.

_____. *Canadian Writers Since 1960: First Series*. Dictionary of Literary Biography 53. Detroit: Gale Research, 1986.

_____. *Canadian Writers Since 1960: Second Series*. Dictionary of Literary Biography 60. Detroit: Gale Research, 1987.

### Criticism

Platnick, Phyllis. *Canadian Poetry: Index to Criticisms, 1970-1979 = Poésie canadienne: Index de critiques, 1970-1979*. Ontario: Canadian Library Association, 1985.

### Dictionaries, histories, and handbooks

Blouin, Louise, Bernard Pozier, and D. G. Jones, eds. *Esprit de Corps: Québec Poetry of the Late Twentieth Century in Translation*. Winnipeg, Man.: Muses, 1997.

Brandt, Di, and Barbara Godard, eds. *Wider Boundaries of Daring: The Modernist Impulse in Canadian Women's Poetry*. Waterloo, Ont.: Wilfrid Laurier University Press, 2009.

Marshall, Tom. *Harsh and Lovely Land: The Major Canadian Poets and the Making of a Canadian Tradition*. Vancouver: University of British Columbia Press, 1979.

Starnino, Carmine, ed. *The New Canon: An Anthology of Canadian Poetry*. Montreal: Véhicule Press, 2006.

Stevens, Peter. *Modern English-Canadian Poetry: A Guide to Information Sources*. American Literature, English Literature, and World Literatures in English: An Information Guide Series 15. Detroit: Gale Research, 1978.

### Indexes of primary works

Fee, Margery, ed. *Canadian Poetry in Selected English-Language Anthologies: An Index and Guide*. Halifax, N.S.: Dalhousie University, University Libraries, School of Library Service, 1985.

McQuarrie, Jane, Anne Mercer, and Gordon Ripley, eds. *Index to Canadian Poetry in English*. Toronto: Reference Press, 1984.

## ENGLAND

### Bibliographies

Case, Arthur E. *A Bibliography of English Poetical Miscellanies, 1521-1750*. London: Oxford University Press for the Bibliographical Society, 1935.

Dyson, A. E., ed. *English Poetry: Select Bibliographical Guides*. London: Oxford University Press, 1971.

### Biographical sources

Fredeman, William E., and Ira B. Nadel, eds. *Victorian Poets Before 1850*. Dictionary of Literary Biography 32. Detroit: Gale Research, 1984.

_____. *Victorian Poets After 1850*. Dictionary of Literary Biography 35. Detroit: Gale Research, 1985.

Greenfield, John R., ed. *British Romantic Poets, 1789-1832: First Series*. Dictionary of Literary Biography 93. Detroit: Gale Research, 1990.

_____, ed. *British Romantic Poets, 1789-1832: Second Series*. Dictionary of Literary Biography 96. Detroit: Gale Research, 1990.

Hester, M. Thomas, ed. *Seventeenth-Century British Nondramatic Poets: First Series*. Dictionary of Literary Biography 121. Detroit: Gale Research, 1992.

Quinn, Patrick, ed. *British Poets of the Great War: Brooke, Rosenberg, Thomas: A Documentary Volume*. Dictionary of Literary Biography 216. Detroit: Gale Group, 2000.

Sherry, Vincent B., Jr., ed. *Poets of Great Britain and Ireland, 1945-1960*. Dictionary of Literary Biography 27. Detroit: Gale Research, 1984.

_____. *Poets of Great Britain and Ireland, Since 1960*. Dictionary of Literary Biography 40. Detroit: Gale Research, 1985.

Sitter, John, ed. *Seventeenth-Century British Nondramatic Poets: Second Series*. Dictionary of Literary Biography 126. Detroit: Gale Research, 1993.

_____. *Seventeenth-Century British Nondramatic Poets: Third Series*. Dictionary of Literary Biography 131. Detroit: Gale Research, 1993.

_____. *Eighteenth-Century British Poets: First Series*. Dictionary of Literary Biography 95. Detroit: Gale Research, 1990.

_____. *Eighteenth-Century British Poets: Second Series*. Dictionary of Literary Biography 109. Detroit: Gale Research, 1991.

Stanford, Donald E., ed. *British Poets, 1880-1914*. Dictionary of Literary Biography 19. Detroit: Gale Research, 1983.

_____. *British Poets, 1914-1945*. Dictionary of Literary Biography 20. Detroit: Gale Research, 1983.

Thesing, William B., ed. *Late Nineteenth- and Early Twentieth-Century British Women Poets*. Dictionary of Literary Biography 240. Detroit: Gale Group, 2001.

_____. *Victorian Women Poets*. Dictionary of Literary Biography 199. Detroit: Gale Research, 1999.

### Criticism

*Guide to British Poetry Explication*. 4 vols. Boston: G. K. Hall, 1991.

### Dictionaries, histories, and handbooks

Courthope, W. J. *A History of English Poetry*. New York: Macmillan, 1895-1910.

Garrett, John. *British Poetry Since the Sixteenth Century: A Student's Guide*. Totowa, N.J.: Barnes & Noble Books, 1987.

Mell, Donald Charles, Jr. *English Poetry, 1660-1800: A Guide to Information Sources*. American Literature, English Literature, and World Literatures in English: An Information Guide Series 40. Detroit: Gale Research, 1982.

Smith, Eric. *A Dictionary of Classical Reference in English Poetry*. Totowa, N.J.: Barnes & Noble, 1984.

Woodring, Carl, and James Shapiro, eds. *The Columbia History of British Poetry*. New York: Columbia University Press, 1993.

### Women writers

Chapman, Alison, ed. *Victorian Women Poets*. Cambridge, England: D. S. Brewer, 2003.

Dowson, Jane, and Alice Entwistle. *A History of Twentieth-Century British Women's Poetry*. New York: Cambridge University Press, 2005.

Gray, F. Elizabeth. *Christian and Lyric Tradition in Victorian Women's Poetry*. New York: Routledge, 2009.

Jackson, J. R. de J. *Romantic Poetry by Women: A Bibliography, 1770-1835*. Oxford: Clarendon-Oxford University Press, 1993.

## IRELAND

### Biographical sources

Sherry, Vincent B., Jr., ed. *Poets of Great Britain and Ireland, 1945-1960*. Dictionary of Literary Biography 27. Detroit: Gale Research, 1984.

_____. *Poets of Great Britain and Ireland Since 1960*. Dictionary of Literary Biography 40. Detroit: Gale Research, 1985.

### Dictionaries, histories, and handbooks

Broom, Sarah. *Contemporary British and Irish Poetry: An Introduction*. Illustrated edition. New York: Palgrave Macmillan, 2006.

Hogan, Robert, ed. *Dictionary of Irish Literature*. Rev. ed. 2 vols. Westport, Conn.: Greenwood Press, 1996.

Schirmer, Gregory A. *Out of What Began: A History of*

*Irish Poetry in English*. Ithaca, N.Y.: Cornell University Press, 1998.

Tuma, Keith, ed. *Anthology of Twentieth-Century British and Irish Poetry*. Annotated ed. New York: Oxford University Press, 2001.

**Women writers**

Colman, Anne Ulry. *Dictionary of Nineteenth-Century Irish Women Poets*. Galway: Kenny's Bookshop, 1996.

McBreen, Joan, ed. *The White Page = an Bhileog bh'an: Twentieth-Century Irish Women Poets*. Cliffs of Moher, Co. Clare: Salmon, 1999.

Weekes, Ann Owens. *Unveiling Treasures: The Attic Guide to the Published Works of Irish Women Literary Writers: Drama, Fiction, Poetry*. Dublin: Attic Press, 1993.

NEW ZEALAND

Keown, Michelle. *Pacific Islands Writing: The Postcolonial Literatures of Aotearoa/New Zealand and Oceania*. New York: Oxford University Press, 2007.

Marsack, Robyn, and Andrew Johnstone, eds. *Twenty Contemporary New Zealand Poets: An Anthology*. Manchester, England: Carcaret Press, 2009.

Sturm, Terry, ed. *The Oxford History of New Zealand Literature in English*. Auckland: Oxford University Press, 1991.

Thomson, John. *New Zealand Literature to 1977: A Guide to Information Sources*. American Literature, English Literature, and World Literatures in English: An Information Guide Series 30. Detroit: Gale Research, 1980.

SCOTLAND

Gifford, Douglas, and Dorothy McMillan. *A History of Scottish Women's Writing*. Edinburgh: Edinburgh University Press, 1997.

Glen, Duncan. *The Poetry of the Scots: An Introduction and Bibliographical Guide to Poetry in Gaelic, Scots, Latin, and English*. Edinburgh: Edinburgh University Press, 1991.

Mapstone, Sally, ed. *Older Scots Literature*. Edinburgh: John Donald, 2005.

Martin, Joanna. *Kingship and Love in Scottish Poetry, 1424-1540*. Farnham, Surrey, England: Ashgate, 2008.

*Scottish Poetry Index: An Index to Poetry and Poetry-Related Material in Scottish Literary Magazines, 1952- . Edinburgh: Scottish Poetry Library, 1994-2000.

Thomson, Derick S. *An Introduction to Gaelic Poetry*. 2d ed. Edinburgh: Edinburgh University Press, 1989.

WALES

Conran, Anthony. *Frontiers in Anglo-Welsh Poetry*. Cardiff: University of Wales Press, 1997.

Jarman, A. O. H., and Gwilym Rees Hughes, eds. *A Guide to Welsh Literature*. 6 vols. Cardiff: University of Wales Press, 1992-2000.

Lofmark, Carl. *Bards and Heroes: An Introduction to Old Welsh Poetry*. Felinfach: Llanerch, 1989.

Williams, Gwyn. *An Introduction to Welsh Poetry, from the Beginnings to the Sixteenth Century*. London: Faber and Faber, 1953.

*Maura Ives; updated by Tracy Irons-Georges*

# GUIDE TO ONLINE RESOURCES

WEB SITES

The following sites were visited by the editors of Salem Press in 2010. Because URLs frequently change, the accuracy of these addresses cannot be guaranteed; however, long-standing sites, such as those of colleges and universities, national organizations, and government agencies, generally maintain links when their sites are moved.

## Australian Literature

http://www.middlemiss.org/lit/lit.html

Perry Middlemiss, a Melbourne-based blogger, created this useful resource about Australian writers, including poets, and their works. It features an alphabetical list of authors that links to biographies and lists of their works. The site also provides, for some of the listed works, links to synopses and excerpts.

## The Cambridge History of English and American Literature

http://www.bartleby.com/cambridge

This site provides an exhaustive examination of the development of all forms of literature in Great Britain and the United States. The multivolume set on which this site is based was published in 1907-1921 but remains a relevant, classic work. It offers "a wide selection of writing on orators, humorists, poets, newspaper columnists, religious leaders, economists, Native Americans, song writers, and even non-English writing, such as Yiddish and Creole."

## The Canadian Literature Archive

http://www.umanitoba.ca/canlit

Created and maintained by the English Department at the University of Manitoba, this site is a comprehensive collection of materials for and about Canadian writers. It includes an alphabetical listing of authors with links to additional Web-based information. Users also can retrieve electronic texts, announcements of literary events, and videocasts of author interviews and readings.

## A Celebration of Women Writers

http://digital.library.upenn.edu/women

This site is an extensive compendium on the contributions of women writers throughout history. The "Local Editions by Authors" and "Local Editions by Category" pages include access to electronic texts of the works of numerous writers. Users can also access biographical and bibliographical information by browsing lists arranged by writers' names, countries of origin, ethnicities, and the centuries in which they lived.

## Contemporary British Writers

http://www.contemporarywriters.com/authors

Created by the British Council, this site offers profiles of living writers of the United Kingdom, the Republic of Ireland, and the Commonwealth. Information includes biographies, bibliographies, critical reviews, and news about literary prizes. Photographs are also featured. Users can search the site by author, genre, nationality, gender, publisher, book title, date of publication, and prize name and date.

## LiteraryHistory.com

http://www.literaryhistory.com

This site is an excellent source of academic, scholarly, and critical literature about eighteenth, nineteenth, and twentieth century American and English writers. It provides numerous pages about specific eras and genres, including individual pages for eighteenth, nineteenth, and twentieth century literature and for African American and postcolonial literatures. These pages contain alphabetical lists of authors that link to articles, reviews, overviews, excerpts of works, teaching guides, podcasts, and other materials.

## Literary Resources on the Net

http://andromeda.rutgers.edu/~jlynch/Lit

Jack Lynch of Rutgers University maintains this extensive collection of links to Web sites that are useful to researchers, including numerous sites about American and English literature. This collection is a good place to

1401

begin online research about poetry, as it links to other sites with broad ranges of literary topics. The site is organized chronologically, with separate pages about the Middle Ages, the Renaissance, the eighteenth century, the Romantic and Victorian eras, and twentieth century British and Irish literature. It also has separate pages providing links to Web sites about American literature and to women's literature and feminism.

## LitWeb

http://litweb.net

LitWeb provides biographies of hundreds of world authors throughout history that can be accessed through an alphabetical listing. The pages about each writer contain a list of his or her works, suggestions for further reading, and illustrations. The site also offers information about past and present winners of major literary prizes.

## The Modern Word: Authors of the Libyrinth

http://www.themodernword.com/authors.html

The Modern Word site, although somewhat haphazard in its organization, provides a great deal of critical information about writers. The "Authors of the Libyrinth" page is very useful, linking author names to essays about them and other resources. The section of the page headed "The Scriptorium" presents "an index of pages featuring writers who have pushed the edges of their medium, combining literary talent with a sense of experimentation to produce some remarkable works of modern literature."

## Poet's Corner

http://theotherpages.org/poems

The Poet's Corner, one of the oldest text resources on the Web, provides access to about seven thousand works of poetry by several hundred different poets from around the world. Indexes are arranged and searchable by title, name of poet, or subject. The site also offers its own resources, including Faces of the Poets—a gallery of portraits—and Lives of the Poets—a growing collection of biographies.

## Representative Poetry Online

http://rpo.library.utoronto.ca

This award-winning resource site, maintained by Ian Lancashire of the Department of English at the University of Toronto in Canada, has several thousand English-language poems by hundreds of poets. The collection is searchable by poet's name, title of work, first line of a poem, and keyword. The site also includes a time line, a glossary, essays, an extensive bibliography, and countless links organized by country and by subject.

## The Victorian Web

http://www.victorianweb.org

One of the finest Web sites about the nineteenth century, the Victorian Web provides a wealth of information about Great Britain during the reign of Queen Victoria, including information about the era's literature. The section "Genre & Technique" includes poetry.

## Voice of the Shuttle

http://vos.ucsb.edu

One of the most complete and authoritative places for online information about literature, Voice of the Shuttle is maintained by professors and students in the English Department at the University of California, Santa Barbara. The site provides countless links to electronic books, academic journals, literary association Web sites, sites created by university professors, and many other resources.

## Voices from the Gaps

http://voices.cla.umn.edu/

Voices from the Gaps is a site of the English Department at the University of Minnesota, dedicated to providing resources on the study of women artists of color, including writers. The site features a comprehensive index searchable by name, and it provides biographical information on each writer or artist and other resources for further study.

## Western European Studies

http://wess.lib.byu.edu

The Western European Studies Section of the Association of College and Research Libraries maintains this collection of resources useful to students of Western European history and culture. It also is a good place to find information about non-English-language literature. The site includes separate pages about the literatures and languages of the Netherlands, France, Germany, Iberia, Italy, and Scandinavia, in which users can find links to electronic texts, association Web sites, journals, and other materials, the majority of which are written in the languages of the respective countries.

### ELECTRONIC DATABASES

Electronic databases usually do not have their own URLs. Instead, public, college, and university libraries subscribe to these databases, provide links to them on their Web sites, and make them available to library card holders or other specified patrons. Readers can visit library Web sites or ask reference librarians to check on availability.

## Bloom's Literary Reference Online

Facts On File publishes this database of thousands of articles by renowned scholar Harold Bloom and other literary critics, examining the lives and works of great writers worldwide. The database also includes information on more than forty-two thousand literary characters, literary topics, themes, movements, and genres, plus video segments about literature. Users can retrieve information by browsing writers' names, titles of works, time periods, genres, or writers' nationalities.

## Canadian Literary Centre

Produced by EBSCO, the Canadian Literary Centre database contains full-text content from ECW Press, a Toronto-based publisher, including the titles in the publisher's Canadian fiction studies, Canadian biography, and Canadian writers and their works series, *ECW's Biographical Guide to Canadian Novelists*, and *George Woodcock's Introduction to Canadian Fiction*. Author biographies, essays and literary criticism, and book reviews are among the database's offerings.

## Literary Reference Center

EBSCO's Literary Reference Center (LRC) is a comprehensive full-text database designed primarily to help high school and undergraduate students in English and the humanities with homework and research assignments about literature. The database contains massive amounts of information from reference works, books, literary journals, and other materials, including more than 31,000 plot summaries, synopses, and overviews of literary works; almost 100,000 essays and articles of literary criticism; about 140,000 author biographies; more than 605,000 book reviews; and more than 5,200 author interviews. It also contains the entire contents of Salem Press's MagillOnLiterature Plus. Users can retrieve information by browsing a list of authors' names or titles of literary works; they can also use an advanced search engine to access information by numerous categories, including author name, gender, cultural identity, national identity, and the years in which he or she lived, or by literary title, character, locale, genre, and publication date. The Literary Reference Center also features a literary-historical time line, an encyclopedia of literature, and a glossary of literary terms.

## Literary Resource Center

Published by Gale, this comprehensive literary database contains information on the lives and works of more than 130,000 authors in all genres, in all time periods, and throughout the world. In addition, the database offers more than 70,000 full-text critical essays and reviews from some of Gale's reference publications, including *Contemporary Literary Criticism*, *Literature Criticism from 1400-1800*, *Nineteenth-Century Literature Criticism*, and *Twentieth-Century Literary Criticism*; more than 7,000 overviews of frequently studied works; more than 650,000 full-text articles, critical essays, and reviews from about three hundred scholarly journals and literary magazines; more than 4,500 interviews; and about five hundred links to selected Web sites. Users can retrieve information by browsing author name, ethnicity, nationality, years of birth and death; titles of literary works; genres; selected literary movements or time periods; keywords; and themes of literary works. Literary Resource

Center also features a literary-historical time line and an encyclopedia of literature.

## MagillOnLiterature Plus

MagillOnLiterature Plus is a comprehensive, integrated literature database produced by Salem Press and available on the EBSCOhost platform. The database contains the full text of essays in Salem's many literature-related reference works, including *Masterplots*, *Cyclopedia of World Authors*, *Cyclopedia of Literary Characters*, *Cyclopedia of Literary Places*, *Critical Survey of Poetry*, *Critical Survey of Long Fic-* *tion*, *Critical Survey of Short Fiction*, *World Philosophers and Their Works*, *Magill's Literary Annual*, and *Magill's Book Reviews*. Among its contents are articles on more than 35,000 literary works and more than 8,500 poets, writers, dramatists, essayists, and philosophers; more than 1,000 images; and a glossary of more than 1,300 literary terms. The biographical essays include lists of authors' works and secondary bibliographies, and hundreds of overview essays examine and discuss literary genres, time periods, and national literatures.

*Rebecca Kuzins; updated by Desiree Dreeuws*

# TIME LINE

| | |
|---|---|
| c. 670 | Cædmon, the first English poet, composes "Hymn," which combines the meters of Nordic heroic poetry with the subject matter of the Scriptures. |
| c. 1000 | *Beowulf*, an Old English epic heroic poem, is composed by an anonymous writer. |
| c. 1205 | Layamon composes *Brut*, the first major literary work written in Middle English and the first English-language version of the stories of King Arthur and King Lear. |
| July 20, 1304 | Petrarch is born in Arezzo, Tuscany (now in Italy). His work will include vernacular poems in which he celebrates his ever-lasting love for a woman named Laura. |
| 1320 | Hafiz, the master of the *ghazal*, or lyric poem, is born in Shīrāz, Persia (now in Iran). |
| c. 1320 | Dante creates his masterpiece, the three-volume *La divina commedia* (*The Divine Comedy*, 1802). This work describes the poet's journey through the three realms of the Christian otherworld—Hell, Purgatory, and Paradise. |
| 1387-1400 | Geoffrey Chaucer writes *The Canterbury Tales*, a collection of comic stories told by a group of pilgrims. |
| c. 1400 | The Pearl-Poet composes *Sir Gawain and the Green Knight*, one of many medieval poems concerning King Arthur and his knights. |
| 1570 | Scottish writer Robert Henryson publishes *The Morall Fabillis of Esope, the Phyrgian* (also known as *Fables*, twelve shorter poems of uncertain attribution). These didactic poems retell thirteen of Aesop's animal fables. |
| 1572 | John Donne is born in London. He will become the best-known of the Metaphysical poets, a group of seventeenth century English writers that includes George Herbert, Andrew Marvell, Thomas Traherne, Henry Vaughan, Richard Crashaw, Abraham Cowley, Sir William Davenant, Sir John Suckling, and Thomas Carew. |
| 1590 | Edmund Spencer creates *The Faerie Queene*, his allegorical tribute to Queen Elizabeth I. |
| 1595 | *Defence of Poesie* by Sir Philip Sidney is published. In this work of Renaissance literary criticism, Sidney argues for the superiority of poetry over any other aesthetic pursuit. |
| 1609 | William Shakespeare's *Sonnets* are published. In addition to being one of the world's greatest dramatists, Shakespeare wrote some of the greatest love poems in the English language. |
| August 6, 1637 | Ben Jonson, the founder of English neoclassical poetry, dies in London. Jonson's verse imitates Roman classical forms and subject matters, foreshadowing a style that would be more commonly employed by eighteenth century British poets. |
| 1660-1700 | "The Age of Dryden," during which the prolific John Dryden writes and translates numerous works of literature. His two hundred poems are composed in a variety of genres, including odes, verse epistles, satires, and religious poetry. |
| 1667 | The first books of John Milton's *Paradise Lost* are published, with the remaining volumes released in 1674. This work is arguably the greatest epic poem in English. |
| 1712 | Alexander Pope publishes his mock-epic poem *The Rape of the Lock*. |
| 1751 | Thomas Gray's poem "Elegy Written in a Country Churchyard," one of the most popular works of British literature, is published. |

| | |
|---|---|
| 1786 | The Kilmarnock edition of Robert Burns's *Poems, Chiefly in the Scottish Dialect*, is published. The poetic works of Burns, who is regarded as the national poet of Scotland, include more than three hundred songs about eighteenth century life in that country. |
| January 22, 1788 | Lord Byron is born in London. His creation of the defiant and brooding "Byronic hero" would exert a profound influence on nineteenth century Romantic sensibility. |
| 1794 | William Blake publishes *Songs of Innocence and of Experience*. Blake was one of the earliest English Romantic poets. |
| 1798 | William Wordsworth and Samuel Taylor Coleridge anonymously publish *Lyrical Ballads*, a collection of their Romantic poetry, which includes the first appearance of Coleridge's poem *The Rime of the Ancient Mariner*. In his preface to the collection, Wordsworth argues that primitivism—the belief that there is an intrinsic "state of nature" from which humankind has fallen into wickedness—is the basis of Romanticism. |
| 1817 | John Keats publishes his first volume of poetry. Keats would die before his twenty-sixth birthday, but in that brief time he would produce some of the greatest Romantic poetry in the English language. |
| July 8, 1822 | Percy Bysshe Shelley drowns in a boating accident in Italy, less than one month before his thirtieth birthday. One of the premier English Romantic poets, Shelley used a wide variety of stanzaic patterns and poetic forms in his work. |
| 1842 | Robert Browning publishes *Dramatic Lyrics*, which includes "My Last Duchess," one of his best dramatic monologues. |
| 1850 | The first of the four versions of "The Blessed Damozel" is published in a British magazine. The ballad's author, Dante Gabriel Rossetti, is also a painter and a member of the Pre-Raphaelite Brotherhood of artists. Rossetti's poetry, with its use of medieval settings and painterly detail, exemplifies the Pre-Raphaelite style of art and literature. |
| 1850 | Elizabeth Barrett Browning publishes *Poems: New Edition*, which includes *Sonnets from the Portuguese*. |
| November 5, 1850 | Prince Albert selects Alfred, Lord Tennyson, to replace William Wordsworth as England's poet laureate. The appointment is announced after *In Memorium* (1850), Tennyson's elegy upon the death of his friend Arthur Henry Hallem, was published and became an instant best seller. Tennyson will hold the position of poet laureate for the next forty-two years. |
| 1867 | Matthew Arnold publishes "Dover Beach," which makes reference to the Victorian debate between religion and science. |
| 1898 | Thomas Hardy publishes the first of his eight volumes of poetry, *Wessex Poems, and Other Verses*. |
| 1907 | Rudyard Kipling receives the Nobel Prize in Literature. |
| 1913-1930 | Robert Bridges is poet laureate of the United Kingdom. |
| April 23, 1915 | Rupert Brooke dies while performing his military service during World War I. During this year, Brooke's collection *1914, and Other Poems*, which features five sonnets glamorizing the fate of martyred soldiers, is published. |
| 1922 | T. S. Eliot's *The Waste Land* is published. In this influential work, Eliot describes human alienation in the years following World War I. |

| | |
|---|---|
| 1923 | Irish poet William Butler Yeats is awarded the Nobel Prize in Literature. |
| 1936 | The publication of *Twenty-five Poems* establishes Welsh writer Dylan Thomas as a significant poet. |
| 1936 | Patrick Kavanagh publishes his collection *Ploughman, and Other Poems*. Kavanagh will become a major figure in the second generation of the Irish literary revival. |
| October 17, 1938 | Les A. Murray is born in Nabiac, New South Wales, Australia. His work will earn him the distinction of being Australia's major poet and also one of the finest poets of his generation writing in English. |
| 1958 | Irish poet Thomas Kinsella receives the Guinness Poetry Award for *Another September*. |
| 1965 | Philip Larkin receives the Queen's Gold Medal for Poetry. |
| 1966 | *The Circle Game*, a collection of poems and the first critically acclaimed work by Canadian writer Margaret Atwood, is published. |
| 1969 | Stevie Smith receives the Queen's Gold Medal for Poetry. |
| 1972-1984 | John Betjeman is poet laureate of the United Kingdom. |
| 1975 | French-Canadian poet Anne Hèbert receives the Governor-General's Award for *Les Enfants du sabbat* (*Children of the Black Sabbath*, 1977). |
| 1976 | Australian poet A. D. Hope receives the Christopher Brennan Award in recognition of his lifetime literary achievement. |
| 1993 | Thom Gunn receives the Lenore Marshall Poetry Prize from the Academy of American Poets for *The Man with Night Sweats*. |
| 1994 | *Poetry Canada Review* ceases publication. The magazine was founded in 1978 by Clifton Whiten in order to publish and review poetry from across Canada. |
| 1994 | Paul Muldoon receives the T. S. Eliot Prize for *The Annals of Chile*. The annual award is given to the best new poetry collection published in the United Kingdom or the Republic of Ireland. |
| 1994 | Irish poet Eavan Boland and American poets Linda Hogan and Jack Gilbert are among the five recipients of the Lannan Literary Award for Poetry. |
| 1995 | Irish writer Seamus Heaney receives the Nobel Prize in Literature. |
| 1998 | Ted Hughes receives the T. S. Eliot Prize for *Birthday Letters*. The annual award is given to the best new poetry collection published in the United Kingdom or the Republic of Ireland. |
| 2001 | Canadian poet Anne Carson receives the Griffin Poetry Prize for *Men in the Off Hours*. |
| September 15, 2001 | Scott Simon of National Public Radio reads W. H. Auden's poem "September 1, 1939" (with many lines omitted). The poem is relevant to the terrorist attacks on September 11, 2001, and will be widely circulated and discussed. |

*Rebecca Kuzins*

# MAJOR AWARDS

## CHRISTOPHER BRENNAN AWARD

*First awarded in 1974, the Christopher Brennan Award (formerly the Robert Frost Prize) recognizes an Australian poet for lifetime achievement. The Fellowship of Australian Writers sponsors the award, which is named after the poet Christopher Brennan.*

1974: R. D. Fitzgerald
1976: A. D. Hope
      Judith Wright
1977: Gwen Harwood
1979: Rosemary Dobson
1980: John Blight
1982: Vincent Buckley
1983: Bruce Dawe
      Les A. Murray
1988: Roland Robinson
1991: Elizabeth Riddell
1992: R. A. Simpson

1993: Geoffrey Dutton
1994: Judith Rodriguez
1995: Robert Adamson
      Thomas Shapcott
1996: Dorothy Hewett
1998: Jennifer Maiden
1999: Kevin Hart
2001: Dorothy Porter
2003: Philip Salom
2004: Kris Hemensley
2006: Geoff Page
2008: John Kinsella

## T. S. ELIOT PRIZE

*Administered by the Poetry Book Society, this annual award is given to the best new poetry collection published in the United Kingdom or the Republic of Ireland.*

1993: Ciaran Carson—*First Language*
1994: Paul Muldoon—*The Annals of Chile*
1995: Mark Doty—*My Alexandria*
1996: Les A. Murray—*Subhuman Redneck Poems*
1997: Don Paterson—*God's Gift to Women*
1998: Ted Hughes—*Birthday Letters*
1999: Hugo Williams—*Billy's Rain*
2000: Michael Longley—*The Weather in Japan*
2001: Anne Carson—*The Beauty of the Husband*

2002: Alice Oswald—*Dart*
2003: Don Paterson—*Landing Light*
2004: George Szirtes—*Reel*
2005: Carol Ann Duffy—*Rapture*
2006: Seamus Heaney—*District and Circle*
2007: Sean O'Brien—*The Drowned Book*
2008: Jen Hadfield—*Nigh-No-Place*
2009: Philip Gross—*The Water Table*

## GOVERNOR-GENERAL'S AWARD IN POETRY (ENGLISH)

*Presented by the Canada Council for the Arts annually to the best English-language book of poetry. The award, first presented in 1937, was for poetry or drama, but it has been given for only poetry since 1981.*

1981: F. R. Scott—*The Collected Poems of F. R. Scott*
1982: Phyllis Webb—*The Vision Tree: Selected Poems*
1983: David Donnell—*Settlements*
1984: Paulette Jiles—*Celestial Navigation*
1985: Fred Wah—*Waiting for Saskatchewan*
1986: Al Purdy—*The Collected Poems of Al Purdy*
1987: Gwendolyn MacEwen—*Afterworlds*
1988: Erin Mouré—*Furious*
1989: Heather Spears—*The Word for Sand*
1990: Margaret Avison—*No Time*
1991: Don McKay—*Night Field*
1992: Lorna Crozier—*Inventing the Hawk*
1993: Don Coles—*Forests of the Medieval World*
1994: Robert Hilles—*Cantos from a Small Room*
1995: Anne Szumigalski—*Voice*
1996: E. D. Blodgett—*Apostrophes: Woman at a Piano*

1997: Dionne Brand—*Land to Light On*
1998: Stephanie Bolster—*White Stone: The Alice Poems*
1999: Jan Zwicky—*Songs for Relinquishing the Earth*
2000: Don McKay—*Another Gravity*
2001: George Elliott Clarke—*Execution Poems*
2002: Roy Miki—*Surrender*
2003: Tim Lilburn—*Kill-Site*
2004: Roo Borson—*Short Journey Upriver Toward Oishida*
2005: Anne Compton—*Processional*
2006: John Pass—*Stumbling in the Bloom*
2007: Don Domanski—*All Our Wonder Unavenged*
2008: Jacob Scheier—*More to Keep Us Warm*
2009: David Zieroth—*The Fly in Autumn*

## GOVERNOR-GENERAL'S AWARD IN POETRY (FRENCH)

*Presented by the Canada Council for the Arts annually to the best French-language book of poetry. The award, first presented in 1959, was for poetry or drama, but it has been given for only poetry since 1981.*

1981: Michel Beaulieu—*Visages*
1982: Michel Savard—*Forages*
1983: Suzanne Paradis—*Un Goût de sel*
1984: Nicole Brossard—*Double Impression*
1985: André Roy—*Action writing*
1986: Cécile Cloutier—*L'Écouté*
1987: Fernand Ouellette—*Les Heures*
1988: Marcel Labine—*Papiers d'épidémie*
1989: Pierre DesRuisseaux—*Monème*
1990: Jean-Paul Daoust—*Les Cendres bleues*
1991: Madeleine Gagnon—*Chant pour un Québec lointain*
1992: Gilles Cyr—*Andromède attendra*
1993: Denise Desautels—*Le Saut de l'ange*
1994: Fulvio Caccia—*Aknos*
1995: Émile Martel—*Pour orchestre et poète seul*
1996: Serge Patrice—*Le Quatuor de l'errance,*

followed by *La Traversée du désert*
1997: Pierre Nepveu—*Romans-fleuves*
1998: Suzanne Jacob—*La Part de feu*, preceded by *Le Deuil de la rancune*
1999: Herménégilde Chiasson—*Conversations*
2000: Normand de Bellefeuille—*La Marche de l'aveugle sans son chien*
2001: Paul Chanel Malenfant—*Des Ombres portées*
2002: Robert Dickson—*Humains paysages en temps de paix relative*
2003: Pierre Nepveu—*Lignes aériennes*
2004: André Brochu—*Les jours à vif*
2005: Jean-Marc Desgent—*Vingtièmes siècles*
2006: Hélène Dorion—*Ravir: Les lieux*
2007: Serge Patrice Thibodeau—*Seul on est*
2008: Michel Pleau—*La Lenteur du monde*
2009: Hélène Monette—*Thérèse pour joie et orchestre*

## GRIFFIN POETRY PRIZE

*The Griffin Poetry Prize is given by Canada each year, beginning in 2001, to collections by one living Canadian poet and one living international poet writing in the English language. Lifetime Recognition Awards to poets from all countries and languages were added in 2006.*

2001: Anne Carson—*Men in the Off Hours* (Canada); Nikolai Popov and Heather McHugh, translation of *Glottal Stop: 101 Poems by Paul Celan* (international)

2002: Christian Bök—*Eunoia* (Canada); Alice Notley—*Disobedience* (international)

2003: Margaret Avison—*Concrete and Wild Carrot* (Canada); Paul Muldoon—*Moy sand and gravel* (international)

2004: Anne Simpson—*Loop* (Canada); August Kleinzahler—*The Strange Hours Travelers Keep* (international)

2005: Roo Borson—*Short Journey Upriver Toward Oishida* (Canada); Charles Simic—*Selected Poems, 1963-2003* (international)

2006: Sylvia Legris—*Nerve Squall* (Canada); Kamau Brathwaite—*Born to Slow Horses*

(international); Lifetime Recognition Award, Robin Blaser

2007: Don McKay—*Strike/Slip* (Canada); Charles Wright—*Scar Tissue* (international); Lifetime Recognition Award, Tomas Tranströmer

2008: Robin Blaser—*The Holy Forest: Collected Poems of Robin Blaser* (Canada); John Ashbery—*Notes from the Air: Selected Later Poems* (international); Lifetime Recognition Award, Ko Un

2009: A. F. Moritz—*The Sentinel* (Canada); C. D. Wright—*Rising, Falling, Hovering* (international); Lifetime Recognition Award, Hans Magnus Enzensberger

2010: Karen Solie—*Pigeon* (Canada); Eilean Ni Chuilleanain—*The Sun-fish* (international); Lifetime Recognition Award, Adrienne Rich

## GRACE LEVEN PRIZE FOR POETRY

*The Grace Leven Prize for Poetry was established in 1947 by William Baylebridge in the name of his benefactor. The award is given to "the best volume of poetry published in the preceding twelve months by a writer either Australian-born, or naturalised in Australia and resident in Australia for not less than ten years."*

1947: Nan McDonald—*Pacific Sea*

1948: Francis Webb—*A Drum for Ben Boyd*

1949: Judith Wright—*Woman to Man*

1951: Rex Ingamells—*The Great South Land*

1952: R. D. Fitzgerald—*Between Two Tides*

1953: Roland Robinson—*Tumult of the Swans*

1954: John Thompson—*Thirty Poems*

1955: A. D. Hope—*The Wandering Islands*

1957: Leonard Mann—*Elegaic, and Other Poems*

1958: Geoffrey Dutton—*Antipodes in Shoes*

1959: R. D. Fitzgerald—*The Wind at Your Door: A Poem*

1960: Colin Thiele—*Man in a Landscape*

1961: Thomas Shapcott—*Time on Fire*

1962: R. D. Fitzgerald—*South-most Tree*

1963: Ian Mudie—*The North-Bound Rider*

1964: David Rowbotham—*All the Room*

1965: Les Murray and Geoffrey Lehmann—*The Ilex Tree*

1966: William Hart-Smith—*The Talking Clothes: Poems*

1967: Douglas Stewart—*Collected Poems, 1936-1967*

1968: David Campbell—*Selected Poems, 1942-1968*

1969: Randolph Stow—*A Counterfeit Silence: Selected Poems*

1970: Bruce Beaver—*Letters to Live Poets*

1971: James McAuley—*Collected Poems, 1936-1970*; Judith Wright—*Collected Poems, 1942-1970*

1972: Peter Skrzynecki—*Head-waters*

1973: Rodney Hall—*A Soapbox Omnibus*

1974: David Malouf—*Neighbours in a Thicket: Poems*
1975: Gwen Harwood—*Selected Poems* (1975)
1976: John Blight—*Selected Poems, 1939-1975*
1977: Robert Adamson—*Selected Poems*
1978: Bruce Dawe—*Sometimes Gladness: Collected Poems, 1954-1978*
1979: David Campbell—*The Man in the Honeysuckle*
1980: Les Murray—*The Boys Who Stole the Funeral*
1981: Geoffrey Lehmann—*Nero's Poems: Translations of the Public and Private Poems of the Emperor Nero*
1982: Vivian Smith—*Tide Country*
1983: Peter Porter—*Collected Poems*
1984: Rosemary Dobson—*The Three Fates, and Other Poems*
1985: Robert Gray—*Selected Poems, 1963-1983*; Chris Wallace-Crabbe—*The Amorous Cannibal*
1986: Rhyll McMaster—*Washing the Money: Poems with Photographs*
1987: Elizabeth Riddell—*Occasions of Birds, and Other Poems*
1988: John Tranter—*Under Berlin*

1989: Dorothy Hewett—*A Tremendous World in Her Head*
1990: Les Murray—*Dog Fox Field*
1992: Kevin Hart—*Peniel*
     Gary Catalano—*Empire of Grass*
1993: Philip Hodgins—*The End of the Season*
1995: Kevin Hart—*New and Selected Poems*; Jemal Sharah—*Path of Ghosts: Poems, 1986-93*
1997: John Kinsella—*The Undertow: New and Selected Poems*
2001: Geoff Page—*Darker and Lighter*
2002: Kate Lilley—*Versary*
2003: Stephen Edgar—*Lost in the Foreground*
2004: Luke Davies—*Totem*
2005: Noel Rowe—*Next to Nothing*
2006: Alan Gould—*The Past Completes Me: Selected Poems, 1973-2003*
2007: Robert Adamson—*The Goldfinches of Baghdad*
2008: Alan Wearne—*The Australian Popular Song Book*
2010: Judith Beveridge—*Storm and Honey*

## NEUSTADT INTERNATIONAL PRIZE FOR LITERATURE

*Awarded biennially since 1970, this award sponsored by the University of Oklahoma honors writers for a body of work.*

1970: Giuseppe Ungaretti (Italy)
1972: Gabriel García Márquez (Colombia)
1974: Francis Ponge (France)
1976: Elizabeth Bishop (USA)
1978: Czesław Miłosz (Poland)
1980: Josef Škvorecky (Czechoslovakia/Canada)
1982: Octavio Paz (Mexico)
1984: Paavo Haavikko (Finland)
1986: Max Frisch (Switzerland)
1988: Raja Rao (India)
1990: Tomas Tranströmer (Sweden)

1992: João Cabral de Melo Neto (Brazil)
1994: Edward Kamau Brathwaite (Barbados)
1996: Assia Djebar (Algeria)
1998: Nuruddin Farah (Somalia)
2000: David Malouf (Australia)
2002: Alvaro Mutis (Colombia)
2004: Adam Zagajewski (Poland)
2006: Claribel Alegría (Nicaragua/El Salvador)
2008: Patricia Grace (New Zealand)
2010: Duo Duo (China)

## NEW SOUTH WALES PREMIER'S LITERARY AWARDS

*Established in 1979, the New South Wales Premier's Literary Awards includes the Kenneth Slessor Prize for poetry.*

1980: David Campbell—*Man in the Honeysuckle*
1981: Alan Gould—*Astral Sea*
1982: Fay Zwicky—*Kaddish, and Other Poems*
1983: Vivian Smith—*Tide Country*
1984: Les A. Murray—*The People's Other World*
1985: Kevin Hart—*Your Shadow*
1986: Robert Gray—*Selected Poems, 1963-83*
1987: Philip Hodgins—*Blood and Bone*
1988: Judith Beveridge—*The Domesticity of Giraffes*
1989: John Tranter—*Under Berlin*
1990: Robert Adamson—*The Clean Dark*
1991: Jennifer Maiden—*The Winter Baby*
1992: Elizabeth Riddell—*Selected Poems*
1993: Les A. Murray—*Translations from the Natural World*
1994: Barry Hill—*Ghosting William Buckley*
1995: Peter Boyle—*Coming Home from the World*

1996: Eric Beach—*Weeping for Lost Babylon*; J. S. Harry—*Selected Poems*
1997: Anthony Lawrence—*The Viewfinder*
1999: Lee Cataldi—*Race Against Time*
2000: Jennifer Maiden—*Mines*
2001: Ken Taylor—*Africa*
2002: Alan Wearne—*The Lovemakers*
2003: Jill Jones—*Screens Jets Heaven: New and Selected Poems*
2004: Pam Brown—*Dear Deliria: New and Selected Poems*
2005: Samuel Wagan Watson—*Smoke Encrypted Whispers*
2006: Jaya Savige—*Latecomers*
2007: John Tranter—*Urban Myths: 210 Poems*
2008: Kathryn Lomer—*Two Kinds of Silence*
2009: L. K. Holt—*Man Wolf Man*

## NOBEL PRIZE IN LITERATURE

*Awarded annually since 1901, this prize is given to an author for his or her entire body of literary work. The list below includes only the poets who have been so honored.*

1901: Sully Prudhomme
1906: Giosuè Carducci
1907: Rudyard Kipling
1913: Rabindranath Tagore
1923: William Butler Yeats
1945: Gabriela Mistral
1946: Hermann Hesse
1948: T. S. Eliot
1956: Juan Ramón Jiménez
1958: Boris Pasternak
1959: Salvatore Quasimodo
1960: Saint-John Perse
1963: George Seferis
1966: Nelly Sachs
1969: Samuel Beckett

1971: Pablo Neruda
1974: Harry Martinson
1975: Eugenio Montale
1977: Vicente Aleixandre
1979: Odysseus Elytis
1980: Czesław Miłosz
1984: Jaroslav Seifert
1986: Wole Soyinka
1987: Joseph Brodsky
1990: Octavio Paz
1992: Derek Walcott
1995: Seamus Heaney
1996: Wisława Szymborska
2005: Harold Pinter
2009: Herta Müller

### POET LAUREATE OF THE UNITED KINGDOM OF GREAT BRITAIN AND NORTHERN IRELAND

*The British Poet Laureate, originally an appointment for life, is now a ten-year term. John Dryden was the first official laureate. Carol Ann Duffy, in 2009, became the first woman appointed to the position.*

1591–1599: Edmund Spenser
1599–1619: Samuel Daniel
1619–1637: Ben Jonson
1638–1668: William Davenant
1668–1689: John Dryden
1689–1692: Thomas Shadwell
1692–1715: Nahum Tate
1715–1718: Nicholas Rowe
1718–1730: Laurence Eusden
1730–1757: Colley Cibber
1757–1785: William Whitehead
1785–1790: Thomas Warton

1790–1813: Henry James Pye
1813–1843: Robert Southey
1843–1850: William Wordsworth
1850–1892: Alfred, Lord Tennyson
1896–1913: Alfred Austin
1913–1930: Robert Bridges
1930–1967: John Masefield
1967–1972: Cecil Day Lewis
1972–1984: Sir John Betjeman
1984–1998: Ted Hughes
1999–2009: Andrew Motion
2009        : Carol Ann Duffy

### QUEEN'S GOLD MEDAL FOR POETRY

*A special committee, selected and chaired by the British poet laureate, selects for this medal a poet from any nation or realm of the British Commonwealth.*

1934: Laurence Whistler
1937: W. H. Auden
1940: Michael Thwaites
1952: Andrew Young
1953: Arthur Waley
1954: Ralph Hodgson
1955: Ruth Pitter
1956: Edmund Blunden
1957: Siegfried Sassoon
1959: Frances Cornford
1960: John Betjeman
1962: Christopher Fry
1963: William Plomer
1964: R. S. Thomas
1965: Philip Larkin
1967: Charles Causley
1968: Robert Graves
1969: Stevie Smith
1970: Roy Fuller
1971: Stephen Spender

1973: John Heath-Stubbs
1974: Ted Hughes
1977: Norman Nicholson
1981: D. J. Enright
1986: Norman MacCaig
1988: Derek Walcott
1989: Allen Curnow
1990: Sorley Maclean
1991: Judith Wright
1992: Kathleen Raine
1996: Peter Redgrove
1998: Les Murray
2000: Edwin Morgan
2001: Michael Longley
2002: Peter Porter
2003: U. A. Fanthorpe
2004: Hugo Williams
2006: Fleur Adcock
2007: James Fenton
2010: Don Paterson

## QUEENSLAND PREMIER'S LITERARY AWARDS

*Inaugurated in 1999, the Queensland Premier's Literary Awards are a leading literary awards program within Australia, with prizes in more than fourteen categories. The Arts Queensland Judith Wright Calanthe Award is given each year for the best poetry collection.*

2004: Judith Beveridge—*Wolf Notes*

2005: Sarah Day—*The Ship*

2006: John Kinsella—*The New Arcadia*

2007: Laurie Duggan—*The Passenger*

2008: David Malouf—*Typewriter Music*

2009: Emma Jones—*The Striped World*

2010: Peter Boyle—*Apocrypha*

# CHRONOLOGICAL LIST OF POETS

This chronology of the poets covered in these volumes serves as a time line for students interested in the development of poetry in Great Britain, Ireland, and the Commonwealth from the seventh century to modern times. The arrangement is chronological on the basis of birth years, and the proximity of writers provides students with some insights into potential influences and contemporaneous developments.

## BORN UP TO 1500

Cædmon (early seventh century)
Cynewulf (757)
Layamon (c. 1200)
Gower, John (c. 1330)
Langland, William (c. 1332)
Chaucer, Geoffrey (c. 1343)
Pearl-Poet (fl. latter half of the fourteenth century)
Lydgate, John (1370?)
Henryson, Robert (c. 1425)
Dunbar, William (c. 1460)
Skelton, John (c. 1460)
Heywood, John (c. 1497)

## BORN 1501-1600

Wyatt, Sir Thomas (1503)
Surrey, Henry Howard, earl of (1517)
Sackville, Thomas (1536)
Gascoigne, George (c. 1539)
Breton, Nicholas (c. 1545)
Ralegh, Sir Walter (c. 1552)
Spenser, Edmund (c. 1552)
Greville, Fulke (October 3, 1554)
Sidney, Sir Philip (November 30, 1554)
Lodge, Thomas (1558?)
Greene, Robert (c. July, 1558)
Chapman, George (c. 1559)
Southwell, Robert (1561)
Daniel, Samuel (1562?)
Constable, Henry (1562)
Drayton, Michael (1563)
Sidney, Sir Robert (November 19, 1563)
Marlowe, Christopher (February 6, 1564)
Shakespeare, William (April 23, 1564)
Campion, Thomas (February 12, 1567)
Nashe, Thomas (November, 1567)

Davies, Sir John (April, 1569)
Dekker, Thomas (c. 1572)
Donne, John (between January 24 and June 19, 1572)
Jonson, Ben (June 11, 1573)
Drummond of Hawthornden, William (December 13, 1585)
Herrick, Robert (August 24, 1591)
Quarles, Francis (1592)
King, Henry (January 16, 1592)
Herbert, George (April 3, 1593)
Carew, Thomas (1594)

## BORN 1601-1700

Davenant, Sir William (February, 1606)
Waller, Edmund (March 3, 1606)
Fanshawe, Sir Richard (June, 1608)
Milton, John (December 9, 1608)
Suckling, Sir John (February 10, 1609)
Crashaw, Richard (c. 1612)
Butler, Samuel (February 8, 1612)
Cowley, Abraham (1618)
Lovelace, Richard (1618)
Marvell, Andrew (March 31, 1621)
Vaughan, Henry (April 17, 1622)
Newcastle, Margaret Cavendish, duchess of (1623)
Cotton, Charles (April 28, 1630)
Dryden, John (August 19, 1631)
Etherege, Sir George (c. 1635)
Traherne, Thomas (c. 1637)
Sedley, Sir Charles (March, 1639)
Behn, Aphra (July?, 1640)
Rochester, John Wilmot, earl of (April 10, 1647)
Oldham, John (August 9, 1653)
Finch, Anne (April, 1661)
Prior, Matthew (July 21, 1664)
Swift, Jonathan (November 30, 1667)

Congreve, William (January 24, 1670)
Addison, Joseph (May 1, 1672)
Watts, Isaac (July 17, 1674)
Young, Edward (July 3, 1683)
Gay, John (June 30, 1685)
Pope, Alexander (May 21, 1688)
Thomson, James (September 7, 1700)

## BORN 1701-1800

Johnson, Samuel (September 18, 1709)
Gray, Thomas (December 26, 1716)
Collins, William (December 25, 1721)
Smart, Christopher (April 11, 1722)
Goldsmith, Oliver (November 10, 1728 or 1730)
Cowper, William (November 26, 1731)
Chatterton, Thomas (November 20, 1752)
Crabbe, George (December 24, 1754)
Blake, William (November 28, 1757)
Burns, Robert (January 25, 1759)
Bowles, William Lisle (September 24, 1762)
Wordsworth, William (April 7, 1770)
Scott, Sir Walter (August 15, 1771)
Coleridge, Samuel Taylor (October 21, 1772)
Southey, Robert (August 12, 1774)
Landor, Walter Savage (January 30, 1775)
Lamb, Charles (February 10, 1775)
Hunt, Leigh (October 19, 1784)
Byron, Lord (January 22, 1788)
Shelley, Percy Bysshe (August 4, 1792)
Clare, John (July 13, 1793)
Hemans, Felicia Dorothea (September 25, 1793)
Darley, George (1795)
Keats, John (October 31, 1795)
Hood, Thomas (May 23, 1799)

## BORN 1801-1850

Mangan, James Clarence (May 1, 1803)
Beddoes, Thomas Lovell (June 30, 1803)
Browning, Elizabeth Barrett (March 6, 1806)
FitzGerald, Edward (March 31, 1809)
Tennyson, Alfred, Lord (August 6, 1809)
Hallam, Arthur Henry (February 1, 1811)
Browning, Robert (May 7, 1812)
Lear, Edward (May 12, 1812)
Brontë, Emily (July 30, 1818)

Clough, Arthur Hugh (January 1, 1819)
Arnold, Matthew (December 24, 1822)
Patmore, Coventry (July 23, 1823)
Allingham, William (March 19, 1824)
Meredith, George (February 12, 1828)
Rossetti, Dante Gabriel (May 12, 1828)
Rossetti, Christina (December 5, 1830)
Carroll, Lewis (January 27, 1832)
Morris, William (March 24, 1834)
Thomson, James (November 23, 1834)
Swinburne, Algernon Charles (April 5, 1837)
Hardy, Thomas (June 2, 1840)
Hopkins, Gerard Manley (July 28, 1844)
Bridges, Robert (October 23, 1844)
Stevenson, Robert Louis (November 13, 1850)

## BORN 1851-1900

Wilde, Oscar (October 16, 1854)
Housman, A. E. (March 26, 1859)
Yeats, William Butler (June 13, 1865)
Kipling, Rudyard (December 30, 1865)
Æ (April 10, 1867)
Mew, Charlotte (November 15, 1869)
Belloc, Hilaire (July 27, 1870)
De la Mare, Walter (April 25, 1873)
Service, Robert W. (January 16, 1874)
Thomas, Edward (March 3, 1878)
Masefield, John (June 1, 1878)
Colum, Padraic (December 8, 1881)
Joyce, James (February 2, 1882)
Pratt, E. J. (February 4, 1882)
Lawrence, D. H. (September 11, 1885)
Sassoon, Siegfried (September 8, 1886)
Muir, Edwin (May 15, 1887)
Sitwell, Edith (September 7, 1887)
Brooke, Rupert (August 3, 1887)
Eliot, T. S. (September 26, 1888)
Gurney, Ivor (August 28, 1890)
Rosenberg, Isaac (November 25, 1890)
Aldington, Richard (July 8, 1892)
MacDiarmid, Hugh (August 11, 1892)
Owen, Wilfred (March 18, 1893)
Graves, Robert (July 24, 1895)
Jones, David (November 1, 1895)
Clarke, Austin (May 9, 1896)

Blunden, Edmund (November 1, 1896)
Bunting, Basil (March 1, 1900)

**BORN 1901-1920**
Smith, Stevie (September 20, 1902)
Day Lewis, Cecil (April 27, 1904)
Birney, Earle (May 13, 1904)
Kavanagh, Patrick (October 21, 1904)
Betjeman, John (August 28, 1906)
Empson, William (September 27, 1906)
Auden, W. H. (February 21, 1907)
Hope, A. D. (July 21, 1907)
MacNeice, Louis (September 12, 1907)
Spender, Stephen (February 28, 1909)
Fuller, Roy (February 11, 1912)
Durrell, Lawrence (February 27, 1912)
Layton, Irving (March 12, 1912)
Prince, F. T. (September 13, 1912)
Thomas, R. S. (March 29, 1913)
Reed, Henry (February 22, 1914)
Thomas, Dylan (October 27, 1914)
Hébert, Anne (August 1, 1916)

**BORN 1921-1940**
Davie, Donald (July 17, 1922)
Larkin, Philip (August 9, 1922)

Abse, Dannie (September 22, 1923)
Beer, Patricia (November 4, 1924)
Middleton, Christopher (June 10, 1926)
Logue, Christopher (November 23, 1926)
Tomlinson, Charles (January 8, 1927)
Kinsella, Thomas (May 4, 1928)
Montague, John (February 28, 1929)
Gunn, Thom (August 29, 1929)
Hughes, Ted (August 17, 1930)
Pinter, Harold (October 10, 1930)
Silkin, Jon (December 2, 1930)
MacBeth, George (January 19, 1932)
Hill, Geoffrey (June 18, 1932)
Cohen, Leonard (September 2, 1934)
Harrison, Tony (April 30, 1937)
Murray, Les A. (October 17, 1938)
Heaney, Seamus (April 13, 1939)
Atwood, Margaret (November 18, 1939)

**BORN AFTER 1941**
Ondaatje, Michael (September 12, 1943)
Boland, Eavan (September 24, 1944)
Fenton, James (April 25, 1949)
Carson, Anne (June 21, 1950)
Muldoon, Paul (June 20, 1951)
Ní Dhomhnaill, Nuala (February 16, 1952)

# INDEXES

# GEOGRAPHICAL INDEX OF POETS

*Critical Survey of Poetry*

# CATEGORIZED INDEX OF POETS

*The Categorized Index of Poets covers three primary subject areas: Culture/Group Identities, Historical Periods/Literary Movements, and Poetic Forms and Themes.*

## Cultural/Group Identities

## Historical Periods/Literary Movements

## Poetic Forms and Themes

**AESTHETIC POETS**

Coleridge, Samuel Taylor, 276
Meredith, George, 890
Rossetti, Dante Gabriel, 1065
Swinburne, Algernon Charles, 1227
Wilde, Oscar, 1303
Yeats, William Butlre, 1330

**AGE OF JOHNSON.** *See*
**JOHNSON, AGE OF**

**AUGUSTAN AGE, ENGLISH**

Addison, Joseph, 7
Collins, William, 287
Cowper, William, 320
Finch, Anne, 491
Gay, John, 512
Gray, Thomas, 542
Johnson, Samuel, 700
Pope, Alexander, 1005
Prior, Matthew, 1026
Swift, Jonathan, 1218
Thomson, James (1700-1748), 1260
Watts, Isaac, 1297
Young, Edward, 1349

**AVANT-GARDE POETS**

Joyce, James, 719

**BALLADS**

Allingham, William, 23
Auden, W. H., 47

Coleridge, Samuel Taylor, 276
Finch, Anne, 491
Gower, John, 525
Graves, Robert, 534
Hardy, Thomas, 579
Hood, Thomas, 650
Kipling, Rudyard, 760
Masefield, John, 885
Meredith, George, 890
Prior, Matthew, 1026
Rossetti, Dante Gabriel, 1065
Scott, Sir Walter, 1087
Service, Robert W., 1099
Southey, Robert, 1171
Stevenson, Robert Louis, 1201
Suckling, Sir John, 1206
Swinburne, Algernon Charles, 1227
Tennyson, Alfred, Lord, 1236
Wordsworth, William, 1310

**BEAT POETS**

Gunn, Thom, 560
Larkin, Philip, 786

**CAROLINE AGE**

Butler, Samuel, 180
Carew, Thomas, 208
Cowley, Abraham, 312
Crashaw, Richard, 337
Davenant, Sir William, 362
Donne, John, 405
Drummond of Hawthornden, William, 424

Fanshawe, Sir Richard, 481
Herbert, George, 617
Herrick, Robert, 626
Jonson, Ben, 711
Lovelace, Richard, 827
Milton, John, 905
Quarles, Francis, 1031
Suckling, Sir John, 1206

**CAVALIER POETS**

Carew, Thomas, 208
Davenant, Sir William, 362
Herrick, Robert, 626
Jonson, Ben, 711
Lovelace, Richard, 827
Milton, John, 905
Waller, Edmund, 1290

**CELTIC REVIVAL.** *See* **IRISH LITERARY REVIVAL**

**CHILDREN'S/YOUNG ADULT POETRY**

Allingham, William, 23
Belloc, Hilaire, 73
Bowles, William Lisle, 119
Carroll, Lewis, 213
De la Mare, Walter, 398
Fuller, Roy, 500
Graves, Robert, 534
Hughes, Ted, 686
Kipling, Rudyard, 760
Lamb, Charles, 768

# *Critical Survey of Poetry* Series: Master List of Contents

*The* Critical Survey of Poetry, Fourth Edition, *profiles more than eight hundred poets in four subsets:* American Poets; British, Irish, and Commonwealth Poets; European Poets; *and* World Poets. *Although some individuals could have been included in more than one subset, each poet appears in only one subset. A fifth subset,* Topical Essays, *includes more than seventy overviews covering geographical areas, historical periods, movements, and critical approaches.*

## AMERICAN POETS

# BRITISH, IRISH, AND COMMONWEALTH POETS

# EUROPEAN POETS

# WORLD POETS

# TOPICAL ESSAYS

## CUMULATIVE INDEXES

# SUBJECT INDEX

All personages whose names appear in **boldface type** in this index are the subject of articles in *Critical Survey of Poetry, Fourth Edition*.

*Abdelazar* (Behn), 70

"Abou Ben Adhem" (Hunt), 698

*About Love* (Montague), 921

*About the House* (Auden), 53

*Absalom and Achitophel* (Dryden), 438

**Abse, Dannie**, 1-7; *Arcadia, One Mile*, 4; "Funland," 4; *New Selected Poems*, 5; *Running Late*, 4

"Absent-Minded Beggar, The" (Kipling), 765

Accentual meter, defined, 1378

Accentual-syllabic meter, defined, 1378

**Addison, Joseph**, 7-13; *The Campaign*, 11; "A Letter from Italy," 10

"Adlestrop" (Thomas), 1255

*Adonais* (Shelley), 1123

Æ, 13-17; *Homeward*, 15

"Aella" (Chatterton), 241

Aesthetic poets. *See* Categorized Index

"African Eclogues" (Chatterton), 239

"After Speaking of One Who Died a Long Time Before" (Colum), 295

"Against Fruition" (Suckling), 1210

*Against Love Poetry* (Boland), 116

*Age of Anxiety, The* (Auden), 52

*Alaham* (Greville), 558

*Alastor* (Shelley), 1117

Aldington, Edward Godfree. *See* Aldington, Richard

**Aldington, Richard**, 17-23; "Choricos," 20; "Eumenides," 21, *A Fool i' the Forest*, 21; *Pinorman*, 19

*Alexander's Feast* (Dryden), 440

Alfred, Lord Tennyson. *See* Tennyson, Alfred, Lord

*Alice's Adventures in Wonderland* (Carroll), 215

Allegory, defined, 1378

"Allegro, L'" (Milton), 908

**Allingham, William**, 23-30; *Blackberries Picked Off Many Bushes*, 29; "The Fairies," 23; *Laurence Bloomfield in Ireland*, 28; *William Allingham*, 27; "The Winding Banks of Erne," 23

Alliteration, defined, 1378

Allusion, defined, 1378

"Altarwise by Owl-Light" (Thomas), 1249

*Ambarvalia* (Clough), 269

"Amber Bead, The" (Herrick), 629

*America* (Blake), 99

*American Scenes, and Other Poems* (Tomlinson), 1271

Amis, Aphara. *See* Behn, Aphra

"Among School Children" (Yeats), 1342

*Amoretti* (Spenser), 1198

*Amours de Voyage* (Clough), 270

Anacrusis, defined, 1378

Anapest, defined, 1378

Anaphora, defined, 1378

*Anathemata, The* (Jones), 709

*Anatomy of the World, An* (Donne), 414

*Ancient Lights* (Clarke), 264

"And Death Shall Have No Dominion" (Thomas), 1249

"Andrea del Sarto" (Browning), 164

"Anecdotes, The" (Durrell), 454

*Angel in the House, The* (Patmore), 987

*Animals in That Country, The* (Atwood), 41

*Annunciations* (Tomlinson), 1274

*Annus Mirabilis* (Dryden), 436

"Anonymous: Myself and Panguar" (Muldoon), 942

"Anthem" (Cohen), 274

"Anthem for Doomed Youth" (Owen), 982

*Anti-Basilisk, The* (Middleton), 903

Aphra Bayn. *See* Behn, Aphra

*Apocalypse* (Lawrence), 801

Approximate rhyme, defined, 1378

*Arbor of Amorous Devices, The* (Breton), 127

*Arcadia, One Mile* (Abse), 4

Archetype, defined, 1378

"Argument of His Book, The" (Herrick), 628

"Arms" (Beer), 64

"Arms and the Boy" (Owen), 981

**Arnold, Matthew**, 30-37; "Dover Beach," 35; "The Scholar-Gipsy," 34; "Stanzas from the Grande Chartreuse," 35; "Thyrsis," 34; "To a Friend," 33

Art for art's sake, 721, 1305

"As I Walked Out One Evening" (Auden), 51

"As the Team's Head-Brass" (Thomas), 1254

*Ash Wednesday* (Eliot), 466

Astrea. *See* Behn, Aphra

*Astrophel and Stella* (Sidney), 1130

"At Rhodes" (Durrell), 454

"At the Great Wall of China" (Blunden), 107

**Atwood, Margaret**, 37-46; *The Animals in That Country*, 41; *The Circle Game*, 40; *The Door*, 45; *Interlunar*, 44; *The Journals of*

Theme, defined, 1390

"They" (Sassoon), 1084

"They flee from me, that sometime did me seek" (Wyatt), 1326

Third person, defined, 1390

"13,000 People" (Lawrence), 800

"This Last Pain" (Empson), 473

"This Lime-Tree Bower My Prison" (Coleridge), 279

**Thomas, Dylan**, 1245-1252; "Altarwise by Owl-Light," 1249; "And Death Shall Have No Dominion," 1249; "Over Sir John's Hill," 1250

**Thomas, Edward**, 1252-1256; "Adlestrop," 1255; "As the Team's Head-Brass," 1254; "No One So Much as You," 1255

**Thomas, R. S.**, 1257-1260; *H'm*, 1259; *Laboratories of the Spirit*, 1259; *Song at the Year's Turning*, 1259

**Thomson, James (1700-1748)**, 1260-1264; *The Castle of Indolence*, 1263; *Liberty*, 1262; *The Seasons*, 1262

**Thomson, James (1834-1882)**, 1264-1268; "The City of Dreadful Night," 1267; "The Doom of a City," 1266; "In the Room," 1266; "Philosophy," 1266; "A Voice from the Nile," 1267

*Through the Looking-Glass and What Alice Found There* (Carroll), 217

"Thyrsis" (Arnold), 34

*Tides* (Montague), 917

*Timber* (Jonson), 713

*Time in Armagh* (Montague), 922

*Time's Laughingstocks, and Other Verses* (Hardy), 585

"Timon" (Rochester), 1052

"Tintagel" (Reed), 1046

*Titanic, The* (Pratt), 1019

"To a Friend" (Arnold), 33

"To a Lady, Asking Him How Long

He Would Love Her" (Etherege), 478

"To a Man on His Horse" (Prince), 1023

"To a Very Young Lady" (Etherege), 478

"To Any Reader" (Stevens), 1203

"To Autumn" (Keats), 740

"To Blossoms" (Herrick), 634

"To Carry the Child" (Smith), 1169

*To Circumjack Cencrastus* (MacDiarmid), 850

"To Dives" (Belloc), 78

"To Hedli" (MacNeice), 860

"To His Coy Mistress" (Marvell), 880

"To His Love" (Gurney), 570

"To His Mistress Going to Bed" (Donne), 411

"To Liber" (Sedley), 1096

"To M. S. Killed in Spain" (Fuller), 501

"To My Brother" (Fuller), 501

"To My Dear Friend Mr. Congreve" (Dryden), 440

"To My Wife" (Pinter), 1004

"To Penshurst" (Jonson), 716

"To Poesy" (Owen), 980

"To the King, on the Taking of Namure" (Congreve), 299

"To the Memory of Mr. Oldham" (Dryden), 439, 972

"To the Nightingale" (Finch), 494

"To the Virgins, to make much of Time" (Herrick), 632

*Tombs of the Kings, The* (Hébert), 607

**Tomlinson, Charles**, 1268-1277; *American Scenes, and Other Poems*, 1271; *Annunciations*, 1274; *The Door in the Wall*, 1275; *The Flood*, 1274; *Jubilation*, 1275; *A Peopled Landscape*, 1271; *The Return*, 1274; *Seeing Is Believing*, 1271; *The Shaft*, 1274; *The Vineyard Above the Sea*, 1275; *The Way In, and Other*

*Poems*, 1273; *The Way of a World*, 1272; *Written on Water*, 1273

Tone, defined, 1390

"Tonight at Seven-Thirty" (Auden), 53

Topographical poetry. *See* Categorized Index

*Torse Three* (Middleton), 900

*Touch* (Gunn), 564

*Towards the Last Spike* (Pratt), 1020

**Traherne, Thomas**, 1277-1283; *Centuries of Meditations*, 1279; *Christian Ethicks*, 1280; *Traherne's Poems of Felicity*, 1281

*Traherne's Poems of Felicity* (Traherne), 1281

*Transitional Poem* (Day Lewis), 387

"Traveller, The" (De la Mare), 403

*Traveller, The* (Goldsmith), 522

*Treatise of Civil Power, A* (Hill), 649

"Tree, The" (Finch), 493

"Tretis of the Tua Mariit Wemen and the Wedo, The" (Dunbar), 447

"Trial of a City" (Birney), 89

"Triptych" (Reed), 1046

*Triumph of Love, The* (Hill), 647

*Trivia* (Gay), 517

Trochee, defined, 1390

*Troilus and Criseyde* (Chaucer), 249

*True Stories* (Atwood), 44

Truncation, defined, 1390

Tudor age. *See* Categorized Index

"Twickham Garden" (Donne), 413

"Two Experiments" (MacBeth), 842

*Two-Headed Poems* (Atwood), 44

"Ultima Ratio Regum" (Spender), 1187

"Ulysses" (Tennyson), 1239

"Under Ben Bulben" (Yeats), 1347

*Undertones of War* (Blunden), 107

*Underwoods* (Stevenson), 1204

*Undesirables* (Gunn), 566

United States. *See* Geographical Index